Eastern
Europe
and
Communist
Rule

J. F. Brown

Eastern Europe and

Communist Rule

J. F. Brown

Duke University Press   *Durham and London*   *1988*

© 1988 Duke University Press
All rights reserved.
Printed in the United States of America
on acid-free paper ∞
Library of Congress Cataloging-in-Publication Data
appear on the last printed page of this book
Parts of, or ideas in, chapters 1, 2, and 3 appeared
in chapters 1, 2, and 8 of Lincoln Gordon, *Eroding
Empire: Western Relations with Eastern Europe*
(Washington, D.C.: Brookings Institution, 1987), and
in chapter 2 of Richard D. Vine, ed., *Soviet-East
European Relations as a Problem for the West*
(London: Croom Helm, 1987). Ideas and some sec-
tions of chapter 10 appeared in chapter 8 of Martin
McCauley and Stephen Carter, *Leadership and
Succession in the Soviet Union, Eastern Europe
and China* (London: Macmillan, 1986). The opening
parts of chapter 5 are based on material in chap-
ter 7 from Lawrence L. Whetten, ed., *The Present
State of Communist Internationalism* (Lexington,
Mass.: Lexington Books, 1983).

For Margaret with love

Contents

Acknowledgments

My first thanks are due to the American Council of Learned Societies and to The Ford Foundation which provided grants enabling me to write this book. Dr. Jason Parker of ACLS and Dr. Enid Schoettle of Ford have been kind, helpful, and patient, and I am grateful to both.

I owe a special debt to my friend Ken Jowitt who, at a critical time, showed what friendship was about.

In the preparing and writing of the book several people gave invaluable help. My friend and old colleague Charles Andras was always there with help and wise counsel. The following also rendered help in a variety of ways: Eva Lengyel, Anneli Ute Gabanyi, Rada Nikolaeva, George Slavov, Iwanka Rebet, Maria Rerrich, Barbara von Ow, Louis Zanga, Zdenko Antic, Ron Asmus, Cam Hudson, Ross Johnson, Roman Stefanowski, Keith Crane, Vladimir Sobell, Robert Hutchings, Herbert Reed, Jozsef Szabados, Vladimir Kusin. My thanks go to them, as to the sections of the Radio Free Europe Library and Research Department in Munich whose archives I freely exploited. While preparing this book I also became, like thousands before me, a devotee of the London Library. My gratitude, too, to the cheerful and efficient ladies of the Oxford Secretarial Centre who typed the manuscript in various phases of its struggle.

Duke University Press, in the persons of Richard Rowson and Bob Mirandon, has been generous, patient, and resourceful. I am most grateful to the institution and the gentlemen concerned.

My daughters, Alison and Julia, and above all my wife, Margaret, sustained me when things were not going well. They can have no idea what I owe to them. Thanks are totally inadequate in cases like this. But I give them just the same.

J. F. Brown
Oxford, September 1987

Foreword

In this book I take a retrospective look at Eastern Europe over roughly the four decades of its communist history, with special reference to the past quarter century. I have not attempted a history of Eastern Europe over these years. Rather I analyze what seem to me the most important events, developments, and underlying trends.

The book is based on more than a quarter century of discussing Eastern Europe, writing, ruminating, arguing, and worrying about it. All this may not have made me much the wiser, but it has made me aware of how much there is to know. It has also given me some idea of the region's complexities based on different and quite contrasting histories.

This book covers Yugoslavia and Albania as well as "the Six." Including these two bloc-free countries involves difficulties of analysis and organization. It certainly inhibits generalization, although this, in itself, may not be a bad thing because writers ignore the big differences among all the East European countries at their peril. But it is best that Yugoslavia and Albania be included. For one thing, they look like they are becoming—each in its own way—"newsworthy" countries. And Yugoslavia, at least, though its political relevance for them may have declined, still provides scope for instructive comparison and contrast with the states of the Soviet alliance.

There is no overriding theme to this book. To have imposed one would have meant dallying with the schematic. But there are several intertwined motifs running through it. They include:

1. The distinctiveness of the East European countries despite the standardizing tendencies of their governing systems.

2. Nationalism and the power of the historical legacy.

3. "Spontaneity" in all walks of public life and its threat to the system.

4. The impact of the invasion of Czechoslovakia on East European political life. Its link with Solidarity in Poland.

5. The effect of the "decade of détente" in the 1970s.

6. The apparently inexorable economic decline and the growing ecological danger.

7. The "incompatibilities" in the East European polities.

8. The unmistakable reemerging of a class system.

9. The Soviet Union's continual dilemma in Eastern Europe.

10. The need for, and the danger of, systemic change.

There is more to Eastern Europe, of course, than ten motifs. But they point to underlying trends that no observer can ignore. It is to be hoped, too, that the following pages will pose for the reader some questions and even provide a few answers about Eastern Europe. Above all, it aims to set Western readers thinking about a region that is part of our own heritage, a vital factor in East-West relations, and bounteously rewarding in its own right.

1 The Course of Political Development

The aim of this opening chapter is to point out the main aspects of Eastern Europe's political development during the course of communist rule. The treatment must needs be brief; perhaps for some it will seem cursory. But it is hoped that the different chapters on individual countries will make up for such deficiencies. It is, after all, the variety of East Europe that remains the region's most striking characteristic, its patchwork quilt of nations, histories, and cultures. One ignores this national distinctiveness in Eastern Europe at one's own cost. No analysis of the region can be made without accepting its fundamental importance. The chapters on the eight different countries, therefore, represent the core of this book.

Still, an awareness of Eastern Europe's variety need not preclude generalizations or observations with a transnational application. The eight countries concerned all had the Soviet system imposed on them in the four years after the end of World War II—the same governing ideology, governmental institutions, economic, legal, and social systems. And, though each country soon began to shape the imposed superstructure in its own image, certain similarities continued to persist. Also, though societal reactions to the superstructure and to those imposing it markedly differed throughout the region, they form reliable premises for comparison, as do the efforts of the different regimes to cope with them.

Despite the manifold differences between the *trees*, an East European *wood* has existed, therefore, for some forty years, with Soviet-style communism as its common element. But an overview chapter can only put up signposts through the wood. It is the trees that make the wood, just as it is the individual countries that make up Eastern Europe.

Changes to the Map

For the purposes of this book Eastern Europe is taken as meaning eight communist countries. Six of these are members of the Soviet-dominated alliance: Bulgaria, Czechoslovakia, the German Democratic Republic, Hungary, Poland, and Romania. Two became independent: Yugoslavia after 1948 and Albania in the early 1960s. The generalizations that are made in this chapter apply mostly to the first set of countries—those that have remained Soviet-dominated. In opposing ways the course of Yugoslav and Albanian development has been quite different from that in the other countries. But not entirely so; certain similarities exist. But unless specifically named, they should be excluded from the following review.

First, a brief look at the political map. In some parts of Eastern Europe this has changed radically in the twentieth century, and in others it has barely altered. Bulgaria and Hungary emerged as dissatisfied from World War II as they had from World War I. During World War II many of their irredentist ambitions had been temporarily satisfied only to be thwarted again by their final defeat. Romania had lost Bessarabia and northern Bukovina to the Soviet Union in 1940, and its prospects of ever recovering these territories were remote. Compared with 1918, therefore, Romania was somewhat slimmer. But as long as it recovered all of Transylvania—which it did—the Romanian nation could live with the loss of Bessarabia and northern Bukovina. Albania for part of World War II had become greater Albania with the addition of the predominantly Albanian Kosovo and part of western Macedonia. But this had been part of the Axis Powers' Balkan dispensation and could not survive the defeat of Germany and Italy. Irredentist sentiments persisted, but since its birth as a state in 1913 Albania has had to be more interested in survival than expansion. Yugoslavia had been dismembered during World War II but was fully restored after it. It was in the northern part, or "tier," of Eastern Europe where the map was basically changed. The old Central Europe was altered beyond recognition by the division of Germany, the ramifications of which appeared in the ensuing years. In addition, parts of the old German Reich were lost to Poland and the Soviet Union. The divided parts of what remained took totally different courses. The larger became the frontline bulwark of the Western alliance, a model democracy, and a booming economy. The smaller became a Soviet appendage, first a liability, then a powerful economic asset. But, even more important than what it is, is what East Germany came to signify: the emasculation of German power. The German Democratic Republic was, therefore, Russia's greatest historic gain from World War II.

The frontiers of Poland were also drastically altered. Large tracts of territory, almost all of it historically disputed with Russia, were lost to the Soviet Union. As "compensation," Poland gained valuable eastern parts of the old German Reich. Czechoslovakia lost Ruthenia, which was of little importance, to the Soviet Union but regained Sudetenland, which it had been forced to surrender at Munich, as well as the part of Slovakia it had lost to Hungary and the area of Tešin that Poland had taken after Munich.

Ethnic Upheavals

But though large parts of Eastern Europe's national-territorial map may have remained the same, its ethnic composition changed radically. Two peoples that had traditionally dominated many spheres of its public life—the Germans and the Jews—practically disappeared. The latter were lost through the Holocaust, the former through the total defeat of the Reich and subsequent mass expulsions. Only in Romania did a sizable German minority remain, but this dropped from some 730,000 before the war to about half that number after it. In Hungary some 200,000 Germans remained by the time the expulsions stopped. These have steadily been assimilated. In Romania, on the other hand, many Germans by the end of the 1970s wished to leave and go to the Federal Republic. The German presence in Eastern Europe will probably, therefore, become almost totally extinguished in the course of the next century.

But, though the disappearance of the Germans and Jews may have mitigated the minority problem in Eastern Europe, it by no means removed it.[1] Nor, for that matter, did the Soviet-imposed communist revolution that swept over Eastern Europe in the few years after World War II, although the revolutionaries concerned considered it axiomatic that it would. Indeed, the national minorities problem, in itself just a segment of the whole question of nationalism, was to reemerge strongly and add a new and disturbing dimension to the complexities of contemporary Eastern Europe (see chapter 14). The most serious problem affected that large segment of the Hungarian nation (over 3 million) which the Treaty of Trianon had forced to live outside the boundaries of the truncated Hungary the treaty had allowed to survive the end of World War I. But toward the end of the period under review the Turkish minority in Bulgaria and, in a quite different way, the Muslim Albanians in Yugoslavia were both a reminder that the legacies of history—in both these cases of the Ottoman domination in south-eastern Europe—were far stronger than the ideological panaceas that had been supposed to remove them.

The Phases of Development

Had the Red Army not been at the Elbe by the end of World War II, had the Soviet Union not even existed, there would still likely have been revolutions of sorts in Eastern Europe after 1945. The nature of Soviet domination, the egregious errors made by their local satraps, the man-ifest failure to satisfy popular and national aspirations and, hence, the widespread rejection of communist rule—all tend to distract atten-tion from the inequities and iniquities of life in most of the interwar East European states. Hugh Seton-Watson's study of Eastern Europe between the wars—contemporaneous and fresh, the view not favor-ably tinted by the knowledge of what was to happen later—demon-strates quite forcefully that in every country the most radical change would have been necessary.[2]

The type of radical change all these countries were to experience was, however, hardly suitable in terms of their histories, predilections, aspirations, or needs. Models other than the Soviet Union would have been vastly more acceptable, as the course of history in Finland, Aus-tria, and even Greece has shown. But the East Europeans—as defined in this book—have had to cope with the incompatible. How they have done so is the story of the last forty years of their history.

Roughly speaking, this story so far has gone through five separate phases and since 1985 has entered on a sixth. There is nothing neat and packaged about these phases: in some countries the one has almost imperceptibly run into the next. Some countries have been well into one phase before others have passed through the preceding one. The whole picture is one of irregular, uneven movement, confused and often confusing. But close examination reveals discernible tendencies, and it is from these that conclusions can be drawn and generaliza-tions made.

The *first* phase—from 1945 to 1948—was the pre-Stalinist phase. It was a period in which, under the shadow of Soviet dominance, all the East European states (East Germany, for obvious reasons, excluded) enjoyed at least a pretense of democracy.[3] The vicissitudes of this short period, in which only in the Czech Lands of Czechoslovakia (not Slovakia) could communism claim really impressive electoral support, are irrelevant here. What is relevant, though, is the behavior of most of the communist parties in the region during this period. *Before* they achieved political mastery they erected policy platforms—in agriculture, for example, or relating to nationalization in industry—that barely distinguished them from some of their agrarian or democratic socialist opponents. Much of this sweet reasonableness was, of course, spurious, designed to win votes and lay their own bogey. But more significant in this connection were the early symptoms of what Zbigniew Brzezinski once called "domesticism" in the period immediately *after* the communists had gained overriding control.[4] What characterized several of these, now ruling, parties was not, of course, any independent behavior toward Moscow but what must have looked from Moscow like a preoccupation with the affairs of their own countries and an apparent readiness to use specific solutions for specific problems. This is what disturbed Stalin, who became less and less satisfied with his satellites' protestations of loyalty and their claims to be operating within an orthodox framework. The climax came, of course, with the break with Tito in 1948. But Tito's was only the extreme case of "domesticism." Gomułka in Poland and Traicho Kostov in Bulgaria both showed symptoms of it, for which the former was to pay with eight years of disgrace, the latter with his life.[5] Even Georgi Dimitrov, who as former secretary-general of the Comintern should have known better, was making unmistakably Bulgarian noises in Sofia and allowing his enthusiasm for Balkan federation to run far ahead of what Stalin had in mind. For this he was humiliated by the Soviet leader, both in public and in private, and eventually he was summoned to Moscow to die in mysterious circumstances in 1949.[6] A man like Dimitrov, of course, a programmed Stalinist, surely considered that he was doing only what Stalin wanted. But the paranoia in the Kremlin was such that it was the very enthusiasm with which Dimitrov returned to things Bulgarian after so long an exile that aroused suspicion.

Stalin founded the Cominform in 1947 precisely to check these signs of "domesticism" (or spontaneity), but it was the break with Tito that moved him from persuasion to compulsion. While every effort short of invasion was used to destroy Tito, every leader throughout Eastern Europe suspected of independence or even "autonomy" of mind was physically or politically liquidated. The Stalinist *Gleichschaltung*, applied in the Soviet Union itself in the 1930s, was now ready to be spread to Eastern Europe.

But before going on to this, it is worth stressing the importance of the factor that did most to accelerate it: the break with Tito. As Yugoslavia seems now to be sinking deeper into the morass of ethnic divisiveness and economic crisis and has so clearly failed to meet the high standard it set for itself, it is easy to forget the incalculable importance of what it did in 1948. It shattered the myth of communist unity almost before the communist bloc itself had been established, setting both a precedent and a level of aspiration for others. Just to have *attempted* what Tito did was a historic act. To have *succeeded* represented leadership of a truly historic order.[7]

What is also worth stressing is that, though it was submerged in the rest of Eastern Europe after 1948, "domesticism" by no means disappeared without trace. It was subsequently to resurface in more permissive periods throughout the next forty years. Much of East European communist history can, in fact, be considered in terms of recurring "domesticism," or spontaneity, a theme with many variations. The great explosions of 1956, 1968, and 1980–81 were aspects of "domesticism." But so were the quiet changes, often almost imperceptible, that have affected various aspects of political, economic, social, cultural, and legal development in every East European country. It is these developments, like grass forcing its way between flagstones, that have inexorably modified, or East Europeanized, the Soviet model and mores first imposed. That is why Eastern Europe is nothing like the Soviet Union and why there is as much difference between the GDR and Bulgaria as there is between Norway and Greece.

But little of this seemed likely between 1948 and 1953 when latter-day Stalinism was being thrust on Eastern Europe. This Gleichschaltung constitutes the *second* historical phase after 1945.

This period, despite all the changes mentioned above, has left its indelible mark on Eastern Europe. It introduced political institutions, an economic structure, and a bureaucratic habit of mind. Even more profound were the momentous social changes it set in train: massive industrialization, huge migrations from rural to urban areas, agricultural collectivization and the breakup of the old peasant culture. These changes continued, and for a period even accelerated, after Stalin's death. They are still continuing. They would have occurred without Stalin. All he did was to give them ruthless efficiency, an inhuman character, and, above all, the pervasive terror to which his name is permanently and inseparably linked. After Stalin's death in 1953 the process of dismantling not so much the base as the superstructure of his legacy began, and the pall of terror was gradually lifted. This was soon to lead in 1956 to an open disavowal of his methods of rule (though not its substance) by Khrushchev at the Twentieth CPSU congress. And in Eastern Europe it was to lead to the Hungarian Revolution and the Polish October.

Communist Eastern Europe's *third* phase began with Khrushchev's new policies after the disasters of 1956. Actually these were a continuation of what Malenkov and Khrushchev himself had initiated after Stalin's death. Now, after the repression in Hungary and the narrowly averted need for it in Poland, these policies simply wanted broadening and applying more urgently. They involved (1) strengthening bloc cohesion mainly through the new Warsaw Treaty Organization (founded in 1955; see chapter 2) and a resuscitated Comecon (founded in 1949; see chapter 4), emphasizing cooperation rather than Stalin-like compulsion; (2) a degree of domestic autonomy for the individual East European regimes to make necessary local adaptations and to acquire a legitimacy in the eyes of their peoples so lacking under Stalin. Indeed, it was the provocative lack of any kind of legitimacy that led to the disruptions in Poland and Hungary in 1956. And what this domestic autonomy was to lead to was the kind of "domesticism" displayed before 1948.

During this phase there also occurred the Great Schism between the Soviet Union and China, and it was this that facilitated not only the defection of Albania in 1961 but also the steadily growing autonomy carved out by Romania in intrabloc and foreign policy. But, most important, it was this phase that witnessed the birth and growth of what in 1968 became the Prague Spring. This movement of reform accelerated after the ousting of Khrushchev in October 1964, partly because of the momentum it was constantly acquiring, partly because of the relative inexperience of the new Soviet leadership and its preoccupation with shoring up its own domestic position.

In retrospect, it was the middle 1960s that probably saw the high point of East European political development under communist rule. The Eastern European states gradually became able to assert, if not their national identity, then at least their distinctiveness to a degree impossible under Stalin. Moscow never intended, of course, to allow them anything more than a semblance of independence. Any illusions on this account Khrushchev sought to dispel immediately. Still, he did much to foster a situation in which Eastern European leaderships, the composition of several of which he helped to change, developed some degree of autonomy and even some degree of bargaining leverage in their relations with the Soviet Union. The Eastern alliance began to assume at least some of the features of stress, strain, and bargaining that have characterized the traditional alliances of history.[8]

The autonomy developed by the Eastern European states served to quicken the stimulus for change at the domestic level, especially when sweeping domestic change, set off by de-Stalinization, seemed likely in the Soviet Union itself. The degree of domestic change in Eastern Europe varied considerably from state to state. Many factors affected these differences. Perhaps the most important were the level of economic advancement, public pressure, and the degree of self-confidence of the ruling elite. Sometimes the very autonomy that the various leaderships now enjoyed served to prevent rather than promote serious change, as in Romania, in Czechoslovakia before 1962, and in Poland after 1958. But domestic needs, plus the innovative examples of the Soviet Union, produced considerable domestic reform and experiment in Eastern Europe—important steps toward viability and the first faltering steps toward the legitimization of communist rule.

The *fourth* phase was ushered in by the Soviet-led invasion of Czechoslovakia in August 1968 that crushed the reform movement there. This act was perhaps the main watershed in communist Eastern European history so far; it signified that the Soviet leadership was not prepared to allow domesticism to go so far as to basically change or regenerate the Stalinist institutional system. For this system, despite all the modifications, had stood intact since 1953. What followed August 1968 were Soviet attempts to impose closer control in its alliance, again by strengthening Comecon and the Warsaw Treaty Organization as well as by imposing tighter bilateral ties. These were accompanied by a latter-day "counterreformation" stressing the basic tenets of ideological orthodoxy. There was a concentrated effort both to reideologize public life and to depoliticize it.[10] It was nothing like the Gleichschaltung of the Stalinist period. Considerable domestic latitude for each country was still allowed. But the inviolability of party supremacy and the total unacceptability of any kind of political pluralism narrowly circumscribed any freedom of action—even assuming the East European leaderships, most of which had been thoroughly alarmed by the Prague experiments, had been willing to use it.

What was permitted, even encouraged, under the new dispensation was economic modernization and a "consumerist" policy aimed at raising the popular standard of living. This latter policy was at least partly designed to keep the masses quiet and dull their political aspirations. For about half a decade this new policy, closely linked with the name of Brezhnev, seemed to work well. Nowhere more so than in Poland, which had seen its once popular leader, Gomułka, toppled by worker riots at the end of 1970, and where the need for rapid rises in the standard of living was particularly acute. The new Polish leader, Edward Gierek, seemed to be achieving precisely that, with the aid of massive injections of Western credits, plus Soviet trade subsidies. Indeed, recourse to Western credits, freely available, became an important part of the economic policy of every Eastern European country, except Czechoslovakia, whose post-invasion regime tended to take an almost paranoid view of any Western intrusion.

But the promising situation of the early 1970s was not to last long. The undoubted prosperity that had been achieved was hit by Western recession and inflation (a sign in itself of the growth of East-West economic relations). But it was more severely affected by major increases in the prices of Soviet oil and other raw materials imposed in 1975 and occasioned by the huge rises in the world price of oil imposed by the OPEC cartel. The ability of the East European regimes to cope with the sudden crisis was impaired by the general inflexibility of their economic structures, which made them slow to adapt to new changes and needs. The result of this combination of factors was a reversal in the rise of the standard of living, growing economic inefficiency, and an accumulation of debt that appeared impossible to repay. A crisis was brewing in the second half of the 1970s that the East European leaderships seemed powerless to prevent.[11]

The situation in Eastern Europe at the end of the 1970s, therefore, hardly fulfilled the promise of the early years of the decade. Indeed, it presented such a contrast that one can justifiably speak of a new *fifth* phase in the course of postwar history. In Hungary, the exemplar in economic reform and political relaxation, the rise in living standards had halted and was even going into reverse. In Romania, under Ceaușescu's personal misrule, both the economic and the psychological condition of the population had deteriorated to almost unbearable levels. Czechoslovakia and the GDR, overall the most advanced of the East European states, also saw living standards decline or stagnate. The former could boast of a low hard-currency debt but of little else; indeed, the longer-term Czechoslovak economic prospects looked extremely bleak. The GDR, on the contrary, had a large Western debt but was making major economic reorganizations designed to increase economic efficiency. It had, moreover, the strong pillar of West German economic aid on which to lean.

Not surprisingly, it was Poland where the explosion came. The Polish economy began to sag dangerously in 1977, and it was only a matter of time before Gierek, who had misled both Soviet and Western leaders with his air of confident ability, fell into the kind of disgrace that had enveloped his predecessor, Gomułka. This came in September 1980 after the third disastrous attempt in ten years to increase the prices of food—a measure that, like the others, may have been economically justified but was fraught with political dangers. The first attempt in 1970 had led to Gomułka's fall and Gierek's rise. The second, in 1976, was the first real indication (largely ignored) that the house Gierek had built was made of cards. The third attempt was one of the immediate reasons for the rise of Solidarity.

Solidarity was one of the most remarkable developments in modern European history.[12] Its direct precedent was, of course, the riots of 1970. But those riots were mainly confined to the Baltic coastline and were violent and bloody. Solidarity began in Gdansk, soon spread to Szczecin and the entire Baltic coast, but then quickly enveloped the whole of Poland. And it was a peaceful movement. It also quickly became a *national* movement against the ruling regime with the aim, not specifically of toppling it, but of extracting far-reaching concessions from it. But the concessions demanded became such that no regime could agree to them and remain communist. This is what the moderates in Solidarity realized and why they sought to contain or to fudge the demands being made. But the movement, especially when faced by a regime patently insincere in its dealings, acquired an ever-quickening momentum. Now, in retrospect, the confrontation that eventually came in December 1981 seems to have been inevitable. When it did come, organized Solidarity was smashed with remarkable skill and speed, and with a minimum of casualties. But resistance in various degrees, shapes, and forms was not broken in Poland. Solidarity became firmly entrenched in Polish history as a set of values and a way of life. As such, it will never be eradicated. Moreover, the general ineffectiveness of the Jaruzelski regime, highlighted by incidents like the murder of Father Popiełuszlo in October 1984 (see chapter 5), caused the gulf between rulers and ruled to widen for a time rather than narrow after December 1981. Many Polish moderates, who saw little point in overt resistance, were looking forward resignedly to the next explosion in Poland rather than looking back to the last one.

Solidarity then was a distinctly Polish phenomenon. But in one key respect it had a consequential link with the Prague Spring of twelve years earlier. The two movements had basically different origins and characters. Whereas the Prague Spring was essentially a movement originating and led from within the party and the ruling establishment, only subsequently engulfing large sections of the population, in Poland it was the reverse. Solidarity originally was a mass societal movement of reform that only later spread to the basic party organizations. But in a sense the fate of the Prague Spring made Solidarity's specific form inevitable. The Soviet-led invasion signaled that Moscow was not prepared to tolerate basic reform from within: no party would be allowed to transform itself and the system it both led and represented. The only alternative, therefore, was that regeneration must come from *outside* the system, from society itself, and *against* the system if necessary. This point was made strongly by several Polish intellectuals in the second half of the 1970s. Events in recent Polish history, of course, notably the disappointments with Gomułka after 1956 and with Gierek after 1970, must have led many Poles to the same conclusion, anyway. But the same Polish intellectuals were insistent that it was the Soviet invasion in 1968 against a Czechoslovak regime sincerely bent on basic renewal that provided a new dimension to the whole question of change in Eastern Europe.[13]

A *sixth* phase in East European communist history appears to have begun with the accession to the Soviet party leadership of Mikhail Gorbachev in 1985. The possibilities arising from this are discussed in chapter 2. It was not clear what new elements would be permanently added to the East European scene as a result of the changes in Moscow. But it was already abundantly clear that Gorbachev regarded change as essential in Eastern Europe. The question was how deep and comprehensive the changes would be and to what extent he would realize that the Soviet–East European relationship was also part of the same question of change. If he did come to this realization and was willing and politically able to initiate meaningful change, then would the volatility of the East European situation allow that kind of controlled, regulated change on which even the most liberal Soviet leader would insist? It is too early to say; in any case, the interaction between Gorbachev and Eastern Europe will probably be a lengthy one—with several distinct phases of its own.[14]

Expected Leadership Changes

Few could have failed to notice the striking contrast in age and length of service between the new Soviet leader and Eastern Europe's own leaders. In 1987 Gorbachev was fifty-six and had been in office more than two years. By contrast, most East European leaders were—or should have been—thinking about their successors. Zhivkov, Kádár, Honecker, and Husák had all either reached or were nearing seventy-five. Ceaușescu, for long the Benjamin of the East European leaders, was approaching seventy. Only General Wojciech Jaruzelski, who owed his position to a bizarre combination of circumstances, was still in his early sixties. Zhivkov had been party leader for thirty-three years, Kádár for thirty-one. While Gorbachev could claim two years' service, the six leaders of the Soviet Union's East European allies claimed a combined total of over 125.

The only certainty emerging from these statistics is that at least four Soviet–East European allies could soon be experiencing a leadership succession. Whether this would involve a crisis was by no means sure. In the past most communist leadership changes have either resulted in or from crises. It would seem, however, that preemptive care has been taken more recently to avoid the classic upheavals. The Brezhnev-Andropov-Chernenko-Gorbachev progress of death and succession was incident-free by the standards of thirty years before. Much earlier, in 1965, Ceaușescu's succession after the death of his predecessor, Gheorghiu-Dej, was smooth, although he had later to neutralize several of his rivals. So, apparently, was that of Ramiz Alia after Enver Hoxha in Albania in 1985. Now it appeared that both Kádár and Honecker were trying to ensure that their departures create no power vacuums in which factionalism could thrive (see chapters 6 and 7). But try as he might, no leader could ensure a stability from beyond the grave. The chances were that, in one or more of the countries affected, power struggles of some intensity would ensue. In any case, however smooth the transitions appeared to be, the new incumbent would need time and skill to familiarize himself with the complexities of his office and to reshape the governing cadres in a form acceptable and loyal to himself.

Just as important as the domestic implications of East European leadership changes (in fact, inextricable from them) was the fact that Gorbachev, as Soviet leader, would of necessity be involved in them —and at a relatively early stage in his career. He would naturally be interested that the leadership changes proceeded with as few disruptions as possible. But even more important was the fact that the new leaders who were to emerge in Eastern Europe would be those with whom Gorbachev would probably work for a long time. It was crucial to him, therefore, that the "right" men be chosen. That made it necessary for him to interfere in East European affairs earlier and more intensively than he might otherwise have thought desirable. All East European leaders, of course, have had to go through some form of Soviet vetting. It would be in Gorbachev's interest to see that his vetting was even more thorough than usual.

The picture presented by Eastern Europe to the new Soviet leader could hardly be a reassuring one. True, no part of the region was in a state of disruption and, such was the numbing effect of the crushing of Solidarity, this need not be feared for some time. But none of the present or previous leaderships had attained anything like that degree of legitimacy that would be reassuring to a Soviet leader.

Tests of Legitimacy

What constitutes legitimacy is a question to which many answers have been given. In the East European case any legitimacy for a ruling elite would need to embrace the following:

1. A policy consonant with the national traditions and aspirations of the bulk of the population.

2. A commonly shared ideology or set of values between rulers and ruled.

3. A minimum and increasing standard of welfare and prosperity.

4. The creation of conditions for social and professional mobility.

5. An increasing degree of freedom of expression and association —political, social, economic, and religious.

6. A general belief that the condition of society will steadily improve.[15] Obviously these points could be debated, amended, or refined almost endlessly. But they do offer a rough and reliable guide to what legitimacy is, or should constitute, in the East European context. The relative importance of these points can vary considerably according to national attitudes and with different historical periods. For example, the Soviet regime enjoys a considerable legitimacy among large sections of its population, although it hardly fulfills all the desiderata mentioned above, something of which numerous Soviet citizens are well aware. This is mainly because, largely through the epic of World

War II, communism was reinforced by nationalism. Whether this mutual interaction is as strong among the new generation is open to question.

In the East European case—involving several quite different countries—the position is much more complex. In the *East German* case, despite the almost frantic efforts of the GDR regime to foster a distinct sense of nationality and its quite striking success in raising living standards, there was little evidence of the development of a new nationalism, as opposed to a certain feeling of distinctiveness. In fact, the nationalism of most East Germans is traditional German nationalism (see chapter 7). And as long as no change occurs there is little point in discussing the subject further. If a state remains artificial —and the test here is whether the population thinks it is artificial or not—then its government hardly begins to be legitimate. In *Poland* the very mention of the subject would arouse derision, scarcely less before December 1981 than after. And yet, even in Poland, the new Gomułka regime did enjoy a certain legitimacy during October 1956 and for a short time after. So, perhaps, did Gierek immediately after December 1970 (see chapter 5). In *Czechoslovakia* the short-lived Dubček regime enjoyed a legitimacy, whereas the Husák regime, despite its successful "consumerist" policy, certainly did not. In Slovakia, though, if still enjoying only a partial fulfillment of their nationalist aspirations, many of the population were prepared to grant the Bratislava government at least a degree of acceptance that could lead to some kind of legitimacy (see chapter 9). In *Hungary*, because of the unique tragedy of the 1956 revolution and the astonishing metamorphosis of János Kádár from traitor to *pater patriae*, the regime did come to acquire some legitimacy, reinforced by its policy of economic reform and a certain "atmospheric" relaxation. But this legitimacy pivoted almost entirely on Kádár. And—to repeat—Kádár in 1987 was seventy-five and his prestige was plummeting (see chapter 6).

Romania has been a case of dissipated legitimacy. With the deepening unpopularity of Ceauşescu, it was easy to forget that for some three years after his accession to power in 1965 he aroused optimistic expectations among many Romanians. This was not simply because of his defense of Romanian national interests against the Soviet Union, but also because on the domestic front promising reforms were set in motion (see chapter 8). In his courageous defiance of the Soviet Union's invasion of Czechoslovakia in August 1968 he undoubtedly had the majority of his countrymen behind him, understandably nervous though they were. That was Ceauşescu's peak. Subsequently, all was decline and degeneration. The nationalist-oriented policy continued, and the years since 1968 were punctuated by periods of tension with Moscow. But economic mismanagement forced Romania back some way into an undesired degree of dependence on Moscow, especially in the energy sector, and often the anti-Soviet stance has seemed to many of its subjects anti-Soviet posturing. Thus many Romanians, originally enthusiastic about Ceaușescu's nationalism, now weighed this dwindling asset against his mounting liabilities. They had even begun (most reluctantly) to envy the situation even in *Bulgaria* (not to mention Hungary).

In Bulgaria, though assessments of popular moods are particularly difficult, there seemed little doubt that the regime had come to enjoy, not legitimacy, but a passive acceptance. This was not so much due, as many observers would have it, to any widespread Bulgarian love of Russia. A hazy pro-Russian sentiment certainly still existed, although it was less among the young than the old, and, in any case, there was often a general embarrassment at the extravagant servitude displayed by the Bulgarian regime toward Moscow. Of much greater concern to many Bulgarians was how their regime conducted itself in relations with the "old enemies"—Serbia, Greece, and Turkey. Here there is no servitude; sometimes, rather, in the case of Yugoslavia, a provocativeness over Macedonia that amounts to a form of surrogate nationalism. This goes down well with many Bulgarians; so apparently do the recent efforts forcibly to assimilate the large Turkish minority in Bulgaria itself. A more healthy nationalism was shown in the support of the efforts of Zhivkov's daughter, Lyudmila, to publicize in the West the great historical creations of Bulgarian civilization—and to make Bulgarians aware of them, too. As for economic prosperity, the Zhivkov regime's record has been generally good. In the mid-1980s, however, the Bulgarian economy was in the most serious difficulties, and there were grave doubts whether favored economic treatment from the Soviet Union would continue. The regime's quest for legitimacy would suffer severely if these difficulties were not overcome (see chapter 10).

The *Yugoslav* and *Albanian* leaderships have at least shared something in common with the Romanian: they have tapped, and in turn been sustained by, the sources of nationalism in their countries. In Eastern Europe forty years of communist rule and Soviet presence have only helped maintain nationalism as the prime political characteristic of every society. Failure to satisfy nationalist aspirations has doomed most regimes to an irremediable lack of legitimacy. But Tito and Hoxha, by their defiance of Moscow in defense of the sovereignty of their own countries, did enjoy a considerable legitimacy, which Hoxha certainly hardly deserved through any other aspect of his rule. Later Yugoslavia's integrity was to be undermined and its sovereignty threatened—by nationalisms from within. But, as will be seen in the country chapter on Yugoslavia (chapter 11), it was fear of the Soviet Union that survived as the strongest unifying force in the federation.

A real and lasting legitimacy encompassing all the above-mentioned criteria can almost certainly never be achieved. It is doubtful indeed whether any Western democratic system has achieved all six to a satisfactory degree. Certainly no East European government in the precommunist era between the two wars did so. But after forty years of communist rule the most depressing aspect about Eastern Europe is that in some countries governmental legitimacy seems further away than ever.

The quest for a genuine legitimacy will be frustrated so long as the East European societies are offered no possibilities of influence or participation in a genuine political interaction. Some form of political pluralism, therefore, is essential, either through a multiparty parliamentary system or through the party sharing its power with other public organizations such as trade unions or umbrella organizations embracing various societal interest groups. Richard Lowenthal has rightly contended that this is a sine qua non for a lasting legitimacy.[16] The Czech reformers of 1968 seemed to realize this, as do radical reformers now in Hungary and Yugoslavia. In Poland, of course, with the power of the Catholic church, a form of pluralism or duality of power actually exists, though hardly by courtesy of the communist authorities. For it to exist elsewhere would require a fundamental break with Leninist tradition, practice, and ideology, of which the monopoly on authority by the party is the main buttress. Any alteration of this in Eastern Europe, therefore, would be the result of only a more basic transformation not to be expected.

Ideology and Orthodoxy

The Leninist tenet of party supremacy has remained alive and well in Eastern European regimes. But what of Marxism-Leninism as a whole? Ideology in the sense of Marxism-Leninism being a way of life, a code of civic conduct, an exclusive guide to political action to be preached with proselytizing zeal and practiced with ascetic application is dead in Eastern Europe. This is assuming it ever was fully alive. Perhaps it was only alive in the underground parties between the two world wars and in the Comintern schools in the Soviet Union so vividly described by Wolfgang Leonhard.[17]

But as a general weltanschauung it did survive for a quarter of a century after World War II. It survived Stalin because many continued to think that Stalinism was a perversion rather than a logical conclusion of Marxism-Leninism. Revisionist reformers set about redefining the ideology and sought to implement their own respectable versions in Yugoslavia after 1950 and in Hungary and Poland in 1956. The most comprehensive and successful effort appeared to have been made in Czechoslovakia during the Prague Spring. But this was crushed by the Soviet Union supported, with varying degrees of enthusiasm, by all but one of its junior partners. The Soviet Union had, therefore, not only said no to self-regeneration; it had finally condemned the ideology to death. It had been moribund enough before then, but some of the finest people in Eastern Europe still believed in the ideology to the extent that they thought it might be revived, if in an entirely different form.

Since then the communist ideology has suffered nothing but rejection and contempt from the vast majority of East European citizens. This includes Yugoslavia, where the deepening disappointment with the new system Tito tried to build left a mood of ideological rejection not as virulent as, but not very dissimilar from, the rest of Eastern Europe. But for bureaucracies searching for reassurance—as all in Eastern Europe are—even a fossilized or rejected ideology has still had its uses, if not as a religion then as a ritual of government. As such, it provides focus and cohesion; it is also a ready-made mythology. The ideology also provides the language, or at least the semantics, by which the ruling elites communicate with each other. It has also provided the rationale by which the ruling elites seek to justify their power (to whom is another matter). In the years before communism became a ruling system, ideology had been seen as something enabling power to be implemented. Subsequently, ideology became the means by which power was justified.[18]

But it also went deeper than that. Among many East European party apparatchiks as late as the mid-1980s ideology, though dead or moribund, had left here and there an indelible impression. Even the more sophisticated viewed the history of their own country, for example, in often simplistic Marxist terms. Some also saw international relations and politics in terms of the struggle between "capitalism" and "socialism." They also viewed the victory of "socialism" as inevitable. Ethically, most of them would also defend the notion of the means justifying the ends in the struggle, domestic and international, for the "triumph of socialism." (Just as many of those who had rejected "socialism" now saw nothing wrong with using the same notion to bring about its defeat.) For such men and women ideology was, therefore, more than a convenience. It was a tablet of stone that had profoundly influenced their way of thinking. It might no longer be a living guide, but it was still a basic primer. It had affected the heart more than the mind—and the marrow of the bones more than either. It has provided both facade and fundamentals for many members of the ruling elites.

Circles of Vested Interests

The ruling elites are, of course, the pillars of the governing system in both Eastern Europe and the Soviet Union. They can be roughly divided into five elites: political, economic, cultural, professional, and military.[19]

The *political* elite has remained the most important, even after forty years of communist rule. Its base is the party bureaucracy in the provinces and at the center. Many of its members have had various levels of party schooling, and some have had Soviet training experience. It was from their numbers that the top leadership has always been mainly drawn.

But as the economies of the different communist countries developed in complexity, the *economic* elites began to assume an even greater importance. They can be divided into two categories. The first, usually of the older generation, were essentially members of the political elite who had received some (often very little) economic training and then moved into senior economic positions in either the party or state bureaucracy or directly in the economy. The real economic elite was mainly composed of younger experts or technocrats, often with only formal political training. In every East European country, even the least developed, these experts had begun moving into senior positions by the early 1970s at the latest. Most were patriotic and what might be deemed "progressive" in the sense of being receptive to ideas promoting efficiency. Many of them, though, were by no means anti-Soviet. In fact, many had had part of their training in the Soviet Union and, after returning home, kept the ties with their Soviet alma mater and their fellow alumni. They had made most progress up the ladder in Hungary. But in the GDR and in Poland many real economic experts have encroached on positions that had previously been the preserve of the economically varnished political elites.

The *cultural* elite covers a wide spectrum of different pursuits: teachers of all grades, men and women in the creative and performing arts, the media, party agitation and propaganda officials. Many of these are party members; most teachers, for example. But some, like writers, men and women of the theater, or artists, need not be party members, although, unless they achieved a rare excellence in their calling, it was materially better for them if they were.

The *professional* elites are composed of doctors, dentists, lawyers, engineers, accountants, etc.—not to mention the battalions of sportsmen and women. These provide rare and much sought after services and, directly or indirectly, have been well rewarded for their services. Most have been party members, but a considerable number were not, especially in Poland.[20]

Finally, there is the *military*. The question of the loyalties of the East European military in the event of a Warsaw Pact—NATO conflict has been the subject of much speculation in recent years, and this has inspired study of the sociology of the new officer class. It is a matter not directly relevant here. What is necessary, however, is simply to stress the role of the officer corps, not only as a pillar of communist power in Eastern Europe but also as its ultimate local guarantor. In every country the vast majority of officers have been party members.[21]

Members of these different elites—party or nonparty—constitute what in Western terminology has become known as the establishment. Many of them are (or have been) critical of their regimes and even of the system, and many have been active in efforts to reform it. But all have had a vested interest in its survival, and even among the most dissatisfied there have been many preferring a bad system to a different system. Very few, except perhaps for a few figures on the fringe of the cultural establishment, would knowingly endanger the system. It is not so much a question of loyalty to it as needing to be convinced that its overthrow would not endanger, even sweep away, the comfortable niches they have carved out for themselves.

Further from the centers of power than these elites are numerous citizens, including many workers, well-off collective farmers, artisans, and latter-day private entrepreneurs, who, critical though they also may be of the regime, would hesitate to see it replaced. They all constitute the relatively large number of people who, in varying degrees, have a "vested interest" in the survival of the regime. Many vociferously complain about the regime, not only at home but to relations, friends, and even strangers in the West, often giving the impression that an outbreak of revolution at home is hourly to be expected. But when in their own countries, with the task of "managing" for themselves and their families, it is their involvement with the system rather than their alienation from it that more often dictates their thoughts and actions.[22]

"Alternative" Politics and Culture

The willy-nilly involvement of many East Europeans in, or with, their governing system has applied mainly to those citizens who have reached and passed the "age of maturity." But since the early 1970s, especially among the youth of Eastern Europe, new concepts of counterculture and alternative living styles have developed that reject as far as is possible (in many cases only as far as is comfortable) any involvement with the governing system. This is a transnational phenomenon that has had its origin in Western Europe and the United States. Indeed, much of the East European version has been derived from its Western model (see chapter 13). But in the East this phenomenon developed in a quite different systemic context than in the West.

The Western political systems might fret over the refusal of countercultural youth to become involved. But these systems have usually been flexible enough to accommodate all but the most extreme expressions of youthful rebellion or withdrawal. In the East, however, noninvolvement was initially less excusable and comprehensible even than opposition. Regimes that aspired to be totalitarian (whether they are or not is another—arid—question) have no place for countercultures or alternative ways of living. But after Stalinism the regimes had deprived themselves of the one weapon that could effectively combat such heresies: terror. The heresies, therefore, grew until by the middle of the 1980s they were widespread. (So widespread, in fact, that the regimes' strategy toward them seemed to be altering.) Without terror the external ideological uniformity that had previously existed could not be enforced. Nor, as was becoming increasingly obvious, could the doubters be won over by the example or the exertions of "real, existing socialism" in practice.

But those who rejected the system in this way presented no immediate danger to regimes harassed by mounting economic problems or direct challenges to their authority. A hands-off official attitude thus appeared to be developing, in spite of the regular propaganda railings against the "new parasites." This had gone furthest in Poland, after the demoralization of the defeat of Solidarity, but it was also apparent in Czechoslovakia, Hungary, and the GDR. It could become an important feature of East European social-political life.

More immediately alarming from the official point of view were the religious and "single-issue" groupings—for example, on ecological questions—that began to emerge in the 1970s. They reflected that spirit of "spontaneity," which even a diluted Leninist regime like the Yugoslav regarded as a mortal threat. The countercultures and alternative modes of living also reflected "spontaneity," but only passively. The much greater youthful interest in religion, however, whether organized through the churches or more individually or independently (see chapter 3), was "spontaneity" of a more active and challenging kind. In Hungary and Czechoslovakia there was an undoubted increase in religious "activism" from the beginning of the 1970s, some of it partly a reaction to the crushing of reform communism in 1968. Most of it was under the Roman Catholic rubric, but in Hungary there was also some regeneration in the Lutheran and Calvinist churches.

In the GDR, although there were few signs of any religious reawakening as such, the Evangelical church became a center for single-issue groupings. It was these, in the GDR and elsewhere, that were probably regarded as the most dangerous of all. They involved an active interference in the issues and policies of the day—the environment, for example, nuclear energy (especially after Chernobyl), and, particularly in the GDR, military service and the alleged militarization of society. Such groups were particularly active in Yugoslavia where the restraints on society were usually fewer. But they also became active in Hungary, causing considerable embarrassment on occasion to the Kádár regime, as well as in Poland and Czechoslovakia.

These societal groupings had become established in Eastern Europe by the middle of the 1980s and were likely to proliferate. They grew mainly because the prevailing political process, wedded inseparably to one-party democratic centralism, could not absorb or satisfy them. August 1968 and then the crushing of Solidarity in December 1981 appeared to have killed the last hopes of this changing. And too little was still known of Mikhail Gorbachev to be sure that he would encourage this kind of change.

Again, these groupings had also grown because—simply put—there was no terror. Perhaps the most important change of all to come over East European life since Stalin's time was the easing of the grip of terror associated with his name. Obviously this is a generalization needing some qualification. The security apparatus in all countries throughout the region was in good repair and far from inactive. In varying degrees every East European state could still be described as "lawless" because the processes of law were, when deemed necessary, subordinated to the exigencies of the political process. In some countries, notably Romania, individual acts of terror were still far from uncommon in the 1980s. In the GDR the very presence of the security forces had an intimidating immediacy. In some countries they occasionally acted out of control; the most publicized case was the murder of Father Popiełuszko in Poland in October 1984. But by and large most East European citizens felt much more secure and less frightened than they had for nearly forty years.

In Hungary there had been a general political and psychological relaxation since the early 1960s. Visitors to Jaruzelski's Poland as early as 1983 were astonished by the freedom of speech and movement allowed. In Yugoslavia after Tito's death in 1980 the official nervousness was reflected in an increasing repressiveness against political dissent. The number of political prisoners rose. But all this had to be seen against a background of freedom of the press, speech, debate, and movement, which continued to be quite extraordinary for a communist state. In the GDR the police, despite their pervasiveness, tolerated much more than they did twenty years before. In Romania and Bulgaria the situation was much less comfortable, but even there, despite periodic lapses, it had apparently improved. In fact, it was a distinguished Romanian scholar, though mindful of the police vindictiveness at home, who in private conversation explained a serious strike by miners in the Jiu Valley in 1977 with a simple generalization: "People aren't frightened anymore." And, once nations have broken through the fear barrier, it is not easy to set them behind it again.

Rulers and Ruled

If the people are not frightened anymore, then some regimes should be more frightened than ever. During the Solidarity episode, for example, and the worker riots that had toppled Gomułka ten years before, every East European regime must have felt more than a fleeting insecurity.

But at the end of 1981 they must have taken heart from the efficient swiftness with which Solidarity as an organization was crushed. Indeed, in terms of ability to cope with internal disturbance, every regime was probably better equipped than ever by the mid-1980s. The Soviet Union must also have derived satisfaction from the efficiency of the Polish army and security forces in December 1981. With such a performance from the local, national forces of coercion, it was always possible that Soviet troops would not be needed again in Eastern Europe! Not only that: the Soviets had some reason to hope that East European society as a whole had been numbed and unnerved by the ease with which Solidarity was put down. They might no longer be frightened, but at least their confidence might never extend to the foolhardiness of mass defiance of authority.

By the late 1980s, therefore, rulers and ruled in Eastern Europe were prepared to concede something to the other in the interest of a modus vivendi. But the modus vivendi was precarious indeed. It was considered by many to depend on the regimes' ability to restore economic progress, above all in the standard of living. And the economic future was very uncertain.

Some observers question the validity of the dichotomy between rulers and ruled, society and the state.[23] Few would argue a complete commonality of outlook and interest between the East European citizens and their governments, although some would claim that this is growing. But more would argue that the complex interaction of the different strata that constitute both "state" and "society" in East Europe so blurs the distinction as to undermine it. Similarly, the extent to which the different vested interests in Eastern European societies have in preserving the system is a decisive aspect of commonality. This may be so. But, though there are many people outside the regime establishment whose interests may serve to *stabilize* the regime, this does not mean that the same interests serve to legitimize it. Moreover, complex though East European societies and attitudes may have become, old attitudes toward authority have remained similar and simple. As much as ever in the checkered history of Eastern Europe, the notion of "them" and "us" has still remained the outstanding feature of public life. Even in Hungary, despite the undoubted popularity of Kádár for many years, that distinction has persisted too glaringly to be missed. Precommunist history may indeed have engendered it. But the communist experience has done nothing whatever to mitigate it.

The notions of "them" and "us," therefore, still remain. But some intelligent citizens in Eastern Europe, especially in Czechoslovakia and Hungary, were by the early 1980s beginning to question the cohesiveness of *society* (of "us") in their country. In Hungary it was agreed that a combination of regime *divide et impera* policy toward the different societal strata and divisive forces unleashed by the New Economic Mechanism had made deep inroads into the nation's cohesiveness. In Czechoslovakia the same result was said to have been mainly caused by the Soviet-led invasion in August 1968 and the opportunism it engendered (see chapter 9). It is difficult to judge how well based or how impressionistic such views were. Just when in history had society been cohesive, anyway? But the fact that many people held these views was in itself a factor of some political importance.

Party and State

As the earlier discussion about the ruling elites suggests, the regimes themselves were becoming more complex and socially differentiated. Some aspects of social differentiation are described in chapter 13. But divisions within the regimes based on what was once called "factionalism," though still persisting, appeared to be more superficial in the 1970s and the 1980s than they had once been.

The first great division had been between "home" communists and "Muscovites" in the late 1940s and during the 1950s. After 1948 this became an open struggle that ended decisively in the latter's favor. After Stalin the "home" communists were rehabilitated, although "Muscovites" often still played important roles, especially in party life. The struggle was now more between "hard-liners" and "reformers": the Polish October was probably the earliest example of this. This struggle went on throughout the 1960s, its center transferring to Czechoslovakia.

After the Soviet-led invasion of Czechoslovakia, intraregime divisions on policy grounds became more blurred. This was because, after the limits of reform had been so sharply circumscribed by August 1968, there was far less political animation in Eastern Europe as a whole. In Hungary, where reform continued, there continued to be some animation; differences persisted between advocates and opponents of reform and among those favoring different degrees of reform. Elsewhere there were few basic issues in the 1970s around which factions in the old sense could form. But differences over questions of tactics, clashes of personality, and over considerations of power continued as before.

Purges continued, but they were less dramatic than before, and the penalties for losing were less severe.

But during the 1970s the question of the relationship between party and state reemerged in a potentially acute form. It was, of course, the party that was still proclaimed as supreme. But the exact nature of the relationship had never been redefined with success after Stalin's time. As early as 1952, at the Yugoslav sixth party congress, the party's role was defined as that of formulating policy and then one essentially of guidance. Implementation was the job of the state apparatus. As discussed in the chapter on Yugoslavia, these decisions always worried Tito, who basically remained a Leninist. They also worried many Yugoslav party officials who saw their influence and even their jobs endangered.

In the Soviet-dominated countries the issue was never faced so directly. But uneasiness about the party-state relationship persisted. After Stalin's death the posts of party leader and prime minister were now divided as a gesture against the personality cult. The initial apparent supremacy in the Soviet Union of Georgi Malenkov, who assumed the post of premier, even led to expectations that the state apparatus might gain in power and influence. But the party in the Soviet Union soon reasserted its power under Khrushchev. He later assumed the premiership as well, thus uniting the two bureaucracies at the very top. But his example was followed in Eastern Europe only by Zhivkov and Kádár. Later, when Brezhnev added the office of head of state (but not the premiership) to his party leadership, his example was followed more generally, though not everywhere. All the party leaders—except Gomułka, Kádár, and the errant Enver Hoxha—also became heads of their respective states. (Apart from anything else, it was a convenient institutional device for ceremonially conscious leaderships in the age of détente to enable the "real" heads of state to meet foreign dignitaries without protocol difficulties.)

But the party-state relationship was not just a problem at the very top of the hierarchy. If anything, it was even more serious lower down—at the local administrative level where the two bureaucracies were duplicated. Even in relatively small districts there was inevitably a party committee and a people's, or local government, council. The relations between these two types of bodies must often have caused problems for practical politicians, let alone ideological theorists. Gierek in Poland and Ceaușescu in Romania tackled the problem by combining the local party secretary posts with that of the local council chairmen. But though this may have done much to reduce personal tensions, it did not come to grips with the problem of the two bureaucracies and the many doubts as to who was responsible for what.

When Gierek replaced Gomułka at the end of 1970 he sought to define the relationship between party and state in much the same way as the Yugoslavs had in 1952. The state should implement; the party should initiate. It sounded a plausible enough distinction with no doubt the added advantage as far as Gierek was concerned that, if disaster occurred, it would be the state and not the party that got the blame.

What eventually happened was rather different, and the difference could lead to a profound shift of power in Poland as well as elsewhere. In April 1981 a Polish party commission was set up, chaired by then Central Committee secretary Tadeusz Grabski, to examine progress in the inquiries into the political responsibility of party and state leaders for the catastrophe that had engulfed the regime. What emerged from the evidence was that, in some respects, the government, under Premier Jaroszewicz, had not only had more responsibility but also more power and influence than the party under Gierek.[24] There could well have been a political reason for this. According to Romuald Spasowski, a former deputy Polish foreign minister who defected while ambassador to Washington in December 1981, Jaroszewicz, the old "Muscovite," was trusted by the Russians; Gierek, the old "Frenchman," was not.[25]

Soviet personal preferences may explain something; but perhaps not everything. The power of the state bureaucracy could partly have been due to the reemergence in the state apparatus of a well-qualified technical bureaucracy. The need for such a bureaucracy had grown immeasurably as the economy had become more complex and sophisticated and as its interaction with the developed Western economies increased during the 1970s. The party hierarchy simply could not present nearly as many suitably qualified personnel. It remained largely a political and ideologically oriented body, and many senior party officials had little to offer except some administrative ability and an influential constituency. Gierek had brought several economic officials with him from Katowice to Warsaw when he assumed power—the "Silesian Mafia"; some were competent, others not. But he could not hope to influence, through these men, the whole economic bureaucracy.

Eventually, of course, the disasters that overtook the Polish economy were no advertisement for the ability of the technical officials in the Polish government hierarchy. But the majority of these officials were not to blame for what befell their country. The important thing was their steady accretion of power. And what was happening in Poland was being replicated elsewhere. In Hungary the economic positions in the state apparatus were mostly being filled by officials of real ability right up to the prime minister. The same was true of the GDR and to a lesser extent of all the other countries. It was certainly true in Yugoslavia at both the federal and republican levels.

This growing need for expertise as the economy becomes more demanding and as the computer revolution slowly but inexorably encroaches could modify the old nomenklatura system in both Eastern Europe and the Soviet Union. The nomenklatura system has always been a concomitant of the party's supremacy and recognized authority. But in a situation where the authority and even relevance of the party were now being eroded in such important sectors, the invidiousness and sheer inefficiency of the nomenklatura would emerge more clearly than ever. But the nomenklatura was the basic institution of apparatchik privilege. In terms of "withering away" it would probably be the last.

The Military's Role

Eventually this threat to its very relevance could be the most serious danger to the communist party. More immediately, however, the power of the military could be the more obvious constraint on the party's power. The spectacular role played by the military in Poland under General Jaruzelski already raised the specter of the "man on horseback" cantering through a region in which, historically, he was by no means a stranger.[26] And, though Poland after 1981 has provided the most telling example of military power yet seen in communist East Europe, there were other examples of the importance of the military. In Yugoslavia the people's army is widely seen as the ultimate bond of unity, and at the tenth congress of the League of Yugoslav Communists in 1974 this role was recognized by the army's being given three standing representatives in the party presidency.[27] In Romania in the winter of 1986 a despairing Ceaușescu put army officers in charge of some of Romania's energy plants.

There have also been examples (or suggestions) of the army opposing rather than supporting civil authority. In Albania, for example, the defense minister and his chief of staff were purged in 1974 for allegedly opposing government policy. There was a small-scale army conspiracy against Todor Zhivkov in 1965.[28] In 1972 General Ion Şerb was arrested in Romania apparently for passing information to the Soviets. In February 1983 there also were reports in the Western press of an abortive military coup against Ceauşescu.[29]

The military in Eastern Europe is undoubtedly an important political factor. But what is debatable is not so much its importance as its independence. Taking East European history since 1945, it has been not its independence but its *subordination* that has been its strongest characteristic. It remains, as December 1981 in Poland showed, the guarantor of the existing order, not its challenger. And the more powerful it becomes in that capacity, the more civil authority will appreciate it. As for the Soviets, the more efficiently the East European military can keep order the less they themselves need to be concerned. In times of future crisis they would be spared the task of having to restore order themselves. They have had to do this twice: Hungary 1956 and Czechoslovakia 1968. They have narrowly escaped having to do it twice in Poland: in 1956 and 1981. They might be prepared to see the East European military become a bit more powerful than they would ideally like if they felt that they themselves would have no need to step in again. Expediency might, therefore, stretch Soviet tolerance.

A New Unorthodoxy?

But toward the end of the 1980s what concerned the growing number of would-be reformers in Eastern Europe was whether the Soviet Union would show any tolerance of *them*. By reformers here are meant those advocating some systemic political and economic change. Would the Gorbachev leadership accept that the situation in Eastern Europe demanded change to such an extent? Is that what Gorbachev had meant when he spoke of "radical reform" at the Twenty-seventh CPSU congress?

Advocates of systemic reform existed in every East European country. But only in Hungary, Poland, and Yugoslavia were they vocal or even visible. They differed among themselves in many respects as they responded to different circumstances, but they were united in the conviction that the system in Eastern Europe was at an impasse both economically and politically. The viability and even the survival of the system depended on its transformation. Economically they stood for measures that had already become familiar. They could be subsumed under the term "market mechanism." Politically their ideas were newer and more daring. They advocated the toleration of dissent and legitimate pressure groups inside the party, the building up of the power of the trade unions, of parliament, and of other organizations as "complementary" loci of power. In short, they advocated a political pluralism, but one still vaguely (and somehow) under the party aegis.

Some of their economic ideas might coincide with what Gorbachev had in mind at the Twenty-seventh CPSU congress. Their political ideas would almost certainly not. In the prevailing context they were subversively revisionist, and from the Soviet point of view they were as objectionable and almost as risky in independent Yugoslavia as in satellite Hungary. They were, after all, a "threat to socialism," and for any Soviet leadership such a threat in Yugoslavia could eventually be as serious as any such threat in Hungary.

They would also involve revising Leninism—its fundamentals not just its marginalia. And revising Lenin would eventually mean repudiating him. By chipping away at the pedestal on which they have placed Lenin, the communists would lose their heritage. Much of that heritage has gone already. Stalin in the Soviet Union, Bierut in Poland, Novotoný in Czechoslovakia, Rákosi in Hungary—these and many lesser gods have had to be cleared from the communist pantheon. Because the losses have been so embarrassing, those gods remaining have had to be revered all the more. None more so than Lenin. If he begins to lose his infallibility, then the whole system is in jeopardy. It loses both its assumptions and its pretensions.

The more sensible among the purveyors of the new political ideas have been aware of these dangers. Their strategy seemed to be to proceed as unobtrusively and decorously as possible—trying to appear as harmless as possible. They saw two dangers. The first, of course, was regime suppression. The second, based on precedent, was the momentum reform acquires once a breakthrough has been made. For the present, the first danger was greater than the second. But the more level-headed reformers had learned from the East European experience that, in systems supposedly subject to objective laws, the unexpected happens with disconcerting frequency.

2 Soviet–East European Relations

Victory in World War II made the Soviet Union what tsarist Russia had been after the middle of the eighteenth century: a great power. Its power rested on several pillars: military strength, its reputation as victor over Nazi Germany, the then extensive attractions of communist ideology, and its dominance over Eastern Europe.

It is the last pillar that concerns us here. Eastern Europe was considered crucial by the Soviet Union in 1945 and is still so considered. No other region has been looked upon as so vital to its interests. This has not meant that Eastern Europe was always on the top of its agenda of concerns. But it has meant that the Soviet Union's predominance in the region was, and remains, nonnegotiable. Eastern Europe is more than a sphere of influence; it is much more an area of control.

This importance of Eastern Europe from the Soviet perspective cannot be explained by any single factor. Several factors, some of them interacting, can best explain it. Indeed, Soviet policy toward Eastern Europe can be viewed in terms of the relative weight given by successive Soviet leaderships to these different factors at given times.

Briefly, Moscow's perceptions of Eastern Europe's value have been:[1]

1. As a *defensive* glacis. Obviously, this mainly applies in the military sphere, but more recently it has also acquired an ideological aspect in that Eastern Europe has been partly seen as a protection for the Soviet Union against Western liberalism—especially by ideological conservatives. In the event, of course, Eastern Europe has proved less of an ideological moat than a conveyor belt—of both Western sedition and its own.

2. As a basis for an *offensive* strategy. This "springboard" function of Eastern Europe has had three aspects: (a) Ideological: here Eastern Europe is seen as both the vanguard and the first fruits of the world

communist movement—an example for the rest of the world to follow. (b) Military: either for purposes of intimidation or aggression, Eastern Europe is seen as an essential forward base. (c) Political: Eastern Europe is seen as a suitable base for initiatives designed to manipulate Western Europe, especially the Federal Republic of Germany.

3. As the nucleus of an international bloc of political and diplomatic support in world politics. The building and expansion of an ostensibly allied grouping of states was considered essential if the Soviets were to be viewed by world opinion in the same light as the United States.

4. As a source of Soviet political and ideological legitimization. This closely interacts with some of the preceding perceptions. But there is evidently a Soviet conviction that the continuing allegiance of Eastern Europe and the preservation there of a system basically similar to its own is essential, not only for the Soviet system's domestic legitimacy, but also for its overall standing and reputation. Thus the ignominy incurred from periodic repression in Eastern Europe is seen as less damaging than basic changes in the system that could make such repression unnecessary. It is this factor that, more than anything else, has made any ideas about the Soviets tolerating any Finlandization of Eastern Europe basically unrealistic.

5. Originally, as a source of economic exploitation. This is now part of history. But even now the question of whether Eastern Europe is an economic asset or liability to the Soviets is much more complex than would at first appear.[2] Eastern Europe, however, has long since ceased to be the bounteous source of loot it was in Stalin's time. Until about 1954 it played a considerable role in the postwar recovery of the Soviet Union.[3]

6. As part of the Soviet heroic mythology. Eastern Europe was the base from which Hitler attacked the Soviet Union. But much more important, it was the last region to be "liberated" before the final defeat of Nazi Germany. As reflected in Brezhnev's emotional outburst to the Czechoslovak leaders in August 1968, many Russians regard the blood spilled in those last weeks of world war as giving them almost a proprietory interest in Eastern Europe. It is a Russian emotional factor not to be taken lightly.[4]

These, then, have been the main Soviet perceptions of the importance of Eastern Europe. Obviously, they are not all of equal importance, and the order in which they have been given above is not intended to reflect their relative weight. Nor have all maintained the same level of importance over the last four decades. And, to repeat, these perceptions are not mutually exclusive. In fact, some are difficult, if not impossible, to separate.[5]

The Special Importance of the GDR

In trying to identify the shorter-term Soviet perceptions of East-Central Europe it is easy to overlook the historical dimensions of the situation that Soviet power has created. It is in this connection that the special importance to the Soviet Union of the German Democratic Republic must be stressed.[6] It was the division of Germany after World War II and then the (almost literal) cementing of that division by the creation of the GDR that constituted the single best Russian historical gain from World War II: the emasculation of German power. Thus one of the most basic historical security ambitions of Russia had been satisfied.[7] The GDR has emerged in the course of forty years as a strong economic power—not just by East European, but by world, standards. This is a remarkable achievement. The GDR's importance, however, is not so much in what it is, or in what it has achieved, but in the strengthening of Russian power that its mere existence signifies. This distinction between existence and significance has led to much international ambivalence about the GDR. For what it *is*, the GDR is often viewed with disdain as an artificial creation with rulers sometimes inhumanly repressive. But for what it *signifies* in terms of European and even world stability, it is largely viewed, if not with satisfaction, then at least with a considerable relief.

The views of Germans, East and West, are discussed in chapter 3. By the rest of Europe—again both East and West—and by many Americans, the GDR is mainly seen as an imperfect but fairly effective means of maintaining a status quo that, if disturbed, could have serious international repercussions.[8] The Soviet Union, it is true, may originally have toyed with the idea of a reunited, neutralized Germany. Occasionally since then it appears to have refloated the notion under different guises. It was implicit in the Rapacki Plan, for example. But the Soviet Union, of all countries, would countenance nothing but the idea of a castrated Germany. Moreover, whatever diplomatic gains the Soviet political leaders might see deriving from any change in the status quo, the Soviet *strategic* interest in Central Europe would seem to make this an issue in which the military could well have the decisive—and conservative—voice.[9]

The future of the GDR, therefore, and hence the division of Germany, seems assured for the foreseeable future. It will remain one of the great paradoxes of our time. More palpably than any other member of the Soviet alliance—except perhaps Mongolia—the GDR is both the creation and protectorate (however vigorous) of the Soviet Union. Yet it is accorded an almost universal toleration for what it avoids rather than for what it represents or has achieved. It is an artificial national entity performing an international service, essentially negative but deemed highly necessary.

It is this character and function of the GDR, even more than its economic power and potential, that makes it the Soviet Union's most important satellite. Poland, of course, is much larger, with over twice the population and territory. Its subordination to Moscow does indeed remove the challenge of an historically defiant adversary. But it is the character and function of the GDR that makes Soviet control over Poland all the more essential. Since 1945 Poland has been the path to the GDR and to mastery in Central Europe. And it was this aspect of Poland's importance that, perhaps as much as anything else, made it essential that Solidarity be crushed in December 1981. For had Solidarity been allowed to take root in Poland, the very survival of the GDR would have been open to question, and this the East German leaders seem to have recognized from the very beginning of Solidarity's short existence. The GDR would have been itself cut off from the Soviet Union, its creator, protector, and main source of economic sustenance. Even worse: with the Federal Republic of Germany (FRG) on one flank, with all its gravitational pull for most East Germans, and a democratizing Poland, on the other, the East German regime doubtlessly felt (and doubtlessly was) in a state approaching siege. The Solidarity episode is far too often seen as one involving only the Soviet Union and Poland. The crucial East German dimension is often ignored.[10]

Northern and Southern Tiers

From a Soviet point of view all parts of Eastern Europe are important, but some are more important than others. The region divides itself in this context into two fairly well-definable areas that for convenience have been called the Northern and Southern Tiers. From a strategic and geopolitical point of view it is the Northern Tier comprising Poland and Czechoslovakia as well as the GDR on which the Soviets have concentrated. The vital importance of the GDR and Poland are obvious. Czechoslovakia's strategic importance has also long been recognized. Even before it came into being, Bismarck himself is recorded as averring that control of Bohemia meant control of Central Europe. Hitler pointed to its location as justification of his annexation in 1939. One of the main reasons for the Soviet invasion in August 1968 was military and strategic, as indeed was the Soviet-inspired coup twenty years earlier. Control of Czechoslovakia was necessary to protect Soviet gains in East-Central Europe against possible allied attack from West Germany and to protect the newly acquired gain of East Germany. It was necessary also to prevent the formation of a broad pro-Western wedge in the heart of Europe made up by Czechoslovakia and Austria. Of the two, Czechoslovakia was strategically the more important. Its acquisition was, therefore, inevitable. (Had it *not* occurred, Austria, for its part, would never have been granted independence in 1955.) And after its acquisition, equally inevitable was not only the Soviet determination to keep it but also to prevent any reversion to a Western orientation, something the Prague Spring of 1968, though ostensibly a communist movement, essentially represented.[11]

All three countries, therefore, have been strategically crucial for the Soviet Union. But they have also disposed of by far the greater part of Eastern Europe's economic strength, wealth, and population. The GDR and the Czech Lands of Czechoslovakia (Bohemia and Moravia) have been easily the most industrially advanced parts of Eastern Europe, while Poland, with valuable raw materials and a rising young population, has had a potential outstripping most countries in any part of the continent.[12]

Southeastern Europe has never had such value—militarily, economically, or even strategically—despite the undoubted value of Yugoslavia's coastline, Albania's proximity to Italy, and Bulgaria's adjacency to the two volatile Western allies, Greece and Turkey. Moreover, Soviet control over this area has been gravely weakened. The defection of Yugoslavia in 1948, of Albania in 1961, and the degree of autonomy Romania has achieved and maintained since the early 1960s have left Bulgaria as Moscow's only true dependency in the region. These defections in southeastern Europe were facilitated mainly by geography, with Romania's impunity so far mainly accountable by its being a negligible threat to Soviet security.[13] In the Northern Tier there have been no such geographical difficulties, and its importance to Soviet security is apparently considered just as important as it ever was in Moscow. The contrast between Soviet military passivity in Yugoslavia and Albania and their military decisiveness—true, after much deliberation and with great reluctance—in the GDR (1953), Czechoslovakia (1968), and Poland (by proxy in 1981) has often been noted and is not difficult to explain. In Hungary, too, in 1956, the Soviet response was decisive. Hungary is, strictly speaking, not a Northern Tier country. Soviet military strategy places it in the Southern Tier. But in no other sense can it be considered a southeast European or Balkan country. Nor does Moscow regard it as such. It is essentially middle European, with a gravitation toward Austria and Germany. As a connecting link with the northern and southern parts of Eastern Europe, its situation is, of course, vital. But in terms of relations, and particularly confrontation, with the West it has never been as important as the GDR, Poland, and Czechoslovakia. This may partly explain the degree of latitude it has been allowed in domestic reform. In 1956, however, it far overstepped the bounds of the permissible, and its geographical location presented no difficulties of coercion.

The course of history in southeastern Europe, therefore, has followed a quite different course over the last forty years from the countries of the Northern Tier. The question being raised in the late 1980s, however, was whether the situation could soon present Moscow with chances to make up lost ground. This question was being raised most seriously about Yugoslavia.[14] The fact that the country survived Tito's death without immediate or early disintegration perhaps induced in many outside observers—and perhaps in many Yugoslavs, too—a complacency that subsequent events confounded. Economically, politically, and in matters regarding nationalities, the deterioration began to accelerate alarmingly. Instability in a multinational state is not in itself a condition that need cause much alarm; it is a common, almost natural, situation. It is when the line is crossed between instability and disintegration that the alarm should be raised. And Yugoslavia by the mid-1980s might have seemed perilously near that line. Some competent observers (including well-wishers) were saying the line had already been crossed (see chapter 12). Albania, for its own part, survived the death of Enver Hoxha in April 1985 with apparent quiet and stability. But, though the leadership under Ramiz Alia was honoring Hoxha's legacy of avoiding entangling alliances, Albania would sooner or later be faced with the agonizing and divisive foreign policy decision of the choice of future allies, since the isolationism attempted after the break with China in 1978 can hardly be viable over the long term[15] (see chapter 12).

Assuming, therefore, that the Soviet Union was in itself in a position to take advantage of opportunities presented, it would seem that Yugoslavia and Albania could be attractive propositions. Military intervention was presumably not being contemplated: nothing would serve to unite Yugoslavia more than the threat of Soviet invasion. What might be contemplated, though, was economic and political penetration of both countries, with Yugoslavia, of course, as the main target. As for Romania, there was no reason to believe that the malaise produced by Ceauşescu's misrule would be reversed. The nationalist anti-Soviet (and occasionally anti-Hungarian) card he still played with customary caution and skill. But it was meeting with nothing like the response it had fifteen to twenty years before. In any case, economic mismanagement alone might possibly force the Ceauşescu regime into a more accommodating political posture vis-à-vis Moscow.

All three independent or dissident Balkan communist countries, therefore, presented Moscow with clear opportunities. Any noticeable increase of Soviet presence or influence in any or all of them would, of course, alarm other countries in the area, at least one of which, the Greece of Andreas Papandreous, had already been inclined to tilt eastward in the trappings of foreign policy.[16] Athens could well realize the dangers of playing with fire in the event of a partial Soviet return to Belgrade, or even Tirana. Italy would certainly respond nervously, and NATO as a whole could see its whole position in the southeast Mediterranean threatened. But the Soviets, unless their foreign initiatives had become cautious to the point of being calcified, might well calculate on an ephemeral and ineffectual Western response, that alarm would not be a prelude to action, and that after the initial Western fury the rationalizations of appeasement would assert themselves. There were indeed few indications on the Western side to indicate that these calculations would be wrong.

Thus though the Northern Tier still retained its primacy of importance for Moscow, real chances seemed to be beckoning in the Southern Tier. The former was still of greater significance, but the latter now seemed the region of greater opportunity.

The Mechanics of Soviet Control ≥

Before discussing some aspects of Soviet policy toward Eastern Europe it is as well to recall the main instruments of control, information, and communication at Moscow's disposal in its relations with its client states in the region. These instruments are both multilateral and bilateral. The main multilateral instruments are the Council for Mutual Economic Assistance (Comecon) and the Warsaw Pact. Comecon is discussed in chapter 4. The Warsaw Pact will be discussed later in this chapter.

Obviously the most potent instrument is the number of Soviet troops stationed in each country. In the GDR there are believed to be about 400,000; in Czechoslovakia some 60,000; in Poland some 30,000, mainly for communications purposes; and in Hungary about 50,000. Their presence is regulated by bilateral treaties with the Soviet Union, which also has general long-term bilateral treaties of cooperation with all its East European allies.[17]

Other more direct and immediate instruments of control, information, and communication may be listed as follows:

1.   The Soviet state security (KGB) agents in the different East European countries.
2.   Warsaw Pact advisers and military intelligence (GRU) agents.
3.   CPSU representatives reporting to the Central Committee department in Moscow responsible for relations with ruling parties.

Part of the functions of the Soviet embassies in East Europe are well enough known, particularly those of the ambassador. Often they have more viceregal than representational functions. Andropov's active role in Budapest during the Hungarian Revolution received retrospective publicity immediately on his being appointed Soviet party leader. Successive Soviet ambassadors to Bulgaria have had their interference in Bulgarian domestic affairs paraded with seeming pride by the domestic media. Throughout Eastern Europe there have been examples similar to the Bulgarian. Petr Abrasimov in the GDR, the fluently Polish-speaking Stanislav Pilotovich in Poland, and Stepan Chervenenko in Czechoslovakia all actively and blatantly interfered in domestic affairs. Chervenenko's clumsy attempts in August 1968 immediately after the invasion to form a "revolutionary" government are well described by Zdeněk Mlynář.[18] As for Abrasimov and Pilotovich, they summoned local ministers and party leaders and made official visits without even informing their hosts of what they were doing. In fact, it was this viceregal behavior that led to their undoing. An outraged Gierek used his waning influence with Brezhnev to get Pilotovich recalled in 1978. And Honecker, who had apparently always resented Abrasimov's behavior, secured a change of ambassador after a visit to Moscow in early 1983.

Finally, there has been the direct communication between Moscow itself and the different East European capitals. This takes place at many levels, from that of party leaders or prime ministers down to relatively junior state or party department heads. In view of the volume of cooperation of all kinds between Moscow and its partners, it can be assumed that this form of communication is brisk indeed and is often two-way rather than solely initiated from Moscow. Sometimes the traffic will be direct, from one official to another; sometimes the concerned embassy or consulate acts as middleman.

The most intriguing variant of this direct contact with Moscow is the unofficial contacts that undoubtedly exist. It is these contacts that often give rise to the wildest speculation, with the speculations often being in inverse ratio to the knowledge about them. Nearly all the speculation, therefore, can be discounted, but over the last thirty years some reliable firsthand evidence has emerged. There is little doubt, for example, that hard-line elements in Czechoslovakia in 1968, like Vasil Bilak and Alois Indra, found ready ears in Moscow and Kiev.[19] Circumstantial evidence suggested that Stefan Olszowski, the ranking reputed hard-liner in the Polish leadership, was, after December 1981, favored by a group in the Soviet leadership. It was almost certain that some Soviet leaders had direct contacts with GDR Defense Minister Heinz Hoffmann and security chief Erich Mielke. The rumors about such intra-alliance groupings and pairings have been endless. The dubiousness, even absurdity, of many rumors should not obscure the plausibility, even probability, of some. In periods of leadership uncertainty or disarray, either in Moscow or any East European capital (or both), such alignments have assumed great importance.

The Warsaw Pact

The Warsaw Pact—or, more correctly, the Warsaw Treaty Organization (WTO)—was established on 14 May 1955. It was to last for twenty years, but its prolongation was assured for another ten years provided no moves were made to dissolve it at least one year before the expiration date. In 1985 it was renewed on the same basis as it had been founded. Its founder members (there have been no additions) were the Soviet Union, Albania, Bulgaria, Czechoslovakia, the GDR, Hungary, Poland, and Romania. Albania formally left the pact in 1968 after having been at odds with it for several years. The revolutionary government in Hungary tried to leave in 1956 but was suppressed by the Soviet invasion.

The pact was created one day before the signing of the Austrian State Treaty, which gave Austria independence with neutrality, and five days before the entry of the now sovereign West Germany (the Federal Republic of Germany) into the North Atlantic Treaty Organization (NATO). It was ostensibly, therefore, the counterweight to a Western alliance that had been immeasurably strengthened by the addition of the FRG. Indeed, the preamble to the Warsaw Treaty cites as *casus foederis* the existence of a "remilitarized Western Germany" and its integration into the "north Atlantic bloc."[20]

The role of the Warsaw Pact in East-West military relations is outside the scope of this study. But what is of direct concern is the pact's role in Eastern Europe itself as an instrument of integration in both the military and political sense. For several years, however, the pact, rather like its economic counterpart, Comecon, remained mainly inactive. It was only in the early 1960s that it began acquiring real military and political content. Warsaw Pact military maneuvers were first held in 1961 and became a regular feature of its operations. The Soviets also began delivering more modern equipment to the East European armies.

Politically, the pact was still slower in developing. Khrushchev appears to have had this political development in mind in 1964 when ruminating about the need for greater foreign policy coordination in the bloc.[21] But, as Robert Hutchings points out, the pact's Political Consultative Committee (PCC), supposed under its statute to meet twice a year, met only six times in the first ten years of its existence (1956–65). In 1965 Brezhnev repeated his predecessor's call for closer foreign policy coordination within the framework of the pact[22] and was reportedly met with countersuggestions from both Romania and Czechoslovakia calling for a greater East European voice in decisionmaking.[23]

Subsequently, it was in the framework of a "joint action" of the Warsaw Pact that the Soviet Union and four of its allies—Poland, the GDR, Hungary, and Bulgaria—invaded Czechoslovakia in August 1968. But the invasion was actually conducted as a Soviet military operation led by the commander-in-chief of Soviet ground forces.

Just a few months after the invasion of Czechoslovakia, at the March 1969 meeting of pact leaders in Budapest, significant changes were announced in the pact's structure. Probably the most important aspect of these changes was the creation of three new bodies: the Committee of Defense Ministers; the Military Council; and the Committee for the Coordination of Defense Technology. All of the new bodies and the changes were military. There was no effort to implement the idea of a political-civilian coordinating body for foreign policy.

The Committee of Defense Ministers was to serve as the supreme military consultative organ of the pact and was to be composed of the members' defense ministers. Since 1971 it has usually met once a year. Formally at least, this was a Soviet concession to the East Europeans since their defense ministers, previously subordinate to the Soviet commander-in-chief of the pact's joint command, were now officially catapulted to the level of the Soviet defense minister. Little is known about the Military Council, which apparently meets twice a year. It evidently has consultative and recommendatory functions, is dominated by Soviet officers, but consists also of a senior field officer or flag officer from each of the East European members. The Committee for the Coordination of Military Technology coordinates military research and is charged with standardizing equipment and weapons systems. It contains East European representatives but, again, is dominated by Soviet officers.

The addition of these three bodies was designed, at least in part, to give the East Europeans a greater sense of participation—and coresponsibility—in Warsaw Pact policy and action. As such, they were an important part of the Brezhnev leadership's general policy of "togetherness" between Soviets and East Europeans after August 1968.

But such organizational changes could not hide overwhelming Soviet dominance. As Hutchings puts it:

> Within the command and consultative bodies of the Warsaw Pact, Soviet dominance is assured not only by the political and military preponderance of the USSR, but also by the overwhelming presence of Soviet officers in key positions. The Warsaw Pact commander-in-chief and chief-of-staff (and first deputy commander-in-chief) are Soviet generals, the former also serving as head of the Military Council. The Committee for the Coordination of Military Technology is headed by a Soviet general, the Joint Secretariat by a Soviet deputy foreign minister. There is a Soviet deputy chief of staff, a Soviet inspector general and a Soviet assistant commander-in-chief for logistics; and Soviet officers command Warsaw Pact ground, air naval and air defense forces.[24]

In addition, a Soviet military liaison mission is attached to each East European ministry of defense, headed by an officer of field rank with numerous Soviet army, naval, and air force officers. All this constitutes part of the Soviet mechanics of control in Eastern Europe.

But it should be emphasized that the joint command of the Warsaw Pact forces, headed by its Soviet commander-in-chief, exercises administrative jurisdiction over the Warsaw Pact "Joint Armed Forces," which are specifically assigned to these forces by the East European governments concerned. East European military forces generally remain under the control of their national governments, and even those specifically assigned to the Warsaw Pact are ultimately responsible to their own governments. (The notable exception is the East German forces, which are ultimately under the control of the Warsaw Pact joint command.)

To quote Hutchings again:

> Thus the grand total of fifty-four non-Soviet divisions [i.e., the East European divisions] can in no way be counted in overall Warsaw Pact operational strength, if for no other reason than the fact that mobilizing these forces (assuming this could be done at all) would be such a cumbersome undertaking that the "surprise factor," so essential to Soviet military doctrine and practice, would be lost. As far as can be ascertained, Soviet war planning is predicated, not on mass Warsaw Pact mobilization, but on the transfer to a unified command of a relatively small number of specially designated East European formations, those included in the "first strategic echelon" and maintained at high levels of combat readiness.[25]

But, finally, it must be stressed that in case of war the Warsaw Pact military structure and all its trappings would apparently simply melt into the Soviet high command. Organizationally this would be simplified by the fact that its commander-in-chief and chief of staff also serve as Soviet first deputy defense minister and first deputy chief of the Soviet general staff. Even in peacetime some East European key military units —air defense units, Polish and East German naval units, most long-range bomber squadrons—are directly controlled by the Soviet military. The Warsaw Pact, therefore, has remained "in essence an administrative organization—not—an operational military command in the usual sense of the term."[26]

The Soviet Dilemma in Eastern Europe

Soviet relations with the East European countries operate on two levels: the *national* (direct) and the *domestic* (indirect). The national level involves relations between the Soviet Union and any given East European country, through whatever channel—party, state, intelligence services, military, personal groupings, etc. The domestic level involves relations between the ruling elites of each East European country and society in that country. The two levels are obviously far from being mutually exclusive.

The Stalinist system in Eastern Europe between 1948 and 1953 was mainly designed to further a process of Gleichschaltung on both these levels: at the national level through the imposition of leaderships trusted (or less mistrusted than others) by Moscow; and at the domestic level through revolutionary transformation laying the foundations for socialist development.[27]

Since Stalin the main general aim of Soviet policy toward Eastern Europe has been to find the right balance between cohesion and viability. *Cohesion* in this context means a situation where—allowing for some degree of diversity caused by differing local conditions—there is a general conformity of both domestic and foreign policies as well as an identification of the institutions implementing these policies in both the Soviet Union and its East European dependencies. *Viability* can be defined as a degree of confidence, credibility, and efficiency in the East European states that would increasingly legitimize Communist rule there and consequently reduce the Soviet need for a preemptive preoccupation with the region.[28]

The Soviet Union has never been able to find the right balance between the two. From Moscow's point of view the two postulates of cohesion and viability are complementary and interacting. They are not subject to separation. They are not exclusive; the one should not exist without the other. Recent East European history, however, has tended to show cohesion predominating over viability—with the cohesion produced by actual or threatened coercion. This has been due to a general popular rejection of Soviet hegemony and the system and values associated with it, a rejection that has necessitated various degrees of repression either directly by the Soviet Union or by the local governing elites whose rule is guaranteed by it. The attainment of viability, and the legitimacy ensuing from it, would necessitate three types of basic change: (a) economic reform, (b) a reform of political institutions, and (c) changes in the relationship with the Soviet Union.

These three conditions have never been met anywhere in Eastern Europe. For a brief deceptive period in Poland in 1956, Czechoslovakia in 1968, and Poland again in 1981, it may have seemed possible to some that they might be. But the processes that seemed to be pointing in the required direction were cut short by erosion after 1956, invasion in

1968, and repression in 1981. They were cut short because they showed the Soviets' dilemma in Eastern Europe, which is that viability, and the consequent legitimization and consensus between rulers and ruled, can be achieved only on terms that are inconsonant with their rule, as conceived and exercised since World War II.

Viability Under Khrushchev?

The point was made in chapter 1 that it was probably in the 1960s that several of the East European regimes came closest to acquiring a degree of legitimacy vis-à-vis their own populations. This was because they were inclined, and felt free enough, to work toward that degree of viability that is indispensable for legitimacy. It occurred in what can be called the Khrushchev period in Eastern Europe.

The upheavals in Hungary and Poland in 1956 had occurred because of the unviability of Stalin's system and because nothing basically new had been established in its place. And it was this omission, after 1956, that Khrushchev sought to rectify. Within a year of the Hungarian Revolution and the upheaval in Poland, his leadership had been both recognized and apparently consolidated in the Soviet Union; an outward appearance of unity had been created in the world communist movement. He could now turn his attention to creating a new system in Eastern Europe.

Against a theoretical background of newly enunciated principles of equally governing relations between socialist states, Khrushchev saw the Council for Mutual Economic Assistance and to a lesser extent the Warsaw Pact as the main institutional tools to weld a new and less brittle cohesion between the Soviet Union and Eastern Europe and among the East European states themselves. But Khrushchev, much more than his predecessor and more than any of his successors so far, saw the importance of viability as well as cohesion. Perhaps there was no conscious design or calculation in what he did. Even more than most political leaders he seemed to depend on a few (usually sound) rudimentary notions of what was required, and then on any number of improvised (and sometimes unsound) means of trying to do it. But whatever the inexactness of his conceptualization and the vagaries of his execution, Khrushchev both pursued policies and generated an atmosphere that broke the rigid frame of Stalinist conformity. His aim was to make the communist system more viable, more legitimate, and more attractive to its own citizens and to those laboring under other systems.

After the very uneven process known as de-Stalinization in Eastern Europe, which occurred in the 1950s, the most noticeable, positive reform measures of the Khrushchev era were those affecting economic structure, planning, and policy, which took place in the 1960s. Practically every country was affected by these measures, and in view of the close interaction between Khrushchev's leadership in Moscow and Eastern European reform, it was hardly coincidental that the go-ahead signal for them was given by the publication of the Liberman proposals in the Soviet Union in 1962 (see chapter 4). Reform blueprints or series of single measures for greater economic efficiency subsequently appeared in the GDR, Czechoslovakia, Hungary, and Bulgaria, and even the Polish and Romanian leaders were constrained to make some efforts at piecemeal change.

These reform measures—again, an illustration of growing diversity—met with different fates in different countries. In the GDR and Hungary they were to achieve some success; in Czechoslovakia they were an important ingredient in the heady mixture of the Prague Spring of 1968; in Bulgaria they were hardly given a chance to operate before they were withdrawn. But just as important as their degrees of success or failure were their embryonic and potential effects on the political and social life of the countries involved. Even the more cautious of these reforms, because they departed from the old command economic system, tended to encourage change in other branches of public life as well. This is what bold and perceptive reformers realized and sought to accelerate; it was also what perceptive and apprehensive party apparatchiki realized and sought to brake. In spite of this resistance to change, some embryonic form of political life began to reemerge. This was particularly the case in Czechoslovakia (not to mention the distinctive case of Yugoslavia, which was developing its own system in a completely different environment). In Czechoslovakia the existence of social and professional interest groups came not only to be recognized (they had always existed) but also to be quietly accepted, and, as a result, the leading role of the Communist party, the fundamental power of Marxism-Leninism, began to be slightly and quietly modified. As the amount of leeway grew for the interaction between various interest groups, so the party's direct and total control over public life tended to diminish, despite all the official disclaimers that anything of the sort was happening. The degree of such development must not, of course, be exaggerated. What is really being discussed here is more the potential than the actual, and, except for

Yugoslavia, it was only in Czechoslovakia and perhaps Hungary that the signs referred to above were becoming clearly visible. But, for all its limitations, the emergence of pluralism in some Eastern European states was a political fact of life of increasing importance in the 1960s.

Khrushchev lost power in October 1964, but the developments that began in Eastern Europe during his period of rule continued for several years after. In this sense the Khrushchev era in Eastern Europe ended in August 1968 rather than October 1964. The momentum of what had begun during his rule increased after it, and had he remained in power no one would have tried harder to check it than he. He allowed forces to be set in motion that he appears to have seriously underestimated. One of these was certainly that of Eastern European nationalism—a strange miscalculation for a man politically groomed in the Ukraine; another was the threat to Communist party absolutism by other political, economic, social, and cultural forces within some Eastern European societies. Thus forces that were first considered feasible to harness for purposes of legitimizing communist rule were found to be so strong as to undermine the legitimacy they had been intended to strengthen.[29] In the pursuit of viability, the goal of cohesion was made less attainable. Under Khrushchev Soviet control in Eastern Europe eroded in three specific cases. One was the rather special case of Albania, whose leaders, from nationalistic motives, took advantage of the Sino-Soviet dispute and exchanged Moscow's tutelage for that of Peking.[30] More important were the cases of Romania and Czechoslovakia. In the former, national autonomy developed into a nationalist Romanian policy, repudiating Soviet hegemony, not openly as in the Albanian case, but steadily through the skillful manipulation of various factors, of which the Sino-Soviet dispute was perhaps the most important.[31] In the Czechoslovak case, domestic reform rushed headlong toward a repudiation of all known variants of the communist system itself.[32] Both processes were set in motion during the Khrushchev era and were made possible by it; both accelerated after his departure.

There were several reasons for this acceleration after 1964, of which perhaps two were preeminent. The first was the lack of decisiveness on the part of the Soviet leadership in Eastern Europe for about three years after Khrushchev's fall from power. The most striking example of this was in relations with West Germany, the most serious European foreign policy issue the Soviet-led alliance had to face throughout the 1960s. The overtures made to Eastern Europe by the Kiesinger-Brandt coalition in late 1966, including the offer to establish diplomatic relations, appear to have caused serious indecision in Moscow resulting in disarray in the ranks of the Soviet allies themselves. Apart from Romania, which reacted with positive alacrity, there seems little doubt that Hungary and Bulgaria were prepared to respond favorably to the West German initiative. But Soviet hesitation resulted in Ulbricht and Gomułka assuming a totally disproportionate influence on alliance decisionmaking in this context.[33]

Subsequently, when Romania independently established diplomatic relations with Bonn in early 1967, the rest of the alliance closed ranks to reject the West German overtures, and Moscow then assumed the lead in a strong anti-West German campaign. But in the months of December 1966 and January 1967 East Berlin and Warsaw seemed to wield the decisive influence. This was but the most conspicuous example of a vacuum in Soviet leadership, greater even than that which occurred after Stalin's death. In a way this was perhaps understandable; the new Soviet leadership was too preoccupied with consolidating its power in the Soviet Union itself to be able to think and act decisively in Eastern Europe.

The second important reason for the acceleration of processes that had begun before Khrushchev's fall was simply that the seriousness of the consequences and implications of some of them could not be realized until much later. The most obvious case of this was the transformation in Czechoslovakia. This slowly began in 1963, or even earlier, although its explosive significance did not really become evident until early 1968.

But even allowing for the difficulties in anticipating the course of developments in Czechoslovakia, there remains more than a suspicion of Soviet indecisiveness. For anyone who watched the careering of events in the Prague Spring, the hesitance of the Soviet leadership emerges as a factor in the equation. Moscow left no doubt as to what it did not like in the Czechoslovak situation but considerable doubt about what it was prepared to do about it. Whatever the reasons for this hesitation—internal divisions, broader policy considerations—it was an important factor contributing to the eventual Czechoslovak tragedy.

Cohesion Under Brezhnev

The steps Khrushchev took in Eastern Europe ushered in the era associated with his name. The Soviet-led invasion of Czechoslovakia marked the end of that era and the beginning of a new period in which the relationship between cohesion and viability strongly tilted back in favor of cohesion. The trauma of Czechoslovakia itself, the disruptive potential the Prague Spring had for other parts of Eastern Europe and for the Soviet Union itself, convinced the Soviet leaders that the spirit of innovation and experimentation, of reformation, that had been abroad in Eastern Europe during the sixties had to be substantially curbed. The situation, as they saw it, now demanded a counterreformation, the reinstitution of orthodoxy, as a means of restoring control over Eastern Europe and buttressing the Soviet Union itself against the dangers inherent in the pre-August Czechoslovak developments.[34]

But the need for immunization against any possible reemergence of the "Czechoslovak virus," urgent and immediate though this was, was not the only factor prompting the Soviet leadership to restore cohesion and orthodoxy in Eastern Europe. It was probably coincidence that the Warsaw Pact's declaration in Budapest in March 1969, renewing the call for international relaxation and the convening of a security conference in Europe, was issued only a few weeks before the deposition of Alexander Dubček in Czechoslovakia in April, the political consummation of the military repression of the previous August. But this close chronological proximity does serve to emphasize the linkage between the Soviet determination to stamp out contamination in Eastern Europe, its own sphere of influence, and at the same time to take all possible steps to guard against the dangers of contamination from the West, which closer relations, under the rubric of Brezhnev's Westpolitik, presented. Both they and all the Eastern European leaders were aware that the *very existence* of Western Europe was a destabilizing element in Eastern Europe and that any real interaction between the societies of Eastern and Western Europe might well lead to a new and more dangerous instability.

Détente, therefore—the pressure for it, the perception and the prospects of it—was certainly a strong additional motivation in the Soviet drive for cohesion in Eastern Europe. The almost simultaneous issuance of the Budapest Declaration and the replacement of Dubček by Gustáv Husák in Prague symbolically dramatize the linkage between the trauma over Czechoslovakia and the fears attendant on international relaxation.

It is also tempting to posit another linkage here, highlighted by another event that occurred at almost exactly the same time in 1969 as these events in Budapest and Prague: the clash on the River Ussuri between Soviet and Chinese forces. This incident, which took place on Soviet-held territory disputed by the Chinese, led to dead and wounded on both sides and threatened a war between the two countries. Its impact on the Russian psyche was considerable.

Obviously in the case of war with China, or the perceived imminence of it, any Soviet leadership would have to decide on the best means of ensuring stability in Eastern Europe. It would presumably be realistic enough to assume that this was a factor that had to enter into its calculations. And, given the Brezhnev leadership's determination to restore cohesion in Eastern Europe, if Ussuri was interpreted in Moscow as a possible prelude to a general conflict with China, it would certainly be plausible to add this factor to the two already mentioned as an important, even crucial, motivation for the safety precautions that were taken in Eastern Europe. But seriously though Ussuri was taken in Moscow, prompting, as it did, the large-scale transfer of Soviet troops to the eastern parts of the Soviet Union, there is no convincing evidence that it was taken so gravely as to warrant the switch to a war-footing strategy that would also have involved policy in Eastern Europe. Ussuri and the Chinese threat, therefore, could not realistically be seen as part of the linkage motivating Soviet policy in Eastern Europe from 1969 onward.

There were many who feared immediately after August 1968 that the crushing of the Czechoslovak experiment might bring back something akin to Stalinism in Eastern Europe itself and in the Soviet Union's relation with it. No such regression was attempted. What evolved instead was a complex effort to promote cohesion through comprehensive integration. With its own powerful armed forces and, through the Warsaw Pact, its control over the Eastern European military, with the invasion of Czechoslovakia as a reminder of its ultimate willingness to use them, the Soviet leadership embarked on a policy designed eventually to create a situation in which the circumstances that led to the necessity for invasion would no longer arise. The ideological and legalistic underpinnings of both the invasion of Czechoslovakia and the subsequent policy were provided by the so-called Brezhnev Doctrine that proclaimed the fate of socialism in one country as the business of every other socialist country.

Integration is a term that, in the Soviet–East European context, is most often associated with economics. And the Soviet Union's efforts, mainly through Comecon, to exploit its own and its allies' economic strength and potential have continued to be the most important aspect of its integration policy. These efforts are discussed briefly in chapter 4.[35]

But the integration concept now went much further and wider. There was now greater stress on political, cultural, ideological, and, of course, military integration. In fact, the Brezhnev leadership appears to have been more aware of the unifying potential of the Warsaw Pact than Khrushchev ever was. The regular summit meetings of party leaders represented only the apex of a whole pyramid of varied types of meetings, at senior, intermediate, and junior levels of the various hierarchies, that now took place with great regularity.

On the face of it this Soviet method of consultation might have looked like a genuine conciliar system, an appearance strengthened by the fact that many of the various meetings now being held took place in East European cities and were presided over by East European officials. But it was not a genuine conciliar system: consultation there certainly was, but it was not joint consultation. The inequality of the partners was accepted, and both discussion and decision proceeded on that basis. This is not to deny that serious discussion might have taken place and that sometimes the directed consensus wanted by the Soviets was difficult to reach. The Romanians certainly balked at many attempts to reach decisions they opposed. They developed a policy not to attend meetings where decisions might be taken infringing on their notion of sovereignty, and at meetings they attended their delegates sometimes refused to accept the otherwise general consensus.

Nor were the Romanians entirely alone in disagreement. It became evident from the Hungarian economic press, for example, that in various Comecon meetings the Hungarian delegates put forward specific points of view—currency convertibility, enterprise-to-enterprise cooperation—that were at variance with those of the Soviets.[36] So, presumably, did the Poles and the East Germans from time to time. It could also be assumed that in matters of lesser importance to the Soviet Union, its delegates allowed a real "sense of the meeting" to prevail or occasionally allowed themselves to be dissuaded from their original viewpoint. A rigid, domineering approach at all levels, on all matters, would have been counterproductive. Moreover, one important use of comprehensive consultation by the Soviets was to keep track of allied thinking on a very wide range of subjects. To do this, the occasional opportunity for dissent and self-interest had to be allowed. But on subjects in which the Soviet leadership saw itself vitally or seriously concerned, the consensus had to be directed, and what distinguished the Romanians' posture regarding the Soviet consultative method was their readiness to differ with the Soviets on precisely such matters.

It might be noted in passing that the system of "directed consensus" was, as Giuseppi Boffa points out, the most recent and rather tattered survivor of the old Comintern tradition.[37] The Comintern was disbanded by Stalin in 1943 and then partially replaced by the Cominform in 1947. After the Cominform was dissolved in 1956 Moscow began to depend on another unifying institution, the international communist conference. This met with little success either on a regional or global level. Only three world conferences were held, the last being in 1969.[38] The last European conference was held in East Berlin in 1976.

The new strategy of "directed consensus" did not mean that the Soviet leadership eschewed direct pressure when that was considered necessary. There was evidence of this in the removal of Walter Ulbricht, the East German party leader in the spring of 1971, and in the pressure on Romania and Yugoslavia the following summer. There was also reason to suspect some direct interference in some aspects of Polish domestic policy. Some of the personnel changes in Hungary and the shifts in policy emphasis in the early 1970s were reflections of the Soviet will. The Soviet leaders, therefore, had not assumed the role of hidden persuaders, but they genuinely tried to make the Soviet–East European interaction one where direct pressure was less needed than it was in the first generation of communist rule.

The Soviet attitude toward the Hungarian economic reform (New Economic Mechanism — NEM) is discussed in chapter 6. But it deserves some passing mention here. It could indeed be cited as something of an exception to the generalizations made above. But there seems little doubt that the NEM began in 1968 under a cloud of considerable Soviet suspiciousness, which only grew after the invasion of Czechoslovakia. The Hungarians, however—and here Kádár's stature and persuasiveness must have played a key role—must have convinced Moscow of its relative harmlessness. Their main arguments presumably were (a) Hungary was not taking the Czechoslovak road in 1968 i.e., was not straying into basic political reform as well; (b) it was not asking for any revision of relations with the Soviet Union.

But Soviet suspicions continued and were at least partly responsible for the "shelving" of the reform in the early 1970s and for the demotion of leading reform officials. Later, the Soviet economy was beginning to deteriorate to the point where some parts of the Hungarian experiment, especially agriculture, started to acquire some attractiveness for the Soviet leadership. This was at the beginning of the 1980s. In the meantime, in the face of mounting economic difficulties and perhaps taking advantage of an apparent lack of concern in Moscow in Eastern Europe (discussed below), the Hungarian leadership had mounted a new reform campaign.

Viability Through Consumerism?

Brezhnev's new post-1968 policy began badly. Order was speedily restored in Czechoslovakia in the course of 1969, but at the end of the following year riots broke out on the Baltic coast in Poland and the Polish party leader, Władysław Gomułka, who had once seemed a pillar of stability throughout Eastern Europe, was thrown from power. For a few days it appeared possible that the Soviets would have to do what they most wanted to avoid: invade another East European country.

In the event, the Polish upheaval and the replacement of Gomułka by Edward Gierek led not only to much-needed relief for Soviet policy in Eastern Europe but also raised the hope of a longer-term success.[39] Fears that the mood of the Polish workers who had toppled Gomułka could prove contagious prompted other East European leaders to concentrate more on raising living standards. Gierek himself set out to mollify the national temper in Poland by a series of important concessions, and his example was to some extent followed. "Consumerism" became a basic part of economic policy.

In the GDR it had, in fact, become accepted even before the Polish upheavals. It was also implicit in the Hungarian NEM. It was to become a basic part of the Husák regime's "normalization" policy in Czechoslovakia. It was also embraced in a typically massive Bulgarian way at the end of 1972. Only in Ceaușescu's Romania, with its leader's almost messianic urge toward full industrial development, did it fail to become such an integral part of official policy, though even there the real incomes of most of the population for a while showed signs of improving. The motivation of "consumerism" was largely political, but it was facilitated by such economic factors as cheap raw materials, especially supplies, massive Western credits, and a favorable international climate.

"Consumerism" turned out, however, to be both deceptive and short-lived and hardly survived into the second half of the 1970s. The drastic increase in the price of Soviet oil deliveries to Eastern Europe,[40] prompted by the far more drastic increase in oil prices on the world market, and the international trade recession these increases caused shattered East European hopes of economic progress and prosperity. Western credits, which had been seen as the key to import-led growth and were to be repaid by East European exports to the West, proved to be a millstone every year heavier and more impossible to shake off. The engulfing disasters would have seriously damaged the most flexible and skillfully operated economic structures. As it was, the East European economies in the 1970s had become less flexible. (The exception was the Hungarian, but this also was to become seriously affected.) By 1978 "consumerism" seemed the foolish fancy of long ago. The reality now was the vain struggle to try and make ends meet.

The Soviet reaction to this developing crisis was marked by a lack of decisiveness similar to that of ten years before but in stark contrast to the energy and decision of the first half of the 1970s. It can best be explained by a combination of several factors. One was the undoubted success of the Soviet normalization campaign itself. It produced a calm deceptive to the Soviet leaders as well as to many Western observers. For the Soviets this led to a costly complacency. Obviously, Eastern Europe continued to be for them ultimately their most important geopolitical, strategic area. But this did not prevent Eastern Europe from being "taken for granted." After all, its two recent trouble spots now presented an almost optimistic picture. Gierek, indeed, seemed to have solved the Polish problem, while, riding on the despondent apathy of the Czechoslovak population, the Husák regime seemed to have normalized the situation with remarkable speed. With Eastern Europe quiescent, therefore, the Moscow. leadership could concentrate on those global ambitions, initiatives, and confrontations that characterized Soviet policy in the 1970s. Eastern Europe, which thirty years before had seemed such a global gain, now appeared a stable, small appendage in terms of a worldview motivated not so much by an ideological messianism as by national interests.

Finally, toward the end of the 1970s the physical enfeeblement of Brezhnev and the decline in energy of the leadership as a whole may have had some effect on Soviet decisiveness in Eastern Europe. It is difficult to see how an energetic Soviet leader could have ignored the danger signals multiplying from Poland, for example, after 1978.[41] Brezhnev, therefore, from a Soviet point of view, must take some considerable blame for two of the major upheavals in East European history since World War II: the Prague Spring and the rise of Solidarity —the one because of inexperience, the other because of degeneration.

After his visit to Prague in December 1967 he apparently still considered the Czechoslovak crisis as one affecting the top leadership alone, and in Poland, despite all the signs to the contrary, Gierek could still convince him the situation was under control. Thus, as the two great crises of Soviet domination in Eastern Europe since 1956 began to unfold, Moscow tended to dismiss them as nothing out of the ordinary. It does not speak highly of the efficiency of the Soviet mechanics of control and information, discussed earlier, if such blunders were allowed to happen.

Soviet Crisis Management: The Case of Solidarity

There is no doubt that Soviet domination in Eastern Europe since World War II has provided the region with a certain stability. But before thinking in terms of a Pax Sovietica the following jarring facts are worth noting.

First, two countries, Yugoslavia and Albania, have left the Soviet alliance. *Second*, there have been six major domestic crises requiring the use of force for order to be maintained. These were:

1. The East Berlin Uprising in June 1953.
2. The Polish October of 1956. The prelude to this had been in the Poznan riots in June when fifty-three workers were killed. In October itself confrontation between Polish and Soviet forces was only narrowly averted.
3. The Hungarian Revolution, October–November 1956.
4. The Prague Spring in Czechoslovakia, 1968.
5. The Baltic riots in Poland, December 1970.
6. Solidarity in Poland, 1980–81. +1976?

These crises were not random occurrences. They should be seen as symptomatic not so much as the failure of Soviet rule *in* Eastern Europe but more as of its incompatibility *with* Eastern Europe. The crises before Solidarity are very much part of history, as is the Soviet response to them.[42] The Soviet response to Solidarity, however, though by no means ignored in the bevy of books that have appeared since December 1981, is worth a brief discussion in the context of this chapter.

The Soviet leadership appeared quite unprepared for the fall of Gierek in September 1980. It was familiar enough with Poland probably not to be too shaken by the eruption of strikes on the Baltic coast. But Gierek's fall and—much more important—the formal acceptance (no matter how insincere) of a free trade union by the Polish authorities shook Moscow out of its complacency. The latter was quite unacceptable. Involving as it did the heresy of *dvoevlastie*, or dual power, it struck at one of the basic pillars of the Soviet system and of "real socialism." But, though shaken, the Soviet leadership might well have been convinced that this was simply a passing phase, that the party with the aid of the police would soon regain control of the situation.

This probably explains Soviet calmness in the first weeks of the crisis and their willingness to rely mainly on financial aid to restore the situation. As in Czechoslovakia in 1968, so in Poland in 1980, Moscow's initial perception of the situation was mistaken. The Czechoslovak crisis was seen as one confined to the party leadership; the Polish was seen as economic, involving wages, prices, availability of goods in the shops, etc. A 450 million ruble long-term credit in hard currency was given in September 1980 and new Soviet loans shortly afterward. In fact, in the winter of 1980–81, Soviet money almost literally poured into Poland. Some Western observers even put the total of Soviet assistance as high as nearly $5 billion.[43] Complacency, therefore, was the first Soviet response to the crisis. The second was economic help.

There then followed two more types of response, both of a threatening nature: the one political; the other military. These responses were not compartmentalized: the economic, the political, and the military overlapped. While the money was pouring in, therefore, the Soviets began to join the East Germans and the Czechoslovaks in vehement criticisms of Polish developments. As early as November 1980 there were hints in the Soviet media about the possibility of invasion, and these took on a more concrete form at the beginning of December with a buildup of Soviet troops on both the Soviet and East German side of the Polish frontier. But the crisis seemed almost immediately to be defused by the Warsaw Pact summit in December, i.e., while the military buildup was still taking place, which affirmed support for Kania, the new Polish party leader, and agreed that his new leadership should be given time to bring the situation under control.

Soviet media criticism resumed in earnest only when the union Rural Solidarity was established for the peasants at the end of January 1981. This, combined with the apparently increased state of military readiness on Poland's frontiers, renewed fears of an invasion.[44] But this was followed in February by the appointment of Defense Minister Wojciech Jaruzelski as premier, a move that led to considerable softening in the Soviet attitude and to a mood of optimism in Poland itself.

The military presence, however, was kept up, this time in the form of Warsaw Pact exercises in March on Polish, East German, Soviet, and Czechoslovak soil. There followed two developments that may have caused the real turning point in Soviet attitudes, bringing a conviction that the deterioration in Poland would have to be forcibly stopped. One was the Polish regime's perceived "capitulation" to avert a general strike after the Bydgoszcz incident in March (see chapter 5), which involved the beating up of several unionists in what was clearly a police provocation. The second was a Polish party Central Committee plenum, also in March, which revealed the weakness of the leadership and strength of reform pressure inside the party itself. The fierceness of the Soviet reaction to these two events reached a new tone and level, probably because it was now the party also that was being contaminated. (The methods used showed some similarities with those used against the Dubček leadership in 1968.) In early June 1981 a letter was sent from the Soviet to the Polish Central Committee, personally criticizing both the Polish party leader Kania and the premier Jaruzelski and setting out Soviet concerns in detail.[45] (The difference with 1968 was that then the most notable warnings were multilateral, signed by all but one of Czechoslovakia's allies; in 1981 the official warnings came from Moscow alone.)

Soviet reaction to the extraordinary ninth congress of the Polish party in July 1981 was relatively mild, especially in view of the unorthodox procedural departures adopted there. But, though it began radically, the congress ended conservatively, and it was the manner of its conclusion that may have appeased Moscow. The Solidarity congress in September gave no such cause for relief. The Soviets were particularly incensed by this congress's "Appeal to the Peoples of Eastern Europe," and the fierce criticism of this was followed by a joint Soviet party and government declaration, presented by the Soviet ambassador at Warsaw, Boris Aristov, "on behalf of the highest party and state leadership of the USSR." It protested against what it called the "unchecked growth of anti-Sovietism" in Poland and was weightier and blunter than the Central Committee complaint in June.[46] Moscow's campaign was escalating. The next step toward the climax of the crisis was the removal of Kania in October from the party leadership and his replacement by Jaruzelski, now first party secretary, prime minister, and minister of defense. The final step was the "declaration of war," or the state of emergency, by Jaruzelski on 13 December 1981.

This narrative, sketchy though it is, might give some idea of both the complexity and the gravity of the Polish situation and the seriousness of the crisis with which the Soviet Union was faced. Perhaps the challenge to Moscow was less direct and overt than in Hungary in 1956, when the Nagy government proclaimed neutrality and announced withdrawal from the Warsaw Pact. But it was more complicated, more prolonged, and more difficult to counter. The final denouement, strikingly successful though it turned out to be, must have been considered enormously risky. The chances of failure, of the army refusing to obey orders, were after all considerable, whereas in neither Hungary nor Czechoslovakia were there any doubts what the outcome would be. It was, therefore, the most difficult crisis Moscow has yet had to face and one where the outcome was least predictable.

The array of responses necessitated by the complexity of the Solidarity challenge was admirably described as early as July 1981. Though written five months before the final blow fell, it could apply perfectly well to the whole period of the challenge:

> The diversity of Soviet tactics and methods employed . . . in confronting the problem of Poland can easily appear bewildering for its sheer scope; expressions of support and confidence, media criticisms, bilateral meetings, a Warsaw Pact summit, the unilateral mobilization of Soviet armed forces and their subsequent partial demobilization, joint exercises, economic assistance, publicity given to hard line party forums, restrictions on travel and tourism, visits by Party delegations of various kinds and at various levels, and a letter from the CPSU Central Committee. . . . This is not to say they have always known how to achieve their objectives —hesitation, uncertainty and even confusion have sometimes seemed to lie behind their tactical shifts—but the objective has always been kept in sight.[47]

This last sentence is of basic importance and is relevant to all the major East European crises the Soviet Union has faced. Moscow was definite enough on what it objected to, and firm on its objectives. But the pursuit of these objectives was often anything but calculated, inexorable, or even consistent. The array of tactics often revealed not so much resourcefulness as vacillation. Such vacillation in both 1968 and 1981 led many Czechoslovaks and Poles, as well as many outsiders, to believe that the Soviet Union would not in the end act decisively. In both cases they were tragically mistaken, and the main lesson of 1968 and 1981 must be that, as long as the Soviet Union has the capacity, it will also eventually have the will to act in crises of such magnitude.

One other factor must be emphasized. When referring to Soviet "vacillation" one should be sure what they were—or what they were not—vacillating between. They were *not* vacillating between repression and acceptance. This applies both to their reactions to the Prague Spring and to Solidarity. In August 1968 there almost certainly were divisions in the Soviet Politburo over whether to invade or not.[48] But those against invasion preferred other, less direct methods of coercion. So it was with Solidarity. The Soviet leadership was presumably undecided between (a) direct invasion, (b) letting the Polish military do the repressing, or (c) an indirect means of undermining Solidarity. Such indirect means both in 1968 and 1981 extended over a range of possibilities, most of which were economic. But the question of *accepting* the Prague Spring or Solidarity would never have crossed the minds of any Soviet leaders.[49]

East European Leverage on the Soviet Union

Even in the most unequal alliance the weaker members have leverage. The Soviet Union may dominate Eastern Europe, but the Eastern European countries have, from time to time, been able to exercise a considerable bargaining power. This bargaining power has been difficult, if not impossible, to measure. It has all too often been impossible to detect. In the case of Romania it was evident enough, but, apart from this, it has had to be inferred or deduced. But there can be little doubt that this leverage has existed and continues to exist.

These are several sources of political leverage, depending on the particular type of relationship involved:

1. Economic strength. This would obviously apply to the GDR and, despite its deterioration, still to Czechoslovakia. The Soviet Union depends to a considerable degree on the machinery, consumer durables, and sheer know-how that these countries export. So does the alliance as a whole, although its dependence has decreased as industrial development in all the countries has proceeded.

2. The ability to turn elsewhere, diplomatically and economically. It is the GDR that has this leverage in its unique relationship with the Federal Republic. It might simply be registered here that the Soviet Union itself derives indirect benefit from this East-West German link, thereby strengthening even further this East German source of leverage. But this leverage had its limits. The GDR's abil-

ity to turn to the Federal Republic has always been limited.

3. The performance of extraneous tasks furthering the cause of Soviet foreign policy. Obviously the GDR with its burgeoning military, political, and economic activity in Africa is, again, the most noteworthy case here.[50] Czechoslovakia, though recently slackening its foreign aid, would also apply.[51]

4. A domestic weakness threatening collapse. This is a classic source of leverage and a major recourse of many small and weak countries. In East Europe it has usually been in evidence immediately after violent upheavals that have shaken communist rule and Soviet domination. Examples are Kádár's Hungary after 1956 and Gierek's Poland after 1970; Husák's Czechoslovakia after 1968; and Jaruzelski's Poland after 1981.

5. Soviet indebtedness to a leadership that has restored order after such upheavals or to one on which Moscow has "gambled" in the hope that it could restore order. Again, all the examples cited above would be applicable here, and the Soviets have almost always chosen soundly in crisis situations like these. (Their only disaster was Gerö in Hungary in 1956 to replace Rákosi prior to the revolution.) The most striking recent example of this potential for leverage at present is, of course, Jaruzelski.

6. A weak, new, or indecisive leadership in Moscow. Andropov was simply new. All three adjectives probably applied to the Chernenko leadership. Now Gorbachev is simply new. But he is neither weak nor indecisive.

7. A strong leadership firmly in control of a viable economy and body politic. No East European state since World War II has ever been in such an enviable position—at least for a sufficient length of time. The Kádár leadership in Hungary may have come close to it in the late 1960s and early 1970s and probably used its leverage to be able to persist with the NEM after 1968.

Such a schematic listing of the different types of leverage, which are by no means exclusive, may be useful, but it can give little idea of the complex set of relationships every East European country has with the Soviet Union. It might, however, convey an aspect of these relationships that is vitally important: unequal though the alliance may be, the East European states cannot and should not be treated as inanimate objects within it. An analysis of Soviet policy toward Eastern Europe under communism illustrates this point. The Soviet Union may have been dominant, but it has by no means been a case of *Moscow locuta causa finita*. For the Soviets the East European problem has always been there, and it has grown rather than diminished.[52]

It would have been a much bigger problem had the East European leverage been concerted rather than single and disunited. Soviet rule in Eastern Europe has always been difficult, but it has been made easier by the national enmities, jealousies, and rivalries that have dominated so much of the region's history. These have persisted as strongly as ever under communism, and one of the few senses in which Soviet rule has been stabilizing has been that it has prevented them from boiling over into conflict. But the nationalism of most East Europeans has often seemed as much internally directed as externally against the Soviet Union.[53] And it is likely to remain so in the short-term future. For example, Hungarian relations with both Romania and Czechoslovakia will continue to be soured by the minorities problem; the GDR's distrust of Poland is deep-seated enough to be chronic; Yugoslavia could become rent by national divisions. In this regard the Soviet leaders and their East European counterparts both have a vested interest in keeping things that way. In fact, by exploiting historic grievances against other East European countries and steering them away from the Soviet Union, some East European leaderships can even gain a spurious legitimacy. Such an atmosphere has given the Soviet leaders breathing space, enabling them, in fact, to contemplate the possibilities of *divide et impera*.

Soviet Choices

The radicalism of Soviet leader Gorbachev's pronouncements from the beginning of 1987 naturally led to much speculation about the impact of his policy on Eastern Europe. While there was no necessary connection between the Soviets' domestic policy and the policy they might pursue in Eastern Europe, it was difficult, from past experience, to envisage no linkage at all. More relaxation, democratization, and decentralization within the Soviet Union could lead to similar changes in Eastern Europe. They might also lead to more leeway for the countries concerned in the pursuit of their own internal affairs. At work here would be not so much a deliberate policy as a habit of mind, an attitude of governance that tolerates, even encourages, a degree of autonomy that is perceived as strengthening rather than weakening the organism as a whole.

It was difficult to say whether Eastern Europe had now embarked on an uninterrupted course of meaningful reform. Doubtless, there were grounds for optimism, despite the disappointing precedents since Stalin's death in 1953. But until the debate and the doubts cleared it was worth remembering some relevant factors:

1. Gorbachev's reform inclinations were still meeting with strong opposition within the Soviet Union itself.

2. In Eastern Europe his calls for reform were probably as divisive as they were in the Soviet Union. Beneath a general pro forma approval there were real differences about the type and the pace of changes needed—indeed, whether any change was needed at all. Opinions differed from regime to regime and within individual regimes. The East German leadership politely but firmly indicated that it was impervious to the clamor for change. In Czechoslovakia the reform issue seemed to recall for some the trauma of 1968, as seen by Vasil Bilak's first negative reaction. But the discreet reformists in Prague were doubtless heartened by the news from Moscow. In Budapest all reformists, bold as well as discreet, were relieved and encouraged by the new trends. In Poland a relationship of confidence was developing between Jaruzelski and Gorbachev. The Polish leader embraced the new Soviet course, and now it would be seen whether he had the strength, will, and skill to implement a Polish version of it. As expected, Ceauşescu rejected any suggestion of being influenced by Soviet reform, but the Bulgarian leader, Todor Zhivkov, appeared to embrace reform enthusiastically.[54]

3. The most important factor of all concerned the repercussions that reform could have in Eastern Europe. The winds blowing from Moscow could have profound and disruptive effects. They could set in motion forces difficult to guide, check, or stop. Again, despite all the differences, the analogy with the situation after Stalin inevitably asserts itself. True, the events of 1953–56 could never happen again. But something similar to them and to Czechoslovakia in 1968 (or even Poland in 1970) might happen. From past experience the Soviet leaders, however new they might be, must be aware that there is nothing more intoxicating in Eastern Europe than the heady brew of reform.

4. Finally, though it was still too early to speak of any "Gorbachev policy" toward Eastern Europe, a dichotomy could be detected in what appeared to be his attitude toward the region. On the one hand, he favored economic and even some political reform. On the other hand, he seemed obviously at pains to strengthen "coordination" (read Soviet control) in Comecon, the Warsaw Pact, and alliance affairs gen-

erally. The leeway Eastern Europe might get in internal affairs might, therefore, not extend to external affairs. Gorbachev may see these two aspects of policy as complementary. But the experience of the past forty years would indicate they were contradictory. Moreover, Gorbachev had given no indication that he was prepared to soften the growing Soviet economic "hard line" toward Eastern Europe, which demanded that the allies share more justly the economic burden of the alliance. In this issue lurks the danger, not so much of contradiction, as of societal instability in Eastern Europe.

The more Gorbachev tries to solve the East European problem, the more he is likely to be impressed by its intractability. Any policy is bound to reveal inconsistencies that could ruin it. Brezhnev may have dimly realized this after his burst of activity in Eastern Europe between 1968 and 1975. Gorbachev may eventually do the same. And beset by the huge domestic and global problems he will face, he may be overtaken by the "Brezhnev progression" in Eastern Europe sooner than many people think. The erstwhile activist gradually settles for peace and quiet, and Soviet policy settles for the uneasy calm. Whatever he does he will be anxious to avoid the damning indictment of Malenkov in a secret memorandum sent from Moscow to several East European parties in 1955. "The policy of Malenkov," it said, "aside from the harm it threatened in Soviet domestic matters, concealed serious dangers for the countries of the people's democracies and for the relations of the Soviet Union with these countries...."[55] More than thirty years later the pitfalls were still there.

3 Relations with the West
and the Impact of Détente

This chapter will concentrate on the attitudes of the East European states and societies toward the West and the mutual relations that waxed and waned after 1968. (At the end it also will contain a review of American policy toward Eastern Europe.) Just as the realities of communist rule demand that Western policy toward different countries in the region be conducted on both the state and societal level, so the same differentiation is needed in analyzing East European attitudes toward the West. Indeed, it is precisely in this differentiation that sharp distinctions as well as subtleties of perception are essential.

East European regimes have tended to view links with Western governments in an essentially tactical way: as means of economic support; as instruments of legitimization vis-à-vis their populations; sometimes, as Romania has most conspicuously done, to expand their maneuverability in relations with Moscow. But in Romania's case there has also been for many years a conscious defiance of Moscow. Other East European countries, while not wishing to stray outside the parameters of the permitted, have nevertheless sought to *diversify* their foreign relations and not let them be exclusively dominated by Moscow. No regime has ever sought a full rapprochement with the Western powers, not only because the Soviet Union would not permit it, but also because it would eventually develop into a threat to the very survival of the regime concerned.

But within the East European regimes themselves there have often been differences of opinion or emphasis regarding relations with the West. During the years of détente in the 1970s many of the East European *economic* elites saw relations with the West as advantageous per se and not simply as a means of developing their own national economies. This was particularly the case in Poland and Hungary, and possibly in the GDR. Many members of the *cultural* elites saw contact with the West, not simply in terms of opportunities for travel, but as means of broadening their intellectual horizons.[1] As already mentioned, members of the *political* elites saw expanding Western relations as giving their country more leeway in foreign policy as a whole. In the special case of Yugoslavia views on foreign policy tended to mirror domestic differences. In the continual struggle between party and technocrats it was the latter who tended openly to espouse better relations with the West. Party officials, though cherishing Yugoslav independence from the Soviet Union, often tended to stress better relations with the East, precisely because the technocrats looked the other way. As for Yugoslav intellectuals, their orientation and basic sympathies were largely Western.

Among East European *societies*, many citizens have tended to see "the West" in idealized terms of liberty and prosperity—what they considered the antithesis of the situation at home. This has often been a blanket sentiment, but where the distinctions among societal attitudes in Eastern Europe have often applied has been in the historical context. Obviously, the ruling and educated classes of the Czech Lands, Poland, Hungary, and Croatia had an affinity with—or in most cases sought to imitate—their counterparts in Western Europe. (The same, of course, could be said about the ruling class in St. Petersburg, a considerable number of whom were often of German origin.) More comprehensively, the westward gravitational pull of Roman Catholicism gave almost the whole populations of Central and Eastern Europe a sense of common belief and culture with several Western nations. Milan Kundera and György Konrád, a Czech and a Hungarian, have recently written passionately about the cultural affinity of Central European intellectuals with the West.[2] Here, a fairly sharp contrast needs to be drawn with southeastern Europe, where the religious, cultural, and social affinities were more with Constantinople, Kiev, or Moscow. Europe was, for the Balkan peoples, a vague concept, anyway. There was little knowledge of, or distinction between, the various countries of Europe. In Bulgaria, for example, before World War II relatively few regarded themselves as being European at all. A youngster going to a university in, say, Leipzig or Paris was said to be "going to Europe" for his education.

So much, then, for the cultural division between Central and southeastern Europe. But returning to Central Europe, the question must still be asked just how far down the intellectual and social ladders this feeling of mutuality with Western Europe extended. Obviously, the mass of nineteenth- and early twentieth-century Polish, Hungarian, or Czech peasants or workers were hardly animated about European cultural unity as Kundera and Konrád are now and their predecessors once were. For the masses, the West meant *emigration*, a source of escape from the miseries of their existence. And, despite some Polish worker emigration to the mines and heavy industries of Germany and France, the West for them meant *America*. Thus for millions of "ordinary" people in East Central Europe, and many parts of southeastern Europe as well, America entered popular mythology and psychology as the land of hope and promise in a way no other Western country could ever do.

(There has always, of course, been mass emigration from Western and Northern Europe to the United States—on a scale much larger than from Eastern Europe. Yet the feeling there for America has not been so strong or friendly. In fact, trans- and cisatlantic bickering often seems to have been the predominant feature in relations between the United States and Western Europe. The main reason for the difference appears to lie in the comprehensively better conditions Western Europeans have always enjoyed. The American "myth" has been much stronger in Eastern Europe, and the Statue of Liberty has symbolized much more. Still, even when allowing for the contrast, the deep historical reservoir of *societal* sympathy for the United States in Western Europe should not be forgotten. The sympathy is to be found mostly among the "lower social orders" whose views have often been ignored, unrecorded, or misunderstood.)

For many years, then, to a small group of East-Central European intellectuals, the West meant the almost exclusively European historical and cultural tradition. For an infinitely greater number of what are now called East Europeans the West meant not only the hope of America but the contact with it through relatives and fellow villagers who had gone there.

After some forty years into the communist era in Eastern Europe, some of these historical generalizations need to be modified. Soviet domination has undoubtedly made many East Europeans more, not less, conscious of their "European-ness." And this now applies to many southeastern Europeans as well. The gulf in this respect, therefore, between the Northern and Southern Tiers of Eastern Europe is much narrower than ever before. Again, quoting perhaps the most extreme example, many Bulgarian intellectuals set great store by Western connections, and the Bulgarian Academy of Sciences, though still (perforcedly) orientated toward the Soviet Union, developed fruitful contacts with Western academic institutions during the détente of the 1970s.

But, again, as the relative political and cultural importance of Western Europe, on the one hand, and the United States, on the other, has undergone a profound change, so "the West" has become rather different in the eyes of most East Europeans. First, the distinction between Western Europe and the United States became blurred as the United States began making a strong impact on the East European mind. Then, as military, political, and even cultural supremacy clearly moved across the Atlantic, the United States replaced Western Europe as the leader and torchbearer of the West. There are many examples to prove this, one of the most potent being the dramatic rise of English to the position of premier foreign language throughout Eastern Europe. And, of course, as international relations became polarized, with the superpower relationship as their determinant aspect, the sheer, multifaceted power of the United States greatly enhanced its significance. Finally, just as American culture and scholarship began to dominate the attention of East European intellectuals, so American sub- and countercultures began to prove irresistible to millions of East European youth *throughout* the region. This is a matter for some concern among their elders—and not just those in the communist establishment. But it is a phenomenon that shows no sign of receding. For most young people in Eastern Europe, Radio Luxemburg with its saturation pop music remains the most popular Western broadcasting station.

The emergence of American dominance in East European popular awareness needs to be stressed because it is an important factor that tends to get ignored in the natural (and justified) excitement about the "European-ness" of the *whole* of Europe and the growing awareness of this concept in Eastern Europe. It is, indeed, difficult to miss this feeling. The enthusiasm for a united Europe, which was commonly found in continental Western Europe in the early 1960s, has largely faded. Much of it has passed to Eastern Europe where the worsening situation has bestowed on it almost the lure of the impossible dream. Despite the emergence of the United States, there still also remains some strong residual sentiment for individual West European countries. France is the main beneficiary of this sentiment—most noticeably in Poland and Romania. Austria evokes nostalgic memories and a current wistfulness. Rome, as the citadel of Catholicism, has remained an inspiration for many, perhaps more than ever with a Pole on the throne of St. Peter and with religion more than holding its own in Eastern Europe. Conversely, there was originally a strong antipathy in Poland, the Czech Lands, and parts of Yugoslavia (though by no means all of Eastern Europe) for West Germany as the perceived successor to the Nazi tradition. This also began to recede. Western Europe, then, has retained a great importance in the minds and imaginations of many East Europeans. And in physical terms, of course, it is accessible to them in a way the United States never will be.

But, without denigrating Western Europe's importance, West Europeans (and Americans) have had to get accustomed to the fact that the United States is no longer the far-off land of hope to which East Europeans emigrated. The vicissitudes of international power, the cultural and educational progress of America, its mass appeal, and the many-sided revolution in communications, all have precipitated the American presence into Eastern Europe, made America itself less remote, and strengthened East European awareness of it. That has been the most important development in popular, societal, East European conceptions of the West in the last half-century.

State Relations and the Importance of West Germany

But despite this historical and growing contemporary American importance, East European contacts on the *state* level have become more numerous with Western Europe than with the United States.

These contacts were slow in developing after World War II, for which there were three main reasons:

1. The nervousness and insecurity of the East European regimes. These regimes were new, and they had been imposed by the Soviet Union. They had no desire to engage in self-undermining relations with Western powers.

2. The Soviet Union, which controlled them, had no desire to expose them to Western influences. Here Soviet attitudes were coincidental with those of the East European leaders. After Stalin's death this iron curtain did begin to be raised slightly, but the Hungarian Revolution and the Polish October of 1956 showed the new Soviet leadership just how volatile the situation was and how careful they had to be. The Soviets have always been concerned about Eastern Europe's relations with the West. Even Yugoslavia, independent since 1948, has always had to show restraint and care in how far it developed its Western orientation.

3. The attitude of the West German government was an inhibiting factor. West Germany had no foreign policy till it became a sovereign state in 1955 as the Federal Republic of Germany, and it naturally took time before it acquired confidence and perspective. In any case the new Federal Republic's main concern was reunification, which, to the government of Chancellor Konrad Adenauer, meant total ostracism of the new German Democratic Republic—founded in 1949. According to the so-called Hallstein Doctrine (named after a senior Bonn foreign office official) the Federal Republic could not enter into diplomatic relations with any state recognizing the GDR. This introduction was waived by Adenauer himself in 1955 in the case of the Soviet Union, but it was to continue for another twelve years for the East European socialist states.[3] Thus these states were prevented from developing relations with the West European state that, by history, geography, and growing economic power, was the most important to them.

The basic importance of the Federal Republic in the whole East-West equation was shown in the first five years of its existence by two occurrences. The first was the Rapacki Plan of 1957 put forward by the then Polish foreign minister, Adam Rapacki. Basically the plan called for the neutralization of a broad stretch of Central European territory including the two Germanies.[4] In the early 1980s Rapacki's proposals were often wistfully remembered by many West Germans (though not by many Poles) in the light of the INF controversy in the Federal Republic. Some tried to resurrect them as yet another example of Eastern reasonableness, Western intransigence, and "what might have been."[5] Such retroactive yearnings can be disposed of quickly. The Rapacki Plan was one in a long list of Soviet efforts—direct or inspired—to weaken the Western alliance through undermining or manipulating the Federal Republic. As such, it is an excellent illustration of one of the Soviet Union's main aims in Central Europe and of its concept of the importance of Eastern Europe (see chapter 2).

The *second* was the signing of the Treaty of Rome, also in 1957, establishing the European Economic Community. This was to have important and probably unforeseen repercussions for the German Democratic Republic. Bowing to Bonn's insistence that the two Germanys be considered one country, a protocol to the Treaty of Rome gave the GDR tariff-free access to the Federal Republic and, therefore, an economic foothold in the Common Market itself. This was to bestow on the GDR bounteous rewards it could hardly have expected and which the behavior of its government in no way led it to deserve.[6] They have been the envy of its East European allies and have contributed to (without entirely explaining) the GDR's economic successes.

The Federal Republic of Germany soon established itself as having a key importance in Western relations for the East European states. At the beginning its own East European policy revolved solely around East Germany and the quest for reunification. For several years the Hallstein Doctrine symbolized its essential negative approach to this whole issue. But in the 1960s, though the quest remained the same, the course changed. The other East European countries were no longer rejected because of their alliance with the GDR. Bonn now began a slow and hesitant courtship of them to try to isolate the GDR.[7]

The early response to this courtship demonstrated not just how important but also how *divisive* the Federal Republic was in Eastern Europe. This was first seen in the mixed reactions to the so-called Erhard "peace note" of March 1966. Adenauer's successor as chancellor, Ludwig Erhard, and his foreign minister, Dieter Schroeder, hesitantly began the Federal Republic's active Ostpolitik and the "peace note" in question was sent to the Soviet Union and its East European clients suggesting a new start in mutual relations. (This had been preceded by the exchange of trade missions between Bonn and all the East European capitals—a concrete symbol of West Germany's growing economic importance.)

The Soviet Union, Poland, and Czechoslovakia rejected Erhard's overture in no uncertain terms. Hungary did so in less than certain terms, while Romania and Bulgaria chose not to reply to the note at all. (At least no reply was ever published.) Romania had already established itself as the maverick of the Warsaw Pact and was soon after to establish full diplomatic relations with Bonn. But the silence of Bulgaria, considered by many to be Moscow's most subservient satellite, was remarkable. While showing obedience to the Soviets, it unmistakably conveyed to Bonn Bulgaria's wish for better relations when the conditions were more auspicious.[8]

For most of the 1960s, as West German policy toward Eastern Europe was developing only slowly, French policy, under President de Gaulle, was developing with characteristic flamboyance. De Gaulle's pan-European concept certainly included a role for Eastern Europe. While accepting the hegemony of the Soviet Union in Eastern Europe, de Gaulle was aware that the stability of that hegemony would depend on more freedom for the satellites. This was the message he took with him on his visits to Poland in 1966 and Romania in 1968. In Poland it was courteously rejected, ostensibly on the grounds of the continuing German menace. In Romania he was preaching to the converted until the May uprising in Paris necessitated his early, humiliating return. But de Gaulle had gone—and this was no coincidence—to the two most Francophile states in Eastern Europe that clearly considered France at that time not only the most compatible but also the most "concerned" Western country. In this they were certainly not alone. It was only after the drama of de Gaulle was over and as West German economic supremacy began to be universally clear that this notion lost its credibility. But it was impressive while it lasted. De Gaulle was rapturously received in Poland, recapturing popular affection for France and restoking the fires of Polish nationalism. It was a brief revival of France's great prestige in Eastern Europe, which had been terribly damaged at Munich in 1938 and even more so with the defeat of 1940. But it changed basically little in France's East European relationships.[9]

The Attraction of Austria

Austria lies in the heart of Central Europe. Its capital, Vienna, was once the capital of an empire that included, partly or wholly, five contemporary East European communist states: Hungary, Czechoslovakia, Romania, Poland, and Yugoslavia. Austria today is a neutral, independent, and democratic country whose population of about 7.5 million is smaller than that of any East European country except Albania. It achieved its independence in 1955 through the greatest diplomatic concession ever made by the Soviet Union. Under both conservative and social democratic governments it has achieved a level of prosperity and social welfare that makes it the envy of many countries in the world.

More recently its reputation in the West has become somewhat tarnished. The Waldheim affair and the lack of sensitivity it showed; the recrudescence of right-wing nationalism; the big cracks in the economic prosperity and the social welfare edifice—all these indicate deep-seated weaknesses and problems that Austrians themselves must tackle. But they are not likely to cause Austria much damage in the East unless they are allowed to go unrealized or unchecked for a very long period.

There is little need to dwell on Austria's historical relevance, or its geographical proximity to Eastern Europe. While the various nationalisms over which the Habsburg monarchy so uneasily ruled were the basic reason for its eventual downfall, some of the links forged during the time of empire were not so easily broken. And now that many parts of the Habsburg empire are under communist rule, and all except the Yugoslav parts under Soviet domination, the attractions of Austria have perceptibly increased rather than declined. Something more than nostalgia is at work here. It is a historical factor magnified by the present situation of Eastern Europe and relevant to East European aspirations. It is not quantifiable, but few would doubt its existence or impact.

Influence can be wielded either by example or exertion. In Austria's case it is the example it sets, the sheer fact of its presence and achievements rather than any conscious Ostpolitik that has had the more decisive role. Vienna, so easily reachable geographically, has become a magnet for most Hungarians and many Czechoslovaks and Poles. Austrian television and radio, though designed exclusively for domestic consumption, have a large following in those areas of Hungary and Czechoslovakia where they can be received. Television, with its more decisive impact, has the more dedicated audience. But Austrian media generally have become a feature of life in communist Central Europe, and the historical interaction between Austria and its neighbors is illustrated by the coverage the Austrian media give to East European developments. Television coverage from Vienna, for example, in both quantity and quality, is generally the best in the Western world.

For most East Europeans the attractions of Austria are in the mind—in their spiritual, political, cultural, and economic aspirations. Austrians, they often ruefully feel, could also have become what they are. Austria could have become part of the Soviet empire, an insignificant part at that. Austria might even have been partitioned, as Germany was. But by a political miracle it was allowed to go free, the only restriction being a neutrality that to any East European would be a bearable deprivation indeed. For nations that, because of their present, see the past in terms of what might have been, Austria is not only what they feel deprived of, but also what they aspire to. It may be the object of envy, but that envy is not tinged with dislike, rather with a certain hope. This hope may be unrealistic, but to many East Europeans even an unrealistic hope has a sustaining quality that makes the present reality the more endurable. And the gravitation toward Austria is somehow a sublimation of, or compensation for, their being tied to the Soviet Union. Austria, in this context, is an escape from the reality that overcame them forty years ago. For at least two countries— Hungary and Czechoslovakia, and also for some Poles—Austria is also an *economic* yardstick. Most Hungarians and Czechs, for example, measure their present material condition not against what it was previously and certainly not against that prevailing anywhere else in the communist bloc but by that prevailing in Austria. (Similarly, East Germans measure theirs by the Federal Republic.) And when comparing economic progress most older Czechs ruefully recall that before World War II many parts of Bohemia and Moravia were more advanced than most parts of Austria.

No one is affected more by the pull of Austria than Hungarians. Here the Habsburg connection is an obvious factor, with its comprehensive impact on the Hungarian habit of mind and way of life. Perhaps three historical aspects are particularly relevant. First is the fact that, in spite of all the bitterness that existed between Vienna and Budapest, Hungary after 1867 was a considerable imperial power in its own right, with the Hungarian nation not just a *Staatsvolk* but a *Herrenvolk* in considerable parts of Eastern Europe and the Balkans. Second, in their association with Austria all Hungarians were united in the same state, a state that was then dismembered by the 1920 Treaty of Trianon. Finally, in the discreditable and nightmarish post-Habsburg interlude between 1918 and 1938, Hungary and Austria shared the status of pariah, and many Hungarians, susceptible to the growing notion that theirs had become a historically "rejected" nation, were almost pathetically grateful to Austria for not "ganging up" on Hungary as Czechoslovakia, Romania, and Yugoslavia did in the "Little Entente."

Nor was the connection broken after 1945. Many would agree with former Chancellor Kreisky's view that the granting of Austrian independence in 1955 was an important factor (not the only one) in hastening the restlessness that led to the Hungarian Revolution a year later.[10] And after "normalcy" had been restored in Hungary, the Kádár leadership not only sought to improve relations with Austria at the state level but, wisely realizing that relations at the popular level made a most effective safety valve, gradually lifted the iron curtain separating the two countries.

The interaction of peoples that developed from these modest and hesitant beginnings has been extraordinary. It became more intense, friendly, and many-sided than at any time in history—much more so than during the Dual Monarchy, perhaps more so than between any two Western countries. Many more Austrians visit Hungary than Hungarians Austria, this being largely due to financial reasons and the residual travel restrictions imposed on Hungarian citizens. But nearly

300,000 Hungarians came in 1984. The figure for Austrians visiting Hungary, however, was nearly 2 million.[11]

Austria, therefore, has been a powerful attraction to many East Europeans for what it is, where it is, and what it once was. Despite its carefully preserved neutral status and its friendly state relations with the East, its very existence and its success are a challenge to the ruling order there. For the populations of Eastern Europe Austria today enjoys an affection and respect much greater than in the great days of the Habsburgs.[12]

The Vatican and the Condition of Catholicism in Eastern Europe

Rome is a unique city. Nowhere more so than in the fact that it contains within its walls three separate institutions each conducting its own foreign policy: the Italian state, the Italian communist party, and the Vatican. The most crucial East European country for the state of Italy is neighboring Yugoslavia just across the strategically vital Adriatic Sea. The Italian Communist party (PCI) became the standard-bearer of Eurocommunism, the impact of which in Eastern Europe is discussed later. But most relevant in our context has been the so-called Ostpolitik of the Vatican and its interaction with the situation of the Roman Catholic churches in Eastern Europe.

Just as it is often overlooked that the West German Ostpolitik (slowly) began with a reluctant Konrad Adenauer in his last years, so it is similarly overlooked that it was Pope Pius XII who, perhaps even more reluctantly, recognized in *his* last years that events were forcing the Vatican into some relations with the East European communist regimes. The situation of the Catholics and their church in Eastern Europe was demanding it. With Pius's successor, John XXIII, the need for action was not just understood but energetically acted upon. Contacts with Poland, Hungary, Czechoslovakia, and Yugoslavia, the main Catholic countries in Eastern Europe, were quickly established, and the Vatican-communist dialogue began. What followed was the eighteen-year period of "the Pauline diplomacy" in Eastern Europe, a diplomacy that, despite the death of Paul VI, its founder, and the almost immediate accession of Pope John Paul II, still dominates Vatican policy.[13]

This diplomacy derived from the principle that the essential organizational basis of the church was its bishops. Without bishops the

Roman Catholic church, in Eastern Europe or anywhere else, would disintegrate. And since disintegration was to be avoided at all costs, agreements with the communist authorities to allow empty dioceses to be filled was essential. From this it followed that negotiation and compromise were necessary, and that the policy of small steps was unavoidable. Under Paul VI a group of able diplomats emerged who became experts on both the overall situation in Eastern Europe and in dealing with the communist authorities there.

The policy that emerged toward Eastern Europe, inspired by Paul VI, has often been criticized as naive and unrealistic, ingenuously allowing the church to be manipulated, even humiliated, by the East European regimes. Alternatively, it has been dismissed as realistic to the point of cynicism, disregarding the ultimately spiritual aspects of the church and ignoring the ideological incompatibility between Christianity and communism. The results of the Pauline policy have also been called into question.

These criticisms are not totally baseless. It did appear sometimes that the Vatican was oversolicitous in seeking accommodation—most notably over the agreement to exile József Cardinal Mindszenty to Vienna in 1975 after his nineteen-year residence in the American embassy in Budapest. The concessions made by the regimes were often tardy and meager. But, against this, the Pauline diplomats could argue the following: (1) papal policy is set against the aspirations of the long-term, not the hopes of the short term; (2) the situation of the church overall in Eastern Europe—in Hungary, Poland, and Yugoslavia (though not Czechoslovakia)—has improved; (3) no basic church position has ever been surrendered. In general, the Pauline "philosophy" of diplomacy was summed up in the privately expressed opinion of one of its ablest practitioners: that to get only 50 percent of what is hoped for is still better than 40 percent. These are formidable arguments, but when Paul VI died in 1978 and was succeeded, after the brief interval of John Paul I, by the Polish John Paul II, who had served his whole priesthood in an embattled church, there was some doubt whether the previous diplomacy would be continued.

Pope John Paul II brought to the Vatican from his native Poland an intimate knowledge of communism in action and all layers of communist bureaucracy, together with charisma, spiritual enthusiasm, and a strong sense of political and social justice. He was quite different from Paul VI and his Italian advisers in style, temperament, and outlook. Instinctively, he was impatient with the niceties of diplomacy. He was a man of mass, almost messianic, appeal, seeking to breathe new life and spirit into the church and what many considered its bureaucratic ways of government. He was also a pastor and man of action.[14]

After his accession in 1978, therefore, there was not one Vatican Ostpolitik approach, but two—the pope's and that of the diplomacy inspired by Paul VI. John Paul II, however, tried hard to bridge the two, to make them complementary rather than in contradiction. He kept the old Pauline team intact and actually appointed Cardinal Casaroli, the chief Pauline diplomat, as head of the Congregation of State, the Vatican's unofficial "prime minister." And, in general, the two approaches worked fairly well together. Continuity was largely preserved. But there were differences of emphasis and style.

Some Vatican diplomats, for example, appear to have considered the pope's attitude toward church-state relations in Czechoslovakia too direct and lacking in subtlety. The persecution of organized religion there since 1968 was of a viciousness unknown in Eastern Europe since Stalin's day. This persecution was accompanied, again in the Stalinist manner, by the setting up of a pro-regime priests' organization, Pacem in Terris. Probably 15 percent of all Czechoslovak priests joined Pacem in Terris, which was led by Bishop Vrana of Olomouc. In 1982 the Vatican issued a decree forbidding the clergy to engage in political activity. This was at first thought to be directed mainly, if not exclusively, toward Latin America. But a papal spokesman made it clear that it also applied to Pacem in Terris.[15] Obviously, no one in the Vatican failed to consider this a disreputable organization. But some felt that such a direct assault on it only aggravated a delicate situation and reduced the chances of improving church-state relations, especially in the crucial sphere of the appointment of bishops. Only three of Czechoslovakia's thirteen dioceses had fully consecrated bishops, a state of affairs already existing for over ten years because of the inability of the Czechoslovak government and the Vatican to agree on suitable candidates. (In all the East European states, including Poland, the government has at least the right of veto in bishops' appointments.)

Opponents of the pope's directness in Czechoslovakia might seek vindication in the fact that, at the end of 1986, the situation regarding bishops was still the same, and other aspects of church-state relations, despite an occasional flicker of hope, still showed no progress. The Czechoslovak government did allow celebrations marking the 1,100th anniversary of the death of St. Methodius at Velehrad in Moravia in

1985. (The government hoped—mistakenly as it turned out—to secularize and politicize the celebrations to its advantage.)[16] But, in addition to refusing permission for the pope to come, it denied entry to both Cardinal Koenig of Vienna and the Polish primate, Cardinal Glemp. Cardinal Casaroli did, however, attend as the pope's representative and had talks with Czechoslovak representatives, including the president and party leader, Gustáv Husák, himself. These talks could eventually bear fruit and, if they did, could be seen as proof of the efficacy of patient diplomacy rather than the direct action manifested in the attack on Pacem in Terris.

Pauline diplomacy could point to its biggest success in Hungary. There its most solid achievement was the agreement with the regime on the appointment of bishops, the first breakthrough being as early as 1964. All Hungarian dioceses came to be filled, and a limited number of Catholic orders were allowed to operate. Anxious for domestic calm and Western approval, the Hungarian authorities followed a skillful policy that brought considerable dividend and little danger. Budapest became the Vatican's favorite communist capital. But many Hungarians continued to feel that the price the church had to pay for its tranquility and concessions was too high. In practice, they would argue, the Hungarian authorities were considerably less than tolerant on vital issues like religious instruction and toward priests who spoke up on public and social issues. They blamed the Hungarian bishops— with one or two notable exceptions—for being too pliant. Their chief target of criticism was the primate himself, László Cardinal Lékai, who was known for his anxiety not to disturb relations with the regime— even to the point of publicly endorsing some of its foreign policy and domestic initiatives. Pope John Paul II himself at first seemed to share these reservations about Lékai. He wrote the Hungarian bishops a letter at the beginning of 1979, implicitly criticizing the degree of their cooperation with the authorities.[17] During a visit by Lékai to Rome the following April, however, he demonstratively praised the Hungarian primate. Some construed this as a sign that the pope had altered his view and had come to realize the solid achievements made by Lékai's approach.[18] More probably he had not changed his mind but, aware of the speculation caused by his letter, wished to reassure Lékai personally by praising his career and publicly acknowledging the difficulties the Hungarian church had survived. Lékai died in the summer of 1986 and was succeeded by Archbishop László Páskai. Some Hungarians wished for a more assertive posture now, but few were hopeful.

The Vatican's relations with Poland have been in a category of their own, partly because Polish Catholicism is unique, partly because of the nationality of John Paul II. For two decades, between the death of Pius XII in 1958 and the accession of the present pope in 1978, these relations were characterized by the high degree of independence enjoyed by the Polish church, under its then primate, Stefan Cardinal Wyszyński. At that time church-state relations in Poland were almost entirely an internal Polish matter. This independence was enhanced by the stature, growing experience, ability, and success of Wyszyński.[19] In the light of his later dominance it is worth recalling that during the reign of Pius XII his reputation had not been so high. He was remembered by senior Vatican officials as having signed in 1950 the agreement between the Polish church and the communist state that some thought conceded too much.[20] Vatican hostility subsequently diminished as the courage and wisdom of Wyszyński's action became evident.[21] Under Pope John XXIII after 1958 all doubts about the Vatican's total support disappeared. Even after the accession of John Paul II in 1978, with his natural concern for Poland, and even with his own obviously weakening health, Wyszyński's authority did not diminish. It was only after his death in 1981 that the pope personally became so directly concerned with Poland.

The new pope's involvement in Poland was deepened by the grave crisis caused by the rise and fall of Solidarity and, simultaneously, by questions concerning the ability of Wyszyński's successor, Josef Cardinal Glemp. The pope's attitude toward, and relations with, Glemp is a subject that attracted much speculation. The lurid gossip on the fringes of the Vatican about the pope's outspoken disapproval of Glemp could be discounted. But so could the counterclaims of implicit trust between the two men and mutual understanding, right from the beginning, about church policy in Poland. The pope clearly saw the need to demonstrate his trust and faith in Glemp's leadership and did so on several occasions. Yet there seemed little doubt that he was more enthusiastic than Glemp about the Polish national spontaneity exemplified by Solidarity and less distrustful of some of Solidarity's intellectual guides.[22] He must also have been unimpressed by a seeming lack of consistency in many of Glemp's utterances. But on the basic point of policy toward regime and resistance in Poland, there may have been little disagreement. There was certainly no disagreement on the overriding need to show unity—between pope and primate, between primate and the Polish episcopate, and among the episcopate itself.[23]

Great efforts were made to demonstrate this unity; and the realization of its need tended to reinforce it. Church unity, therefore, especially between pope and primate, became an important political factor on the Polish scene. But also important was the persistent popular suspicion that this unity was contrived rather than genuine, that the pope's instinct was for a stronger assertion of national rights than Glemp's. Glemp, after his early hesitancy, did begin to show more firmness and resolution, but suspicions remained. He remained a primate few Poles could feel proud of.

The differences between John Paul II and Cardinal Glemp may, therefore, have been exaggerated, even sensationalized. But, despite all the disclaimers, few ever doubted that differences existed. In a way these differences were similar to those between the pope and the Pauline diplomats in the Vatican itself. Glemp, longtime secretary to Cardinal Wyszyński, had little pastoral experience and even less pastoral instinct. He was a scholar, administrator, and negotiator, bent on easing the situation of the church in small steps and by compromise if necessary. Keeping in mind the difference of degree, there were similarities between him and Cardinal Lékai in Hungary. The pope was primarily the pastor with his appeal to the masses. His overall appraisal of a given situation might be similar to, or identical with, that of Glemp and the Vatican diplomats. But this appraisal was imbued with an emotion they did not share.

Obviously, both approaches had their place. As already mentioned, Pope John Paul II did try to make them complementary and has generally been successful. There need be nothing contradictory in seeking to strengthen the church organization and its hierarchy while appealing to the masses at the same time. In Poland, Slovakia in Czechoslovakia, and Croatia in Yugoslavia, the two aims could be self-reinforcing because of the intimate links between church, people, and national feeling. The church was also seen now as the most powerful obstacle to communist totalitarian goals. As long as it remained so, there was no danger of contradiction. But the restlessness of many Polish clergy against a hierarchy they regarded as not militant enough could eventually create serious problems for the church in Poland despite its traditional discipline.

In the Czech Lands and Hungary the hierarchy was in much greater danger because it lacked any historical identity with the nation. The Catholic church in both these countries, especially perhaps in the Czech Lands, was historically a symbol of foreign—Habsburg—domination. In Hungary only about two-thirds of the population are Roman Catholic in any case. In the Czech Lands, though almost 90 percent are believing, nominal, or lapsed Catholics, whatever nationalism exists is associated with the traditional Hussitism that was virtually wiped out by the Czech defeat at the Battle of the White Mountain in 1620. There was a real problem of identification with the masses, therefore, that did not exist in Poland.

One of the most important centers of Catholicism in Eastern Europe is Croatia. Hence the Vatican has always paid particular regard to the condition of the church there, to church-state relations, and to its own relations with the state authorities in Zagreb, the capital of Croatia, and with the federal authorities in Belgrade.

Relations between Croatian church and state got off to the worst possible start after World War II because of the atrocities committed after 1941 in Croatia by the Nazi puppet Ustasa regime of Ante Pavelić, which murdered hundreds of thousands of Serbs and Jews. This regime had specifically identified itself with Catholicism. The Archbishop of Zagreb, Aloysius Stepinac, though wanting an independent Croatia, had objected to the crimes of the Pavelić regime. But some of his activities had lacked political sensitivity, and other Croatian and church dignitaries in Yugoslavia generally had collaborated either with Pavelić or the occupying Nazis.[24] This all gave the new Tito regime, at that time as Stalinist and militantly anticlerical as any, the pretext for a harsh persecution of the Catholic church. Stepinac was tried in 1946 for supporting the Pavelić regime and, in a clear miscarriage of justice, was found guilty and sentenced to sixteen years' imprisonment.

In 1953 Pope Paul XII made Stepinac a cardinal, an action strongly resented by Tito. But because of its break with Stalin in 1948, its need for Western help, and its own developing liberalism, the Yugoslav government set aside its severity toward the church. The freedom and condition of both the church and its flock improved appreciably, and Croatia and Slovenia, the two overwhelmingly Catholic republics of the Yugoslav federation, steadily became models of good church-state relations for the whole of Eastern Europe.

Negotiations between the Vatican and the Yugoslav government for the normalization of relations began in 1963, and further concessions were made to all the churches in Yugoslavia between 1964 and 1966. Finally in 1971 Belgrade and the Vatican agreed to full diplomatic relations.

It was ironic that shortly after this high point of good relations the

situation began to deteriorate. Croatian public sentiment had continued to be dominated by nationalism, ranging from a wish for complete
independence to a much greater degree of sovereignty within the
Yugoslav federation. As discussed in chapter 11, Croatian nationalism
both in the Croatian communist party and outside it could have led to
civil war in December 1971, had not Tito taken firm steps to prevent it.
After the purging of the more prominent (or suspected) nationalists
from the party ranks and the banning of the militant nationalist lay
organization, Matica Hrvatska, it was the Catholic church that came to
be regarded by many Croatians as the repository and bastion of the
Croatian national heritage.

The reputation of the church in Croatia in the 1970s began steadily
to grow. This was not solely because of its identification with nationalism. As the luster of the communist ideology began to dim—again, the
situation was similar to that in other parts of Eastern Europe—more
and more young Croatians became drawn to the church. This tendency was doubtlessly hastened by the growing dogmatism of the
Croatian communist party. Many of the young now stood for Croatia
and Christianity (probably in that order), and this was what the Croatian church stood for (mostly in the reverse order). The party simply
could not compete.

This was the basic reason for the growing antagonism of the party
and the tension that ensued in the late 1970s and the early 1980s.[25]
The Croatian church was attacked for nationalism, "clerical fascism,"
and hostility to the state. After a period of better relations in which the
Yugoslav head of state, Cvijetin Mijatović, was received in the Vatican
by Pope John Paul II at the end of 1980, the Zagreb authorities stepped
up their attacks.[26] The Stepinac case was exhumed in a renewed effort
to tar the dead prelate with the Ustasa brush.[27] The occasional priest
was tried and jailed and many more pilloried in the press. There can
be little doubt that the activities and especially the utterances of many
clerics in Croatia would have been found objectionable by even the
most liberal lay authority. Some embodied a hatred for Serbs that
showed that the spirit of Ante Pavelić had not yet been exorcized.
There were examples of political tactlessness on the part of even senior
churchmen. But, all in all, the cases of genuine offense were few, and
the party machine in Zagreb sought to generalize or magnify them. A
projected papal visit for the 1,300th anniversary of Croatian Christianity, which was massively celebrated in September 1984, had to be called
off because the lay authorities did not have the will to overcome the

myriad of bureaucratic difficulties.[28] It was somehow systematic of the dead end into which church-state relations had blundered.

But the Croatian church, under the robust leadership of Franjo Cardinal Kuharić, continued both to survive and thrive. And in spite of the bad relations with the Zagreb party and authorities its condition remained relatively enviable. The federal authorities in Belgrade knew that Yugoslavia's reputation in the West depended considerably on the Croatian church remaining in good health. The big question for the future, however, was whether the republican authorities in Zagreb realized this—or whether they cared. It was, after all, what Zagreb did that counted.

Just as the young in Croatia were being drawn to the church, there were also unmistakable signs of youthful religious revival, especially in Hungary and the Czech Lands. (This is also discussed in the chapters on the two countries concerned.) The revival has taken several forms, one of which is a renewed interest in Catholicism itself. In the Czech Lands the strengthening resolve of the aging primate, Cardinal Tomášek, sparked the loyalty and affection of many. The St. Methodius ceremonies in Velehrad in Moravia in 1985 attracted a very large following. There were several reasons for this revival, among which disillusionment with communism as an ideology and the need for a counterweight to it were probably the most important. But the Catholicism that was emerging was generally of an individualistic, spontaneous kind tending to reject organization and formal structures. It had little affinity for the traditional Catholic hierarchical system. In Hungary it had already caused some consternation among senior church officials. And it often saw its inspiration in the message and manner of Pope John Paul II, rejecting, or ignoring, what it considered to be religious "formalism." In the Czech Lands, too, there were signs of this Catholic spontaneity, often with ecumenical leanings. Though on a far smaller scale, it had similarities with the restless movements of the church in other parts of the world. Thus, the Roman Catholic church, which has been remarkably successful in surviving and repelling communism, could be faced by a growing problem with the younger generation among its own ranks. It could also be a problem more difficult to manage than the direct persecution it had endured under communism. It could make Vatican policy all the more difficult to formulate, articulate, and implement. Christianity might be reviving. But was the church in its old traditional form not also endangered by this revival?

Reactions to Eurocommunism

The Soviet determination to prevent the recurrence of another Prague Spring, and the emphasis on cohesion after August 1968 (see chapter 2), both attested to that suspicion of ideological nonconformity that has plagued Soviet relations with Eastern Europe since 1948. Whether Yugoslav or Polish revisionism, Hungarian "counterrevolution," or Czechoslovak reformism—all have met with the same negative Soviet response. It is a response that may have prevented the development of a viable system in Eastern Europe and a more satisfactory relationship between the Soviet Union and its allies. But it has not been entirely irrational: a basically conservative, defensive Soviet regime has feared the eroding qualities that change could have on the acceptance of its legitimacy and authority both at home and abroad.

As seen in this context, therefore, Soviet nervousness over Eurocommunism that began in the early 1970s took on a double dimension. They resented the loss of control over several important West European parties. But, more crucially, they probably feared that the impact of Eurocommunism on Eastern Europe could lead to a Czechoslovakia all over again. (After all, the ideas of the Prague Spring had contributed much to the ideological arsenal of Eurocommunism.) It was only logical for the Soviet leaders to assume that the most powerful communist party in the West (the Italian) in alliance with one of the most prestigious (the Spanish), fitfully supported by the best-organized (the French), could have some erosive influence on the East European political elites. While Moscow might endure the loss of control over these three parties, it could not tolerate the spread of their heresies to its allies.

Very briefly, the Eurocommunists, particularly the Italian and Spanish leaders, criticized "real" (i.e., Soviet-type) socialism on the following grounds: (1) its rejection of pluralism in public life; (2) its lack of internal party democracy; (3) its failure to separate the functions and responsibilities of party and state in government; (4) its use of trade unions solely as a transmission belt; (5) the paucity of independence that the Soviet Union accorded other states and parties; (6) the Soviet tendency to make their own state interests synonymous with the interests of communism as a whole.[29]

This was a severe enough indictment, and there is little doubt that many Eastern European communists would subscribe to most of it. There was little doubt, also, that many intellectuals were particularly interested in the Eurocommunist phenomenon. But it would seem that relatively few East Europeans considered it relevant to their particular problems of the 1970s. Particularly in Prague it evoked a sense of déjà vu. In fact, in Czechoslovakia, one of the salient features of Eurocommunism was probably more readily apparent than in other East European countries: that the basic tenets of Eurocommunism originated not in Western but in Eastern Europe, where they had already been tried but never tolerated. Eurocommunism presupposed the reforming of the communist system from within, as had the Prague Spring. But, as has been argued in chapter 1, the Prague Spring was the system's last chance to redeem itself. Eurocommunism was based on the acceptance of certain values and beliefs, a political and moral motivation, and a belief in certain possibilities that no longer seemed to apply in Eastern Europe.[30] It was also based on the fundamental acceptance of an ideology that had already become largely rejected.

The question of any possible impact of Eurocommunism on the reforms in Hungary and later on the renewal in Poland in 1980 and 1981 must, of course, be raised. Regarding Hungary it need only be said that reform there began in the early 1960s or even the late 1950s. The New Economic Mechanism had been prepared and introduced long before the loose tenets of Eurocommunism had been formulated under that label. As for Poland, the rise of Solidarity was a protest against the communist system as practiced in Poland and, as seen by the publication of its "Theses" in April 1981, its ideological underpinnings obviously considered any form of communism as basically irrelevant. As for the belated reform of the Polish party itself, it is true that this embodied some of the basic Eurocommunist tenets, and it was strongly supported by the Italian party (PCI). But there is no evidence at all suggesting that its inspiration derived from Eurocommunist sources. It was rather much more likely that it stemmed solely from those indigenous sources in Polish communism that were frustrated in 1956 and 1970 but had always remained not far below the surface of party life.

The Eurocommunists, particularly the Italian communists, strongly supported the "renewal" process in Poland—both the development of a pluralistic public life and the reforms suggested within the party itself. In fact, the PCI, and Enrico Berlinguer personally, had always attached great value to as full relations as possible with as many East European parties as were willing.[31] Relations were close with the Polish party under Gierek as well as with the Hungarian party under

Kádár.[32] Relations were maintained, however, even with the East Germans and Bulgarians whose opposition at times was more robust. (Only with the Czechoslovak party under Husák was there practically no contact.) It would seem that the Italians and the Spaniards assiduously cultivated the East European parties in the hope perhaps of influencing them, but probably more of supporting and publicizing any reform currents alive within them. This, in turn, probably explained the efforts Berlinguer in particular made to maintain the links with the CPSU. A break with Moscow would have meant a break with most of Eastern Europe.

The relations of the PCI and the Spanish party (PCE) with the Yugoslavs and, though less so, with the Romanians have continued to be close and relaxed. Indeed the PCI's relations with the League of Yugoslav Communists have been the fullest it has enjoyed with any party. Here it has not only been independence, but also the Yugoslavs' relative flexibility on political, ideological, and economic issues that led to close relations. Good Eurocommunist relations with Bucharest have rested solely on the Romanian party's independence from Moscow, Ceauşescu's domestic policy being hardly one with which they would wish to be associated.

It was partly the Soviets' concern over the possible inroads of Eurocommunism that prompted them to initiate the European conference of communist parties that finally met in East Berlin in June 1976. But this was not the only reason. East Berlin 1976 should probably be seen as the concomitant to the Helsinki CSCE conference of 1975, discussed later. Each was designed in its own way to consecrate Soviet supremacy: in the case of Helsinki over Soviet gains as a result of World War II; in the case of East Berlin over the whole European communist movement. In both cases, however, the Soviets appear to have miscalculated: to get either conference they had to make concessions, making the prize they won considerably less valuable than they had hoped.

In the case of East Berlin the basic mistake the Soviets appear to have made lay in their determination to induce the Yugoslavs to participate. For this they were eventually forced to pay the price the Yugoslavs were demanding, which was that the consensus rule be adopted, i.e., there should be no statement without unanimous consent. In all it took twenty months of preparation before the parties finally met in East Berlin, and during this period an alliance was forged between the Eurocommunists—the Italian, Spanish, British, Swedish, and, though with diminishing fervor and conviction, the French—and the Yugoslavs and the Romanians, mainly on this principle of consensus. In the end the CPSU was faced, rather as in the case of Helsinki, with the prospect of concession or no conference.

The document finally agreed on at East Berlin was a lowest common denominator document—so bland that everybody could agree. It was not binding; it was not even signed; it contained no general line, no ideological commitments. There was no mention of any special status for the CPSU or of "proletarian internationalism," and strong emphasis was laid on independence, equality, and noninterference. True, some of the Soviet Union's anti-Western foreign policy principles were approved, but this must have been cold comfort for Moscow after the losses it had suffered.[33]

After East Berlin the Soviets set about trying to salvage something from their defeat. For example, they strongly reasserted the principle of proletarian internationalism and pointedly strengthened their bilateral links with the loyalist parties that had supported them at East Berlin. Among these the most vociferous in their support were the Czechoslovaks, the East Germans, and the Bulgarians. The Poles and Hungarians, though supportive, were less conspicuous in the campaign for "real, existing socialism" against heresy, but it was the Polish party that agreed, presumably under considerable Soviet pressure, to cosponsor the April 1980 Paris conference of European parties. This was the Soviets' most important attempt to recoup the losses of East Berlin, and it was hosted by the French party, whose defection in the meantime from the Eurocommunist ranks had been an undoubted success for Moscow. But the conference turned out a fiasco. The Yugoslavs and the Romanians, as well as several West European parties, did not go. The divisions of East Berlin were only confirmed by the absences from Paris.

At the beginning of the 1980s, just when it seemed that the dynamism in the Eurocommunist movement was weakening, mainly because of the total defection of the French and the serious splintering of the Spanish party, the events in Poland served to give it a new temporary lease on life. Though it would be a misunderstanding to assume that Eurocommunism as such influenced these upheavals, their interaction could still be profound. The PCI's acrimony with the Soviets and their allies over the cause of Polish discontent, its character, and how to handle it showed, as it had in the case of Czechoslovakia in 1968, that developments in Eastern Europe most clearly revealed the basic differences between the Eurocommunist ethos and that of the "real, existing socialism."

But in the mid-1980s Eurocommunism became more of a memory than a current factor. The PCI was now concentrating not on Eurocommunism but what was being called the "Euro-Left," a combination of pluralistic communist parties and left-wing social democrats. It had expressed its sense of outrage over the destruction of Solidarity in Poland and had generally remained true to the principles that had evoked sympathy among many East Europeans. Several East European parties—especially the Yugoslav—continued to have excellent relations with it. But its presence was decreasingly felt, and its impact, never great, was less than ever.

The Onset of Détente

The following section does not try to narrate the détente process as it involved the East European states. Rather it gives the author's views on how détente affected the relations of some of those states with the Western powers, how it affected aspects of internal development in Eastern Europe, and how it affected East European relations with the Soviet Union. It is best to begin with the *economic* aspect of détente.

The economic division of Europe after World War II was best symbolized by Stalin's establishment of Comecon in 1949 (see chapter 4). Comecon symbolized the almost complete transformation of East European commerce that took place as a result of World War II and subsequent Soviet domination. In the interwar years the commerce of the East European countries that emerged from the Paris peace treaties was almost completely oriented westward—by no means to their total benefit. Trade with the Soviet Union was negligible; in the case of some countries it was nonexistent. Soviet domination now led to a reversal of this situation and, in its early years, to an economic exploitation that made the region's interwar exploitation by Western economic interests look mild in comparison. But this reversal was not to remain total for very long, and one of the most important aspects of East European history from the end of the 1960s has been the *partial* shift back to economic relations with the West—especially Western Europe, and most especially with West Germany.

Political relations developed along with economic relations. Several Western countries were involved in the process, but the most dramatic change was signaled by the now uninhibited reentry into Eastern Europe of the Federal Republic and eventual West German domination of the state-to-state détente process. This was facilitated by the interaction of the West German Ostpolitik and what became known as the new Soviet Westpolitik. With the former the name of the German Social Democratic chancellor, Willy Brandt, became intimately associated; with the latter that of Leonid Brezhnev.

But as indicated earlier, the Federal Republic was not welcomed with open arms by the whole of Eastern Europe—and here the distinction between Northern and Southern Tiers again asserts itself. Hungary, Bulgaria, and Romania, all three German allies in World War II, had no difficulty adapting themselves to the West German presence. In fact, they did so with alacrity. So did Yugoslavia, which, though it had suffered grievously at the hands of the Third Reich, now saw better relations with Bonn as an important political and economic buttress.[34] But with Poland, Czechoslovakia, and the GDR there were both old scores to settle and new difficulties to overcome. Ironically, it was with Poland that progress was quickest. The recent past had not been forgotten in Poland, but the communist leaders in Warsaw were Polish enough to know that Poland's raison d'état might have most to fear from a German-Russian rapprochement—the so-called Rapallo complex. Poland was therefore quick to anticipate developments between Bonn and Moscow by declaring its own readiness for the normalization of relations with the Federal Republic. This it did with Gomułka's speech in May 1969, just two months after the Warsaw Pact summit meeting in Budapest that marked the beginnings of Soviet rapprochement with Bonn.[35] The Polish normalization treaty with West Germany was signed in December 1970, just four months after the Soviet–West German treaty in August of that year.

The tactics of both the GDR and Czechoslovakia were quite different. The fear of West Germany that had actually hastened Warsaw's move for normalization only served to delay the responses of East Berlin and Prague. The GDR, insecure to the point of paranoia in its relations with the Federal Republic, now saw the stability it felt it had achieved through the building of the Berlin Wall in 1961 seriously threatened. Czechoslovakia was doubtless mindful of the experiences of World War II, although the Husák regime was even more mindful of the Prague Spring and what it perceived as the dangers of Western contamination.

But the GDR's attitude represented a greater obstacle to the new Soviet policy than the Czechoslovak. Prague could wait, but East Berlin could not. Pressure was, therefore, applied on Ulbricht, and his continued obstinacy caused his elegant dismissal in May 1971. In

September of the same year the Four Power Berlin agreement was signed. Its main effect on East-West German relations was that it allowed much freer access than before for West Germans to visit relations in the GDR.[36] But the most important agreement between the GDR and the FRG was the "Basic Agreement" (*Grundvertrag*) signed in December 1972.

As David Childs puts it:

> The Basic Treaty gave the SED (Socialist Unity—Communist—Party) what it had been after since 1949 and what Bonn had always denied the GDR—the recognition of its separate existence and of its full equality with the Federal Republic. Bonn still refused to recognize the GDR as a foreign state under international law. But the treaty made it respectable for all the other Western states, in NATO and outside it, to recognize the GDR, and a wave of recognitions began.[37]

The Czechoslovaks delayed the final signing of their normalization treaty with Bonn until December 1973, ostensibly on the issue of whether the Munich agreement, which dismembered the First Republic in 1938, should be regarded as null and void from the very point of signing (ab initio), as Prague argued, or as no longer having any validity, as Bonn argued. The issue was finally resolved after six rounds of talks, which began in March 1971. But, although the issue involved more than legal semantics, had the will been there on the Czechoslovak side it could have been settled much earlier. What worried Husák was the West German foot in the door. He may well have hoped that by delaying agreement long enough the whole process of détente might in the meantime be reversed.[38]

By the time Prague and Bonn signed their normalization treaty East-West détente was in full swing. It involved not only Western Europe but the United States and Canada, too. Improved political and cultural relations were certainly involved, though the picture here was uneven. Generally speaking, the Western states improved relations in both these spheres with Poland, Hungary, Bulgaria, and Romania, and, of course, with Yugoslavia; with the GDR and especially Czechoslovakia less so. (With Albania not at all.) But the main interest lay in the economic sphere. Eastern Europe's economic-technocratic intelligentsia now received full backing in their foraging from their political superiors, who, in turn, saw no signs of discouragement from Moscow. On the contrary, no matter how disconcerted some Soviet leaders may have been by the westward gravitation of their allies, Moscow, after all, appeared to be a full partner in the détente process.

The culmination of the détente process was the Final Act of the Conference on Security and Cooperation in Europe (CSCE) in Helsinki in July–August 1975.[39] Both the motives and the merits of Helsinki have been fiercely debated in the West. At one end of the spectrum it has been praised as a Western diplomatic success, at the other end as a Western diplomatic and moral betrayal, with the Soviets as the cynical victors and the hapless East Europeans as the losers. It was the Soviets who had pressed for the conference for almost ten years, and eventually they had got what they wanted.

Looking back at the 1970s it seems necessary to distinguish the formalities of détente, as dramatized in such spectaculars as the Helsinki conference, from its realities. The formalities should have been an expression of the realities but instead tended to assume an importance of their own, which they soon lost. The publication of the final Helsinki Agreement, full of the noblest sentiments about multiple freedoms in the Soviet and East European press, was in reality an act of cynicism and was regarded as such by the populations of the countries concerned. As for the "follow-ups" to Helsinki—the plenary meetings in Belgrade, Madrid, and Vienna, and the more specialized meetings in Stockholm, Bern, Budapest, and elsewhere—these may have been useful as signifying that contacts have not broken down altogether. But they became a boring charade, divorced from the realities of the situation, scrambling after meaningless consensus (though not always finding it),[40] and deservedly consigned to the minutiae columns of even the most comprehensive Western newspapers.

The symbols persisted, therefore, long after the realities changed. But the realities of détente in the 1970s were by no means as tilted in the Soviets' favor as many have insisted they were. Their economic effect could bring long-term benefits for the Eastern European economies. It is true that, from the contacts that developed, the Soviet Union gained access to valuable technology and technical information via Eastern Europe as well as directly. But just how much and how valuable this was is better left to experts or polemicists.[41] The whole Western credit policy may have brought little but debts for some of the debtor countries, but it was not without considerable advantage for others.[42] But, more generally, what the economic aspects of détente did was to bring the West into Eastern Europe in a much more comprehensive way than ever before. Some of the shorter-term effects of this might have been economically painful, but the eventual advantages could be considerable. The hard medicine the International Monetary Fund (IMF) began to administer in the 1980s might also bring results both for Yugoslavia and perhaps for Poland also. Had the eager creditors ten years earlier been more insistent on good husbandry before they showered Eastern Europe with petrodollars, some of the worst effects might have been avoided. But this was perhaps impossible to expect at the time. Perhaps lessons were later learned. The debt crisis made the West intimately involved with the economics of Eastern Europe. The involvement may have been unwilling on both sides, but eventually it might not be unrewarding for either side.

Détente's Political Impact

The political impact of détente in Eastern Europe revolves around the question whether it resulted in more political relaxation, no matter how marginal, for the societies concerned, and, if so, to what extent was this the result of regime responsiveness or of societal pressure.

No general answer can be given to the first question; it depended on the country concerned. In *Romania* the situation of society—politically and psychologically—deteriorated during the 1970s, this despite the improving relations between the Ceauşescu regime and the Western powers for most of the decade. *Czechoslovakia* hardly applies here since the Husák regime mainly stayed outside the détente process. In *Bulgaria* there was some political relaxation and, especially under Lyudmila Zhivkov in the second half of the 1970s, considerably more cultural freedom. But this was probably more due to Zhivkova's unique personality than to anything else. In *Yugoslavia* five years of virtual liberalism after the fall of Alexander Ranković in 1966 deteriorated in the 1970s, but this was due mainly to the real dangers of disintegration the Yugoslav federation faced. In *Albania*, the self-appointed pariah, rigidity, even terror, within the party increased as policy and personal conflicts continued. But life became somewhat easier for most Albanians, if for purely domestic reasons. At the other end of the spectrum no country engaged as enthusiastically in the détente process as *Hungary*, and few would disagree that the impact of this process was beneficial for society. And these domestic benefits of détente were largely the result of regime policy in Hungary rather than any direct societal pressure (at least in the immediate sense; ultimately much of the regime policy of concession dates back to the very pressure exerted by society in 1956). For the Kádár regime détente simply caused the policy already begun ten years before to accelerate.

The most complex and controversial cases in this regard concern the *GDR* and *Poland*. So nervous was the leadership in the GDR about its Basic Treaty with the Federal Republic that, for it, the domestic dangers seemed to outweigh the great international advantages mentioned earlier. They were too much for Walter Ulbricht, and though Honecker, his successor, was obviously prepared to live with the treaty, he seemed ready to take any precaution against its perceived risks. Hence the stress on *Abgrenzung* (or delimitation) from the Federal Republic. Hence also the ideologically motivated nationalization of much private and semiprivate property, the stepped-up spying on the citizenry, the even greater barbarity at the border against those trying to escape. Honecker, as the former party secretary for security and the man who supervised the building of the Berlin Wall in 1961, seemed ideally suited for repression and little inclined toward political relaxation. In cultural matters he was at first inclined to benevolence. But it was a watchful benevolence, and when by 1976 a real cultural ferment had developed in the GDR he responded by expulsions and deprivations of citizenship that in turn led to further disaffection among the cultural milieu.[43] There was pressure also from other sections of society —workers, pacifists, the churches, the youth generally (see chapter 7). By the second half of the decade the regime was on the defensive. But its response was considerably more civilized than many expected. There were some arrests, but expulsion to West Berlin and the Federal Republic was the main punishment. In the meantime, though the possibilities of travel to the West were for many years strictly limited for all but East German pensioners, few limitations were placed on travel the other way. In 1980, the peak year, 3.5 million visits from the Federal Republic and 2.6 million visits by West Berliners were recorded,[44] and the television transmissions from the Federal Republic, worrisome though they became, were still allowed unhindered entry.

The GDR was, therefore, a considerably livelier place at the end of the 1970s than at the beginning, with society much less afraid and more assertive. Regime policy or public pressure? Probably something of both—with the regime having to concede much more than it originally intended but finding it could both do it and survive. In overrating the dangers of détente it had underrated itself. It had both acquired more international respectability and maintained domestic stability, and, financially, it had done very well indeed.

In *Poland* there was considerable relaxation in both the political and cultural spheres throughout the 1970s (see chapter 5). There were several reasons for it: (a) the assertiveness of Polish society, especially the impressiveness of worker muscle that had toppled Gomułka and left no doubt that it could topple his successor if and when required; (b) a certain "live and let live" tolerance on the part of the Gierek leadership; (c) a gradual weakening of party discipline and morale resulting in further relaxation of control; (d) the détente process that brought Poland into the mainstream of East-West rapprochement and encouraged a regime sense of "international respectability," for which some internal relaxation was essential.

This last factor was reinforced by the evident concern in some regime circles that attempts to tighten controls over society could lead to Western credits being curtailed.[45] It was the interaction of all these factors that, though not fully accounting for the emergence of Solidarity, certainly helped to facilitate it. It is difficult to say which factor was the most important, but Warsaw's desire to "keep on the right side" of the Western powers undoubtedly played its part.

The impact of détente, therefore, showed yet again the distinctiveness of the different East European states and societies concerned. Moreover, the détente factor could never be considered except in combination with the others. It probably tended to incline the regimes to better behavior. But it was never powerful enough to neutralize factors working in the other direction—as in Romania, for example. On the other hand, it greatly strengthened and accelerated the effectiveness of factors working in the same direction—as in Hungary, especially, but also in Poland.

Détente's Impact on East European–Soviet Relations

Détente tended to project the East European states as members—no matter how junior—of the East-West relations process. It raised their international standing and, by doing so, raised problems for the Soviet Union in its relations with them.

For many years the Western diplomacy of the East European states was fully controlled by the Soviet Union. Control was exercised directly and indirectly. In the first case, depending on the demands of the situation, one, more, or all of the East European states (Yugoslavia after

1948 and Albania after 1961 excepted) followed or participated in Soviet foreign policy initiatives. The most spectacular example was probably the Khrushchev-led parade of communist leaders at the United Nations in New York in 1960. In the West European context the moves against the new Federal Republic of Germany in the late 1950s are perhaps the best known. The indirect, proxy, or orchestrated methods were more interesting. They could be seen when an East European state launched an initiative clearly inspired by Moscow; obviously to Moscow's advantage; sometimes, though not always, also in the national interest of the state concerned. Here a division of roles usually took place.

To take specific examples: the proposals for cooperation toward a nuclear-free Balkans put forward by the Romanian premier, Chivu Stoica, in 1957 and 1959, followed by the more extensive proposals for disarmament by the Bulgarian leader Todor Zhivkov in 1960[46] and, more recently, by Zhivkov again in the early 1980s[47] — all these moves can be taken as examples of the second, indirect, or proxy method. They were all in the Soviet interest, but it could also be argued that they generally conformed with the historic and longer-term interests of the states concerned. They also gave Romania and Bulgaria a role to play, as well as a certain prominence that they doubtless enjoyed. Romania was soon to make this role at least a semi-independent one. Bulgaria remained a loyal dependency of the Soviet Union, but even in its case there was sometimes a lingering suspicion that it tended to cross the limits of authority Moscow laid out for it (see chapter 10). On the Northern Tier probably the best example was the Rapacki Plan. Here a Soviet foreign policy stratagem could be genuinely identified with the Polish national interest because, if it had been successful, it would have neutralized what must have been perceived by many Poles —communist and noncommunist alike—as a new German threat looming so soon after the defeat of the old one. Within the framework of a Soviet initiative, therefore, the Poles' "own" interest was being served.

But this cozy situation from the Soviet point of view did not continue long after détente arrived on the international scene. It has already been mentioned how, during the first rustling of détente in 1966, even Bulgaria seemed reluctant to follow the Soviet lead in rejecting West German advances. Soon Romania, in one of its greatest gestures of defiance to Moscow, established diplomatic relations with Bonn in February 1967. Two years later Poland, with quite different motives from Romania, probably sought to preempt what it feared might be a new Russian-German Rapallo by itself offering normalization with Bonn, something Gomułka had implicitly rejected when suggested by de Gaulle in 1968. Ulbricht, as already mentioned, could not bring himself to digest détente and had to be retired.

The readiness with which most East European states made and then multiplied their contacts must have caused some nervousness in the Kremlin. But Moscow gave no obvious signs of discouragement. The Soviet leadership may have been confident that, despite the apparent relish and spontaneity with which some of their clients were exploiting the new Western conection, they could be reined in whenever the need arose. In this their confidence turned out to be exaggerated.

"Damage Limitation" as Détente Wanes

At the end of the 1970s and in the early 1980s the superpower relationship suffered three shattering blows. They were:

1. The Soviet invasion of Afghanistan in December 1979.
2. The crushing of Solidarity in Poland in December 1981.
3. Soviet reaction to the installation by the Federal Republic, along with Britain and Italy, of new medium-range ballistic missiles—the INF controversy. Less shattering, but by no means without their impact, were also two personal factors:

    a.   The assumption of power in the United States in January 1981 by Ronald Reagan, who was perceived as an opponent even of negotiations with the Soviet Union and whose early rhetoric did little to correct that perception.

    b.   The long, eroding enfeeblement and eventually the death of Leonid Brezhnev in 1982. No matter how self-serving Brezhnev's interpretation of détente may have been, his death only augmented the apprehensiveness already pervading the world situation.[48]

It was these factors that were largely to destroy the American-Soviet relationship. But as superpower relations deteriorated rapidly, those between the two halves of Europe were not nearly as seriously affected.

Over Afghanistan practically the whole globe joined the United States in its sense of outrage, but there was little support for the practical steps that the Carter administration wished to take in retaliation. There was little solidarity among the NATO allies. In fact, Afghanistan increased allied disunity rather than unity. Most West Europeans refused to see the issue as either a threat to global peace or to détente. If anything, it tended to strengthen Eurocentricism rather than weaken it. As for Moscow's allies, there were indications of distinct uneasiness in at least three of them—Poland, Hungary, and, of course, Romania—over the Soviet action and a fear it could endanger East-West relations. It was a development that led to some West European illusions about a unity of European interest, with the two halves of Europe forced together by the irresponsibility of their two patrons. This was nonsense. What did happen was that, because of Afghanistan, the East Europeans had to be more circumspect in pursuing their relations with Washington and Wall Street. But even here there were nuances. Romania, always the exception, still maintained correct relations with the United States, although these were now becoming much less cordial because of Bucharest's lamentable record on domestic human rights. Hungary also continued to make clear its wish for good relations, and even the GDR quietly signaled that it had no wish to return to the days of no relations. Still, Afghanistan tended to put Washington off-limits for Moscow's allies, and this only made Western Europe more attractive to them than before.

The military coup in Poland under General Jaruzelski in December 1981 again found the Soviet Union in the dock, now along with the Polish regime, with the Americans again pointing the accusing finger.

As for the West Europeans, if Afghanistan had been too far away for commitment, Poland was too close for comfort. Genuine outrage at what happened soon spent itself in Western Europe and, especially in the Federal Republic, tended to be replaced by:

1. Fear that the Polish situation could lead—*or could have led*—to war in Europe.
2. Confusion over the motives of General Jaruzelski in crushing Solidarity. Was he patriot or janissary?
3. Concern or exasperation with the American reaction, which many Europeans felt would only exacerbate a situation to which they were more exposed than the Americans. Many Europeans also thought that such a situation in the hands of a man like Reagan could lead to disaster.
4. A resigned acceptance to the fact that Poland, like the rest of Eastern Europe, was in the Soviet sphere of influence and—as in Hungary in 1956 and Czechoslovakia in 1968—Moscow could get away with anything there, since to try to stop it could lead to nuclear war.
5. A hope—not entirely unreasonable at the time—that some or many

of the freedoms gained in Poland would eventually be preserved, if in a different form. This was sometimes accompanied by criticisms of Solidarity that it had gone too far in its demands and of the Polish nation as a whole for its alleged historic lack of moderation.[49]

Like Afghanistan, therefore, Poland worsened rather than improved Western European relations with the United States and only deepened the splits in the alliance. It was more serious than Afghanistan since Poland was in Europe and many Europeans—even those without personal prejudice against Reagan—considered that Washington did not adequately realize the sensitiveness and gravity of the situation. This view was most prevalent in the Federal Republic, where genuine apprehensiveness and concern were often mixed with a blithe optimism about the outcome of Polish developments and sometimes even a tortuous attempt to rationalize or defend the Soviet action. In Western Europe generally there was a conscience-troubled relief over Poland.

East European reactions to the suppression of Solidarity are discussed in chapter 5. As for relations with Western Europe, December 1981 tended to reinforce the effect Afghanistan had already had in making Eastern Europe's relations closer with Western Europe. Its adverse impact on American relations with the Soviet Union was much greater than that of Afghanistan. Good relations with the United States, therefore, became even less of an option than before (although both Hungary and even the GDR continued to flag their good intentions). The corresponding reaction was for the East Europeans to intensify their efforts to improve relations with Western Europe. "Europeanness" was the order of the day, and the Soviets had no objection to it because it generally served their anti-American purpose.

Moscow's relaxed attitude was specifically due to the persisting hope of achieving two aims: (1) to prevent the implementation of NATO's 1979 dual-track INF decision involving the stationing of cruise missiles in several West European countries and of cruise and Pershing II missiles in the Federal Republic; and (2) to deepen and widen the split between Western Europe and the United States.

At the beginning of the 1980s both these aims had looked realistic. But within a couple of years they looked much less so. In Britain the Conservative government under Margaret Thatcher was firmly committed to the Atlantic alliance, and specifically to the American tie. France under the socialist Mitterrand was more Atlanticist and anti-Soviet than under its previous, right-wing government. Italy's Atlanticist resolve appeared to be strengthening, and the socialist victory in Spain failed to promise any Soviet gains in the Iberian peninsula. Only in the Balkans, where the new Greek government under Andreas Papandreou had come to power on an anti-Western platform, had Soviet strategic and diplomatic opportunities seemed to be brightening. But despite anti-American and pro-Soviet gestures, Papandreou showed no sign once in power of leaving NATO or the European Community. Even the American bases in Greece seemed to be given a new lease on life.

Finally, the biggest hope of all turned into disappointment. The Federal Republic—the key, despite itself, to Western unity—returned the Christian Democrats to power in early 1983, and by the end of the year the first Pershings and cruises were in place. In Britain the Conservatives were returned to power stronger than ever, and the cruises were installed there, while in Italy a Socialist premier was not to be drawn away from NATO decisions by either threats or blandishments.

It was then that Moscow abandoned (or temporarily shelved, as it was later to turn out) its grand design and the "European cooperation" policy it had pursued since 1969. The United States remained, of course, the chief pariah on a global scale, but in Europe the Federal Republic, for long the object of Moscow's blandishments, now became the target for its venom. The other West Europeans did not escape lightly, but the main wrath was reserved for Bonn. Old charges of German "revanchism" were unearthed and the bust of "der böse Deutsche" dusted off. Détente, which for several years the Soviets had been preaching was indeed divisible, became indivisible again.

This was the critical point for the détente between the two halves of Europe. Now that the Soviet Union had so demonstratively turned its back on Western Europe, especially on West Germany, it expected a similar about-face from its junior partners.

Turning inward and "socialist self-sufficiency" became the order of the day. Perhaps with stronger, more united, and vigorous leadership in the Kremlin the rebuff over IMF might have been met more positively —with, say, some counterproposition or assertive counteraction. But, from the calcified leadership existing then (this was still pre-Gorbachev) a thoroughly negative response was perhaps all that could be expected.

The Soviet leaders can hardly have been so purblind as to expect enthusiastic and prompt East European alignment with the new policy. But, in the event, neither they nor probably the majority of East Europeans (nor the most informed Western observers) could have expected the tepidity, deviousness, or plain defiance of the response from several of the capitals concerned.

The Soviet Union, therefore, after November 1983 retired, like Achilles, to sulk in its tent. But not all its East European clients, except for Czechoslovakia, which had never left its tent, were prepared to do the same. Poland found itself in a special situation. It castigated the West for its alleged "interference" after martial law was imposed, yet it moaned over the West's decision to withdraw the economic concessions the Polish economy had previously enjoyed.

Three East European states were obviously unwilling to retire to their tents. They were Romania, Hungary, and the GDR. Yet a fourth, Bulgaria, made its unwillingness less obvious, but it was always there to be inferred. The dispute that followed was unique in the history of Soviet–East European relations.

Dr. Johann-Georg Reissmuller, the highly respected West German commentator, summed up the situation as follows: "In the Soviet Union's front yard it is not so much that a small block has been formed of countries with generally the same outlook. It is much more a case of some states having found parallel interests in one aspect of foreign policy. Therefore, one cannot speak of any special alliance. But the fact of three of its allies pursuing the same self-willed course carries for the Soviet Politburo the whiff of 'fractionalism.'"[50]

In terms of confrontation the dispute that took place in 1984 was one between East Berlin and Moscow. But, as Ron Asmus has pointed out, its "theoretical parameters" were staked out in Budapest.[51] This was done by Mátyás Szürös, Central Committee secretary responsible for relations with other communist parties, in a lecture published in January 1984.[52] Szürös, the Hungarian, preached the familiar Romanian sermon about each party having to decide its policy for itself, according to its own perceptions of its interests. He was later to make a name for himself by repeating such sentiments several times, and by urging the rights and the importance of small nations. Basically he was to say little that the Romanians had not been saying since 1964, but the fact that now a Hungarian official was saying it gave the issue a new importance and freshness—not least because on intrabloc and foreign policy Kádár had always been careful to follow the Soviet line.[53]

It was shortly before the publication of Szürös's theoretical formulations that Honecker made his practical remark about the need to "limit the damage" done to relations between the two Germanies as a result of Bonn's missile deployment.[54] He followed up his remark by a number of practical concessions, especially with regard to emigration to the Federal Republic, which left no doubt about his seriousness. But at this stage Honecker was not ostensibly defying the Soviet line because nobody (perhaps least of all the Soviets themselves) seems to have known what their line was. (This was yet another example of the Soviet lack of decisiveness in Eastern Europe at times of misunderstanding or crisis.) With Moscow apparently undecided, the way was open for polemics among the East Europeans themselves. The Czechoslovak party daily *Rúde Právo* indirectly but obviously waded in against Szürös,[55] who was not slow getting into print to defend himself.[56] It was only in April that Moscow began making clear, not only its new anti-West German policy, but also its opposition to both Hungarian principles and East German practice.

What followed was open dispute between Moscow and East Berlin. The GDR authorities continued their verbal restraint toward Bonn, maintained their policy of concessions, stepped up their plans for a Honecker visit to the Federal Republic in September 1984, and received, in July, the second major West German loan inside thirteen months (see chapter 7). Two days after the announcement of the second loan *Pravda* strongly attacked relations between the two Germanies and, by implication, reprimanded the Honecker regime.[57] It followed with a similar reprimand a few days later, by which time *Neues Deutschland*, the East German party daily, had defended itself with a reply of its own and by publishing two articles from the Hungarian press defending East Berlin's position.[58] The sparring continued practically throughout August, and, in an unmistakable gesture, Honecker flew to Bucharest toward the end of that month to attend the Romanian Liberation Day ceremonies. He was easily the highest-ranking East European visitor present.

But he was not prepared for the culminating act of defiance, which would have been to go ahead with the planned visit to the Federal Republic in September. In early September it was announced that the visit had been "postponed." Just a few days later the Bulgarian leader, Todor Zhivkov, called off his own visit to Bonn after the visit to Sofia of a Soviet delegation led by Mikhail Gorbachev. (Only Ceauşescu, inured and resistant to Soviet opposition, went ahead with his already planned visit.) Subsequently, relations between Bonn and East Berlin cooled (although they never froze), and the Soviet Union appeared to have restored some sort of order.

Several points emerge from this intrabloc imbroglio of 1984. They are:

1. The continuing importance and divisiveness of the Federal Republic in Eastern Europe as a whole.

2. The fact that the most popular and "legitimizing" policy for the GDR was one involving closer relations with the Federal Republic, that Honecker realized it and was prepared to act on it.

3. The Hungarian determination to maintain good relations with the West and to clothe it with a theoretical justification despite opposition from Moscow.

4. The lack of decisiveness of Soviet policy at a critical period. This was by no means new, having occurred in 1956, 1968, and 1980 in Poland, to mention only three of the most notable occasions.

5. The interacting nature of Eastern Europe's policy with the West and with the Soviet Union. To quote Asmus again, "although the 'special relationship' between the two German states had served as a catalyst, the real issue at the heart of this dispute went much deeper and touched upon the interests of the entire bloc."

6. The eventual ability of the Soviet Union to get its way when determined to do so.

Three years later, in 1987, in a much different international climate and under a much different overlord in Moscow, Erich Honecker did visit the Federal Republic. It was a triumph for both himself and the GDR. But the point about Moscow's ultimate authority had been reaffirmed.

It is this point that has constituted the basic and ultimate truth about Eastern Europe for forty years. Détente—in this case exemplified by the inter-German relations in 1984—has so far exhibited a chronic tendency to turn on itself. It bares the dichotomy between Soviet and East European interests and threatens Soviet control in Eastern Europe itself. Sooner or later it founders on Soviet determination and power.

Is it not more cruel than kind, therefore, for the West to cultivate good relations with willing East European states, especially since the West has neither a big enough stick, nor enough carrots, nor enough will, to induce Moscow to extend, or even cut, its curbing leash? The best answer to this legitimate question is that Eastern Europe cannot be excised from any East-West equation. Unless the West deliberately built its own wall of exclusion it could not stop that westward gravitation to which all East European countries are now subject. From time to time that gravitation may end in frustration or even tragedy. But it reappears very soon, and its tendency is to accelerate. And though they are fully aware of the risks involved, the East European peoples, pressing their governments to comply, would not have it otherwise.

American Policy Toward Eastern Europe

America's first exposure to East Europeans came in the last two decades of the nineteenth century when tens of thousands of the "huddled masses" began passing through Castle Garden or Ellis Island on the way to playing their invaluable part in the building of the United States. In 1914, the first year of World War I, immigrants from Eastern Europe accounted for at least 300,000 out of the all-time annual peak of 1.2 million.[59]

Direct American interest in Eastern Europe at the official level was dramatically exhibited by President Wilson at the Paris peace negotiations at the end of World War I. Five of Wilson's Fourteen Points concerned Eastern Europe and were predicated on the principle of national self-determination, a principle based on the American notion of international justice and on sympathy for the historically oppressed nations of the region, but one that inevitably led to the oversimplification of a most complex situation.

But though the political map of post-World War I Eastern Europe was largely drawn up on the basis of Wilson's principles, the United States did not remain on the international scene to monitor or even guarantee them. Wilson was repudiated; the United States lapsed into neutralistic normalcy and stayed there till December 1941. When it emerged from World War II it was the dominant international power, the unquestioned leader of the free nations in a polarized world. Now it could not avoid Eastern Europe, on whose self-determination it had insisted some thirty years before, but which was already being obliterated by Soviet power and ambition.

It is pointless here to stir up the pools of Yalta and Tehran. The acrimony over the Western mistakes allegedly made there is totally incommensurate with their scant relevance today. What matters here is that in 1945, and for over a decade to come, the United States was the only Western power to be a factor in East European developments. The formerly great West European powers—Germany, Italy, France, Great Britain, and Austria—either had difficulties themselves in resisting communist subversion or were at best only slowly recovering from the economic and psychological damage of war.

They were able to recover largely through American vision, decisiveness, and generosity. By the end of 1948 Western Europe (including Greece and Turkey) was safe from the Soviet danger. What had seemed at least a possibility in 1945—Soviet subversion of parts of Western Europe—had been avoided. Moreover, in 1948 the Soviet Union itself suffered its first great postwar reverse—the loss of Yugoslavia. Policy-makers in Washington now had more time and more calm in which to frame a policy toward Eastern Europe.

As Lincoln Gordon writes, the main factor that has shaped American policy toward Eastern Europe since World War II has been its "critical position—in the global super-power confrontation, including its direct relationship to the security and political orientation of Western Europe."[60] As additional factors of less importance, Gordon lists the influence of organized ethnic groups in the United States (although only the huge Polish community is very impressive in terms of numbers) and "the idealistic pursuit of the universal desiderata of national self-determination and respect for human rights." These last two factors, continues Gordon, "have (however) often been decisive on specific issues within a broad line of policy."[61] He rightly rejects the importance, at least up to now, of the American economic interest in Eastern Europe. "The scale of these interests," as he says, "is comparatively small and their impact on policy making only marginal."[62]

The Principles and Objectives of Policy

The United States has never accepted the validity or the permanence of Soviet domination over Eastern Europe or the forced imposition of communist rule there. It stands for self-determination and the right of East Europeans to choose their own kind of government. But it accepts the realities of the East European situation and of Soviet power, interests, and sensitivities there (see chapter 2). It has never seriously sought to challenge the Soviet Union's hold directly, even when it possessed unrivaled military superiority in the first decade after 1945. This is true in spite of the "rollback" rhetoric and robustness for a short period before Stalin's death in 1953.

This tempering of eventual aim with indefinite constraints on its fulfillment leaves the United States with little room for maneuver in its East European policy. But it has generally sought to edge toward the long-term goal of internal democratization and the slackening of the Soviet grip through a policy aimed at "transforming" power relationships within the East European states themselves and in their relationships with Moscow. Though the United States is aware that the meaningful political developments in the communist world would always be endogenous, it was never prepared to sit back and be an idle spectator to the course of Eastern Europe's progress. Here its policy is different from that of most West European countries, which, at least in the political sphere, have preferred a role of minimal interference or penetration. This minimal policy, its defenders argue, is more effective because it does not unnecessarily or prematurely arouse Soviet fears. By the same token, it is claimed that it mitigates the risks to international peace.[63] Generally, the West Europeans argue (despite an often more lively rhetoric in Paris and London) that the best way to change the status quo is to accept it, while the Americans maintain that the best way of changing it is by eroding it—but gradually, almost imperceptibly.

The American Strategy

In its strategy of erosion the United States has generally used three main methods:

1. The insistence on conducting foreign policy with the different East European states at two levels: the state level and the societal level.

2. Differentiation, or scaling, the benevolence of American treatment of an individual East European country according to its domestic policy and/or its foreign policy, particularly toward the Soviet Union.

3. The consideration of Eastern Europe (or, more accurately, the individual East European states) as an entity in its own right and not as a Soviet appendage, particularly rejecting the contentions that any significant movement in Eastern Europe must be dependent on Soviet initiative, example, or permission.

All three methods need explaining. The difference between the state and societal levels in diplomacy is self-evident. The state level means the gamut of government-to-government contacts that correspond to "diplomatic" or "state relations" between sovereign states. Societal relations involve direct or indirect relations between the government and groups or individuals of one country with the society of another country; it is sometimes called "public diplomacy." Between democratic states such societal relations proceed with the permission, blessing, or active encouragement of all parties concerned. Authoritarian or aspirant-totalitarian governments resent such contacts, however, often regarding them as a threat or unfriendly interference. Most East European governments (not to mention the Soviet) still do so, although more recently the Hungarian government has shown a wise tolerance of many forms of societal contacts with the West. The most officially resented of American societal contacts with East Europeans are the broadcasts of Radio Free Europe. This station regards itself as speaking not so much in the official interests of the United States as in the interests of the East Europeans themselves and has been remarkably successful over the years in attracting and keeping large audiences. Another example of American "societal diplomacy" with Eastern Europe has been contacts with "dissidents" of various kinds, especially in Poland since the crushing of Solidarity in 1981.

As in several other respects, West Germany finds itself at the other end of the spectrum in regard to policy at the societal level. Most prominently under the Social Democratic–Free Democratic administration of the 1970s, but also under the Christian Democratic–Free Democratic administration of the 1980s, it has tended to avoid the more open types of contact with East European society. This is logical in view of the whole thrust of Ostpolitik since the late 1960s and its stress on government-to-government relations. The West Germans regard their approach as more effectively humane, especially in relations with the GDR, which dominate their Ostpolitik; repression has been much more widely eased and permission to settle in the Federal Republic much more generously given, it is claimed, through unpublicized official contacts than headline-grabbing derring-do on behalf of human rights. Because of the very existence of the GDR, of course, Bonn's policy has entailed special characteristics, and on the question of societal contacts and human rights most West European countries have gone along with the United States in pursuing a quite vigorous policy.

Differentiation was a term already used to describe American policy in the early 1960s, but it became widely used only in the 1970s. Differentiation would have made no sense anyway before the end of the 1950s, until some East European regimes began distinguishing themselves from others by the liberalization of their domestic policies and/or by the first signs of thinking for themselves in their relations with Moscow. Those countries that were perceived as doing one or both were "differentiated favorably" by the United States from the others in political and cultural but mainly in economic policies. Those countries that did neither, especially those that demonstratively eschewed both, have been "differentiated unfavorably" by Washington.

Differentiation was one of the main subjects of a speech given by Vice-President George Bush in Vienna in September 1983. It was a strident speech, embarrassing both his Austrian hosts and those East European governments he was anxious to "differentiate favorably" from the others. But for the purposes of explaining differentiation it was plain enough. Said Bush: "Our policy is one of differentiation—that is, we look to what degree [East European] countries pursue autonomous foreign policies, independent of Moscow's direction, and to what degree they foster domestic liberalization—politically, economically and in their respect for human rights." He continued: "The United States will engage in close political, economic and cultural relations with those countries such as Hungary and Romania which assert greater openness and independence. We will strengthen our dialogue and cooperation with those countries." Bush concluded:

> We will not, however, reward closed societies and belligerent foreign policies—countries such as Bulgaria and Czechoslovakia, which continue to flagrantly violate the most fundamental human rights; and countries such as East Germany and, again, Bulgaria which act as proxies for the Soviets in the training, funding and arming of terrorists, and which supply advisors and military and technical assistance to armed movements seeking to destabilize governments in the developing world.[64]

As already mentioned, "differentiation" is best reflected in economic policy. The best-known and most important form of "positive differentiation," i.e., favorable policy for good behavior, is the accordance of MFN (Most Favored Nation) treatment to the country concerned. MFN status means that the goods exported to the United States are not subject to the quite severe tariff levels raised as long ago as 1930 by the Smoot-Hawley Act. In a sense this privilege may not amount to much since the American share of total East European trade with Western industrial countries has amounted to no more than 10 percent, and the Western share overall of East European trade is relatively small.[65] Still, MFN conveys an advantage, and, for both its economic worth and its political symbolism, it is eagerly sought after by *all* the East European states. Though less important than MFN, substantial credits from the Export-Import Bank to buy American industrial goods and from the Commodity Credit Corporation to buy agricultural supplies are also granted. In the 1970s American commercial (i.e., nongovernmental) banks provided commercial credits for several East European countries (though, taken together, West European credits were much larger), and during the East European balance-of-payments crises of the early 1980s "differentiation" could be brought to bear in helping to reschedule the debts of some East European countries.

Poland, Romania, and Hungary have been by far the main beneficiaries of differentiation, although other countries, including the nefarious GDR and Bulgaria, also received large (nonofficial) commercial credits in the 1970s. Poland received MFN as early as 1960 in response to the Polish October of 1956 and the promising beginnings of Gomułka's rule. Romania received it in 1975 and Hungary in 1978. It was gratefully received—there can be no doubt about that. But in all three cases the glacierlike slowness of the American perception and the American executive-legislative process is evident. By 1960, for example, Gomułka had long cast aside his reformer's mantle and was behaving like a true reactionary—and a loyal Soviet ally to boot (see chapter 5). By 1975 the doubts about Ceauşescu's domestic policies had become gloomy certainties (see chapter 8). He still sought as much independence as possible from the Kremlin—one of the two differentiation criteria —but, still, a pat on the back would have looked better five years earlier.[66] Even in the case of Hungary, the liberalizing domestic policies had begun ten or even fifteen years before. But at least Hungary got MFN when it was still deserving it. In the case of both Poland and Romania the awards had very much of a retrospective look.

As MFN can be given, so also it can be taken away, as was the case with Poland in 1982 after the crushing of Solidarity and the imposition of martial law. A reward for good behavior thus became a sanction for bad. In the face of oppression in Poland, the United States found itself engaged in a series of punitive acts—political, economic, and cultural —for the first time against an East European country. (These followed closely on the sanctions against the Soviet Union for the invasion of Afghanistan at the end of 1979.) The effectiveness of the sanctions against Poland are referred to in chapter 5. While apparently damaging to some extent the already ravaged Polish economy, they appear to have had little effect on the course, or even the pace, of Polish domestic policy. Had they been part of a concerted Western policy and action they might have been more generally effective. Still, some gesture of outrage from Washington against the destruction of democracy in Poland was probably essential for both international and domestic consumption.

Finally, to the third method in the American strategy—treating Eastern Europe as an entity in itself. The element of key importance here has been the rejection of the notion that ultimately what happens in Eastern Europe depends on what happens in the Soviet Union. Since the invasion of Czechoslovakia in August 1968, which saw the Soviets destroy an East European regime's attempt to regenerate itself, this has become a notion widely accepted in the West. The destruction of Solidarity in Poland in 1981 only strengthened it. Again, it was always one of the premises of the West German Ostpolitik and, although it is not as clearly articulated by the Christian Democrats as it was by the Social Democrats, it has had widespread backing in political circles in Bonn as well as among the population as a whole. In other West European countries there is also a muted or tacit acceptance of this premise, despite the occasional rhetoric to the contrary. It derives not from any fainthearted unwillingness "to stand up to the Russians" but rather from what those who accept it consider to be a humane and realistic understanding of the situation. It also became accepted by some circles in the United States, but it has never become formally incorporated into American policy. Obviously, Washington accepts the fact and the implications of Soviet domination—above all, Moscow's ultimate ability to obstruct the course of events in Eastern Europe. But it does not see Moscow as either originating or dictating events, or as having the right to do so. Any other course would be seen by East Europeans as condemning them to a fatal helplessness. Most thoughtful East Europeans do see what happens in the Soviet Union as being of essential relevance to their own countries. Hence their enthusiasm for Gorbachev in the late 1980s. But that does not mean that the same East Europeans see themselves as having no role to play at home except as conveyors, purveyors, or adapters of the Soviet model, always looking over their shoulders at the orchestrators in Moscow.

The Phases of American Policy

Though the ultimate objective of American policy in Eastern Europe —self-determination through an erosion of the status quo—has generally remained the same since World War II, this does not mean that different periods have not had different rhetoric, emphasis, and nuance. In fact, in the early postwar period, up to 1956, it seemed that interference rather than erosion might become the main means of trying to gain Washington's ends.

The cold war in Europe had, as already mentioned, taken a favorable turn for the United States by the end of 1948 after the tense years since the end of the war. Even Stalin's empire itself showed signs of crumbling. After the brilliant Soviet subversion of Czechoslovakia in February 1948, there had come the stunning loss of Yugoslavia, the veritable jewel in the new imperial crown. It was probably this unexpected bonus that spurred an increased confidence in Washington. First Tito was given economic, military, political, and psychological support, invaluable in helping him withstand the East bloc boycott and the attempts to subvert him immediately after 1948. But American hopes appear to have gone further. A National Security Council paper of December 1949 suggested that, Western Europe having now apparently been secured against communism, it might be time to assume a more offensive posture with regard to Eastern Europe, to "do more to cause the elimination or at least the reduction of predominant Soviet influence in the satellite states of Eastern Europe." Freedom for Eastern Europe was the ultimate goal, but the interim aim was "to foster a heretic drifting away process" leading to "schismatic communist regimes."[67] What was meant, of course, was Titoism. Communism itself was not the interim target. On the contrary, national communism was the interim goal.

However overconfident these suggestions came to look in retrospect, they were sober indeed compared with the rhetoric that was being splashed about in public with regard to Eastern Europe. These were the days of the "rollback of communism" and the "liberation of the captive nations," totally unrealistic slogans being mouthed by leading politicians against a background of frenetic anticommunism that was soon to acquire its McCarthyite tinge. Actually, the whole "rollback" notion had very little substance. True, it spawned Radio Free Europe in 1949 and appears to have inspired amateurish CIA attempts to liberate Albania between 1950 and 1952 (monitored by Kim Philby). But it had little impact on actual American policy, which became guided by prudence and a realistic view of the power situation in Eastern Europe.

The Soviet suppression of the workers' rebellion in East Germany in 1953 should have been sufficient damper on any American crusading in Eastern Europe. But it was the unhindered suppression of the Hungarian Revolution by the Red Army that finally brought Americans, as well as the East Europeans themselves, to realize the basic Western inability to interfere directly in a region where the Soviets would use force if they felt they had to.[68]

After the suppression of the Hungarian Revolution the cold war imagery gradually died down. "Rollback" became a thing of the past, almost a dirty word from a bygone era. But it took several years for new thinking to be articulated. In 1961, however, Zbigniew Brzezinski and William Griffith published their seminal article, "Peaceful Engagement in Eastern Europe," in *Foreign Affairs*.[69] Essentially, they preached erosion in Eastern Europe. Again, in retrospect their goals seem optimistic. Undoubtedly influenced by the beginnings of domestic liberalization in some East European countries, the continuation of de-Stalinization by Khrushchev, the advent of the Sino-Soviet schism and the room for maneuver this might give some East European states, Brzezinski and Griffith were apparently confident of an indefinite liberalizing trend leading eventually to the Finlandization of Eastern Europe. Brzezinski, later at the State Department, gave vogue to the expression "bridge building," a process by which the West might, with sympathy but also with circumspection, aid the endogenous processes of Finlandization in the different East European countries. Brzezinski had later to temper his optimism about the speed of these processes, and the invasion of Czechoslovakia delivered what then seemed a knockout blow to his hopes. But August 1968 scattered rather than destroyed the centrifugal forces in Eastern Europe. Within a few years, as Brzezinski and others always predicted, these forces had regrouped and were on the move again. Brzezinski may have been premature in some of his expectations, but nobody has understood the basic forces at work in Eastern Europe better than he and nobody has done more to keep Eastern Europe, qua Eastern Europe, within the purview of American attention.

During the Nixon-Kissinger era (1969–74, or until 1977 to allow for President Ford) the overall substance of American policy toward Eastern Europe may not have changed, but its manner and emphasis certainly did. Basically, Nixon and Kissinger saw the region more in what are usually called realpolitik terms than either their predecessors or successors. They did much to "normalize" and expand state relations with most of the East European countries—at the political, economic, and cultural levels. But the concentration was mainly on the state level, very little on the societal level. President Nixon's unprecedented visits to Eastern Europe—to Romania in 1969, Yugoslavia in 1970, and Poland in 1972—though received with popular enthusiasm, were primarily designed to remind Moscow that Eastern Europe was a source of Soviet vulnerability as well as strength. This is not to disparage the policies of those years. East-West détente, for which Kissinger in particular worked so hard, did achieve considerable success, some of which has been lasting. American–East European state relations greatly increased in volume and kind, the high point being the culmination of the CSCE process at Helsinki in 1975. The general balance for the United States and the East European states of this process was favorable. And the closer state relations did have an extensive spin-off at the societal level in the fewer restrictions on travel as well as in other aspects of human rights. But the *motives* of the Nixon-Kissinger policy tended to be different. The whipped-up commotion over the so-called Sonnenfeldt Doctrine aside,[70] it would not have been difficult seeing Kissinger's policy leading to a decline of American official interest in the fate of East Europeans if the prospect of a comprehensive breakthrough in U.S.-Soviet relations had appeared likely.[71]

The Carter-Brzezinski tandem that took to the road at the beginning of 1977, with Brzezinski as National Security adviser, at once emphasized more strongly the societal level of American–East European relations. And within the framework of the differentiation concept there was considerably more emphasis now laid on domestic liberalization in addition to autonomy in foreign policy. In his memoirs covering his years in the White House Brzezinski made clear that his basic attitudes toward the region had not essentially changed. American policy should "advance the larger goal of gradually transforming the Soviet bloc into a more pluralistic and diversified entity."[72] As Lincoln Gordon argues, this was essentially the long-term objective of all American policy, but it was often the *emphasis* given to such sentiments that made the policy sound novel. Similarly, Brzezinski stressed that "evolutionary changes" were "more likely to occur first in Eastern Europe" than in the Soviet Union.[73]

Many of the Carter administration's actions toward Eastern Europe can be seen in the light of Brzezinski's concepts—the presidential visit to Poland, immediately followed by the return of the crown of St. Stephen to Hungary (with all its historical symbolism and emotionalism) in 1978, and the more down-to-earth granting of MFN status to Hungary in the same year. There was also the strong American interest in the CSCE follow-up meeting in Belgrade, also in 1978, which, rather than the formality the Soviets apparently expected, turned into an embarrassing indictment of the East bloc's human rights record.

It was also during the Carter administration that the Gierek bubble in Poland burst, and widespread dissent grew again in Polish public life, leading to the rise of Solidarity. The Carter administration, backed and sometimes prodded by the Polish-American lobby, gave moral and material support to the course of democratization in Poland. Solidarity was established in August 1980 just a few months before Carter lost the presidential election and he and Brzezinski went out of power. But even before they did the first ominous signs appeared of the Soviet refusal to accept the revolution that was taking place. At least the Carter administration, and Brzezinski in particular, were spared the agony of office as Poland headed for the disaster of December 1981.

Many feared, and some hoped, that a basic change in American policy would be ushered in by the Reagan administration. Certainly, judging from the president's own political reputation, some of his pre-White House utterances, and the political profiles of many of his entourage, such a change would have surprised few. Previous policy was indeed rather agonizingly reappraised, but in the end differentiation, the key East European issue at risk, was retained, as spelled out by Vice-President Bush in his Vienna speech. In this speech Bush also indirectly confirmed the continuation of the administration's listing of East European countries as to their behavioral merit in American eyes. This list was begun under Nixon in 1973 and continued, though with more flexibility applied, under Carter, under whom it fell into two groupings. Romania, Poland, and Hungary occupied the upper division, and the GDR, Czechoslovakia, and Bulgaria the lower division. After December 1981 Poland fell precipitously off its perch, and the disasters of Ceauşescu's personal misrule must often have brought Romania perilously close to plummeting. This list may have had its uses, but many observers always considered it pointless and schematic. If Eastern Europe had consisted of, say, eighteen countries, all well and good. But only six hardly seemed worth the elaboration.

Reagan, then, continued the main lines of American policy in Eastern Europe, and his restrained handling of the Polish crisis dispelled the doubts about his moderation in action. But his administration also made clear its strong interest in relations at the societal level and left Moscow and the ruling East European regimes in no doubt about American interest in more domestic liberalization and its concern for ordinary East Europeans.

Finally, a word about the diplomats who implement American policy —the officials in the State Department in Washington and in the field in Eastern Europe itself. The United States is lucky to have men and women of such quality and ability working for it. Almost without exception they are notable for their intelligence, understanding, and dedication. There may have been cases among them of "localitis"—too much concern for their country of posting and not enough balanced appraisal of it. But these have been few. Even the politically appointed ambassadors have often been better than they might have been—with the odd catastrophic exception. The American diplomatic corps in Eastern Europe has done much to keep its country's prestige aloft.[74]

East European Perceptions of Policy

Western policymakers constantly need to be sensitive to East European perceptions of their policy. Obviously this applies to policymaking for any part of the world, but in the case of Eastern Europe the need is particularly great. Despite the liberalization that has taken place in all the countries since 1953, none of them is yet an open society in anything like the Western sense. For long periods of their history, in some cases stretching over centuries, these nations have been occupied or dominated by others. Society was forced to become secretive or conspiratorial. The authorities were "them" as distinct from "us." Things were never, or seldom, as they appeared to be—or at least were not perceived as being. These are characteristics relevant for every aspect of East European public life, not just to the impact of Western policy. But in Eastern Europe they are taken for granted; by Westerners they may not be. Moreover, the East Europeans' suspicion of authority, though mainly directed against their own governments, extends in some degree to those they find more sympathetic—like Western governments. This includes Western political systems that most East Europeans wrongly identify with governments.

It is especially difficult with the American political system, its division between executive and legislature and especially its tradition of openness, all conducted under a glare of media publicity that often fails (or refuses) to distinguish the wheat from the chaff. (This is partly because the chaff makes better headlines but partly because of the general ignorance about Eastern Europe.) On top of it all is the besetting sin of all foreign policymaking in democratic societies, especially the American—difficulty in long-term planning.

In view of all these difficulties it is surprising that American policy toward Eastern Europe has been so consistent! But the point is that many East Europeans—accustomed in their own body politic to see basic change implied by nuance, stress, or even silence, seldom prepared to allow for accident or chance, distrustful of public pronouncements, cynical over official reassurances, receptive to rumor—have not realized, or accepted, that it has been so consistent. Many persisted in believing, for example, that Helmut Sonnenfeldt was enunciating a new policy for Eastern Europe in 1976 detrimental to them. The fact that neither Richard Nixon nor Ronald Reagan reflected in their East European policies the anticommunist rhetoric they brought to the White House was regarded by many East Europeans as classic cases of opportunism or betrayal. And, needless to say, the remarks of many members of Congress are considered (with bemusement) as being official American pronouncements.

There is probably little that can be done about these misperceptions. Certainly the American system is not going to change just to improve communication with Eastern Europe. Nor should it. But in view of the misunderstandings that have arisen, it is perhaps not too much to ask the small number of public figures interested in East European affairs, especially in Congress and the media, to watch their words with a view to how East Europeans might read and heed them.

That being said, there can be no question that, with all its imperfections of procedure, the United States is seen by Eastern Europeans as having a crucial role in the region. Through its proximity and expanding economic role, the Federal Republic may be more directly influential in some respects. But no Western country has anywhere near the same credibility, in terms of overall power and commitment, as the United States. This can never be replaced; nor could it be diminished without serious repercussions. The next decade may be the most crucial for the American presence and the most severe test of its policy and commitment. The Gorbachev impact on Eastern Europe is bound to be considerable. It may unwittingly set in motion movements leading to unforeseen destinations. Or it may fairly soon result in unfulfilled popular expectations with ensuing crises similar to, perhaps greater than, those that have occurred in the past. America, therefore, could be more needed than ever.

4   An Economic Overview

The chapters in this book dealing with the individual East European countries contain varying amounts of economic discussion and detail. The aim there is to show how economic development has interacted with the general development of the country concerned. In each of the country chapters the background is mainly political. No one, however, would deny the crucial importance of economic considerations in Eastern Europe's development. They have affected the individual countries in different ways. Hence the need to discuss them in the differing contexts of each country's history and recent development. But there is also a need for an economic overview that discusses common factors. This chapter tries to do this. It will concentrate on *seven* aspects of the East European economic situation: the economic system and its reform; general economic performance since the beginning of the 1970s; recent developments in agriculture; the Soviet–East European trade relationship; the energy situation; Comecon since 1968; and future prospects. The treatment is, of necessity, brief—too brief for the importance of the subject. But all that can be attempted in this book is a general view of Eastern Europe's economic progress and perhaps a more precise picture of the economic predicament with which it appears to be faced.

The Economic System and Its Reform

Forty years after World War II and at least thirty-five after the imposition of communist power, the economic structure and mechanisms in every East European country, with the partial exception of Yugoslavia, were basically the same as they were at the beginning. The system that

Stalin's proxies imposed had survived into an era when its obsolescence became ever more apparent.[1]

The basis of the Stalinist system was a central planning agency (GOSPLAN was the Soviet prototype) staffed by a bureaucracy that inexorably grew. This central planning agency ultimately controlled the operation of every factory or enterprise in the economy, often down to the most minute detail. The enterprises' financial operations were supervised by the central state bank, which collected data on the value of inputs and the output of the individual enterprises. The financial activity of the enterprises was very strictly controlled. Foreign trade was conducted by a state monopoly in a way that completely cut off domestic prices from world prices.

Prices were established centrally as were wage rates. Housing, health services, transportation, and educational facilities were supplied by the state. The state subsidized basic foodstuffs, housing, and clothing.

The basic structure of the Stalinist system was relatively simple, although its daily operation involved the most complicated routine. This was mainly because of the intricacies of the planning system. The planning bureaucracy did what the market does (or is supposed to do) in Western systems. The decisions of the central authorities were passed down through officials of the large number of ministries responsible for the different sectors of the economy to the enterprise directors. These directors had to operate through a layer of plans: long-term (fifteen to twenty years), medium-term (five years), and short-term (one year) plans. Just as they received orders passed down from the central planning authorities and the ministries, so they (the managers) were supposed to pass up information to the officials to help them make their relevant decisions and recommendations.

This in very brief outline was the system that had operated in the Soviet Union since the early 1930s. It was associated with the huge quantitative success the Soviet economy had achieved and had the added prestige of its wartime achievement and experience. In Eastern Europe it was arbitrarily imposed and slavishly copied regardless of its compatibility with a situation totally different in scale, economic background, and resources. Its disadvantages applied very much the same everywhere but were more immediately apparent in the more advanced Northern Tier of East European countries than in the less developed south.

But, in all the countries the sheer weight of the planning superstructure and apparatus was stifling. The difficulty of finding even partly

qualified personnel to staff the ministries, committees, and departments, especially in the first decade of communist rule, was also very
serious. It was not surprising that, despite their initial refusal, all the
communist regimes had to accept the services of some of the prewar
"bourgeois" managers and technicians. But even more serious than
the structure were economic processes operating through it. Alan
Smith has conveniently summarized the four main objections to the
system:[2]

1. The "ratchet" effect. This worked both ways. Planning authorities,
especially in the first twenty years or so when sheer volume of production amounted to almost an obsession; automatically added a few
percentage points to the previous year's output. The enterprise directors, for their part, used their intimate knowledge of their own performances to knock off something from their annual achieved production
reports to the higher authorities. The aim was a lower and hence an
easier production target and, of course, to neutralize any higher target
imposed by the authorities. It was the classic bureaucratic battle in a
new setting.

2. A chronic seller's market. In this system the planners, the enterprise managers, and the work force are lined up together against the
consumer (who is hardly a consumer in the Western sense, anyway).
Their first concern is meeting the plan targets because that brings
bonuses; failure to do so brings penalties.

3. The emphasis on gross output. This tends to make everyone concerned ignore the costs as well as the quality of production. It also
discourages attention to assortment and variety.

4. A lack of stimulus to innovate. The prevailing system seems to be a
"safe" one for all concerned, at least in the short term. There is a
disincentive to innovate since this could result in not meeting the set
targets. Moreover, the whole system, psychologically, politically, and
economically, is set against experiment and the independence of
thought it assumes.

Finally, there was the question of the priorities of economic policy in
such a system. The almost exclusive priority was that given to heavy
industry. In fact, economic development came to mean progress in
heavy industry, described by Smith as "the most critical feature of the
system imposed on East European countries." And heavy industry
meant the metallurgical, machine tool, and engineering industries.
(Later the petrochemical industry could be added.) These industries
became virtually synonymous with socialism. The GDR and Czecho-

slovakia already had an established heavy industrial base, but the other socialist countries felt obliged to catch up. Huge complexes were built that became symbols of a country's striving for, and dedication to, "socialism." The Nowa Huta complex near Cracow in Poland; the Dunaujvaros (originally Stalinvaros) complex in Hungary; Kremikovtsi in Bulgaria; Galaţi in Romania; all these became expensive and inefficient monuments to the Stalinist economic concept. The irony was that in the less developed East European countries like Bulgaria and Romania—Albania and parts of Yugoslavia may be included here— they also tended to become symbols of national prestige and progress. This was especially true in the case of Romania where Soviet objections to Galaţi in the early 1960s on the grounds of bloc integration requirements aroused the sentiment that brought on the Romanian "national deviation."

Emphasis on heavy industry and sharp increases in the volume of production were also responsible for what has become one of the greatest disasters of all in communist East European history: the damage to the environment. This is discussed at some length in chapter 13, but mention must be made of it here. For far too long economic policy was conducted with total disregard for its ecological effects. Only when it appeared to be almost too late was some attention—alarmed in some cases, grudging in others—paid to it.

The emphasis on heavy industry also strengthened Eastern Europe's dependence on the Soviet Union, which became virtually the sole supplier of the energy and other raw materials required. Eastern Europe, except for Polish coal and Romanian oil and natural gas, was poor and vulnerable in energy and raw materials. It was also poor in the technology required for heavy industry, and this originally had to be obtained mainly from either the Soviet Union or the West. Generally, though, the new system at first produced impressive quantitative results, especially in the less developed countries. But "extensive growth" demanded continual supplies of new labor using essentially the same technology, techniques, and production methods. Although the growth within the system may for a time have been rapid, the system itself was static —and extremely wasteful in terms of labor, environmental costs, plant, energy, and other raw materials. Continued output depended on continual input. Innovation and productivity for a long time were almost totally ignored.

In the GDR and Czechoslovakia the diminishing returns of this model soon became evident. Later this was true of the intermediate countries, Poland and Hungary. By the mid-1960s the need for change was perceived even in Bulgaria. A little later the same applied to Romania, which had still been able to resort to a fairly large pool of labor in the countryside. In Yugoslavia, where the dichotomy between relative advancement and backwardness operated within one state, the tension between their conflicting demands became evident in the 1960s when the changes that were deemed beneficial for Slovenia and Croatia were seen as discriminatory and dangerous by the other republics.

Varieties of Reform

The Stalinist system briefly described above continues to have relevance. Though widely repudiated in theory, it has often remained the yardstick by which new economic models have been judged. And many aspects of it remain in practice. In Romania it persists essentially unchanged.

Its shortcomings were so manifest that attempts to reform it began very early. Leaving aside Yugoslavia, the first real efforts were in Poland for a brief period after October 1956. Had they been allowed to progress and be implemented, the proposals of Oskar Lange and his brilliant group of associates might have changed the whole course of East European history. But the political and psychological conservatism that remained strong throughout the 1950s simply quashed the Polish reform proposals. The economic weaknesses they had been intended to ameliorate were not quashed, however, and in the early 1960s modified versions of reform appeared in several countries. Their appearance had been facilitated by developments in the Soviet Union, and the specific green light for reform is thought to have come from an article by Professor Yevsai Liberman in *Pravda* in 1962.[3] But hopes for reform in the Soviet Union faded after the measures of 1965 were discontinued. They were essentially Khrushchevian in spirit, and without Khrushchev they were lost in the wave of conservatism that had engulfed him in October 1964.

These reforms are discussed in several places in this book. Their common features—again mainly to use Alan Smith's categorizations—were:[4]

1. The introduction of the "trust" or "association" as a new intermediate layer of management between the ministry and the enterprise. A "trust" or "association" was made up of several enterprises. There was, therefore, some decentralization "down" from the top, but the individ-

ual enterprises now had a new layer of management (and bureaucracy) between them and the top. Still, the new structure did make for more efficiency, especially because the trust managements could now treat several enterprises as a single unit.

2. Getting away from exclusive use of the gross output concept toward a definition, however crude, of net output, with profit or value added. More attention, through bonuses or higher prices, began to be paid to quality.

3. Considerable reductions in the number of central planning indicators.

4. Greater enterprise (or "trust") freedom: (a) to make contracts for raw materials and spare parts (although these were still subject to central approval); (b) in the disposal of the wage fund, meaning that the number of employees and the amount of their wages could be set more freely, although the wage fund was still fixed centrally.

5. Changes in the price system. The wholesale price system was reformed to take into account capital charges. Though retail prices were still largely fixed, a small degree of leeway was introduced for some prices to move within a set range and for a few even to float freely.

These changes were common to all the reform proposals of the 1960s. They would generally fall into the first of Morris Bornstein's two categories of East European reform—"administrative decentralization." This merely involves the devolution of decisionmaking. Bornstein's second category, "economic decentralization," involves the introduction, however partial, of the market mechanism.[5] The allocation of resources through administrative means is replaced by allocation through markets, with enterprise decisions now being more influenced by financial instruments like prices, taxes, and subsidies.

It was the aborted Czechoslovak model of 1968 that really met Bornstein's requirement for true economic decentralization and reform. (Many aspects in the Yugoslav structure and system over the years would also come close to doing so.) Czechoslovak market socialism would have meant the abolition of all annual plans and enterprise indicators. The enterprises would have been governed by the market in determining inputs and outputs. They could go anywhere in the country, and eventually outside it, to obtain supplies. Domestic prices would be influenced by world market conditions. Industrial democracy was to be achieved through freely elected workers' councils deciding on amounts to be allocated to wages, investments, and social facilities. Central planning would be responsible solely for long-term macroeconomic targets and would seek to influence enterprise decisions only through financial instruments.[6]

After the invasion of Czechoslovakia this reform model was excoriated as capitalistic and counterrevolutionary. Any other model with even the vaguest similarities to it was bound to be subject to the most critical scrutiny. It was all the more extraordinary, therefore, that the Hungarians persisted with their own New Economic Mechanism (NEM). Conversely, the Hungarian awareness that the climate demanded caution may have inhibited them from applying their reform as fully as they could (or should) have.

The very title of the Hungarian reforms, New Economic Mechanism, reflects the prudence of the times. The reforms made by the NEM were similar in some respects to the Czechoslovak, but they were less decisive than the latter showed signs of being. Their aim may have been to eventually transform the system, but as they were applied they appeared to be bent mainly on merely reordering it. The main features of the NEM are described in the country chapter on Hungary (chapter 6). It contained genuine "economic decentralization," to use Bornstein's terminology, in that it dispensed with annual plans and resorted to guiding enterprises toward centrally planned targets by means of financial instruments such as credits and taxes. Like the Czechoslovak reform, it sought to remove the insulation of domestic prices from world prices, and Hungarian enterprises were given more freedom to conduct foreign trade without having to go through the ministry of foreign trade. This attempt to bring some interaction between domestic and world prices was an essential step in bringing a socialist economy out of its cocoon of unreality in which all had begun and in which most of them were to remain.[7]

The Polish economic reforms that were supposed to begin operation in 1982 under the name of Reformed Economic System (RES) were, on paper, some of the most radical reforms ever touted in the history of Eastern Europe. They are only referred to in passing in the country chapter on Poland because they had been so ineffectively and halfheartedly applied as to have little or no effect on Polish developments as a whole. It was very doubtful, in fact, whether they would ever be applied in toto.

Their main characteristics, at least on paper, were:[8]

1. The independence of enterprises, based on the much-publicized "3 Ss principle"—independence, self-management, and self-financing.

Enterprises could choose what to produce and how to produce without direction from the central authorities. Workers' incomes were to be based only on the financial results achieved by the enterprises in the management of which the work force was to be given a big say through freely elected workers' councils.

2. Greater flexibility in the price system and the encouragement of competition, allowing even for bankruptcies. Domestic markets would be open to foreign competition.

3. Much less detailed central planning. As in the Hungarian case, central plan indicators would be used much less and financial instruments more in order to steer enterprises toward the required performance.

4. The widespread use of the media, trade unions, professional bodies, the Sejm (parliament), and other public bodies to publicize and debate economic questions and have influence on the planning center in its choice of economic decisions. This is a good example of the merging of the economic and political, and an embryonic political pluralism was evident in this proposal similar to that being debated in Hungary (see chapter 6) and Yugoslavia (see chapter 11).

One observer has pointed to the influence of Oskar Lange and the erstwhile Warsawian (later Oxonian) Włodzimierz Brus in these proposals.[9] They were exciting proposals, and they illustrated the type of reform thinking common, not just in Polish, but in other East European circles at the turn of the 1980s. But, given the political environment in which Poland would be obliged to operate for many years to come, they were totally unrealistic. The fine print to these proposals gave the regime authority to delay their implementation indefinitely, and the part referring to political pluralism sank into the morass of public life after the declaration of martial law in December 1981. These proposals, however, were worth bearing in mind. If the situation in Eastern Europe ever became auspicious enough for real reform, they might be dusted off and put to work—not only in Poland but elsewhere.

The only other reforms worth mentioning in this brief appraisal are the Bulgarian and the East German, also referred to in chapters 10 and 7, respectively. Neither was anywhere near as far-reaching as the Hungarian in practice or the Polish on paper. The record of both countries in economic reform is broadly similar: both made starts in the 1960s and then both decided against reform—the Bulgarians in 1968 and the East Germans two years later. Both subsequently had second tries at the end of the 1970s and in the 1980s. Both aimed at overhauling rather than transforming the old system, although aspects of both would find themselves in the no-man's-land between Morris Born-stein's two categories. The East German reform was more coherent and consistent than the Bulgarian, which gave enterprises incentives to maximize profits but, at the same time, could not get away from the concept of compulsory planning targets. After a good economic run for several years, the Bulgarians were facing a serious economic future by the middle of the 1980s. Partly under Gorbachev's prodding they were showing signs in 1987 of implementing imposing reform propos-als. As for the East Germans, after the serious difficulties of the early 1980s, they were doing better. At the eleventh SED congress in April 1986 they exuded confidence. But they, too, faced longer-term difficul-ties that might dent their complacency and induce them to contem-plate more meaningful changes.

The East European performance in economic reform has been con-siderably more enterprising than the Soviet. Still, well over thirty years after his death, Stalin would have had no difficulty in recognizing the system he bequeathed in 1953. They were still mainly "centrally directed, administrative economies, the principal defect of which (was) a lack of spontaneity and a relative slowness to identify and to react to changes in world market conditions and technology."[10]

The reasons for their lack of real progress are discussed explicitly and implicitly in several parts of this book. The basic dilemma about economic reform was the fear of the political consequences it could have for the ruling elites as well as the effects it could have on society. It was not a question of reform just threatening the political bureau-crats. It also threatened, more immediately and directly, the "econ-ocrats" (the economic bureaucrats), and it was the "econocrats" who were in an ideal position to delay, hinder, discredit, even destroy the work of the reformers. (The one exception may have been Czechoslo-vakia in 1968, although the period was too short for conclusions to be drawn, and, in any case, some of the top Czechoslovak leaders did not understand the implications of much of what was going on around them.) In Hungary and even in Yugoslavia the issue of political plural-ism to go with economic reform was pressing. As for Poland, General Jaruzelski had proposals for both political pluralism and economic reform prepared in November 1987 when they were rejected by popu-lar vote in an unprecedented national referendum.

A report issued after a meeting organized by the Feltrinelli Founda-tion in Milan in October 1983 on reform in Eastern Europe summed up the problem well. It referred directly to the Soviet Union but could have been referring equally well to Eastern Europe. Its pinpointing of the social consequences is particularly instructive.

> At the origin of the blocking of economic reform in the USSR a decisive consideration was the fear of the destabilizing effect that it might have in the social sphere, through the weakening of some principles that help to maintain consensus around the regime —substantially stable prices, job security, and so on. These are considered to be principles that cannot be given up, even if citizens have to pay for them through very modest salaries, inefficient services, and shops that are often half-empty and in any case stocked with low-quality products. To this is added the certainty that in any case economic reform would require a political price (decentralization of decisionmaking power) that the regime does not want to pay or is incapable of paying.[11]

The dilemma was deepened by the opinion held by many that political pluralism was not just a likely *consequence* of economic reform (if the latter is left undisturbed) but that it was an essential *prerequisite* for economic efficiency. This case is powerfully argued by Włodzimierz Brus, among others. He sees "the lack of political pluralism" as "the major cause of blockage of information flows in Eastern Europe, and hence the major cause of misallocation of resources on a long-term scale."[12] Although by no means against the market mechanism, Brus disapproves of too much dependence on it in making "long-term allocative decisions." He believes in the value of long-term planning, provided influences and pressures can be brought to bear to prevent it from becoming autocratic and hence arbitrary. If not, he argues, then this "autocratic syndrome goes a long way toward explaining not only the imprecisions but also the lack of elementary coordination in the construction and implementation of plans." The ensuing "planned chaos," and "particularly the investment cycles peculiar to this form of socialism, seem to be firmly rooted in the political system."[13]

Many "junior" members of the political elites in Eastern Europe and the Soviet Union were recognizing this by the middle of the 1980s. Some of their seniors also were probably aware. But when they would be able to bring themselves to act on it was another question. What it involved was basic changes in both the political and educational systems, as well as the economic. Above all it was necessary to lose that totalitarian fear and distrust of societal *spontaneity*. It would require a change of psyche and mentality that, if it were to happen at all, would happen slowly—perhaps too slowly for economic salvation. It involved risks for both the Soviet Union's weltanschauung and its raison d'état. But the penalty for not taking them would be inexorable and would probably accelerate systemic decline.

Economic Performance

The political stabilization in Eastern Europe that the Soviet Union deemed so necessary after the Prague Spring was greatly assisted by economic circumstances. Cheap energy, mainly from the Soviet Union, Soviet subsidies in East European trade (to be discussed below), an expanding global economy presenting Eastern Europe with attractive markets both in the developed countries and in the Third World —these were some of the elements promising a favorable phase in the East European economy.

Such phases in the past had been characterized by investment cycles followed by periods of stagnation. In such phases plan targets are greatly increased and central budgetary impediments to spending reduced. The result is a plethora of investments initiated both centrally and locally by the enterprises themselves. The 1970s saw this familiar characteristic at work to a degree unknown since the early 1950s.[14] The most spectacular example was in Poland (see chapter 5). At the same time both nominal and real wages tend to rise rapidly. As the number of investments increase, so does the demand for domestic construction services. A boom atmosphere pervades. In Poland the atmosphere in the early 1970s was positively euphoric. But in such a situation potential hard-currency exports are usually diverted to the home economy to stoke up the boom. The result is a strain on the balance of payments as the demand for hard-currency imports continues while exports to hard-currency areas diminish. This goes on until the balance of payments becomes so adverse that the central planning authorities order a "cooling off." This means stopping further investment projects and has often meant abandoning some of those under way until equilibrium in the balance of payments is restored. The lack of any coordination of the boom also means that some vital resources (e.g., energy) are in excess demand causing disruptions in production or even the failure to bring large investment projects on line. A good example of this lack of coordination was during the Polish boom in the early 1970s when the shortage of batteries and tires meant that tractors from modernized plants could not be delivered despite their being desperately needed.

What was new about the investment boom of the 1970s was the ready availability of huge amounts of hard-currency credit from Western governments and especially from Western private banks. The volume of these credits increased dramatically in 1973–74 after the first OPEC price explosion that increased oil prices by about 400 percent. The oil-exporting countries found themselves with huge savings on their hands, and they put them to use in the international capital markets. Huge amounts of money became available for borrowing at lower rates of interest than had hitherto applied. Most of the loans contracted went to the newly industrializing countries (NICs), but huge sums were also loaned to Eastern Europe. It has been estimated that between 1973 and 1978 the gross hard-currency debt of Eastern Europe had increased by 480 percent, some 93 percent of this increase being in commercial debt.[15] (For a country-by-country development of East European indebtedness since 1970, see appendix III, table 18.)

It was the ready availability of so much cheap credit that lengthened the investment cycles in all the countries of Eastern Europe. The balance of payments difficulties could be hidden, or their reality postponed, by borrowing. The "stop-go" economic strategy of all the regimes prior to the 1970s now appeared to have been replaced by possibilities of a permanent "go." Western loans not only directly facilitated investment but also enabled the planning authorities to increase the percentage of utilized national income earmarked for investment. The relevant ratios for Poland in 1976 and Romania between 1976 and 1980 even exceeded the levels for the Stalinist period in the early 1950s.

There was, of course, some rationale—even a theory—behind all this helter-skelter. The strategy of "import-led growth" and modernization would, it was argued, result in the manufacture of sophisticated products from imports of the latest technology. These products could then be exported to the West and help pay off the debts incurred. The idea was simple and not without sense, if it were tempered with moderation. But few countries did apply it with moderation except perhaps Czechoslovakia, which, in view of its aging industrial base and infrastructure, might well have been a bit bolder in Western capital markets. At the other end of the spectrum Poland was the example of credits becoming a speeding carousel from which it was difficult to alight. Romania, with its huge borrowing after 1978 to pay the rapidly rising costs of imports of oil to feed its massive petrochemical industry, presented the best example of the dangers during this heady period of putting too many eggs in one basket.

And, as it turned out, the hoped-for rewards from import-led growth did not materialize. Manufacturing exports to the Western countries hardly grew at all, and in the case of the GDR and Czechoslovakia they actually dropped slightly. Thus while more and more agricultural products and raw materials, which were normally exported to the West, were being kept at home to meet rising consumer expectations and the demands of the investment boom, very little was being exported in their stead.

The Soviet Shocks

But one of the main reasons why the rewards from import-led growth did not materialize was the shock administered by the Soviet Union with its price increase for oil and other raw materials. The complex question of Soviet economic relations as a whole with Eastern Europe is discussed later in this chapter; but the oil price increase fits conveniently here in the context of sudden international trade disturbances.

Prices in trade among Comecon countries between 1958 and 1975 were regulated by an agreement signed in Bucharest in 1958, which became known as the "Bucharest formula." Prices between two partners were based for a five-year period on the *average world market price* for the commodity concerned in the *preceding five-year period*. The price thus fixed remained the same for five years regardless of what then happened in the meantime to the price of that commodity on the world market.

But when world prices of oil increased so rapidly after 1973 it was inevitable that the Soviets would invoke the small print in the "Bucharest formula" allowing for adjustments in case of unexpected developments. By March 1974 the official Comecon price of oil was 80 percent below the world price. Moscow forced its partners to agree to a special price increase for 1975 and then to a new formula for 1976 onward allowing for *annual adjustments* in prices based on average world market prices for individual commodities in the preceding five-year period. What this meant in practical terms was that Soviet oil to Eastern Europe doubled in price between 1974 and 1976, and between 1974 and 1983 it increased more than 400 percent. In 1985 the East Europeans were shipping nearly 50 percent more goods to the Soviet Union for the same quantity of goods they had received from it ten years earlier.

Most experts agree that, generally, the East Europeans were let off lightly by the Soviets with the new price formula and that overall they continued to derive large benefits from the Soviet connection. But there is no doubt that the oil shock of 1975 added further to the burdens that their own domestic mistakes and the growing debt with the West were causing.

Facing the Recession

Though faced with mounting trade deficits and mounting debts, most of the East European states did little or nothing about them for several years. (Romania was something of an exception here because, as stated in chapter 8, for a considerable time its foreign trade situation appeared healthy and its borrowing small.) The reasons for this inaction stemmed from both the objective difficulties inherent in the East European systems and the subjective attitude of the political leaderships. In both their structure and planning system the East European economies have been slow to respond to relatively fast-moving changes. "On the demand side," as Laura D'Andrea Tyson says, "declines in export demand stemming from world market conditions did not influence the level of domestic output, because supply availabilities rather than demand conditions determined output levels." And, she continues, "there was no dearth of domestic demand to absorb the output made available as a result of exogenous decline in foreign demand."[17]

On the *supply* side there was also a lack of response. The worsening trade situation did not have the contractionary effect in the East European economies that it has, in similar conditions, in the more responsive market economies. In the latter, as energy and raw materials become more expensive, domestic production tends to drop because it has become less profitable. Such market considerations make little or only slow impact on centrally planned systems. Moreover, such a policy means lowering consumer supplies, and there were obvious political reasons for not doing this. Not only had the prosperity in the early part of the 1970s encouraged higher consumer expectations, but also the memory of the Prague Spring and, especially in this context, the Polish upheavals of December 1970 were still fresh in the minds of both regimes and populations.

The result generally was a passive reaction to an oncoming crisis the dimensions of which were so huge that they may even have numbed the responses of those concerned. Many competent East European economists saw the crisis coming, but such was the political and popular pressure against facing reality that they were either overruled or chose to keep quiet. It was, however, easy to understand a psychosis reflected in the argument that once borrowing had begun it was better to continue it until it began to pay off through increased exports. And when exports were very slow in increasing, hopes could linger for a long time that the corner could still eventually be turned. Soon the interest payments had reached a level where new loans had to be taken to service previous ones. As each new one was taken, the spiral of debt was given an extra twist.

The climax came in 1978 when Western creditors became seriously alarmed at the volume of debt, not only in Eastern Europe but also worldwide, and at the growing unlikelihood of it being repaid. Borrowing conditions, therefore, became much tighter, repayment periods shorter, and the rates of interest higher. And all this occurred at a time when Eastern Europe was having to borrow more, not so much now to continue the boom, which was rapidly evaporating anyway, but to stop living standards from crashing and to service the existing debt.

Then came the serious worsening of the world trade situation with the second OPEC price explosion toward the end of the decade. Eastern Europe was already on the downhill slope, but this only made the descent steeper and the fall quicker. The subsequent five-year planning period, beginning in 1980, saw more sober expectations in every country.

The plans became much more modest and reflected the adverse conditions already prevailing. But in 1981–82 came the great East European debt crisis. Western creditors stopped lending. Poland and Romania had to ask for debt rescheduling, and both Hungary and the GDR found themselves in a liquidity crisis. In 1982 the Soviet Union also, apparently reneging on a pledge made by then Premier Kosygin in 1979 that oil supplies would be maintained,[18] announced a 10 percent cut for the GDR, Czechoslovakia, and Hungary.

The response of all the governments to this now multiple crisis was to impose austerity, mainly in the form of cutting imports. In most countries considerable publicity was also given to the need to increase exports as well to find the domestic resources needed to complete at least the most important investment projects. But it appears that considerable prudence was exercised in both regards. The general decline in living standards had been felt since the turn of the decade, although more so in a country like Poland than, for example, the GDR or Bulgaria. The regimes, therefore, desisted from taking more measures that would starkly depress living standards. Again, there were differences, with Ceauşescu, for example, being prepared to impose burdens on his people to an extent that the Bulgarian, Polish, and East German leaderships would not. Food and consumer goods were, therefore, not exported to the degree possible (although most East Europeans, especially Romanians, would have been surprised to hear this), and fewer resources than could have been were actually diverted to completing investments. But even so the bite into living standards was sharp enough. Shortages, higher prices, and then the disastrous energy cuts in southeastern Europe, partly resulting from extraordinarily severe weather, combined to make, not one, but several winters of discontent for most East Europeans in the early 1980s.

From the Brink

The determination of East European countries to reverse the deteriorating terms of trade with the West and at least to recover some creditworthiness met with some success. Most of them ran trade surpluses with Western countries after 1981, with Poland and Romania, the countries worst affected by the debt crisis, recording the best statistical results in this regard. Bulgaria and Hungary were exceptions, but both did well in their trade with developing countries, with Bulgaria's Western balance also being helped by good earnings from tourism. By the middle of the 1980s most had recovered their creditworthy status. Only Poland and Yugoslavia had failed to make impressive progress in reducing their hard-currency debts. Hungary and Romania were by now both members of the International Monetary Fund (IMF), as was Yugoslavia, and Poland finally became a member in 1986. The IMF demanded rigorous financial policies with which both Hungary and Poland tried to comply. Romania rejected the IMF proposals as encroachments on its sovereignty but nevertheless tried to implement policies similar in spirit. Eastern Europe's reputation in the financial world was beginning to rise, if partly because creditors now realized that the region's problems were small compared with those of Third World debtors. Thus Eastern Europe was partly rehabilitated—with a speed that left many surprised. After the calamities of the early 1980s many expected that it would be a generation before the West would resume lending—if it ever did. But in this respect the international financial system, not to mention Eastern Europe itself, showed a surprising resilience. The wave of lending was, of course, nothing like what it had previously been. But Hungary, for one, confidently borrowed over $3 billion in 1985, and even Romania, which had earlier demonstratively rejected more borrowing, took $150,000.[19] Romania, however, experienced another repayments crisis in 1986, and its case only showed how precarious this East European financial recovery was.[20]

The Soviet Union also played its part in preventing Eastern Europe from being totally engulfed. It did not, as some Western creditors had apparently anticipated, act as an umbrella for East European economies encountering repayments difficulties. Nor did it show much consideration in 1982 when it cut its supplies of oil. Moreover, the deterioration in Eastern Europe's real terms of trade with the Soviets was a reason for the crisis of 1981 and 1982. But Moscow helped considerably by allowing the East European countries to run deficits in their trade with the Soviet Union. For many years before 1975, when the Soviets increased their prices for oil and other raw materials, the East Europeans had generally had surpluses in their trade with the Soviet Union. But with the steadily increasing prices of Soviet energy supplies this situation was reversed. By the end of the 1970s some of these deficits had become very large. Normally, according to the procedures of intra-Comecon trade, imbalances should be settled immediately. By allowing deficits to mount, therefore, the Soviets were in effect granting credits to the East Europeans at a time when the Western credit lines were cut.[21] (Again Romania was the big exception here, largely because of its independence in oil supplies until the early 1980s.)

Generally, after the crisis of 1981–82, the Soviets also sought to ease Eastern Europe's financial situation by accepting increased imports of machinery and manufactures that would have been difficult to offload elsewhere.[22] These concessions on trade deficits may not have been decisive rescue instruments, but without them the situation would have been even worse.

Thus a number of reasons conspired to pull Eastern Europe back from the brink, and relief may have been the predominant feeling midway through the 1980s. Still, the results for the quinquennial planning period 1981–85 (see appendix III, table 13) made for dismal reading.

None of the countries achieved its Net Material Product (NMP) growth target, although the East German performance was good. The general reduction in the rates of growth for a whole decade since 1976 was striking. The nadir of fortunes was, not surprisingly, in 1981 and 1982. In 1981 Czechoslovakia, as it had done some twenty years earlier, actually achieved a negative growth, although it was tiny compared with the 12 percent negative growth for Poland, a disaster that pulled the whole Eastern European performance into negative figures for the first time. From then on there was general improvement with some exceptions. East German growth in 1981, for example, was well below both its usual level and the East European performance as a whole for that year. In 1985 the Bulgarian performance was notably poor, largely, it seems, because of the severe weather in southeastern Europe, a fact that makes the claimed Romanian growth rate of nearly 6 percent look hard to believe. Hungary, too, suffered a bad year in 1985.

In general, the performance for 1985 throughout the region was disappointing, the upturn of the previous two years not being maintained. Some Western experts attributed this new downturn to the fact that the considerable savings in energy and raw materials that their situation forced on the East Europeans in 1983 and 1984 were not (or could not be) maintained in 1985. Another cause, at least for Bulgaria and Romania, was the weather. The situation in Romania was probably the most worrying in the whole of Eastern Europe, not even excluding Poland, and it remained to be seen from future results both there and in Bulgaria to what extent the calamitous year of 1985 could really be blamed on the weather.

A Note on Agriculture

Agricultural collectivization involved a political, economic, social, and cultural revolution the effects of which will last much longer than a mere generation. Here it is possible to deal only with a few of its more important economic effects, but its broader significance has a bearing on all aspects of East European history since 1945.

Toward the end of the 1980s the collectivized system of agriculture had been fully in operation in Eastern Europe for about a quarter of a century. Bulgaria had become almost totally collectivized by 1958, and within four years Czechoslovakia, the GDR, Hungary, and Romania had followed suit. Poland remained virtually uncollectivized, as did Yugoslavia. Right from the beginning Bulgaria adopted the full *kholkhoz* system, while the others had usually begun with lower and looser forms of collectivization before going over to the kholkhoz system. The GDR, in particular, had progressed very slowly in this regard, and it was not until 1976 that the land was totally collectivized according to the full Soviet pattern. In the 1970s Bulgaria took socialization a step further by establishing Agro-Industrial Complexes (see chapter 10). The other countries have generally stayed with the collective system, although with some variations. Generally, East German collectives have been the largest, averaging about 5,000 hectares, and Romanian the smallest, averaging about half that size. State farms, supposedly the highest form of socialist agriculture, also exist in all of the countries, in Czechoslovakia and Romania using up to 30 percent of the arable land. They have invariably received the lion's share of investments.

The second great revolution that has affected agriculture since 1945 has simply been its diminishing importance in the economies of all the countries concerned. Until the mid-1960s, in terms of both share in total employment and in share in the gross national product, agriculture was the largest economic sector in several of the East European countries. But in all the countries concerned the number of people engaged directly in agriculture has sharply declined. As might be expected, the reductions have been greatest in Bulgaria and Romania, which were overwhelmingly agricultural. In both these countries the percentage halved between 1965 and 1982; in 1982 in Bulgaria it stood at 22.7 percent and in Romania 28.3 percent. In a country like the GDR, on the other hand, which had been industrialized before 1945, the drop was only from 14 percent to 10 percent.[23]

As for contribution to the gross national product, as might be expected, the biggest falls were again in Bulgaria and Romania. The interesting anomaly, however, was Hungary where the percentage share was almost the same in 1982 as it had been in 1965. The main reason for this was the remarkable success—discussed at the end of this section—achieved in Hungarian agriculture since the early 1970s.

The Effects of Collectivization

The initial object of collectivization was not so much to improve agricultural performance as to break up the traditional peasant way of life and to provide labor and capital for industrialization. It was this and the ruthless suppression of opposition to it that gave collectivization the foul reputation from which it never subsequently recovered. Nor was the odium of its introduction mitigated by any efficiency in its operation in the early years. Its bad results were caused by many factors, some general and others local. Probably the most important were (1) continuing low investments while industrialization was still continuing; (2) peasant noncooperation and unfamiliarity with the new ways of life and work into which they had been pitchforked; (3) local managerial incompetence; (4) bureaucratism and centralized planning.

By about the middle of the 1960s, however, the grave weaknesses of agriculture, the greatly increased demand for food, the concern about social unrest if the demand were not met, as well as the hard-currency possibilities for food exports, led to some sharp increases in investment, especially in the less-developed countries of southeastern Europe. These increases, however, began to drop off in the second half of the 1970s and into the 1980s as serious economic problems overtook the region. Moreover, agriculture's share in total investment still remained relatively small and in most countries has been much smaller than agriculture's percentage contribution to the Gross National Product. (Table 19 in appendix III shows gross fixed agricultural investment and its share in total investment.) Thus, though after the mid-1960s it might no longer have been true, as it once undoubtedly was, to say that the "essence of collectivization has been to take the most possible out of agriculture while putting the least possible into it,"[24] there remained the strong suspicion that in most countries agriculture was the lowest priority, and therefore the weakest link, in the whole economic process.

Still, some of the results showed that collectivized agriculture benefited from the attention it did get. Indeed, some results were quite remarkable. Yields, for instance, which twenty years before had, with the partial exception of the GDR and Czechoslovakia, been very low, had greatly improved by the beginning of the 1980s. Wheat yields had doubled in Hungary and Bulgaria, as had maize yields in Hungary, Bulgaria, and even Romania. Milk yields had almost doubled in Hungary. Comparisons with Western Europe were not all to Eastern Europe's disadvantage: in wheat yields, for example, the GDR, Czechoslovakia, Bulgaria, and Hungary were all about level with or even better than the West European average; in maize and milk Hungary was better.[25] In general, Western Europe was still much superior, but at the end of the 1950s, say, few would have thought it possible that Eastern Europe could ever have approached even some of its levels.

All the countries of the region have made efforts to increase annual production to keep up with the fast-growing consumption of meat. An increase in general food consumption is characteristic of all industrializing countries, but the very high consumption of meat, especially in Poland, has remained an East European characteristic not shared by societies in either Western Europe or North America. Production of meat, except in Hungary, has simply not been able to keep pace with demand, especially in situations where its price has been artificially kept down by very large government subsidies. The East European countries, again except for Hungary, have all made expensive imports of feed, paid for in hard currency, from the West. But this has not been solely to supply the domestic market. All the East European countries had become net exporters of meat by the end of the 1970s. In fact, a small but important trade link had been forged with the West in this regard. Feed was imported and meat exported. It was estimated that 25 percent of Czechoslovak meat exports resulted from grain and protein feed imports. For the GDR the share was reckoned at 20 percent, much of its feed grain coming from the United States.[26]

Not unnaturally the Soviet Union began to resent this kind of cooperation between Eastern Europe and the West. In the early 1980s its net meat imports roughly equaled the total of East European meat exports, some of which went to the Soviet Union but much of which went to the West.[27] These were just the kind of "hard" goods the Soviets were now pressing their partners to send to them in return for energy and raw materials. But meat was a good hard-currency trade item for the East Europeans, and they would be very loath to give it up.

After a quarter of a century East European agriculture was undoubtedly showing strengths. Its weaknesses were both human and material. Though private agriculture in Eastern Europe before World War II, and in Poland and Yugoslavia after it, was plagued by various problems and was often grossly inefficient, land ownership alone often provided the peasants with enough incentive to work hard, if often not very profitably. Nowhere in Eastern Europe, except partly in Hungary, was that private incentive adequately replaced. In Romania, indeed, the regime seemed sometimes to have done its utmost to strew disincentives in the path of the socialized peasant. But Romania was only the most glaring example of a general trend. One of the main disincentives throughout the region has always been low procurement prices, which have often lagged considerably behind costs for fuel, fertilizer, machinery, and various other inputs. Many collectives either actually lost money or made very little profit.

Agriculture, whether private in Poland and Yugoslavia or socialized elsewhere, also suffered from a poor infrastructure. Transport and communications, generally, in the countryside, as well as storage facilities, have often been grossly inadequate. The latter have often been the main reason why 25 percent of the gross harvest output is said to have been regularly lost. On the farms themselves mechanization, though adequate or even impressive in purely statistical terms, has been of a low standard of efficiency. Many tractors, for example, have always been either antiquated or broken down, and supplies of spare parts often nonexistent.

As for human resources, collectivization itself saw to it that these were greatly reduced in numerical terms. In view of the historical overpopulation in the countryside this, in itself, was no bad thing. Urbanization and the development of industry would have caused an exodus from the countryside, anyway. Moreover, even as late as the mid-1980s East European agriculture was still overmanned by the standards of Western Europe and North America. But, generally, the young and the energetic had drifted to the towns, and for many years the average age of workers on the collectives hovered around or over fifty years.

One welcome change was the improvement of personal incomes and living standards over the years. Again, the two neighboring countries, Hungary and Romania, also supplied the contrast in this context. In Hungary material conditions on the better collectives were unprecedentedly prosperous and better than the city average. In Romania living standards rose slowly and erratically, and the disincentives referred to above reduced morale to the point where many peasants perceived themselves as continually being worse off. In Czechoslovakia and the GDR there was evidence, as there was in Hungary, suggesting that, in the early 1980s, the average was somewhat higher than the average nonagricultural labor income.[28] In Czechoslovakia a visitor traveling in 1978 was assured several times—not only, it should be said, by regime officials—that the peasants generally were "doing very well" out of collectivized agriculture.

The Private Plots

Many East European peasants would have been doing considerably less well, as would the economy as a whole, but for the production from private plots on the collective farms. Generally these only covered half a hectare and the peasants had free use of what was produced on them. They fed themselves and sold the rest. Over the years private plots have suffered various disabilities and forms of discrimination. But, largely because of the proprietary instinct that they tap, they have been extraordinarily productive. They cannot usually compete with the socialist sector in extensive or industrial crops and have concentrated on fruits, vegetables, milk products, eggs, and meat. They have produced a disproportionately high percentage of these products for the amount of land they cover. Some statistics for Hungary are given in chapter 6. Those for Bulgaria are also impressive. Situated on 13 percent of the country's arable land (often not very good land), Bulgarian private plots accounted in 1982 for 25 percent of gross agricultural production, out of which came 33 percent of all vegetables, 51 percent of all potatoes, and 37 percent of all fruit.[29]

The authorities, whether central bureaucrats or collective farm managers, have constantly and justifiably complained that the peasants spend too much time on their private plots. Farming on the collective sector had become just another job—and many peasants now preferred it that way. But on the private plots that extra effort was applied. And this sometimes led to what in Eastern Europe are often euphemistically referred to as "administrative measures." In Romania, private plots have until recently been subject to severe controls, presenting another unfortunate example of the Ceaușescu regime's determination to discourage the entrepreneurial inclinations of the Romanian nation. But in neither Czechoslovakia nor the GDR have they been given much encouragement. In Hungary and Bulgaria, on the other hand, they have fared much better. But, whether encouraged or discouraged, their production records have been outstanding and even in Czechoslovakia and the GDR the regimes were quietly signaling, by the end of 1985, that the days of severe discrimination might be over.

Socially and culturally, as well as economically, the phenomenon of the private plots showed that, however different the times and habits, the attachment of most East Europeans to the land has not basically changed. There was also abundant evidence of this *throughout* society. A very large number of East Europeans have still retained a connection with the land. Many who work in the towns commute daily from the countryside. Many go home for the weekends. The better-off have cottages in the country. Even in the towns miniature private plots have appeared, often out of the most unpromising bits of turf. The figures given for Hungary in chapter 6 could be duplicated throughout the region. The old adage about being able to take the boy out of the country but not the country out of the boy is still truer in Eastern Europe than in most places.

Transplanting the Hungarian Example?

Because of the economic difficulties all the East European countries face, it is likely that more pragmatism in agriculture will prevail in the future both regarding the private plots and the collectivized sector itself. No regime can afford the kind of social disturbances arising from agricultural scarcities that are directly in its power to avoid. (Even the Ceauşescu regime lifted restrictions in the early 1980s on the amount of livestock a peasant family could privately own.)

Inevitably, therefore, the Hungarian model and its successes have been the subject of much speculation in terms of whether they can be imitated, adapted, or even directly transplanted. Obviously some aspects of it have been suitable for export, but any transfer of it in toto or even in considerable part would face very great difficulties. And those parts that could be transferred could hardly be expected to achieve the same results as they did in the specific Hungarian setting. The Hungarian model, as the distinguished German agricultural scholar Karl-Eugen Wädekin says, "represents a whole [system] of interrelated measures, which in their total come close to what indeed might be called a reform within a Communist system, and, at the same time, they are specifically Hungarian in several of their aspects."[30] Wädekin goes on:

> Neither the tolerance toward the private sector, nor the opening up of cooperation with Western firms, which has led to the widespread adoption of Western technology and the spreading of technical innovations . . . , nor the flexible ways in entering export markets are alone sufficient explanations of the Hungarian success. There are other elements of great importance that allowed for the successful application of these approaches: abstention from setting plan targets in physical units and substituting them with highly aggregated, annually corrected and not absolutely mandatory ones (i.e. targets), combined with leaving considerable decision-making powers to farm managers. . . . In that same sense, a sizeable decompression of the domestic political atmosphere . . . also exerted a positive influence. . . . Last but not least, this rather consistent reform has been continued for roughly two decades. . . .[31]

Wädekin here not only succinctly itemizes the main features of the Hungarian model but wisely stresses the setting in which they were implemented. Unless a setting of reform, receptiveness, and relaxation can develop elsewhere—and they must develop in other countries in their own distinctive ways—then the good in the Hungarian model will remain largely confined to Hungary.

The Soviet–East European Trade Relationship

For many years a simplified view of "who/whom" with regard to Soviet–East European economic relations prevailed in the West. "Who was exploiting whom?" While there was general agreement that, during Stalin's time and probably for a short time afterward, Soviet exploitation of Eastern Europe existed on a massive scale, informed opinion subsequently agreed that the Eastern European states were steadily becoming an economic liability for Moscow. Opinions differed over how much of a liability, but there seemed to be few serious efforts to identify and quantify the degree of asset or liability involved. The notion of a reciprocal relationship, no matter how approximate, was seldom entertained.

This is not to disregard or denigrate the valuable work professional economists were doing. It is simply that the general observer of Eastern Europe was unaware of all the complexities involved and, therefore, inclined to make invalid assumptions. It was not until the 1970s that this situation changed. The enormous growth of Eastern European hard-currency indebtedness in the West prompted interest in exploring the region's economic relations as a whole, including commercial and financial relations with the Soviet Union. Interest was further stimulated by the increase in Soviet oil and raw material prices for Eastern Europe in 1975. It led to inquiry not just into the differences between the Soviet and world prices but into the whole question of Soviet pricing and subsidization in trade with Eastern Europe. And the work involved had become much easier thanks to intelligent handling of the computer revolution.

The importance of such inquiry can hardly be overestimated. Eastern Europe is economically dependent on the Soviet Union. Nearly all its energy and raw material supplies are of Soviet provenance, and the Soviet Union has been the main export market for all the countries of the region. The terms on which these economic relations are conducted are, therefore, crucial toward understanding the real nature of the overall relationship. It is all the more unfortunate, therefore, that though the computer may have made inquiry easier, it has not led to anything like unity in the findings the experts have produced. There is agreement, though, on one basic point: that the Soviet Union has indeed incurred opportunity costs in its economic relations with Eastern Europe. But then the differences take over, differences so enormous as to leave general practitioners groping in a fog of specialist expertise. Still, old assumptions and even certainties have been overturned and there is more clarity than before.

Loans and Subsidies

The question of East European deficits was touched on earlier. The remainder of this section will cover Soviet ruble loans and trade subsidies.

In his valuable study of Soviet economic policies toward Eastern Europe, Keith Crane shows that there was a huge increase in the volume of Soviet credit granted in the crisis years of the early 1980s.[32] The size of the loans to Poland was to be expected, but they were almost as big to the GDR until 1984, and they were also large to Bulgaria. Moreover, as Crane points out, the Soviets incurred large opportunity costs when granting these ruble loans. First, the nominal interest rates on these loans was about 2.5 to 3 percent, which was relatively very advantageous for the borrower. Second, because of the pricing system in trade between the Soviet Union and Eastern Europe, the latter has enjoyed a trade subsidy in repaying the loans. The goods they used to repay the loans were worth considerably less than the goods they received on credit, and the Soviets were the losers by the amount involved.

Soviet Trade Subsidies

Assessing the benefits to the East Europeans involved in Soviet ruble loans is a matter of relatively little controversy among experts. The same cannot be said, however, about the question of Soviet subsidies in trade with Eastern Europe. It is a field in which no one can ignore the work of two American economists, Michael Marrese and Jan Vaňous. Their findings aroused great controversy. But they usually kept the initiative in the ensuing controversy, and many contributions by others to the debate were in the form of responses to them.

Marrese and Vaňous basically asked whether the Soviet Union would have got more out of trade with the West, settled in dollars, than it did out of trade with Eastern Europe, settled in transferable rubles. (*The "foregone gains" issue.*) The prices paid to or received from the West represented the Soviets' opportunity cost. Hence to get the difference (or the amount the Soviets are losing) East European trade should be repriced and revalued at those hypothetical dollar prices. At the heart of the issue has been the undeniable fact that Soviet exports to Eastern Europe, especially in energy and raw materials, are "hard goods" in terms of their relatively high value on the world market, while East European exports are mainly "soft goods" of low quality and value on the world market. Marrese and Vaňous established a methodology based on a series of estimates and assumptions and came to the conclusion that the opportunity cost involved in the Soviets' trade with Eastern Europe between 1970 and 1984 was about $110 billion (1984).[33]

Most economists have rejected these figures as too high. Some idea of the size of the discrepancy between experts can be derived from the fact that, while Marrese and Vaňous estimate that Soviet foregone gains between 1972 and 1974 increased by 5.2 billion transferable rubles, the estimate by Raimund Dietz, the noted Austrian economist, was only 2.6 billion transferable rubles—or exactly half.[34] Other authorities, like Paul Marer and Jozef van Brabant, questioned the findings of Marrese and Vaňous but did not differ so radically with them as Dietz.[35] An unabashed tyro like the present writer cannot begin to decide between the warring experts. The truth, most experts would agree, almost certainly lay between the Marrese-Vaňous estimates and those of Dietz. They would also agree that a better way of assessing dollar-ruble exchange rates for some aspects of intra-Comecon trade was essential for arriving at more accurate estimates.

This is a debate that will continue even in the new situation of much lower oil and other raw material prices after 1985, which in many respects made the former debate obsolete and academic. In the meantime, for their part, most East Europeans would have greeted the Marrese and Vaňous findings with some incredulity. They would even have been inclined to reject Dietz's figures as far too high! Most Soviet citizens, on the other hand, especially Russians, would probably consider Marrese and Vaňous as too conservative. Each side in the Soviet–East European divide is convinced the one is exploiting the other. Such is the nature of the fraternal socialist alliance.

Those who could afford a somewhat more detached view must, however, accept that Soviet subsidization has been considerable, higher than many had previously suspected. Why, then, were the Soviets prepared to do it? Some observers concluded that the reasons were mainly economic, designed perhaps in part to ease the crippling burden of energy payments for the East Europeans. It is difficult, though, not to conclude that these subsidies were part of the economic price Moscow was prepared to pay for relative stability in Eastern Europe, i.e., that they were basically politically motivated. Marrese and Vaňous have argued this point, and they were probably right. This is not to say that the subsidies developed in the way the Soviets wanted or expected. They probably began as part of an overall package of indirect economic support with which Moscow was prepared to burden itself to try to secure peace and quiet. But the Soviet leadership had little or no idea how the different parts of the package would grow.[36] Other parts were the ruble loans and the practice of allowing the East Europeans to run up deficits. The Soviets appear to have granted this latter concession extensively to all countries in distress since the middle 1950s. These included Poland and Hungary in 1956 and 1957, Czechoslovakia in 1968, Poland in 1971, and several countries, especially Poland, again in the 1980s.[37] But the trade subsidies have been the most regular, ongoing form of financial aid and certainly the most complex to assess. They presumably grew in a way nobody expected, and, because they were difficult to check or control, they accumulated formidably over the years.

Finally, if Moscow has used economic instruments for political purposes, has it used them to reward and to punish as well as to preempt or avoid? Bulgaria would certainly seem to be a case of virtue rewarded (see chapter 10). As for punishment, many East Europeans are convinced that this has been an integral part of Soviet policy, and, in view of the difficulties the Soviets have from time to time faced, it is hard to imagine that so powerful a weapon has not been sometimes used to coerce or, at least, to try to "induce." Romanian leaders, especially Ceauşescu himself, strongly implied as much in the 1960s.[38] In the case of Albania before the break with Moscow in 1961 the pressure was blatant, and there were also suspicions of it in Poland in 1981.[39] The Romanians have also not been accorded most of the general advantages in trade that the other members of Comecon have enjoyed. But the Soviets can hardly be accused of "victimizing" Romania in this regard. As for the other countries, though suspicions may abound, there is precious little direct evidence. (The 10 percent oil cut in 1982, for example, can hardly be seen as deliberate punishment.) The available evidence, in fact, tends to point the other way, with Soviet anxiety about a country leading to more aid rather than less. The Soviet Union has never been a charitable organization. But, since Stalin, it has realized that Eastern Europe has had to be handled with care, and its economic policy toward it has reflected this caution.

The Energy Situation

It is hard to believe that up to 1955 the Soviet Union was a net importer of both solid and liquid fuels from Eastern Europe or that for much of the 1960s Eastern Europe remained a net exporter of the same to Western Europe. The energy problem only began for the region as a whole when it passed a (fairly early) stage on the road to industrialization and its own domestic resources could not keep pace. At the same time the development of oil fields and natural gas reserves in the Soviet Union enabled it to supply Eastern Europe with all its needs, and then pipelines were built to overcome the problems of transportation. Between 1960 and 1970 East European imports of Soviet crude oil rose from 7 million to 35 million tons.

But increases like these, plus the growing importance of oil for the East European economies, might tend to distract attention from the continuing importance of coal. (Romania is again the exception here. It had traditionally depended not on coal, but more on its own large supplies of oil and natural gas.) Coal has continued to be the main source of energy for all the other East European countries.[41] But by the middle of the 1970s most East European economies had become vulnerably dependent on Soviet oil. All oil imports were not used directly in the domestic industrial process. But the amounts that were not were used as exports for vital hard currency.

This crucial Soviet role continued throughout the 1970s into the 1980s. But for a time in the early 1970s it had appeared that Moscow was prepared to abdicate this role and allow—even encourage—the East Europeans to look to world markets for the increased supplies of oil they would undoubtedly need. (This was in spite of the fact that earlier fears of reduced quantities of Soviet oil available for export had been removed by the opening of new fields in Siberia.) The Soviets were apparently not preparing to supply Eastern Europe at anywhere near the rate of increase it had done even in the 1960s. Initial projections were that East European imports would rise by only 3 percent during the 1976–80 planning period as against 10.6 percent in the first half of the decade.[42] Various reasons for this change have been suggested: that East European demand subsequently turned out to be much bigger than the Soviets anticipated; that this was a Soviet response to East European reluctance to invest in extraction in the Soviet Union; that the Soviets suspected oil was not as indispensable as the East Europeans were saying. It has also been suggested that, after the crushing of reforms in Czechoslovakia, it was politically safe to let the East Europeans loose on the world energy markets. At any rate, the Soviets seemed willing to considerably step up their supplies of natural gas but not of oil.

The Arab oil embargo in 1973 and then the quadrupling of prices completely changed the situation. The East Europeans were thrown at the mercy of the Soviet Union, which now disposed of unprecedented economic leverage. Cut off from the world market because of the soaring prices, the East Europeans (except the Romanians) were more dependent on Soviet oil than ever, which even after 1975 continued relatively cheap. They were also now less able to resist Soviet pressure to invest in their extractive industries. Moreover, as the East European economies expanded in the 1970s, stimulated by Western credits, their demand for energy increased—partly to reexport oil products to gain hard currency to pay debts. Between 1971 and 1975 Soviet exports of energy to the region increased by 9.6 percent and between 1976 and 1980 by 6 percent. During the latter period the Soviets shipped 370 million tons of crude oil and oil products, 98 billion cubic meters of gas, 57 billion kilowatt hours of electricity, and 41 billion tons of coke and coal.[43]

The Question of Prices

These few figures dramatically project Eastern Europe's economic and, by extension, political dependence on the Soviet Union. As already mentioned, it was in the middle of the 1970s that the Soviets increased the price of their energy supplies to Eastern Europe. The "Bucharest formula," in operation since 1958, was abandoned and a five-year moving average adopted with one year being dropped annually and a new one added. The price doubled between 1974 and 1976, and between 1976 and 1983 it increased fourfold.

It still remained lower than the OPEC world price. Everyone seemed agreed on that. But the question of how much lower has, as in the case of Soviet trade subsidies, caused controversy among economists. In terms of official prices the Soviet price of oil had crept up to 90 percent of the world price toward the end of the 1970s. With the second OPEC price explosion of 1979, however, it was reduced to less than half the world price in 1980. But as world prices quickly went down, the two sets of prices were about equal in 1984, and the Comecon price had surpassed the world price by the last quarter of 1985.[44] But apparently it was not as simple as that, since relating the official Comecon price to the world price at the official dollar/ruble exchange rates distorts the picture. At a more realistic exchange rate the East Europeans were probably still doing much better out of the Soviet oil trade than many people thought.[45]

But, inevitably, there were factors on the other side to be taken into account. The East Europeans, reportedly, had to buy "soft" goods from the Soviets at inflated prices in partial compensation for the bargain they got on the oil prices. Any quantities of oil they got above contract they had to pay for in hard currency at world market prices. (The Romanians were purchasing all their Soviet oil on these conditions, although their imports were still small.) Moreover, despite the standard Comecon price formula, prices to individual countries varied considerably, mainly according to the types and quality of the goods bartered to the Soviet Union in exchange for the oil, and to the extent that each country invested in Soviet oil production itself.[46] Finally, the East Europeans were having to invest heavily in the joint Comecon energy development projects in the Soviet Union such as the Orenburg natural gas pipeline.

East Europeans could also point out, especially as of 1982 when the 10 percent cut in deliveries occurred, that the Soviet Union had become an unreliable supplier. (Subsequently supplies to Bulgaria were also reported to have been trimmed.) In fact, comparing supplies in 1983 with those in 1981 it can be estimated that the reduction for Czechoslovakia was nearly 12 percent, for Hungary nearly 10 percent, even for beleaguered Poland about 7.5 percent, and for the GDR as much as 24.7 percent.

The drop for the GDR seems punitive, and the East Germans may well have considered it so. But the Soviets could well have concluded that neither they nor others needed so much oil. By the early 1980s the East Germans were reported to be making a profitable trade in buying large quantities of oil and selling much of it to the West. During this period 30 percent of the GDR's exports to the OECD countries consisted of energy. According to the West Berlin-based Institute for Economic Research, in 1984 the GDR imported 23.9 million tons of crude oil of which it used only about 10 million tons domestically. The rest was exported. Out of these total imports of 23.9 millions, the Soviets supplied 17 million tons, or 7 million tons *more* than the East Germans directly needed domestically.[47] In such circumstances the Soviets could be excused for taking a harder attitude toward East German appeals for more supplies. Czechoslovakia and Hungary also conducted the same kind of business but on a much smaller scale. But it was the Bulgarians who, relatively, conducted the biggest business of all in oil exports to the West. In 1983 more than 60 percent of Bulgarian exports to the West consisted of crude or refined oil products, four-fifths of which originated in the Soviet Union.[48] The Bulgarians, therefore, could not justifiably have felt victimized when Gorbachev in 1985 reportedly began to query this blatant case of favoritism. Nor, apparently, was all the oil reexported by the East Europeans supplied over contract by the Soviets and hence paid for in hard currency. Some must have been delivered contractually. (The Bulgarians are reported to have received *all* of their oil at contract prices.)

The Soviet Union could, therefore, in some respects feel aggrieved. It could also accuse the East Europeans of being profligate users of energy in their own industries (although the Soviets themselves were probably the worst offenders here). In 1982 the East European consumption of energy was twenty-eight barrels of oil equivalent as against twenty-five barrels for the countries of the European Community, although the latter had a 30 percent higher per capita income. And between 1979 and 1985 the same West European countries reduced total energy consumption by over 10 percent, while energy consumption in Eastern Europe actually increased by 0.4 percent. In 1978 West Germany consumed from 28 to 56 percent less energy per dollar of industrial output than all members of the Soviet bloc.[49]

These are just a few illustrative figures collected by Keith Crane showing the East European backwardness. It is a problem recognized by economists throughout Eastern Europe, but relatively little had ever been done to tackle it. The GDR and Czechoslovakia had probably tried the hardest. But, no matter how hard they might try, the East Europeans were in a dilemma. In the case of the East Germans and the Czechoslovaks, for example, conserving on imported oil was throwing them back more on their domestic supplies of brown coal. This was not only inefficient but a notorious polluter, compounding the already horrendous ecological situation in parts of these two countries. For some East European countries nuclear energy had seemed the answer.

Already by 1985 about 30 percent of Bulgaria's power requirements was supplied by nuclear energy. It was scheduled to become an important energy supplier, but the Chernobyl disaster of April 1986 must have increased public unease as well as pressure for greater safeguards (see chapter 13).

Difficulties in Supplies

As for the future, it was likely that the Soviet oil supply cuts of 1982 would provide a pointer to it. The Soviets subsequently indicated that its oil supplies had reached their limit and the East Europeans had become resigned to it. The basic reason for this was the anticipated leveling off in Soviet oil production. Earlier predictions of an almost catastrophic decline were modified, but no one expected output to increase substantially. Even if it did, the world market price for oil, though it might ease upward after the lows of the middle 1980s, might never reach the heights of the 1970s. The Soviets, therefore, seriously hurt on the world market in 1985 and 1986, would want to export correspondingly more to hard-currency areas. But the overriding dilemma remained: Moscow had always to be careful lest anything they did in the economic sphere spilled over into the political and social. The right balance would always be difficult to achieve and always easy to upset.

Generally, though, it seemed very likely that East Europe had to prepare itself for much more natural gas from the Soviet Union in the 1990s. Unless, of course, with Soviet permission and perhaps even prompting, they began looking more to the world market for oil now that the prices had dropped so dramatically. As already mentioned, the Soviets had apparently contemplated this in the early 1970s. If it were actually to happen in the late 1980s it could mean the beginnings of a revolution, first economic and eventually political. Again, the political dilemma asserted itself. What might seem economic relief for Moscow could begin to unravel the web of economic and political relationships the Soviet Union had been spinning for thirty years or more.

Comecon

The Council for Mutual Economic Assistance (Comecon, CEMA, or CMEA) was founded at the beginning of 1949 apparently as Stalin's response to the Marshall Plan for Europe and partly as means of establishing greater coordination and Soviet control, especially after the defection of Yugoslavia in 1948. Its existence, however, was little more than a formality for several years. Each of the East European communist states built industry in autarkic fashion, and there was little thought of economic cooperation beyond the most basic kind.

It was Khrushchev in the late 1950s who saw both the necessity and the opportunities of an economic organization facilitating greater cooperation, specialization, and eventually a form of integration. This had now acquired an urgency caused only partly by the establishment of the European Economic Community in 1958. Economic development and postwar reconstruction had now reached the point where primitive autarky was seen as increasingly wasteful. But, perhaps most important of all, Comecon and the Warsaw Pact (as discussed in chapter 2) had become key instruments in securing greater Soviet control in Eastern Europe after the debacles in Hungary and Poland in 1956.

In 1960 Comecon first got its charter, and two years later its means and ends were outlined in "The Basic Principles of the International Socialist Division of the Labour." Economic and technical cooperation between the member countries was to be deepened, the national plans of the different countries coordinated, and the "international division of labour" improved. It was also clear that one of the main aims was to equalize the economic development and levels of the different members.[50]

Just as clear was the stress on national sovereignty. There was to be no supranationalism, and each member retained the right of veto. But even before the publication of the "Basic Principles" in 1962 an argument had developed that was to show how contradictory some of these principles were. The argument led to what became known as the "Romanian deviation," one of the most important developments in East European communist history. It arose from the initial demand of Czechoslovakia and the GDR, eventually supported by the Soviet Union, that the international division of labor be used to justify a developmental status quo, with the industrialized members of Comecon continuing with their all-round industrial programs while the less-developed states carry on mainly with agriculture, food processing, and some consumer goods for the whole of the bloc. Thus, as soon as Comecon began showing signs of life, the basic conflict of its existence was revealed. Between the developed Northern Tier and the undeveloped Southern Tier there was a gulf that no common ideology could narrow.

The "Romanian deviation" was the main outcome of this basic conflict of interest, and it is quite probable that Bucharest's opposition was supported by countries like Hungary and Bulgaria, which, in this context, were in a similar situation—especially the latter. (Albania would also have been, but it was already in the throes of its own "deviation" from the Moscow norm.)[51] It is easy to overlook what a serious obstacle to coordinated action Romania's opposition signified. It was the second largest and second most populous East European country and the richest in natural resources. Therefore when it forcefully made actual the potential contradiction between national sovereignty and the international division of labor, Comecon faced a major crisis that was more political than economic. Khrushchev, characteristically, did not seek to avoid the crisis but countered by suggesting some kind of supranational planning and decisionmaking body for Comecon. (In 1964 he was also hinting at a supranational body to coordinate bloc foreign policy.)

Khrushchev's proposals, rather than forcing a solution, only deepened the crisis as the Romanians maintained their opposition, showing extraordinary diplomatic skill in doing so. The dismissal of Khrushchev in October 1964 probably avoided a major confrontation between him and the Romanian leadership. Subsequently, after a serious clash between the new Soviet leaders, Brezhnev and Kosygin, and the new Romanian leader, Ceauşescu, over Soviet centralizing plans for the Warsaw Pact, the Romanian question and, with it, the question of Comecon reorganization were shelved as the Czechoslovak crisis approached.

Brezhnev's New Approach

After the invasion and the "normalization" of Czechoslovakia, the Brezhnev leadership looked to Comecon and the Warsaw Pact, as Khrushchev had done after the upheavals of 1956, as the main instruments for a new cohesion. Its designs for, and through, Comecon were enshrined in the "Comprehensive Program" of 1971. (Full title: "Comprehensive Program for the Further Extension and Improvement of Cooperation and the Development of Socialist Integration by the Comecon Member Countries.") This document tried to take into account the different stages of development of the economies of the member states and the need to harmonize and equalize them. It also spoke of initiating programs of joint investment and for the exploitation of energy resources in the Soviet Union. Politically it sought to circumvent the difficulties implicit in the national sovereignty principle, at the same time promoting Comecon as an instrument of coordination and even of integration.

The "Comprehensive Program" got around the national sovereignty issue and the single veto paralysis by adopting the "interested party" principle. Thus unanimous approval and unanimous participation were jettisoned. A country not wanting to join in a project simply did not participate but could not veto it. Romanian recalcitrance was, therefore, neutralized. The Soviets knew that Romania simply could not refuse cooperation in all Comecon joint schemes, and indeed Ceauşescu was soon emphasizing Romania's readiness to participate in several of them. But on the basic point at issue in the early 1960s—a supranational authority—the Romanians had got their way and the Soviet Union was not to return to the subject. Instead Brezhnev, through the manifold types of cooperation provided for in the "Comprehensive Program," sought to build integration from the "bottom up" rather than from the "top down" as Khrushchev had apparently attempted. Integration was to become something organic not imposed (see chapter 2).

At the same time the new Soviet approach to integration rejected the market mechanism and market notions like comparative advantage and relative scarcity. The implication and significance of this rejection are discussed later. Here it need only be said that in making this decision Comecon was also rejecting the most effective long-term means of achieving real integration. The cumbersome bilateralism of trade through barter was left essentially undisturbed. The introduction of the transferable ruble also left the character of this trade untouched. It hardly lived up to the notion of "transferable" anyway. A surplus in trade with one country still could not be used to buy in a third country. The transferable ruble remained, therefore, very little more than a unit of account. The prices used by the Comecon countries in their mutual trade have always been derived from those obtaining on the world market, a fact that underlies another basic contradiction in the whole of Comecon cooperation. The market mechanism and its rules are rejected on ideological grounds, and the Soviet Union has periodically led drives for regional self-sufficiency; yet Comecon price levels are derived from the very system that is economically, politically, and ideologically rejected.

Joint Investments

The Comprehensive Program sought to hasten the cooperation-coordination-integration sequence by means of joint economic planning—long-term as well as short-term—and joint production ventures, embodied during the 1970s in new "target programs" in key areas of economic activity. Nine large joint investment projects were begun after 1972, eight of which had become operational by the end of the decade. Probably the most spectacular was the Orenburg natural gas pipeline in which all members participated, although Romania had only a limited role. Others deserving mention were the Ust Ilimsk cellulose mill, the Kiembaev asbestos plant, and the Vinnitsa-Albertirsa electric power transmission line. Eight out of these nine projects were in the Soviet Union. None was in Eastern Europe: the ninth, a nickel and cobalt production complex, was in Cuba. It is worth noting that Romania participated in all but two of these projects. Czechoslovakia, one of the most dependable of the Soviet Union's allies after 1968 and a strong advocate of integration, was the only nonparticipant in the Ust Ilimsk cellulose mill.[52]

These joint investment projects were a new feature in Comecon's history and must be distinguished from the joint enterprises, the first of which dated back to 1954. These latter were mainly bilateral and the best known was probably Haldex, an enterprise for processing coal products, founded in 1959 and operated jointly by Poland and Hungary. Most projects did involve the Soviet Union, but they were by no means as Soviet-dominated as the joint investment projects. Though most of the investment projects were agreed to in the first half of the 1970s, they became operational only in the second half. They were linked to long-term "target programs," as well as to the "Coordinated Plan for Multilateral Integration Measures, 1976–1980." Not only were all but one located in the Soviet Union, but they were also Soviet-controlled as to conception, planning, production, and distribution. They reflected not just the well-known fact that the Soviet Union disposed of the overwhelming mass of raw materials in Comecon but also the emerging Soviet determination that their partners must share in the increasing cost of extracting and processing them. Nor did it go unnoticed in Eastern Europe that, though these may be "joint" ventures, their facilities were solely owned by the Soviet Union. The East Europeans simply supplied part of the labor and capital and received supplies of the raw materials concerned. The question whether they received a "just return" was one which worried many East European officials, including even the Czechoslovak premier, Lubomir Štrougal, who in 1976 proposed what he delicately called a "principle of equivalence."[53]

East European coolness to the joint investment projects, together with the difficulties in both completing them and then getting them to work effectively, appears to have reduced Soviet enthusiasm for them. But under the influence of the new OPEC oil price explosion at the end of the 1970s the Soviets were determined that they should not go entirely unrecompensed for supplying their partners with relatively cheap energy and other raw materials. They refrained—though the temptation must have been great—from changing the oil price formula, operating since 1976, yet again. But they got the East Europeans to agree to the principle of general "multilateral investment cooperation," which ensured investment coordination in key sectors of the individual economies. The aim was to upgrade the quality and value of manufactured goods exported by Eastern Europe to the Soviet Union in exchange for oil and other raw materials. This had always been a sore point with the Soviets and in the 1980s was to become one of their main preoccupations in their dealings with the East Europeans.

Basic Failures

By any standards Comecon has had some impressive statistics to its credit. In 1985 60 percent of the trade of its member countries was conducted within its confines, and the volume of the trade turnover among its members had increased thirty times since 1950. It had a huge research establishment, and several of the joint investment projects mentioned above were impressive enough, despite technical difficulties and East European suspicions. Some progress had also been made in specialization—for example, Bulgaria in forklift trucks and various kinds of electronics, and Hungary in its famous Ikarus buses.

In addition, a country like Bulgaria had been helped through Comecon to a degree of economic modernization it would never have achieved on its own. Whether the other southeast European communist countries, Yugoslavia, Albania, and Romania—the first never a member, the second only effectively till about 1960, the third often only a nominal member—would have been better off with full membership is debatable. In some respects Romania might have been, while Yugoslavia, which to some extent changed both its principles and practices to take advantage of the Western connection, almost certainly would not. As for Albania, the economic succor it received from China was probably not such as could have replaced the benefits it would have derived from Comecon. Inside Comecon its industrial progress might have been just as impressive, while the living standards of its citizens would probably have been considerably higher.

But in spite of its achievements and its blessings, Comecon, by the standards of progress accepted in the West, has been a failure. As Daniel Franklin has written:

> Comecon suffers from the problems usually associated with this form (i.e. the system of central planning)—irrational prices, shortages, mistrust of outside supplies leading to autarkic behaviour, lack of market stimulus leading to poor quality and low levels of innovation, separation of producer and consumer, crippling bureaucracy etc.—with many of the difficulties compounded by barriers which inevitably arise between 10 sovereign states keen to protect their national interests. In particular the prices in each country are not only distorted (in that they reflect neither scarcity, nor utility, nor real costs), but the distortions are different in each country. This makes it immensely difficult to establish what, precisely, constitutes a fair exchange among the members.[54]

This is a formidable indictment indeed—and an accurate one by the market-orientated approach used in the West. Comecon has been notoriously unsuccessful as a trading area designed to promote maximum efficiency.

An "International Protection System"

But the question remains whether Comecon was ever supposed to be what observers in the West—and a growing number in the East, it must be said—thought it should be. Vladimir Sobell, a Czech-born economist, has argued strongly in his book *The Red Market* that Comecon integration was never designed as a "tool for maximizing productive efficiency." Eastern planners, he argues, "do not see foreign trade as a desirable pursuit in its own right but merely as an additional source of supplies, the volume and composition of which is contingent on the requirements of the production plan." Comecon he sees as an "international protection system" (IPS), which he distinguishes from an "international trade system"

(ITS), which (in many respects) the European Economic Community is. Sobell amplifies his distinction between the two types of organization:

> [An] IPS may be defined as an international system of commodity exchange whose purpose is not the maximization of benefits of comparative advantage, but the protection and expansion of production, the regulation of which is not by prices reflecting relative scarcities but by bilateral and multilateral intergovernmental agreements reflecting political aspirations. In contradistinction, [an] ITS may be defined as an international system of commodity exchange whose purpose is the derivation of the benefits of comparative advantage, whose terms are determined by prices reflecting relative scarcities, and where the extent of the protection of production (or subsidy to depressed areas) is subject to bilateral and multilateral politically inspired agreements.[55]

Sobell then enters an interesting caveat to the argument that, despite much talk of multilateralism within Comecon, what really predominates is a persistent and all-embracing bilateralism. In one respect he sees this bilateralism as being "animated by covert multilateral relationships." The key to understanding this is the division of items exchanged in intra-Comecon trade into "hard" and "soft" goods. ("Hard goods," by which are usually meant fuels and raw materials, are goods that suppliers could always sell more of; "soft goods" are those that suppliers find hard to get rid of at the going price—or for what the partner is prepared to barter for them.) The shortage of "hard" goods in Comecon and the shortage of markets for "soft" goods create a multilateral interdependence, since any Soviet decision regarding the allocation of "hard" goods has a multifaceted impact on the Soviet Union and especially on its East European partners. To quote Sobell again, a "preferential allocation of such commodities to one country has repercussions throughout the system because the remaining countries are compelled to seek their supplies elsewhere and on stiffer terms."[56]

In this sense, therefore, there is a considerable degree of multilateralism in Comecon. Furthermore, taking Comecon as an "international protection system" rather than an "international trade system," Sobell argues that Comecon also has always had a considerable degree of integration—at least of a kind. Looking at Comecon through a Western prism, it appears there can never be real integration until there is supranational planning (or a real market, or both). But need the absence of a supranational institution preclude a process—a slow, fitful process—of coming together? All the interdependent relationships existing within Comecon represent an extension of the domestic plans of the member economies into "the inter-grouping dimension" that steadily assumes more importance. Therefore, "the mesh of such relationships may," according to Sobell, "be identified as the 'single plan' of Comecon."[57]

This attempt to see Comecon development from a different perspective is enlightening since it explains the economic, as well as the political, rationale behind many of the decisions that have guided its progress. Finally it gives, not a theoretical, but an actual model for Comecon. The Khrushchev notion of a supranational planning authority was another model that foundered on political or nationalist opposition spearheaded by Romania.

A third model would involve the introduction of the market mechanism, bringing Comecon much closer to the Western notion of an "international trade system." It was advocated by economists in Hungary and, to a lesser extent, in Poland in the 1970s and the 1980s. This would involve decentralization, price reforms, and a genuinely convertible ruble. It would also allow direct business relationships between individual enterprises in the different member countries. It was favored by Hungarians because it was compatible with their own newly introduced New Economic Mechanism, or at least with the goals they had in mind for it. The insuperable difficulty, of course, lay in all the other member countries being centrally organized in the Soviet fashion. It would need a transformation of every economy along Hungarian lines to enable a market-guided Comecon to work. And any change along those lines has been ideologically unacceptable up to now.

Mounting Problems

Comecon, therefore, has persisted with its well-worn system. But by the end of the 1970s its difficulties were mounting. The spectacular joint investment projects, Brezhnev's "hallmark," were not as successful as had been hoped. The economies of some of its members were faltering badly. Energy and raw material supplies did not look as assured as they once did. Acrimony grew and mutual recriminations seemed to be multiplying. The line of division was not just between the Soviets, on the one side, and the East Europeans, on the other. The East Europeans were often dissatisfied with each other, and the old cleavage of interest between Northern and Southern Tiers was as clear as ever. There were also problems relating to the non-European members —Mongolia (joined 1962), Cuba (1972), and Vietnam (1978). The Cuban drain was resented by the East Europeans, but there was much more concern over what the membership of Vietnam might involve—not just economically, but politically and militarily.

Past practice suggested that these mounting problems needed a Comecon summit to help resolve them. It was finally held in June 1984, some fifteen years after the previous one. (The "Comprehensive Program" was approved in 1971 at a council meeting of premiers, not at a summit. It had been suggested at the Comecon summit, including party leaders and premiers, in 1969.) This extraordinary delay was presumably due to an initially preoccupied, subsequently enfeebled, and ultimately unstable Soviet leadership not wanting to discuss and tackle problems so difficult and divisive.[58]

It was an irony, therefore, that the summit was eventually held when Chernenko was Soviet leader and that it featured a stern Soviet lecture to the Eastern Europeans about their economic "responsibilities." The meeting approved a document, or "Basic Guidelines," which reflected a hybrid approach. It did not seek to change the conservative or "international protection system" character of Comecon, but at the same time it at least mentioned notions like enterprise-to-enterprise relations and even commodity-monetary relations. But the main point in the document was that no basic changes in structure and practice would be contemplated in the near future. As for the lecture to the East Europeans, its sentiments were not new, but they had never been expressed as forcefully in public as this. The relevant (and oft-quoted) passage in the document was as follows:

> To create economic conditions ensuring the implementation and continuation of deliveries from the USSR of a number of types of raw materials and energy carriers to satisfy the import requirements in volumes determined on the basis of coordination of plans and long term accords, the interested Comecon member states shall gradually and consistently develop . . . their structure of production and export and carry out all the necessary . . . capital investments, reconstruction and rationalization of their industry with the aim of supplying the USSR with the products it needs, in particular foodstuffs and manufactured consumer goods, some

types of construction materials, machines and equipment of a high quality and of the world technical level.[59]

This hard Soviet line was maintained at a Comecon council meeting of prime ministers in Havana in October 1984. It was essentially an expression of Soviet exasperation at what they considered the self-seeking behavior of their East European liabilities. The combination of international and local conditions had led, they considered, to their being increasingly exploited by the East Europeans. It also reflected Moscow's concern at the Western contacts of the East Europeans and probably the growing resentment in the Soviet Union itself over the better living standards the East Europeans continued to enjoy. The directness of the above-quoted passage, which was, after all, part of an *agreed* document, gives some idea of what the debates over the issue must have been like and of what the Soviets' *original* suggestions might have been.

The Soviets could complain, as they had always done. But what did they intend doing? They appeared to be demanding changes involving enormous difficulties in reorienting attitudes and restructuring practices. Even more important, the economic, social, and political consequences in Eastern Europe of a drastically new Soviet policy might be very dangerous. The anticipation of such consequences could, therefore, as they apparently had in the past, stay the Soviets' hand. This was part of the Eastern Europeans' leverage in their relations with the Soviet Union. But they must nevertheless have resigned themselves to a more difficult economic relationship with Moscow, especially under the energetic leadership of Mikhail Gorbachev. The East wind was becoming colder, and the East Europeans were having to brace themselves for it.

Gorbachev's New Look

Gorbachev's first important policy act within the Comecon framework was to get the premiers of the member countries to approve in December 1985 the "Comprehensive Program for Scientific and Technical Progress" to the year A.D. 2000. Such a program was necessary, said Gorbachev at the meeting, to ensure "technological independence from and invulnerability to pressure and blackmail on the part of the imperialists." The program itself contained some of the points made in the new CPSU program approved in February 1986. Productivity, for example, was to be doubled by the end of the century, and savings were to be made in the use of energy and raw materials. The program itself covered five main topics: electronics, automation systems (mainly robots), nuclear energy, the development of new materials and technology, and biotechnology. A new Comecon international organization, "Interrobot," was to be established to develop new generations of robots and programmable machine tool systems. In the nuclear field more efficient fast-breeder nuclear reactors were to be developed. In short, Gorbachev's "Comprehensive Program" was supposed to herald the scientific and technological revolution for Comecon.

It bore the hallmarks of Gorbachev: energy, speed, and determination. It also reflected his awareness of the revolutionary nature of the new technology and the crucial urgency it gave to the need for modernization. But it was also a political document, as he himself admitted. For the new technology, and the enormous lead the West possessed in it, represented yet another danger to cohesion in Eastern Europe. The technical elites of Eastern Europe had, largely through the openings created by the détente of the 1970s, been exposed to, and thoroughly impressed by, Western methods and technology. They became more aware than ever of Western superiority. Gorbachev was also aware of this superiority, of its temptation for Eastern Europeans and the political dangers of that temptation. The "Comprehensive Program," therefore, was a major effort to preempt this danger.[60]

Factors for the Future

The economic situation in Eastern Europe toward the end of the 1980s outwardly looked better than it had at the beginning. But the improvement appeared to be only a temporary respite. The longer-term outlook was probably bleaker than it had been at any time since 1945. This was because some of the pillars on which previous progress had been built were now weaker and because some of the assumptions influencing previous economic strategy were no longer fully accepted.

The most crucial of these assumptions had been:

1. The domestic availability of labor and raw materials to maintain an extensive system of industrial growth. This foundation had long since disappeared in the Northern Tier. It had almost disappeared in Romania and Bulgaria also—not to mention Yugoslavia.

2. The centralized structure of economic planning and direction that had been tolerable and, in some cases, even effective in a situation of extensive growth had become manifestly counterproductive in a situation of intensive growth. Throughout Eastern Europe, therefore, there was a need for economic reform embodying the kind of principles at work in Hungary. But the ideological and political constraints on this kind of reform were still great. It was in any case imperative that the Hungarian experiment be seen to be succeeding. In the first half of the 1980s it was doing just the opposite—to the consternation of reformers and the glee of conservatives.

3. The Soviet Union was unwilling and/or unable to supply Eastern Europe with the energy and raw materials it needed or was likely to need.

4. The Soviet Union also seemed inclined to adopt a much more rigorous attitude to its economic relations with Eastern Europe generally.

5. Economic relations with the West could continue to decline because of continuing debt repayment problems, drastic curtailment of Western credit, and lack of East European competitiveness. Essential Western technology and know-how could, therefore, be withheld.

Any one of these factors occurring singly would be serious enough. Altogether, they seemed to put Eastern Europe at an unbearable disadvantage. They could possibly be a spur to greater initiative by the East European leaderships themselves. The demands of intensive growth at home might lead to economic reforms embracing market principles. Soviet restrictions on energy and raw material supplies, coinciding with a new situation of favorable world prices, could induce efforts to find new sources elsewhere. A more international orientation could also lead to greater Western technology. But, again, the kind of self-help and Western contacts needed involved political factors affecting not only the Soviet Union but the relations between the regime leaderships and their societies in Eastern Europe itself. The economic situation in Eastern Europe has always been a hostage to political considerations. It was likely to remain so. Gorbachev wanted viability in Comecon and seemed ready for basic reform in its workings. But he was moving into unmapped and dangerous territory.

5 Poland

The greatest challenge to communist rule in Eastern Europe has come from Poland. It is true that, at least since the imposition of communist rule, Poland has not yet been invaded by Soviet troops, as Hungary and Czechoslovakia were. Nor, despite the bloodshed of 1956, 1970, and 1981–82, inflicted by Poles on Poles, has there been anything like the repression during or after the Hungarian Revolution or the East German uprising of 1953. In terms of historical impact Tito's break with Stalin was a more important single factor than any episode in recent Polish history. But in terms of a consistent, sustained rejection by much the greater part of Polish society of communist attempts at domination for forty years, a period during which this rejection has spilled over into violence several times, there is no record in Eastern Europe to match that of Poland.

There are several explanations: the indomitability of the Polish nation, without which it could hardly have survived the colonizations of the nineteenth century; its sustaining hatred of Russia; the role of the Roman Catholic church in its national history and culture; the Westward cultural and spiritual gravitation of most Poles, a process in which the Church has played a dominant role; the incompetence of Poland's communist rulers; and the size and strategic importance of the country itself, which, though militating against any likelihood of achieving real independence from Moscow, has given Polish society a self-confidence and bargaining leverage the smaller East European nations simply have not possessed.[1]

Finally, the Poles have acquired a sympathy in the West—both in Europe and the United States—not possessed by any other East European nation. This is due to a combination of Polish immigration, heroism in World War II, and a collective Western guilt over the failure to do anything effective to help Poland either in 1939 or in 1945 and after. It is a matter for debate, of course, how much this Western sympathy has done for Poland over the last forty years. Precious little, most Poles might say. But in combination with other factors, at least *American* interest might have deterred the country's Soviet and Polish rulers from policies that could have made the situation worse. It may, for example, have helped to ease pressure on the church and deter efforts toward the socialization of agriculture.

The sustained national challenge to Soviet-imposed rule has not been reflected in a permanent state of open rebellion. Indeed, there have been numerous variations on that theme of "organic work" that was a feature of partitioned Poland in the nineteenth century. The rebuilding of the country after the devastations of World War II, the development of the newly acquired Western territories, the exploitation of natural resources, the triumphs of Polish culture and scholarship, all these, despite the official propaganda, were not so much communist as national successes in which society played its full part and in which it took pride. All of this, of course, involved some degree of cooperation with the communist authorities, between society and state. Indeed, many Polish communists, including high-ranking dignitaries, have viewed Polish achievements more from a national than from an ideological perspective. But, whereas in other communist countries in Eastern Europe, not to mention the Soviet Union, the regimes have succeeded, in varying degrees, in dominating, infiltrating, decimating, or corrupting society, in Poland society has remained largely intact, firm, and independent—and, in a basic sense, dominant. This is not to say that Polish society is immune from the grave social and moral dangers that beset all societies, east and west. Far from it. It means that Polish society has been more resistant than most, and it, rather than the Polish regime, has set the essential tone and pace of public life.

Nowhere else in Eastern Europe has communist rule been so thin or shallow; nowhere has it been regarded with such a curious combination of hatred, contempt, and amusement, and, at least until the declaration of martial law in December 1981, with that lofty good humor that stems from the certainty of natural superiority. Societal opposition has mostly been tempered by a realism easy to overlook. Much has been written, correctly, about Polish romanticism and volatility, but one of the predominant characteristics of Polish society under communism has been the awareness that the Polish nation was, in the last analysis, on its own, and the acceptance of the geopolitical realities of Soviet dominance and its implications for Poland. This point needs stressing right at the outset since it has often not been appreciated in the West, especially during the brief history of Solidarity in 1980–81. Then Poles were criticized for "going too far," for "a lack of responsibility," etc. These charges need to be repudiated. Solidarity did contain some elements that lacked moderation. But what stands out about the movement as a whole was its restraint in the face of the frustration accumulated, and the disappointments experienced, by the nation over thirty-five years and in the face of the regime's manifest reluctance to fulfill the agreements it signed in August 1980.

The Gomułka Illusion

But restrained though most of Solidarity's policies and actions were, the very fact of its birth was due to the Poles' determination not to be deceived again by their rulers. They had already been deceived twice. Their first illusion was Władysław Gomułka. No survey of the Gomułka period as a whole (1956–70) will be attempted here. It began with high hopes for a decisive turn in communist rule in Poland and, indeed, in the history of Eastern Europe as a whole. It ended in a bloody debacle in the industrial towns on the Baltic coast, in which scores of Polish workers are believed to have been killed, and in a serious disillusionment about the "reformability" of communist rule.

Actually, disillusion with Gomułka had begun very early, only about two years after the Polish October. And well before the end of the 1950s most of the achievement and all the promise of 1956 had been dissipated. Yet amid all the dissatisfaction with Gomułka it is easy to forget some of the qualities he possessed. His courage, for example, was never in doubt, either when he was being hounded from the party leadership the first time in 1948 in a situation that, for all he knew, could have led to his execution, or during the frantic negotiations with the Soviet delegation, led by Khrushchev, in Warsaw in October 1956. Some of his speeches between October and December 1956 exposing and denouncing the extent and manner of Stalinist domination were outstanding in their concern for Polish integrity and outrage at its violation.[2] Some of his subsequent activity and his capitulation to Soviet dictates make it difficult to describe him as a Polish patriot, but there was always a "distinctive Polishness" about him that elicited some respect. Finally, he had a modesty and a personal integrity that, though often demonstrated in a perverse way, stood out in direct contrast with the lack of it demonstrated by his successor, Edward Gierek.

It was not so much, therefore, that Gomułka was deceiving the Polish people in 1956 as that they were deceiving themselves. They thought he would both lead and symbolize a process of transformation of the system. He saw himself as preserving it. Certainly he was against its Stalinist deformations, of which he himself had been a victim. But, far from being a "liberal," he was a dogmatic supporter of traditional communist institutions, and he could be ruthless enough when defending them. He was a blinkered champion, for example, of the leading role of the party and of central planning, two tenets of orthodoxy the Polish October initially seemed set to modify. It quickly became evident that there was a basic incompatibility between him and the Polish nation: their hopes pointed in one direction, his prejudices tugged in the opposite. To cap it all, Gomułka as a leader was incompetent. His strength of personality and character could not compensate for this deficiency. He possessed neither intellectual ability, nor political flair, nor administrative nor economic expertise. Scouring the whole East European scene these last forty years it is difficult to find a leader less competent.

He had two basic disadvantages. One was lack of education, although this need not have been a crippling disability. In any case, whereas most of the "Muscovite" communists (those trained for long periods in the Soviet Union) had had an education of sorts, with many of them being well educated, most "home" communists (those without any extended Moscow experience) had not. János Kádár, for example, turned out to be a leader of consummate ability, and many other poorly educated "home" communists revealed considerable talent. Perhaps more serious was the fact that Gomułka's political evolution was retarded or even "frozen" by his (first) fall in 1948, which kept him out of circulation for eight years. He, therefore, missed any active participation in the "thaw" after Stalin's death and the ferment in Poland that culminated in the Polish October and his own return. Gomułka seemed never to have lost the characteristic values and limitations of an underground communist fighter in peace and war. The only obvious parallel to this (interrupted) career of Gomułka, is that of Gustáv Husák, who was out of circulation the whole of the 1950s, although in circumstances far worse than in Gomułka's disgrace. Husák, though a victim of Stalinism like Gomułka, could never, also like Gomułka, repudiate its basic institutions (see chapter 9). The two men were different in many respects: Husák is an intellectual and a man of real political skills. But their main roles in East European history are strikingly similar: both led their countries away from the threshold of hope and progress back into the wastes of "normalization," reaction, and despondence.[3]

The End of Gomułka

It must have appeared to many Poles that the "normalization" that superseded the excitement of the Polish October would go on indefinitely. By the mid-1960s it had drifted into a "normalcy" that was an almost eventless continuum of failure. A practically inactive captain, Władysław Gomułka was on the bridge of a ship of state that was not just in the doldrums but, as the more perceptive saw, was slowly sinking.

But the sinking could be a long process, and in the meantime life for many had its consolations. In the first place, despite the disappointment and retrogression after 1956, Gomułka resisted any attempts to put the clock back entirely. The Polish people, unlike the Hungarians, were not defeated in 1956, and they would not have tolerated total reaction, anyway. A considerable degree of personal freedom was allowed—or, more correctly, was claimed unopposed by Polish society. The church, whose Primate Stefan Cardinal Wyszyński had played a key role in society's backing of Gomułka in 1956, was being constantly pinpricked by administrative chicanery. But though Gomułka clearly saw the church as his main institutional and ideological adversary, he hesitated to confront it openly. Despite its almost constant (and justifiable) complaints of harassment, it came to enjoy a remarkable amount of freedom—for which it never ceased to be duly ungrateful.

Life was tolerable. But there was an uneasy stagnation about Poland in the 1960s that was in direct contrast to the situation in most of the other East European countries. For example, in 1961, as Poland was sinking firmly into its post-October malaise, Czechoslovakia, awakened by the Twenty-second CPSU congress, was slowly beginning on the reform path that led to the Prague Spring in 1968. Society in the GDR, recovering from the shock of the Berlin Wall in August 1961, settled down into an unglamorous routine that produced an impressive economic development. Hungary, with its unwritten compact between rulers and ruled born out of the revolution and its suppression, was also accelerating its progress toward higher economic standards and a better way of life. Romania was caught up in the excitement of defying the Soviet Union, and its domestic situation was (deceptively) looking better. Even Bulgaria presented a picture of more hope and movement than Poland. As for the communist states outside the alliance, Yugoslavia seemed on the way to liberalism and prosperity, and even Albania, though presenting no hopeful domestic picture, had attracted world attention by discarding Soviet domination and accepting Chinese patronage.

Poland was, therefore, very much the exception. Beneath the stagnation, public life was festering, and it was out of this festering that grew the malignancy of March 1968. The previous January the Warsaw authorities had seen fit to take off a production of Adam Mickiewicz's famous nineteenth-century play "The Forefathers" (*Dziady*). The play had strong anti-Russian overtones, which enthusiastic audiences had no difficulty fitting into a contemporary context. The withdrawal of the play was met by boisterous student demonstrations. These were then used as a pretext by the police to begin a brutal repression of students, a persecution of many intellectuals branded as "revisionists," and an anti-Jewish campaign that had some of the characteristics of a classic pogrom.[4]

The repressions of March 1968 were dominated by General Mieczysław Moczar, minister of the interior and acknowledged leader of a network of wartime underground figures popularly known as the Partisans. This was a hard line, anti-Semitic group, highly suspicious of "Muscovite" communists, both because many of them were Jewish and because of the persecution many of the Partisans suffered at their hands during the Stalinist period. It was mainly this hostility toward "Muscovites" that gave the Partisans an aura of nationalism they cleverly exploited. Moczar, by skillful use of patronage and conspiracy, was able to bring the police and internal security forces (but not the armed forces) under his control. He also enjoyed considerable support in the media, which was harnessed to effect in 1968.[5]

This Partisan group was just one of the regime factions that had formed in the 1960s, but it enjoyed the advantage of operating conspiratorially. The other factions were must less virulent.[6] They included a large but inchoate "worker" group represented in the Politburo by Gomułka himself and his close associates. There was also a large and influential group of "pragmatists" who looked to Edward Gierek, Politburo member and party chief in Silesia. What appeared to be Gierek's "modern" outlook, technocratic bent, and efficient administration in

Silesia attracted supporters from all over Poland. Managers, technical experts, economists, and many skilled workers, they were a most useful adjunct to Gierek's home power base centered on the coal-mining community from which he himself sprung. Finally, there was a dwindling group of communist "revisionist" intellectuals, who had wielded considerable influence in the run-up to the Polish October in 1956. But their influence declined steadily. Their political patrons were purged, and worker sympathy eroded rapidly. But basically their decline was due to the fact that communist idealism was fast disappearing and the importance of ideology was changing. It was ceasing to be an inspirational or creative force or even a guidance for rule. It was becoming mainly a ritual; what was happening in Poland was happening in the rest of Eastern Europe (see chapter 1). But perhaps it began earliest in Poland, accelerated by the disappointments of 1956. The Polish October after all, though it could not have happened without worker muscle, was initiated and sustained by intellectuals. The October, therefore, was both climax and anticlimax. From then on the intellectuals' standing with the regime declined as their own disillusion with it rose. And their disillusion did not stop there; it extended to the whole communist ideology that many of them had once embraced so eagerly.

By the beginning of 1968, therefore, these were the principal factions inside the regime. Another force, which later was to assume a crucial role, was the military. But in 1968 it played no role. The Polish armed forces had just passed through their most important phase since the communists came to power: they had become derussified.[7] More than any other East European military the Polish had been dominated by Soviet officers who had assumed practically every key position, including that of the ministry of defense, taken in 1949 by Marshal Konstantin Rokossovsky, a Red Army commander of Polish descent. One of the lasting achievements of the Polish October was to begin the shedding of these foreign bodies. Rokossovsky was replaced by Gomułka's ally Marian Spychalski, and the general replacement process was virtually completed by about 1966. In 1968 General Wojciech Jaruzelski became minister of defense. Though Soviet-educated and trained, Jaruzelski's appointment was not considered the result of Soviet pressure (though Soviet approval for it and satisfaction with it can be assumed). In fact, Jaruzelski, despite his Soviet background, was considered a patriotic Pole, and, despite his having for the seven years prior to his appointment been head of the Main Political Administration of the armed forces, was considered at the time an apolitical, professional officer who would keep the military out of politics.

In retrospect, the March "events" of 1968 were essentially an attempt by the Moczar group to take advantage of the crumbling of Gomułka's position to stake its claim to power. This did not necessarily mean overturning the party leader straightaway. It meant capturing the political initiative and preempting any move on the part of Gierek, regarded generally as the natural and inevitable successor to Gomułka. The rallying cries of the Moczarites were nationalism, anti-intellectualism, and anti-Semitism.

It was a shaming episode for many Poles. Anti-Semitism quickly became predominant. After the Holocaust the size of Poland's Jewish community had shrunk from over 3 million to about 15,000. But some of these Jews occupied prominent positions in scholarship, journalism, and the more intellectually demanding positions of the party and state apparatus. After March about half the number left Poland, thrown out of their jobs and humiliated by anti-Semitic hysteria.

Not all Moczar's victims were Jews. They included, for example, the famous philosopher Leszek Kołakowski, who left Warsaw and settled in Oxford. But the majority of them were Jewish. Nor was the campaign against them conducted in a vacuum. Moczar and his collaborators knew when they were striking a chord familiar in Polish history. It may have been Gomułka himself who (uncharacteristically) initiated the campaign after the Arab-Israeli Seven Day War the previous summer in 1967 when, in a choleric outburst, he referred to a potential Zionist "fifth column" in Poland. But the following March it was clear that Gomułka was not in control of the situation. There was some support for the anti-Semitic campaign among workers, peasants, and a considerable section of the intelligentsia. The harping by sections of the press on the iniquities of many communist Jews in the early postwar years covered a basic anti-Semitism with a cloak of justification, even respectability. And in a situation as sordid as this it was unfortunate for the good name of Poland, and of itself, that the Roman Catholic church chose to remain silent— on the grounds apparently that it was all an internal party matter. A few words from Cardinal Wyszyński may not have stopped the campaign, but they would have unequivocally dissociated the moral authority of the Polish nation from it. Without those words the church condemned itself to continued suspicion about its own anti-Semitic past, one which Wyszyński's successor, Cardinal Glemp, subsequently did little to dispel with his ill-chosen criticisms of some of Solidarity's intellectual advisers.[8]

In retrospect it can be argued that the Gomułka era effectively ended in March 1968. The political and moral authority he had once enjoyed was gone. What was left for the next two and a half years was a propping-up operation. But it is doubtful whether Gomułka would have been granted even this respite had it not been for the situation in other parts of the Soviet bloc. Poles generally enjoy a cheerful provincialism that ignores or despises what goes on in the communist world around them. But even they could not escape the impact of the Prague Spring. It affected Polish political life in several ways during 1968. First, the intoxicating events in Prague influenced the Warsaw student milieu (as it influenced the Belgrade students), raising the level of restlessness and dissatisfaction with their own situation. And, in turn, this restlessness partly prompted the viciousness of the police reaction against the students. Communism was being threatened not just in Czechoslovakia, so the argument went, but the virus was also spreading to Poland. Gomułka's later insistence, along with Ulbricht, that the Czechoslovak reform movement be put down, by force if necessary, was also the result of his fear of contamination—as well as being a sign of his own weakness.[9] Finally, the immediate aftermath of the invasion of Czechoslovakia brought a strong Soviet stress on stability that probably kept Gomułka in power. Brezhnev was alarmed and in no mood to experiment. At the Polish United Workers' party congress in November 1968 he was, therefore, present to demonstrate Soviet support for Gomułka and the status quo.

Gomułka was eventually unseated, ironically enough as a result of a belated effort to emerge from his sloth and do something—in this case to tackle Poland's growing economic problems. He was at last forced to listen to the pragmatic economic officials who had for several years been seeping into senior regime positions. These were recommending a series of reforms involving sharp decreases in food subsidies, hence sharp increases in prices of basic foodstuffs. These were an economic necessity but also a serious political risk. Gomułka took the risk a few days before Christmas in 1970, the season dearest to his Christian and convivial countrymen, and the risk became catastrophe.

The tragic chapter that followed is so well known that it need not be recounted here. Some salient points, however, are worth noting about the workers' riots on the Baltic coast that followed the price rises in December 1970. The *first* is that the number of casualties was greater than in any other episode in East European history since the Hungarian Revolution. It was also greater than in any subsequent violence, at least in the northern part of Eastern Europe. The official death toll was put at forty-five, but reliable unofficial accounts put it considerably higher. The *second* is that the military was also used against the workers in Gdansk—a point to bear in mind in the light of events in December 1981. The *third* is that the disturbances were almost entirely confined to the Baltic coastline, establishing for that area of Poland the reputation as a powder keg and leaving embers of resentment that were to be rekindled ten years later.

Finally, there is still the question of the extraordinary timing of the announcement of the price increases to be considered. Less than a week before the price increases were announced in December 1970, Poland and the Federal Republic of Germany signed their historic "normalization of relations" agreement (see chapter 3). This involved a de facto recognition by Bonn of Poland's new western border on the Oder-Neisse gained as a result of World War II as compensation for large territories in the East annexed by the Soviet Union. Until this treaty with Bonn, the Soviet Union had been seen as the sole effective guarantor of the inviolability of these borders, while the West Germans had been officially depicted, not only as not recognizing the Polish right to them, but also as being ready to seize them back if ever the opportunity arose. Most Poles recoiled at the notion of Russia as protector, but the Germans were historic enemies and the horrors of the wartime occupation had made the Poles fear and distrust them even more. Now, however, with the signing of the treaty with Bonn and the gestures of Chancellor Brandt, the "good" German, the situation appeared dramatically altered—politically and atmospherically, if not legalistically.

Some observers at the time tended to see this national sense of relief as an important contributory cause of the rioting that greeted the price increases. The German revanchist danger had passed; hence the Polish raison d'état no longer needed the Soviet underpinning; hence one major psychological obstacle to the full expression of the popular will had been removed. Perhaps. But a corollary to this argument would be that, had the price increases been announced, say, two weeks earlier (i.e., before the agreement with Bonn), then the reaction might have been less turbulent. It would be sounder to try to analyze the situation not through the instincts of the populace but through the motives of the regime. Gomułka and his advisers may well have grossly miscalculated the effect of the normalization treaty by assuming that the popular euphoria would be such as to enable them to get away with both the price increases and their timing. It is true that the price increases were part of a reform package due to start operating on 1 January 1971. Hence there was a certain urgency. But it is difficult to believe that even a leader as insensitive as Gomułka would have inflicted such a pre-Christmas punishment on the public without having already offered what he considered a powerful sweetener in the form of German recognition of the Oder-Neisse frontiers.

Public bitterness, however, was such that the sweetener was nowhere near sweet enough. It was simply irrelevant. It is more correct, therefore, to speak of the price increases being announced by the regime less than a week after the signing of the treaty with the FRG rather than the Polish public reacting violently to the price increases less than a week after the treaty. Both statements are true; what they imply, however, is quite different.

Beginning of the Gierek Era

It was the riots on the coast and the bloody way they were repressed that led to the almost immediate fall of Gomułka. But basically his fall was due to the discredit into which he had steadily sunk. In the regime and in society (and in Moscow) he had lost all credibility.

Gomułka is unofficially reported to have asked for Brezhnev's support during the food price riots in December 1970. But he had by now—as opposed to immediately after August 1968—become a liability to the Soviet leadership in its efforts to promote a new stability and consensus after the Prague Spring. Besides, helping Gomułka could have meant another Soviet invasion only two and a half years after Czechoslovakia. The dangers, therefore, in deserting him were deemed less than those of trying to keep him. Thus Gomułka became the second of three long-standing leaders to be overturned in three years in Eastern Europe's Northern Tier or Triangle. Brezhnev did nothing to save the Czechoslovak leader, Antonín Novotný, in January 1968. Gomułka went in December 1970, and Walter Ulbricht was to be eased out of the East German party leadership in May 1971. The enforced departure of these three leaders in so short a period reflected the serious instability in this area so crucial to Soviet power.[10]

Edward Gierek was himself one of the reasons why the Soviets were prepared to let Gomułka go. By the end of 1970 he had majority support in the party. The public appeared even anxious to give him a try. There was, therefore, an air of certainty about his succession. And, apart from the mood of "anybody but Gomułka," Gierek seemed to have positive attractions as well. As mentioned earlier, he was credited with running an efficient administration in the Katowice voivodship of Silesia, where he also enjoyed a genuine popularity. Not just the workers but the better-educated also welcomed his arrival. They saw him as a reform-minded and modernizing leader. Ten years later, when Gierek was shunted aside in disgrace, it may have been painful to remember all the qualities attributed to him when he came to power. The truth was that Gierek combined his real abilities with a strong element of the confidence trickster. He could make a good impression not only in the Gdansk shipyards, immediately after his appointment, but also in Moscow, Bonn, Paris, and Washington. History may condemn him as a mountebank, a machine politician right out of a socialist Tammany Hall. But history must also admit that his contemporaries—partly because they wanted to be—were fooled for years.[11]

There could be no doubting Gierek's political adroitness. His immediate task was to shore up three political fronts more or less simultaneously. The first was with the rebellious workers. This he did in dramatic meetings with strikers' representatives and by reluctantly canceling the price increases that had led to Gomułka's downfall.[12] The second front was in the Kremlin, and Gierek was able to build a workable subordinate relationship with Brezhnev. But the Soviet leaders never fully trusted him, however useful and welcome he was to them at the end of 1970. He had spent his youth and politically formative years in France and Belgium; his family had been one of the thousands of Polish families that had migrated to the French and Belgian coalfields. This tended to make him instantly suspect in Moscow. Even more serious was the fact that he had been propelled into office by a popular revolt from below. He was, therefore, the beneficiary of precisely that societal spontaneity the Soviets feared and distrusted. They tended to trust the new premier, Piotr Jaroszewicz, an old "Muscovite," more than him.[13] But they soon realized that, unlike Dubček had surprisingly turned out to be in Prague, Gierek was no threat. He may have begun as Moscow's problem but soon became a safe satellite. Eventually, like his predecessor, he was to become Moscow's liability.

Gierek's third front was inside the Polish party itself. He could comfortably control every grouping except Moczar and the police faction. With Moczar he struck up a temporary alliance of convenience that involved putting him in both the Politburo and the Secretariat. But it was an uneasy alliance, with the restless Moczar unwilling to rest on what he had already achieved.

Moczar looms large in the recent history of Poland, not because of his contribution but his threat. He had five main characteristics: a thirst for power; a conspiratorial restlessness and resilience; leadership qualities; an intelligent political opportunism—occasionally statesmanlike, always demogogic; and a readiness to use the means of violence or coercion at his disposal. He attracted not just the police roughs, educated or uneducated, of whom there were plenty, but also a number of intellectuals who sympathized with his professed nationalism and what they considered his ability to cut through the bureaucracy and *Schlamperei* impeding efficient government. His type was not unknown in other parts of Eastern Europe. Moczar had some similarities with the Yugoslav Alexander Ranković, purged in 1966 (see chapter 11).

Though it was clear that Moczar's alliance with Gierek could not last, the circumstances of his speedy downfall remain unclear. In May 1971 Gierek suddenly left a Czechoslovak party congress in Prague and sped to Olsztyn in northern Poland where he nipped in the bud what was apparently an attempt at a coup by Moczar.[14] (He then returned to Prague.) A tightly kept silence surrounded the whole affair, but Moczar virtually disappeared from public life, and his removal from the Politburo and Secretariat at the sixth party congress in December 1971 followed as a matter of course. He was pushed to the edges of public life as president of the Supreme Chamber of Control, a parliamentary watchdog committee. He also lost his chairmanship of the Polish war veterans' association (acronym ZBoWiD), which had been his main power base. But he was not to be written off permanently. By the end of the 1970s when the extent of corruption in the Gierek regime was becoming known, Moczar first emerged as the champion of public probity and, then, after the rise of Solidarity and the fall of Gierek, as a potential system savior. He returned to the Politburo under Kania and was tipped by many as the next party leader. But he was caught between the deep dislike harbored for him by General Jaruzelski and the wave of now freely expressed aversion of both party apparatchiki and members. At the extraordinary party congress in July 1981 he disappeared from the Politburo and from public life with very slender prospects of another return. He died in late 1986.

Gierek's Early Promise

Even before he had established full control, Gierek began to initiate changes and make promises affecting most areas of public life. Indeed, it became hard to recall even a few years afterward the sense of movement and expectation that gripped the country during 1971 and the contrast it presented with the decade of stagnation under Gomułka.

It was in the political sphere that perhaps the most intriguing promises were made. The party, for example, was to withdraw from direct control or interference in the economy, leaving the field to the state apparatus. It was to devote itself instead to overseeing and guidance. The party "leads and inspires the nation"; the government "governs the country." (The statements in this regard were similar to those first made in Yugoslavia nearly twenty years earlier; see chapter 11.) Inner-party democracy was to be established. The powers of the trade unions were to be considerably increased, with the right of veto granted at the local level. Genuine workers' councils of the kind established after October 1956, and terminated by Gomułka in 1958, were to be restored. Popular criticism was not just to be introduced but actively encouraged. The whole emphasis was on democracy and dialogue.

The above is just a representative sample of the promises being made in the political sphere. They were also accompanied by strong hints in the media and directly from some of the new leaders that they would be guaranteed by *institutional* reforms. Some hoped that the sixth party congress in December 1971 would approve such an institutional framework. In the event, the congress did practically nothing. It particularly disappointed those workers who had taken the promises of more independent trade unions seriously. The particular insistence, therefore, by Lech Wałęsa and his union committee in Gdansk in the summer of 1980 on written assurances for free unions should be traced back to this sense of betrayal in 1971. Many of the shipyard workers had personally experienced the promises, expectations, and disappointments of that year. Some were also old enough to remember the disappointments of 1956.

In the economic sphere considerably more was done. Economic priorities were changed, with more now being allocated to agriculture and the food and consumer goods industries. Foreign trade was reorganized, giving greater freedom to industrial exporters and importers and more realism to the foreign exchange system within which they operated. In April 1972 a commission charged with suggesting proposals for the "improvement of the system of planning and management" (everywhere, even in Hungary, the word "reform" was avoided at this time) published its findings. It recommended some of the measures operating in Hungary since 1968. The most important was a considerable reduction in the number of central planning indicators.[15] The wage system was also to be changed, allowing more flexibility at the lower level and putting greater stress on incentive schemes and payment by results. More flexibility was also to be allowed in price formation, which, together with certain other changes, was designed to make industrial managers more responsive to changes in market conditions.

But these suggestions, though pointing in the right direction, were timid and unimaginative in terms of the expectations aroused and the demands of the economic situation. Moreover, the decentralization they involved was not to go right down to the enterprises but to huge, newly organized industrial combinations (*Welkie Organizacje Gospodarcze*, or Large Economic Organizations—WOGs).[16] In this respect the reform was similar to the early reforms in Czechoslovakia and the East German reforms of the 1960s. The WOGs, like their counterparts in other East European countries, were an intermediate level of management between the central bureaucracy and the enterprises. Thus, while there was some decentralization from the ministries down to the WOGs, there was, from the enterprises' viewpoint, a huge new obstacle of bureaucracy between them and the ministries.

Still, the proof of the new pudding would be in the eating. The new scheme, with all its limitations, would have been an improvement and could have been refined and adapted as time went along. But this pudding was not even for the eating. A few pilot schemes were set up, official interest and media publicity then began to fade, and by 1975 the whole project had sunk into the sand. Everything was back to the safe haven of orthodox communist planning.

The sector of the economy that demanded the promptest attention was agriculture. There had been a sharp increase in the demand for food (especially meat), the prices had had to be refrozen as a result of popular pressure, and there was a lot of excess purchasing power in the economy. It was essential, therefore, to stimulate production. The regime wisely increased the purchasing prices and abolished the system of compulsory deliveries. It introduced, though with a number of important modifications, the state social security system for private peasants and appeared to take steps to encourage the integration of peasant holdings, often unproductively scattered in small strips of land. It also showed some inclination to start manufacturing the smaller types of agricultural machinery private peasants could use on their small holdings. Distribution of land to private peasants from the State Land Fund also increased.[17] (Previously the state farms had been the main beneficiary of grants from this fund—a clear discrimination against private farming, which accounted for about three quarters of Poland's total arable land.)

But, again, the promise in agriculture, as in other parts of the economy, turned to disappointment in a few years. From 1975 there was increased stress on socialist agriculture and during the 1970s the total amount of arable land covered by the private sector declined somewhat, although this still remained by far the largest sector with output proportionately much greater than that of either the state or the tiny collectivized sector. Moreover, the discrimination against the private sector was now increased to an unprecedented degree. The generous policy of land grants begun by Gierek was reversed in favor of the socialized sector, and the amounts of seed grains, credits, investments, and machinery began to be curtailed. The intention of squeezing out private farming over the long term seemed clearer than ever.

Reasons for the Reversal

Why, after so much early promise, the reversal? One explanation offered is Soviet interference. Andrzej Korbonski has put together interesting evidence tending to suggest this might have been the main factor. The key event in this context could have been the visit by Gierek to Moscow in late 1973. Some Polish sources were convinced that he was warned by Brezhnev about the course Poland was taking. Certainly 1974 was the year, as Korbonski points out, when the change of course away from reform became absolutely clear.[18]

There is an East European tendency to be paranoid about Soviet interference, domination, and exploitation. (Professor Korbonski is obviously not included in this generalization!) And there has certainly been enough of all three to make this understandable. But to blame Moscow for everything is almost as naive as exculpating it from everything. It can also mean providing the Eastern European regimes with an alibi they often do not deserve. But in this particular case there are grounds for suspecting the Soviet factor. Moscow's trust in Gierek, as mentioned earlier, may always have been tempered by a close watchfulness. Premier Jaroszewicz and the many conservatives still in the regime may well have been part of that watchfulness. Moreover, as early as March 1971 the Soviets despatched Stanislav Pilotovich, a Polish-speaking White Russian, as ambassador to Warsaw. Pilotovich saw his role as that of viceregal watchdog. He interfered in practically everything, making himself particularly unpopular among the cultural milieu. Pilotovich's ambassadorial role can be compared with that of the better-known Petr Abrasimov in East Berlin. Both were to suffer the double indignity of being unofficially declared personae non gratae by their exasperated host governments and then being duly recalled by Moscow —unprecedented occurrences in fraternal diplomatic history.

It should also be recalled that in 1972 the Hungarian authorities practically discontinued the New Economic Mechanism (NEM) begun four years earlier. (It was resumed in earnest only in 1978.) Senior officials associated with the NEM were dismissed (see chapter 6). It was later confirmed that the change of both policy and personnel was due chiefly to Soviet pressure. It is not unreasonable to assume, therefore, that what happened to Hungary also happened to Poland. The fear in the Kremlin of a new Czechoslovakia must still have been considerable, despite the successes of the post-1968 consolidation drive. To the Soviet leaders Gierek's Poland could have been showing those ominous signs of spontaneity they had been so slow to perceive in Czechoslovakia. It was time, therefore, to make the new Polish leadership familiar with the old facts of East European geopolitical life.

One aspect of Gierek's early policy that could have disturbed some Soviet leaders was his initial encouragement of private agriculture. The tolerance since 1955–56 by the Soviets of private agriculture in Poland is often cited as an example of their permissiveness in situations where they have no alternative. This is true. But it is not so much *private* agriculture the Soviets have tolerated as *noncollectivized* agriculture. They understood the disastrous consequences of trying to force Polish peasants into kholkhozes. But they also understood the serious ideological and political consequences of efficient, prosperous private farms helped by a socialist state. Short-term support they would tolerate because not to do so might lead to shortages and upheavals. But long-term support, "consecrating" an institution the Soviet communists so massively and bloodily destroyed in the 1930s—that was neither a political nor an ideological option.

Soviet interference, therefore, is arguable; it may have played its part in taking the bloom off Gierek's early promise. But it was almost certainly not the sole explanation. To take the case of agriculture, the strong reservations of all but the most "liberal" Polish communists with regard to private ownership must be taken into account. Apart from the deeply ingrained ideological animosity toward kulaks (an animosity even the Yugoslav communists could not shake off; see chapter 11), there was the particularly Polish aversion against any possible development of a clerical-peasant alliance. The Polish communists had failed in the late 1940s and early 1950s, when the circumstances were the most propitious, to break either the church or the peasantry. The church emerged stronger than before. The relatively few peasants who had been pressed into collectives had mostly deserted them well before October 1956. Gomułka wisely made no attempt to reintroduce collectivization. But the state neither helped the private peasants nor allowed them to utilize their freedom fully. Part of this refusal was "instinctively ideological." But part may also have been due to a fear of a yeoman peasantry backed by the church developing into a powerful social and even political force. The regime settled, therefore, for a policy that would keep the free peasantry alive but only just so. Whatever the political grounds for this, it was a recipe for economic disaster.

In the case of economic reform generally, it may also be assumed that its discontinuance was not simply due to a nervous ringmaster, Brezhnev, reining in the galloping pony, Gierek. There was nothing from Gierek's record in Silesia, successful though it was, to indicate any interest in systemic change, or even radical change within the system. He took over in Warsaw in a situation where the economy was in a parlous state and public opinion thoroughly roused. Both demanded action, and his almost feverish early activity might simply have been responses to them.

But then in 1971, immediately after the new leadership took power, the economy took a sharp turn for the better and continued to improve for about five years. This was due partly to a series of very good harvests, Soviet hard-currency help, and the revamping of investment priorities. The rate of real growth went up about 10 percent annually until 1975, and Poland, which had previously lagged behind all other East European countries in increases in real wages, now began to overtake them.[19] In a few years the economy emerged from depression under Gomułka into a euphoric boom under Gierek. Why change the system when it was doing so well?

Moreover, what seemed the ideal substitute for real reform now appeared in the form of Western credits. These were becoming available in prodigious amounts at low interest rates. Both Western private banks and governments were not just willing but anxious to lend. They offered all the East European states a chance for big investments and higher living standards with apparently no self-help required on their part. Every government in the region, except the Czechoslovak, took advantage of this opportunity. Eventually, though, Poland was to become the biggest debtor of all, the total eventually amounting to over $35 billion (see chapter 4). Western credits seemed to offer a shortcut to success without the need to cope with reality.

The Path to Destruction

Well before 1975, the halfway mark in Gierek's decade of power, it was clear that what mainly concerned him, despite his earlier posturing as tribune of the plebs, was control over the party. He sought to achieve this by two methods: first by centralizing party power; second, by making the rewards for party service and loyalty as generous as possible. All this was contrary to what was at first promised. At the beginning it was promised that the party and state, the trade unions and the organs of local government, were going to be invigorated. But these promises were soon forgotten—at least by those who made them. What was invigorated even further was the concept of nomenklatura, the list of positions to be filled exclusively by party members. It was the club of members filling these positions—and they were only a handful of total party membership—that wielded the real power. And it was its members who got the real privileges. "The party takes care of its own" was a popular but loose saying throughout Eastern Europe. It was loose because the ordinary rank-and-file member was not very well taken care of when compared with the relative few in the nomenklatura. Again, the original promise was different; everyone was to be rewarded according to his work. But this was yet another of the promises forgotten by all but the millions to whom they were made.[20]

For Gierek the concentration of power became not so much a policy as a mania. In 1971, for example, the party organizations of the large economic organizations (WOGs) were placed directly under the Central Committee staff, bypassing the normal chain of command.[21] Between 1973 and 1975 a total reorganization of local government was carried out, the most prominent aspect of which was the breaking up of the old seventeen voivodships, the largest unit of local government, and the creation of forty-nine new ones.[22] The biggest single effect of the whole reform was the weakening, through decimation and fragmentation, of the medium level of party officials in the provinces. The county and district party leaders now became, ex officio, chairmen of the counterpart local government council. The two offices were combined—as they were in Romania, where Ceaușescu had an equal passion for concentrating power. In effect, the party as a whole was weakened rather than strengthened. The very large increase in the number of territorial units of local authority—voivodships, counties, and districts—concentrated power at the center but divided and demoralized the provincial party apparatus.[23]

Gierek was probably acting from personal experience here. He had been first party secretary in the Katowice voivodship, probably the most powerful in Poland because of its economic weight. He had built up formidable power in relation to the Warsaw center, so much so that in the early 1960s, when disintegration of the Congo was briefly capturing the media headlines, Katowice became known as the Polish "Katanga" and Gierek—perhaps not entirely to his liking—the Polish "Moise Tshombe." He was now determined, therefore, not to let any more Katangas develop or any new Tshombes appear. But what Gierek did not apparently realize was that concentrating power at the center also meant isolating it. And it also meant weakening the provincial apparatus. Both were to have the most serious consequences. The growing remoteness at the center was probably partly responsible for the first great political disaster of the Gierek regime: the food price increases of 1976 that had to be rescinded within twenty-four hours because of violent popular reaction.[24] It was Gierek's remoteness from grass-roots opinion that presumably caused his huge miscalculation. But the serious weakening of the provincial party apparatus could also have been partly responsible for the culminating disaster: the rise of Solidarity. Had the party apparatus not been as weakened and demoralized, it might have been able to check the groundswell that culminated in the formation of the free trade union.

Gierek's reorganizations, therefore, weakened the party. But what totally *discredited* it was its rampant corruption, the blatant self-enrichment of the nomenklatura club at all levels. It is impossible to tell whether Poland in the 1970s was any or much worse in this matter than other East European countries or the Soviet Union itself. It is a feature of public life in every country. In communist Europe, however, a combination of an overt political caste system, widespread and chronic consumer shortages, and an often impenetrable bureaucracy tend to stimulate the venal tendencies more than in societies less afflicted by such handicaps. There is also the "insecurity of tenure" factor. The higher one rises in the hierarchy the more perilous the future becomes; the more likelihood there is, in fact, of a sudden fall into oblivion. It is much better than in Stalin's time, but a man's career can still be short, his future bleak. Public careers can be short in other systems, too. But whereas in the Western system an erstwhile officeholder usually goes, without disgrace, to posts in other branches of society, often more remunerative, in communist countries the only way to go is down—often very far down with no easy landing. In terms of housing, pension, and other privileges many still do better than the vast majority of citizens. But by their own past standards they and their families are pauperized—and often ostracized. To insure themselves against this fate many of them take the opportunity to "put something on one side," either in cash or in kind, villas being a favorite example of the latter.[25]

Again, Poland was no exception in this regard. But corruption there became known worldwide because the rise of Solidarity caused the books to be opened. They riveted public attention on the likes, for example, of Maciej Szczepański, a Gierek lackey from Katowice who became head of state radio and television and whose spectacular wallowings in the fleshpots of office made communist Warsaw look like imperial Rome in one of its most permissive periods. More serious, if less colorful, was the mentality reflected by Gierek himself. It was not simply one of easygoing tolerance, though that was certainly one of his characteristics. It was more a deliberate encouragement to senior party cadres to take care of themselves, a latter-day "sultanism," as one scholar, evoking Max Weber, has described it.[26] This was aimed at securing their loyalty. It was the cronyism of the Katowice party machine elevated to the national level, and in marked contrast, indeed, to the austere simplicity of his predecessor, Gomułka.

The Magic Carpet of Credits

But the exposure of this corruption and of the other deficiencies in Gierek's rule was for the future. For a few years there seemed to be nothing but success and confidence, both based on an economic progress that seemed indefinite. And the motor of this progress was Western credits.

As discussed in chapter 4, there was little wrong with the thinking behind Western credits. The machinery and equipment acquired on credit would, as Włodzimierz Brus points out, give the economy the boost toward modernization, and the credits would eventually be repaid by exporting products of the new technology. This would "help in restructuring industry by placing more emphasis on technologically advanced sectors like electronics and modern food processing and some branches of light industry."[27] Had some realism and moderation been preserved, import-led growth might have brought the Polish economy into an age of stable prosperity. As it was, it pushed it deeper and deeper into the mire. In the first place, because the whole idea of economic reform was shelved early on, the new strategy had to operate in a faulty structure. The result was incompatibility. But even this might not have been so glaring had some control been exercised over the rate of borrowing. Rates of investment in fixed assets soared far higher than planned. Far more technology was imported than could be used, and the resulting strain became excessive. (Similar situations were, of course, being repeated throughout most of Eastern Europe; see chapter 4.) In Poland the numerous lobbies vied with one another in concocting new investment projects requiring Western loans. Individual enterprises were considered backward if they did not order the latest sophisticated Western equipment.

What followed was an industrial free-for-all in which original plans, ambitious enough, were disregarded almost as soon as they were approved. The biggest investment project of the 1970s, the Huta Katowice metallurgical combine, a massive hulk of Stalinist pork-barreling by Gierek, was not even originally in the five-year plan for 1971–75. There were many "plan-as-you-go" projects, not originally planned but fitted uncomfortably into what was left of the planning process. The Polish economy was in a permanent state of intoxication. Some Polish observers were already referring to it as "cowboy economics." Borrowing begat more borrowing. Once the basic investment units were imported, they then required a continuing flow of parts, components, raw materials, etc. A considerable percentage of borrowing in the West was actually occasioned by these requirements. The Polish regime, therefore, found itself on an ever-accelerating carousel from which it could not escape.

By the middle of the 1970s the carousel did what the Cassandras both inside and outside Poland had predicted. It did not just slow down, it broke down. The result was an economic slump of unprecedented magnitude for a socialist state. Afflicted, if indirectly, by the world oil price explosions of the 1970s, which raised the raw material prices it paid the Soviet Union and reduced Western demand for Polish exports, Poland had no choice but to put tight curbs on its ramshackle economy. The authorities had to drastically reduce both borrowing abroad and spending at home. First to be neglected was the infrastructure, although the effects of this could be hidden for some time. But very soon numerous and often very expensive projects had to be discontinued. It has been estimated that these by 1980 amounted to about half the total national income. Most of them had been built with the new technology. Thus the real opportunity Poland had at the beginning of the 1970s to modernize its economy had been squandered in a spectacular and disastrous way.

Gierek's Last Phase

In June 1976 the Gierek regime resorted to what many observers had predicted would be inevitable: a new attempt to raise prices on basic foodstuffs. This was even more necessary now than in 1970. The government was spending more on food subsidies than ever before; incomes were rising rapidly, and the disproportion between the money in circulation and the consumer goods available had grown. If any meaningful relationship between prices, costs, and availability was even to be approached, then the price increases were necessary.

The outcome was not just Gierek's first great political disaster; it was the beginning of his downfall. Without direct warning, prices went up an average of 60 percent. There were immediate strikes throughout the country, and the price increases were almost immediately withdrawn. Like Gomułka in December 1970, Gierek had grossly miscalculated the public mood. He assumed that the appreciable rise in living standards over the past five years would make the workers more charitably disposed than six years before. Gierek overestimated his own popularity, and this illusion was apparently fostered by the poor advice coming up from the weakened provincial party apparatus. He made no attempt to prepare public opinion. Obviously in a situation of scarcity advance notice of price increases could lead to disaster. But a skillful "softening-up," the kind that later was to characterize Kádár's price increase tactics in Hungary (see chapter 6), a show of candor with the public and a calibrating of the price increase, might have avoided what followed. As for the Polish public, its reaction probably had two main causes. First was the sense of having been deceived, a shock that rearoused all the basic suspicions of communist rule. Second was the frustration of their rising expectations. Gierek was being made to pay for the "miracle man" image he had been pleased to promote.

He never recovered from this debacle. Just as March 1968 led to Gomułka's downfall, so June 1976 led to Gierek's. But while Gomułka's fall shook the system to its foundations, it did not change it. Gierek's fall was part of a popular process that actually overturned party supremacy.

He might have recovered from the June 1976 disaster had the economy taken an upswing or even had it simply leveled off. But it continued to deteriorate rapidly, and as it did so public disillusion grew. The whole tawdriness of Gierek's rule was revealed, and the popular support he had once undoubtedly enjoyed melted into cynicism. Nor did opposition remain passive. It took an active turn and, for the regime, an ominous character. For the first time since 1956 intellectuals and workers began to coalesce. This was due primarily to the work of a group of intellectuals who now spearheaded the opposition. Actually, Gierek had had a foretaste of such opposition in December 1975 when fifty-nine prominent intellectuals signed a protest against proposed changes in the constitution "consecrating" not only the leading role of the party but also the country's membership of the Soviet alliance. The protest, which did succeed in getting some of the offending passages modified, was more like a full democratic manifesto than a single issue complaint. As Leszek Kołakowski has written: "Coming after a period of passivity, the statement was the first open act of democratic opposition to totalitarian—albeit inefficient and clumsy totalitarian—rule."[28]

After June 1976, and specifically as a consequence of police brutality and the victimization of many striking workers, the Workers' Defense Committee was formed, referred to by its acronym KOR. It included about thirty intellectuals, some of them already prominent, others initially less so. They formed contacts with many workers and, because of their devotion and sincerity, won the respect of even more. Broadening their activities, they became an open, peaceful opposition democratic movement. Jacek Kuron, a once idealistic communist, and the young historian Adam Michnik became the most active and best publicized of the group. Kuron was a brilliant publicist and always retained a small dedicated following. But he often offended or disconcerted the broader public with suggestions or strategies that lacked both consistency and clarity.

Alongside KOR there sprouted other opposition groups of which the Movement for the Defense of Human and Civil Rights (ROPCiO) was the best known. ROPCiO made a stronger appeal to Polish history and nationalism than KOR and quickly attracted much support, significantly among young people.[29] Another smaller group, the KPN (Confederation for an Independent Poland), was even more nationalist, the statements of some of its members sometimes casting doubt on their democratic convictions.[30] Soon opposition in Poland became a patchwork quilt of political views and ideological patterns. But despite all their differences these groups were united on one thing: opposition to the regime.

It is also worth recalling here that the growing opposition in Poland had its impact in other countries of Eastern Europe. The most noteworthy was in Czechoslovakia where Charter 77 was formed in 1977. It was still active ten years later. But also in Romania, Hungary, and the GDR there were smaller and generally more temporary opposition activities. Even in Bulgaria there were a few signs of restlessness. None of this, of course, can be directly traced to the rebirth of opposition in Poland; nor was any of it on anywhere near the Polish scale. But it was evidence that, throughout the region, the passivity that the economic boom of the early 1970s had fostered was being replaced by manifestations of opposition or suspicion.

The Polish Revolution

Historical analysis often tends to impart an inevitability to events not evident to those who lived through them. "Prerevolutionary situations" are recognized more by historians than by contemporaries.

So it was in Poland. By as early as 1978 the weaknesses and failures of the Gierek regime were obvious to any Pole. But few, if any, would have predicted its total demise. Gierek, for his part, despite (or because of) his failures at home, was very active in international diplomacy, seemingly making himself indispensable to the cause of East-West détente. He had become a friend of both the West German Chancellor, Helmut Schmidt, and the French President, Valéry Giscard d'Estaing. With a Soviet leadership preoccupied with global concerns and less inclined than earlier to pry too closely into the internal affairs of its East European clients, he appeared to be on reasonably good terms. But in any case, even when there was speculation about his regime's future, it was simply in terms of the conventional game of spotting his successor. His most dangerous rival seemed to be Stefan Olszowski, an able, opportunistic politician, erstwhile Moczarite, later to be economic reformer, then hard-liner after December 1981, and finally forced retiree under Jaruzelski. But Gierek was still strong enough to rusticate Olszowski to East Berlin as ambassador in 1980.[32] As late as the spring of 1980 anyone suggesting a mass societal revolt against the prevailing system would have been dismissed with derision.

The August revolution in Gdansk in 1980 began quietly, almost casually. It followed small-scale strikes in Lublin and other centers protesting a new round of relatively small price increases imposed by a regime that was now economically desperate. The spark in Gdansk itself was small enough: the arbitrary sacking of a diminutive woman crane driver, Anna Walentynowicz, a sturdy fighter for the rights of labor. But once the shipyard workers took up her cause their deep sense of frustration and accumulated grievance surfaced irresistibly. They were led by Lech Wałęsa, as unlikely a hero as this nation of heroes had yet produced. Against them was an enfeebled regime that they forced to negotiate. And the very fact that negotiations were begun meant the strikers had won their first battle. A regime that even *aspires* to be totalitarian never regrets, never explains, never apologizes—and never negotiates.

The history of Solidarity has already been told many times, in most cases very well.[33] It will not be repeated here because the present writer has no new light to shed on an already brilliantly illuminated episode. What might be more appropriate would be briefly to stress certain key aspects and ask—perhaps answer—key questions.

The most basic fact about Solidarity has already been mentioned. The revolutionary idea of a free trade union, negotiating equally with the communist regime, was born of the disappointments of 1956 and 1970. Now the workers were prepared to face defeat, with all the consequences that defeat might entail, but they were not going to be deceived again. And, once they had set foot on this road, the only way to go was forward. They could neither go backward nor leave the road.

They were ready for this because seldom for more than three hundred years had the Polish nation been more self-confident. On 16 October 1978, Karol Cardinal Wojtyła, archbishop of Cracow, was elected pope. It is difficult to describe the pride, joy, patriotism, romanticism, sense of fulfillment and justification with which this news was greeted by the Poles, including many of the more than three million members of the communist party. Ten months later, in June 1979, all these emotions found expression during Pope John Paul II's triumphal visit to his native country. This pope showed how many divisions he had! And apart from boosting the confidence of his compatriots, the pope's visit also helped make the situation in Poland the concern of the whole civilized West. It was over a year before the strikes began in Gdansk. They might well have begun without the pope's visit. But they would hardly have been carried through with the same determination and boldness of aim.

As for the church in Poland itself, however, the response of its leadership to the Gdansk strike as well as some of its behavior throughout the Solidarity episode was often characterized by a lack of customary decisiveness. This was in marked contrast to the sureness of touch it had shown for a full quarter of a century before. The church had acquired a role in Polish public life that, ironically, was perhaps greater in the communist period than it had been before. It became Poland's alternative government and only moral authority. But now the great Primate Stefan Cardinal Wyszyński was seriously enfeebled and was to die in May 1981. His initial response to the strike was unenthusiastic to the point of discouraging, couched in a manner that made it all too easy for the regime media to distort.[34] Shortly afterward, it is true, the Episcopate as a whole issued a long statement much more reassuring to the strikers, and Wyszyński himself in a meeting with Wałęsa was to leave no doubt where his sympathies lay.[35] But the initial response led to considerable speculation as to just what the primate's real grasp of the situation was.

The reaction of many Catholic intellectuals was much more enthusiastic, and several of them immediately went to Gdansk, placing themselves at the disposal of the strike committee. Among the most prominent were Tadeusz Mazowiecki and Bohdan Cywiński, both well-known lay Catholic editors. The cooperation between men like them —and they were to be joined eventually by numerous others—with the strikers was greatly eased by the fact that some of the early strike leaders, especially Wałęsa himself, were devout Catholics and inclined to moderation. Subsequently, Wałęsa was to be sharply criticized by some of his colleagues for what they considered too much deference to both the church itself and his lay Catholic advisers.

But these Catholic advisers did not have the field to themselves. Also seeking influence at the court of Solidarity were the intellectuals from KOR. Many of these had been helping persecuted workers and their families for several years and considered themselves as well equipped to help the strikers as their Catholic counterparts. While there was little open rivalry between these two groups—indeed, some relations between individuals were warm and close—they generally considered themselves separate from each other. Some lay Catholics around Solidarity distrusted some KOR members, notably Kuron, as did many members of the church hierarchy. Indeed, some of the latter, while applauding Solidarity, were apparently of the view that, since the church was no longer the only institution in Poland claiming mass support and on which anticommunist attitudes could focus, it must seek by all means to influence the burgeoning new institution. And the fact that several KOR members were former communists—and Jewish to boot—only seemed to make the task more urgent. Cardinal Glemp, who became primate of Poland in May 1981, on the death of Wyszyński was to make little effort to disguise his distaste for KOR. He showed little of the graciousness displayed, for example, by the partly Jewish Michnik. Once a fierce anticlerical, Michnik became an admirer of the church's role in Polish history and wrote movingly to that effect.

Solidarity, therefore, did not lack for advisers. But how influential were they? Did they really do what they set out to—calm passions and balance emotion with reason? This very aim might be seen as reflecting a certain condescension toward their "charges," assuming a lack of restraint among the unschooled and bitter Solidarity worker representatives. In the event, most Solidarity worker representatives, above all Wałęsa, did show maturity and moderation. (Wałęsa became a charismatic leader capturing world sympathy.) Only in the very last phase, between September and December 1981, did prudence and restraint begin to wear thin. The regime's lack of sincerity was a great provocation, and there appears to have been a deliberate policy of trying to goad Solidarity into an unreasonableness that would somehow justify the later suppression. What is still not entirely clear is what role Solidarity's different intellectual advisers played in this last phase. The lay Catholics apparently sought to check emotions, while Kuron and others seemed more bent on rationalizing them. Certainly toward the end of Solidarity, its leadership presented a picture of almost unseemly disarray.

The situation was made more complicated by the new primate's lack of ability and authority. Glemp was Wyszyński's nominee, and many came to regard this as the only disservice the latter ever rendered to Poland. Glemp was essentially an administrator and scholar with very little pastoral experience. He lacked stature and presence and frequently displayed an embarrassing political ineptitude. There was, however, a dogged perseverance and courage about him that gradually won respect. He was never slow to criticize the regime when it violated basic freedoms and decencies. His relations with the pope were for some time a matter of colorful speculation and a fertile field for Vatican gossip-mongers (see chapter 3). What might safely be said is that the pope agreed to his appointment out of respect for the late Wyszyński and that, once appointed, Glemp received his loyalty and support. The pope also supported—or initiated—the church's post-December policy of noninterference in overtly political affairs; non-provocative criticism of the martial law regime of General Jaruzelski; strong defense of human rights; and speaking up for the Polish *pays réel*. In the essentials, therefore, the pope supported Glemp. As for Glemp's failings, he was after all the only primate Poland had.

Similarly, the Polish episcopate, despite the personal reservations of some, rallied round Glemp out of loyalty and obedience. Many parish priests, however, chafed at the restraints church policy imposed on them. They were dedicated Solidarity supporters, close to their flock. It was they who found it hardest to obey the new primate and who were often more critical of him (publicly and privately) than most of the regime media.

The party during the Solidarity crisis stumbled from ineffectiveness into impotence. Gierek's successor, Stanisław Kania, however well meaning, was totally unable to handle a situation that to an apparatchik like himself must have seemed barely imaginable. The new prime minister, Józef Pinkowski, was incapable of ever addressing himself to the country's ruinous economic situation. For a while Kania elicited some grudging sympathy for an apparent straightforwardness. But he was presiding over a disintegrating party, and, to add to his problems, some party organizations in the provinces began to urge drastic reform of the party itself, just as the Czechoslovak party had done in 1968. This aspect of the Solidarity period is sometimes overlooked. The fever in Polish society did indeed spread to elements in the party. And the party center felt threatened by some of the proposals coming from the provinces and actively discouraged them.[36]

These efforts at party reform were at one end of the whole spectrum of regime response to Solidarity. At the opposite end were the police activities designed to make unworkable the agreements that had spawned Solidarity in August 1980. These included provocations against groups of trade union activists, the most serious of which was at Bydgoszcz in March 1981 where several workers were badly beaten, and the mounting of a defamation and disinformation campaign against the Solidarity leaders and advisers. This latter was often accompanied by demagogic statements purporting to support "sensible" reforms and condemning the iniquities of the Gierek regime. The aim was obviously to steal Solidarity's thunder. The resilient Mieczysław Moczar, during his brief return to the Politburo, was at the hub of some of this activity.[37] Between these extremes of regeneration and defamation were a few party officials who initially negotiated with Solidarity with some sincerity and tried to hammer out some modus operandi based on compromise. The best known of these was undoubtedly Mieczysław Rakowski, long-time editor of *Polityka*, perhaps the best and liveliest political magazine in the whole communist bloc. Rakowski was made a vice-premier and chief regular negotiator with Solidarity. Eventually, many of his former associates came to despise him for holding on more tenaciously to power than to principle. His behavior after the imposition of martial law tends to justify this severity. Certainly Rakowski failed dismally in the task he considered himself so well suited to perform. At the beginning he may well have thought some compromise possible. But as the negotiations with Solidarity began to show the incompatibility between the two sides, what became most evident about Rakowski was his self-esteem, his lust for power and prominence. What seems to have soured him most was the singular lack of deference the Solidarity negotiators showed for him.

In February 1981 General Wojciech Jaruzelski, already minister of defense, was made prime minister in place of the hapless Pinkowski. Few men in recent history have taken office amid such hope and approbation. He had acquired an excellent reputation as defense minister; he was considered a patriot; and he was known for a formidable personal integrity and austerity. Both the church and Solidarity welcomed him as the man who might bring both sides together and lead them out of the crisis. His appointment also appealed to the romantic side in many Poles. The nation in crisis was turning to its army! Jaruzelski was only the most recent in a line of soldiers called upon in Poland's hour of need. Such sentiments did not survive his military coup on 13 December 1981. From Polish hero Jaruzelski became Soviet janissary. His education from an early age and subsequent military training in the Soviet Union were remembered, while his gentry birth in Poland was forgotten. The several years he spent as the Polish military's chief political officer were now emphasized, the many years previously spent as officer of the line ignored. The one myth that, more than anything else, had enshrined him in the hearts of his countrymen—that he had refused to use troops against strikers in 1976—was exploded. New stories were quickly circulated arraigning him with a lifetime of treachery against Poland.

Such disillusionment was understandable in the traumatic weeks after the imposition of martial law. Even years later it was still too early for a balanced assessment of this enigmatic personality. In the controversy over *what* he did on 13 December 1981 the reasons *why* he did it are considered secondary.

Was it an act of repression against the Polish nation by the Soviet Union and its Polish puppets of whom he was the leader? Or was it an unavoidable act that not only saved Poland from Soviet invasion but also the rest of Europe from a new East-West crisis possibly leading to war? Obviously the vast majority of Poles and many people in the West—particularly the United States—strongly held the first viewpoint. Many in Europe, especially in West Germany, inclined to the second, which in the case of many did not preclude sympathy for the Poles and condemnation of the Soviet Union and the communist system generally (see chapter 3). But its adherents stressed geopolitical realities and considered that any disturbing of them, particularly in such a crucial case as Poland, could lead to a general calamity. To them, therefore, General Jaruzelski's motives were not of primary importance. Whatever they were, the results of what he did were good, better than the alternative, even eventually for the Polish people. Similarly, for the vast majority of the Polish nation, which deplored his action, his motives were of little importance. The personal riddle of Jaruzelski, therefore, was no nearer solution because the ultimate political effect of what he did was so sharply disputed.

Before December, though, Jaruzelski gave no hint of the controversy he was later to rouse. He seemed the main pillar of whatever stability remained in Poland, a figure of trust and confidence. His appointment as party leader to replace Kania in October 1981 was welcomed mainly on those grounds. His unprecedented accumulation of power was seen, not as a threat, but as a reassurance.

One of the most keenly discussed questions Jaruzelski has prompted concerns when the plans for the December coup were actually prepared. Some have thought the answer to this might also go some way to ascertaining his motives. The earlier the plans can safely be dated, the stronger the evidence that everything was conspiratorially prearranged. So the reasoning goes. But, actually, such speculation could turn out to be pointless. What matters is not when Jaruzelski laid his plans but when he decided to implement them. Any regime chief, particularly one coming from the military, would be expected to devise contingency plans in such a volatile situation. Those sources who insist that preparations began early in 1981, i.e., very soon after Jaruzelski assumed the premiership, or even earlier may well be correct. But this in itself, while it may serve to corroborate other evidence, hardly proves anything.[38]

The most crucial question of all regarding Solidarity is whether at any time a satisfactory compromise between it and the regime was possible. Timothy Garton Ash, an expert with a deep knowledge of the Polish scene, argues that this might have been possible in the first few months of Solidarity, provided the West had offered large-scale economic aid and credits (in short a Marshall Plan for Poland). This massive aid would have had reform and good husbandry strings attached. Solidarity's existence would have been assured but in a way least damaging to Soviet interests. The chances of success would have been small but still realistic enough to have been worth trying. As it was, the chance was missed and there was subsequently no hope, barring the miracle that never occurred.[39]

The real question here concerns the threshold of Soviet tolerance at any particular time and, hence, how large the framework for maneuver is inside the Soviet bloc. This is referred to briefly in chapter 2. Here it needs simply be said had the Soviet Union been prepared to accept, or be seen to be accepting, the permanence and, therefore, the legitimacy of an institution like Solidarity, then it would have been signaling to the world, to Eastern Europe, and to its own population, that a basic shift, not only in its own policy but also in its own character, had been made. And, applied to Poland, this would have meant that Moscow was prepared to give up its security position in Central Europe. As argued in chapter 2, a Soviet-controlled Poland is essential not just to the security of the GDR but to its very survival. In a situation of weakness a Soviet leadership might have been prepared to go through the motions of tolerating an institution like Solidarity. But that would only have been a cover or delaying tactic. Beneath the cover, or after the delay, the inexorable undermining operation would have begun. Similarly, if the Soviet Union had, for whatever reason, thought better of invading Czechoslovakia in 1968 this would not have meant it would have accepted the Prague Spring. Moscow would simply have used every undermining tactic against Dubček short of invasion—and eventually it would have succeeded. There is no reason to think it would have been different with Solidarity.

Military Rule

The military coup of 13 December 1981 was a brilliantly conducted operation. It achieved surprise (how total is not clear) and almost immediate success with the minimum number of casualties.

The coup had obviously been prepared well in advance; hence it was all the more remarkable that such tight secrecy about it was kept. But this was not the sole reason for the surprise. Equally important was the attitude of the Solidarity leadership and of most Western observers—complacency or a mind-set that refused to consider massive repression. For several months the question of the reaction to Solidarity by the Soviet Union and the Polish regime had been discussed. The use of the Polish armed forces was one of the possibilities most seriously considered. This had been dismissed by many as unlikely because of the widespread belief that, when faced with the crucial decision, the bulk of the military would opt for the nation and would not suppress fellow Poles. An attempt to use the military, therefore, would enhance the dangers of a bloody civil war that the Soviets would not allow. In any case, Solidarity would call a general strike that could bring Poland to a standstill. Anything short of a Soviet invasion was, therefore, ruled out, and, as time went on, many considered this less likely. The Soviets in December 1980 and then the following February had, through threatening military movements, made as if to invade and then held off. The danger of their now doing so was thought to have receded.

But the military coup took place after all. Jaruzelski was prepared to take the most serious risks, pressed by a Soviet leadership desperately anxious to avoid trying the job themselves. But he must have had the assurance that the Soviets would invade if he looked like failing.

In the event, he owed his success to a move few in either Poland or outside had apparently anticipated. This was the complete cutting off of telephonic and telegraphic communications within Poland and between Poland and the outside world. Solidarity, therefore, and the whole of Polish society were fragmented and cut off from mutual contact. Some rudimentary counterplans against this strategy had evidently been drawn up, but they were useless in the new situation. Solidarity as an organized force, therefore, was soon reduced to helplessness. Practically its entire leadership and thousands of sympathizers were shipped off to prisons or internment camps. It was this—the loss of Solidarity's communications and its leadership—that caused resistance to collapse relatively early. Plus, of course, the fact that the armed forces obeyed orders, and that in the notorious ZOMOS Jaruzelski found his perfect means of restoring and maintaining order. It was these forces, some 70,000 of them, rather than the army (which stayed mainly in the background) that broke organized Solidarity.[40]

The ease with which it was all done surprised everyone. For many Poles themselves it was a source of chagrin and even humiliation. Some East Europeans derived *Schadenfreude* from the fact that, as they saw it, the "arrogant" Polish nation had been put down by a mere handful of their own countrymen. Indeed, much of Eastern Europe's reaction to the whole Solidarity story reflected anything but human concern and sympathy. All the regimes obviously viewed Solidarity with mounting anxiety, but Romania and Yugoslavia insisted, as they had done over Czechoslovakia in 1968, on the principle of noninterference. Among the East European peoples historical attitudes asserted themselves strongly. For many East (and West) Germans, for example, Solidarity had been yet further evidence of Polish anarchy and disinclination to work. Most Czechs, whose historic dislike of Poles was reinforced by their role in the invasion of 1968, wished Solidarity ill from the start and scarcely hid their satisfaction when it was struck down. Other East Europeans, like the Hungarians, who historically have a sympathy for Poles, were disturbed over Solidarity because they considered it would present the Soviets with the opportunity, not just of coercing Poland, but of "cracking down" on them as well. Significantly, it was the Romanians who seemed less perturbed by this possibility, presumably thinking that for them things could hardly get much worse anyway. Most Bulgarians were simply not interested.

The Failure of Reconstruction

In the years since the coup Poland has virtually stood still. Immediately after December 1981 the very few Solidarity leaders who escaped imprisonment went underground and built an impressive network soon covering the whole country. Its main aim was to keep the spirit of resistance alive among the almost 10 million workers who had belonged to Solidarity, and in this it succeeded admirably. Solidarity continued to remain powerful as a symbol of freedom, of a system of values, and of a way of life. It was in this sense that resistance to the Jaruzelski regime remained strong. Different groups advocated different gradations of resistance—from those still ready for active, nonviolent resistance in the form of token strikes and demonstrations, to those who still made financial contributions to Solidarity but thought all forms of active resistance useless and even self-defeating.

Gradually, however, many citizens were pushed into some cooperation with the regime. The new official trade union organization, for example, which the regime established in 1982 to replace Solidarity, steadily increased its membership; already by early 1984 the regime claimed it stood at 4 million.[41] To attract recruits it occasionally showed surprising signs of independence—many more than other East European trade unions. It also disposed of the usual patronage of perquisites and privileges.[42] Most Polish workers, however, continued to despise it. Most intellectuals, too, refused to cooperate with the regime, and the few who did were considered pariahs. But nowhere was opposition to the Jaruzelski regime stronger than among the youth. In 1956 the youth had generally been enthusiastic about Gomułka. As they grew older their attitudes changed to cynicism. A partly new generation welcomed Gierek in 1970 but with less enthusiasm than their predecessors had shown fourteen years earlier. Now youthful contempt for Jaruzelski remained as strong and as implacable as ever. In fact, in youth circles anticommunism was now de rigueur. In their idealistic anger they could not compromise with Jaruzelski, the man who, as one student privately put it, had "attacked the spirit of Poland." They were determined to show everyone that he had still not destroyed it.[43] Many left Poland and more were anxious to do so.

In such a climate of opinion it was the church that gained in loyalty. The traditional guardian of the nation now reverted to its old status of Poland's sole independent and popular institution. In this sense, therefore, the church was the beneficiary of Solidarity's demise. That this should occur so quickly was perhaps surprising in view of the ambivalence with which Glemp greeted the Jaruzelski coup in December 1981. At that time he gave the impression that he at least understood the reasons for it and was certainly less than generous in his attitude to the fallen Solidarity. In the months that followed he viewed the activities of the underground Solidarity with a reserve that, even allowing for his difficult situation, embarrassed many church dignitaries by its tactlessness. Later, however, his hold was to become firmer and his touch more sure.[44]

But Glemp was not the whole Polish church. And the institution the vast majority of Poles now increasingly identified with was more robustly represented by the legions of local parish priests. These men were no longer just representatives of the church: they became leaders of the nation, of the *pays réel*, now that Solidarity was overturned and Lech Wałęsa with its other leaders spirited away. Despite all the injunctions about the church not interfering in politics, many priests became totally involved in the concerns of their parishioners. And that meant politics. Father Jerzy Popiełuszko, murdered by security agents in October 1984, paid for his dedication with his life. Others were persecuted or harassed. The church, therefore, in the person of these battalions of clergy, rallied to the nation. And these men brought the church its own reward in devotion and gratitude. Many bishops, too, though they had to express their views more discreetly, pressed for a stronger stand for those principles of which both the church and Solidarity had been an expression. The declarations of the episcopate now carried increasing authority, especially when it was becoming clear that the promises made by Jaruzelski and his spokesmen immediately after the coup were not being kept.

But there were also deeper reasons for the loyalty the church inspired. These lay in the traditions of the church, its unbreakable link with Poland's past, and with the very survival of the nation. They also lay in its own mystique, the hold and spell it exercised. And, by sublime coincidence, the personification of that mystique in this time of national travail was sitting on the throne of St. Peter. When John Paul II visited his native country a second time in 1983 the poignancy of the situation overflowed in waves of devotion that engulfed the whole nation. The pope himself had the immensely difficult task of giving heart to the nation while at the same time conveying the need for restraint. He performed it with great skill, but part of his success was also due to the instinctive understanding the masses had for his situation, and for their own.

The waxing of church influence only threw into bold relief the waning of party power. Within the regime the military had replaced the party. Before December 1981 there had been considerable public satisfaction over this development. The eclipse of the party seemed somehow to take communism out of the regime. The three main actors in public life were now acceptable: the church, Solidarity, and the army. All were at least Polish, something the party was not perceived as being. This satisfaction became for many a hope that the future of

Poland might henceforth be decided by the interaction of these three institutions. And even though it was the army that ultimately destroyed Solidarity, a few Poles still, immediately after the coup, apparently harbored illusions that the country might be effectively and equitably ruled by an arrangement between it and the church. Jaruzelski's speech declaring martial law and the Polish episcopate's first reaction to it evidently gave some credence to the idea.

But any illusions that remained were dispelled soon afterward. The means the military used to suppress Solidarity were hardly compatible with any cooperation, or even toleration, from the church. In any case, dominant though the army was, it gradually became clear that one of the eventual aims of the new regime was to bring back the party, hobbling though it might be, to the center of the political stage. The military were not in politics to stay indefinitely. No basic change in the system was to be allowed that would involve the withering away of the party. In terms of sheer power relationships this might have been the logical course in Poland. But it would have presented such a threat to the Soviet system, in Eastern Europe and the Soviet Union itself. Moscow was thankful for the military's ability to come to the aid of the party. But it should not become a permanent fixture.

Bringing back the party was, therefore, an important task for the martial law regime. The officers were to return to their barracks as early as the situation allowed. But how soon that would be depended on the speed with which "normalization," after December 1981, proceeded. And, unlike in Czechoslovakia, where it proceeded with considerable speed, in Poland it went very slowly, at times almost imperceptibly. Poland was quickly "pacified," but "normalization" was different. In this context "normalization" can be defined as the achievement of a degree of acceptance by the majority of the population of the new power relationship, enabling public life to be resumed according to patterns previously established. It remained doubtful whether such normalization would ever be attained.

This was partly due to Jaruzelski's failures as a politician. In the first place he found difficulty in "projecting" himself. He was very shy and spurned the publicity-seeking in which some other communist leaders —none more so than Gierek—have heavily indulged. Among a nation that responds to warmth and human sympathy Jaruzelski appeared to have neither. The Poles, of course, would not readily have been inclined to take to a man whom they saw as crushing their freedom. But Kádár, in even less promising circumstances, achieved this in Hungary. The comparison may be misleading, but few would deny that Jaruzelski's personality has been an encumbrance to the "normalization" campaign. He came to be less hated as the years wore on. In fact, many were grudgingly prepared to grant him more respect than any of his associates. But he could not develop this into anything like a positive image.

His lack of personality was matched by his second great handicap: his lack of political skill. This showed itself both in his early relations with Moscow and his performance on the domestic scene. Few East European leaders ever appeared to have had as much bargaining power with Moscow as Jaruzelski did after December 1981. The Soviets were rid of Solidarity; and not a single Soviet soldier was used. It may be true that gratitude has never been an outstanding characteristic of the Soviet Union—or of any great power. It is also probably true that the Soviets, despite that enormous relief, felt some embarrassment over the new political situation that now prevailed in Poland. But after allowing for all such reservations, the Soviets knew that Jaruzelski was indispensable not just on 13 December 1981 but also for some time in the future. This gave Jaruzelski leverage. But there were few signs he was prepared to use it.

On the domestic scene there was precious little sign of that strong leadership that he had earlier seemed to personify. For several years his regime presented the picture of an uneasy coalition, with hardliners opposed to reforms and police elements more interested in avenging themselves on society than protecting it. The murder of Father Popiełuszko was only the most extreme example of police criminality. And the way this case was handled was an example of Jaruzelski getting the worst of all worlds. There was a deep suspicion in Polish society that the order for Popiełuszko's murder had come from high up in the regime. (This was one of the more rational of the suspicions circulating.) Jaruzelski moved to counter this and showed firmness in bringing the culprits to trial and giving the trial in early 1985 considerable publicity. But the prosecution used the trial only partly to try the accused. It used it mainly to attack the church. For the public, therefore, the satisfaction of seeing guilty police officers condemned was greatly reduced by the way the trial had been conducted.[45]

The first five years of Jaruzelski's regime were studded with such inconsistencies. The far-reaching amnesty in July 1984, for example, was followed by arrests that soon sent some of the most prominent opponents back into jail. A promising situation for Jaruzelski resulting from the Sejm (parliament) elections in October 1985, in which underground Solidarity's calls for a boycott had nowhere near the effect it had hoped, was spoiled by purges of university rectors that further enraged the vast majority of intellectuals and students. Relations with the church also deteriorated for a time after what should have been a reassuring election result.

The third great failure of the Jaruzelski regime was in economic policy. Here the legacy of the Gierek regime, together with the sullen uncooperativeness of many workers, except in the pampered coal industry in Silesia, were too much for a leadership so lacking in resolve. The hard-currency debt climbed to well over $30 billion, and the problem became not so much trying to repay the capital but on getting the interest repayments rescheduled. The economic sanctions applied by the U.S. government also hurt the economy considerably,[46] but they would have counted for little if progress could have been made on the economy as a whole. With active opposition crushed, the regime was able to impose very stiff price increases, and this tended to reduce consumer demand. Optically, therefore, one aspect of the situation improved because in the course of 1984 the long food lines in front of shops got steadily shorter. But the supply situation continued very serious. Thus Jaruzelski was deprived of one of the most powerful means for "normalization" that Husák had used successfully on Czechoslovakia some ten years before: plentifully stocked shops. Jaruzelski could not sweeten his normalization with "consumerism."

These economic failures were taking place against the background of a steadily deteriorating quality of life. The whole economic, social, and cultural infrastructure was rotting. Standards of hygiene, the water supply, transport and communications, hospitals and medical services, schools and kindergartens—all were in serious decline in many parts of the country. The economy was simply not generating enough wealth to tackle these problems. In any case, in view of the other priorities, it would take decades or a colossal disaster before money was available for them.

As for economic reform, it was virtually at a standstill for several years. An ambitious plan of reform was to have been introduced in 1982, which allowed for considerable enterprise autonomy and worker democracy, along with the introduction of some elements of the market mechanism. On paper it was probably more reformist than any other system in Eastern Europe except the Hungarian, which it resembled in several respects (see chapter 4). But though workers' councils were introduced in many factories beginning in 1983, little else appeared to have been achieved. Bureaucratic inertia and downright hostility seem to have been responsible for this ineffectiveness, plus a reluctance on the part of many officials and managers, otherwise sympathetic to reform, but who thought the economy was just too fragile to take the measures that it needed! In the middle of the 1980s Jaruzelski's economic reform seemed to many to be going the same way Gierek's had by the middle of the previous decade.

Poland, therefore, drifted for a number of years. Yet it was by no means a scene of unbroken harshness and repression. Compared with almost every other East European country it had undeniably "liberal" aspects. There was practically no bar, for example, on travel abroad. Foreign correspondents reported freely, and Poland's own press was often very outspoken. The Polish people felt no inhibitions when it came to speaking openly. The astonishing Lech Wałęsa, Nobel Peace Prize winner in 1984, who since his release from detention in 1982 had even increased in stature and authority and was certainly the most popular and respected man in Poland, did have restrictions placed on some of his activities that he parried with skill and good humor. But the very fact that he could still act openly as the symbol of Polish resistance was itself a sign of the paradox of post-December Poland: the population could still inhibit the regime, and there was little the regime could do to impress them. For them the cup was never even half full; it was always totally empty. They might accept all Jaruzelski had to offer, but they would never respond to it in the way he hoped and in the way he seemed genuinely to believe he deserved.

Indeed, the picture Poland now presented was one of two societies —the "official" and the "alternative." The "official" consisted of the regime establishment and the large number of people who, willingly or unwillingly, cooperated with the regime to some degree. The "alternative" society, in which youth played a disproportionately large role, had its own media, literature, and cultural and educational activities. It avoided contact with the "official" society as far as was ever possible. In a sense two societies had always existed in communist Eastern Europe. But never had the chasm between the two been as wide as it was now in Poland, and never had the "alternative" society been so well-organized and so self-sufficient.

In this connection it is worth quoting a passage from a report of a "workshop" on Poland conducted in Washington, D.C., by the Rand Corporation in early 1987:

The Polish opposition has produced a wealth of underground papers and publishing houses. In 1986 alone, 20 new titles appeared. There are about 600 underground papers at present, 400 of which have been issued continuously since 1982. Approximately 20,000 people are involved in distributing the underground press. Twelve major underground publishing houses have formed a syndicate. An underground bank pays advances for books, and an underground insurance company pays compensations in case of arrest or confiscation of equipment. There is also a network of clandestine lending libraries. Radio Solidarity can be heard in various parts of the country on frequencies of the official radio and television. Use of audio and especially video cassettes has revolutionized the underground media. The number of video recorders in the country rose from zero in 1983 to 350,000 in 1986. The underground press has also produced over 400 satellite television antennas to date.[47]

Statistics like these were part of Jaruzelski's awesome task. But by the beginning of 1987 the situation seemed to be changing. For one thing, Jaruzelski seemed to be gaining in confidence. In November 1985 he had become head of state, giving up the premiership to Zbigniew Messner, a competent economics professor, but retaining the party leadership. In June–July 1986, at the tenth Polish United Workers' Party congress, his position inside the regime was visibly strengthened by a ringing endorsement from Soviet leader Gorbachev. It was now up to Jaruzelski to exploit this support. He fully endorsed Gorbachev's reform policy, and the question now was how much of it would he try to adapt for Poland.

In September 1986 Jaruzelski made his boldest move of all by freeing *all* of Poland's 225 political prisoners, including Zbigniew Bujak, leader of underground Solidarity since December 1981, who had only been arrested a few months before. This was certainly a sign of the regime's increasing confidence and proof of the *organizational* weakness of Solidarity, which had been evident for some time. It might also have been the beginning of further concessions to the Polish population.

But there remained the two essential concessions neither Jaruzelski nor any other leader could make. There could be no early basic economic improvement. Indeed, all the signs pointed to stagnation or even further deterioration. More important: under the present Soviet-type system there could be no institutional pluralization of political life and real dialogue with society. This is what Solidarity symbolized and stood for. Without it the prison gates in Poland that had just let the political prisoners out would become revolving doors letting some of them back in. And, until it showed signs of appearing, the abilities of the Polish nation would never be harnessed or its spirit appeased.

The pope's third visit to Poland in June 1987 dramatized the chasm that still existed between the concessions the regime was prepared to make and the aspirations of society, as voiced by John Paul II. The latter, though mindful as always of the geopolitical restraints, was talking about more freedoms. The regime was talking about fewer restraints. The difference was lost on nobody.

But Jaruzelski persisted, within his own limits and those he perceived as set by the situation, to cast about for measures that would alleviate economic conditions and involve society at the same time. In the second half of 1987 his experts at last elaborated a plan of genuine economic reform that included many of the features of the aborted 1982 measures. (The impact of Gorbachev was plain to see!) In the hope of involving society Jaruzelski then ordered a referendum for the end of November, in effect asking the public whether it wanted a deep-going reform that would include steep price increases and a short-term austerity. The public answered no. The entire situation was unprecedented. It revealed a number of things, the most important being how little Jaruzelski had progressed in six frustrating years.

6   Hungary

In 1986 Hungary marked the thirtieth anniversary of the Revolution; the regime celebrated the occasion in one way, the majority of the population (undemonstratively) in another. The recollection of those nineteen days in October–November 1956 reminded, not only Hungary, but the rest of Eastern Europe and the world of the heroic courage of a nation pushed beyond endurance by the system forced on it after World War II. The official communist version of the events of 1956 continues to be that they were a "counterrevolution," a cruel distortion that the vast majority of Hungarians, including many communists, have always rejected.[1] But this official designation of the revolution is simply one aspect of that make-believe quality in Hungarian public life evident ever since 1956.

This make-believe quality essentially arose from the unwritten "compact" or acceptance of limitations imposed by the Kádár regime on the Hungarian population after the revolution. It was imposed on the people rather than in any way agreed, since the nation had been both defeated and shattered, physically and spiritually, by the revolution. And the aftermath of the revolution was quite protracted, with the former premier, Imre Nagy, being executed not until June 1958, a move apparently followed by a final wave of persecution.

The compact after 1956, therefore, could not have been more one-sided. But it reflected the acceptance by the new Kádár regime of the necessity, or the inevitability, of a *two-sided* relationship, and the admission that two sides did exist. In effect, this meant a tacit repudiation of the classic ideological insistence that no two sides could exist. Of course, the class enemy still remained, and the designation of 1956 as a "counterrevolution" reflected the official view that this enemy had been strong enough to mount a violent challenge. But the fact that after the revolution the Kádár leadership was prepared to see the governance of a socialist state in terms of a contractual relationship, no matter how one-sided and ill-defined, meant a major retreat from accepted orthodoxy. Implicit in the new relationship was another retreat from orthodoxy: the regime's willingness to see society withdraw from active politics in return for its own efforts to supply adequate standards of consumer and welfare provisions.[2]

Obviously the Hungarian regime would never admit to such ideological retreat. Official propaganda continued to expound the classic tenets of Leninism, but regime policy on this basic question of relations with society ignored them. Nothing summed up János Kádár's retreat from doctrinal orthodoxy more than his famous exhortation to the nation in 1961: "Whoever is not against us is with us."[3] These few famous words have generally been seen as reflecting the human, conciliatory, and politically farsighted policy for which Kádár himself has become noted. They are certainly this; but they also imply the abandonment of communist proselytizing zeal in favor of a philosophy of live-and-let-live that cut across all accepted notions of ideological purity and agitprop ethos. Kádár, it should be stressed, was not offering any changes whatever in the structure of power. The Leninist institutions have remained as intact in Hungary as they have anywhere else. But these institutions have been managed differently—more flexibly, humanely, and often more humorously. The rigors of socialism have been replaced by its relaxation. That difference is the essence of what has become known as "Kádárism."

Kádár's policy was to unfold gradually. "Kádárism" was not contained in any one holy writ. At the beginning he himself probably had little idea of the detailed course he would take. But he knew the direction in which he wanted Hungary to move. He may not have been sure of the methods to be used. He did know, though, from the years of Stalinist rule under Mátyás Rákosi before the revolution and, above all, from the revolution itself, what methods must *not* be used. The Hungarian nation could not be pushed too far—even in its shattered state after 1956. Its "character" as well as the "political culture" that had nurtured it had to be taken into account. The latter might historically have been the birthright of a privileged few, but the former was the property of the whole nation. It was Kádár's merit that he was fully aware of this and hence of the need to promote not only a sense of security from the arbitrary police repression that had characterized Stalinist rule, but also an atmosphere of psychological relaxation in which the memories of the recent past would ebb away and the abilities of the nation would be fostered. "Kádárism," therefore, was not only "goulash" communism. It also involved a healthy respect for the talent, the character, and the courage of Hungarians.

But what of the nation? What did its new "apoliticism" involve? Basically, looking back on the tragedy of 1956, it meant "never again": therefore, the acceptance of Soviet domination, socialist rule (but to be diluted as far as possible), and Hungary's raison d'être within the Soviet-led alliance. After these basic premises it was a matter of individual interpretation and behavior. Some chose active cooperation, even identification, with the regime. For others, it was to be an energetic exploitation of the material opportunities offered by the regime, without any corresponding identification with it. These comprised the huge constituency Kádár had in mind when he made his "he who is not against us . . ." speech. (There were also to be many citizens who would have exploited the material opportunities but could not do so. They were to be shouldered aside as life grew more competitive.) Finally, there were those whose "cooperation" with the regime was simply confined to doing nothing against it. Some of these were intellectuals who became worried by what they considered to be the basic assumption of the 1956 compromise: that not only society's acceptance, but even its cooperation, could be bought. The Hungarian nation, they came to argue, was corrupted by the contract. The heroism of the revolution had given way to the amoral opportunism implicit in Kádárism. By the time the thirtieth anniversary of the revolution came this group and the attitude it represented had become a factor of importance in public life that neither the regime nor the society at large could ignore. Its members considered Kádárism and the way of life it stimulated as worse than make-believe. They saw it as an historic and all-consuming hypocrisy. The serpent had offered Eve the apple, and she had indeed taken it.[4] These views will be considered later. At the beginning of the story, however, in the early 1960s, the fact of overriding importance was that the Hungarian nation was gratified at being offered anything at all.

Kádár's Consolidation of Power

The three decades after the revolution were dominated by János Kádár. And it was during this period that he underwent one of the most astonishing political metamorphoses in modern history. From the despised "traitor" of 1956 he evolved into a figure of respect, often of admiration, even affection. More important, in a system that had perforce to depend on people rather than institutions to guarantee its gains, Kádár was often seen as the guarantor of the progress achieved since 1956 as well as the assurance that there would be no retreat from it. Never was this more evident than after the fall of Nikita Khrushchev in October 1964. There was genuine fear in Hungary that Kádár, so closely linked with Khrushchev, would soon follow.[5] Subsequently he became the eponym of "Kádárism"—the socialist "good life" based on success and relaxation. Later still when economic adversity replaced prosperity and when the situation in Moscow became less predictable, he was seen as the guardian of whatever stability remained and the reassurance against things getting worse. Finally, almost inevitably for such longevity, he aroused impatience rather than admiration. But by this time his place in history was secure.

Kádár was by no means unknown before 1956, but few who knew him would have suspected him of being the material of which such a metamorphosis could be made. But, personally, he soon showed he had that wit, warmth, and humanity to which his compatriots so readily respond. He also revealed an unsuspected political skill in handling the Hungarian public, his colleagues, and his ultimate controllers in Moscow. He has lacked charisma or dynamism, but has compensated with skill, timing, perceptiveness, and shrewd human judgment. He has been prepared to take risks (his whole policy being the biggest risk of all), but he always seemed to have prepared his path of retreat. His sureness of touch was often uncanny. But most important of all was his ability to project calm and confidence. Finally, his very longevity was reassuring. He was less heroic or charismatic than Tito, but he came to mean almost as much to the politics and confidence of his own country as even Tito did to his. In the early years of communist power Kádár brought ignominy on himself: he persuaded his friend Lászlo Rajk, executed in 1949, to confess, in the interests of the party, to the monstrous charges against him;[6] he betrayed the revolution in 1956; he acquiesced in Imre Nagy's execution in 1958. Yet only ten years after the revolution he was beginning to be seen by many as *pater patriae*. After thirty years he was a great Hungarian historical figure.

Kádár has owed much to his ability to win the confidence of successive Soviet leaders. In the extraordinary circumstances in which he came to power his links with Khrushchev were bound to be close. For a short time Kádár was totally dependent on Khrushchev's support. But the dependence was not all on one side. Khrushchev was new and still by no means secure in the Soviet leadership. Before the Twentieth CPSU congress in 1956 he had rivals in the leadership, and, after his onslaught on Stalin at the congress, opposition to him or uncertainty about him grew. The Polish October and especially the Hungarian Revolution, seen by many as the consequences of his de-Stalinization policy, might well have led to his downfall. Any man chosen by him to lead the postrevolution Hungarian regime must have been looked on askance by many. The amount of leverage Kádár had with Khrushchev, therefore, was in direct proportion to the latter's considerable investment in him.[7] Soon afterward, Khrushchev's position was secured by his victory over the "antiparty" group in 1957, and the degree of his dependence on Kádár's success in "normalizing" Hungary decreased accordingly. But it did not disappear: he still had a political investment in Kádár's success. And it was this that made his support for Kádár's reform program all the more enlightened, although it is doubtful whether he would have felt confident enough to do so before the antiparty group in Moscow was purged.

Support from Khrushchev was essential for Kádár in his first few years of power, essential for the implementation of his policy in the face of hard-line domestic opposition. But as Kádár's support and confidence grew, he became less dependent. Khrushchev became less a crutch and more of a guarantee. But just how important this guarantee was perceived to be was seen at the time of Khrushchev's fall in October 1964. Yet, once Kádár had safely negotiated the transition in Moscow from Khrushchev to Brezhnev, his stature in Hungary actually grew. He was seen less as a Soviet client and more as a Hungarian leader, more macro- than microdependent.

His relations with Brezhnev appear to have been generally excellent; temperamentally the two seemed to have been highly compatible. Kádár also grew in Brezhnev's esteem as a figure of continuity and sanity. Their relationship was not one of unbroken agreement. Kádár apparently doubted the need for the invasion of Czechoslovakia.[8] Brezhnev doubted the wisdom of the Hungarian economic reform. His opposition led to it being virtually shelved from 1972 to 1978.[9] But despite the difficulties Brezhnev (or any other Soviet leader) might have with Kádár, he was sure of one thing: eventually Kádár would obey. He had that quality of ultimate loyalty that every Soviet leader since Stalin has looked for in Eastern Europe. (Stalin demanded reflexive loyalty.) As for

Kádár, he has occasionally been suspected of exaggerating the danger of Soviet interference to cool the ardor of reformist spirits at home, just as Tito was suspected of doing in Yugoslavia. Manipulating Soviet domination is a useful expedient for any East European leader—as long as it is not done too often.

With Brezhnev's successor, Andropov, it was claimed that Kádár was on good terms. Ambassador to Hungary during the revolution, Andropov was intimately connected with the circumstances bringing Kádár to power. Later, as a Central Committee secretary for relations with ruling parties, he maintained his links with Hungary, as presumably he did during his fifteen years as head of the KGB. But Hungarian satisfaction at Andropov's appointment was cut short by his untimely death. Little, apparently, was expected in Budapest of Chernenko. But Chernenko did not live long enough to show either vindictiveness or magnanimity. As for Gorbachev, though the possibilities arising from his elevation will be discussed later in this chapter, it should be said here that he was initially welcomed by almost all shades of opinion in the Budapest political establishment.

Reform as a Way of Life

From 1968 onward the history of Hungary has been dominated by the reform prosaically (and prudently) known as the "New Economic Mechanism" (NEM). The NEM has had ramifications extending into all parts of Hungarian society, its significance far transcending the economic domain. It became not so much a program of economic reform as a way of life or a habit of mind.[10] It was associated with softening the rigors of life under socialism and dispersing its gloom. Westward travel (for those who could afford it) became an integral part of this way of life. And presiding over this—modestly and, until the situation demanded otherwise, self-effacingly—has been Kádár.

It was nothing new in Soviet-dominated Eastern Europe for economic reforms to symbolize or set off a liberalizing of public life as a whole. The Prague Spring was originally motored by the economic reform proposals of 1964. Similarly, the economic reform proposals associated with the Polish October in 1956 were in the context of demands for many-sided change. But the Polish reforms were still-born, the Czechoslovak cut short by the Soviet-led invasion. In the Hungarian case the economic reforms have been regarded as an ongoing feature of public life. And even when they were interrupted in the

1970s the psychological relaxation they had ushered in still continued. What has probably made Hungary unique in this respect is the fact that a much longer period of political relaxation preceded the introduction of the economic reform and provided a solid basis for it, able to survive any interruptions it might suffer. It had generated a momentum of its own. Besides, it prepared and sustained that degree of credibility without which no economic reform can work effectively. And it never passed that point—as the political relaxation in Czechoslovakia did—where it threatened the basic political practices and institutions regarded as essential to the preservation of the Soviet-type system.

The NEM did not spring like water out of the rock on 1 January 1968. Some, indeed, put the beginnings of reform as far back as 1957 with certain policy and bureaucratic changes mainly affecting agriculture and the food industries.[11] This was well before political relaxation could even be contemplated, about a year in fact before Imre Nagy and his companions were executed. It was also two years before the agricultural collectivization began.

It is perhaps this event—the agricultural collectivization process —that can be considered the real watershed in Hungarian history since the revolution. It began in 1959 and was carried out in three annual stages ending in 1961. It met with little resistance from a peasantry that, though largely inactive in the revolution and hence not as emotionally shattered as the rest of the nation, simply regarded what was happening as inevitable. Collectivization was considered by the regime the essential backdrop to the politics of reform and relaxation. Though apparently only after considerable debate, the postrevolution regime was not prepared to tolerate private agriculture. The post-October Polish regime had little choice because the private peasants in Poland were much stronger than in Hungary and were supported by a powerful, authoritative, national church, something the Catholic church in Hungary had never been. Only about two-thirds of the Hungarian population were considered even nominally Catholic, and the Hungarian church had, in any case, like the Czech, been traditionally identified more with Habsburg dynastic interests than with national aspirations. It is almost certain, also, that, whatever the hesitations in Budapest, the Soviet Union would not have allowed the survival of a free Hungarian peasantry. A free peasantry in one country (Poland) could be shrugged off as an anomaly. In a second it could set a fashion.

The completion of collectivization in 1961, then, was like clearing

the decks for action, the action being the attempt at national reconciliation. This involved more than conciliatory statements: in practice it
meant the continuing purge of dogmatists, for whom the emerging
postrevolutionary policy was a betrayal, the general amnesty for political prisoners in 1963, the abolition of the system of internal exile and
internment without trial, a reduction in the number of forced labor
camps, and the elimination of the jamming of Western radio broadcasts. In addition, a liberal travel policy was initiated that allowed
growing numbers of Hungarians to travel to the West. (At the beginning
many travelers visited only relatives in the West. Some of these later
were the victims of locust-like descents that they ruefully described as
"Kádár's revenge.")

These gestures were accompanied by what William F. Robinson calls
a "remarkable flowering of free criticism and enquiry"; and Robinson
continues, "numerous and relatively far-reaching debates took place
among scholars, scientists, specialists, journalists, writers, managers,
trade union leaders, and lower ranking trade union officials." It was
these debates, he says, that were the most impressive, "for here was an
application of the Kádár doctrine of participation and enlightenment
that was well suited to the times and the needs of the country."[12]

Similar tolerance was shown toward the newly collectivized peasants. Whereas it had traditionally been communist tactics to exploit
economic and class differences in the countryside, now that collectivization had been completed it was Kádár's policy to stress the concept
of a unified peasant class. He strongly urged that there should be no
vindictiveness toward former kulaks. Class background and past
grudges could now be forgotten. There was also to be more democracy
inside the newly established collectives and—most important of all
for the peasants themselves—private plots were to be protected and
production on them encouraged.[13] It was this benevolence toward
private plots that did much to make the collectivization under Kádár
more palatable and has over the years had a considerable share in the
success of Hungarian agriculture and the relative content on the
collectives.

There can be no doubt that Kádár's policy of conciliation owed
much to the second bout of de-Stalinization introduced by Khrushchev
at the Twenty-second CPSU congress in 1961. It gave Kádár the moral
support and the political authority for what he was doing. It was also
an important factor in the growing legitimization of his rule. But growing legitimization among society did not necessarily mean total accep-

tance within his own party. One month after the revolution had been crushed the party's membership had shrunk to just under 38,000. As a result of crash recruiting campaigns, by the middle of 1962 it stood at over half a million.[14] The Hungarian Socialist Workers' party had had to be reborn without those who had disfigured the reputation of its predecessor before 1956. But though the men judged guilty after 1956 may have gone, there were still many others who objected to the character and pace of Kádár's new course. The turning point in the struggle within the party was the eighth congress in November 1962 when several of Kádár's prominent followers were promoted to senior positions.[15] Among the new Central Committee secretaries was Rezsö Nyers, who was later to be known as the "father" or "spiritus rector" of the NEM. It was this victory by Kádár, which in turn had been made possible only by the Twenty-second CPSU congress, that enabled him finally to get rid of his unofficial deputy, György Marosán, who had apparently been intriguing against him. Marosán himself was a volatile, unpredictable personality, and his own political constituency was small.[16] But the very fact that the man generally recognized as number two in the regime, whatever his personality, could be involved in intrigues against his leader showed that opposition was still not to be discounted.

Nor were the shocks to end there. A far greater one occurred in October 1964 when Khrushchev was ousted from power. The Hungarian leader's political guarantor had departed just when Kádár's new course seemed to have come through its initial difficulties and to be safely on its way. A brief period of hesitation also followed in which domestic opponents of the new policy hoped for a signal of support from the new Brezhnev-Kosygin leadership. But they got nothing of the sort. In 1965 the Soviets themselves began a series of (short-lived) economic changes obviously prepared when Khrushchev had still been in power. The signal from Moscow that counted, therefore, was one of encouragement for economic reform. Subsequently, the new Soviet leadership was mainly preoccupied with domestic concerns, the most immediate of which was the consolidation of its own power. In any case, the East European country that began to demand the new Soviet leaders' attention was not Hungary but Czechoslovakia.

The Beginnings of the New Economic Mechanism

The Hungarian reformers were, therefore, able to press ahead, and a Central Committee plenum in May 1966 set the stage for the formal opening of the NEM for 1 January 1968. This coincided with the downfall of Antonín Novotný in Czechoslovakia, his replacement by Alexander Dubček, and the ushering in of the Prague Spring. Events in Czechoslovakia apparently caught the Soviet leaders unaware. Brezhnev had visited Prague early in December, considered the ferment there a matter of leadership politics, and refused to intervene. Presumably, therefore, he saw no danger in what was being prepared in Hungary. Only later, when the full danger of the Czechoslovak situation became apparent, could misgivings also have grown in the Kremlin about the situation there.

These voices probably became louder and more clamorous after the invasion of Czechoslovakia in August 1968 and when Moscow was preparing its "counterreformation" in Eastern Europe (see chapter 2). But, in spite of this, the Hungarians continued full steam ahead after August 1968. Nor were the misgivings confined to the Soviet Union. Vasil Bilak, the conscience of neo-Stalinism in "normalized" Czechoslovakia, was, for example, a constant critic of the NEM, as were some leading politicians in the GDR. In keeping with the codes of fraternal behavior these criticisms were never, or only rarely, publicized, but reports of them were frequent and reliable enough.[17]

One may assume that the Czechoslovak and East German critics had their backers in Moscow itself. But Kádár had several arguments with which to allay the Brezhnev leadership's fears. In the first place, the NEM had actually begun several months before the invasion of Czechoslovakia. Hence, it would not be a simple task to discontinue it. Politically it would also be highly embarrassing for Moscow to be stigmatized with another negative act of interference in Eastern Europe so soon after August 1968. Second, there was the respect Kádár enjoyed in Moscow: he had "normalized" Hungary; he had taken part in the invasion of Czechoslovakia, though it had been against his better judgment, proving his ultimate loyalty to the alliance; he was developing a good personal and working relationship with Brezhnev.

Kádár could also point to the fact that the new regulations coming into force in January 1968 were not all that revolutionary. They involved the abolition of many of the former central planning indicators and the consequent large-scale shift of many management responsibilities from the center to the enterprises themselves. The central plan now specified only global growth figures—national income, domestic consumption, industrial and agricultural production, construction, and real incomes —and was not binding on individual enterprises. At the same time there were major reforms in the price system: 50 percent of all prices were now to be determined by market forces, and a semifree market was introduced in the industrial sector. Efforts were also made to co-opt economic specialists and to give them a stake in the system in much the same way Ulbricht had done in the GDR in the 1960s (see chapter 7).

The essence of these measures had been contained in the first Czechoslovak economic reform proposals of 1964 and the embryonic Bulgarian reform the following year. As a safety net, those parts of the regulations on the decentralization of Hungarian industry were accompanied by "temporary measures" designed to offset the dangers of too abrupt a change in practice. But they also had the effect of preserving some characteristics of the old command economy that the NEM in theory was out to change. In addition, they helped to bolster the "tradition" of factory managers in a socialist system looking to the center for guidance.[18]

The NEM, therefore, implied no ideological earthquake. But the Soviet leadership, though permissive, must have retained some worries. The "counterrevolution" had only been twelve years ago. The 1964 Czechoslovak reform, harmless though it may have looked in relation to what happened afterward, had started the avalanche. As for the Bulgarian reforms, the Zhivkov regime had prudently got cold feet and rescinded them in July 1968, one month before Czechoslovakia was invaded.

In the event, the Soviet misgivings persisted. The Hungarian NEM was to be a victim not so much of the aftermath of the invasion of Czechoslovakia but of the new offensive for coordination and "directed consensus" in Eastern Europe. This began in earnest at the beginning of the 1970s and had its first major expression in Comecon's Comprehensive Program for Socialist Integration approved in 1971. One year later, at a Hungarian Central Committee plenum in November 1972, the first steps were taken signaling the slowing down and part reversal of the New Economic Mechanism.

The main personal victim of this reversal, Rezsö Nyers, was later to confirm what many had suspected at the time: that the Soviet Union had warned Kádár about the "liberal" character of Hungarian developments. But many Hungarians had begun to have misgivings, too, both inside and outside the party. Though the conservative, or "dogmatic," faction had been defeated decisively in terms of political power, it still had nuisance value and was now joined by some Kádárites concerned about the political and social impact of NEM. The most notable of these was Béla Biszkú. A loyal supporter of Kádár and considered by many as his eventual successor, Biszkú had a strong power base in the police and security apparatus, as well as among party cadres. He was a Politburo member and secretary for personnel, organization, and security. He was an intelligent, capable executive who won considerable respect, as Kádár himself did, through his modest way of life. During the 1970s he became the focus of both outright anti-NEM sentiment (which was small) and the widespread concern that the regime might be deserting the working class. If not capitalism, then capitalist instincts were creeping back into Hungarian society under the guise of the NEM. Many workers, though also loyal to Kádár personally, were beginning to think the same and were putting pressure on their trade union representatives. And in the much freer atmosphere that had been developing in Hungary for over a decade, criticisms like these could be voiced and they made their impact. Many workers were beginning to realize a basic characteristic about the NEM: that it both caused and solidified social inequalities.

The November 1972 Party Central Committee plenum, obviously acting under both Soviet and domestic worker pressure, ordered a wage increase for well over a million of the lowest-paid workers. The following year another increase was ordered. Socially there was much to be said for a centrally directed wage increase; economically it went directly against the basic principles of the NEM; politically, therefore, it was a serious setback for reform and reformers. The same plenum also approved a decision putting fifty large enterprise corporations directly under the control of the Council of Ministers, a clear reversal of the NEM spirit of 1968.[19] The personal consequences were quick to follow: Nyers and György Aczél were dismissed from the Secretariat. The removal of Nyers was clearly a consequence of the partial reversal in economic policy. But in some ways Aczél's removal was just as significant.

Himself an intellectual (of Jewish origin), Aczél was the senior party official for culture and ideology. He was prepared to allow a considerable degree of cultural freedom and of leeway in party debates. Although he was later to be criticized by many Hungarian intellectuals (both establishment and dissident) for what they considered his excessive "prudence" and even cynicism, he usually held their respect both for his own intelligence, his accessibility, and the permissiveness of his policy. Most preferred him to any other senior official and were noticeably nervous whenever the possibility of his removal was rumored.

Such rumors were frequent since Aczél had many enemies in Moscow as well as in Budapest. But he was highly valued by Kádár, who protected him whenever possible. Though removed from the Secretariat in 1973, he remained in the Politburo. He was still, therefore, the "overlord" of the cultural-ideological field, though removed from the everyday supervision of it.

The significance of this demotion lay in the fact that, whereas Nyers was regarded as the symbol of the economic dangers said to be presented by the NEM, Aczél was made the scapegoat for its political, ideological, and cultural spillover. At the November 1972 plenum "certain party organizations" were criticized for allowing open dissent. Among ideological purists in Moscow, Prague, and East Berlin (not to mention Budapest itself) this must have sounded disconcertingly like the Prague Spring, the trauma of which was still fresh in the mind.

Retreat and Recession

But apart from Soviet hostility and domestic opposition, and the possible interaction between the two, economic factors also began to weigh heavily against the NEM. The most important was undoubtedly the repercussions of the first world oil price explosion of 1973. They came from both East and West. At the beginning of 1975 the Soviet Union altered the base of calculation of its oil prices to Eastern Europe (see chapter 4) resulting in an average increase of about 120 percent. At the same time the recession in the West, which was becoming for Hungary an essential market, was sharply reducing demand for Hungarian hard-currency exports, the prices for which, in any case, suffered a sharp drop. It has been estimated that as a result of price changes on the world market, Hungary lost a whole year's national income between 1973 and 1983.[20]

That the Hungarian economy suffered from these external factors there can be no doubt. Where there is some question is over whether the reforms already in operation since 1968 (despite their never being fully implemented) helped, through their flexibility, to prevent even worse injury. It is argued by NEM proponents that the reforms did help, and they would also argue that had the NEM not been shelved for more than five years the seriousness of the phase through which the economy passed after about 1978 could have been avoided or at least mitigated. Be that as it may, the Hungarian economy reverted to greater centralization and more price controls after 1972. It also joined the East European queue for Western credits. This was partly to try to offset the deterioration in the terms of trade and partly to modernize with Western technology. By 1980 this hard-currency debt had reached $9.1 billion gross, compared with $1 billion in 1970.[21] At the same time the terms of trade with the Soviet Union began to deteriorate rapidly: in 1982 the Soviet trade surplus with Hungary was nearly $600 million.[22]

In view of these severe blows falling in a relatively short period, it is not surprising that Hungarian prosperity and economic performance sharply declined. In the late 1960s and early 1970s the economy had scored impressive gains resulting in sharp increases in the overall standard of living. It was during this period that Hungary acquired its reputation as the consumer showpiece of Eastern Europe (displacing Yugoslavia), which it was to retain ever since despite the emerging weaknesses. These weaknesses became apparent about the middle of the 1970s, and they had not been cured a decade later. In the second half of the 1970s Hungary's average annual GNP growth rate was only 2.3 percent. Only Poland and Czechoslovakia were lower. Between 1970 and 1975 it had been 3.4 percent. The first half of the 1980s were worse, and in 1981 and 1983 negative growth was recorded. The economy went through a liquidity crisis in 1982 and had to get Western credits enabling it to pay the interest on its hard-currency debt. Hungary was forced to sharply reduce its investment program—as well as the import of consumer goods. Real wages were no higher in 1986 than they had been ten years before, and there was an estimated annual inflation rate of 7 percent in the first half of the 1980s.[24] Amid the optical consumerism that so dazzled Western (not to mention Eastern) visitors to Budapest, the government was forced to initiate a program of special import curbs in 1982, which, as will be seen later, was to aggravate the already considerable social and even political tensions. (These curbs were finally lifted in 1985.)

These, then, in brief outline, were the economic as well as the political difficulties that began to crowd in on the Hungarian authorities in the middle of the 1970s. Taken together—with the Soviet displeasure predominating—they made retreat from reform scarcely avoidable. The recentralization of economic controls was accompanied by increased repression in the cultural and scholarly sphere, a familiar enough syndrome throughout East Europe, though it was still mild by the general standards of the region. In the wake of Aczél's removal several prominent reform sociologists lost both their jobs and their party cards. The most notable was András Hegedüs, the erstwhile premier from the days of the revolution in 1956. Hegedüs's metamorphosis—from Stalinist whiz kid to mature reformist sociologist—perhaps exceeds even Kádár's in dramatic effect.

One of the remarkable aspects of this "retrenchment," however, was that it was carried on so undemonstratively. So much so that for some Hungarians (and some outside observers) it was almost over before they realized its real extent and character. In fact, many Hungarians began to feel a real change for themselves—and this was for the worse—only when reform was *resumed* and when its painful aspects began to bite some of the more vulnerable sections of society. During the period of retrenchment itself the momentum of the previous prosperity still worked its way through. Looked at in retrospect, and with the benefit of informed revelations, the period of doldrums seems quite well defined. But, living through it, its contours were much less clear. This was largely because, except for a very few, the psychological relaxation that both preceded the reform and came to be associated with it continued and for many was even amplified. The economic aspects of NEM may have been largely rescinded. But the NEM as a way of life continued largely unopposed.

The Second Reform Wave

The retrenchment lasted above five years. During this period the economic situation of all the East European countries worsened. This was partly due to mismanagement and the rigidity of the economic structures in all the countries concerned. But it was more immediately due to the deterioration of the economic situation at the international level. Most East European countries, poor in raw materials anyway, were victims of a hostile global process. As for the prospects, if anything they looked even worse, especially in the energy sphere. Most observers could see the situation moving toward the second great oil price explosion at the end of the 1970s, the effects of which would be just as serious as those of the first. Hungary seemed in an especially precarious position. Considered the most impoverished of all East European countries in natural resources, with between 40 and 50 percent of its national income derived from foreign trade, it was the most vulnerable of all to the vagaries of international commerce and finance.

Its leaders decided that the only hope of eventually mastering these problems was to continue and expand reform. As one official with a flair for American idiom put it privately, they chose to "try and fight their way out of trouble." From an economic standpoint the choice was probably inevitable. But politically and socially it was fraught with difficulty. The conservative forces that had received their satisfaction in 1972 now had to be forced or persuaded to restrain themselves while a new reform offensive was mounted. There was apparently considerable debate over the issue, the strongest argument for reform being that, while improvement through change might be far from sure, deterioration through doing nothing was certain.

But Kádár was too experienced not to have sounded out Moscow before making his final decision. What caused this same Soviet leadership to change its mind? First, they may finally have become persuaded of the political harmlessness of what the Hungarians were proposing. Conversely, they needed no persuading of the seriousness of the economic situation facing Eastern Europe. But there may also have been less specific reasons for Soviet acceptance. These are discussed more fully in chapter 2. Briefly, there was a growing satisfaction, even complacency, about the stability in Eastern Europe, a growing preoccupation with global and East-West problems with a corresponding neglect of immediate regional ones. Eastern Europe was still regarded by the Soviet leadership as the most important single region within the purview of its power considerations. But, at least for the time being, it was not the most urgent.

As usual, policy changes were heralded or symbolized by personnel changes. The most important this time was the departure from the Secretariat of Biszkú in 1978. Biszkú's removal brought two officials to the limelight who were to play important roles over the next few years. Károly Németh, an all-round apparatchik with experience in both agriculture and the Budapest party committee, took over party personnel and organizational affairs. At the same time Ferenc Havasi took over responsibility for implementing economic reform. Németh, who was initially believed reluctant toward reform, was to be named deputy party leader to Kádár in 1985. He had become known for a certain run-of-the-mill forcefulness.[25] But it was Havasi who grew in stature and became known both inside and outside Hungary for his championing of reform.[26]

The wave of reform that began in about 1978 is sometimes referred to by experts as the third wave, the first having been begun at the end of 1956 and the second in 1968. Some call it the "reform of the reform," an expression frowned on by the leadership. It introduced deeper structural changes than ever before. A price reform was initiated, extending the one of 1968. Second, a series of institutional reforms were introduced: some large state industrial monopolies were broken up into smaller units to encourage competition; industry branch ministries were merged into one ministry. This not only cut down bureaucracy and red tape; it also made enterprises less dependent on government direction, since it had been these specialized branch ministries that had exercised most of the control. Furthermore, the "second economy" became in effect legalized, and private plots in agriculture were given a further stimulus.

The "second economy" has received such publicity and played such a key role that it demands special attention. Most of its activity embraces work by small businesses, mainly in the service sector that up to the beginning of the 1980s had been neglected in Hungary. But the twelfth party congress in 1980 set in motion legislation designed to change this situation. New regulations published the following year allowed small businesses to be operated by state firms, small cooperatives, "professional cooperative groups" (PCGs), and "economic work communities" (EWCs).[27] In addition, purely private firms were to be allowed to operate in all fields of economic activity. The "professional cooperative groups" are specialized units having an independent financial status within a cooperative business. Their equivalent in the state sector are the "economic work communities." These are small groups of up to thirty workers who set up a private business in a state factory. They are active in the repairing and servicing of machinery, cleaning and painting, and, on the production side, in die cutting and tool making. They are employees of the factory concerned, use the factory's machinery, and do this private work (at least in theory) in their spare time. What usually happens is that the members of the EWCs—and they often are the most energetic workers—give some of the hours to the EWC that they used to give to the factory as overtime. But their productivity is generally considerably higher when wearing the EWC cap and their rewards greater. As for the factories, their managers generally approve the system as an efficient means of maintenance and service.[28]

The importance of the EWCs and the PCGs should not be exaggerated. By the end of 1985 the EWCs, for example, employed only 140,000 people, over half in Budapest, and their statistical impact on the economy was minimal.[29] But in their service and maintenance capacity their impact was greater than mere figures might suggest. The same can be said about the unprofitable state enterprises like restaurants and food stores leased by private artisans who can employ in all up to ten workers.

As for private firms, this was a sector in which Hungary up to the early 1980s had made very little progress. In 1981 only 3.6 percent of the total work force was employed in privately owned enterprises.[30] This was about half the percentage for both Poland and the GDR. Since then the percentage has only marginally increased. But private entrepreneurs answer a real need, especially in small towns and in the villages where they are mostly engaged in the service sectors. They do much more for the economy as a whole than the few spectacular entrepreneurs in Budapest, who made quick fortunes (by Hungarian standards) for themselves in the 1980s and who tended to give private initiative a bad reputation among the public at large.

Side by side with this legalized "second" economy is the "black" economy, which is illegal but tolerated. It is this economy that, throughout Eastern Europe as well as in some Western European countries, enables a large number of professional people to live much better than their legal income would allow and gives a decent living to many workers which they would not get if they depended solely on their legal income. Some doctors, dentists, and architects, for example, have earned far higher fees in extra than in normal work, as do workers engaged in the evening hours and at the weekend on building private villas, painting, or bricklaying. This kind of work is illegal because earnings from it go straight into the pocket without being declared to the tax authorities or without necessary permits having been obtained. More insidious, because it obviously crosses the boundary of corruption, is the practice of many doctors, dentists, and others giving a service of demanding *bakshish*, or "sliding money." This is the practice that has also become general throughout Eastern Europe. But in Hungary, perhaps because there is more to buy with the money thus procured, it had become rampant by the mid-1970s.

Amid the economic inconsistencies, disappointments, and downright failures in Hungary since the beginning of the 1960s, the one saving grace has been agriculture. Hungarian agriculture has, in fact, been the most successful in the entire Eastern bloc, including the overwhelmingly private agriculture in Poland. By the 1980s yields per hectare were only slightly under Western averages. The methods employed on a handful of state farms had become famous worldwide. The Soviet Union, as well as China, had sent agricultural study teams to Hungary and imported specialized systems and know-how. And these glamorous successes were not achieved at the expense of the peasants. On the contrary, general prosperity steadily increased. Few, of course, like farmers everywhere, would ever be prepared to admit this, and there have been many justified specific grievances. But few Hungarian peasants would now want to return to the days before collectivization. Some may idealize the past, but most would not give up the practical advantages of the present.

Field crops are generally produced by the state or collective farms; most other produce comes from these two sectors plus the private sector. Only some 12 percent of the arable land is either owned or farmed privately. The private sector consists of a relatively small number of private farms and then the huge number of private and household plots allocated to members of the collectivized sector. It has been officially estimated that about half the Hungarian population is involved, in some way and in some degree, in agricultural production. In fact, only about 26 percent of private producers are farmers; 28 percent old age pensioners.[31] This massive involvement in agriculture has important historical and social ramifications. It also has a considerable impact on the contemporary standard of living.

About a third of Hungary's total agricultural production comes from the private sector, most of it from the private plots on the collectives. The private contribution is mainly in livestock and (overwhelmingly) in fruits and vegetables. It has continued to be indispensable and, although in the course of the 1980s its share in total production began to diminish slightly, there is no doubt that it will remain so.[32]

Meanwhile, the success of the public sector in agriculture has been bolstered by two developments in which Hungary has been at the forefront. The first is the democratization of management and of participation on both the state and the collective farms. The second has been the possibility for both to engage in ancillary production or economic activity. This has tapped great (and often unsuspected) imagination and entrepreneurial talent. Some ventures have ended in catastrophe. But many collectives now have brickworks, cement works, small canning factories, and the like. A few have gone in for petrol stations and snack bars. They make farming more remunerative and for some more attractive. And as such they are an extra strength for the regime in its Sisyphean task of trying to lower the average age in agriculture.

Comprehensive Reform Continues

The government and its economic advisers were far from fully satisfied with the results of the new set of reforms initiated in 1978. There were undoubted successes, but these mainly affected Hungary's position and reputation in international trade. By 1985 the country's international liquidity appeared assured in contrast, say, to the situation of Poland, Romania, and Yugoslavia, still faced with severe rescheduling problems. The crucial year, as already mentioned, was 1982 when Hungary, close to bankruptcy, entered the International Monetary Fund and received emergency credits to meet its repayment obligations. It then steadily regained the confidence of Western lenders and in 1984 was the biggest single borrower among the Comecon countries.[33] Thus, although Hungary did not succeed in cutting its total debt by much, it gained considerable relief by becoming commercially respectable again. In regaining this status it was helped by a great improvement in the hard-currency trade balance, which changed from a deficit of well over a billion dollars in 1978 to a $600 million surplus in 1984. But by the middle of 1986 Hungary was in serious difficulties again with the trade deficit of about $400 million for the half-year.[34]

Hungary's trade difficulties with the West overshadowed its difficulties with the Soviet Union. This is partly because Budapest chooses to talk much less about the latter. In the early 1980s it was able to run up a deficit ranging from nearly 700 million rubles in 1980 to 400 million in 1984—which amounted to a de facto credit.[35] But in 1984 the Soviets insisted that Hungary cut this deficit by about 70 percent. The Soviet Union also made it clear that it wanted to stop paying Hungary in hard currency for a portion of its food imports.[36]

These difficulties with both West and East led to higher inflation, investment cuts, import cuts, and lower living standards. Thus the revival achieved in one branch of the economy, international trade (and this was only temporary), helped to induce severe difficulties in others; and these were the ones that mainly affect the consumer. But the regime was still apparently determined to persist with measures that were essential if the structure and workings of the economy were to be made more efficient. It was a courageous policy because it meant postponing real increases in living standards for some time. The policy involved an effective investment policy to restructure industry further, especially the export industries; and improving the price system by allowing efficient firms to make higher profits that would enable them to invest adequately. The egalitarian-inspired subsidy system that had led to unwarranted support for badly managed firms was to be steadily dropped, with the emphasis put on profitability and productivity. In this connection the government wanted to increase the flow of labor from unprofitable to profitable enterprises. This could, it was conceded, lead to temporary redundancies or even unemployment. But to counter this possibility retraining funds were set up to speed up changes in the labor market.

Finally, the authorities took steps to free the flow of capital throughout the economy. One much publicized step was the establishment of a bond market in 1983 through which a number of local authorities and companies have raised capital. More important, though, were changes in the banking system, involving the creation of two new banks, introduced in 1985, designed to provide more competition for deposits, bond issuance, and leasing deals. Another important step in freeing the flow of capital was announced in September 1986. Three more commercial banks began operations at the beginning of 1987. These three, and the two announced the previous year, were to operate as joint stock corporations with shareholdings split between the state, which would be the majority shareholder, and corporate shareholders from companies and cooperatives.[37]

There was another important change made in 1985 that had political as well as economic aspects and recalled earlier reforms made in Yugoslavia. It involved the employees' right to select their director. For many years Hungary had remained rooted in the one-man-management principle in the economy. But now it was obviously felt there was need to induce, as far as possible, something similar to the sense of participation and identification that existed in the "second economy" or in the private sector. The Ministry of Industry would still appoint the directors of about a hundred key enterprises and public utilities, responsible for about 40 percent of total production. But in other enterprises the employees could elect the managers themselves through elected works councils.[38]

This was an important concession. It was apparently slow in getting started because of a distinct timidity on the part of workers to use their new powers. Those elected to the works councils were not usually workers but, as in Yugoslavia until 1976, technocrats. It was part of a recurring pattern of sectional hesitation in the history of the Hungarian reform. Many managers, for example, were reluctant to use the authority granted to them by decentralization. Some local trade union officials, at least at the beginning, had to be chivvied by Budapest to be more militant. It was taking time for attitudes to catch up with change, especially where instinctive suspicions persisted that the changes might not be permanent or even sincere.

The year 1985 also saw an important reform that was wholly political. This was the law making it mandatory (not optional as previously) in both parliamentary and local elections to have two or more candidates. (In parliamentary elections, however, thirty top regime figures were exempted from having to contest seats.) This reform was put into practice for the first time in the national elections in June 1985.[39] It received considerable publicity in the West, and perhaps inevitably its results were hardly in keeping with some naive expectations. But it was not without effect. Twenty-five candidates who were not the regime's first nominees were eventually elected to parliament. There might well have been more but for the regime's tactics aimed either at getting desirables in or keeping undesirables out. But more important than the final results was the interest, even animation, the new procedures aroused at the constituency level, especially where the officially favored candidate was being vigorously challenged. There appeared to be a general feeling that this was a good beginning. And, most important of all, the elections were followed up by a freer spirit in the newly elected parliament itself. One deputy actually voted against the draft budget bill, and seventy-five declared themselves dissatisfied with a minister's reply to an interpellation. Obviously this was not parliamentary democracy in action. But it was probably not the put-up job some cynics thought it was. It did not yet approach the turmoil of Yugoslav parliamentary life in the 1960s. But, except for fitful examples of parliamentary independence in Poland, it was quite new for the Soviet bloc. At the same time there was an impressive decentralization in local government involving greater self-government and financial sovereignty.

The electoral reform was the clearest example so far of overt political change. But the whole question of political reform had hung over Hungarian political life for almost twenty years. At first it was something to be avoided, especially in protestations being made in an easterly direction toward Moscow. For, keeping in mind the Czechoslovak example, where economic reform had become tangled up with political changes disruptive to the system, the Kádár leadership was anxious to repudiate the linkage between the two made so clearly by Ota Šik as early as 1966. Pace Šik, you could have one without the other! At least, so the Hungarians argued. And for many years after the NEM was introduced in 1968 they tried to prove their contention.

But there had always been reformers in Hungary advocating political as well as economic change despite the dangers of doing so. Some did so because they believed in political reform per se. But others, though aware of the dangers, argued that it was essential for the success of the economic reform itself. They were not necessarily champions of liberal democracy and the multiparty system. But they argued that genuine political pluralism of some kind, some political competition that would break the total monopoly of the party, was necessary, for example, to gain the right degree of access to and dissemination of essential information and for those engaged in the economy to have the required sense of participation and even decisionmaking. This was what Šik had in mind in 1966 and was to elaborate on in his productive exile. Economic efficiency depended on political reform. Moreover, many felt that some political institutional change was necessary to guarantee economic changes already made. The ease with which economic reform had first been partially avoided and then shelved after 1972 provided strong argument for this viewpoint.

Views like these were coming out into the open. They may have been taboo for many years because of Prague 1968 and even Budapest 1956. But the taboos were now wearing thin. The Hungarian revolution might still be casting a long shadow, but it meant little directly to many of the more articulate members of Hungarian society. In fact, it had begun to seem to many no more than an excuse for the fossilization of political and moral standards.

Political reform was, therefore, in the air in Budapest at the beginning of the 1980s. Nor was it confined to the yet small but increasingly vocal "dissident" intellectuals, whose impact will be discussed later. It was also a topic in party circles. Privately, quite senior officials would discuss various proposals for reform, traces of which would occasionally find their way into the media. In this respect the situation was the same as in Yugoslavia, although there the arguments usually had an urgency and an openness absent from those in Hungary. Some of the actual proposals were also similar to those being discussed in Belgrade, Zagreb, and Ljubljana. Usually they favored more power for the trade unions, perhaps channeled through their coordinating body, the central council, or through interest groups operating under the umbrella of the national unity organization, the People's Patriotic Front (PPF).

Toward the end of the 1980s the results were still disappointing for the advocates of political change. Neither the most recent People's Patriotic Front nor the trade union congresses had heralded any important changes, despite some expectations. If anything, there now appeared to be still greater emphasis in the official propaganda on the leading role of the party. Still, some progress was being made. Though no one questioned party supremacy, both the People's Patriotic Front and the Central Council of Trade Unions appeared to have acquired at least a foothold in the decisionmaking process. Even more interesting was the sudden flowering, beginning in 1985, of voluntary associations that, in effect, were embryonic interest groups. This resulted from the easing of the legal restrictions on creating them. The most publicized of these was the environmental group that protested against the Gabčikovo-Nagymaros hydroelectric dam, a joint Czechoslovak-Hungarian venture that many considered ecologically harmful.[40] But there were several other interest groups, the most intriguing being a nudists' association at Lake Balaton, and many professional societies.

Growing Dissatisfaction

When taken together, these economic and political changes did add up to a considerable reform effort. They also reflected a willingness to respond to the needs of the situation and the demands, however inchoate, of the nation. But by the middle of the 1980s the level of societal dissatisfaction appeared to be getting dangerously high. Worse still from the regime's point of view, some of the bonds that had undoubtedly developed between rulers and ruled had become seriously frayed. The peculiar form of legitimacy that Kádár had been able to build after 1956 had begun to erode.

The most serious disaffection was among the workers. Many of that small percentage who, through their manifold activities were fairly well off economically, were physically and often nervously exhausted. The large percentage that simply depended on the wages from their daily work had great difficulties making ends meet. Socialism and private entrepreneurship coexisted on far from amicable terms. In fact, a form of class struggle had developed under socialism. The society could not live off socialism alone, yet the rewards available from private enterprise were disruptive rather than fulfilling. At the same time the earlier successes of the economy had raised expectations that could only be fulfilled for a relative few. The rewards were still available but not, apparently, for the vast majority. There was little solidarity in society, which was anyway still feeling the long-term shock effects of the upheavals of war, industrialization, and the imposition of communism. Workers envied farmers, and farmers envied the better-off workers, who, in turn, were envied by the worse-off workers. They all envied the people in professions, the technocrats, and the managers. Life had also become riddled with corruption (see chapter 13). The plight of the pensioners, practically ignored, was often ghastly (see also chapter 13). One of the deadliest comments on Horthy's Hungary was that it was a nation of 3 million beggars. It had been cruelly resurrected in Kádár's Hungary nearly fifty years later. Hungary was out on its own at the top of the world suicide rate table and had a very high rate of mental illness. Alcoholism had become a very serious problem. Drugs were becoming one.

The greatest specific economic grievance was undoubtedly inflation. Consumer prices rose by almost 39 percent from 1980 to 1985.[41] Feelings on this subject were inflamed by what was becoming an annual round of price hikes. The Kádár strategy on price increases, beginning with the first big increase in 1976, has been vastly more skillful than that pursued in Poland by either Gomułka or Gierek. He gave the public plenty of warning and explanation, with due understanding —often in real concessions as well as words—for the hardships they would cause. The increases were generally effective, as from the beginning of each year when festive libations tend to douse the flames of economic bitterness. But the effectiveness of this strategy was becoming progressively weaker, while the groundswell of dissatisfaction became stronger and more audible. It was sharply reflected at the thirteenth party congress in March 1985 when the national trade union leader, Sándor Gáspár, and the Budapest party leader and later premier, Károly Grósz, strongly urged that economic policy be tempered by greater social consideration.[42] It was also a key issue at the parliamentary elections in June 1985 in which fifteen out of seventeen leading union officials were defeated, presumably because of dissatisfaction at their performance in defending workers' interests.

Close observers who might previously have tended to dismiss this dissatisfaction were now becoming impressed by it. But it had generally not got past the vocal stage. It did not appear as bitter as, for example, in Yugoslavia. There appear to have been small strikes of limited duration but, by the middle of the 1980s, feelings were either being transmitted through the "constitutional" channels available—

party organizations and trade unions mainly—or they were subli-
mated through extra work to make ends meet. But the dissatisfaction
had also begun to spawn a small but active group of intellectual
dissidents.

Hungary's dissidents began to surface shortly after 1968. The most
vocal of them at the start were left-wing sociologists and philosophers
who accused the regime of perverting the true Marxist ideals. These
were centered on the "Budapest School," which took its inspiration
from the great Hungarian Marxist philosopher, György Lukács, and
was now led by András Hegedüs. The most prominent of these dissidents were expelled from the party in 1974. They included György
Konrád and Miklós Harasti, two very able writers, and scholars like
Agnes Heller, Iván Szelényi, Ferenc Fehér, Mária Márkus, and György
Márkus. These earlier dissidents were handled skillfully by the regime:
they were allowed to go and stay abroad but could apparently return
when and if they wanted. Konrád, in particular, took advantage of this
tolerance, spending months at a time in Western countries and then
returning—in spite of voicing a frankness abroad that many thought
deliberately provocative. Subsequently, the nucleus of dissent became
enlarged, and several samizdat publications began appearing irregu-
larly, among the best known being *Beszélö* (The Talker) and *Hirmondó*
(The Messenger). The number of active dissenters grew slowly to about
three hundred, with a total "catchment" following of no more than
10,000.[43]

The movement as a whole (if it can be so described) is a many-sided
one. But it can be divided into the following main sectors: the left-wing
"worker" or "urbanist" group; the "populist-nationalist" group; the
"liberal" group; and a group of economists urging both far-reaching
economic and political reform. But these divisions are not watertight
compartments. The liberal and the economists' group, for example,
have both principles and adherents in common. The "worker" group,
some of whose most important members are Jewish, draws some of its
inspiration and mentors from the Budapest School. All of them draw
on long and honorable Hungarian intellectual traditions. In the 1980s
it was probably the "worker-urbanist" and the "populist-nationalist"
groups that attracted most attention. While it is hazardous both to
define and distinguish between the principles and emphases of the
two groups, it might be said that the urbanists are mainly concerned
with domestic considerations and what they consider the cynicism,
materialism, and lack of principle of the Kádár regime, which they

accuse of contaminating society with its lack of values. The compromise after 1956 they consider to have been a rotten one that should be replaced by a unity based on liberty and true socialism. Many of the populists would concur with such sentiment, but their distinguishing characteristic is concern for the condition of Hungarian national minorities in Romania and Czechoslovakia and to a certain extent in Yugoslavia and the Soviet Union. The outstanding literary champion of Hungarian minorities abroad was for many years Gyula Illyés. Since his death it has been Sándor Csoóri. The question of the Hungarian minorities is dealt with in chapter 14. It is undoubtedly an issue causing growing anger in Hungary, although how far this has spread beyond the better-educated strata of society remains open to question.

Most Hungarian dissidents are both politically and personally attractive from a Western point of view. They believe strongly in individual freedoms and in the cause of the oppressed everywhere. They are obviously sincere; they take their role seriously but themselves sometimes less so. While some are obviously outside what could be termed the Budapest establishment, many have mixed easily with intellectuals inside it. In fact, the dividing line between intra- and extraestablishment dissent in Hungary has often been hard to draw. Generally, too, the dissidents have been treated tolerantly by a regime sophisticated enough to know that persecution means publicity, on which dissent thrives. The Hungarian leadership has also known that, mainly because of the excellent contacts many dissidents have with the West, any persecution could have serious effects on its own image. But, even so, the record has not been unblemished. There have continued to be cases of brutality, dismissals, refusals of passport, and other forms of harassment. Most of these appeared to have begun about 1982 and in 1986 seemed to be getting rather worse. But there were also remarkable and inspired examples of lenience. László Rajk, son of the interior minister executed by Rákosi in 1949 and afterward fully rehabilitated, thumbed his nose at the authorities by running a samizdat boutique in Budapest for several years. This, however, was closed at the beginning of 1983. But in 1986 Rajk was allowed to go to teach at an American university, and then returned with no difficulty. The best example of all, however, is that of Hegedüs, whose memoirs about the revolution in 1956 were published in the West, and yet he himself continued to live in Budapest, traveling regularly to Vienna and points west.

At the end of 1986 the regime found itself at loggerheads, not so much with the recognized dissidents, but with what is usually regarded in most communist countries as a pillar of the establishment: the official Writers' Union. Meeting in November 1986 union members, after heated debates, elected a new executive board that had very few party members. The vote was partly a gesture against recent regime victimization of certain writers, the suspension of a well-known literary monthly, and clumsy attempts at manipulation and intimidation by the Central Committee secretary reponsible for culture, János Bérecz. But it also reflected a mounting intellectual dissatisfaction that was becoming an even bigger headache for the Kádár regime.

The problem, nevertheless, was still manageable. Most important was the fact that there were still no real intellectual-worker links, which there had been in 1956 and which there had been so recently in Poland. But there was no cause for complacency, and Kádár must have been very much aware that one of Gierek's great mistakes in the second half of the 1970s was to tolerate, partly also for the sake of appearances in the West, the rise of the KOR intellectuals and their cooperation with the workers. Taking the relation between regime and the dissident intellectuals in Hungary as a contest, which it inevitably became, the advantage generally lay with the regime. Through a clever policy of lack of definition, part lenience, and, at least ostensibly, not taking them too seriously, the regime put the dissidents in a state of defensive, humiliated uncertainty. The intellectuals, despite the personal modesty of many of them, saw themselves in the grand Central European tradition of being the conscience of the nation. The regime obviously demurred. And so, for the time being, did most Hungarians.

Along with the intellectual dissidence was the revival of religiousness in Hungary, especially among the youth. This was perhaps more evident in the provinces than in metropolitan Budapest. In some provincial centers and often in some small towns a new youth Catholic and Protestant elite seemed to be emerging. They were not overtly antiregime, but they embraced a weltanschauung quite different from that which the regime propagandized. Their knowledge of the West was often surprisingly deep, and yet their "internationalism" or "ecumenism" was combined with real patriotism. This they shared with many other younger and older Hungarians. It was a patriotism that was often associated with concern about their fellow countrymen in Romania and Czechoslovakia, and there was a danger that it could become dominated by it. But for the present it could exist independently of it. It was indeed often preoccupied with those deeper questions of Hungary's identity and its fate, which Hungarians have always been asking.

A Calculated Risk

Kádár was probably more concerned about future Soviet policy than domestic intellectual or religious dissidents. He had enjoyed good personal and political relations with successive Soviet leaders. The Soviet factor since 1956 had been of greater importance than any domestic pressure in determining regime policy. This was partly why leadership changes in Moscow had been followed probably with more nervousness in Hungary than in other East European countries. Many were asking what Gorbachev's accession would mean for Hungary. Many proponents of reform in Budapest were optimistic, as were their counterparts elsewhere. In the event optimism appeared to be justified, although initially there was considerable evidence suggesting Kremlin disunity on the subject of reform in Eastern Europe. But in 1987 the relief in Budapest was almost tangible. Indeed, there was scope for confusion and disappointment in the jubilation over Gorbachev. While moderate reformers looked to him for reassurance, radical political and economic reformers were looking to him with hope. Some were going to be disappointed if they lost touch with reality.

As for Kádár himself, he may now have been facing a situation that was not without its irony. Gorbachev was not just giving the green light for the NEM but (whether he wanted to or not) appeared to be encouraging those whose ideas of reform went far beyond anything the NEM had ever envisaged. Indeed he was construed by some as encouraging the calls for political pluralism made by men like Imre Pozgai, the head of the national unity organization, the People's Patriotic Front. The personnel changes forced by Kádár in June 1987 seemed to indicate retrenchment rather than movement. György Lázár moved from the premiership and became deputy party leader under Kádár, replacing Károly Németh who became nominal head of state. Grósz became premier. Havasi moved over from directing the reform program to take Grósz's place as head of the powerful Budapest party organization. Bérecz was rewarded for his stand against the writers with full membership in the Politburo.[44]

These moves were more than musical chairs. Havasi's transfer, Bérecz's promotion, and even Grósz's ascent to be premier first seemed to indicate a hardening of the political, if not the economic, line. A cautious Budapest hand cagily called the changes "balanced but inclining toward conservative."[45] But Grósz soon impressed with his vigor, perceptiveness, and managerial boldness. He was obviously an able man, and some saw him as Kádár's successor. He seemed to have what was wanted.

Kádár no longer did. He seemed to have lost his political touch, his management flair, and his mental alertness. By common consent the man who had dominated Hungarian politics for nearly thirty years was past his best. He had begun to lose some of the popularity and even the respect he once enjoyed. His best service now to Hungary, many thought, would be to retire. The public mood was becoming restive. Both workers and intellectuals were expressing discontent. Hungary was moving into a new political situation with which Kádár seemed unable to cope.

7　The German Democratic Republic

The unique artificiality of the GDR makes it difficult to categorize. There are many nations in search of states, but there must be few states in search of a nation. There is certainly nothing like it in what today is loosely designated as Eastern Europe. Czechoslovakia and Yugoslavia may have been artificial creations of state when they were founded after World War I. Many would say they still are. But few would doubt, especially today, the existence of the distinct nations of which they consist.

Moreover, the GDR's artificiality has made it dependent in quite different ways on two quite different states—the Soviet Union and the Federal Republic of Germany. This dual dependence has had many repercussions, not least on the organization of this book. Many of the foreign policy considerations affecting the GDR have had to be included in chapters 2 and 3. This chapter is mainly a retrospective view of East German internal developments, although, as will immediately be seen, it is impossible to divorce these from the external factors. It begins with a few signposts pointing out the unique interaction of the internal and external in the GDR's history and the different phases through which this interaction has passed.[1]

They are:

1. The relationship with the Federal Republic of Germany. By the end of the 1980s this had gone through four phases. These phases, while not rigidly separate, were clearly identifiable:

   a.　The pre-Wall period from 1949–61. This was characterized by flux, uncertainty about the future of the GDR, and of Germany as a whole. But its most obvious feature was the refugee hemorrhage to the Federal Republic, which, between 1945 and 1961, accounted for about 3 million people.

b. Between the building of the Berlin Wall in August 1961 to the "normalization" agreement at the beginning of the 1970s. This was a period of relative "seclusion" for the Ulbricht regime. The Wall and the atmosphere it signified ensured domestic calm in which the East German populace resigned—and partially reconciled—itself not just to belonging to a separate state but to a state that had willfully isolated itself from the other Germany. The regime, for its part, was freed the worry of "destructive subversion."

c. The period of détente, 1972–80. This period was ushered in mainly by the Soviet Union, the Federal Republic, and the United States over the GDR's head and against its will. Ulbricht's opposition led to his removal in May 1971, and the new Honecker leadership found itself at first reacting nervously to the greatly increased contact détente had brought with the Federal Republic at the popular level. The seclusion of the 1960s was over. But as well as danger, détente also brought the GDR the international recognition its leaders had always demanded.

d. The demise of détente after 1980. This set in with the Soviet invasion of Afghanistan, the suppression of Solidarity in Poland, and the INF controversy. The reaction of the Honecker regime was to seek to preserve the best possible relations in the circumstances with the Federal Republic (see chapter 3). This reaction was due to (1) the economically profitable relations with the FRG; and (2) the increased self-confidence of the regime that had coped with both the dangers of détente and of Solidarity in terms of the reactions of its own people.

2. The relationship with the Soviet Union. This has evolved steadily. Though the overall dependency on Soviet power has remained, the GDR has evolved from a condition of total dependency to being the second most important state in the Soviet bloc—economically and militarily. Yet a basic mistrust between the GDR and the Soviet Union has persisted. The Soviet Union is chary of any East-West German contact over which it does not have total control. The GDR resents the Soviet readiness to neglect its interests in the international arena. Still, despite the differences that have developed, the GDR has supported most Soviet policies and initiatives.

3. The East German regime's domestic policy and the interaction with East German society. Here are meant those measures and reactions that in any other East European country would be subsumed

under "domestic situation." But in the GDR the matter is complicated by the fact that much domestic policy and societal reaction have been influenced by the Federal Republic. It would be a mistake, though, to see East German history solely through the prism of East-West relations. Some of it has been influenced by Soviet and Soviet bloc developments. But much has been endogenous. The problem is that it has sometimes been impossible to distinguish between the influences and their origins.

The Internal "Miracle"

It is as well at the outset to stress the remarkable material progress the GDR has made. Without this progress there would have been no basis for its later importance in East-West relations.

The extent of the progress has been astounding to those remembering the circumstances of the GDR's birth. These circumstances are well enough known. Here only two things need be remembered. The first is that for ten years after World War II it was not certain whether this new state would be effectively born at all. Though most of the doubts that ever existed on this subject were due to an interaction of Soviet pretense and Western gullibility, they did saddle the young GDR with early suspicions of impermanence militating against its being taken as a serious European proposition. These suspicions were immeasurably strengthened by the mass migrations to West Germany already referred to—almost all through the Berlin escape hatch.

Second, the economic future of this new territory looked blighted by massive Soviet depredations on its industry and economic infrastructure in the form of war reparations. Certainly no one in the first ten years after World War II could have foreseen the GDR's subsequent development. During this period it was regarded with loathing and derision—certainly in Western Europe and probably in many parts of Eastern Europe, too. It was seen as both repressive and derelict, especially when compared to the Federal Republic. East Berlin and West Berlin seemed to symbolize the antithesis between pauperization with tyranny and prosperity with freedom.

Even in the early 1960s any visitor who could negotiate the grim procedures and visit East Berlin shortly after the Wall was built could be excused for thinking that the squalor and moon landscape desolation were somehow embedded into an East German permanence. But in August 1986, a quarter of a century later, the same visitor could be excused for succumbing, in spite of himself, to the trumpeted notion of an East German "economic miracle." The restoration and reconstruction had indeed been extraordinary, much of the new construction impressive if not pleasing. East Berlin in the middle of the 1980s still did not give the atmosphere of a real metropolis (which West Berlin still somehow did), but it decisively repudiated the image of the GDR's first years.

Appearances were backed by solid achievement. By the end of the 1960s the GDR had displaced Czechoslovakia and Poland to become the Soviet Union's most important economic partner. During the 1970s it evolved from regional to global significance, becoming one of the world's ten most industrialized countries. It had diplomatic relations with over 130 countries. In Africa and other parts of the Third World its military, technical, and economic advisers had made a considerable impact. In the heavily politicized world of sport its athletes, representing a country of only 17 million inhabitants, had made a colossal impact.

It is necessary to record these achievements—not, of course, with the hyperbolical ululations of the East German propaganda apparatus —but with a sobriety tinged with respect. In concentrating on the GDR's problems of identity and legitimacy, its almost obsessive inferiority complex toward its Western neighbor, and the vicissitudes through which its relations with that neighbor have passed, it is easy to overlook the power and importance the GDR has acquired on its own account.

Several reasons have been advanced for the GDR's successes. They mainly involve popular moods, regime policies, national character, good fortune, and the twin buttressing from the Soviet Union and the Federal Republic.

The decisive popular mood was one of constructive resignation after the building of the Berlin Wall in 1961. The possibility of migration to West Germany had now been cut off for all but the heroic or suicidal few. Now, instead of three alternatives, there were two: to work or to resist. The East German population chose the former. In no way was it dedicating its efforts to the new socialist fatherland, as official propaganda was to proclaim, but to its own individual survival and then well-being. In the GDR in the early 1960s there may still have been many convinced communists to whom the first socialist Germany in history meant something (a quarter of a century later there were far fewer). But they were an insignificant fraction of the population. In fact, in the 1950s and into the 1960s, there was more public spirit in the capitalist Federal Republic than there has ever been in the socialist GDR. But, no matter how much their motives may have differed at different times, the work forces of both Germanies brought to their task a discipline, skill, resourcefulness, and efficiency that history had come to expect from them.

The East German population also combined this efficiency with a passiveness that has characterized the GDR since the worker riots of 1953. This passiveness can be explained by:

(a)   the memory of those riots themselves
(b)   the resignation induced by the Wall
(c)   the fact that the approximately 3 million people who left before the Wall probably embodied the most active oppositional spirit anyway[2]
(d)   the presence in the GDR of between 300,000 and 400,000 Soviet troops
(e)   the efficiency and ubiquity of the East German security apparatus
(f)   the domestic policies first of Walter Ulbricht and then of Erich Honecker that tended to neutralize and even co-opt crucial strata of society
(g)   steady increases in the overall standard of living due to a combination of domestic policy and Soviet and West German assistance.

This passiveness was to play a crucial role in later East German foreign policy. It should not be confused with docility. (The GDR regime had more to worry about with its workers and writers than, for example, the Czechoslovak regime did after 1968.) But it was East German societal passivity during the détente in the 1970s and then during the Solidarity period in Poland that emboldened the regime to try to cling to détente in the 1980s when the cold war reappeared.

With regard to the 3 million East Germans who left before August 1961, it should be stressed that they took away more than just the free spirits that prompted their departure in the first place. They also took valuable economic skills difficult to replace. Their departure, therefore, was a mixed blessing for the Ulbricht regime: what it gained politically, it lost economically, and part of Ulbricht's economic policy in the 1960s can be explained by the need to redeploy and exploit the skills remaining. Among the 3 million defectors was a whole range of skills: managerial, bureaucratic, technical, handicraft, and artisan. The talent that remained was, therefore, at a premium and one of the

GDR's early successes was in harnessing it with such relative effect.

After the building of the Wall in August 1961, Ulbricht could consider the GDR mainly immune from its most lethal danger: the Federal Republic. But the GDR could not be totally insulated from the new currents inside the Soviet bloc itself. A few months before the Wall was built Khrushchev, at the Twenty-second CPSU congress, had launched another de-Stalinization campaign. The Sino-Soviet rift was becoming impossible to hide—even from the public, let alone the party cadres. The effects of de-Stalinization soon began to show in neighboring Czechoslovakia. In Hungary Kádárism was taking shape.

But these currents in the bloc were not strong enough to disturb the internal stability of the GDR that the popular passivity facilitated. There was, however, some restlessness among parts of the working class over high industrial norms and low living standards as well as in the countryside where most of the farmers had been declared collectivized in 1960. There was also a measure of cultural ferment, an obvious spinoff from the twenty-second congress. Professor Robert Havemann, to become the GDR's single best-known dissident, began his "provocative" lectures as early as 1964, for example, and Christa Wolf, one of the greatest postwar German novelists (from either side of the Wall), was making life uncomfortable for cultural policy purists.[3]

But none of the discontent, impatience, or individualism expressed amounted to a threat. In any case the Ulbricht regime did not have to rely solely on historical deterrents to ensure stability. To opposition it responded with outright repression, especially to opposition suspected of having a West German connection. Throughout most of the 1960s there were an estimated 10,000 political prisoners to attest to this.[4] But the repressiveness was not total. Indeed, the exceptions to it were numerous and important enough to make the GDR now look relatively moderate compared with the 1950s. Professor Havemann, for example, though losing his post at Humboldt University as well as his party membership, was never brought to trial and actually imprisoned. The case of Christa Wolf and others was instructive. Their works aroused controversy that included much severe official criticism, but they were publicized rather than victimized. In broader areas of policy the regime also showed some flexibility. In agriculture it shrewdly responded to rural hostility after collectivization in 1960 by keeping many farms in a loose collective form of organization for several years. This enabled the peasants to keep part of their land and most of their livestock at their private disposal. Full collectivization was not, in fact, completed until 1976.

But it was in the task of securing economic efficiency and higher living standards that the Ulbricht regime showed itself the most flexible and innovative. Quantitatively, the economy was performing impressively. In 1964 East German industry was producing what the whole of the Third Reich produced in 1938. But it was a typically rigid, Stalinist-structured, unsophisticated economy, more and more achieving less and less than its potential. The East Germans, therefore, joined the general East European procession toward reform after the green light had come from Moscow in 1962. They were in fact the first East European regime to do so. In 1963 they announced a whole new system of economic planning and management, to become known as the New Economic System for Planning and Management (NES). It involved considerable decentralization and autonomy at the factory level, much greater expertise in management, more attention to profitability, and freer play for the laws of supply and demand. Both in outline and in many of the details, the New Economic System was similar to the reforms being discussed in Bulgaria and Czechoslovakia.[5] In terms of subsequent economic reforms it may appear rather modest. But in the first half of the 1960s (and certainly in terms of what many observers had expected of the Ulbricht regime) it was almost startling in its boldness.

The NES was accompanied by a strategy of trying to co-opt the growing economic managerial and technical strata into the economic decisionmaking process. The new socialist middle class was granted extensive consultative and often executive powers in the economy. In no sense did they take over the economy, which remained firmly in the hands of the party political leadership. But they were given an important stake in it, and hence in the future of the GDR as a whole. The system that evolved on this basis was aptly called "consultative authoritarianism" by the late Peter Christian Ludz. It offered power, initiative, and responsibility—as well as generous incomes and perquisites—to many of the best brains in the GDR. It also appealed to the historic German dedication to public service and civic conscience. It met with a powerful response. The result was a growing sense of identity with the East German state on the part of the new middle class. Mutatis mutandis, the technocrats became for the GDR what the officer corps had been for Imperial Germany.[6]

Gunther Mittag and Erich Apel, probably the regime's two most senior economic officials, were the architects of the NES.[7] But Ulbricht himself was the principal strategist of the reform policy it symbolized.

A personal assessment of Ulbricht can be found elsewhere.[8] Here it can be simply said that posterity is beginning to appraise him more favorably than his contemporaries did. He was associated with some of the worst aspects of the Stalinist order in Eastern Europe, and the Berlin Wall is considered his monument. An old Cominternist, he was considered loyal above all to Soviet dictates. But before dismissing him as the personification of East European Stalinism par excellence, it is worth remembering the reformist aspects of his domestic policies in the 1960s, above all his economic and social strategies outlined above. He was, moreover, one of the ablest East European leaders since 1945. As for his Soviet loyalties, he was to find these increasingly difficult to reconcile with what he considered to be the vital interests of the GDR.

Ulbricht also considered that the GDR had its *own* contribution to make to what was often called the "treasury of Marxism-Leninism." He never preached or practiced anything at variance with the Moscow line, but, on the other hand, he was not always content to wait for the Moscow lead. In April 1967 he announced a variation on the New Economic System that he called the Economic System of Socialism. This new system was designed to graft on to the NES the latest findings in the "scientific-technological" revolution—of cybernetics, systems theory, etc. They were to be integrated into the GDR's planning process. Ulbricht also had strong views on the social relations prevailing in the GDR: the stage of capitalism had now been passed, and East Germany was in the process of building a human community or *Menschengemeinschaft*.[9] There may have been nothing very original in the ideas underlying either the Economic System of Socialism or the Menschengemeinschaft. But Ulbricht considered that he had the perfect right to fashion these in a particular East German mold. He was eventually to anger the Soviet leadership by his condescending attitude and by his implied claims that in some respects the GDR was ahead of the Soviet Union. There were also several in his own Politburo —not least Erich Honecker—who were disconcerted by his presumptuousness and ideological individualism.[10]

The External Dangers

For about six years after the building of the Wall the East German regime was generally left to its own devices. But it was not totally free from external alarms. The Cuban missile crisis of 1962, for example, raised the specter of a world war in which the GDR would have been one of the first casualties. But the most frightening shape of things to come must have been Khrushchev's overtures to West Germany in 1964 shortly before his fall, overtures crystallizing in the visit to Bonn of his son-in-law, A. L. Adzhubei. For the GDR it was evidence of Soviet unreliability, just as the fall of Khrushchev himself was evidence of Soviet unpredictability. In the Federal Republic, too, the departure of Adenauer, the shedding of the Hallstein Doctrine, and the rustle of a new policy toward the GDR began to cause nervousness (see chapter 3).

By 1967 external factors began to press, and for the next five years they were to expose the GDR's vulnerability once again. Two of these, the Prague Spring of 1968 and the Polish upheaval of December 1970, affected the stability of an alliance that, after all, was the bedrock of the GDR's existence. The third was the gradual but accelerating process of East-West détente that Ulbricht feared could undermine the foundations of that existence.

The Prague Spring was less dangerous to the GDR than Solidarity in Poland twelve years later. But Ulbricht correctly saw it as a possible threat to East German stability and perhaps to its ultimate survival. In fact, moving into the leadership vacuum created by the departure of Khrushchev, he, along with Gomułka, seemed initially to be taking the lead in stressing the danger coming from Prague. These two were reported to have been strong advocates of decisive action in 1968, urging an invasion well before the Soviet leadership could steel itself for the task.[11] Only two and a half years later Gomułka himself was to be driven from power and Ulbricht reminded that, whatever the problems presented by Czechoslovakia, it was Poland that was the GDR's more vital permanent concern.

The real threat from Poland, though, was to be reserved for Ulbricht's successor, Honecker, in 1980–81. What now threatened Ulbricht was the gathering pace of détente and the changes it promised in the European diplomatic landscape. He was old enough to remember the Hitler-Stalin treaty of 1939, even Rapallo in 1922, as well as the vagaries of Soviet and Comintern policies. He had fully realized the dangers to the status quo and was probably surprised by the fact that they had not receded after the invasion of Czechoslovakia. But the invasion had only killed one bird with one stone. The second bird—the détente process—was not killed. On the contrary, it prospered.

It would certainly have been no comfort to Ulbricht to know that many others had made the same miscalculation. None, he would have insisted, would suffer more from it than the GDR. Ulbricht had apparently come to the conclusion earlier that there was a close identity between the interests of proletarian internationalism and those of the GDR. Was not the GDR, after all, not only a product of proletarian internationalism but also one of its great tangible successes? But now the interests of the two seemed to be colliding. At the Warsaw Pact summit meeting in March 1969 the decision was made to resume, in stronger form, the overtures for East-West détente. The references in its final communiqué to the Federal Republic were remarkably restrained, and a call was made to resume negotiations on a conference on European security in particular that had been interrupted by the Czechoslovak crisis.[12] The following May Gomułka, Ulbricht's closest ally of only a few months ago, announced Poland's readiness to begin negotiations with the Federal Republic on the normalization of relations.[13] And in the fall of 1969 a social-liberal government led by Willy Brandt assumed power in Bonn determined to press for normalization with the Soviet Union and Eastern Europe. The Soviet Union responded readily and cooperatively.

The turn of events, it is true, did have some consolations. Brandt's Ostpolitik was not so blatantly aimed at outflanking the GDR as was the policy of his predecessors. Coming after the invasion of Czechoslovakia it recognized that negotiating with East European governments independently of Moscow was futile. It finally repudiated the Hallstein Doctrine, which laid down that no government having diplomatic relations with East Berlin could have them with Bonn, and cleared away virtually all obstacles to the international recognition of the GDR, something the East German regime had been pursuing for years.

The Ulbricht regime certainly wanted international recognition, from the Federal Republic above all. For nothing would solidify the fact of two Germanies more than this. But what alarmed it—and there was no stronger testimony to its continuing sense of weakness—was the unashamed candor of Bonn's new Ostpolitik in its desire for multifaceted official and nonofficial contacts with the GDR. Ulbricht was not prepared to run the risks in return for the political victory of official recognition. He wanted recognition, certainly, but with contacts kept to a minimum, a posture to become known as *Abgrenzung* ("delimitation"). But the Soviet Union, as Angela Stent says, now "considered that the benefits of rapprochement with West Germany outweighed the risks of undermining the GDR's security."[14]

Ulbricht could not agree, and by May 1971 he had become such an obstacle to Soviet policy in Europe that he was ceremoniously pushed aside from the party leadership, though he remained head of state. The treaty normalizing relations between Bonn and East Berlin was signed the following year. He had to be disposed of before it could be signed. His departure was unlamented, neither East Germans nor West Germans regarding it as anything but a welcome break with a discredited past. But his impact should not be underrated. He played the major role in building up the second German state. He also stood up to the Soviet Union in a way few East European leaders have ever done. Coming from any other leader his policy would have been seen as one of nationalism. But the GDR and nationalism seemed incompatible notions. Hence in his differences with Moscow he had practically no popular support in the way Tito, Nagy, Gomułka, Hoxha, Dubček, and Ceauşescu all had. Such was the idiosyncracy of the GDR that, for most East Germans, nationalism meant rejecting their state rather than defending it. They approved what the Soviets were doing in this case.

The Honecker Era

The new party leader, Erich Honecker (born 1912), was nineteen years younger than Ulbricht. Insofar as the term means anything in the GDR, he was a "home" communist while his predecessor had been the "Muscovite" par excellence. A native of the Saarland, Honecker spent ten years in a Nazi prison between 1935 and 1945. He had made his career in the GDR in the regime's youth organization and had later been Politburo member and Central Committee secretary responsible primarily for security matters.

No one who had followed Honecker's early career would have had any idea of the flexible, adventurous leader he was to become. He was considered an efficient, rather colorless apparatchik, ostentatiously loyal to Moscow and a strong advocate of as much Abgrenzung from the Federal Republic as possible. He proved his point on the latter by supervising the building of the Berlin Wall in 1961, the single deed for which he was best known before becoming leader of the SED. Honecker was a *party* man by temperament and experience, most at home with central and provincial apparatchiki, among whom later he was to dispense considerable patronage. Personally, he radiated a Germanic, no-nonsense approach. No one suspected that he would lead the GDR down unexpected paths.

Within eighteen months of his assuming the leadership, the situation of the GDR changed dramatically. In September 1971, after long negotiations, agreement was reached on the status of Berlin and its relations with the West. Some aspects of the agreement must have been profoundly disturbing for the East German leadership. In the first place the GDR, though active in the negotiations, was not a signatory of the final agreement, which was signed by the occupying powers of Berlin: the Soviet Union, the United States, Britain, and France. Second, the unofficial links between Berlin and the Federal Republic, to which the GDR had vehemently objected, were to be maintained and even developed. Third, the Soviets were forced to agree that they, not the East Germans, would supervise the transit links between West Berlin and West Germany. Finally, the Soviets agreed that West Berliners could make regular visits (not just on special holidays as had previously been the case) to East Berlin and to the rest of the GDR.[15]

The West Berliners' response was overwhelming. In the course of 1973 there were 4 million visits from West Berlin, and 3 million West Germans used the transit routes to visit West Berlin.[16] The GDR's seclusion, seemingly assured by the Berlin Wall, had been breached by the Berlin Accords—with the full agreement of the Soviet Union.

But the four-power agreement on Berlin was just the prelude to the Basic Treaty (*Grundvertrag*) between the two Germanies themselves on the normalization of relations. Agreement was finally reached on the treaty in November 1972, shortly before the parliamentary elections in the Federal Republic that brought a big victory for Chancellor Willy Brandt's Social Democratic party. The GDR made important gains from the treaty. It achieved de facto recognition from Bonn, though with the exchange of special missions rather than embassies, and eventually full diplomatic recognition from the world in general. It entered the United Nations in 1973. The West Germans dropped their previous claim to speak for all Germans and in effect recognized the GDR's territorial integrity and sovereignty. But the failure to get full diplomatic recognition from Bonn, as well as any recognition of specific GDR citizenship, were major disappointments. The East Germans were also forced to ease various kinds of contact between the GDR and the Federal Republic. The result was a flood, not only of West Berliners but also of West Germans to the GDR—2.3 million of them in 1973.[17] Nothing like the same concessions, of course, were granted for travel the other way. There were few hindrances for older East Germans, but now, under the rubric of "urgent family need," a trickle of younger ones could now apply for brief visits to the West. If the Berlin Accords had breached the GDR's seclusion, the Grundvertrag had finally broken it.

Honecker's response to this new situation was reflected in both style and policy. He was determined to make the best of both agreements, to proclaim them as victories for both socialism and the GDR. He was also at pains to commend the Soviet Union for standing up so successfully for the rights of the GDR and for yet another diplomatic triumph.

But what the Honecker leadership really thought about the diplomatic revolution that had just taken place was shown by the new emphasis in its domestic policy. As A. James McAdams puts it: "the country's new circumstances . . . called for a new ruling formula. While Walter Ulbricht might once have been able to present the GDR as a totally 'secured' system, isolated from its enemies and free to come up with its own novel solutions to the challenges of socialism, the Berlin accord and the Basic Treaty both demonstrated that East Germany was no longer in such a privileged position."[18] McAdams goes on to say that Honecker now "assumed the defensive posture that was suited to a leader of a penetrated system."[19] Abgrenzung now became a many-sided policy, ideologically and practically. So much so that the leadership virtually declared the GDR in a state of siege just when the portcullis had been lifted and literally millions of West Germans were pouring through the gates.

The grimmest aspects of Abgrenzung were soon to be seen in the sophisticated new border devices for slaughtering would-be escapers. But these, together with a much heightened policy security, were but the outward signs of a new policy stressing all-round vigilance, class struggle, and a rejection of things Western. Ulbricht's old ideas of Menschengemeinschaft were swept aside amid much greater stress on the role of the party. There was also more emphasis than in Ulbricht's last years of alliance with, and obedience to, the Soviet Union. Ideological education was brought even more to the fore, as was paramilitary education in the schools. There was also a tendency to downplay common historical and cultural links with West Germany and to hammer home socialist distinctiveness. Finally, in 1972, all remaining forms of private ownership and semiprivate ownership in the economy were nationalized. This was a policy on which there was virtual unanimity in the new East German leadership. But what was not entirely clear at the beginning was whether Honecker had the necessary personal authority. He evidently soon gained the support of the Brezhnev leadership in Moscow. But in East Berlin the picture was less simple. His main personal rival at the time appeared to be Willi Stoph, premier since 1964, slightly younger than Honecker himself but with a wealth of administrative experience including periods as minister of the interior and of defense.[21] But because of the very nature of the GDR, especially its crucially strategic importance to the Soviet Union, there were other key figures in its ruling elite who had a special relationship with Moscow and hence needed careful handling. One was undoubtedly the veteran Heinz Hoffmann, minister of defense from 1960. Even after Honecker had become undisputed master in the GDR, Hoffmann, combining a forceful personality with his experience and institutional authority, was known for a prickly independence. Only in 1985 when Hoffmann died and Honecker was able to replace him with an old friend, General Heinz Kessler, could he feel more in control of the military establishment.[22] With Erich Mielke, the long-serving minister of state security, Honecker's relationship was even more complicated. Mielke was believed to have owed his prime loyalty to the KGB, and it was certain that Moscow would want a man it could implicitly trust in the Central European spying grounds. Once again, therefore, though Honecker himself had intimate connections and previous experience in security matters, he had to concede Mielke that untouchable quality that stemmed only from a vital Soviet connection.[23]

He had to tread carefully, therefore, in the military and security sectors. Nor did his early efforts to strengthen his regime elsewhere meet with much success. In fact, they led to an important miscalculation that later had to be reversed. Ulbricht's death in August 1973 left the position of president of the State Council (nominal head of state) open. Stoph was appointed to the post—apparently a clear demotion. Similarly, Gunter Mittag, one of the ablest economic officials the GDR had ever had, lost his position as Central Committee secretary and became a first deputy premier. Though less obviously, this was also a demotion since it removed Mittag from his important party post precisely when the authority of the party was being reasserted. Stoph was replaced by Horst Sindermann as premier, and Werner Krolikowski took Mittag's post. Both had been provincial party secretaries—Honecker's favorite clientele. But neither Sindermann nor Krolikowski proved competent in the face of the serious new economic problems caused by the world oil explosion and economic recession. In an extraordinary turnabout in October 1976 they were both dismissed and Stoph and Mittag brought back to their former positions.

With Mittag, it was simply a case of expertise being needed in a right situation. With Stoph, whose abilities were respectable but hardly indispensable, it seems to have been more a matter of Honecker reassuring the older guard of the party while he himself both expanded and solidified his own power. He followed the fashion among Soviet bloc party leaders of taking the position as president of the State Council. This enabled him to represent the regime internationally without undermining protocol, an important consideration now that the GDR had been catapulted on to the world scene. But Honecker next consolidated his party strength at the ninth SED congress in May 1976 by packing a large Politburo of twenty-eight full and candidate members with many of his own supporters. Nine of the new Politburo members had been youth organization officials. They were later to be joined by yet another, Egon Krenz, who also became Central Committee secretary for security matters. Krenz's career had closely resembled that of Honecker, whose protegé and annointed successor he was, by 1985, reputed to be.

Regime Concessions to Society

But before his leadership might have been fully recognized elsewhere, Honecker began to exert it in the economic sphere. In December 1970, already before Ulbricht resigned, the New Economic System was largely discontinued, and many aspects of the economy reverted to the old command system. It was a reversion that did have certain advantages in that Ulbricht's policy had tended to concentrate investment and research on a relatively few large projects. Other projects tended to be neglected and could not meet their production quotas, thereby setting off a chain reaction through many parts of industry. By the late 1960s, therefore, Ulbricht's reform needed reform itself.

But where Honecker's economic policy began pursuing a new path was in the greater stress now placed on living standards, housing, and consumer goods generally. One reason for this change was the fear of any repercussions from the Polish workers' revolt of December 1970 that had toppled Gomułka (see chapter 5). This had varying effects on economic policy throughout Eastern Europe. But there was a deeper, more localized reason for it in the GDR. It should be seen as the other, friendlier side of the Abgrenzung coin, as part of a social contract Honecker was offering to a reluctant East German population that, through West German television and its own numerous contacts with West Germans, could now see what life on the other side of the Wall was really like and that wanted at least some attempt by its own regime to copy it.[24]

Nor was it only the changes in the regime's economic policy that could be explained in those terms. Judging from the shrillness of the Abgrenzung policy, with its stress on ideological purity and conformity, it might have been expected, for example, that cultural policy and policy toward the churches would have been totally rigid. But, as will be seen, Honecker's attitude toward East German writers in the early 1970s was ambivalent, certainly less severe than many expected. And on the far-flung accessibility of West German television programs—a veritable ideological cancer—his approach became relaxed, almost casual. With the East German Evangelical church, although he would have liked an advantageous modus operandi, he was, as will be seen later, eventually prepared to settle more for a live-and-let-live relationship, not without benefit for the church.

The Economy: Policy, Difficulties, and Reform

Honecker's intention to restructure economic priorities was evident in the five-year plan of 1971–76. A considerably greater volume of consumer goods and services were planned for the first half of the decade, and an ambitious housing construction campaign was launched. At the same time there was a corresponding cut in industrial production and investment.

But it was only two years into the Honecker era that international factors began profoundly to affect East German economic development. In economics as in politics, therefore, the GDR became more clearly than ever the hostage of global events over which it had little or no control. Not all external influences on the East German economy were damaging, of course. The various forms of subsidization from the Federal Republic brought the GDR a unique advantage and partly explains its successful economic progress. While not so important as to make the difference between prosperity and destitution, they have made a valuable cushion for the GDR economy, bolstering it in good times or easing its fall in bad.

But this consistent subsidization did little to help the GDR ward off the dangers resulting from the OPEC oil price explosions in 1973 and 1979–80 and their effect on world trade generally. The change in the Soviet pricing system for oil, effective from the beginning of 1975, hit the GDR perhaps harder than any other East European country. This was because of the GDR's poverty in energy supplies, on the one hand (except for an abundance of inefficient and ecologically disastrous brown coal; see chapter 13), and of the inexorable demands of an advanced economy, on the other. Some 93 percent of the GDR's oil supplies came from the Soviet Union, and after 1975 the Soviet oil bill shot up by more than 100 percent. In the early 1980s the East Germans were paying the equivalent of about $25 a ton for Soviet oil. Honecker himself complained in 1979 that the GDR was having to export three times more produce for a ton of Soviet oil than it had before 1973.[25]

The world chain reaction set off by the oil price explosion also seriously affected the GDR. The recession frustrated East German commercial aims, for one thing. But the most serious consequence was the international hard-currency debt the GDR began to accumulate. This accumulation, facilitated by the glut of petrodollars in Western financial institutions, was partly caused by the need for protection against the rigors of the new international situation and partly by the new policy of import-led growth, which all the East European states except Czechoslovakia were enthusiastically pursuing. Some idea of the growth of the GDR's indebtedness can be gained from the fact that in 1971 its gross debt stood at only $1.4 billion. By 1975 it had risen to $5.9 billion, by 1979 to $10.9 billion, and by 1981 to its highest ever of $14.2 billion.[26] In terms of absolute gross indebtedness, the GDR came third after Poland and Yugoslavia, Eastern Europe's two most insatiable borrowers.

In the early 1980s the difficulties of repayment were to become one of the GDR's most serious economic headaches. With about $4 billion in repayments due between 1983 and 1985 the government was forced to do what most other East European hard-currency debtors were doing: reduce imports and increase exports as far as possible. Here the special advantage it enjoyed through the "West German connection" was very important. The GDR shifted the pattern of its Western trade even more to the Federal Republic, with which the standing "swing credit" provision enabled it to avoid paying hard currency for many West German imports.[27] In 1982, for example, while imports from the other OECD countries fell by over 30 percent, with the Federal Republic they increased from $2.5 billion in 1981 to $2.9 billion.[28]

All the difficulties were to show in the economic results achieved between 1975 and 1985. In the first half of the 1970s the results had been good. In terms of Net Material Product the five-year plan for 1971 to 1975 was actually overfulfilled (5.5 percent achieved against 4.9 percent planned). Such progress, of course, was undramatic indeed compared with the headlong rush of its eastern neighbor, Poland. But

Poland was rushing toward catastrophe, which it had encountered by the time the next five-year planning period was over in 1980. It was, indeed, during the second half of the decade that the impact of the steep downturn in the world economy began to appear in all the European countries, East and West. The East German economy was no exception; in no single year of this planning period was its overall Net Material Product target met, and the overall target of a 5.1 percent increase was met to only 4.3 percent. In 1978, which in Eastern Europe generally was the worst year of the quinquennium, the achievement was only 3.6 percent against a planned 5.2 percent.[29] These results were by no means disastrous. But they were disappointing, and they gave strong arguments to those who had been pressing for major economic reform.

By the end of the 1970s the East German leadership, especially Honecker himself, had become convinced that important operational changes were necessary. The growing indebtedness to the West, a mounting trade deficit with the Soviet Union, the second oil price explosion, and the sluggish performance of the economy as a whole left no doubt that the time for tinkering was past. The Politburo report to a Central Committee meeting at the end of 1979, at the beginning of the second world oil price shock, dramatically summed up the situation: "We are not just dealing with the aggravation of an already complicated situation. A *new* situation confronts us."[30]

Reform and the Living Standard

The East German leadership responded with resolution to this "new situation" by developing what it called the "economic strategy for the eighties." The ten points of this strategy were presented by Honecker to the tenth SED congress in April 1981. They could be boiled down to a few essentials: (1) the acceleration of scientific and technological progress to face the electronic revolution; (2) the cutting down in the use of energy supplies in industry, a sphere in which the GDR, like all the East European countries, was notably profligate; (3) the gearing of investment policy more to modernizing existing plant than to commissioning new projects; (4) the raising of labor productivity. The essentials could all be subsumed under "intensification," propelled from above, and the need for savings in all facets of the economic process was reflected in the elevation of the principle of "cost accountability" to form a trinity with "direction" and "planning" in economic policy generally.[31]

The main aspect of this new strategy was the organizational restructuring of the economy; this was carried through in 1979–80. The previous three-tiered structure of industry, involving the ministry, the associations of enterprises (VVBs, *Vereinigung volkseigener Betriebe*, or Association of People's Enterprises), and the individual enterprises (VEBS —Volkseigener Betriebe) themselves, was altered by abolishing the middle tier of VVBS. (The VVBS had been established under the reforms of the 1960s and had survived their discontinuation.) The individual enterprises were then grouped in 132 larger combines (or *Kombinaten*). Each Kombinat had between twenty and forty factories with an average work force of about 25,000 employees.[32] The new Kombinaten had wide powers and responsibilities.[33] They now incorporated research laboratories and establishments as well as factories making components and spare parts for the main product. In addition, their competences in foreign trade were considerably increased. At the same time direct control from the center, from the economic ministries in East Berlin, was considerably relaxed with more powers devolved to the Kombinaten.

This reorganization and decentralization went a long way to provide the streamlining the leadership wished. It also revealed and unshackled still more managerial talent in the directors of the Kombinaten and their managers.[34] In this sense the new economic strategy was a continuation of Ulbricht's old socioeconomic policy of co-opting and rewarding the economic-technical strata. It was generally agreed by 1985 that the new structure was working reasonably well. It was also attracting considerable attention from both East and West, with the Soviet media pointedly praising it on several occasions.

One aspect that attracted the Soviets was the economic use of manpower under the reorganization, since both theirs and the East German economy had become increasingly short of labor. In this context the Schwedt "Initiative" was particularly relevant. It was an experiment begun in 1979 at a large petrochemical complex practically on the GDR-Polish border. There were not enough workers available to man the planned extension of the complex, so the management launched a drive for the "rationalization of the work force." This meant cutting the work force in the original part of the plant to provide workers for the extension. But the work norms at the original part of the plant allegedly stayed the same, while production and performance generally kept the same level through rationalization, mechanization, and automation. Bonuses were paid for good performance and adaptability, and half the wages fund saved at the original plant went back into the so-called fund for "economic stimulation" (i.e., incentives).

With the introduction of the Kombinaten, the impact of the new economic strategy as a whole, and the single-minded reorientation of Western trade to take advantage of the protective West German link, the East German economy generally did better in the 1980s than any other Soviet bloc economy. In 1982, the bleakest year throughout the region, the growth of the Net Material Product was down to 2.6 percent, but the next year it was up to 4.4 percent. In 1984 it was 5.5 percent, and in 1985 the growth was 4.8 percent in a year that was generally a poor one for other East European countries. In general, East German spokesmen were satisfied when surveying progress during the five-year planning period, in spite of the fact that the average yearly Net Material Product achieved—4.5 percent—was a few decimal points behind the originally planned 5.1 percent.[35]

But there were still serious domestic problems. As a recent paper submitted to the U.S. Congress points out, the most important were:

1. An excessively labor-intensive system of production, as well as lost man-hours from too frequent disruptions of the production process.
2. Low capital productivity.
3. Inadequate application of technology.
4. Spiraling costs of energy resources.
5. Wasteful use of materials.[36]

These problems were persisting despite the regime's awareness of them and some considerable success over the years in alleviating them. One the whole, then, by the standards of Eastern Europe and the Soviet Union, the East German economy was, both materially and managerially, in good shape.[37] But the GDR is not as other socialist countries are. It cannot be satisfied with advantageous comparisons with its socialist allies. Its yardstick is across the Elbe and over the Wall—or at least that of most of its people is. And here the regime has always been in a dilemma. Systemic reform would unquestionably improve the performance of an economy like East Germany's. But even if the East German leaders were ideologically and temperamentally disposed to such reform, they would be inhibited by a consideration unique to the GDR's very existence. Their claim has not simply been that the GDR is the second German state but, more important, that it is the first socialist German state. As such, its "socialism" has to be carefully guarded to distinguish itself from the other, "capitalist," German state. Hence, though systemic reform might be deemed necessary, it could never be allowed to dilute socialism too much.

The East German strategy has been based on modernization and reorganization. As such, it is conservative. There is little of the market mechanism boldness that characterizes the Hungarian, Chinese, or Yugoslav economies. Indeed, the East Germans have tended to be dismissive about the alleged magic of the market. They might also take comfort in the better performance of their "conservative" economy compared with the "liberal" Hungarian (ignoring the benefits of the West German cushion). But by the late 1980s the time seemed not far away when the diminishing returns from their own system would force even them to consider the benefits of the market and not solely its dangers. In a situation demanding reform, reorganization might not be enough.

Finally, a word on the standard of living, the material lot of the ordinary East German. How was Honecker's side of the social contract working? That living standards had improved in the quarter of a century since the Wall and especially during the 1970s could be denied by no one. But they continued to lag considerably behind rises in Domestic Material Product and labor productivity. The increases in net income and in retail trade, the two figures that mainly reflect general living standards, might often exceed the amounts planned. But these planned increases were all too often memorable only for their modesty. Certainly the mass of workers were in the middle of the 1980s still far from getting their proportionate share of the GDR's overall economic growth.

But official statistics can distort in both directions. The actual standard of living was not as rosy as they suggested. At the same time they did not cover the whole gray and black areas of economic activity. These areas had generally the same character and characteristics of their counterparts in other East European countries. But—yet again—in the GDR they had a unique and crucial ingredient: the deutsche mark (DM), the currency of the Federal Republic.

It is impossible even to estimate realistically how many West German marks have been in East Germany, circulating or static, at any particular time. They have entered legally and illegally, in smaller and larger sums. Obviously the GDR authorities have been anxious to lay their hands on as many of them as possible, both by levies on West German visitors (often varied capriciously for political ends) and inducements within the country itself. One of the best-known means of doing this has been through the use of special hard-currency shops, the type all

East European regimes use for the same purpose. "Intershops" have sold top-quality goods only for deutsche marks. (They were originally only for West Germans but were later opened for East Germans with deutsche marks.) To soak up purchasing power represented in the ostmark (the domestic currency) there also exist the "Exquisit" and "Delikat" shops. The former specializes in fashion and clothes, the latter mainly in delicatessen products.[38]

The whole "Intershop" initiative has been a howling commercial success and has satisfied many people. In that sense it can be seen as a ploy in the social contract policy. But the blatancy with which it was operated only exacerbated the divisions in society. The GDR, the saying went, now became divided into three classes: those who had deutsche marks and used "Intershops"; those who had plenty of ostmarks and used the "Exquisit" and "Delikat" shops; and the third and by far the biggest class, those who had no DMs and few ostmarks and could afford to use none of them. Those with relatives or contacts in West Germany obviously enjoyed a considerable advantage. The DM in the 1970s became an essential second currency in the GDR and for some transactions was indispensable. There were reports of some factory workers demanding to be paid partly in deutsche marks, and feelings grew so strong that the number of "Intershops" was reduced in 1977.

The basic demoralization the whole deutsche mark issue tended to induce was, of course, known to Honecker. It is believed to have caused divisions among the top leadership, with Willi Stoph, as to be expected, taking the puritanical conservative line. But Honecker's laissez-faire approach was attractive to the large and growing number of "successful" men and women in the GDR, mainly those in economic management and technocratic positions, but also those in the professions, the arts, and sports. It was yet another aspect of co-opting the socialist middle class that had begun under Ulbricht. If success could be achieved in this, then the concomitant damage of social divisiveness and corruption would simply have to be sustained. The decision in 1980 and 1981 (also rumored to have caused controversy in the leadership) to import several types of Western cars should also be seen in this context. Honecker had begun by indicating bigger material concessions for the workers. To some extent he had made these. But it was the better off who continually seemed to be doing better. This was nothing like the "class war under socialism" that threatened to break out in Hungary. But it was not the socialism on which the GDR was supposed to be based.

The Ambivalent Relationship with Society

The new relationship that imposed itself between state and society with the onset of détente has already been referred to in this chapter. But it is worth discussing more fully since it was probably the main feature of East German public life in the 1970s. First, however, a word about the framework inside which this relationship developed.

Regime control over society in Eastern Europe has, since Stalin, rested on a minimum of provocation combined with the necessary coercive power to be used only when necessary. In the case of the GDR, where the sensitivities of society are deeply affected by the Federal Republic, the need to avoid provocation has been perhaps more pressing than anywhere in Eastern Europe, not excluding Poland. And avoiding provocation is the necessary precondition for seeking legitimization. This has certainly been the case in the GDR.

At the same time the forces of coercion the East German regime has had at its disposal are probably more effective than any other in Eastern Europe. They are, mainly, the security police, or *Staatssicherheitsdienst* (the notorious Stasis), the police force (VOPOS), the workers' militia, and the Peoples Army (the GDR's regular and conscript military). Finally, there are the 300,000–400,000 Soviet troops stationed in the GDR. They try to preserve a discreet presence, but they are too numerous and the GDR is too small for them to stay virtually out of sight, as they can sometimes do in Poland or even in Hungary. They are both the East German regime's ultimate safeguard and its indirect deterrent.

Though by no means inactive, none of these instruments of coercion have been used extensively since the beginning of the 1970s. Far more active have been the various ideological "troops" deployed in the Abgrenzung strategy already discussed. They have had to fight against the three main forms of penetration since détente began: (1) the West German mark; (2) West German travelers; (3) West German television programs.

The hordes of West German visitors—in 1979 they topped 8 million—were very likely the least of the regime's worries. Toward the end of the decade they had been accepted as a feature of East German life, a profitable one for the economy, an irritant for the regime (and often for many of their private hosts) but less a political danger than had been feared. On the other hand, the key role now assumed by the deutsche mark could eventually corrupt the whole East German policy—economically, ideologically, and morally—militating decisively against the GDR's struggle for its own identity.

The most intriguing intrusion was that by West German television. In an earlier part of his career Honecker apparently mobilized large numbers of East German youth organizations in raids designed to deter East Germans from tuning in to West Germany. But in power his youthful enthusiasms were diverted into other channels, and in the course of the 1980s he even gave his blessing to new arrangements enabling the previously benighted residents of Dresden to wallow in the pleasure of this capitalist entertainment. Now, therefore, not just 80 percent but 100 percent of the East German population could clamber through their television screens into the Federal Republic every night, stay there a few hours if they wanted, and then clamber back. It was not the same as visiting, which for many years few could do, but it was the next best thing, and very few refused the opportunity.

The best explanations for the regime's tolerance were (1) it would be immensely difficult, technically, to block the reception of West German programs; (2) if it were possible, it would be a crippling, self-inflicted propaganda defeat to do so; (3) much of West German television, both as information and entertainment, might be seen as condemning the Western way of life; (4) viewing Western television was not just a "safety valve" for East German society but also a gesture of regime understanding for it and of confidence in its own ability to withstand any ill effects. These explanations are not mutually exclusive, but rather mutually reinforcing and add up to a powerful enough reason for the shoulder-shrugging inactivity to which the regime resorted.

Over the short term the policy seemed to do no harm. There was little serious dissension directly attributable to the seductions of West German television. But, inevitably, the West German popular and consumer culture began to play an insidious and important role in East German life, countering both communist ideology and the GDR's separatist pretensions. No one could predict when and how its effects would be felt. But few doubted that eventually they would.

Still, all this was for the future. For the moment, penetration was profitable for the regime and pleasurable for society. There was much less complacency about the impact of the Helsinki Final Agreements of July–August 1975, the culmination of the European cooperation and security negotiations that the GDR, like all its East bloc allies, signed. The impact was immediate, mainly in connection with the emigration issue. In many parts of the GDR silent demonstrations took place invoking some of the articles of the Helsinki Agreements. The East German authorities did eventually become more liberal in their emigration policy. In 1984 emigration peaked at about 40,000. But with an estimate of well over 200,000 filing for emigration, the regime remained niggardly by any human standards and far from the spirit of Helsinki.[39]

Beginning in 1986, however, the regime noticeably began to relax its travel restrictions to the Federal Republic. In that year the number of East Germans below and of retirement age visiting West Germany rose sharply to 575,000. For 1987 it was intimated that at least 1 million East Germans under sixty years of age would be allowed to make the trip. If this continued, it would not be just relaxation but a basic change of policy and an important factor attesting to the regime's self-confidence. The authorities claimed in 1987 that only 0.025 percent of all those visiting the West failed to return. It was also announced that the numbers for legal emigration in the first quarter of 1987—perhaps influenced by the relaxation in travel restrictions—were down almost two-thirds from the first quarter in 1986.[40]

Emigration policy presented the regime with problems. It wanted to seem just generous enough to avoid offending West German political and financial circles and to prevent itself from being carpeted before world opinion for flouting Helsinki. It also wanted to dump onto the Federal Republic as many malcontents as possible, of whom the irrepressible Rudolf Bahro became a newsworthy example.[41] Yet to its own citizens it did not want to signal any major change in policy that might turn the emigration trickle into a tidal wave of demand. It was to become particularly embarrassed by those GDR citizens sitting in at different East European embassies of the Federal Republic and demanding emigration to the FRG. Even a niece of premier Willi Stoph availed herself of this opportunity in Prague in 1984.

It is also in the context of Helsinki that the minirebellion of certain prominent East German writers in the mid-1970s should be considered. Their inexcusable offense was that they took Helsinki seriously enough (or they wished to test the regime's sincerity) to press for a freer cultural atmosphere within the GDR itself and for new avenues of cooperation with their West German counterparts. Their pressure crystallized in 1976 over the case of Wolf Biermann, a troubador of some distinction, who, while on a visit to West Germany, was barred reentry and then deprived of East German citizenship. Many of the most distinguished cultural figures in the GDR, such as Stephan Heym and Christa Wolf, protested against this injustice to Biermann, and there

followed a train of official vindictiveness and chicanery that, well publicized in the Federal Republic, did no little damage to the GDR's
international standing.

There was apparently not as much overt persecution as in Czechoslovakia, but this may have been because of the opportunities to
offload undesirables onto the Federal Republic. More distinguished
figures than Rudolf Bahro ended up, willingly or unwillingly, permanently or indefinitely, in the Federal Republic—writers, for example,
such as Gunther Künert, Jurek Becker, and Joachim Seyppel. These
were men the like of whom a healthy body politic could not afford to
lose. The Federal Republic's gain was very much the GDR's loss.

The Role of the Evangelical Church

What specifically worried the regime about Helsinki were the different
forces of spontaneity it unleashed. This distrust of spontaneity made
the regime's relations with the Evangelical church all the more intriguing. The territory of the GDR is situated in traditionally Protestant
parts of the old Germany. Out of a total population of some 17 million
there are only about 1.3 million Roman Catholics. But there is a much
higher percentage of *practicing* Catholics than Protestants. Of the latter, less than 20 percent are estimated to be practicing. Generally, the
Roman Catholic church has followed the pattern of behavior of minor
churches under communism. Though not tainted with any suspicion
of collaboration with the regime, it has generally remained quiet and
presented few political problems.[42]

For its part, though never a rebellious institution, the Evangelical
church has maintained a firm dignity and spoken out when it felt it
needed to, as, for example, against the introduction of military conscription in 1962. Until 1969 it was institutionally linked and subordinated to the Evangelical church in the Federal Republic, an
association that was a matter of no small concern to the GDR authorities. Since it achieved independent status, however, it has still
derived financial support from the church in West Germany and
remained indirectly influenced by it in a number of ways. For many
years, though, the appeal of religion was declining in the GDR, and
the activity and standing of the Evangelical church declined with
it. Not only was churchgoing decreasing, but so were Christian bap-
tisms, weddings, and other ceremonies.[43] Both ideologically and
politically the regime had reason to be satisfied with both the state

of religion and of the institutions connected with it.

But declining though the Evangelical church seemed to be, several factors conspired to save it from disintegration and extinction. Its reputation had been damaged by its cooperation with Hitler, and in the early postwar years it suffered considerably from this stigma. But it still stayed one of the few links remaining with the all-German heritage. Its ties with the church in the Federal Republic were also an institutional reminder of the notion of German unity. It also had contacts with Protestant churches throughout the world. Finally, in a state governed by a regime that aspired to totalitarianism it remained, however much weakened, an alternative point of loyalty. The regime's attitude toward it was ambiguous: it was wary of the church's very existence yet aware of its potential value. Provided the church were controlled, it would have its propaganda uses both at home and abroad. And as the Honecker regime began its search for historical roots and legitimacy, so the church of Luther took on an added significance and attractiveness.

If the church would cooperate, the pragmatic Honecker was prepared to make concessions. The meeting in 1978 between him and Bishop Albrecht Schoenherr, the then leader of the bishops of the Evangelical church, reflected the desire of both for a better modus vivendi. But the church was to show a resilience and a strength that surprised the regime and frustrated its attempts to use it as a front organization.[44]

The church derived its new strength by taking cautious but firm stands on issues that were assuming political and social significance, especially among the youth of the GDR. The most important of these was the peace issue. Its close involvement originally sprang from the growing militarization of East German life since the early 1970s. Nowhere in Eastern Europe has a more avowed and blatant militarization of young people's lives occurred than in the GDR. Here the likening of communist society to a barracks takes on a very real significance. (Comparisons with Nazi Germany have also been unavoidable.) In September 1978 the regime decided to introduce compulsory military education into the school curriculum for the ninth and tenth grades. This caused considerable unease in society as a whole, and the Evangelical church stepped forward as the best-organized critic of the militaristic tendencies that appeared to be proliferating.[45]

The birth of the East German "peace movement" owed much to the similar, much bigger movement active for several years in the Federal

Republic, thereby providing yet another example of the West German influence and the interaction between the two German societies. But the movement in the GDR developed its own momentum. It was not a creation of the Evangelical church, but the church sought to guide it—and restrain it where necessary. The most important initiative in this context was the call on the regime to institute a "social peace service" as an alternative to military conscription. Modeled on the West German example, this would enable conscientious objectors to military service to perform other social duties for the community instead of being conscripted. The regime first opposed this adamantly, but subsequently indicated that it was prepared to take a tolerant view of applications on an individual basis.[46]

The "peace movement" in the GDR reached its climax, however, over the INF issue—the agreement by several NATO countries to the deployment of new American missiles in 1983 and the Soviet response of stationing new types of their own missiles in both the GDR and Czechoslovakia. The West German decision to deploy Pershing and cruise missiles naturally led to a mushrooming of peace activism in the Federal Republic, and this gave a further impetus to like-minded activists in the GDR. The East Berlin regime was put in a quandary by this development. It strongly supported, of course, the spontaneous peace activism in the Federal Republic and for years had nurtured its own official peace movement, which it duly trotted out on occasions like this one. The official peace movement it could depend on; the unofficial peace movement it could not. For this movement, composed mainly of the young but with citizens of all age groups, was just as concerned about the Soviet missiles in Eastern Europe (especially in the GDR) as about American missiles in Western Europe.

Again, here was something spontaneous, something unprogrammed, and all the more embarrassing because it was over an issue in which the Soviet Union was directly involved. Regime spokesmen, especially Honecker himself, treated the subject with considerable tact in public utterances. But ruthlessness was also shown: the peace movement's slogan of "swords into ploughshares" was virtually banned, and some of the most recalcitrant peace activists were deported to the Federal Republic.

The peace issue may have been the most dramatic in which the Evangelical church was involved—its own determination and the importance of the issue also inspired the Roman Catholic church to some militancy—but it was not the only one. The disastrous deterioration of the environment in some areas of the GDR (see chapter 13) prompted the church to take a stand on this issue as well. It gained public support and respect for doing so since this was an issue on which many East Germans were becoming highly aroused. Abortion and the whole birth control and sexual behavior complex of issues became additional matters for study, discussion, and action. In fact, church halls in many parishes up and down the country—depending on the concern and courage of the local clergymen—became social study centers where the freedom of expression was remarkable. By 1986 the Evangelical church had become a clearinghouse for the consideration of some of the most important issues of the day. It was making its mark as the most important church in public life in Eastern Europe after the Catholic churches in Poland and Croatia. And it was doing this not so much in its religious as in its social capacity.

The Evangelical church had come from the margin to the middle of East German public life. It rarely challenged the regime directly. Sometimes it even seemed rather pliable.[47] There were indeed some bishops more cooperative than others. The same went for the clergy at the parish level. But it was precisely at that level that visitors were most impressed by the growth in stature and prestige of the Evangelical church and of its sense of purpose. Its relations with the state were likely to become more ambiguous and uneasy. This ambiguity was already reflected in its description of itself: "the church in socialism." At first this might sound like a concession to the regime. But it was more subtle and less accommodating than that.[48]

The Quest for Legitimacy and Security

In the second half of 1985 an 839-page book appeared called *Bismarck: Urpreusse und Reichsgruender* (*Bismarck: Archetypal Prussian and Founder of an Empire*). The author was Ernst Engelberg, the dean of East German historians and a first-class scholar by any standard.[49]

The book, which covered Bismarck's career to the founding of the German Empire in 1871, contained a remarkably positive assessment of his career and was favorably received by the (officially inspired) East German critics. Only just over ten years earlier the publication of such a work would have been unthinkable. Until the middle of the 1970s Bismarck had been a cross between evil genius and aristocratic parasite, personifying the absolute antithesis of all the German Democratic Republic stood for. But Engelberg's book was but the most recent example of the massive reappraisal of history going on for about a decade, instigated and eagerly encouraged by Honecker himself. This reappraisal affected many figures in German history associated directly or indirectly with historic Prussia or those territories incorporated into the GDR. These came to include not just "progressive" or "enlightened" military men, like Scharnhorst, Gneisenau, and Clausewitz, but in the late 1970s extended even to Frederick the Great, who along with Bismarck had been held up as the personification of all that was militaristically evil about Prussian history. Frederick's equestrian statue resumed its place in the Unter den Linden, and a favorable biography of him was published, written by another distinguished East German historian, Ingrid Mittenzwei.

The high point of the historical rehabilitation campaign, however, was the commemoration of the five hundredth anniversary of Martin Luther's death in 1983. The event became a state occasion, organized by a committee presided over by Honecker himself. The Great Reformer's positive contributions to both national and international history were now stressed, and the antisocial lapses in his turbulent career were now overlooked.[50] Several giants from German cultural history were also appropriated into the East German pantheon. They included Goethe, against whom it has always been difficult to say much, and even Wagner, against whom it has always been difficult to say little. A bemused East German public could hardly wait for the next historiographical volte-face.

The rehabilitation campaign, which received considerable publicity outside the GDR as well, was a new and highly intriguing aspect of the GDR's quest for the Grail of legitimacy. It was designed to show that, despite its separateness, the GDR did indeed have roots and was the inheritor and the continuation of all that was finest in German history. Its timing was significant, too. It came after several vicissitudes in the GDR's history marked by uncertainty and apprehensiveness. But the GDR had survived. Not only that: it was now an accepted part of the European political landscape—many would have said an essential part. Nobody—not even the West German Christian Democrats—was threatening its existence.

There was another point, too. The Honecker regime had realized that ideology alone was no longer enough. The public needs a sense of history with which it might identify, not just the boringly familiar dialectic it had always, for the most part, rejected. Not that the regime gave any *outward* sign of acknowledging this need. The ideology continued to be purveyed massively, by a huge army of propagandists. But Marx was no match for Luther, nor Engels for *der alte Fritz*. Honecker had to be careful, though. Young East Germans, once initiated into their heritage, might develop too much of a taste for it.

How far then, a quarter of a century after the Wall, had the notion of the German Democratic Republic as a self-sustaining nation-state become embedded in the consciousness of its citizens? By the late 1980s there was little to suggest that it had even penetrated it. Opinion polls could suggest that a considerable majority of East German citizens might support and/or accept the GDR regime, but these meant little. They, and similar polls in other East European states, might fairly accurately represent opinion in the existing context of the communist system and Soviet domination. But here the distinction between aspiration and accommodation needs to be made, especially in the peculiar case of the GDR. Most East Germans aspire to reunification. But most East Germans have already accommodated themselves to the realities of a situation they know is indefinite, perhaps permanent.

But the act of accommodation need not mean resignation. It need not exclude pressure, or faute de mieux aspirations, for as much association as possible with the Federal Republic short of reunification. The notion of confederation is still sometimes floated (Ulbricht used to float it in the 1950s) but it would be difficult to imagine a confederation between two states of such different systems, belonging to two different and adversarial alliances. Perhaps more realistic are the suggestions of growing *Annäherung* (coming closer) between the societies of the two countries within an elastic framework of correct and many-sided cooperation between the two states.

This has seemed to be the most many East Germans were hoping for. Would it help or hinder progress toward a separate nationhood, matching the separate notions of statehood already existing? Over a long period of time it might help. But it was difficult to see it leading to that separate sense of nationhood that has characterized most (but not all) Austrians, for example, since 1955. It could further promote, though, a sense of regional or provincial patriotism, which is already present in the GDR. In time this could solidify into a strong enough feeling of East German distinctiveness that could serve as an ersatz nationalism. A sense of distinctiveness was already present in the late 1980s, and it was partly based on the factual distinctiveness that exists between the two Germanies. The GDR has, paradoxically, retained many more of the traditional characteristics of the old Germany than the Federal

Republic. Though forty years of communist rule are everywhere visible, the GDR was much less Russified than the Federal Republic was Americanized.[51] Erich Honecker remains just as much a German as Helmut Kohl. And East Germany was more likely to retain its "Germanness" if it continued being the German Democratic Republic. It could hardly lose it more quickly than by reuniting with the Federal Republic!

Honecker's Progress

In relations with the Federal Republic Honecker's own policies have often appeared contradictory. While proclaiming and often pursuing the policy of Abgrenzung he has allowed manifold penetration: the deutsche mark, the millions of West German visitors, and unlimited access to West German television. Honecker has also established himself as a pragmatist. But the question arises whether there has been a consistent purpose in his pragmatism or whether it has simply been a series of makeshift moves that have mostly fallen into place.

Probably the best way to understand Honecker's policies is to see him as a political gambler. He took over the GDR when the Ulbrichtian certainties had been shattered, a process in which the Soviet Union, the founder and protector of the GDR, had been intimately involved. In this new situation he had to ensure the durability and viability of his state, leaning on the Soviet Union as little as possible. To do this he was prepared to take huge risks with the East German population, most recently involving their increasing exposure to the Federal Republic itself. To reduce the danger he had at his disposal, of course, all the armory of Abgrenzung and, ultimately, Soviet power. But he also genuinely sought to make life more tolerable in the GDR by raising living standards and by permitting a more relaxed political and cultural atmosphere. He also showed some understanding for the aspirations and frustrations of youth and sought rapprochement with the churches.

It was a gamble that has generally paid off. There certainly was dissent during the decade of détente, causing the regime no little irritation. But it was always containable, never anything like the problem many had expected. Similarly, the GDR survived the Solidarity period in Poland with scarcely a ripple from society.

It was these escapes—fairly easy ones as they turned out to be—that emboldened Honecker, after the virtual collapse of détente in the early 1980s, to try to preserve the relation with the Federal Republic that initially he had feared so much. (This was referred to briefly at the beginning of this chapter and is discussed more fully in chapter 3.) The fact was that détente had been good to the GDR, economically and internationally. The Wall may have been breached, but the state behind it had flourished, not fallen. Instead of concern it began showing confidence, toward both East and West. At no time was this confidence more evident than at the eleventh SED congress in April 1986 with Gorbachev in attendance. In fact, as was later to become evident, Honecker seemed determined to emphasize that the GDR was doing very nicely with its own policies, regardless of what the Soviet Union might be doing itself or want others to do.

But how long would the gamble go on paying off? How long would it take—if ever—for those destructive properties associated with West German penetration to take effect? Could the GDR retain its confidence and its policies during a period of instability that might occur domestically or in the Soviet Union's East European bloc? Would the Soviets ever find themselves insisting that East Berlin choose between Moscow and Bonn on a more protracted basis? Would Gorbachev become impatient with Honecker's intention to stick to his own policies?

Despite all its progress, the GDR's future still depends on questions like these. It is still a uniquely vulnerable state. Perhaps a policy of gamble is the only one for it. But that shows just how vulnerable it is.

8 Romania

Romania's finest hour in its communist history came on 21 August 1968 when its state and party leader, Nicolae Ceauşescu, denounced the Soviet-led invasion of Czechoslovakia that had just taken place.[1] All other East European members of the Soviet alliance had joined the invasion, some with less enthusiasm or fewer troops than others. But Romania had made clear all along that Czechoslovak domestic policy was the Czechoslovaks' own business. No one, therefore, expected Ceauşescu to support the invasion. But few expected him to denounce it when it came. His words, carefully expressed but still courageous, brought his country a worldwide respect it had seldom enjoyed in its history.

Romania had gained a historical reputation for international unreliability. This solidified in the Balkan Wars of 1912 and 1913 and matured in World War I when Romania diplomatically dallied with both sides. It was maintained in World War II when Romania began as combatant on the side of the Axis and then switched to the Allies very late in the war. It is a formidable record by any standard and has helped nurture a deep-seated international prejudice against Romania.

But it is a reputation largely undeserved. Emerging after centuries of Ottoman and Phanariot misrule; its national independence struggle immeasurably complicated by the struggle also for the unity of the two principalities of Moldavia and Wallachia; threatened and/or manipulated by the Great Powers as soon even as it gained its first measure of independence; caught up in a passionately patriotic dispute with Hungary, not simply over the possession of Transylvania but even of the origin of the Romanians living there; above all, constantly the target, and often the victim, of Russian imperialism: with such a background it is hardly surprising that Romanian leaders, of whatever social origin or political hue, have used the arts of diplomacy —sometimes with a Florentine tinge—to keep their country intact and alive. Nor should it be forgotten that in both world wars, though Romania did change sides, its troops often fought with great valor and with huge losses.

There are similarities between Romania and the other Balkan countries that emerged, or reemerged, in the nineteenth century. But, generally, despite their wrongs, Romanians have had less cause to complain about the treatment of history than some of their neighbors. True, they suffered grievously in both world wars and permanently lost territory—South Dobrudja and, more seriously, Bessarabia—in World War II. But even allowing for its daunting diplomatic skill and timing Romania had been extremely lucky in gaining the territories given it by the Paris Agreements after World War I.[2] When one considers totally dissatisfied states like Hungary and Bulgaria and the national troubles of Yugoslavia before and after World War II, then Romania's relative luck can be appreciated. Above all, after World War II Transylvania—the whole of it—was recovered and that to most Romanians was the essential part of the lost heritage.

There is one more historical factor to be recalled. That is the Romanians as a race—their Dacian-Roman origin. There is no doubt that, despite centuries of Slavic, Greek, and Turkish influence, the Romanians are at least partly of Latin origin, stemming from the Roman invasions of the Emperor Trajan at the beginning of the second century after Christ. The language, though studded with Turkish and Slavic words, which linguistic purists have struggled to weed out, is definitely Romance, as is the name of the country itself. Of their Roman origins Romanians have always been proudly aware. After 1970, however, they were exposed to a massive campaign, inspired by Ceauşescu himself, stressing and glorifying their Dacian origin as well. This campaign has had its ridiculous side, including films worthy of the old Hollywood extravaganzas. Such propaganda was greeted by many educated Romanians with a shoulder-shrugging cynicism. But Ceauşescu's campaign was not without its more serious political—even irredentist—aspect. The territory occupied by the historical Dacians was quite large, larger than the territory that became Romanized. It spilled over into Bessarabia.[3]

There are many differences between Romania before and since World War II. There was, for example, even in the worst days of the royal dictatorship in the 1930s much more political liberty in the precommunist era. But anyone viewing the twentieth century from a historical perspective cannot fail to see similarities: the nationalism in domestic and foreign affairs, for example, of Premier Ionel Bratianu in the 1920s and later Gheorghiu-Dej and Ceauşescu, the two main communist leaders; also the diplomatic tactics of the Bratianu family, of Nicolae Titulescu, the interwar foreign minister, of King Carol II himself, of Gheorghe Gheorghiu-Dej, the first communist regime leader, and after 1965 of Nicolae Ceauşescu. Not all these tactics ended with success. King Carol's ended in the tragedy of the Vienna Diktat of 1940, which lost Northern Transylvania to Hungary shortly after Bessarabia and Northern Bukovina had been surrendered to the Russians; Ceauşescu's may yet end in disaster. But the point here is not so much their success as their similarity. Paul Lendvai, in his brilliant book *Eagles in Cobwebs* about Balkan nationalism, juxtaposes a statement on Romanian foreign policy by Titulescu with one by Ceauşescu to illustrate this continuity. First Titulescu in 1936: "We shall never renounce for the sake of the Great Powers, or all the Great Powers together, the principle of equality of states, that is, the sovereign right to decide our fate and to refuse decisions concerning us in which we have been involved without our consent."[4] Second, Ceauşescu in 1967: "The small and medium-sized states refuse to play the role of pawn in the service of the interests of big imperialist powers any longer. They rise against any form of domination and promote an independent policy. By vigorously defending their legitimate rights and interests, the small and medium-sized powers can play an outstanding part in international life; can considerably influence the course of events."[5]

The similarity between, and the courage of, both these statements needs no amplification.

The Dispute with Moscow

It has been a matter of some controversy among observers about when the continuity, so clearly demonstrated by Ceauşescu in the above passage, was taken up by the Romanian communist regime, which was firmly in power by 1948. In other words, there is dispute over when the Romanian "deviation" from Moscow's foreign and bloc policies began. Some have argued that it originally lay in the fact that, unlike in any other East European satellite, Gheorghiu-Dej and his immediate coterie of "home" communists were allowed to stay in power by Stalin, whereas elsewhere it was the "home communists" who were being framed, executed, and replaced by the "Muscovites."

In Romania the "Muscovites" were routed; not executed but sentenced to long prison terms. The difference may lie in a complicated situation that Gheorghiu-Dej exploited skillfully, in the extraordinary luck with which several Romanian leaders have been blessed, and the fact that the top Romanian "Muscovites"—most notably Ana Pauker —were Jewish and, like their counterparts in Czechoslovakia, fell victim to Stalin's last prolonged bout of anti-Semitism. Others have stressed that the Romanian dispute with Moscow began with Khrushchev, with the new Soviet leader's personal dislike of Gheorghiu-Dej and his "Stalinism," plus the fact that Tito, as part of the price of rapprochement with Khrushchev, is alleged to have included the Romanian leader on his "demolition" list, along with such luminaries as Rákosi, Chervenkov, and Hoxha. Gheorghiu-Dej, therefore, like Tito himself in 1948, was forced by the basic instinct of self-preservation to begin his defiance of the Soviet Union.

There may be truth in both these arguments. When historians look for causes, the digging can go very deep indeed. Obviously the historical reasons have their validity. Most observers, though, tend to put the real beginnings of the Romanian "deviation" about 1958 or 1959 when Khrushchev as part of his major overhaul of the Soviet alliance after 1956 toyed with the notion of "supranationalism." His supranationalism would have been confined, at least to begin with, to the framework of the Council for Mutual Economic Assistance (Comecon), established by Stalin in 1949 but revived by Khrushchev after 1956 as a handy instrument for bloc cohesion. What Khrushchev ostensibly wanted was a rationalization and specialization of economic effort within the alliance. (The Soviet Union, of course, excepted; it would—and, of course, could—continue to produce everything.) Prompted, or strongly supported, by the GDR and Czechoslovakia, both industrially advanced countries, pressure was applied on Romania, and probably Bulgaria and Albania, to abandon their ambitious industrialization plans and concentrate on developing their agriculture and food industries.[6]

The emergence of this new Soviet policy roughly coincided with the withdrawal of Soviet troops from Romania in the summer of 1958. (They had been there since the end of World War II.) The reason for this move has remained unclear. The Romanian leadership apparently requested the withdrawal.[7] As for the Soviet side, Khrushchev probably thought it could be turned to good bargaining account in East-West relations. No one after all was under any illusions about Romania's strategic importance. Whatever the reasons, once the Soviet troops had gone, an important psychological barrier to more independent Romanian action had been removed.

Romania's rejection of Khrushchev's proposals for bloc economic specialization should be seen against the background of four factors.

The *first* was purely economic: accepting the Soviet proposal (or directive) would have meant such a massive restructuring of the whole of Romanian economic policy that a long, drawn-out chaos would have been inevitable.

The *second*—and more profound—lay in the Romanian communists' striving for legitimacy. No East European communist movement had been as pathetically weak and unsuccessful before it came to power as the Romanian. Among a nation strongly anti-Russian it could hardly entrench itself by supporting, as it did between the wars, Comintern policy in favor of restoring Bessarabia to the Soviet Union. Among its leaders had been Bulgarians, Hungarians, and Jews. It was commonly regarded, therefore, as both un-Romanian and anti-Romanian.[8] Now in power, Romania's communists ("home" communists, most of them, at the helm) were certainly not insensitive to the historical unpopularity of their predecessors.

The *third* factor—closely linked with the second—was that Romanian hatred for Russia had been still more intensified by the economic exploitation after World War II. All Soviet-occupied countries were exploited ruthlessly, though none, except what is now the GDR, more than Romania, relatively rich in natural resources. With the death of Stalin and the warning signals of Hungary and Poland in 1956, this exploitation was greatly reduced. But it was still fresh in the minds of all Romanians, many of whom, in any case, knew that the exploitation had not ceased till well after Stalin died. For the Romanian leadership to have accepted another and, if anything, more basic and humiliating form of exploitation or discrimination at the hands of the Soviets would have destroyed any hope of the legitimacy it desired.

The *fourth* factor was international; and here Romanian historic skills once again emerged. Certainly by 1958 the Sino-Soviet dispute was becoming known, if not to the world at large then at least to senior officials in all the ruling parties. Albania, at odds with the Soviet leaders for even more basic reasons than Romania, soon took advantage of the dispute by openly breaking with Moscow. Even had the Romanian leaders wished to follow the Albanian example, they must have realized it would almost certainly have led to a Soviet invasion. Instead, they exploited the developing Sino-Soviet rift with great skill, not only to insist that their domestic economic policy continue unimpaired but also to steadily carve out for Romania a position of growing autonomy within the Warsaw Pact alliance. The famous April Central Committee Declaration of 1964 gave the Romanian view of independence, equal socialist relations, and the importance and integrity of small and medium powers with great force and clarity. It would be too much to call it Romania's "Declaration of Independence" from the Soviet Union, as has popularly been done. But in its insistence on Romanian rights, it was both a Romanian nationalist and an essentially anti-Soviet document. It has served as the basic premise on which continued Romanian autonomy in both Comecon and the Warsaw Pact has been founded.[9]

Gheorghiu-Dej died in March 1965. The new party leader, Nicolae Ceauşescu, was only forty-seven years old but had been a Central Committee secretary for thirteen years and a full Politburo member for ten. He had risen through the party's youth organization and had been responsible for political work in the armed forces and then for several years had been secretary for party organization and cadres. He was obviously groomed to be Gheorghiu-Dej's successor, and his elevation came as no surprise. In fact, it appeared to have been the smoothest succession so far in communist politics anywhere. Ceauşescu began his rule full of promise, and in foreign affairs he had the invaluable assistance of Prime Minister Ion Gheorghe Maurer.

Communist prime ministers tend to be forgotten unless they have been men of outstanding ability like Chou En-lai or meet a bizarre and mysterious end like the Albanian Mehmet Shehu. Their fading from memory reflects the basic lack of importance in communist systems of the office they hold. Most have deserved their obscurity. But Maurer is an exception. He was one of the ablest and most interesting of Eastern European communist leaders. Born in 1902 to a Saxon-Romanian father and a Romanian mother of French extraction, he came from a professional family background. A graduate in law, he became known in interwar Bucharest as a defense attorney for left-wing politicians and agitators, and he himself apparently joined the underground communist party in 1936. During the war he helped Gheorghiu-Dej who, when he had achieved the mastery in the regime in the early 1950s, sent for Maurer. The latter served in several missions abroad before becoming foreign minister in 1957. He became nominal head of state in 1958, a full Politburo member in 1960, and prime minister in 1961. His old friend Gheorghiu-Dej recognized both his talents and the need for them.

Maurer gave to the regimes of both Gheorghiu-Dej and Ceauşescu what many would call a touch of class, of which each was in considerable need. At home he commanded respect through his wisdom, stature, leadership qualities, and civility. In foreign affairs he was more than just a good salesman for the communist regime. He showed coolness and skill in alternately defying and placating Moscow and in making Romanian policy credible in the West. He and Gheorghiu-Dej worked well together; he and Ceauşescu less so, and as the latter began evincing those despotic tendencies that eventually became dominant, Maurer's role became humiliatingly circumscribed. His retirement in 1974 only accelerated a degeneration that had already begun. Ostensibly he retired because of the injuries sustained in an automobile accident. But he was known to resent Ceauşescu's style as well as the growing ascendancy of Ceauşescu's wife, Elena, which began to become clear at this time.

But few anticipated degeneration in the first four years of Ceauşescu's rule. Indeed, the August days of 1968 marked the zenith of communist rule in Romania. Frightened though Romanians were of an invasion many feared imminent, they applauded Ceauşescu for his stand just as they had approved the whole course of anti-Soviet defiance that culminated in the denunciation of the Czechoslovak invasion. They were also hopeful that the improvement in their domestic conditions would continue. The supply situation was undoubtedly better. Many political prisoners had already been released; Alexandru Draghici, minister of the interior responsible for—or symbolizing—the terror of previous years, had been purged. Intellectual freedom was broadening. There is no doubt that, though most Romanians may have remained distrustful of the communist regime as a whole, Ceauşescu, the cobbler's son from Scorniceşti, had acquired a genuine respect. What was needed in the 1970s for the legitimacy Romanian communism had so conspicuously lacked was a skillful continuation of the independent foreign policy with genuine domestic reform, efficiency, and enlightenment.

Continuity in Foreign Policy

The foreign policy certainly continued. Even after Maurer's departure in 1974 it showed no sign of slackening in either pace, scope, or skill, and since Ceauşescu presumably now accepted as little advice in foreign policy as he did in domestic, he must take credit for the successes in the one as he must take responsibility for the disasters in the other.

Indeed, after 1974 Romanian cultivation of good relations with the West, particularly the United States, the Federal Republic of Germany, and France, was continued and even intensified. Ceauşescu himself conducted a highly personal diplomacy, visiting these three countries twice during the 1970s, while entertaining many leading world figures. But it was not only the West that Ceauşescu cultivated. A special relationship with Yugoslavia developed—the Belgrade-Bucharest defensive axis. Indeed, the whole world became Ceauşescu's parish. Central and southern America, most parts of Africa, the Near and Middle East, the Far East, there was scarcely a country the indefatigable Romanian leader did not visit. Here there is a very close similarity to the motives that led Tito to help found and lead the nonaligned movement. These motives were preventive and protective—safety from the Soviets. A leader so well known on the world scene, so insistent on the rights of medium, small, and developing nations would be a more difficult target for Soviet wrath. So went the reasoning of both Tito and Ceauşescu. (It also bolstered the immense vanity each man shared.) Ceauşescu would obviously have liked Romania to join the nonaligned movement. But here even Romania's nominal membership of the Warsaw Pact made this impossible, not to mention political prudence. But Romania did achieve "permanent guest status" with the nonaligned movement and sent observers to economic groupings of Third World countries, like the original "group of 77."

Ceauşescu's persistent traveling, *la politique de présence*, also brought some economic results. There seems little doubt that if Romania's defiance of the Soviet Union did not lead to severe economic sanctions per se being taken against it, it did lead to its being denied many of the benefits of socialist community membership. Moreover, some economic blackmail was threatened or even practiced—certainly enough for Ceauşescu to refer to it publicly more than once.[10] The trade picked up from his world traveling, therefore, gave Romania some much needed diversification and was both part compensation for Soviet economic pressure and insurance against any more.

Ceauşescu's global policy had yet another dimension: that of mediation. Few international disputes from 1970 onward seemed able to avoid Bucharest's offer of mediation. Offering itself as mediator was the

Romanian party's original ploy in the Sino-Soviet dispute in the early 1960s. By ostensibly seeking to bring the two sides together it hoped to increase the distance between itself and Moscow. Thereafter this tactic was expanded onto the international diplomatic scene. The Arab-Israeli conflict was one in which Romania, the only Warsaw Pact country with diplomatic relations with both Israel and the Arab states, made serious attempts at mediation at various stages. So with the Vietnamese-Cambodian and the Chinese-Vietnamese disputes. At forums like the follow-up Conference on European Security and Cooperation in Madrid in 1978 Romania was occasionally useful as a conciliating factor, and in the Stockholm conference on confidence-building measures and disarmament in 1984–86 the Romanian delegate presented many suggestions.[11]

During the 1970s the close relationship continued with China, but it was evident that Soviet resentment did inhibit the Romanians from pressing it too far. Ceaușescu's visit to China and North Korea in the summer of 1971 was a case in point. This visit came less than three years after the invasion of Czechoslovakia, when Romanian nonparticipation had so angered the Soviets, and just over two years after the Soviet clash with the Chinese on the Ussuri River in March 1969.[12] For several years after 1971 Romania's interest in China was therefore less than demonstrative. But the good relations were maintained, and Romania received at least some economic benefit from them. After the death of Chairman Mao his short-lived successor, Hua Guofeng, visited Romania in 1978 as well as China's recently acquired friend, the former archfiend Yugoslavia. In 1982 Ceaușescu and a powerful entourage made an extended visit to China and North Korea, and in May 1983 the new secretary-general of the Chinese party, Hu Yaobang, visited both Romania and Yugoslavia. The atmosphere remained warm and friendly. Ceaușescu was well received in China in 1982, and between the beginning of 1980 and May 1983 thirty-four official Chinese delegations were reported as having visited Romania.[13] Ceaușescu himself in May 1983 is reported as having said that Sino-Romanian relations had "withstood many difficulties and demonstrated their durability."[14] It was an accurate appraisal. Certainly in the early phases of its dispute with Moscow, Romania found the Chinese useful and exploited them adroitly. But by the end of the 1970s China's real usefulness to Romania seemed to be over. The situation that had given rise to the relationship had changed dramatically. By 1985, for example, Romanian economic weakness made them more dependent on Soviet trade, especially supplies of oil and other raw materials. Moscow and Peking were also trying, with some success, to improve their relations.[15] China, too, had become quite a different country. In domestic affairs it had become the vanguard of communist reform. Abroad, its unsatisfactory experience with Albania (see chapter 12) must have only strengthened a growing inclination to avoid far-flung adventurism. Finally, Romania itself was no longer the "international attraction" it had been earlier. Its "deviation" had become an accepted and relatively unimportant part of the international scenery. It had certainly not become as contaminating as many had feared (or hoped). And its domestic policy now made it very much a liability rather than an asset. For China and for the United States, both of which once saw it as having nuisance value, it had become something of an embarrassment.

With its nominal allies, the Soviet Union and the other Warsaw Pact members, Romania was consistent in pursuing its policy of cooperation tempered by national interest. For Moscow, of course, a policy based on such a principle was tantamount to one of noncooperation. But generally Romanian-Soviet relations during the Brezhnev period maintained an uneasy calm. Romania had established its limited autonomy during the 1960s, and this had become entrenched through the successful defiance of Moscow over the invasion of Czechoslovakia. But this calm under Brezhnev was punctuated by episodes of tension. The Soviet anger over Ceaușescu's visit to China in 1971 has been mentioned. In 1974 Romania reportedly repeated its call for a rotation of the position of Warsaw Pact commander-in-chief.[16] Probably the most serious dispute of all was the breach in November 1978 over Warsaw Pact members' military expenditures. At a special meeting of the pact's leaders in Moscow Ceaușescu flatly refused to meet Soviet demands to this effect. A clash was also reported over Soviet efforts to persuade their allies to agree to stationing at least token East European forces in the Far East, as a sign of support for Vietnam.[17] On both issues, especially the latter, Romania must have had some allied support, however muted. But Ceaușescu's cardinal sin in this context was his decision to go public with the issue of expenditures immediately on arriving home after his early departure from Moscow. A massive public propaganda campaign was initiated against increases in military expenditure, and, though the Soviet Union was not directly blamed in the course of it, there was no doubt against whom the campaign was directed.[18] Eight years later, in October 1986, Ceaușescu resorted to the bizarre constitutional innovation of holding a referendum on an official proposal to restrict military expenditure. (Needless to say, it was overwhelmingly approved.)[19] Right at the end of 1979 the Soviets invaded Afghanistan, and, again, the Romanian government, though painfully careful in its choice of words, distanced itself from the Soviet action.[20]

Right up to the end of the Brezhnev era, therefore, Romania persisted in its "provocations" and pinpricks. These were tolerated by the Soviets, not because they were incapable of reacting, but because they had concluded that to discipline Ceauşescu—through military, political, or economic action—would cost them more than forbearance. Romania had become a special protégé of the West, particularly of the United States, and the 1970s were, after all, the decade of détente. This did not deter the Soviets from pursuing their own interests in many parts of the world. But, ironically, it did tend to inhibit them with this particular problem in their own backyard. What they apparently banked on in Romania's case was that the deteriorating domestic situation there would not only weaken Ceauşescu internally but would also make him a much less attractive proposition both for other East European states and for his Western patrons. By late into the 1980s this had come to seem a piece of shrewd political foresight. The Soviets could wait, and, after all, Romania's strategic location was the least crucial of any of their East European allies.

Still, Romania always had to carefully guard the elbow room it had won. Although their economic relations with the Soviet Union and the rest of Comecon increased in importance during the 1980s, the Romanians were still careful to resist any idea that smacked of supranationalism or infringement of sovereignty. In the Warsaw Pact they were still refusing to allow pact exercises involving foreign troops on their own soil and confining participation in pact maneuvers generally to staff officers and auxiliary troops. More than once in the 1970s they reportedly refused to allow their territory to be used as a corridor for the passage of Soviet troops to Bulgaria, and this was considered the main reason for the introduction in 1982 of a special ferry service between Illichovsk, near Odessa, and Varna on the Bulgarian coast—a ferry that would bypass Romania. Finally, on the issue Romania deemed most important of all—the right of self-determination and noninterference —there had again been no weakening. Just as Ceauşescu had defended the right of Czechoslovakia in 1968 to conduct its own affairs, so he did with Poland in 1980 and 1981. Though regarding Solidarity as much of an abomination as he had regarded the Prague Spring, he was against any suggestion or threat of outside interference.

In the interregnum between Brezhnev and Gorbachev there was little sign of change in Romania's basic position. Neither Andropov nor Chernenko lasted long enough to make any impact on it. And, though growing economic weakness appeared to have softened the expression of the Romanian policy, its content remained the same. The best example of this was over the Intermediate Nuclear Force (INF) controversy, particularly the decision of the Bonn government to go ahead in November 1983 with the stationing of Pershing II and cruise missiles in the Federal Republic. This was, like Afghanistan, a major issue of contention between East and West in which the Romanian tactic was to reassure the West by not automatically or fully taking the Soviet stand. Neither issue directly threatened or immediately affected Romania, but both were of sufficient concern to both sides to make it in the Romanian interest to try to avoid antagonizing the West without provoking the Soviets. Obviously the Romanian response to INF annoyed Moscow but not to the point where it would make Bucharest's "straddling" tactic unworkable.

Faced by the Soviet government's intention, made clear in November 1983, to deploy additional missiles in Czechoslovakia and the GDR in response to Bonn's decision, and its withdrawal from the Geneva talks, Ceauşescu made no one-sided condemnation of the West's action, as the other East Europeans did. In fact, he criticized both sides and exhorted them to get back to the negotiating table, calling for the destruction of *all* medium-range missiles in Europe. He carefully refrained from blaming anyone but, at the same time, seemed by implication to criticize the Soviet intention of expanding its nuclear arsenal and deploying part of it in Eastern Europe. Romania mostly refused to send representatives to meetings of Central Committee secretaries aimed at coordinating Eastern propaganda on the missile issue. There continued to be none of the anti-Western rhetoric of Soviet or other East European pronouncements on the subject.[21] Subsequently, when Gorbachev emerged as the advocate of meaningful nuclear reductions, Ceauşescu could feel himself vindicated—and relieved that at least one bone of contention with Moscow was being removed.

Degeneration at Home

For almost twenty years after August 1968, therefore, Romanian policy toward the Soviet Union has remained essentially the same. It has needed skill, courage, and nerve. Nor should one attempt to belittle the role of Ceaușescu in either its formation or its implementation. And it is this that has made the contrast with his domestic policy so stark and lamentable. Moreover, Romania's domestic policy has affected the whole perspective in which its foreign policy has been viewed. Domestic mismanagement and decay have steadily lost for Romania the respect its diplomacy originally aroused and have weakened the protective shield it so patiently devised against the Soviet Union and the alliance to which it nominally belongs.

At the risk of oversimplifying a complex process, the following generalization can be made: in foreign policy the communists inherited and continued the best and most skillful characteristics of the old regime; in domestic policy they took over some of the worst and amplified them. Nationalist and resourceful in foreign policy, the Bucharest regime under Ceaușescu became tyrannical and unresourceful at home, with all those characteristics of nepotism, corruption, and indifference to popular needs that had disfigured Romania's prewar governmental systems. Romania came to be considered the worst-governed East European country. Those observers who once argued that Ceaușescu deliberately (and perhaps unwillingly) abjured domestic reform as a protection against Moscow, which, it was maintained, would not have tolerated unorthodoxy at home as well as abroad, soon found this notion untenable as the reality of his rule unfolded. And Ceaușescu's misrule even began to sap the will to independence of many Romanians, who compared their country and its situation unfavorably with Kádár's Hungary.[22]

What steadily developed in Romania during the 1970s can loosely be described as neo-Stalinism without terror. The result was a creeping disintegration. The gulf between regime and society widened to an extent unknown in Eastern Europe since Stalin's day, except for Poland for a period after the imposition of martial law in December 1981. And within both the regime and society divisive, demoralizing forces caused further fragmentation. Ironically, the absence of terror, with all its grimly cohesive properties, may only have served to accelerate the process. The "absence of terror" did not, it should be stressed, mean an inactive secret police (*Securitate*). Both Romanians and visitors have had reason enough to be aware of that institution; and psychiatric wards and labor camps were used for some dissidents. But Stalinism had meant an all-pervading terror affecting every layer of society and every branch of officialdom. It represented the Gulag syndrome. This has not existed in Ceaușescu's Romania. But what did come to exist was an overall suspicion and repressiveness as well as the ever-growing personality cult around Ceauşescu himself. A psychiatrist would be needed to fully explain his personal rule and its style, and a larger book than this one would be needed to do justice to its scope, intricacies, and absurdities. In Europe the personality cult surrounding him could be compared only with that of his two Balkan contemporaries, Hoxha and Tito. In fairness to him, however, he has been spared the murderous paranoia of Hoxha, while in fairness to Tito, he totally lacked the Yugoslav's stature and qualities of leadership. His cult also bore a strong resemblance to the cults of Chairman Mao and North Korea's Kim Il Sung. As his rule wore on and he outlived Mao, Hoxha, and Tito, more and more comparisons were indeed made between Ceauşescu and Kim Il Sung.[23]

The greatest single factor in Romania's internal debacle has been Ceauşescu's capriciousness. No European leader in the second half of the twentieth century has so personified the debilitating effects of power more than he has. An intelligent man, an extraordinarily hard worker, a patriot, not personally cruel (in the sense that, say, Mátyás Rákosi of Hungary or Stalin were); once well intentioned—he has probably remained so in a perverted way—his name has yet become synonymous with many of the iniquities associated with historic tyranny. A willful refusal to take advice; a toleration for nothing but sycophants; a nepotism ever-growing in dimensions; an intolerance visibly hardening as absolute power corrupted absolutely; a self-defeating impatience clamoring for instant success; an inconsistency and unpredictability; a conglomerate of convictions and prejudices; a pretentiousness reflecting little but bad taste; a suspiciousness bordering on paranoia; a wife, Elena, who encouraged the bad and stifled the good in her husband; a self-promoting personality cult the sheer ludicrousness of which insulted, humiliated, angered, or amused most Romanians—it was for these characteristics that Nicolae Ceauşescu would be remembered by most of his countrymen.

But few, if any, of these characteristics were evident in the first half-decade of Ceauşescu's rule. The drama of his defiance of the Soviets in August 1968 has understandably overshadowed the promising impression he had already begun to make in domestic affairs. The political relaxation begun in the last years of Gheorghiu-Dej was continued. The reputation of Gheorghiu-Dej's most famous political victim, Lucreţiu Pătrăşcanu, executed in 1954, was fully rehabilitated. Some of the iniquities of the Gheorghiu-Dej era were admitted or hinted at, and the impression was given that a full de-Stalinization campaign would be mounted involving the posthumous disgrace of Gheorghiu-Dej himself. As for Ceauşescu, he gave the personal impression of all due modesty.

Alexandru Draghici, long-time minister of the interior and the living symbol of past repression, was purged in 1968. On policy questions Ceauşescu and others in the new leadership spoke of reform, if not in precise terms, then with apparent sincerity. Cultural restrictions were noticeably slackened, and many Romanian writers later came to look on the second half of the 1960s as the golden age of communist literature. Bucharest was a capital breathing more freely. For the country as a whole, the indicators were set fair.

Why was this initial promise first discontinued and then reversed? A plausible explanation is that it was part of a skillful strategy of consolidation on Ceauşescu's part.[24] Although his succession to Georghiu-Dej had been expected, the Romanian leadership was still weighted heavily with the associates of his predecessor. It was probably these who insisted on collective leadership, with Ceauşescu only as primus inter pares. Sharing power with him were Chivu Stoica, prime minister between 1955 and 1961 who became titular head of state, Gheorghe Apostol, first party secretary between 1954 and 1955 who was now a first deputy premier, and Premier Maurer. Ceauşescu's first task, therefore, was to neutralize the power of these men and the older guard generally and then bring into the leadership men he could trust.

This he did by both institutional and political means. As early as 1967 he was able to dislodge Stoica from the position of titular head of state and assumed the position himself. Apostol was soon swept from contention and eventually sent packing and grumbling as ambassador to Argentina. Maurer, less vulnerable because of his ability and reputation, stayed until 1974. More important for the future was the establishment at the ninth party congress in 1965 of the Executive Committee, an intermediate body between the Central Committee and the topmost party body. At the same time the Politburo was abolished and replaced by a small Standing Presidium, later to be called Permanent Bureau. (Both the Executive Committee and the Standing Presidium were later considerably enlarged.) All the candidate members of the first Executive Committee were Ceauşescu supporters. By the time of the tenth party congress in 1969 the old guard had been virtually neutralized. His leadership was now secure. Under him were princelings like Manea Mănescu, Ilie Verdeţ, Vasile Patilineţ, Paul Niculescu-Mizil, and Virgil Trofin. Every one of these men was to suffer the whims of his master's caprice, first raised up and then cast down, or aside, in a style of rule that defied both logic and prediction. More serious for Romania's future was his treatment of senior economic officials like deputy premier Alexandru Bîrlădeanu and planning chief Gheorge Gaston-Marin. These were men of high ability, and, perhaps because of this, they were cast aside in favor of men less competent but more pliable.

Ceaușescu's personal and institutional maneuverings, for which he showed a remarkable talent, were important enough, but they affected only the ruling elite. They had little or no direct effect on most of the population. Ceaușescu sought to impress the nation at large—and to discredit the older guard—by hints of de-Stalinization, criticisms of Gheorghiu-Dej's excesses, the removal of Draghici (who was also a personal rival), and promises of reform. The promise of the new dawn put the old regime in a bad light. Thus by the end of the 1970s Ceaușescu had achieved a growing legitimacy on account of both his domestic and his foreign policy. But while the latter was to persist, the former was to prove transient. And, as already mentioned, the disillusion over domestic disappointment came to erode the credit gained from the pursuit of popular policies abroad.

The Rise of the Family

Disillusion on the first count set in early. The tenth party congress in 1969 set the seal on Ceaușescu's political victory, and he was then free to pursue his own course. In June 1971 he made his visit to China and North Korea. This visit first revealed Ceaușescu's predilection for the autocratic, the grandiose, and the totalitarian. On his return, Romania began its own version of the "cultural revolution," the first symptom of erratic tendencies from which both regime and nation were to suffer and that made Khrushchev, with his "harebrained scheming," look almost level-headed. Like Khrushchev, Ceaușescu presumably realized that inertia and complacency were the two besetting sins of the system and its functionaries. They had to be battled constantly. But in Ceaușescu's case, what may have begun as a crusade soon became a retreat into his own personal citadel of despotism, nepotism, and caprice.

His immediate subordinates—those who had both helped him and been raised by him—were the first to experience the idiosyncracies of their master. If they ever had his real confidence, all were eventually to lose it. They were chopped and changed, shuffled and reshuffled like cards in a pack, seldom secure enough to exploit whatever talents they had, and continually frustrated, suspected, or simply disregarded. The whole system lent itself to excessive caution, sycophancy, cynicism, and demoralization.

For much of the 1970s Ceauşescu's leading group was composed of about fifty officials who occupied the top positions in party and state —the "inner nomenklatura." The veterans from the Gheorghiu-Dej era steadily receded from view, although some like Apostol, Bîrlădeanu, Constantin Pîrvulescu, and, allegedly, Ştefan Voitec did not leave before making their own protests against Ceauşescu's methods of rule.[25] (Pîrvulescu's outburst at the twelfth party congress in 1979—in full view of the television cameras—became legendary.) But by the end of the decade it was evident that this inner nomenklatura was itself no longer trusted enough by its leader. Trust and, therefore, power and influence began to be narrowed down to a small core of followers, by far the most prominent of whom was Elena Ceauşescu, who in 1977 was promoted to the Permanent Bureau of the party.

At the same time Ilie Verdeţ and Cornel Burtică were promoted to the Permanent Bureau. Under Ceauşescu Bucharest has been both a rumor-rife and a family-conscious city, the family in question being his own (change the name, and Bucharest was here, of course, reverting to two of its precommunist era characteristics). Both Verdeţ and Burtică, like several other top and temporarily favored officials, found them- selves automatically suspected of being related to the ruling family —the former as Ceauşescu's brother-in-law, the latter as a relative of Elena. However, while good grounds persisted for accepting Burtică's kinship, Verdeţ was subsequently discovered to be innocent of any familial relationship.

The case of Verdeţ and that of Virgil Trofin illustrate Ceauşescu's way with his princelings. In the early years of Ceauşescu's rule Trofin was considered the number two man in the party and was in charge of organization and cadres, a post with great power and influence. He was evidently a man with his own views and probably his own follow- ing. It was probably because of this that he eventually became a victim of Ceauşescu's "rotation" system for cadres. The ostensible aim of rotation was to give cadres all-around experience and to prevent their falling into the rut of inertia that being too long in one post tends to induce. But it was also designed to keep the inner nomenklatura off balance and to prevent any one person from acquiring too much power. Trofin, therefore, rotated in an ever-downward spiral until his final expulsion from the Central Committee in 1981. He reportedly died in 1984. He did not allow himself to be intimidated by Ceauşescu and appears to have retained a degree of rare self-respect. Verdeţ actually became prime minister in 1979 in place of the temporarily ailing Manea Mănescu who had replaced Maurer five years before. (Mănescu was also once believed, apparently incorrectly, to be part of the Ceauşescus' kith and kin.) In 1982, however, Verdeţ began his descent. He was replaced as premier by Constantin Dăscălescu. He subsequently became a Central Committee secretary and then minister of mines, oil, and geology, a political graveyard that Trofin had recently occupied. In June 1986 he was appointed chairman of the party's Central Audit Commission, and this precluded his continuing as a Central Committee member. By Stalinist standards, of course, these men were let down lightly. But this must have been cold comfort to them and to other victims of a despotic Byzantine court system who proved less pliant than they were expected to be.

As Trofin, Verdeţ, and others faded, so it was Elena Ceauşescu who steadily came to the fore, becoming, in fact, the second most powerful person in Romania. In 1979 she became chairman of the National Council for Science and Technology and—more important —chairman of the Central Committee commission for state and party cadres. Later she became the acknowledged senior first deputy prime minister.

But Ceauşescu did not stop at the promotion of his wife. He began elevating his son Nicu to a prominence apparently even less deserved. Born in 1950, Nicu was scarcely out of his teens when he established a reputation as a "socialist playboy," needing parental rescue on more than one occasion from scrapes of his own making. Made a Central Committee member in 1982, he became first secretary of the communist youth organization at the end of 1983, a post that carried with it the position of youth minister in the government. Toward the end of 1984 he became a candidate member of the Executive Committee (now the Political Executive Committee). But in late 1987 Nicu was sent off to the provinces as head of a county organization. For a man of his proclivities it must have seemed like Siberia. But whether Nicu was "finished" or just being "rotated" remained to be seen.

Elena and Nicu were the two most flagrant examples of Ceauşescu's nepotism. Resentment at their preferment was only compounded by their personal unpopularity, which, in both cases, appears to have been thoroughly deserved. But they were not the only ones favored. The numerical strength of the Ceauşescu clan has certainly been exaggerated over the years. As mentioned earlier, people are alleged to have belonged and profited who were later declared innocent of all connection. But there was no doubt that the clan was multitentacled. The Ceauşescus predominated, but Elena's own family, the Petrescus, also had its members at different levels of the hierarchy.[26]

Three of Ceauşescu's brothers held important positions in the government after 1983. Ion was a deputy chief of the State Planning Commission, but the main interest centered on two other brothers, Ilie and Nicolae Andruta Ceauşescu. In 1983 both were promoted, Ilie, a military historian of much activity and mediocrity, to be a deputy minister of defense, and Nicolae Andruta to be a lieutenant-general in the interior ministry. These appointments were connected with rumors of an attempted military coup by some army officers at the beginning of 1983. There was much circumstantial evidence to support these rumors,[27] and their promotions seem to have been a case of resorting to one's family for support and protection in times of crisis. Ceauşescu's two brothers were his own men—more, his own family—in the two ministries that were the most crucial, not so much for his success as for his very survival. Ceauşescu appears to have resorted to "familialization" when he lost trust in the inner nomenklatura. His relations with his subordinates appear to have been caught in a spiral of paranoia and disaffection, fed and speeded by the extremism, absurdity, and failures of his policies. He first resorted to his wife, then to relatives in both his and his wife's families. At the same time the preferment of Nicu, their son, began. Then the key postings of the two brothers. By the end of 1985 the Ceauşescu regime was based less on the inner nomenklatura as on the inner and outer core of the family.

It was a bizarre process to be explained partly by sociology.[28] In Ceauşescu's case the megalomania process must also be taken into account. Active opposition to him over the years appears to have been slight, but there could still have been enough, actual and perceived, to drive him into the arms of his family. The discovery in 1972 of the treasonable activities of General Ion Şerb, who was accused of passing military secrets to the Soviet embassy, could have fueled inordinate suspicions of Soviet intrigue.[29] In the party itself, despite all the sycophancy and the dues paid to the personality cult, there have been cases of opposition. One of the most notable was at the eleventh party congress in 1974, when efforts to make Ceauşescu secretary-general *for life* (presumably aping the Yugoslav example with Tito) were defeated, and the congress ended in some disorder.[30] On several occasions Ceauşescu has also thought fit to complain, not just of sluggishness in obeying his orders, but of opposition to them.[31] And any opposition, however slight or scattered, seemed likely to ratchet the paranoia.

The megalomania kept pace. A cult of personality can be explained in terms of logic and calculation. It need not have a pathological aspect to it. But such a degeneration is difficult to avoid, and in Ceauşescu's case it became its dominant aspect. The heavily orchestrated paeans of praise, the idealized portraits, and the prostrations can better be explained by temperamental vagaries than by any planned striving for political effect or the instinctive adoption of historical or cultural traditions.

Two examples, ascending steeply in degree of megalomania, may be noted. The first was Ceauşescu's chosen regalia when the office of state presidency was instituted in 1974 with himself, of course, as the first incumbent. He appeared in front of the cameras carrying a scepter and sporting a sash of the Romanian national colors. Such an apparition might be explained rationally: that Romania's leader sought to project a sense of historical unity and continuity. But Ceauşescu's subsequent behavior leaves little doubt that, in this patriotic theater, the irrational played a very important role. This example, however, though ludicrous enough, was relatively harmless. The second has been anything but that. In 1984 work began in Bucharest on a monumental civic center dedicated to socialism (and to the personal gratification of Nicolae Ceauşescu). A huge complex of buildings, in classic pharonic style, was planned, with 1990 as the tentative completion date. To make way for this creation a whole city quarter was to be destroyed, including a number of historical and religious buildings, and at least 40,000 residents relocated. The projects could in no way be defended on the grounds of civic planning, as some earlier transformations of other parts of Bucharest could. This project would, when completed, be a monument to vandalism as well as megalomania.[32]

The Economic Deterioration

But the failure of Ceauşescu that has had the greatest impact on the mass of the Romanian population has been in economic policy. Here, his own inclinations fully accorded with the imperatives of primitive communism: human regimentation, heavy industry, "gigantomania," the socialization of agriculture, the ideologically motivated prejudice against private gain.

To take this last-listed imperative first. The Romanians make up an individualistic and entrepreneurial nation. Given a little business freedom within a less suffocating framework, many would have been successful. Their individualism might have been greater than their public spirit, but in the end *everyone* would have gained from their enterprise —not least the state.

Such entrepreneurial freedom might not, of course, have had a huge impact on Romania's longer-term economic progress or on basic questions of economic policy. But the unshackling of small workshops, artisanry, catering establishments, handicrafts, services, and the like would have stimulated economic activity among many Romanians and made the life of many more a great deal more convenient. This, however, would have meant recognizing and truckling to *spontaneity*, which, as mentioned several times in this book, "real, existing socialism" fears and rejects. And, in this respect, Ceauşescu has probably been the greatest "real, existing socialist" of them all. Indeed, much of his political, cultural, and economic policy can be explained by his aversion to spontaneity. In economics this is evident in more ways than his rejection of an effective private business sector. It has meant that no real economic reform, involving decentralization and the market, could be implemented. In agriculture it has meant a deep official suspicion of private plots, of auxiliary activity by the collectives, and of any real degree of management autonomy for the whole of the rural socialist sector. In late 1985 when even the more conservative Eastern European regimes were toying with some notions of economic reform, Ceauşescu ostentatiously made it clear that no marketlike innovations would be tolerated in Romania.[33]

This ideological conservatism by no means implies, however, that Ceauşescu left the Romanian economy dozing in a centralized continuum. Over the years it was in fact the subject of an almost constant organizational harassment. The quest for greater efficiency has been constant. Structures, like people, have been chopped, changed, and then restored. Experiments purporting to establish "collegiality," worker democracy, participation, and a sense of ownership have been introduced with great fanfare and then allowed slowly to sink in the sand. A "New Economic Mechanism" introduced in 1978 was nothing like its Hungarian or even its Bulgarian namesake but was simply another set of tinkering devices.

Ceauşescu appears to have genuinely believed that a sense of common ownership, however distant, and as direct a worker participation as large-scale industry allowed would be motive and incentive enough for a successful economy, whether in industry or agriculture. His was a primitive form of collectivism and one that instinctively shunned any concession to the individual or to private gain.

A principle like this was a passport to disaster. But all Romania's economic misfortunes could not be ascribed to the huge ideological blind spot of its leader. The disaster that overtook the Romanian petrochemical industry in the 1970s is a case in point. In 1965 the decision was made to expand the industry based partly on Romania's own (steadily declining) oil deposits but mainly on imports of then cheap Middle Eastern oil. At the time the decision seemed rational and farsighted. But the whole project was doomed by the OPEC price explosions of the 1970s. In 1980 Romania imported almost 16 million tons of oil, and as late as 1985 the figure was 13.9 million.[34] The whole project caused huge (undisclosed) losses, and by 1981 some 30 percent of the country's refining and petrochemical industry was idle. Mainly because of the rocketing world price of oil Romania began importing small amounts of Soviet oil in 1979, and by 1985 the Soviets were offering 3 million tons.[35] Subsequently the plummeting of world prices in 1985 and 1986 began to make the project look more attractive again, just as it made the increasing imports from the Soviet Union all the more expensive over the longer term. Whether it could ever acquire sufficient momentum to become worthwhile remained, however, very doubtful.

It was largely the need to import large quantities of Middle Eastern oil to feed the new monster that had been created, and the need to borrow in the West to do this, that hastened Romania's economic crisis.[36] In view of Ceauşescu's ideological and economic prejudices it is surprising that economic crisis did not hit earlier in the 1970s than it did. Allowing for some important differences, the Romanian experience was similar to that of Poland. Both countries, especially Poland, went in for import-led growth. But Romania felt the impact of the first OPEC price explosion less than Poland. In the first half of the decade it was still relying mainly on domestic oil. Manufactured exports continued to grow, and refined oil exports in the new high-priced era did well. Romania, in fact, managed to improve its trade position between 1975 and 1978.[37] As for borrowing, the Romanian record still seemed good. By the criteria of creditworthiness such as debt service ratio, debt export ratio, and per capita debt level, Romania was higher than any other East European country except Czechoslovakia. But just as the Polish economy began to show signs of collapse in 1978, so the Romanian began flying danger signals. As Laura Tyson puts it: "By 1977–78 the Romanian economy began to exhibit the traditional characteristics of shortage associated with an excessive investment drive, including disruptions in raw material and fuel supplies, a sharp increase in the number and volume of incomplete investment projects and shortages too in consumer goods markets. . . ."[38] The rate of industrial growth and growth of the national product also dropped sharply. Unfinished investment in the socialist sector more than doubled. Production in some of the major industrial branches plummeted.

It was now that the petrochemical industry project became a nightmare. Between 1976 and 1980 the volume of petroleum imports more than doubled. Nearly all of it came from the Middle East at prices that were skyrocketing. It has been estimated that in 1979 the unit value index for Romanian oil imports rose 55 percent in 1979 and 66 percent in 1980.[39] The miseries of its oil industry were aggravated by the fall of the royal government in Iran and then by the Iran-Iraq war. Both of these events led to a sharp reduction in the volume of oil imports, much of which had been on a barter basis. Domestic oil production also declined steadily after 1976. The foreign trade deficit rose dramatically, and Romania began borrowing heavily mainly to finance the deficits. And it began borrowing heavily when it had become much less advantageous to do so (see chapter 4). In 1977 Romania's gross debt stood at only $3.6 billion and its net debt at $3.4 billion. By 1981 the figures were $10.2 billion and $9.8 billion, respectively, and Romania was unable to meet its obligations.[40] In the course of 1982 it had to make rescheduling agreements with a number of Western banks. Its access to further credit was barred. Romania, with very few reserves, was practically insolvent, and it was this, as well as the international humiliation involved, that caused Ceauşescu to embark in 1981 on a policy of minimizing imports and maximizing exports and thereby steadily paying off the debt. He apparently pursued this with a ruthlessness no other East European country in a similar position could approach. By the beginning of 1986 the net debt was down to about $6 billion. Romania restored its credit rating, and the previous year had actually been welcomed back to the "borrowers' club" by taking out a small Western loan of $150 million. But in May 1986 it suddenly informed its main Western creditors that it was unable to meet its repayment commitments and, in effect, asked for a second debt rescheduling.

Among the reasons cited for this default was the effect on Romanian agriculture of the Chernobyl disaster.[41] Thus the sacrifices the long-suffering Romanians had had to make in the form of constantly increasing food shortages looked likely to continue and become more onerous. It should also be noted that Romanian food exports were not simply going in a westward direction. The need for imports of Soviet oil led to increased food exports to the Soviet Union as well.[42] By the turn of the 1980s the food shortages had become desperate. Rationing of bread and flour was decreed in October 1981, and prison sentences were imposed for hoarding. Heavy price increases in 1982 and 1983 helped relieve the shortage of some foodstuffs but in a way calculated to hurt the worst-off in society.

These miseries coincided with alarming energy shortages, accentuated by severe winters. In the winter of 1982–83 public and shop lighting was forbidden in most towns from relatively early evening. The following winter the situation was even worse, with factory production often coming to a halt. In the winter of 1985–86 heating and lighting in houses or apartments were impossible or forbidden for long periods, and Ceauşescu's desperation was such that he virtually turned the electric power complex over to the military to run.[43] This was not just an abject confession of failure. It was also establishing a dangerous precedent. In what had become the key economic sector the civil regime had confessed its impotence. What had happened in Poland on a countrywide scale over four years before had now happened in Romania in one segment of public life. It invited conjecture dangerous to Ceauşescu and, beyond him, to the whole communist system.

It was a debacle like this that represented the reality of the Romanian economy rather than the overall economic statistics, most of which continued fairly impressive. Throughout the 1970s the alleged yearly rate of growth of the Net Material Product was almost spectacularly high: 11.3 percent between 1975 and 1976 and 7.1 percent between 1976 and 1980—quite the highest in Eastern Europe. In the general regional depression at the beginning of the 1980s the rates sank rapidly to 2.1 percent in 1981 and 2.8 percent the following year. In 1983 they began to pick up, and by the end of 1984 they were over 7 percent again.[44] (Romanian statistics are considered by experts the most unreliable and inadequate in the whole of Eastern Europe. But however inaccurate these figures might be they faithfully indicate an approximate trend.) The longer-term economic prospects were, however, dim in what was after all the richest country in natural resources in Eastern Europe. The prospects for the overall standard of living were still dimmer.

Public Opposition and Dissent

Most observers, bearing in mind the degeneration of Ceauşescu's rule and the rising public dissatisfaction, have pointed to the relative quiescence of the Romanian population. In general, they are correct. In terms of the provocation offered, the response was small. But it was not to be dismissed entirely. From the beginning of the 1970s there were probably more signs of opposition to the regime in Romania than in any other country in the Warsaw Pact, with the towering exception of Poland. It was never such as to pose a serious threat, not even enough apparently to turn Ceauşescu from his appointed path. But some of it must have caused considerable concern. In any case, the same point must be made about Romania as that made for Bulgaria (see chapter 10): it has been a country scantily covered by the Western press, at least after the novelty of the Romanian "deviation" had worn off. It was never so poorly served as Bulgaria, and there have always seemed to be good communications between dissidents in Bucharest and the Romanian colonies in Western capitals, especially Paris. But Western media coverage has remained inadequate, and it must be assumed that much transpires that is never reported.

Societal opposition can be considered in a number of categories:[45]

Workers. Here opposition has generally seemed to be sullen or simmering rather than openly rebellious. But there have apparently been many small strikes or temporary work stoppages. The most dramatic incident appears to have been the strike of some 35,000 coal miners in the River Jiu Valley in August 1977. The stoppage ended only after Ceauşescu's personal intervention, a foray that reflected both his presence of mind and courage. In 1981 in a much less publicized incident Ceauşescu's helicopter was reported stoned by striking miners. In the case of the Jiu Valley it should be noted that the regime's concessions to the miners, in the form of pay and working conditions, was followed by savage Securitate reprisals.[46] Elsewhere there have been sporadic reports over the years of sabotage in large factories, many of which can be discounted. But some were confirmed by reliable sources who usually tended to play down the extent of any damage involved. In November 1987 there were reports of demonstrations and arrests in Brasov. Restiveness was growing, and such outbreaks could increase.

Peasants. There have been no reliable reports of open peasant resistance on a scale worth mentioning. But there is no doubt that passive resistance in the form of withholding food supplies and destroying livestock has been endemic. The regime would do well to watch the countryside. Patient the Romanian peasants may be, but they have a tradition of revolt. There may be still a few who can tell stories about the massive rising of 1907.

Religious. The Romanian Orthodox church has continued for the most part to wallow in comfortable subservience. Striking exceptions like Father Calciu, sentenced to ten years for subversion and inhumanly treated, seemed only to prove the rule. Among other denominations and sects, however, there were signs of lively activities. The Baptists in Romania, numbering about a quarter of a million, have conducted a vigorous life of their own and received succor from their brethren in the United States and elsewhere. (Some of the large supplies of Bibles sent them from the United States were confiscated by the regime and recycled as toilet paper. Initial incredulity about this was dispelled when irrefutable proof actually reached the West.) A bizarre example of religious or mystical deviation was the so-called "Transcendental Meditation" group that included a considerable number of regime officials as well as various intellectuals. It appears to have been a trendy, alienated human collection seeking to sublimate Ceauşescu's Romania in any way it could. It was uncovered with no little embarrassment in 1982.[47]

Intellectual. As with the Orthodox church, so with the vast majority of Romanian intellectuals: with very few exceptions, though despising the regime, they have taken what it offered and remained silent or, tongue in cheek, have bent before the personality cult. A tiny minority, of which Paul Goma, a high-ranking novelist who was allowed to emigrate to the West, was the outstanding example, tried an open resistance that probably reached its high point in 1977. But men like Goma received practically no support. A number of literary works reflected the contempt of their authors for "present-day reality," but, by and large, Romania's writers, many of whom had real ability, showed no inclination to mount even the most figurative barricade. Of any serious attempts to make common cause with workers there was scarcely a trace.

Nationalities. This opposition is covered at some length in chapter 14. Among the German minority, opposition was slight largely because of the growing desire of most Germans to emigrate to the Federal

Republic and of the opportunities for them to do so. With the Hungarians it was different. The opportunities to move to Hungary were far fewer and the desire to remain incomparably stronger. As regime discrimination against them mounted, the Hungarians, therefore, resorted to a resistance that was mainly a form of self-protection. This grew considerably in the second half of the 1970s. Letters and petitions citing discrimination and often violent victimization were smuggled to the West. Several petitions invoked the Helsinki Final Act of 1975 in appealing to Western governments to call Bucharest to account for its violation of both the letter and spirit of that document. Several underground Hungarian journals took up the cause of the minority. Resistance, which received strong *moral* support from across the border in Hungary, persisted.

These, then, were the main types of societal opposition or resistance. Opposition from within the regime itself has been mentioned earlier in this chapter. It is difficult to gauge the extent of military opposition from the paucity of information available. The Şerb case of 1972 was followed by a long period of quiet until 1983 when there was considerable evidence to suggest open dissension among some officers. At the same time General Constantin Olteanu, minister of defense, was promoted to the Political Executive Committee. The same General Olteanu, however, was abruptly dismissed at the end of 1985 just after returning from a visit to Moscow.[48] This inevitably provoked speculation about the general's indiscretions, or even worse. Certainly after 1983 there was continually more evidence suggesting Ceauşescu's dissatisfaction with the military and their dissatisfaction with him.

As for the security services, the increasing number of defections from their ranks to the West presumably reflected considerable dissatisfaction. The most prominent defector was General Ion Pacepa who defected to the United States in 1978. He and other defectors provided lurid details about their former colleagues and about their terrorist activities in the West—often too lurid to be true.

It did seem, therefore, that in the two main forces of coercion at the regime's disposal—the military and the security services—that had previously been considered as strong buttresses of Ceauşescu's rule, there was some degree of instability, uncertainty, or disaffection. Taken together with the growing but still inchoate disaffection within the party itself, it could eventually represent a threat to the Ceauşescu dynasty. It could become that danger from inside that was so much more formidable when there were so few friends outside.

Layers of Isolation

After more than twenty years of rule Ceauşescu's immediate problem appeared to be his physical health. His face, even when touched up for newspaper photographs, indicated a sick man.[49] But, assuming that the denials or reassurances coming out of Bucharest were true, what faced Ceauşescu was a growing isolation. It was isolation at different levels—from Romanian society, within his own regime, from the West, from China, and from the Third World. About his isolation from society little more needs be written. The massive backing he had in 1968 when he defied the Soviets had all but evaporated. True, a threadbare legitimacy still remained, deriving from his unquestioned patriotism and continued insistence on autonomy from Moscow. But it had been wearing fast. He was still an adroit manipulator, however, and he knew how to tap national emotions. His publicity performances after his differences with Moscow at the Warsaw Pact meeting in November 1978 and again in 1986 were ample evidence of this. It may be too much to claim that he simply manufactured crises like these and that they were solely propaganda stunts aimed at shoring up public support. The issue did, after all, appear to be serious enough. But he doubtless used it for all it was worth.

Since national emotion seemed all that was left to him to exploit, there was always the possibility that he would deliberately bring on some confrontation with either the Hungarian or the German minorities. In an age of nationalism and in a region where, in spite of all doctrinal pretensions, it was waxing rather than waning, such a move would elicit considerable Romanian support. The view of most Romanians on the minority issue has often been ignored in the general sympathy felt for the Hungarians in their historic predicament and in view of the ultimate threat to their existence. Romanians generally consider the Hungarians an aggressive nation, and they regard the behavior of the Hungarian minority in Romania as having become more aggressive in recent years. They, therefore, have less sympathy than ever for the rights of the minority—and they never had much (see chapter 14). The issue was one Ceauşescu could use to much propaganda advantage. But the returns derived from it would be finite. What would remain to be exploited after this?

Within his own regime, his isolation was shown by his resort to family. Still, he probably had little to fear. Despite the cynicism and distrust between him and many apparatchiks, there was a mutual interest in survival. If he departed, many who had served him would be vulnerable, especially when so few had ever sought to restrain him. The regime, therefore, had probably settled into a negative cohesion, bound together for the present out of fear for the future.

As for the family, its own cohesiveness would presumably tighten as its isolation grew more evident and as the leader's dependence on it increased in relation to his own isolation. But it faced a precarious future, dependent as it was on a man whose mortality seemed to have become distressingly obvious. Whatever arrangements Ceaușescu might have made for his succession were not likely to remain intact long after his departure. If those arrangements involved any family member —either Elena or Nicu—succeeding him, they would not last at all. They could be contested even before Ceaușescu's death. This possibility seemed to many observers the one thing that could galvanize the groups of potential dissent in the party, military, and Securitate and cause them to coalesce. It could even cause active interference by Moscow.[50] Whichever way, the days of the clan looked numbered, and among the more realistic of them the main concern was probably that they should be let down as lightly as possible.

Ceaușescu's isolation from the West had, ironically, been growing ever since the end of the 1960s when he was at the height of his popularity and acclaim, both at home and in the West itself. This was because Bonn's Ostpolitik, and détente in general, had destroyed Romania's uniqueness in East-West relations. As Western relations with Poland, the GDR, and Hungary proliferated—not to mention those with the Soviet Union—Romania inevitably fell several places in the priorities of the Western states concerned (see chapter 3). Even had Ceaușescu maintained the good behavior of his first few years, Romania's importance and desirability would have diminished. As it was, he proceeded to unfold a domestic policy that thoroughly alienated all but the most eccentric of his erstwhile Western admirers. His nuisance value as the Soviet alliance maverick remained. But even that had diminished. In the case of the Federal Republic he still held the 250,000 Romanian Germans as potential hostages and had to be treated carefully on that score. But for the West generally, Romania had not only diminished in value but had become something of an embarrassment. Nowhere was this more evident than in the United States with its "open house" formation of foreign policy. Romania's most favored nation (MFN) status granted, almost enthusiastically in 1975, became a hotly debated annual issue in Congress, and in early 1986 Secretary of State

George Schultz, while visiting Romania, energetically relayed American concern to Ceauşescu over his persistent denials of human rights.

Romania's isolation from China has been discussed earlier. Similarly, though relations with Yugoslavia were still close, the growing weakness of both countries detracted from the value of their association. Romania's isolation from the Third World was at least as rapid as that of Yugoslavia after Tito's death in 1980, and its relationship, in any case, had never been as close or its standing as high as Yugoslavia's. The offensive in the Third World had developed out of Ceauşescu's own forcefulness, as a further means of political protection from the Soviet Union ("unofficial nonalignment") and for reasons of trade and general economic advantage. But by the late 1980s, though formal relations with most developing countries continued, their dynamism had spent itself. Always a gambit rather than a real policy, with more headlines than fine print, Romania's global pretensions shrank as quickly as Ceauşescu's charisma dimmed.

This left the Soviet Union master of the alliance to which Romania nominally adheres. It was Romania that chose to isolate itself as far as possible from this alliance in the early 1960s. Twenty years later the question being asked centered on how far Romania was now seeking to return from that isolation toward a closer relationship with Moscow. There were, indeed, some indications that prompted this question. Economic relations had grown closer; the Soviet Union had become a supplier of oil; the number of bilateral agreements on economic collaboration had increased considerably. Romania, since the Warsaw Pact imbroglio of 1978, had seemed anxious to avoid *openly* airing its differences with Moscow. But any speculation about Romania returning to the fold was clearly premature. Soviet-Romanian differences still existed, and economic cooperation between the two countries was still well below the level that need involve political surrender. Ceauşescu seemed eager to maintain his distance. Despite the degeneration and disappointment of his rule, he still remained a patriot, and, though he was conclusive enough proof that patriotism alone is not enough, there was never reason to doubt his sincerity. Besides, he was shrewd enough to see that, despite its debasement, patriotism remained his only valuable coin.

And Gorbachev? He visited Bucharest in the summer of 1987—not surprisingly the last Warsaw Pact capital to receive his introductory call. His differences, personal and policy, with Ceauşescu were plain to see. In future there was no reason to expect that he would not play the same waiting game as his predecessors. Gorbachev may have been a man in a hurry, but there were far more pressing issues summoning his haste and vigor. Time and patience were perhaps all he needed in Romania's case.

9 Czechoslovakia

If this book had been written shortly before, during, or shortly after 1968, Czechoslovakia would have dominated it. For one thing, the drama and tragedy of the Prague Spring are the real stuff of which history is made.[1] For another, the Czechoslovak reform movement and the fate that befell it were a watershed in the history of communist rule in Eastern Europe. It showed communism's potential for evolution if the country concerned were left to its own devices. But it also showed the limitations on the exploiting of that potential that the Soviet Union was prepared to impose if it was seen to threaten its imperial position, its international security, and the power and privileges of its ruling elite. As long as the Soviet Union stayed where it was and the way it was, no dependent communist regime would be allowed to regenerate itself in terms of the history and ideals of the country it ruled.

It was an inspiring and exhilarating episode while it lasted. Nor has it disappeared without trace. For its ideals became the forbidden fruit of reformers everywhere. The vehemence with which they were rejected attest to their appeal and relevance. The link between greater personal freedoms, political pluralism, and economic reform—the essence of the Prague Spring—was what every genuine reformer in Eastern Europe after 1968 knew was essential but also knew could not be proclaimed. It was a contradiction well calculated to feed the Czech predilection for rueful irony.

But after the failure of "consumerism" in the 1970s, the subsequent economic depression, the obvious bankruptcy of "real, existing socialism" and the thinking on which it was based, more and more thoughtful East Europeans, inside and outside the political establishment, were quietly turning again to some of the ideas of 1968. What drew them especially was the notion that institutional reform was required to guarantee change. The rise of Solidarity was partly influenced by this idea. In both Hungary and Yugoslavia the same idea was even lapping the shores of public life. The Prague Spring, therefore, whether through demonstrative rejection or stealthy acceptance, remained a force in the politics of Eastern Europe.

It has been in Czechoslovakia itself, however, despite the consistency and courage of a heroic handful, that the Prague Spring has often seemed to come closest to real rejection. And not just by the new ruling elite that emerged after 1968 from the debris of the old. In the collapse of public morale after the invasion some sections of society chose to vent their spleen on the reformers of 1968. They, it appeared, were being held responsible for the present predicament. And the few who still persisted with active dissent were often the target of particular abuse. It was an emotional and all too understandable response. But it resulted in the Czech nation, especially, lapsing again into one of its historical sloughs of despond that, together with a do-nothing regime, made Czechoslovakia a backwater for almost twenty years.

"Normalization"

The popular mood of disillusion and resentment considerably eased the task of Gustáv Husák's reactionary regime in speedily restoring "normalcy." It was an easy one compared with the massive and Sisyphean task facing General Jaruzelski in Poland after the imposition of martial law in December 1981. In Czechoslovakia there was practically no popular resistance. Still, the new Husák regime, which came into power in April 1969, found it advisable to carry out massive purges and dismissals that probably accounted for more than half a million people, among them many of the most qualified political, professional, and military personnel. Order was guaranteed by the civil police and militia, full-time and part-time, the thoroughly purged Czechoslovak armed forces, and, ultimately, of course, by a Soviet military force, "temporarily stationed," as the official media insisted, of between 50,000 to 75,000. These purges were accompanied by political trials involving several hundred of the more prominent, or recalcitrant, supporters of the Prague Spring, and this number would have been much higher but for the emigration of some reform supporters after August 1968.

Whether the dismissals, which deprived Czechoslovakia of so much talent, were really needed on such a scale is open to question. Many of those affected would, with varying degrees of cheerfulness, probably have adapted to the new order and placed their services at its disposal. It was, most likely, the nervousness and vindictiveness of the new Husák regime that made the victims so numerous. The Soviets themselves can hardly be blamed totally. They had suffered a great fright and, wishing to avoid the same experience again, doubtlessly insisted that the bourgeois-democratic "cancer" be cut out. But they can hardly have supervised the purges down to the last detail. Inside the Czechoslovak regime itself Husák stood out against even more severe purges and apparently against show trials of reform leaders like Dubček himself and Josef Smrkovský. And, though Husák cannot dodge the blame for the purges, it was others who set the tone for them. These were men like Vasil Bilak, the Ruthenian who stood for Slovakia and Stalinism, and the Czech Alois Indra, who pressed for "retribution" against Dubček and his circle. And men like these had their counterparts at every rung of the public ladder, men and women who had waited to settle scores or to pursue ambitions.

The massive purges, which lasted about four years, were part of Husák's "normalization." The other part consisted of measures designed to induce the population as a whole to accept the new order and, if possible, to work for it. One of the best commentators on the Czechoslovak situation, Vladimir Kusin, has attributed Husák's successes in "normalization" to what he calls "the 3 Cs": coercion, consumerism, and circuses.[2] Coercion, through purge and vigilance, has just been discussed. By "circuses" Kusin means the "toleration of a widened range of individual entertainment [that] formed another factor in the depoliticization scheme." Here are included pop music (as long as it was tepid enough), Western theatrical and television movies, detective stories, a plethora of cookbooks, and soap opera TV sagas (some of them quite tolerable compared with their capitalist counterparts). More substantial was the regime's material and moral encouragement of house and apartment building and—more important in this context—of weekend dwellings in the country. These latter increased from 128,000 in 1969 to 160,000 in 1973 to 225,000 in 1981 in the Czech Lands alone.[3]

Finally, there was "consumerism." In the late 1960s and the first half of the 1970s Czechoslovakia joined in the Eastern European prosperity. The basis of this prosperity and the most important aspects of it are discussed in chapter 4. Here it need only be emphasized that consumerism was a vital part of the Soviet leadership's post-1968 program for Eastern Europe. Its essential political element was to promote, or restore, stability. It was hardly coincidental, therefore, that Poland, after the riots of 1970 that toppled Gomułka, and Czechoslovakia were to experience big increases in real incomes and living standards. And in both cases the Soviets helped directly with financial aid to maintain living standards in the immediate aftermath of their upheavals,[4] although the aid to Czechoslovakia appears to have been substantially less than to Poland, probably because the economic need was less.

In Czechoslovakia the rise in living standards can be demonstrated by a few figures for the 1970s. Between 1971 and 1975, while real wages rose by a relatively modest 5 percent, personal consumption rose by 27 percent. In 1971 one in seventeen people had an automobile; in 1975 one in ten; in 1979 one in eight.[5]

Certainly Vladimir Kusin's "3 Cs" go a long way to explain the effectiveness of Husák's normalization. But three more factors might also be taken into account. One is the Czech national mood, discussed above. The second is Husák's political skill. The third is the situation in Slovakia that had special characteristics and cannot be squeezed into one comprehensive Czechoslovak frame.

Gustáv Husák

Certainly Husák's leadership cannot be ignored. Moral revulsion at the role he has played since 1968 need not blind one to his political skills, courage, tenacity, and dominant personality.

Had Husák died just before, or even just after, the Soviet-led invasion of Czechoslovakia he would have been remembered as one of the positive figures of recent East European history. An intellectual and a Slovak nationalist, he made his mark in Czechoslovak politics after World War II as an able, ruthless, and rising communist in Bratislava. Two of his closest collaborators were Vladímir (Vlado) Clementis, another Slovak communist who became Czechoslovak foreign minister, and the communist poet, Laço Novomeský. In the Stalinist show trials that were delayed in Czechoslovakia until 1951 and ended only after three years, first Clementis was executed in 1952 and then Husák and Novomeský were sentenced to life imprisonment in 1954. All three were sentenced for "bourgeois" (Slovak) nationalism. Clementis became a Slovak national communist martyr, while Husák gained respect from many Czechs and Slovaks for his courageous behavior in prison.

He was released in 1960 and partially rehabilitated in 1963, though he was not allowed to reenter political life until January 1968. He became something of a popular hero in Slovakia as Slovak demands for federal status grew louder with the slow disintegration of Antonín Novotný's rule. His following among young people was particularly strong and enthusiastic. In 1965 he appeared to be one of the champions, not only of Slovak nationalism, but also of the democratic reforms of the Prague Spring. He also appeared unswervingly loyal to Dubček personally. In 1968 he was made a deputy premier. But on August 23, two days after the invasion, he flew with the then President Svoboda and several hard-line Czechoslovak leaders to Moscow to negotiate with the Soviets. Two days before the core of the reform leadership, Dubček, Premier Oldřich Černík, Smrkovský, and František Kriegel, had been arrested by Soviet troops in Prague and flown to Moscow. It was during the sessions in Moscow when the Soviets dictated their terms to the Czechoslovaks that Husák evidently caught Brezhnev's eye as the man who might take over the new Czechoslovak leadership. At any rate, from then Husák's star was in the ascendant. He immediately became leader of the Slovak party and very soon a member of the Czechoslovak Politburo. In April 1969, when Dubček was finally removed from the Czechoslovak party leadership, it seemed inevitable that it was Gustáv Husák who took his place.

Until his ascent to the topmost position in the land, some points of Husák's career had been similar to those in that of János Kádár in Hungary. Both had been victims of internal party feuding and had been barbarously treated. Both, after appearing to support popular movements, had been earmarked by the Soviet Union to desert them and lead a process of orthodox stabilization. The Soviet Union took a risk with both of them and came to congratulate itself on the wisdom of its choice.

But Kádár, once stabilization had been achieved, embarked on his program of reform, and it was his example that led many to speculate whether Husák would do the same. Several years later speculation had shifted to why he had not done so. Husák not only showed no inclination to follow the Kádár example; his regime had become a champion of unimaginative orthodoxy and indeed a behind-the-scenes critic of Hungarian policy.

There have been two principal reasons for Husák's *immobilisme*. First, his own personality and background. Husák could never break the mold that had shaped him. A member of the provincial intelligentsia of interwar Slovakia, he made a choice early in his life for Leninism, which inculcated a rigid orthodoxy and only reinforced his already existing narrowness of outlook. Ambition, courage, ruthlessness, drive, and a calculating intelligence, these were some of the attributes he combined with a strong and determined character. Without this strength of character he could not have survived his imprisonment in the 1950s. But this long imprisonment may also have retarded or even frozen his political development.[6] (For his similarities in this respect to Gomułka, see chapter 5.) He was a victim of Stalinism and, to his credit, refused to be associated with Stalinist methods of terror when he himself achieved power. But his dogmatic, conservative cast of mind made him insist that the Leninist institutions, which Stalin had developed and then embedded in the system, were untouchable. He opposed what he considered the errors of Stalinism, but not its essence. His political opposition to Novotný derived from this sentiment. But against Novotný he also had the personal score of his own imprisonment and the national score of Slovak grievance to settle. It added up to a formidable bill of indictment against the pre-1968 Czechoslovak regime.

As for 1968 itself, Husák, despite some strongly reformist utterances, was never closely identified with the Dubček reform group, and certainly not with the army of intellectuals straining at the leash. But after the invasion it was not only the Soviets who looked to him to normalize the situation their way; many Czechoslovaks, especially in Slovakia, looked to him to save what could be saved. And in his speeches between August 1968 and April 1969 he gave the impression that this was what he would try to do. In the end, of course, he satisfied the Soviets and disappointed many of his countrymen. In some Czechoslovaks he aroused a hatred that made any balanced appraisal impossible. But perhaps Husák's behavior after 1968 can best be explained not by any principle but rather by ambition—the ambition to take power and then to keep it. His great days were before he came to power. In the eyes of many what he did afterward sullied and then destroyed the reputation he had built.

But to ascribe everything to Husák's personality would be to forget the broader circumstances in which he came to power. In 1968 and 1969 Moscow prescribed a policy of orthodoxy to disperse the national and ideological "heresies" that had gathered in the 1960s. These heresies had been generated by Stalinism and accelerated by the attempts to exorcise it. Czechoslovakia had been the center of disintegration, and Brezhnev needed a leader orthodox, reliable, and capable enough to be considered "safe." Husák was that man.

The circumstances in which Kádár took power in Hungary in 1956 were in many ways similar. What was strikingly dissimilar was the response to them of the then Soviet leader, Nikita Khrushchev. In the immediate post-Stalin situation Khrushchev had staked his political life on a policy of change and more autonomy for the East European satellites. In this he was opposed by strong forces within the Soviet leadership. The disasters in Hungary and Poland in 1956 might have led to a halt in the reform process. But, once order had been restored, Khrushchev did not insist on a new *Gleichschaltung*. In Hungary, at any rate, he was content to let reform resume under Kádár. Thus Kádár came to power when Soviet policy and attitudes were quite different from what they were when Husák came to power in Czechoslovakia. Khrushchev believed reform necessary; Kádár thought so too and produced it. Brezhnev wanted reaction; Husák gave it to him. Even had he wanted to be, Husák could not have become another Kádár. But at least he resisted those, both in Moscow and Prague, who wanted him to become another Rákosi.

The Situation in Slovakia

The history of Slovakia after World War II deserves more treatment than it usually receives.[7] In the minds of far too many, Slovakia as a separate entity hardly exists or, even if it does, it is seen as a similar, if less developed, version of Bohemia and Moravia, the Czech Lands. Many Czech observers themselves, though pillars of liberalism in other respects, have difficulties in accepting the distinctiveness of Slovakia and Slovaks. But it has been a fact of Czechoslovak life ever since the foundation of the First Republic after World War I. During 1968 and afterward this distinctiveness became increasingly apparent. What motivated most Slovaks in 1968 was not democracy but nationalism. Many may even have wanted independence, but most were prepared to settle for federal status for Slovakia. This they got in October 1968, in the only major reform of the Prague Spring to survive, despite serious modifications as early as 1970.[8] Since 1968 many of the burgeoning Slovak political, economic, and cultural elite have been relatively satisfied. Jobs in the growing Bratislava bureaucracy have been plentiful; Czechs, who once dominated Slovak economic and educational life, have virtually disappeared; more jobs were available for Slovaks in the federal bureaucracy in Prague, not a few by virtue of the fact that the Czechoslovak president and party leader was once a strong Slovak nationalist.[9]

Moreover, the post-1968 regime in Slovakia was moderate compared with that in the Czech Lands. This was both because there was considerably less heresy to stamp out and because the ruling team in Bratislava—especially party leader Jozef Lenárt, Premier Peter Colotka, and culture minister Miroslav Valek—imposed normalization with a certain circumspection. It was mainly against religion, in its war against the Roman Catholic church, which had revived strongly before and during 1968, that the Bratislava regime showed a viciousness in deed as well as word. This it often did under the banner of the struggle against "clerical-fascism," still an evocative term in Slovakia for those remembering the puppet Slovak republic in World War II.[10]

But generalization should not lead to oversimplification. It would be as much a mistake to see Slovakia as a benevolently ruled haven of fulfilled nationalism after 1968 as it would be to see the Czech Lands groaning under a Stalinist tyranny. Slovakia is still affected by many decisions taken in Prague, and it is easy to exaggerate the moderation of its regime. The two parts of Czechoslovakia may be distinct, but they are by no means separate, and many educated Slovaks continued to feel a sense of community with their counterparts in Prague. Nevertheless, the attitudes of Czechs and Slovaks toward each other have undergone profound and subtle changes since they were thrown together after 1918. It has always been a complicated relationship. Here, however, one must suffice by saying that by the end of the 1980s the younger generation of Slovaks had lost much of the resentful inferiority complex toward the Czechs that had characterized so many of their elders. They felt (and usually were) equal to Czechs socially and intellectually. They bothered less about Czechs than before, because Czechs were now less relevant. The Czechs, who for centuries had been made to feel inferior to Germans, had tended to compensate in the first republic by feeling superior to Slovaks. But after 1968 their arrogance was steadily transmuted into a resentfulness at their own self-debasement and at the rise in self-esteem of the Slovaks. This resentfulness was only compounded by what they considered the "Slovak ascendancy" under Husák and by the new informal "Proporz" arrangement after 1968 that involved the presence of many more Slovaks in the central government than before. This increase in assertiveness corresponded to the economic progress Slovakia had made. In 1937 the Slovak population represented 26.4 percent of the total population. They received only 15 percent of the total national income and provided only 7.3 percent of the total industrial output. By 1974 Slovakia was responsible for 25 percent of the total industrial production.[11]

The Economic Slowdown

The economic prosperity that aided and abetted Husák's consumerism—as well as his circuses—did not last long. By the middle of the 1970s the economic situation began to look much less propitious. Some of the reasons for this were general, while others applied more specifically to Czechoslovakia. The OPEC price explosion of the early 1970s ushered in an economic recession in Western Europe and the United States, a recession that the second OPEC price explosion at the end of the decade only served to intensify (see chapter 4). This and the Soviet response of readjusting upward its own pricing mechanism hit the two most industrialized East European states, the GDR and Czechoslovakia, the most immediately. By as early as 1980 Czechoslovakia was paying nearly five times as much for a ton of Soviet oil than it had done in 1971 and was importing almost twice as much.[12] And this disability partly caused and fully coincided with a Czechoslovak industrial depression leading to negative industrial growth in 1981 and 1982 and overall negative national income in 1981. The economic situation recalled the beginning of the 1960s (see appendix III, table 14).

Indeed, in key respects it was now worse than it was then. At the beginning of the 1960s Czechoslovak industry and important elements of the economic infrastructure were relatively modern—or, at least, twenty years younger—and the price of Soviet raw materials was low and seemed likely to remain so. Now much of Czechoslovak industry and its infrastructure was that much older, Soviet oil deliveries were that much dearer, and were cut by 10 percent in 1982, anyway (see chapter 4). Moreover, though current supplies had been guaranteed till the end of the 1980s, the prospects looked bleak. Czechoslovak industry had, in any case, always been grossly spendthrift in its use of oil, as had East European industry generally. But the greatest single problem the whole economy faced by the middle of the 1980s was the huge number of unfinished investment projects. At the end of 1981 about 30,000 industrial building sites stood unfinished—tied-up capital representing just over 20 percent of all capital funds in the Czechoslovak economy for that year.[13]

This represented an economic disaster for Czechoslovakia, resulting from an earlier overcommitment to investment. It was investment that was self-financed and, as it turned out, could not be paid for by industrial output and export. Czechoslovakia had been reluctant to indulge in a capital investment drive financed by Western credits as most other

East European states did in the 1970s. After the profligacy of other East European countries, especially Poland, in their use of Western credits, and its catastrophic consequences, the Czechoslovak leaders had prided themselves on their prudence.[14] But foreign credits wisely used might well have avoided the investment impasse in which the economy found itself.

Moreover, a combination of wisely used Western credits and a "New Economic Mechanism," both of which have constituted Hungary's basic economy strategy, might well have secured the Czechoslovak economy by seeing it through its next unavoidable industrial revolution: that of modernization. For by the middle of the 1980s it was this daunting task, in industry itself and its infrastructure, that had to be faced, and it was more urgent for Czechoslovakia than for any other East European country. But it seemed unlikely that the task would be undertaken soon enough or on a scale big enough. For one thing the Czechoslovak regime, like several others in Eastern Europe in the early 1980s, began cutting back on investment funds in order to keep consumption up, as well as to keep sufficient reserves to expend in the energy sector.

But more fundamental was the fear of change that continued to characterize the Husák regime. Its surly return to orthodoxy after the Prague Spring was perhaps understandable enough from its own point of view. And for the first few years it seemed to be doing Czechoslovakia no economic harm. But all too soon, abhorrence of change became an ingrained way of governance. Subsequently it became a national way of life as *immobilisme* filtered down to a population needing little encouragement to lapse even further into sullenness. The regime sank deeper into the rut of its own making. It was a rut it could not even see out of, let alone climb out of. And making sure it tried neither were the custodians of the post-1968 orthodoxy, led vociferously by the aforementioned Bilak, the high priest of Czechoslovakia's counterreformation.

The Prospects for Reform

Throughout the 1970s it was the counterreformational psychosis that held undisputed sway. But three factors were in the making by the turn of the 1980s that pointed toward change. The first two concerned longevity—that of both the Czechoslovak and the Soviet leadership.

The group that took over from Dubček was relatively young. In 1969 Husák himself, born in 1913, was the oldest man in the Politburo after the death of President Ludvík Svoboda in 1975. He was followed by

Bilak, born in 1917. The rest were all born in the 1920s, with the Czechoslovak federal Prime Minister Lubomir Štrougal, born in 1924, one of the youngest. It was a leadership that displayed remarkable durability. Both direct and circumstantial evidence points to serious differences of opinion from time to time. Bilak, for example, in his famous "blue sky" outburst in 1972, was clearly criticizing a Husák remark about the situation now having stabilized and hence a less rigorous approach than before being needed.[15] Lénart and Colotka in Slovakia generally went their own way, and neither had much time for the contentious Bilak. Premier Štrougal often indicated his wish for more boldness in economic policy and was considered the best hope by a growing number of economists who stood, albeit timidly, for reform. Jozef Kempný, like Štrougal, was considered a proponent of a less suspicious attitude toward society, and his ousting from the Secretariat in 1981 may have been one of very few cases where policy differences led to a leadership breach.

But generally the ice that bound and froze the leadership refused to crack. It still refused to crack as late as the seventeenth Czechoslovak party congress in March 1986 when, contrary to many expectations, every member of the existing Politburo was reelected. As mentioned in chapter 2, the main reason probably lay in Moscow rather than Prague, with Gorbachev, again contrary to many expectations, opting for *personal* stability in Eastern Europe at least during the first period of what many expected would be a long leadership. But, despite this continuity, few expected that the now veteran leadership group would enter the last decade of the twentieth century in toto. Age would certainly take its toll. And events themselves would, almost irresistibly, demand changes in personnel as well as policy.

The longevity of the Czechoslovak leadership had been helped by Brezhnev's policy both before and after 1975. Before 1975 he pursued a vigorous orthodoxy. After 1975, as discussed in chapter 2, Moscow began pursuing the manifold ambitions of a global superpower. With Eastern Europe apparently stabilized, it became less preoccupied with the region, less directly interested in the ephemeral or the short term. If the situation seemed quiet, and Eastern Europe's leaders—all of whom except Ceauşescu he trusted—assured him it was quiet, then Brezhnev seemed satisfied. And Moscow had particular reason to be satisfied with the Husák regime. The latter's level of anxiety may have been raised briefly when Andropov succeeded Brezhnev, only to be lowered again by the accession to power of Chernenko. With the arrival of the young, vigorous Gorbachev in 1985, neither Husák nor many of his subordinates could have felt safe, especially when they saw the scattering of Brezhnev's cronies and the steady dismantling of the political machine. The advanced age of Husák and others in the Czechoslovak leadership, as well as the approach of a party congress in 1986, could have given a face-saving pretext for a "new look" in Prague, too. But the party congresses in Czechoslovakia, as well as Bulgaria and the GDR, resulted in such total leadership continuity that it must have been the result of some prearrangement. The period of grace, though, or reprieve, might be only a short one. As if realizing the dangers of this—and faced with an increasingly serious economic situation in any case—Husák signaled some movement toward economic change at the seventeenth party congress. In the summer of 1985 he had ostentatiously spoken against any truckling with the market mechanism.[16] In February of the following year he was talking about the need for meaningful "reform," actually using a word that had been taboo in Czechoslovakia since 1968.[17] Then at the party congress he actually pressed for a modification of the planning system and increased responsibility and power for enterprise managers. He appeared to be taking Czechoslovakia back to those first changes in the Stalinist economic system made in 1958, which were broadened and deepened in 1964.[18] It was not clear what Husák specifically had in mind. But those in Prague who had hoped the subject would go away must have been bitterly disappointed by the vigor with which Gorbachev urged reform in the early part of 1987. It surprised no one that it was Bilak who expressed his faction's dismay in a typically ungracious way. But the situation seemed to be turning against the philosophy of *non movere* so much so that Bilak himself was forced to mind his language. And it surprised no one that it was Premier Štrougal who became increasingly assertive in his demands for change.[19] Pragmatism, nudged by the signs in Moscow, was in the process of disinterment in Prague. By the middle of 1987 there were signs of change; Czechoslovakia, for example, was gingerly negotiating some Western credits and making efforts to increase Western trade contacts.[20] (Already at the beginning of 1986 the state and collective farms had been allowed far greater freedom than previously.[21]) By themselves these moves might mean little. But broader change, motored by Moscow, was being readily embraced by the growing number of reformers and accepted as inevitable by the conservatives.

Personalities and Policies

The reform issue would presumably influence the choice of Husák's successor. When Husák became party leader in 1969 he had several rivals, and for some years afterward the names of Bilak, Alois Indra, and Antonín Kapek, the then Prague first party secretary, were mentioned as possibly replacing him. Husák, however, played his survival politics skillfully both in Moscow and in Prague. He succeeded in neutralizing both Indra and Kapek, and, although Bilak remained as voluble as ever, his credibility as a potential party leader—never strong —sharply declined. In the second half of the 1970s Miloš Jakeš, central committee secretary for the economy and Politburo member, began to be considered as the regime's second most powerful figure and a possible successor to Husák. He had gained prominence as a hard-line apparatchik, but by the late 1980s had acquired a reputation for political suppleness. Some observers saw him now favoring economic reform. Unless this reputation were spurious, he and Premier Štrougal might take the lead in any movement toward reform. But Jakeš, born in 1922, was now approaching the veteran age. As an aspirant for the leadership, he must have been a man in a hurry. As for Štrougal, two years younger, he had been an able and receptive executive but it would surprise many if he were to move from the premiership to the party leadership.

But any Czechoslovak succession would also contain an ethnic dimension distinguishing it from other East European successions. The Czech-Slovak factor would have considerable influence. The next change of Czechoslovak party leader would be the first to have taken place in what might be termed "normal" circumstances since Slovakia acquired federal status in October 1968. (The circumstances of the change in April 1969 from Dubček to Husák were hardly "normal.") The new federal character of the Czechoslovak state, therefore, would affect the division of posts at the federal level, even those at the very top.

While a Slovak of Husák's stature and ability remained leader and as long as the memories of 1968 bound the leadership together, there was likely to be little friction based on Czech-Slovak rivalry. (This held good for the higher echelons, although lower down there was apparently friction enough.) But with the departure of Husák, few Czechs would gladly suffer a Slovak as both Czechoslovak president and party leader again. If Husák were simply to give up the party leadership and remain president—always a possibility on health grounds—then many Czechs would not want another Slovak party leader, particularly to go with a Slovak president. Similarly, many Slovaks would not want to see Czechs as both head of the party and head of government. The opportunities for dispute were legion. And there was no one in sight after Husák with the stature to bridge the jealousies. The aforementioned Jakeš appeared for several years to be the strongest contender for the party leadership. But he was Czech. The best solution would probably be a Czech as president and a Czech and Slovak taking the top party and government posts. But then there would be disputes over which posts. As long as there was, despite federation, a strong central government and a central party, located in Prague, the Czech-Slovak relationship affecting position and patronage, to mention only one issue, would be a problem. And the relationship could have wider ramifications. It could present Moscow with *divide et impera* opportunities if the need to bring Czechoslovakia to heel were ever to arise again.

It might be mentioned here in passing (since the subject is discussed more fully in chapter 14) that the Czech-Slovak relationship is not the only national issue in Czechoslovakia. There is a Slovak-Hungarian problem arising from the presence of a Hungarian minority of some 600,000 in Slovakia. Traditionally, a Slovak nationalist was anti-Hungarian by definition (Gustáv Husák was certainly no exception). Slovakia had been an integral part of Hungary for a thousand years, and Slovaks were often subjected to a ruthless Magyarization and general oppression. With the establishment of Czechoslovakia the roles were reversed, and the Hungarians were subjected to intermittent discrimination of various kinds. After federation, and hence the removal of protection Prague may have offered the Hungarians, there was little doubt that Hungarian minority rights were being increasingly violated. This led to a spirited reaction among many Hungarian Slovaks, popular indignation in Hungary itself, and quiet representations from the Hungarian government. Budapest's anger was not as great over Slovakia as it was over the Hungarians in Transylvania. But it was serious enough, and likely to get more so.

Currents in Society

Husák's methods to ensure normalization in postinvasion Czechoslovakia have been discussed earlier. They had been facilitated by popular disappointment and apathy. It was not surprising, therefore, that whatever societal dissent existed was generally of the sullen, passive variety expressed by internalization and material pursuits. This attitude became noticeable in the first part of the 1970s and has persisted. But some Czechoslovaks at least have refused to wallow in a morass of defeat and consumerism. In a notable article in *Problems of Communism* in January 1985, Gordon Skilling has described the various strands of independent activity that have crisscrossed the Czech Lands since 1975.[22] Charter 77 has tended to dominate this activity and has certainly captured most attention in the West. Beginning in January 1977 with a declaration signed by 241 men and women of assorted political views, its signatory-members had by 1985 grown slowly to about 1,200, of whom 200 had in the meantime emigrated to the West. The Chartists, essentially Czech (mostly Prague) intellectuals, kept alive, often with difficulty, the spirit of Czech democracy. Among their "spokesmen," rotated annually, have been famous and worthy men such as the playwright Václav Havel, the former foreign minister in 1968 Jiři Hájek, and the late Jan Patocka, the philosopher. These were the three original spokesmen, but most of those who have followed, though less famous, have been highly regarded and undoubtedly courageous. From the beginning the regime regarded the Chartists as its main enemy; some of its members were imprisoned and almost all hounded or harassed.[23] In 1979 Charter 77 began publishing "position papers," or "situation reports," on a wide variety of public issues: prison conditions (of which some of its members were only too well aware), scientific research, price rises, school reform, etc. One of its best-known papers was on the disastrous ecological situation in the industrial parts of the Czech Lands, about which public unease, and even regime concern, had been steadily mounting. This paper (actually a study by the Czechoslovak Academy of Sciences) could indeed become the most historic of all Charter 77's publications. The damage being done, not only to nature, but also to human beings in and near the industrial parts of Bohemia and Moravia, has been on a scale that for many makes ecology even more important in the long run than politics or the economy (see chapter 13).

Closely connected with Charter 77, though institutionally separate, was VONS (the Committee for the Defense of the Unjustly Persecuted), which was founded in 1978. VONS issued regular communiqués on cases of persecution of all kinds, and it was not surprising that, even more than Charter 77, it was the object of police curiosity. Over 450 VONS communiqués had been issued by mid-1985.

Preceding both Charter 77 and VONS was the publication of literature under the auspices of several underground publishing houses, of which *Edíce Petlíce* (The Padlock Press) became the best known. Founded by Ludvík Vaculík, one of Czechoslovakia's best writers, a giant of the Prague Spring and later a signatory of Charter 77, the Padlock Press had by 1985 published over 250 volumes. Practically all of this underground literature—known in the West by the generic Russian term samizdat—was produced (for legalistic reasons) on a typewriter with as many carbons as the key pressure would allow, and, like its much more numerous Polish Solidarity counterpart, it often fell short of mechanical perfection. The readership of all this underground literature was very small, but much of it reached the West and was then relayed back to Czechoslovakia by Western radio transmitters. The same went for articles in the considerable number of literary and scholarly journals that also appeared in samizdat. Of these journals, perhaps the best known was the literary *Kritický Sborník* (Critical Review), which appeared about four times annually for several years after 1981. Some of these journals were devoted to politics and economics. It was all a proof of the courage of some of the best minds in the Czech Lands and a sober reminder of what the *pays legal* was losing by depriving itself of their abilities.

Young people in Czechoslovakia, as practically everywhere else, often chose to express their frustrations in music of various degrees of discordance. Rock music became very popular—again, especially in the Czech Lands. It became a vehicle of social and political protest and was supported by distinguished intellectuals like Havel within the country and two writers of world distinction who had gone into exile, Milan Kundera and Josef Škvorecký (see chapter 13). Pop and jazz were also popular, and it seemed in the natural order of things that Marta Kubišova, once the leading female pop singer, was for a time a spokesman for Charter 77.

Some young people—not necessarily excluding some of the rock, pop, and jazz addicts just mentioned—also turned to religion. It would be too much to speak of a "massive" religious revival, but there was little doubt that, beginning in the 1970s, a traditionally free-thinking people like the Czechs was displaying more interest than for many years in organized and unorganized religion (see chapter 3). "Unorganized" here means private, "spontaneous" (almost "do your own thing") religious meetings, which were also common in Hungary and for which the support of the official church was sometimes less than enthusiastic. The organized Roman Catholic church in Czechoslovakia had for years been in a desperate state, with a shortage of over a thousand parish clergy in 1985 and only three out of the country's thirteen dioceses having regular bishops.[24] Indeed, the unrelenting discrimination by the state against the church was one reason for the growth in public sympathy for it. Unlike the Slovak church, the church in the Czech Lands historically never enjoyed much popular national sympathy, being widely regarded as a branch and expression of Habsburg rule. In the First Republic the Catholic church was definitely out of political and intellectual fashion, and its leadership's lack of a firm attitude toward the communist takeover in 1948 did little to enhance its prestige. For many years this lack of firmness in relation to the authorities seemed personified by the aging archbishop, later cardinal, František Tomášek of Prague. But later, stiffened partly by the advent of a vigorous Slavic pope, Tomášek toughened his attitude toward the communist authorities and began to enjoy more popular respect than ever before.

The most striking demonstration perhaps in the entire history of Czechoslovakia of support for the Catholic church came during the celebrations of Saints Cyril and Methodius, the evangelizers of the Slavic peoples, on the 1,100th anniversary of the death of St. Methodius in 1985 (see chapter 3). The state tried unsuccessfully to politicize, even propagandize, these celebrations but was rebuffed by Cardinal Tomášek, the Vatican, and the Czechoslovak faithful who turned out in the tens of thousands at the claimed burial site of St. Methodius at Velehrad in Moravia.[25]

There was no doubt also that Tomášek was receiving strong support from the Vatican, particularly in his resistance to the proregime Pacem in Terris Catholic organization, publicly disowned by the Holy See in 1982 (see chapter 3). By the end of the 1970s Pacem in Terris was claiming allegiance of a third of Czechoslovakia's over 3,000 priests, but that number, if it ever were so high, dropped considerably after the papal disavowal, and Cardinal Tomášek later estimated it to be about three hundred.[26] However diminished its following, Pacem in Terris, with its strong material backing from the regime, remained a threat to the integrity and independence of the church. As for the main Protestant churches, they had been thoroughly neutered early in the communist period and offered little resistance to the regime or promise to the people.

In their humiliating condition the Protestant churches were wont to join inter alia in the regime's periodic massive peace campaigns. But later the regime was to have something less than a monopoly on peace campaigning. Almost from its inception, Charter 77 was active in the worldwide peace movements and had contacts with some peace groups in the West. These contacts sometimes led to difficulties because, though there was the occasional element of naivete among some of these unofficial Czechoslovak peace activists, they were realism itself compared with some of their Western colleagues. They did try to keep the general European peace movement to political neutrality by pointing to the Soviet responsibilities in this regard, by stressing that freedom should accompany peace, as must the observance of human rights, and by rejecting the notion of peace at any price. The principle of peace without appeasement seems to have guided their thought and action.[27]

For many Czechoslovaks, as for many East Germans, the peace movement received added impetus and a new urgency by the deployment of new Soviet missiles on their soil in late 1983. The communist leadership was aware of the disquiet and, like its counterpart in East Berlin, openly admitted it. At the same time both regimes were nervous about popular reaction, and in Czechoslovakia leading Chartists were apparently warned against any public expression of opposition. There was, indeed, widespread public misgiving, of which a petition from Brno reportedly signed by several thousand people was a good example.[28]

An Alternative Culture?

What emerges from this survey of independent currents in the Czech Lands is that very few of them were avowedly hostile to the regime as such. Of course, in a system that aspires to be totalitarian anything that is not supportive can be dubbed hostile, anything nonconformist disruptive. And this would apply particularly in the atmosphere of the Czech Lands after 1968. But even the briefest comparison of Czech samizdat and underground activists with their Polish counterparts would reveal the difference. Though after 1982 much Polish samizdat writing began concentrating on sober analyses of topics of public interest—very much like many Charter 77 publications—the bulk of Solidarity and Polish resistance activity remained openly antagonistic toward the Jaruzelski dictatorship.

In Czechoslovakia the samizdat writers avoided overt opposition to the regime, intentionally and often in a subtle manner. In fact, the independent currents in the Czech Lands mirrored a societal activity common throughout Eastern Europe, certainly in Poland and Hungary. This activity was not so much against the official political culture as trying to form an alternative to it. Increasingly, while the regime establishment was going one way, large elements of society were going another. They were sometimes going not in one, but in several, directions. Official values were considered irrelevant or simply rejected. (This trend in East European societies is also discussed in chapter 1.) By the middle of the 1980s it appeared that Czechoslovakia was leading this trend after Poland. It was more than anything a faute de mieux phenomenon brought on by what was perceived as the hopelessness of the situation.

Just how the Czechoslovak authorities would eventually cope with this development was difficult to say. As discussed in chapter 1, it might be the kind of standoff they would not find intolerable. In the meantime, however, the authorities were not exactly amenable to the independent currents. The discrimination and chicanery against the church have been mentioned. The scale of harassment and persecution against Charter 77 and VONS varied considerably. Prison sentences, house detentions, expulsions, and deprivations of citizenship and the like took place against a background of constant professional victimization. But victimization was sometimes tempered by a certain moderation, a typical Czech reluctance to push things to extremes. It was this characteristic that made life for many less unbearable than it might have been. With the peace movement, the regime tried to squeeze as much propaganda advantage out of it as the opportunities presented, but it hesitated, especially after deployment of the new Soviet missiles in late 1983, to use sharp persecution—perhaps a reflection of its own keen embarrassment. In policy toward the rock and pop manifestations of youth there seemed to be little central direction, with local authorities being left a good deal of discretion. This led to inconsistency: considerable tolerance went side-by-side with thick-headed intolerance. Generally, though, any hints of the political in rock bands' lyrics were persecuted. Within this milieu the authorities knew they were not kicking against public opinion; popular prejudice was almost as great as their own. The life-style, mode of dress, and general appearance of most rock groups, together with a worrying increase in drug addiction in Czechoslovakia,[30] militated against much general sympathy for this expression of youthful independence.

A separate word must be added centering on Slovaks in their environment in Slovakia. The Slovaks were not unaffected by the currents flowing through the Czech Lands. On the contrary. The situation, for example, in Bratislava, though still very different in many ways from Czech cities, had many characteristics in common with them. Some of the youthful currents certainly appeared quite similar. But generally the currents in Slovakia were weaker. Slovak society continued more conservative and inbred than the Czech. There was a general feeling also, mentioned earlier, that what happened in the Czech Lands was no longer relevant to Slovakia. But Slovak patriotism and anti-Czech feeling were still not entirely separated. An American of Slovak birth was astonished on a visit to Slovakia in early 1977 by the first reaction of some solidly anticommunist friends to the foundation of Charter 77. It was, he was told, a Czech plot against Husák!

The main independent current in Slovakia was unquestionably the Catholic church. It was believed by many Slovaks, including some of the younger generation, to be the exclusive embodiment of the true Slovak national spirit. (Protestants and Jews, once the cultural and economic elite of Slovak society and strongly Czechoslovak in orientation, were often considered as "un-Slovak.") The Catholic church was certainly seen by the regime as communism's greatest enemy, and this explained a persecution that had no parallel in the Czech Lands. But between these two antagonistic forces—communism and the church —there now appeared to be a third stratum in Slovakia, most composed of people under forty, who had little time for either. They were conscious of their Slovak nationality, prepared to accept the benefits the state offered in jobs, status, welfare, etc., and taking some pride in the Husák hegemony in Prague. Yet they showed little gratitude to the *system* for what they got out of it; the nonmaterial "appeals" of communism they rejected almost totally. As for the church, though many were indifferent to religion, they tended to marry, bury, and baptize in it, and, though they deplored its clerical-fascist tradition (as some of their elders did not), they respected it as Slovakia's most powerful national institution. This third stratum was neither pro- nor anti-Czech. It was also probably the most susceptible to the societal ideas coming eastward from Prague.

The Prospects

By any standard and on either the state or the societal level, the shorter-term prospects for Czechoslovakia had long begun to look bleak. But there was one brighter prospect: the chances of change were stronger than they had been since the Soviet-led invasion in August 1968. The Czechoslovak leadership could not be far from rejuvenation. There was a new Soviet leader who wanted change. His concept of change might be uncomfortable, but at least he stood for movement and vigor. And at a minimum the Czechoslovak economy needed both.

As to state-society relations, if some sections of society in the Czech Lands embraced the alternative culture in varying degrees and this was to be tolerated by a state that had lost its stomach for ideological combat, then an uneasy but calm stalemate could persist for some time. If under a new generation of political leaders, however, economic reforms were to be accompanied by some political relaxation, then society might generally respond with more commitment or, at least, more engagement. If the church were to hold its ground in Slovakia (which seemed likely), and the Czech church, with Vatican support, continued its own revival, then the autonomy of both might increase.

As for Czechoslovakia's two nations, the Slovak looked healthy and assertive. It had survived ten centuries of Hungarian oppression and was now moving with self-confidence. The future of the Czech nation gave fewer grounds for optimism. It was always to be reckoned that one of those historical troughs of despair into which it was prone to fall might become its permanent resting place. In this context the trend toward an alternative culture could present real dangers. It could lead to the ultimate in privatization: the rejection not only of the present communist state but of all sense of community. This could then lead to such fragmentation as to cause a decline in the sense of identity as a nation. The danger of this happening was greater for the Czechs than for any other nation in what is today known as Eastern Europe.

A danger of such magnitude made the work of movements like Charter 77 all the more important. They were engaged in "preparing and recultivating the soil for future political changes." What these changes were like would, in the words of a Czech who believed in his nation, "in part be determined by the preparatory work in that period . . . that appeared to be a vacuum but that in reality was filled with strivings to preserve, regenerate, and recultivate." It would also be determined by those men and women who "took the path of their civic right and duty, even though to the majority of their contemporaries this seemed merely the dangerous conduct of a handful of fools."[31]

It is easy to dismiss such sentiments as noble but isolated, irrelevant, or even academic. Easy but mistaken. Czech history suggests they be taken seriously. And, if ever the Czechs themselves were to disregard them, their outlook as a nation would be bleak indeed.

10 Bulgaria

In April 1986 at the thirteenth congress of the Bulgarian communist party, Tudor Zhivkov was reelected party leader. He had first been elected to this post at the sixth congress in 1954 and was subsequently reelected no less than seven times. He had been the dean of Warsaw Pact party leaders since the fall of Antonín Novotný in Czechoslovakia in January 1968 and, since the death of Enver Hoxha in April 1985, the longest-serving East European party leader. Between 1962 and 1971 he was also prime minister and since 1971 has also been head of state. Balkan communist leaders, with veterans like Tito and Hoxha, had become noted for their longevity. Zhivkov still had a way to go before he equaled the length of service of either of these. Indeed, he would probably never catch them (both had forty-three years). But for the Warsaw Pact he was building on a record that might never be broken.

The continuity in the Bulgarian leadership has certainly been impressive. But it has not been without disturbance or even danger, especially in the earlier years. For Zhivkov, when appointed party leader, was very much a compromise candidate. The vacancy at the top of the party occurred only because Vulko Chervenkov, Bulgaria's "little Stalin," had to leave either that position or the premiership, in conformity with the separation of state and party functions ordained by Stalin's successors in Moscow. Chervenkov rather surprisingly chose to keep the premiership, presumably because Malenkov, then apparently the strongest of Stalin's successors, had become Soviet premier. It turned out to be a serious mistake, cutting Chervenkov off from his real power base and deepening his vulnerability when his numerous enemies—in Bulgaria itself, Moscow, and Belgrade—began their campaign against him.[1]

But Zhivkov, though a "safe" compromise candidate and overshadowed by rivals more brilliant, was not without experience. Though only forty-three he had fought with the minuscule Bulgarian partisan movement in the war, had been a Central Committee member since 1948, and had held for a time the three posts of head of the Sofia party central committee, of the Sofia branch of the Fatherland Front organization, and of the Sofia city people's council. In 1950 he had moved into the Politburo as a nonvoting member and had become a Central Committee secretary. He may have been short on intellectual ability, but he had political instinct and patience. He also had a Balkan peasant shrewdness that was to become his outstanding political characteristic. It was partly this that enabled him to discern, anticipate, and adapt to the changing personalities and moods in Moscow.

When first elected to the party leadership in 1954 Zhivkov also had three undoubted *political* assets. First, he had already built up a party constituency based in Sofia, which, as the capital, had the most powerful political organization in the country. Second, he was a "home" communist at a time when, immediately after the death of Stalin, "Muscovites" were falling out of political favor throughout Eastern Europe. (Zhivkov's record as a communist partisan in World War II would be a bonus in this regard.) Finally, he was not *directly* connected with the brutal crimes of repression perpetrated by the party in its ascent to power.

Zhivkov in 1954, therefore, was acceptable in both Sofia and Moscow. After 1954 it was Khrushchev and his open de-Stalinization campaign that gave him his first political boost. Khrushchev's "secret speech" denouncing Stalin at the Twentieth CPSU congress in 1956 led to the Bulgarian Communist party's (BCP) own de-Stalinizing April Plenum in the same year. This plenum, still incessantly invoked as one of the great turning points in the party's history, led to the dismissal of Chervenkov from the premiership. Chervenkov for several years after was still to have considerable political and ideological influence, but it was obvious that any return to power by him was highly unlikely.

After 1956 the factionalism in the party if anything increased. Zhivkov's main personal rival was now Anton Yugov, the main "home" communist, who had fallen into the shadows shortly before Stalin died, but whom de-Stalinization had now catapulted to the premiership. Even allowing for the exaggerations in his indictment, it was clear from the charges leveled at Yugov after his dismissal in 1962 that his years as premier had been marked by constant differences with Zhivkov. But even more important than the personal rivalries animating Bulgarian politics was the need for Zhivkov to wrest control of the main institution essential for any regime leader to master before his power was secure: the security apparat. This he was able to do with the purge of Politburo member and longtime interior minister Georgi Tsankov, also in 1962. With the simultaneous purging of Yugov and Tsankov, following the dismissal five years earlier of Politburo member and economic planning chief Georgi Chankov, Zhivkov was well on the way to undisputed power.[2]

The seal on his supremacy was finally set in 1965 after the failure of an army conspiracy against him in April of that year.[3] Much about this bizarre episode is still not clear; the extent of the conspiracy, for example. But there appears to have been some interaction between the officers involved—some of them of field rank—and various local party branches, especially that in Vratsa, north of Sofia. Thus, while the military elements in the conspiracy were mopped up relatively quickly, it took at least two years for the "viper's nest" of Vratsa to be cleared.

But whatever the motives and the strength of the conspiracy, its uncovering and defeat enabled Zhivkov to rule without challenge. He had successfully resisted all threats—personal and institutional. Just as important, he had safely negotiated the dismissal of Khrushchev in October 1964 and his replacement by Brezhnev. This was no mean feat for a satellite leader who had deferred to Khrushchev with an alacrity and ostentation many found excessive. But Zhivkov both read and obeyed the signals coming from the Kremlin, and, close though his relations had been with Khrushchev, the assumption of power by Brezhnev in 1964 began an equally close and apparently friendly association lasting eighteen years.

After his first, very difficult ten years as party leader, for Zhivkov this association was to guarantee his longevity. In fact, most of the political excitement in the Bulgarian regime after that was reflected in the rise of putative heirs to Zhivkov and then their fall into political oblivion. Mitko Grigorov who led the campaign against Yugov in 1962, then Luchezar Avramov, Ivan Abadzhiev, who routed out the conspirators in Vratsa in 1967, up to Alexander Lilov, purged in 1982—these were just the most prominent of the political casualties of over two decades. Whether it was simply their power ambitions that led to their downfall or whether aspects of policy were also involved is not known. It is unlikely, though, that the latter played any great role. More likely was the fact that their apparent emergence as actual or potential "crown princes" attracted enough followers to their side to form the kind of power base that Zhivkov, mindful of the factionalism in the 1950s, could instantly have suspected. Perhaps only in the case of Lilov and the relatively relaxed cultural policy for which he apparently stood did questions of policy play an important role.[4]

The Soviet Connection

Bulgaria has served the Soviet Union with loyalty and with stability. Both are virtues that Moscow is not likely to have underestimated. First, because of the obvious strategic importance of Bulgaria, bordering on two volatile NATO allies—Greece and Turkey—in a region of crucial historical importance to Russia. Second, because the defection of Yugoslavia in 1948 and Albania in the early 1960s, followed by the partial defection of Romania shortly afterward, left Bulgaria as Moscow's only loyal dependency in the Balkans.

The Bulgarian relationship became vital, therefore, for the Soviet Union, and it was one for which it was obviously prepared to pay. It is impossible to put a precise figure on the financial aid Sofia has received from Moscow in the form of trade subsidies, low credit or interest-free loans, concealed credits, and the like. Western economists differ radically in their estimates of Soviet aid to Eastern Europe generally. But in 1984, to quote one example, outstanding Soviet ruble loans to Bulgaria were estimated at over $3 billion, a sum exceeded only by the GDR and Poland. In the same year the Marrese-Vaňous estimate of Soviet trade subsidies to Bulgaria was almost $1.75 billion.[5] By any account, Bulgaria had received, and was continuing to receive, a disproportionately large share of Soviet financial support. Perhaps special mention should be made of the privileges it was reportedly receiving in energy supplies: above-contract amounts of oil not payable in hard currency, for example, much of which was refined in Bulgaria and then sold on world markets.[6]

Despite continuing Bulgarian complaints about too low prices for their farm produce in Comecon,[7] there can be no doubt about the overall material benefits of the Soviet connection. And this has led to considerable speculation about the motives beyond Bulgaria's apparent unflinching loyalty. In the beginning Zhivkov's dependence on Moscow's support for the establishment and maintenance of his position must obviously be considered. So must some of the traditional pro-Russian sentiment explained by history and racial and cultural affinity, which it would be as pointless to deny as it would be facile to exaggerate. Moreover, anti-Yugoslav (or Serb) feeling arising from the

Macedonian dispute is never far below the surface of Bulgarian political life. The Tito-Stalin break, therefore, could have strengthened Bulgarian resolve to remain loyal to Moscow since this may have seemed to have offered the best hope of recovering Macedonia. Then, again, there have been Bulgaria's own economic problems aggravated, especially in the early years, by gigantomanic socialist policies, sheer incompetence, and unproductive experiment.

All these reasons have their validity. Yet there remains the suspicion that a cool calculation played some role with the Zhivkov-led regime, especially as its leader grew in confidence and political experience. From no other source could Bulgaria get the material assistance in the volume and variety it received from the Soviet Union. For the kind of economic development required by the ongoing Leninist view of socialist construction the Bulgarians needed massive help, and the Soviet Union was the obvious source. Bulgarian loyalty, therefore, may have originated in weakness and evolved into habit. But it gained its rewards. And as the importance of Bulgaria to Soviet interests grew beyond anything that could originally have been contemplated, so the Bulgarian leaders themselves probably saw their link with Moscow not solely in terms of dependence but also as a relationship to which both had something to offer and from which both showed profit.

The "Chinese Connection"

And yet, loyalty notwithstanding, the Bulgarian relationship has not been entirely problem-free for the Soviets. The Bulgarian party, for example, took about twenty years after its assumption of power before it could shake off the "left-sectarianism" that had often characterized it during its years of infancy and illegality. This was shown during the second half of the 1950s in an obvious fascination with some of China's experimental "shortcuts" to communism. During this period, for example, Bulgaria had its own "great leap forward" that, like its Chinese exemplar, ended disastrously. There was also some sympathy with the notion of communes, certainly with the trend toward "gigantism" in Chinese agriculture. How widespread the general sympathy for China was in the BCP is impossible to estimate. It seems to have centered on Chervenkov in the late 1950s when he was by now, at least in rank, just an ordinary Central Committee member, later to lose even his party membership. His followers were jocularly dubbed "the Chinese." Some of this pro-Chinese sentiment was probably a legacy of Stalinism, which, repudiating Khrushchev, seemed now to have found safekeeping in China. The same could be said for the BCP's tradition of "internationalism." In practical terms this had meant loyalty to Moscow. But the Moscow of Khrushchev presented a confusing or repellent picture to many "internationalists." That of Mao's Peking was at once more familiar and attractive.[8]

Anti-Yugoslav nationalism also played its part. Yugoslav "revisionism" stood at the other end of the spectrum from Maoism. Khrushchev seemed considerably closer to "revisionism" than to Maoism, and, despite the rebuffs and in 1956 the near-disasters, he seemed determined to court Tito. And Tito's Yugoslavia held Bulgaria's claimed birthright, Macedonia.[9] Thus nationalism and ideology became inextricably intertwined for many Bulgarian communists, as it did for the Hoxha regime in Albania, with Yugoslavia the nexus for both. Many of these Bulgarian communists may have liked to have eventually followed the Hoxha regime into the arms of China, but all except the most romantic and/or obtuse must have realized that Bulgaria's geopolitical location made this impossible. All the same, they were obstinate in their conservatism. When Khrushchev attempted his second big reconciliation with Tito after the CPSU congress in 1961, he had to visit Bulgaria a year later to bolster Zhivkov in his efforts to make the BCP comply.[10] And as late as 1965, according to Zhivkov's own testimony, some of the April military conspirators were imbued with "confused" Chinese sympathies.

After this episode, however, there was little trace of Chinese sympathy in Bulgaria. The Chinese political pendulum in the 1970s swung erratically from left to right, and neither of the two extremes it touched elicited any sympathy in Sofia. Besides, after the Ussuri River clash in March 1969 between Soviet and Chinese troops, relations between Moscow and Peking entered one of their worst phases, and the Brezhnev leadership would not have tolerated any dalliance in a situation like this. Later in the 1980s, when China took Deng Xiaoping's path of systemic reform and excited many actual and potential reformers in Eastern Europe, it had few attractions for Bulgaria. It was, indeed, more typical of the history of Bulgarian communism that China should have had more influence on it when dogmatic and romantic than when pragmatic and moderate.[11]

The Lyudmila Phenomenon

But the attractions of China were not the only problem for Moscow that the Bulgarian communists have presented. Another, bizarre in view of its provenance, was caused by Todor Zhivkov's daughter, Lyudmila.

When Lyudmila Zhivkov died, aged thirty-seven, of a brain hemorrhage in July 1981, she was already minister of culture and a Politburo member. She was proof enough that nepotism need not always deserve total condemnation.[12] But what is relevant here is not so much Zhivkova's extraordinary personality and wide range of sometimes exotic interests, as her zealous cultural nationalism and the responsive chord it struck among many of her compatriots. Her appeal showed—instructively to anyone who had ever suspected otherwise—that Bulgarian nationalism had not been submerged by communism or engulfed by any pan-Slavic tide of enthusiasm. What Zhivkova tried to do with the magnificent cultural-historical exhibitions she organized, the archeological excavations she sponsored, not to mention the massive celebration she inspired of the 1,300th anniversary of the first Bulgarian state in 1981, was to convince Bulgarians—and others—of the worth of Bulgaria's heritage. She may have been seeking to overcome the "defeatist" complex that history had instilled into the Bulgarians or the "national nihilism" about which her father railed so often. There was nothing inherently chauvinistic in her ambition. In the West the masterpieces of Bulgarian art history her exhibitions made available were a revelation. In Bulgaria itself she became probably the most popular political figure since the imposition of communism. Among Bulgaria's cultural milieu she was also popular. Although by no means without personal prejudices and occasional vindictiveness, she was an imaginative patron of modern art and literature and presided over a more relaxed and productive cultural scene.

The Soviets basically disliked Zhivkova because she was a personality with an independent turn of mind. For them she was spontaneous and unpredictable, two of the grisliest adjectives in Moscow's dictionary. More specifically, in stressing the Bulgarian cultural contributions she inevitably—and apparently unhesitatingly—pointed up the primacy of her own country vis-à-vis Russian civilization in several fields in which Moscow had always claimed pride of place.[13] Second, she appeared to emphasize less the specific link of Bulgarian culture with Russia as the Bulgarian link with Europe as a whole. A postgraduate student for several months at Oxford University, she visited the West more often than she did the Soviet Union. The exhibitions she sponsored took place during a period of East-West détente when many Bulgarians, in different fields, were making their acquaintance with the West and were impressed with what they saw. There can be little doubt that Lyudmila caused the Soviets anxiety and that Zhivkov père's affection for his daughter led to occasional strain in Sofia's relations with the Kremlin. Her unexpected death in July 1981 inevitably roused suspicions of KGB foul play. They seem to have been groundless. Still, Moscow must have been relieved. But it can hardly have been pleased by the outpouring of public sympathy at Lyudmila's funeral. It was unquestionably a partly nationalist demonstration. Older Bulgarians compared it with the funeral of King Boris in 1943.

The Path of Reform

But, taking the period since 1945 as a whole, the BCP's fascination with Maoism and Zhivkov's protection of his wayward daughter were, for Moscow, minor irritations when compared with the sustained disobedience of Romania, the periodic upheavals in Poland, the broad menace of the Prague Spring, and the near-disaster of Hungary in 1956—not to mention the defections of Yugoslavia and Albania. Bulgaria has generally deserved its reputation as the most pliant of satellites, posing only tolerable difficulties at home and abroad while, in the main, presenting a showpiece for "real, existing socialism."

At home there have been few recorded instances of societal dissent since the early 1950s, except, perhaps, for some sporadic and poorly reported acts of dissidence in the 1970s. In 1984 and 1985 a number of cases of bombing, arson, and sabotage were admitted, however.[14] These went unexplained, although some connected them with acts of defiance by members of the Turkish minority. In general, however, a note of caution is necessary on the subject of societal dissent. There have been no Western press correspondents stationed in Sofia. For long periods there have even been no local stringers for Western news agencies. The number of Bulgarians traveling to the West has been limited and carefully selected. Individual Western visitors have always been mostly well shepherded. There would need to be, therefore, an incident of major proportions for news of it to reach the West—similar, for example, to the April conspiracy in 1965. And in the case of public dissent Western exposure not only records but often feeds and reinforces. Thus one of the great essentials for dissent to originate, grow, and flourish has been absent in Bulgaria.

What mainly caught the attention, apart from the occasional purge of men too close to Zhivkov, was the economic progress and experimentation through the 1970s and for most of the 1980s. After attaining full power in the late 1940s, the Bulgarian communists embarked on a classic communist industrialization drive largely at the expense of agriculture, which was totally collectivized by the end of the 1950s. Swift progress—even if some if it was more statistical than actual—was inevitable in Bulgarian conditions: except for Albania it was the least industrially developed country in Europe. In the 1950s and 1960s the annual increases of industrial output were mostly in double figures. In the 1970s they dropped to a respectable 7 to 8 percent, and even in the downturn of the late 1970s and early 1980s they registered between 3 and 5 percent. As might be expected, agriculture has fared less well, especially in the 1950s and early 1960s and more recently between the years 1983 and 1985, which, as will be discussed later, saw a general downturn in the whole economy.[15] But taking the two decades from 1965 as a whole, Bulgaria made impressive economic progress. Certainly by the standards of its Balkan communist neighbors, Bulgaria has become and remains fairly prosperous. The contrast between its own economic situation and that of Romania has been drawn by almost all visitors. Indeed, toward the end of the 1970s the point was often made that most visitors who sang the praises of Bulgaria's progress had been to Romania first.

Symbolizing Bulgaria's economic progress has been the fact that, in the framework of Comecon specialization, it has become one of the main producers of various electronic and electrical products like forklift trucks and experimental robots. Bulgaria may still be famous for attar of roses and fine tobacco, but exotic products like these represent not the present and the future but more the link with the past. By 1983 agricultural exports amounted to only a quarter of the whole. Bulgarian exports had become balanced and varied, and they played a key role in one of the most striking economic successes of the early 1980s, which was the reduction of the net hard-currency debt. In 1979 this stood at $4 billion, one of the highest per capita debts in Eastern Europe. By the beginning of 1985 it was down to well under $1 billion.[16]

More striking than Bulgaria's economic progress during the more than thirty years of Zhivkov's leadership have been the number, scope, and variety of the economic reforms (or reorganizations) with which it has experimented. Any attempt to depict Bulgarian communist history as an eventless continuum would be a travesty indeed. First, there were the "Chinese-type" experiments with which the regime flirted in the late 1950s. In the 1960s, after Professor Liberman's "go-ahead" signal from Moscow in 1962, there followed a period of exciting reform discussion and solid reform proposals. Suggestions for self-management were even made by some leading personalities, and, after a series of interesting experiments, an official program for reform, similar to the first reforms proposed by Ota Šik in Czechoslovakia, was presented to the public in 1964. By the Yugoslav and Polish standards of the 1950s, the Czechoslovak standards of the late 1960s, the Hungarian of the 1970s, not to mention the Chinese of the 1980s, the Bulgarian reform might look timid. But providing, as it did, for a fair measure of managerial decentralization, the abolition of some price controls, and some deference to the market mechanism, it represented a considerable breakthrough at the time. The reform, however, was never given a chance because it was never implemented. Not only did it meet the all-too-familiar resistance from the entrenched political and economic apparatchiks, it was also affected by the fall of Khrushchev and the quick petering out of the Soviet reform proposals of 1965. Then came the advent and the arrival of the Prague Spring, and one month *before* its termination by Soviet-led troops (including a flown-in contingent of obliging Bulgarians) in August 1968, the cautious Zhivkov also terminated his own exercise in genuine economic reform.[17]

After August 1968 the very term "reform" acquired a pejorative, political association throughout Eastern Europe. "Reorganization" or "new mechanism" became the more fashionable euphemisms. And in "reorganization" the Zhivkov regime took the plunge by refurbishing the classic Bolshevik notion of agroindustrial complexes and putting it into reality. The aim of these new creations was the "organic unity" of all production derived from, or associated with, agriculture through a vertical organizational structure. The first step toward the new complexes had been—probably unintentionally—made with the large-scale merger of collective farms at the end of the 1950s. Their introduction in the 1970s necessitated a massive reorganization of administrative districts, local government, and party administration generally.[18] The sheer change and dislocation involved were enormous, and by the end of the seventies rural Bulgaria looked much different than it had at the beginning. The Bulgarian experiments were approvingly watched in the Soviet Union, and experiments on similar lines were tried in the Moldavian republic in the second half of the seventies.

The agroindustrial complexes (AICs), as well as their more industrially oriented (though less numerous) counterparts, the industrial-agrarian complexes (IACs), were essentially reorganizations by no means inconsistent with a command-type economy. But by the end of the seventies the Bulgarian regime evidently saw that some qualitative change in the command structure of the economy was necessary if the country's performance was to be maintained in a period of serious economic difficulty. In reaching their decision they were guided—as so often—by Moscow, which had begun to show some strivings itself after economic efficiency after 1978.[19]

It was then that what has become known as the Bulgarian "New Economic Mechanism" (NEM) began to be implemented. It has been introduced in two stages: first in agriculture in the late 1970s and then in industry and other sectors in 1982. Attracting considerable attention in both West and East, it was implemented in piecemeal fashion. It was never very reformist by the standards of the Hungarian New Economic Mechanism, from which it copied the name but not much else. Not surprisingly, the Hungarians themselves were anxious to see similarities, largely because the emergence of a Bulgarian NEM made their own reform seem less vulnerably conspicuous. Few, however, would see much basic similarity between the two reforms. Still, the Bulgarian reform contained elements of decentralization, scope for profit, and free pricing that were all genuinely reformist and certainly made it the most far-reaching reform in Eastern Europe after the Hungarian—more basic than, for example, the East German.[20] One sharp break with Bulgarian communist tradition was the encouragement now being given to small enterprises. The "big is beautiful" psychosis apparently remained no longer sacrosanct in Bulgarian economic thinking.[21]

The Downturn

A keen observer of Bulgaria over many years visited Sofia in 1982 and then again at the end of 1985. The two visits presented sharply contrasting impressions. In 1982 Bulgaria had appeared to be on the crest of an economic wave. The reform had been comprehensively introduced into an economy that still seemed buoyant enough. The public, in the main, seemed not only satisfied but expectant of further progress. Many young people seemed prepared to give the regime the benefit of their doubts. In the cultural field there was considerable freedom. But by the end of 1985 much of this had changed. Bulgaria was suffering a severe economic downturn, with agriculture and the energy supply the main victims. Sofia and other cities were "blacked out" at night to ease energy shortages. (Bulgarians used to sneer at

Romania for this, but no longer.) The mood of optimism and expectancy had been replaced by sullenness and frustration. Cultural policy had become more restrictive. It appeared that the regime's self-confidence, growing throughout the 1970s, had been severely shaken.

Several factors probably caused this transformation. The most important was the economic deterioration. The bad year of 1983 was followed by recovery in 1984, but then in 1985 Bulgaria was hit by one of the severest winters on record. This had followed, and was then followed in turn, by a very dry summer. A serious energy shortage then affected industry, public lighting, and domestic households, where the electric power was sometimes cut several times a day for periods of weeks. There was much complaining and not a little grim humor. In Sofia (as apparently in Bucharest) people remarked that a different kind of snow had fallen that winter: when they put it in front of their electric fires it refused to melt.

Agriculture appeared to have suffered its worst year for many decades, with the main—almost the exclusive—official blame being put on the weather. It was described by one official as having had "no equal this century."[22] Communist agricultural officials, perhaps more than others, tend to lay the blame for failure squarely at the door of the weather—with the credit for success being attributable solely to their own wisdom. The abnormality of the weather was certainly a most powerful factor, not just in agriculture but in the general economic downturn. The mining of coal, for instance, was prevented for a time by freezing conditions, and some idea of the winter of 1985 in southeastern Europe can be got from the fact that coal supplies from the Soviet Union to Bulgaria were disrupted because the Sea of Azov froze over.

But, however powerfully the weather might have struck agriculture, it was not entirely to blame in the nonagricultural sectors. The fact that the economy and its infrastructure could be caught so unaware spoke ill of their efficiency and resilience. Many were waiting to see the economy's performance in the next two or three years (always assuming reasonable weather) before deciding on how basic the deficiencies were. But for several years before 1985 Bulgarian officials, none more than Zhivkov himself, had been complaining about basic faults, especially about the twin evils of low productivity and poor quality. The introduction of the economic reform into industry in 1982 was both an admission of continuing problems and an effort to solve them. At the thirteenth party congress in April 1986 Zhivkov and other leaders dwelt on the need for more economic efficiency and announced considerable extensions of the scope (without changing the basic character) of the existing reform.[24] Just before the congress the prime minister, Grisha Filipov, had been moved to the Central Committee Secretariat and replaced by Georgi Atanasov, a relatively young official whose experience was mainly in organization. The regime, therefore, knew the serious difficulties and confessed them.

But the thirteenth party congress gave little indication of the sweeping reforms that were to be announced in the course of 1987. These involved much greater democracy in the election of party and state bodies, a system of self-management perilously close to the Yugoslav, and a massive reorganization of local government and of the central state apparatus, which in effect meant the abolition of the council of ministers. All of these changes were to take place in an atmosphere of greater social and individual freedom and were to herald a "new socialism."[25]

It certainly seemed that the BCP was outdoing itself, even by the standards of the huge changes at the end of the 1950s and the Agro-Industrial Complex reorganization of the early 1970s. They raised two questions, however.

First, how many of the proposals announced would be implemented, and, more important, how many, even if implemented, would survive? Second, how much of this welter of initiatives was designed to appease Gorbachev and how much to preempt him? Obviously, the initiative (and the pressure) came from Moscow, but were not these new, bewilderingly far-reaching reforms part of Zhivkov's old strategy of leaving his own imprint within the framework of pro-Soviet obedience? Certainly the character and outcome of the reforms would be watched carefully.

One aspect of the new Soviet leader's policy that must have been worrying Sofia was an apparently tougher attitude toward economic relations with Eastern Europe. Even before the death of Brezhnev in 1983 the Soviet Union had been showing a tougher economic attitude toward its East European partners (see chapter 4). The East Europeans were not only being forced to invest more in Soviet or Comecon projects located in the Soviet Union but were being constantly warned that nothing but their best was acceptable as far as their exports to the Soviet market were concerned. This new toughness could have affected the Bulgarians correspondingly more than others since they had often been considered Moscow's most favored ally. But by about the middle of 1985 the Soviets reportedly began reducing their oil deliveries to Bulgaria, thereby reducing the Bulgarians' opportunities of selling refined oil on world markets. This had been much better business than many had realized. In the late 1970s some 60 percent of hard-currency earnings had come from this source (see chapter 4). The role it played also reflected badly on the basic health of the economy, which should have been depending on its manufactures. There were also Soviet complaints about the quality of imports from Bulgaria, and in the summer of 1985 there were obviously serious difficulties in concluding the new agreements between the two countries on economic cooperation for the next five-year planning period. Since nearly 60 percent of Bulgaria's total foreign trade was with the Soviet Union, the difficulties with Moscow could only compound Sofia's economic difficulties.[26]

The Bulgarians seemed unprepared for this situation. For the first time in more than thirty years they might have to stop relying on preferential treatment from the Soviet Union that had been one of the pillars of their economic development. They could react by introducing further, deeper reforms. Or they could nervously pull back to the old orthodox centralism, just as they did in 1968. A third possibility might be that, if the situation were to deteriorate seriously, Gorbachev could soften his approach and restore at least some of the privileges Bulgaria had enjoyed. But, whatever happened, it looked as though a new and difficult phase for the Bulgarian economy was beginning.

Foreign Policy

Bulgarian foreign policy is dominated by the Soviet Union. This has become one of the truisms of the East European situation. Nor in this respect is Bulgaria different from most of its other East European allies. But this domination has not meant that the Bulgarians have been inactive in foreign policy or that, in pursuing their pro-Soviet course, they have invariably ignored their own national interest. Very often, in fact (as also discussed in chapter 3), the initiatives that Bulgaria has pressed for Moscow have also furthered its own raison d'état. For example, the various Soviet initiatives pressed by the Bulgarians from 1960 for military reductions in the Balkans and for various forms of bilateral cooperation could hardly be judged as being other than in Bulgaria's interests. They were certainly not *contrary* to Bulgaria's interest. The same was true with the renewed Bulgarian pressure after 1981 for a nuclear-free zone in the Balkans, with once again the Soviet military and propaganda motives also being painfully clear. Occasionally the Bulgarians, probably more in their own interests than in an excess of pro-Soviet zeal, may have gone beyond their brief, as for example with Zhivkov's proposals in 1959 and 1960 for total disarmament with Greece. At least once, at the tenth Bulgarian party congress in 1971, Zhivkov also seems to have let slip an interest in *multilateral* (not just bilateral) cooperation in the Balkans to which the Soviets have been cool ever since Stalin humiliated Georgi Dimitrov on the subject in 1949.[27] Nor, mentioned in chapter 3, were these suspicions of Bulgarian self-interest confined to the Balkans. The Bulgarians obviously prized their links with West Germany, not to the point of defying the Soviet Union but at least to the point of not enthusiastically supporting it.

But it has been in its bilateral relations with its neighbors that Bulgaria has shown the most vigor and initiative. It has also been in these relations that history has had its clear impact. With Romania, the only neighbor that is a fellow member of the Warsaw Pact, Bulgarian relations have outwardly been surprisingly cordial. This despite the fact that the one country is loyalist, the other a maverick; and also despite the almost continual strain in relations between the two countries since independence from Turkey in the nineteenth century. Zhivkov and Ceaușescu held frequent meetings throughout the 1970s, and, though the number of these subsequently declined, close relations continued. Bulgaria has also refrained from criticizing Romanian policy even at moments of serious tension between Bucharest and Moscow. Perhaps the closeness with Romania was dictated by Moscow so that Zhivkov could remain the link with Ceaușescu. Certainly any Bulgarian defiance of Moscow in this regard can be discounted. But, whatever the motives, good relations with Romania brought to the Bulgarians an extra confidence-bolstering dimension in their diplomatic activity.[28]

Bulgaria's relations with neighboring Greece, whose cultural and religious hegemony in Ottoman times some Bulgarians sometimes resented as much as the "Turkish yoke," have generally been cordial since relations were resumed in 1964. Under the Papandreou socialist government in Greece they have been friendly,[29] but even when the military junta ruled in Athens relations were better than might have been expected.

Relations with Turkey, colored by the "yoke" psychosis from which few Bulgarians have escaped, have also been bedeviled by the problems relating to the large Turkish minority in the country—a living reminder of five hundred years of Ottoman rule. For about a quarter of a century, however, between the end of the 1950s and about halfway through the 1980s, both countries tried to put the past history and their present membership of adversarial alliances behind them. But, as discussed later, the brutal and cynical forced assimilation of the Turks in 1984–85 undid all the good patiently achieved and sowed the seeds of new bitterness (see chapter 14).

Bulgaria's relations with Yugoslavia have been dominated by the Macedonian issue. For many years it was held that the level of Bulgarian polemics and aggressiveness on this issue was a weather vane for Soviet-Yugoslav relations: when these were bad, Sofia beat the Macedonian drum; when they were better, Sofia desisted. For some twenty years after World War II this may have been generally true. But the more the Zhivkov regime began to mount a strenuous campaign to rekindle patriotism and combat "national nihilism" at home, the more it stressed the part Macedonia had played in Bulgarian history. It denied any claim as such to Macedonia, but it also denied the existence of a Macedonian nation. Historical anniversaries, great and small, were ostentatiously celebrated with the lesson driven home that Macedonia had been (and still should be) part of Bulgaria. The centennial of the Treaty of San Stefano in 1978, which had given Macedonia to the new Bulgaria and was then annulled by the Congress of Berlin a few months later, was the most sensitive in this regard. This campaign obviously met with a considerable public response, and the opinion grew that the Bulgarian leadership was now acting on its own over the Macedonian issue. A situation could arise in future, therefore, in which Soviet and Bulgarian policies toward Yugoslavia could be at cross-purposes. If Moscow were determined, it could always presumably discipline Sofia—but only with much more difficulty than before.

Bulgaria's relations with its four neighbors are more important than is often realized. Bulgaria is internationally more isolated than any other Warsaw Pact country. One of its neighbors, Romania, is an unreliable Soviet ally and the other three, Greece, Turkey, and Yugoslavia, have in varying degrees adversarial relationships with Moscow. All three are also historic enemies. Bulgaria, therefore, is exposed, and this exposure may, in itself, go some way to explain its dependence on the Soviet Union. It certainly explains its high level of diplomatic engagement with its neighbors. So do the opportunities that the diplomatic situation in the region present, with its two NATO adversaries hating and fearing each other more than they do either Bulgaria or the Soviet Union.

Bulgaria's conduct toward its neighbors must also be taken into account when trying to assess the opinions of the Bulgarian population about its regime's foreign policy. Many Bulgarians, especially younger ones, are often embarrassed by what they consider the excess of devotion to Moscow. Their patriotism and self-respect are offended by it. Yet there is little opposition to a close relationship with *Russia* partly on ethnic and historical grounds, partly perhaps from the sense of isolation just referred to, partly because Russia was one of the few countries that had never wronged modern Bulgaria (Greece, Turkey, Serbia, not to mention the Western powers, had). The notion of Russia as protector, which was strong in the Balkans in Ottoman times, still has some resonance in Bulgaria. It is by its policies toward its neighbors, therefore, that a regime in Sofia is judged, and by this account the Zhivkov leadership has come off reasonably well. What is most important for Bulgarians is that in no sense has it given anything away. In relations with its neighbors, therefore, Bulgaria under Zhivkov has developed a policy of "surrogate nationalism," replacing, or compensating for, its allegiance to Moscow by a firmness and genuine nationalism closer to home.

International Odium

There has certainly been nothing in Bulgaria's policy toward its neighbors since World War II that would feed the historical inferiority complex from which the Bulgarians as a nation have suffered since independence in 1878. This began to develop immediately after the first flush of independence when Bulgarians considered that the Congress of Berlin in 1878 cheated them out of their historic lands and, therefore, of historic fulfillment. It deepened as a result of efforts to win back those lands, which led to catastrophe in the second Balkan War, World War I, and finally in World War II.

For nearly forty years after World War II Bulgaria reverted to its familiar international backwater status. But two events in the 1980s pitchforked it back into the headlines in a manner well calculated to resurrect the traditional inferiority complex of its citizens. One was the "Bulgarization" of the Turkish minority in Bulgaria itself, mentioned earlier in this chapter and discussed more fully in chapter 14. The other was Bulgaria's alleged involvement in the assassination attempt against Pope John Paul II in 1981. The brutal name-change operation in 1984–85 directed against the Turkish minority was slow in attracting world attention, and the commotion it did cause was always muted. But it did Bulgaria's reputation great harm. Nor could the international opprobrium be heaped solely onto the regime. The Bulgarian people themselves, the majority of whom strongly supported the move against the Turks, also received their deserved share. Their attitude may have been understandable, but even those in the outside world with pro-Bulgarian sympathies—precious few at the best of times—found it inexcusable.

As for the alleged involvement in the attempted murder in St. Peter's Square—the "Bulgarian connection," as it became known—the Bulgarian defendant was after all acquitted for lack of evidence in the spring of 1986, a decision that satisfied everybody and nobody. But as the case developed, both inside and outside the Rome courtroom, it put the spotlight on many less than gentlemanly activities of the Bulgarian secret service. These included drug smuggling, gunrunning, assistance to terrorism, and various alleged assassinations.[30] Nobody would claim that such activities were the exclusive preserve of the Bulgarians. But their disclosure in the context of the papal assassination attempt trial made lurid press copy, and, unfair though it was, some of the sins of the regime were visited onto the population.

These disclosures also reflected a new aspect of Bulgaria's contemporary situation that may have gone largely unnoticed. Since the beginning of the 1960s Bulgaria has been the gateway to Europe for the more than a million Turks and their families working and living in different Western European countries. The Turks are very much back in Europe —but this time in Western rather than Eastern Europe and in a considerably less exalted status than before. To get there and back the vast majority of them go through Bulgaria. In 1985, 2,690,546 Turks crisscrossed Bulgaria.[31] The overwhelming majority are on lawful business. But a tiny minority are on errands less innocent. These constitute a new underworld with headquarters in Sofia and often with heroin as its currency. It would hardly have been surprising for the Bulgarian secret service not to take an active interest in this bizarre, promising, and dangerous opening. Sofia used to be a sleepy capital. It was now on its way to becoming a headquarters of crime.

A Zhivkov Balance Sheet

Zhivkov may have been confirmed in his positions at the thirteenth party congress in April 1986, but it was only a matter of time before, partly or wholly, he left the scene. A new pretender was emerging in the person of Chudomir Alexandrov, born in 1936, Politburo member and Central Committee secretary for organization and cadres. Ognyan Doynov, for several years one of the most powerful economic officials, was also favored for very senior status. But in view of the history of "coming men" in the Zhivkov regime, it would be a bold man who would heavily bet on either of them.

But ending where this chapter began—with Zhivkov—it is worth listing the main features of a rule that has lasted well over three decades. At the end of the 1980s half Bulgaria's population of some 9 million would have known or remembered no other leader. His record was their total public experience. Its main characteristics have been:

1. Loyalty to Moscow, regardless of who has been in power there.
2. A "surrogate" nationalism, mainly evidenced in periodic confrontation with Yugoslavia over the still emotive Macedonian issue and "equal-footed" relations with both Greece and Turkey.
3. A growing determination to force Bulgaria's minorities into an integrated unitary state, culminating in the forced "Bulgarization" of the Turkish minority in 1984–85.
4. Economic progress and gradually rising living standards.
5. A willingness to experiment boldly in economic and administrative organization.
6. Strong central control over cultural and intellectual life.
7. Political "conservatism."
8. The emergence of a technical intelligentsia—created, nurtured, even pampered by the regime—acutely conscious of a need for Western contracts in the modernization of their country.
9. The rise and fall of several putative "crown princes."
10. The phenomenon of Zhivkov's daughter, Lyudmila.
11. The steady evolution of Zhivkov himself as a national leader and, despite his loyalty to Moscow, with a tendency to self-assertion.

It is a better record than many who knew Bulgaria in the first years of the communist takeover would ever have expected. It has been marred, of course, by many failings, none greater than the fact that the Bulgarian people themselves have not had a real chance to hand down a verdict on the record themselves. But in the twilight of his era Zhivkov, according to his own lights, could look back with some satisfaction.

When he looked forward, however, he could not fail to see dangers. Internationally there was the danger of Bulgaria's reputation. It was urgently necessary to make up for the recent damage. Closer to home the possibility of a harder Soviet line toward Bulgaria had to be taken seriously. The economic situation seemed to be getting more difficult. Finally, at home itself there was the question of succession. It was getting high time for a Bulgarian crown prince—Alexandrov or whomever—to be given security of tenure. This might not prevent anarchy after Zhivkov's departure, but at least it might mitigate it.

11 Yugoslavia

Forty years after its break with the Soviet Union in 1948 Yugoslavia seemed to many to be close to disaster. The mood of the population was a compound of cynicism, pessimism, resentment, and sheer indifference. Those Westerners who perceived the strategic importance of Yugoslavia, and thus of its political and territorial integrity, watched its degeneration with concern and despair. The Soviet Union, on the other hand, presumably viewed it with a hopeful interest. For Yugoslavia had always been an important factor in East-West rivalry. Since 1948 and the break with Stalin the mere existence of an independent Yugoslavia had been a net advantage to the West, despite all the vicissitudes of Yugoslav policy. Now, however, that advantage, already depreciated, looked as if it could be eventually lost altogether as the domestic situation lurched from bad to worse. And, if that advantage were to be lost, the balance of power in southeast Europe could be seriously affected.

The Yugoslav crisis was multifaceted. It was composed of interacting factors difficult to separate. Some were mutually reinforcing, and such was the complexity of the Yugoslav situation that the factors tended to fade indistinguishably into each other.

The factor most evident to any visitor and most keenly felt by many Yugoslavs was that of economic decline. Over 1 million of the country's domestic work force—about 20 percent—were unemployed. (Another 1 million were working in the West, their remittances one of the two life belts of the whole economy; the other was Western tourism.) Real incomes were estimated to have declined by more than 40 percent since 1980. Inflation was estimated to be over 120 percent. Yugoslavia's hard-currency debt, largely accumulated in the 1970s, was still over $20 billion.[1] The country more than once had been to the edge of bankruptcy. Assistance from the International Monetary Fund and the diminishing patience of its Western creditors were helping to pay the interest or to postpone repayment schedules. Between 1981 and 1983 there had been some improvement in overall productivity and in the balance of trade and payments positions. But this hardly eased the overall seriousness of the general situation, which after 1984 went sharply into reverse anyway.

The clearest social effect of this deterioration was on workers' morale and their confidence in the efficacy and durability of the unique Yugoslav system of self-management. Like most of their counterparts anywhere else, the Yugoslav workers would tolerate, even support, a system as long as it was productive and well-paying. And for about two decades, despite the unevenness, self-management had generally met these demands. It gave Yugoslavs an opportunity for political, economic, and social participation in the life of their country that no communist state has ever come near to matching. The economic and social character of the country was transformed, the standard of living rose rapidly, choice on the market was almost unimaginably widened, making Yugoslavia appear a veritable socialist paradise. And this mood of satisfaction and relative optimism induced many workers to approve of the self-management system: the sense of equality it conveyed, of enterprise independence, even of the enhanced dignity of labor.

Ideologically as well as economically, therefore, many had seemed ready to accept the Yugoslav socialist road.[2] But during the 1980s, after the preceding half decade of accelerating economic downturn, it was hard to find anyone with a good word for it. Now self-management was being viewed as a sham, enriching and empowering the managerial and technical classes and pauperizing the workers. (In Slovenia, by far the most economically advanced republic, a skilled worker was taking home only some 60,000 Dinars in 1985 — about $220 per month — while his counterpart in backward Macedonia, in the south, was getting no more than half that amount.) Moreover, the bureaucracy and delay, the endless meetings and difficulties in reaching decisions, all of which were implicit in the self-management system, became now the objects of bitter scorn rather than of the good-humored ridicule of the past. In 1985 there were about seven hundred recorded strikes, some of them quite long and very bitter. This was twice as high as in 1984 and an all-time record.[3] In the spring of 1987 there was a veritable strike epidemic.

At the other end of the economic and social spectrum were the managerial and technical classes, far fewer, of course, than workers or peasants despite the burgeoning of the previous quarter of a century. (They should be distinguished from the relatively small number of entrepreneurs who, operating in a legal no-man's-land, made fortunes out of loopholes in the law, as did their counterparts in pre-Jaruzelski Poland, Hungary, and the USSR.) Most managers and technocrats continued to earn and live well, though many not as well as they were suspected of doing by the workers.[4] Many had suffered, relatively, because of the economic depression, especially those south of Yugoslavia's great dividing line, an area comprising Bosnia-Herzegovina, the southern part of Serbia, Montenegro, Macedonia, and—most deprived of all—Kosovo, with its huge majority of Albanians.

But worse than the economic setbacks was the loss of self-confidence many members of these classes had suffered. With the introduction of self-management, of the market mechanism, decentralization, and the prosperity that once seemed inseparably linked with them, they had grown in power, wealth, and assurance. Many had also come to believe in their own potential, and in that of the system that had allowed them to develop it. They compared themselves favorably (and complacently) with their counterparts in Soviet-controlled Eastern Europe. Now, however, the system seemed to be crumbling beneath them. The confidence of many changed to cynicism, as well as to a *sauve qui peut* mentality that only accelerated the decline it had originally helped to induce.

Nowhere, however, was loss of confidence more apparent than among party members. Reference will be made later in this chapter to some of the vicissitudes of party power. It is sufficient at present simply to register this basic fact of generally low morale. Party power was by no means broken in Yugoslavia. But the locus of its power had changed dramatically over forty years, from the federal center in Belgrade to the republican and provincial capitals. This was part of the process, first of decentralization from the center, then of true federalization, finally to an unofficial and precarious confederalization—a process that has been one of the main themes of Yugoslavia's development since 1948.[5] Depending on the republican capital concerned, therefore, the party could still be strong—or very strong in some. Nowhere was it impotent except at the federal level, where all forms of authority—moral, economic, and political—had sharply declined.

But the shock of decentralization, the weakening of party police power in the 1960s and 1970s, the failure of Tito's efforts to restore party federal authority after 1971, all these had tended to put the party on the defensive in Yugoslav public life. The different republican parties could still assert their authority, often in a repressive way; the Croatian party became the best example of this. But this repressiveness was at least partly the result of a nervousness and uncertainty about the role it was supposed to play.

The death of Tito in 1980 was also a hugely important psychological factor.[6] It was, in fact, Tito's longevity (he was born in 1892) that kept many of the cracks papered over in the edifice he had built. Once he died they appeared, widened, and deepened. His death meant not only the departure of the man who personified the postwar Yugoslav state. It also brought home to everybody that the days of the very capable leadership generation that came to power after World War II were finally over. Now there seemed nothing but mediocrity—and transient mediocrity at that. Second-rate, gray personalities now took the stage, allowed to hold office for seemingly the briefest of possible terms.[7] Their brevity of tenure (perhaps merciful in some cases) was the result of a complicated party and state system elaborated by Tito himself to help stem the centrifugal ethnic forces threatening to engulf Yugoslavia. Tito's system was not only demonstrably failing to do this: in the specific party context it was deepening the uncertainty among rank-and-file members about both the present and the future.

But it was the relationship between the different nationalities that continued to be Yugoslavia's special, basic, and most intractable problem. The differences in economic and cultural level between the northern republics of Slovenia and Croatia and the others were perhaps greater than they had been in 1945. Some of the northerly parts of Serbia, including the Vojvodina with its 20 percent Hungarian minority, were quite prosperous and relatively advanced. But some southern parts of Serbia were very backward, with the largely Muslim and Albanian province of Kosovo the most backward part of all Yugoslavia, more backward even than Macedonia, Bosnia-Herzegovina, and Montenegro. The differences persisted despite strenuous efforts to reduce them, efforts that seemed to exacerbate rather than mitigate the political and economic problems of the country as a whole.

In 1981 rioting in Kosovo caused some deaths and many injuries. Subsequently the smoldering hatred between the Serbs in Kosovo and the awakening Albanian majority continued (see chapter 14). In Croatia separatist sentiment also remained strong despite the great latitude confederation allowed. Great resentment against the Serbs persisted, with the situation gravely complicated by the presence in Croatia of about 800,000 Serbs out of a total population of under 5 million. Among Yugoslavia's 4 million Muslims there was a growing assertiveness. But the nationalist manifestation many considered the most ominous was the so-called "Serb backlash." This phenomenon could be explained by a frustration at the progressive reduction of Serb power and influence in Yugoslavia as a whole. The domination so evident in the interwar kingdom had been gradually whittled away. The physical size of interwar Serbia had been greatly reduced in the postwar federation by the creation of the republics of Macedonia, Montenegro, Bosnia-Herzegovina, and the autonomous authority granted Vojvodina and Kosovo. The Serbian grip on the federal strongholds of power like the government, secret police (UDBa), party, and the military had been greatly reduced, as had the federal authority itself. Finally, there was the humiliation in Kosovo, the cradle of Serb history, culture, and mythology. Here the despised Albanians were inexorably pushing the Serbian remnant out and proclaiming their own nationality and authority.[8]

But the nationalist resentments in Yugoslavia did not just poison the political, cultural, and social atmosphere. They also had crippling economic effects. Once the economic difficulties of Yugoslavia started being defined not simply in territorial but also in *ethnic* terms—and in the postwar period this was not until the early 1960s—then the task of creating a unified, or common, Yugoslav economic system became virtually impossible.[9] Each component of the federation, especially Slovenia and Croatia, as the most advanced republics and the biggest hard-currency earners, insisted on treating itself as a separate, practically sovereign economic unit, concerned about the Yugoslav economy as a whole only when discernible advantage could be got from it. This national separatism was enhanced by the self-management system that produced economic fragmentation and enterprise independence. By 1985, therefore, a unified Yugoslav economic system was further away than ever. There were now too many vested interests in keeping Yugoslavia fragmented, even though many agreed in the abstract that some economic recentralization was needed.[10] And —returning to the basic national jealousies—one powerful reason why there was little practical support for recentralization was the fear that strengthening the federal center really meant strengthening Serbia. For all Yugoslavs (obviously including Serbs) Belgrade was less the capital of Yugoslavia than the capital of Serbia. Central power meant to all Yugoslavs (this time excepting the Serbs) Serbian power.

It was not surprising that the accumulation of such serious domestic weaknesses had led to a sharp decline in Yugoslavia's international standing. Though it accelerated after Tito's death, this decline had begun even earlier. True, Yugoslavia still kept a certain prestige among older age groups for its defiance of Stalin in 1948, but this was a steadily depreciating asset. Its stand against the Soviet-led invasion of Czechoslovakia in 1968 and against the military coup in Poland in 1981 also elicited respect. But the towering prestige Tito's Yugoslavia enjoyed in the Third World in the 1960s and early 1970s as one of the founders of the nonaligned movement was largely a thing of the past. Western Europe and the United States still appreciated Yugoslavia's key importance in the East-West rivalry but resented its continual need for financial help and despaired of ever seeing again the money it had borrowed. Yugoslavia's weaknesses had become plain for all the world to see. It could no longer afford the luxury of a far-flung international policy. The goal now was not influence but survival.

The Ethnic Dimension

In brief outline such is the state of Yugoslavia. Speculation about its failure had turned to fear for its future. Why and how did this decline occur? They are difficult questions. As with the factors of the crisis, so with the reasons for them: the problem is not so much identifying as delineating them and assessing their relative importance. What follows is an attempt to do this, performed with considerable trepidation.

The basic reason for Yugoslavia's decline lies in its national or ethnic differences, differences so great that they have virtually amounted to general mutual incompatibility. The vast majority of its population is indeed Slavic, but a common Slavdom is no guarantee of cohesion, a truism buttressed by other examples in Eastern Europe. Historical experience counts for vastly more than common ethnicity, sometimes to the point of obliterating its relevance. As mentioned earlier, history divided Yugoslavia roughly into two: into a "Habsburg" Catholic north and an "Ottoman" south. The north was composed of Slovenia and Croatia. These two parts had important differences; in one respect they were like the differences between the Czech Lands and Slovakia. Slovenia, like the Czech Lands since 1618, had been ruled by Austria. Croatia, like Slovakia, had been ruled for a thousand years by Hungary.

The type of rule exercised by the two Habsburg ruling states differed considerably, not least in the manner of its application. But it was basically similar, and this similarity became clear by any comparison with the other parts of what was to become Yugoslavia. Here, too, there were broad cracks in the homogeneity. Turkish rule was uneven. What became Montenegro partly escaped it altogether because of the difficulty of its mountainous terrain. The numerous Muslim converts in the southern part of the Balkan peninsula were not treated by the Turks as subject peoples. Then again, Serbia gained its freedom early in the nineteenth century. Macedonia and what is now Kosovo had to wait till the twentieth. Bosnia, formerly Turkish, was occupied by Austria after 1878. After 1918 all these territories became part of Serbia in the new Yugoslavia. For the non-Muslims in this southern part of Yugoslavia the dominant religious and cultural influence was Byzantine. This was an important positive element most South Slavs had in common. But they also had other elements in common—much less positive—that they owed to Turkish rule. The most relevant of these was a lack of public spirit, civic conscience, or even political awareness.

It would need a study in depth to describe what these differences of history meant to the two parts of Yugoslavia.[11] They produced differences in philosophy, attitudes to life, in the governing process as well as in the economic level. These, in turn, became irreconcilable and antagonistic. Slovenes and Croats, representing a higher civilization and enjoying a far higher material standard of living, despised their southern compatriots after 1918. But the Slovenes, numbering just over 1 million when Yugoslavia was founded and well under 2 million by as late as 1985, saw no viable alternative for themselves alone and generally supported the notion of Yugoslavia. The Croats, on the other hand, numbered well over 4 million and had a keenly developed sense of national pride. In the new Yugoslavia after 1918 this pride became directed against the dominant Serbs, with whom an increasingly hostile relationship was complicated by the large Serb minority within Croatia itself. As for Serbia, it dominated the first Yugoslavia. The royal house was Serbian, and the Yugoslav organs of government, including the military, were monopolized by Serbs. The Serbs, in some respects, became the new imperialist power in the Balkans, considering this to be their just rights since they had led the fight for the new Yugoslavia. But despite their power, their great historic role, and their pretensions, the Serbs were never quite numerous enough to become an effective *Staatsvolk*, or "nation of state." The Croats were too strong and determined. It is this Croat-Serb antithesis that was, and has remained, the most serious stumbling block for real South Slav unity.

In World War II Croat-Serb animosity exploded into some of the most atrocious violence even the Balkan peninsula had ever known. During that period Yugoslavia went through both a civil war and a struggle for independence from the Axis powers. The communist-led Partisans won both, and Tito, the Croat-Slovene "quintessential" Yugoslav, now sought to establish a governing system that would secure the "unity and brotherhood" of the Yugoslav people. His solution was federalism, socialism, and, after 1948, independence from Soviet control. It was backed up by a self-confident ruling elite, the top echelon of which contained many men of real ability. In the country as a whole, tired of war and shocked at the violence it caused, there was a willingness (brought of resignation) to try to live together. The Yugoslav idea had always had its supporters.[12] Now there were many more in all parts of the country who passively accepted it.

The task of making it a viable reality was to prove impossible. For some twenty years after 1945 there was the illusion of success, but then the same antagonisms began to be expressed, if in different forms. In a way it was the very success of postwar reconstruction and the preservation of independence after 1948 that gradually pushed these antagonisms back to center stage. The memory of war faded; a new generation grew up that did not experience or remember the past; the perils of construction and the Soviet menace had been overcome. (And, like all younger generations, the more they heard about it from their elders the more they rejected the past—partly because they had not lived through it.) Unity seemed less vital than two decades before. The historical pattern of the Balkans could reassert itself. And, as it did, so certain unpleasant truths about the new Yugoslavia began to be first realized and resented. The most important was that, despite federation, a disproportionate amount of power in all branches of government was still held by Serbs. Thus, as mentioned earlier, the federal government steadily became synonymous for many Yugoslavs with Serbian power. It was inevitable, of course, that many federal posts should be held by Serbs simply because of Belgrade's location, and it was this that prompted many Yugoslavs to question the wisdom of retaining Belgrade as the Yugoslav capital. Would not Jajce in Bosnia, for example, where Tito founded his first wartime government, have been preferable? The logistic problems of converting this, or any other, obscure town into a capital would have been immense. But they might not have been insuperable. Almost any solution would have been better than having the federal capital identified with Serb power. But ultimately it might not have mattered.

The Serbs, of course, were content—at least relatively and temporarily—with the way things were. Until the mid-1960s the federal government had strong powers, as did the League of Communists of Yugoslavia (LCY, the party). In the background was the military, with its officer corps some 70 percent Serb.[13] Finally, there was the all-pervasive federal security apparatus (universally known as UDBa), Serb-dominated, the creation of Alexander Ranković, who was popularly identified with Serb nationalism, party dominance and discipline in the Leninist vein, antireformism, and strong-arm tactics. Ranković was for many years minister of the interior, a center of power that continued after him to be dominated by his supporters. In 1964 the post of Yugoslav vice-president was created, especially for him, in recognition of his seniority over everybody but Tito. Even more important, he had been organizational secretary of the party since 1957, a responsibility that gave him power over all important party appointments. Obviously Tito was master—and Ranković always remained personally loyal to him —but in the day-to-day running of the country Ranković wielded most of the power. As long as he did so, Serbian interests and superiority seemed safe.

Self-Management and the Political Struggle

But by the early 1960s resentment at this situation was to become more confident, real, and articulate. It was expressed both politically and economically. In fact, it was about this time that the ethnic, political, and economic dimensions of the Yugoslav problem became inextricably intertwined. A few years later cultural nationalism became another important ingredient. And it was into this complex and divisive situation that the uniquely Yugoslav self-management system was injected and expanded.

This system has been the subject of the most intense study.[14] What is relevant here is not so much the system itself as its impact on the situation and the political controversies it spawned. There is no doubt it introduced pluralistic tendencies in Yugoslav life that were to take hold and become ineradicable. Indeed, after its formulation and application in the 1950s, a part of Yugoslavia's subsequent political history can be explained by the conflicts in attitudes toward it. Thus self-management became not just the hallmark of Yugoslav socialism worldwide but the touchstone for domestic politics as well. There was a group—and it persisted—whose Leninist principles and instincts felt betrayed by it and who opposed it from the start. At the other end of the spectrum there was Milovan Djilas who, even before his downfall in 1954, saw it as the motor for further and wider reform. (Later Edward Kardelj, who after Djilas became the chief regime ideologist and later Tito's right-hand man, saw it as a means of unifying the state in the face of centrifugal nationalism.)

Before describing the course of the political struggle in Yugoslavia one outstanding characteristic should be stressed. That is the often strong ideological coloration of Yugoslav reform. In fact, many of the reformers were anything but pragmatists. They were certainly less pragmatic than some of the conservatives. Nowhere is the fallacy of automatically identifying reformism with pragmatism seen more clearly than in communist Yugoslavia. The whole self-management system in its various stages of conception and implementation was hidebound with doctrinaire concepts, as were the different constitutions promulgated and then discarded. Nor was this solely due to the rise and preeminence of Kardelj, the supreme pedant despite all his qualities. Djilas, the reformer turned iconoclast, was very much the nonpragmatic idealist. And among those who remained within the system it often seemed never to occur to many that politics might be the art of the possible. (The contrast with the Hungarian reformers after 1968 is very clear.) Tito, it is true, remained a pragmatist, but, except in crises, he was content to leave most of the domestic affairs of Yugoslavia to others.

Under the lofty Tito maneuvered the groups that were to be the main factors on the Yugoslav political stage. By the early 1960s they could be roughly divided into "conservatives" and "liberals."[15] This division was not just over the extent of self-management; it covered economic issues, the differences over investment policy and income distribution, and the questions of what kind of further reform, if any, was necessary. It was now that the ethnic, political, and economic factors of public life merged almost indistinguishably into one another. The most important single issue debated in the 1960s was that relating to control and distribution of investments: should the main power belong to the federal government, the republics, the communes (the most important organ of local government), or the enterprises?

Ostensibly this was an economic question, but it was also inescapably ethnic and political. Generally, the liberal forces—and there were many gradations (and fluctuations) of them—favored decentralization from the federal center. The more liberal the proponents, the further they wished to decentralize. As could be expected, the stronghold of liberal opinion was in the northern, economically advanced republics of Slovenia and Croatia. As the main money earners for the Yugoslav federation as a whole, these two republics resented the fact that they were making very high (as they considered) financial contributions to the federal center only for much of the money concerned to be distributed in investment to the underdeveloped southern regions. Many of these investments, they often correctly argued, were politically rather than economically motivated. "Political factories" were springing up; investments were duplicated and wasted.

In the 1960s the conservatives' stronghold was Serbia. Their argument for directed investment from the federal center to the underdeveloped south was not solely ethnically or emotionally motivated. It also had some economic rationale. Centrally directed investment and the subsidization of new industries and an economic infrastructure in the southern regions, it was argued, were legitimate and necessary until these regions had attained a level of economic development that would enable them to be more self-sufficient. Until that time came it was only right that Slovenia and Croatia should pay more than "their share" to the federal center for distribution southward.

If this economic argument could have been separated from the mainstream of the controversy, it would have been recognized by many as having some validity. But it tended to get submerged in the welter of emotional excess, ethnic chauvinism, and self-serving prejudice. Thus the regional issue continued to undermine Yugoslavia. The struggle between the "have" and the "have not" republics has never been settled. In years of prosperity its weakening effects could be contained; they could not be contained in times of depression and impoverishment.

Decline of the Party

This division between north and south, however, was not as simple as might have appeared. It was complicated by the historical antipathies in some southern republics toward Serbia, and this once again revealed one of the tragic ironies of Yugoslav history: rather than being the unifying force it always wanted to be, Serbia has been a divisive element, both its past and its present arousing resentment or fear. In the struggle between "liberals" and "conservatives," between "haves" and "have nots," Serbia aspired to be the leader of the southern grouping of conservative, poorer republics against Slovenia and Croatia. But only the Montenegrins, an essentially Serb nation, would consistently support Serbia. (This, in itself, was something of an embarrassment for the Serbs because there has always been a universal resentment over the obvious economic and political favoritism extended to Montenegro at the federal level. Both in federal spending and in the number of senior offices held at the center, especially in the party, security, and the military, Montenegro, for reasons of its history of independence, alliance with Serbia, proportionally large number of communists, and sheer assertiveness, was always in a privileged position.) There was considerable fear of Serbia in Macedonia, the autonomous province of Kosovo, and among the Croats and Muslims of Bosnia-Herzegovina. Macedonia and Kosovo, in the interwar royal Yugoslavia, had been an oppressed part of Serbia. Kosovo remained so; and in Macedonia some of the younger leaders even tended to support the Croats against the Serbs on certain issues.[16]

Another vital, identifiable issue dividing conservatives and liberals concerned the role of the party (LCY). It was ostensibly political but, again, had ethnic and economic ramifications. As early as the sixth party congress in 1952, the one that set Yugoslav politics on its unique road, the party's role had been described as being that of a guide, a teacher, using influence not coercion. This was different from the Leninist stress on the party's universal leadership, direction, and control that obtained in the Soviet Union and its satellites and that had been the classic concept with which all Yugoslav communists at that time had grown up. The new description was ambivalent enough for differing interpretations. In many parts of public life the Leninist spirit and methods continued unimpaired. But many communists were puzzled by the new formulations, and those inclined to reform naturally tended to put a liberal construction on them. Thus there began a period of uncertainty resulting in the loss of confidence in the party as a whole. Many years afterward Tito was to say that he had "never liked the sixth congress," referring obviously to this crucial ambivalence.[17] At heart, Tito remained a Leninist. But his thinking here, as in most cases, was not doctrinally motivated; it was political and strategic. He saw the party as being the centrally directed institution that would keep Yugoslavia together. Yet its leading role began to be eroded, by what must have seemed in retrospect a fatal formulation, as early as 1952.

The Great Reforms and Western Migration

The first period of liberal-conservative strife was settled—and the whole course of Yugoslav history changed—between 1963 and 1966 in favor of the liberals. The new Yugoslav constitution of 1963 gave much greater power than before to local enterprises, communes, and other self-managing associations throughout Yugoslavia. The trend in this respect was strongly toward decentralization, and this culminated in the great reform measures of July 1965, always referred to as "the Reform." Already in 1964 there had been some decentralization of the banking system, savings and investment, and a further introduction of the market mechanism. The 1965 Reform introduced basic changes in both the primary and secondary distribution of the national income and in foreign trade. The market now became the predominant mechanism through which the economic life of the country was conducted. The primary distribution of national income was changed by revising the existing price ratios through differentiated increases in prices. The main yardstick was now the world price of the item concerned, translated into the new parity of the dinar. Secondary distribution was greatly reduced by cutting taxes. The main aim here was to reduce the state's share of the net income of enterprises throughout the country from about 50 percent to about 30 percent. The tax cuts were facilitated by eliminating the federal center's role in investment. Subsidies for weak industries and for exports were eliminated.

These changes established the basic pattern for the economic process, a pattern that was to remain permanent. But the Reform spurred another development that was also to have a profound effect on Yugoslav life. Two years earlier, in 1963, the federal government had lifted all restrictions on migration to the West. But it was the economic rigors introduced by the measures of 1965 that started the great migration westward. Many enterprises went bankrupt, while others carried out mass dismissals to stay alive. Furthermore, news of job opportunities, high wages, and decent conditions, especially in the Federal Republic of Germany, soon got back. The numbers of migrants increased. There was already a long tradition of emigration from the Yugoslav lands—to the United States, Australia, Latin America. But there had never been anything like this short-distance, short-term migration. By the end of the 1970s there were over 1 million Yugoslav workers in Western Europe, mainly in the Federal Republic. Their impact on their homeland was great and varied. Economically it was beneficial. It greatly eased the worsening unemployment situation in Yugoslavia itself, and, by the end of the 1970s, Yugoslav workers were sending home between $2 billion and $3 billion a year in remittances to their families. When (and if) the migrant workers came home for good they brought with them all (or some) of the money they had saved and deposited in Western banks. That this could involve large amounts indeed is shown by the fact that the bank accounts of Yugoslav workers in the Federal Republic alone were said to amount to $7 billion in 1977.

The Western migration also had a very strong social and political impact. It contributed enormously to the modernization, the "Westernization," and often to the aggravation of Yugoslav life. Returning or vacationing migrants built houses, large, comfortable, and with every convenience. They often drove impressive Western cars. Not for them the backwardness and *Schlamperei* of their boyhood and girlhood years! In the West, too, they had seen a freedom of political life unknown at home. More important, many had taken part, however remotely, in free trade union affairs not fettered as they were at home. Most of them returned as free spirits, glad to be home but dissatisfied with much they saw, an uncomfortable element for political as well as social conservatives.[18]

The Fall of Ranković

The Reform of 1965, therefore, had its indirect as well as direct influences. But not before the very strong opposition to it was defeated or intimidated. Because of the very decisiveness of the reformers' victory and their support, however hesitatingly from Tito, this opposition had to be covert and indirect, taking the form usually of delaying tactics. Not all of those previously considered as conservative joined this opposition. Many may have had serious reservations about the extent and depth of the Reform, but they accepted the party's and, above all, Tito's decision. Those ready to defy the Reform did so out of much the same interacting reasons already mentioned. The common denominator of opposition was probably an orthodox Leninism and its tenets of the leading role of the party and central planning. But there was also a strong ethnic tinge to it, and this was Serbian nationalism. At the apex of this opposition stood Alexander Ranković, combining Leninist orthodoxy with Serbian "hegemonialism" and disposing of great influence and patronage. Only Tito could break Ranković. This he did, decisively, in July 1966. In the biggest political earthquake since 1948, Ranković was stripped of all his posts and expelled from the party. Many of his supporters in Serbia and other republics were removed amid astonishing revelations about secret police (UDBa) activities—including the bugging of Tito's own quarters. In this respect, Yugoslavia, despite its "separate road," showed itself very similar to the rest of Eastern Europe and the Soviet Union. Indeed, the exposures of secret police power had come considerably earlier in the Soviet-controlled countries as a result of a de-Stalinization the Yugoslavs thought they had never needed.

It was the fall of Ranković that enabled the Reform to blossom. Perhaps most important of all was the freer atmosphere that now prevailed with the virtual collapse of UDBa power at the federal level. But Ranković's fall also had less wholesome effects. It gave a great impetus to anti-Serb nationalism everywhere (except in Montenegro). Indeed, among the two most anti-Serb nations, the Croats and the Albanians of Kosovo, it was this nationalist virulence that became uppermost. This was obvious to visitors in Croatia at the time. Kosovo, up to then, got practically no visitors, but the Kosovars' sense of a changed situation was shown in a number of demonstrations in the province. What released this Albanian assertiveness, however, was not just the perception of Serb decline. Pride in being Muslim was also growing and was to increase during the 1970s with the resurgence of Islam worldwide.

But there was also a third factor in Kosovo with the most dangerous implications of all: the existence, survival, and independence of neighboring Albania. In a peninsula where race prejudice is endemic, the Albanians were historically the most despised and downtrodden of nations. This they continued to be, but an independent Albania and a more powerful Islam have at least given them the will to rage against their status.

Moreover, while Albania itself was a thoroughly obscure Soviet dependency, it had little influence in Kosovo. But the very act of throwing off Russian control in the early 1960s put the question in many a Kosovar's head as to why he could not do the same with the Serbs. Even with Serb domination, the Kosovo Albanians still had several advantages over their kinsmen across the border under Enver Hoxha's tyranny. Their standards of living and education were, for example, better, in spite of their being the worst in Yugoslavia itself. But these factors counted for little against the psychological dimension that came into Albanian life in Kosovo in the 1960s. Few wanted incorporation into

Albania, and the Tirana regime was careful to avoid openly espousing it.[19] But during the 1970s and 1980s the demand for separate republican status for Kosovo became more clamorous. From the Albanian viewpoint it was justified and made superficial political sense. But there were three big reasons for its continued rejection. First, many of the 300,000 to 400,000 Albanians in neighboring Macedonia and Montenegro, most of them in areas adjacent to Kosovo, would presumably want to join any new republic. Second, once the process of ethnic-territorial restructuring started in Yugoslavia, it could lead to the steady unraveling of much of the whole federation. Many of the very large Serb minority in Croatia, for example, would want incorporation into Serbia itself. Bosnia-Herzegovina, composed of Muslims, Serbs, and Croats, could even disintegrate entirely. Third, the loss of Kosovo could provoke the final explosion of frustration in Serbia proper. Nothing would be likely to exacerbate Serb resentment more than the loss of the emotion-drenched territory of historic Serbia to the Albanians.[20] Kosovo, therefore, must wait—perhaps indefinitely. After all, along with the other Serbian regional province of Vojvodina, it has had since 1974 practically all the powers of a full republic, including that of veto on the federal level. But the discontent and tension in Kosovo did not diminish. The bloody rioting in 1981, following Tito's death the year before, was just another warning of a rising self-awareness that no repression could crush.

Back on the federal level, the fall of Ranković was immediately followed by important organizational reforms in the party, mainly designed to prevent the concentration of power that had taken place under him. But after all the changes had been made the same dilemma over the party's role, caused by the ambivalence of 1952, remained. Edward Kardelj referred to the party having to steer between the Scylla of impermissible interference and the Charybdis of political impotence. But at the federal level it was drifting much closer to Charybdis than to Scylla. The central authority became seriously weakened to the benefit of party leaderships at the republic level. Further down the hierarchical level the local party organizations were becoming more independent in defying policies higher authorities in their republic tried to impose on them. The press also was increasingly lively. The parliamentary scene, after the reforms of the electoral system in 1963, became astonishingly animated at the federal level.[21] It reached its apogee at the republic level almost immediately after Ranković's fall when the Slovene government actually resigned after defeat in a vote in the parliament in Ljubljana. Public life generally was jolted by the Belgrade student disturbances of May 1968. These, in part, owed their origins to developments outside Yugoslavia: in Western Europe, Czechoslovakia, and Poland. But they could hardly have occurred had the domestic political situation not been propitious. However, the way the disturbances were ended, through the dramatic intervention of Tito himself in which he ostensibly showed an understanding for the students' motives, also gave many Yugoslavs the assurance that, whatever the crisis, Tito would master it.

But all this exuberance had a darker, perilous aspect. The greatly increased political and economic freedom was leading to more rather than less nationalist assertiveness. Liberals had always argued that comprehensive reform would tend to weaken the appeal of nationalism. Vladimir Bakarić, the most able and respected figure in Croatia, was saying in 1966 that nationalism would become "question number one" if the battle over reform were not won quickly. But the battle had been won, and nationalism was not only question number one but also seemed further away from being answered than ever. Bakarić, therefore, was wrong. But how much more wrong had Tito been four years earlier when he had flatly declared: "We have solved the national question"?[22]

The Croatian Crisis and Aftermath

The issue was fed by an economic situation that, despite—or, as many would argue, because of the Reform—was getting worse. Inflation was increasing perceptibly and, by the end of the 1960s, was about 15 percent, starting that vicious spiral that in fifteen years would take the percentage into three figures. Moreover, although support for the Reform had come mainly from Slovenia and Croatia, some of its consequences worked against these two republics. One was the fact that it had made the banking system extremely important. Bank funds began to take over from the federal government as the main source of investment in the economy and housing. The federal banks that supplied most of this credit began to show themselves as insensitive to the problems and needs of the enterprises as the state had been.[23] But most galling of all, especially to Croat national sentiments, was that most of the big banks were in Belgrade, unaffected by the decentralization that had been taking place.

The foreign currency issue, always the subject of disquiet to the

Croats, also began to assume an ominous importance. The Croats pressed for the right of each republic to keep a much higher share of the foreign currency it earned. Western tourism was becoming a multibillion business, and Croatia, especially its Dalmatian coastline, was getting the lion's share of the tourists' hard-currency spending, only to have to hand a large part of it over to the federal treasury. The demand for a higher share of this (or virtually all of it) was to become the ostensible cause of the great Croatian crisis of December 1971.

Depending on whether one took the conservative or liberal approach to the great issues of Yugoslav public life, the Croatian crisis, which began very early in 1970, either refutes or confirms the view that reform defuses nationalism. The conservatives needed only to point to the situation in Kosovo and Croatia, and they were now being joined by many who had once supported reform and hailed the fall of Ranković in 1966 but who now saw things as getting out of control. They wanted some federal recentralization that would not endanger the political and economic freedoms already won. The more hard-core conservatives wanted to get back to Leninism and the manifold centralization that term implied. The liberals, on the other hand, especially those in Zagreb, argued that the reforms had not gone far enough and that the national question would not be solved until reformist demands had been met. The Croatian leaders, while making the currency issue their main specific demand, wanted more constitutional changes designed to weaken the federal center still further. In party affairs, like some Czechoslovak reformers, they wanted to erode Leninism further by relaxing the rules of democratic centralism. Even after a party decision had been taken, those against it should be allowed to maintain their dissenting views. At the local political level, outside the party, elections should be more democratic. Ordinary workers in the factories should get more powers at the expense of party and/or trade union officials and the managerial-technocratic strata. Finally, conservatives, i.e., those who did not agree with one or more of the preceding parts, should be purged. (That was where the liberalism of the liberals stopped.)

These demands were radical enough at the time. But they were not wholly confined to Croatia. Some were being made by the burgeoning liberal wing in the Serbian party and the reformist group of the Macedonian party in Skopje, not to mention the majority in the Slovene party. What distinguished the demands in Zagreb was that they were permeated with Croatian nationalism. It may have been true that the most prominent new leaders of the Croat party, Mika Tripalo, Savka

Dabčević-Kučar, and Pero Pirker, did not see themselves primarily as nationalists and honestly believed they could control the separatist passions that were rising. But in retrospect it seems clear that they could never have channeled the flow of Croat nationalism but would eventually (even quite soon) have been engulfed by it. They claimed that they could only control Croat nationalism if they spoke for it. In the event it was another organization, the Matica Hrvatska, a national cultural body with a distinguished history, and not the party that captured nationalist passions and loyalties. It quickly became an alternative political authority in Croatia, riding the crest of nationalism.

The story of the Croatian crisis is well known. It ended quickly and surprisingly peacefully in December 1971 when Tito made his historic threat to use armed force—and subsequently indicated that the Soviet Union had offered its own "help," too. The Croat leadership was purged, and some Matica Hrvatska leaders were arrested, as were the leaders of the student strike that ushered in the last stage of the crisis. All this is familiar enough. What is still disputed by some, however, is what the crisis was really about. Was the movement in Croatia mainly democratic because the emergence of Matica Hrvatska heralded real pluralism and an alternative option? Would the fulfillment of reasonable Croatian demands have taken the edge off nationalist intemperance? Many Croatian intellectuals made these claims after the crisis was over, and some of them were undoubtedly sincere. They point to the onset of the "Leninist reaction" once the crisis was over, mainly in Croatia and Serbia, but also to a lesser extent in Macedonia and Slovenia. This they cite as proof that the struggle was really about "liberalism" and "conservatism" in the political or economic sense, with nationalism only a side issue.

These arguments have a certain plausibility but are unconvincing. What predominated in Croatia in 1971 was an infectious nationalism. Had it gone unchecked, civil war would probably have followed. The first victims would have been the Serbs in Croatia. This would have caused Serbian retaliation even if the federal authority had been unable to act. The whole Yugoslav federal system would have been endangered. The Soviet Union would have had the opportunity to interfere in a number of ways—not with any open aggression but with the "sly infiltration and subversion" one Yugoslav official spoke to Dusko Doder about.[24] The Croatian crisis was not about the peaceful evolution of Yugoslavia—or even of Croatia—but about its survival or destruction.

It was the gravest crisis since 1948. Tito met it with his customary nerve and decisiveness—remarkable for a man nearly eighty years old. But Tito, though always in possession of strong nerves, seemed to reserve his decisiveness for crises only: during the war, in 1948, in 1966, and then 1971. (Only during the Hungarian Revolution in 1956 did there appear to be doubt and fumbling for a few fateful days.) But in less heroic times hesitation and inconsistency were Tito's characteristics. He had a sharp political sense but sometimes allowed himself to be persuaded into doing, or accepting, things apparently against his better judgment. For long periods he was, of course, engaged in foreign affairs, leaving the nitty-gritty of domestic affairs to others. Besides, though every inch a dictator, he was prepared to be advised, persuaded, or dissuaded. He was also refreshingly ready and self-confident enough to admit his mistakes. But—and 1971 was a good example—he sometimes allowed events to drift toward crisis without trying to check them. And in the Croatian case he even gave the principal actors the wrong impression that he would tolerate what they were doing. After the crisis he was determined not to allow a repetition and had his own views on how this should be done. If he had previously given the impression that he was tolerating "liberalism," now he left no doubt that he was moving toward the "conservatives."

As mentioned earlier, Tito was by instinct a Leninist, and it was to Leninism he attempted to revert after December 1971. This meant first that the more prominent liberals *outside* Croatia also had to go. The purge affected both Slovenia and Macedonia, but Serbia was affected the worst. The Serbian purge was important for two reasons. First, the Serbian leadership in the late 1960s and early 1970s had become, as an evident reaction to the Ranković years, not only liberal in political and economic outlook but also the least nationalist that any Serb leadership could possibly be. The new president of the party, Marko Nikezić, a former Yugoslav foreign minister, and the party secretary, Latinka Perović, were the leaders of an emerging group of relatively young politicians who might have modified the natural Serb tendency toward hegemonistic nationalism and therefore mitigated the anti-Serb prejudice in the rest of the country. By forcing these people out of political life in 1972, however, Tito was actually promoting Serb nationalism. Second, for the first time on a vital issue, Tito had difficulty in getting his way over the Serbian leadership purge. Many Serbian Central Committee members opposed his will at a Serbian Central Committee plenum in October 1972 when Tito forced Nikezić and Perović out. Some supported the liberal line, but even more resented what they thought an interference in Serb affairs. Tito met the challenge with his usual frankness and eventually won. But the all-powerful, all-knowing image had been slightly dented.

The purge of the Serbian liberal leadership took place amid an extensive propaganda campaign stressing the party's leading role, Leninism, and Tito's leadership. But, apart from the personnel changes, there was little effort to turn the clock back, especially with regard to decentralization from the federal center to the republics. Any such intention, in fact, would have been made all the more difficult by a constitutional amendment of 1970 that formally allocated prime sovereignty to the six republics and two autonomous provinces and all powers of government not specifically allocated to the federation. These federal powers were foreign policy, national defense, measures necessary to ensure a unitary Yugoslav market, common monetary and trade policies, the ensuring of ethnic and individual rights, and "the principles of the political system." But, as has been pointed out, even on these points long haggling was sometimes necessary, with always the possibility of a veto.[26] In financial matters the only direct and exclusive sources of income for the federal government would be customs duties and state stamp taxes. The rest of the federal government's income would be the subject of negotiation between it and the republican governments. The amendment of 1970 was approved well before the Croatian crisis came to its climax. It would probably not have been approved had such a crisis been foreseen; almost certainly not *after* such a crisis. But, once approved, even with the Croatian crisis fresh in people's memory, it could hardly be withdrawn.

In fact, decentralization was carried further by the new constitution of 1974. A massive document, more a primer for living than for lawmaking, it simply made Yugoslavia a de facto confederation by reducing the federal structure "almost entirely to an apparatus for agreement" among the republics and provinces.[27] It also gave the two Serbian autonomous provinces of Kosovo and Vojuodina the right of veto in federal decisionmaking.

The New Self-Management

At the same time important changes were being prepared in the system of self-management. They were finally formulated in the law of 1976, with the ostensible aim of making self-management more a concern and privilege of the workers. The main unit of self-management was now to be the Basic Organization of Associated Labor (BOAL), taking the place formerly held by the enterprise. There could now, in fact, be several BOALs in one enterprise, according to the type and place of work of the members concerned. At the end of 1985 there were about 30,000 BOALs in the whole of Yugoslavia, and 365 in the federal railway system alone.[28] These were autonomous administrative and financial units governed by workers' councils and were responsible for wages, production, prices, markets, credit policy, and questions relating to capital. As the basic units in the self-management system, they sent representatives to the highest unit of the system at the communal level. In a drastic move to enhance worker status, the managerial and technical staffs were no longer allowed to stand for election to the workers' councils. Thus the managerial-technocrat stranglehold on the self-management system was formally broken.

What was the real aim of these very important changes? The official explanation was that it was at last to give the workers what self-management was supposed to give them in the first place—real authority and real responsibility. Many workers, however, had a less favorable explanation. The new measures, they complained, so fragmented self-management as to make it impotent. They saw it, therefore, as a conspiracy to destroy the system in the context of a retreat from reform toward party control and centralism.[29] Tito and the regime leadership, the argument went, hesitated to assault the system frontally, so they resorted to undermining it under the guise of perfecting it. There was yet a third explanation: that it was an attempt by the party to break the power of the managerial-technocratic class in public life as a whole. Not only would individual enterprises be harder to manage because of the ubiquitous and proliferating BOALs, but also the barring of managerial and technical personnel from places on works councils was an obvious attempt to reduce their status.

There is something to be said for all three of these contentions. Kardelj, himself, seems to have believed that the more deeply the self-management system penetrated, the more democratic the whole system would be. He also believed, as did Tito, that self-management was the only effective weapon against ethnic particularism. But they turned out to be almost totally wrong. The fragmentation went beyond all reasonable bounds. More chaos rather than more democracy resulted. And ethnic particularism also continued unabated.

Moreover, if the leadership were truly concerned about the workers coming into their own, why were there no arrangements for technical advice or managerial, legal, and technical expertise to be put at their disposal? Many works councils were now left to founder out of sheer ignorance and lack of experience on the part of their members. Finally, the managers and technocrats certainly had a point in the suspicions of malicious intent. Over the previous thirty years they had emerged as a rival class to the party bureaucracy at all levels—federal, republic, and local. This was, at least partly, an attempt to put them in their place. But, as things turned out, worker ignorance and apathy under the new system was even greater than under the old. In many parts of the economy, therefore, managers and technocrats continued to exercise much influence behind the scenes.

The Succession Issue

Tito was eighty-two when the 1974 Constitution was promulgated. His physical energy and mental alertness were still remarkable, but it was obvious he could not go on much longer. He was clearly concerned about his succession and must have been just as concerned about the paucity of leadership talent among the upcoming generation. There was nothing like the abundance of talent once at his disposal. The main reason for this was chance: some generations of leadership are more talented than others. But another was the steady loss in power and prestige of the federal center. As decentralization to the republic level progressed, a career at the center lost its attractions. Most ambitious politicians now sought a career in Zagreb, Skopje, or other republic and provincial capitals, or, in the Serbian case, in the Serbian republic administration in Belgrade. A few years (not too long) at the federal center in Belgrade might be considered important, but mainly as a stepping stone in a career "at home." This naturally tended to encourage a narrow, provincial outlook militating against the broad-minded outlook Yugoslav leadership so sorely needed.

Tito must have realized the seriousness of the problem. But he did nothing to ease it by his attempted "return to Leninism" after the Croatian crisis and his purge of some of the younger liberals, some of whom could have been potential leadership material at the federal level. Obviously neither the highly intelligent Mika Tripalo nor any of the Croat leaders during the 1971 crisis could be eligible. But the purged liberal Serb leadership could have produced likely candidates. Krsto Crvenkovski, the Macedonian leader, politely but firmly sidelined in 1972, was also a man of stature. There were others, too, who had not had time to make a name, but who could have done so had the political climate and the course of Yugoslav history been more propitious.

The national dimension was a third, seriously limiting factor in the succession issue. Not only would any new leadership group have to have the "right" ethnic balance, i.e., the one that would cause the least national jealousies, but the "topmost" leader, or even the accepted primus inter pares (presuming these familiar concepts of leadership were still relevant), would have to be of a "neutral" nationality. That meant he could not be a Serb or a Croat. In the case of the former, the general fear and distrust of Serbs was too great; in the case of the latter, the Serbs would not accept yet another Croat, because Tito, himself, was considered a Croat (when stripped of his Yugoslav aura). Again the "Serb syndrome" was paralyzing the workings of state.

For a few years in the 1970s, however, it did seem that Tito was grooming a successor with both the right political and ethnic credentials. Stane Dolanc was Slovenian, tough, capable, a believer in federalism and in a strong party line.[30] He came to the fore in 1972, after the purge of liberals and, after Tito, he was the main figure in the "return to Leninism" campaign. In 1972 he cosigned a letter with Tito on strengthening the role of the party and in 1974 was made secretary of the party executive committee. Dolanc seemed to personify the "Slovenian solution": he was neither Serb nor Croat. Historically, too, Slovenia had favored the Yugoslav concept. Culturally and economically it was the most advanced part of the country.

But by 1978 Dolanc's momentum seemed to have slowed. Perhaps revelations about a brief membership of a Nazi youth organization in wartime Slovenia crippled his chances. Perhaps the abrasive elements in his personality offended too many colleagues, and Tito still had time to head off the danger. Whatever the reasons Dolanc, though he continued active in top federal bodies, receded from the limelight. But in October 1978 the situation was radically changed by the publication of the "standing rules" for collective leadership. The clearest aim of these new rules was not to promote any one man but to prevent anybody from gaining too much power after Tito's death. These rules were the work of Tito himself. They were, logically, an extension of the constitutional provisions of 1974 and sought to establish and preserve a strict equality between the Yugoslav nations in party posts and in the executive organs of federal government.

Their main innovation was the consecration of the rotation system, mooted four years before. The posts of president of the Yugoslav state and of the Yugoslav party were to be rotated annually on an ethnic basis. Therefore a new head of state and party leader, from a different republic or province than the previous one, would be elected every year. At the level of federal government it was felt that more continuity and stability were needed. Federal prime ministers were to rotate every four years (i.e., every legislative term) according to republic or province, while all other federal ministers could hold office for two terms, (i.e., eight years).[31] The first federal prime minister under this new dispensation was the Montenegrin Veselin Djuranović. He was succeeded in 1982 by a Croat, Mrs. Milka Planinc, whose efforts were dedicated mainly to the unsuccessful struggle against economic decline. In May 1986 she was replaced by Branko Mikulić whose Croat blood was presumably considered diluted by his Bosnian provenance. Mikulić had briefly taken Dolanc's place as executive committee secretary before collective leadership was introduced. A forceful man, an advocate of more strength for the federal center, and certainly no liberal, Mikulić seemed determined to halt Yugoslavia's economic decline and to use to the full what remained of federal power.

Compared with twenty years before, there was now little of this power left. But in matters affecting Yugoslavia's external relations, defense, and international finance, federal power was vital still. Moreover, continuity in Belgrade did represent a stabilizing factor and symbol. The federal center still had *some* uses, therefore. The question was whether it could now attract ministers and administrators. Even more important was the question whether the republics would allow the center enough latitude to tackle the economic problems briefly referred to at the beginning of this chapter. By the end of 1986 the signs were definitely that they would not. Mikulić was more formidable than Mrs. Planinc.[32] Indeed, though under the rotation rules Bosnia-Herzegovina's turn to fill the premiership came after that of both Slovenia and Vojvodina, the two last-named deferred to Mikulić on the grounds of his ability and experience. (He was, after all, the man credited with making the Sarajevo Winter Olympics of 1984 such a success!) This showed both respect for Mikulić and an awareness of how serious the situation was. But even so, the vested interests against Mikulić were awesome.

Within only a year of assuming power Mikulić must have realized the near-impossibility of his task. If anything, the crisis had worsened. The mood of the workers, expressed in a wave of strikes in most parts of the country, had become ominous. There seemed no improvement in sight, and Mikulić's reputation correspondingly suffered. To top it all, the worst financial scandal in the history of communist Yugoslavia broke in the summer of 1987. It involved "Agrokomerc," one of the biggest agro-industrial manufacturing enterprises in the country, which, even more unfortunately for Mikulić, was located in Bosnia. For years "Agrokomerc" had been issuing promissory notes to the tune of an estimated $400 million with no collateral. The perpetrators of the racket, some of them colorful characters indeed, were not lining their own pockets but seeking to spread the notion that "Agrokomerc" was a thriving concern. The scandal, which cost a federal vice-president and scores of others their jobs, somehow symbolized the whole shoddy and rickety edifice that the Yugoslav economy had become.

The Military Factor

Tito died in 1980. He had dominated his country's history for nearly forty years. But he had failed in his main aim of creating a united Yugoslavia. The very fact that he himself had come to be considered the most powerful unifying factor in Yugoslav life was itself a reflection of his failure. He had failed to create the necessary mechanisms and generate the right atmosphere for a federal, socialist Yugoslavia to exist without, or independently of, him. The expression "Tito's Yugoslavia" became not simply journalists' shorthand: it was an accurate description of the state he led. Perhaps this mutual identification was harmless, even necessary, in the early years of the new Yugoslavia. This was a state, after all, that did not grow organically as many European states had done. Tito realized this well enough, and he appears also to have grasped some of the essentials of nation-building. He both established a myth and the leadership personality (himself) to go with it. His Yugoslavia was born of a momentous wartime victory, the defiance of Stalin in 1948, the brilliance of the first leadership generation, as well as his own greatness. But more was needed for the new state to be both durable and viable. Tito's recipe was socialism, tempered by self-management and federation. Neither produced the magic formula, and his departure from the scene left many Yugoslavs wondering whether there was any formula for Yugoslavia at all. More: it left many Yugoslavs not caring.

With Tito gone, many of those who *did* care saw the military as the one cohesive factor remaining, a view shared by many Western observers. The army, it was argued, was the one central, avowedly

Yugoslav element remaining. It was well equipped to act as both a coercive and a cohesive force. It was responsible and self-disciplined. And it was the only major institution in Yugoslav public life where there was no self-management.

These generalizations are partly true but warrant closer examination. In case of outside attack one can assume that the military would lead a general all-national defense. (A nationwide defense system was established in 1969, immediately after the Soviet-led invasion of Czechoslovakia.) But an attack by Soviet or Soviet-led forces—and it is difficult even to imagine an attack from any other source—is highly unlikely in any foreseeable future. Much more topical is the possible role of the military as the defender of the internal order and integrity of the Yugoslav state.

Tito threatened to use the military in the Croatian crisis of 1971. He subsequently made it clear that he regarded the armed forces as being there to defend Yugoslavia from internal as well as external danger. Even at that time, however, there was controversy over any internal military role. Bakarić, second to none in his determination to preserve Yugoslavia, thought that it could bring civil war.[33] While Tito was alive, and almost certainly in the Croatian crisis, the military could probably have been used for any internal purpose, with its loyalty and discipline remaining intact. But after Tito's departure the prediction of Bakarić would probably have turned out correct.

It is difficult to see the Yugoslav army being used to coerce, say, an individual republic without serious defections by troops from the republic concerned and perhaps by troops from other republics. Use of the army against Serbia, for example, is practically unthinkable. Any attempted move against Croatia would, since Tito, result in massive Croat defections, not just from Croatian regiments per se, but also from Croatian troops in Bosnian-Herzegovinian regiments. The only probable exception to this generalization would be if coercion were seen as required against the Albanians of Kosovo. Serbian and Montenegrin troops would respond with alacrity to such a call. Others might be less enthusiastic but would hardly balk at the prospect. And the possibility that such a move might lead to war with Albania would hardly discourage anybody.

The Soviet Shadow

The only cohesive factor (or prospect) remaining, would appear to be fear of the Soviet Union or, more correctly, fear of falling again under direct Soviet control. The depth of anti-Soviet feeling was always difficult to gauge. The anti-Soviet emotion invariably displayed, for example, on sporting occasions where Soviet teams participated has always been genuine enough. It may also be taken as a pointer to how most Yugoslavs would behave were there an overt Soviet threat. But the real danger has always been of a progressive internal disintegration being manipulated by skillful Soviet diplomacy, tactics, and covert interference —the "sly infiltration," as it was described to Dusko Doder.

The number of disaster scenarios that could be depicted for Yugoslavia is almost endless. But it hardly requires the fantasy of an unhinged mind to imagine a situation developing in Croatia, for example, where separatist tendencies revived, captured control of the government, and threatened secession from Yugoslavia if certain (impossible) conditions were not met. The weak federal government would be offered help by the Soviet Union. The situation, in this respect, would be similar to 1971 when, according to Tito, the Soviets did offer help.[34] But, instead of being led with determination by a Tito, as it had been in 1971, the federal authorities this time might be powerless to act. As for the Western powers, even if they were of a mind to, they could not help as quickly or efficiently as the Soviet Union could interfere. There might then be some temptation for Belgrade to accept "limited" help from Moscow. Once that was given—or even accepted in theory or principle—the days of Yugoslav independence could be numbered. Alternatively, if in a thoroughly chaotic Yugoslavia a secessionist Croatian government declared that socialism was endangered inside its borders, then Soviet help might be offered to Croatia against the federal government.[35] This, of course, would be more serious. Yugoslav integrity and independence would be directly threatened. A casus belli would have emerged that, step-by-step, could lead to confrontation between the Soviet Union and the Western powers, primarily the United States.

These are simply some examples of cases where the Soviets could intervene in a Croatian context. In less immediately threatening ways they could also help stoke the fires of growing *Serbian* resentment. Some might argue that the Soviets have entirely lost any proprietary interest in Yugoslavia. But such a view seems to reflect complacency when the activities of the huge Soviet embassy in Belgrade are considered, as well as the various forms of political, military, and economic activity in which it indulges—not to mention the operations of the KGB. The supposition must remain that the Soviets view Yugoslavia as an errant or prodigal son who might one day be induced to return to the fold, and should be quietly encouraged to do so. In a speech (which greatly disturbed the Yugoslavs) in Belgrade in 1971, Brezhnev referred to Yugoslavia as being in the same "socioeconomic world grouping" as the Soviet Union.[37] Five years later he had moved from the inclusive to the patronizing: "It has recently become fashionable to slander our good relations with [Yugoslavia] and to spread the most absurd fabrications about them. The authors of these fairy tales try to depict Yugoslavia as some kind of poor, defenseless Little Red Riding Hood whom the terrible rapacious wolf—the Soviet Union—threatens to tear to pieces and devour."[37]

Though ostensibly designed to reassure, it was sentiment and expressions like these that worried the Yugoslavs. They expressed the true Soviet feelings about Yugoslavia much more than the terminology of the 1955 Belgrade and 1956 Moscow Declarations in which Moscow had recognized Yugoslavia's "special road." Whatever Gorbachev's policy is to Yugoslavia he will doubtless express himself somewhat more tactfully than Brezhnev.

In turn, the Yugoslav attitude to Moscow seems always to have been colored by the need to react against this proprietary Soviet attitude. Tito at first thought he could influence Khrushchev, but subsequent events proved him wrong. Later, some observers saw a pattern in Yugoslav-Soviet relations, an interaction between a harder political line at home and an improvement in these relations. Events did seem to lend this view some credence. The years between 1961 and 1964, for example, saw Khrushchev making strong efforts to repair the harm done in his relations with Tito; at the same time there was more emphasis on central control, and planning, and the leading role of the party in Yugoslavia itself. Even more striking was the similar convergence some ten years later after the Croatian crisis. Tito's purge of liberals and attempts to reinstate Leninist purity in political life were immediately followed by an obvious warming of relations with Moscow expressed by a top-level exchange of visits and the Soviet promise in 1972 of a mammoth credit.[38] (The credit, however, never fully materialized.)

Obviously, these developments were not entirely coincidental. But they should not lead to far-reaching conclusions. It should be remembered that the Yugoslav leaders—none more so than Tito—were communist in ideology and outlook. The assertion of independence in 1948 and the break with Stalin never altered that. Thus everything they did, however "unorthodox," had to be placed within a communist framework. It also meant that, despite their fear of it, they sometimes tended to gravitate toward the Soviet Union almost by instinct. Certainly on most global issues they supported it. On some, like the Arab-Israeli war of 1967, the raison d'état of both demanded mutual support for the Arab states. But on the many other issues, where no Yugoslav state interest was involved, they usually supported the Soviet Union on broad ideological grounds.

In doing so, the Yugoslavs appeared ready to offend Western, particularly American, opinion. But when it came to issues affecting "socialist relations," which to them meant the right of independence from the Soviet Union, there was no doubt where they stood. They bitterly opposed Soviet interference in Czechoslovakia and (indirectly) in Poland; also in Afghanistan. Even during the period of their own hostile relations with Peking, they defended China's right of independence. Later when the Chinese attitude changed, relations became much warmer, with Tito making a triumphant visit in 1977. Indeed, if a generalization can be hazarded at all, it is as follows: on global issues Yugoslavia has usually supported the Soviet line, on important issues involving "socialist" relations, whether state or party, Yugoslavia has opposed it, because this was necessary to preserve independence. In this attitude the Yugoslavs have been very similar to the Italian communists, with whom they have always maintained close relations. But the similarity ends there. The Italian communist leaders are Western —by habit, instinct, values, and choice. The Yugoslav communists are Eastern and Balkan, heirs to a different set of values. Their natural gravitation is eastward.

Yugoslavia's relations with the West should be seen in the light of its relations with the Soviet Union. Belgrade certainly sees the West as a very vital trading partner. In this connection the comprehensive agreement with the European Community in 1970 was of crucial importance, both commercially and politically. Indeed, the early 1970s, which were crisis years politically, were good years economically and marked a new phase in Yugoslavia's economic standing.[39] It was no longer overwhelmingly an exporter of raw materials but with some success was exporting to the West finished products of some sophistication.

It was also becoming a shipbuilder of world recognition. The "developed" West's share of Yugoslavia's foreign trade in 1971 stood at nearly 53 percent of exports and nearly 66 percent of imports.[40] But then, as Rusinow puts it, some Yugoslav leaders "began to lose their nerve,"[41] preferring the safer haven of Soviet and Comecon trade to the more dangerous waters of Western competition. The Soviet Union, as early as 1971, again became Yugoslavia's number one trading partner and in 1972 came the promise of the huge Soviet loan. This was immediately followed in 1973 by the first world oil crisis, which began Yugoslavia's steady economic decline.

Subsequently, Yugoslav commercial policy was to follow a dual track. The volume of its trade in both percentage and volume continued to shift eastward. But Western *borrowing*, in which the Yugoslavs had always indulged, now increased very sharply indeed. This occurred for two reasons. First, the money was readily available in the West. Second, with the continuing decentralization of the domestic economy generally, local enterprises could now negotiate Western loans with totally inadequate control exercised over them. The result was an uncontrolled borrowing spree that in a few years resulted in the $20 billion millstone round the neck of the Yugoslav economy.

But while economic reasons certainly explain the Yugoslav shift back toward the East in commerce, they do not fully account for the Yugoslavs' hesitation in the early 1970s to take the opening to the West that seemed to be offered them. This was partly due to an intuitive, ideological, and political hesitation about getting too "involved" with the West. There was a genuine fear that underdeveloped Yugoslavia could not compete. There were also fears of getting too close to "capitalism," the product of the same a priori socialist mentality that led Yugoslavia generally to lean toward the Soviet Union on many global issues.[42] And, considering this basic attitude, the Yugoslav leaders' concern about closeness to capitalism was becoming understandable by the beginning of the 1970s. The rapidly increasing number of Yugoslav workers in the West were already having their impact. Knowledge of and fascination with the West increased (the latter even more than the former). It was considered time, therefore, to sound the official warning. The irony was that, during the 1970s, the Yugoslav leaders themselves became, through the contracting of loans over which they had no control, more beholden to the West than ever they had dreamed in their worst ideological nightmares.

Yugoslavia, therefore, became part of a modern, global financial problem, and it was no comfort to its leaders to be told that, from a world perspective, its debt was inconsiderable. For Yugoslavia it was huge and it sapped confidence and eroded independence. And this kind of financial involvement with the West only served to lengthen, not shorten, the Soviet shadow.

The Prospects

This chapter began with a brief description of Yugoslavia's present situation and continued with an attempt to analyze how and why it came about. It has spent much time in the 1960s and the early 1970s because it is then, especially in the decade between 1964 and 1974, that the basic explanations for what followed are to be found. It is pointless to speculate whether the past could have been different. More to the point is what the future might be.

If toward the end of the 1980s the Yugoslav present was grim, the future looked even worse. Economically Yugoslavia seemed so crippled that it was doubtful it would ever walk without crutches again. The reasons for this, already intimated, were far from being wholly economic per se. The only way toward economic salvation—though this alone would not ensure it—was through a unified Yugoslav market. But the obstacles to creating this market had grown rather than receded, and there seems little likelihood of their being reduced. The tragedy of Yugoslavia was that the golden mean between centralism and devolution, without which no successful federation is possible, had not been found. The decentralization that began in the 1960s generated an unstoppable momentum. The more the republics received, the more they wanted and the less they conceded. The Serbs, the largest and historically the greatest of the Yugoslav nations, represent not just the biggest symbol of national difficulties but also the insuperable obstacle to their solution. It is an impasse from which there seemed no escape. At the end of 1985 the Serbian authorities tried to get rescinded the right of veto at the federal level enjoyed by Kosovo and Vojvodina. They argued that these were parts of Serbia and their right of veto violated Serbian sovereignty. They were strongly rebuffed, and this only added to their bitterness. The danger of Serbia going through something like the Croatian crisis of 1971 could not be excluded. And this time there would be no Tito to tackle it. More recently it was the situation in Slovenia that was causing heads to shake and sometimes minds to boggle. In 1986 and 1987 a permissive and obviously conniving government in Ljubljana was condoning youthful acts of lèse-majesté against the memory of Tito and the dignity of Yugoslavia that could well become the Yugoslav mode in a fairly short time.

Could Yugoslavia survive? Subsumed under this general question were three specific ones.

(1) Could it resist disintegration?

(2) Could it remain independent of the Soviet Union?

(3) Could it persist with a relatively humane and reformist socialist concept?

The third specific question had always in the past been a matter of some doubt. The Partisans were never particularly humane to their opponents during the war, or immediately after it. Many of the "Cominformists" who resisted the break in 1948 were treated atrociously. Up to 1966 the security apparatus was feared throughout Yugoslavia. During the same period the large Albanian majority in Kosovo was repressed and humiliated. After the turn of the 1980s police activities perceptibly increased. Croatia probably became the most repressive republic in the whole federation, persecuting intellectuals as well as trying to intimidate the Roman Catholic church (see chapter 3). But there were growing examples of intellectual persecution in all the republics, the most notable and grotesque of which occurred in Serbia in April 1984.[43] But for about fifteen years, between 1966 and 1980, Yugoslav citizens enjoyed freedoms that, accepting the "socialist" framework as unavoidable, were quite remarkable. In the 1980s they began to be eroded. Later on in the decade they still remained relatively impressive. But they were shrinking.

Can Yugoslavia resist disintegration? It was probably not so much a matter of resisting it as of not succumbing to it. Yugoslavia could drift for many years, even generations, in the same doldrums. There could be ebbs and flows in a gradually deteriorating situation, which inertia itself might well maintain almost indefinitely. Indeed, in some respects, the situation was somewhat misleading in its grimness. As in Hungary, the economic situation of many families was eased by second and sometimes even third jobs. Many families still had contacts with the land that helped their food provisions. Low morale and resentment need not degenerate into violent irresponsibility. Besides, on an overall labor front as fragmented by the self-management system as Yugoslavia's, it was very difficult to organize a strike movement along the lines, say, of Solidarity in Poland. Strikes in abundance could continue, and there could well be outbreaks of local violence and terrorism. But unless the forces of coercion lost all self-confidence, these should be handled quite efficiently. In the meantime the economy could take its periodic upturns, as it did in 1982 and 1983; remittances from abroad, though reduced, might continue, as will income from tourism. A certain level, however low and unsatisfactory, could be maintained. With all the latent human and economic resources at its disposal, Yugoslav society could endure much.

Politically, much would depend on how the Belgrade center performed what had now become its main domestic task: to facilitate relations between the different republics and autonomous provinces. The dangers inherent in the centrifugal character of Yugoslavia have been stressed often enough in this chapter. But there have been times, especially after the great Croatian crisis, when federal coordinating mechanisms worked relatively well for a time. Perhaps they could be allowed to work efficiently when the atmosphere was not so crisis-laden. There have also been a few examples of the federal authority still pushing through essential legislation in the interests of economic sanity, as in control measures in 1985 over foreign loan transactions and the disposal of hard-currency earnings. Many sensible proposals from the center, such as the economic stabilization package in 1983, became victims of the battle of national self-interest. But the few that got through gave some reason to hope that the decline might be contained. The battle between "conservatives" and "liberals" that began in the 1960s was still going on. The issues changed, but the attitudes remained the same. In the 1980s a veritable plethora of proposals for further political pluralization were coming from the "liberals" together with a tough economic package to restore economic stability. The "conservatives" generally opposed both. It was to be hoped that viable compromise rather than paralyzing division would prevail. But the hopes for any breakthrough solution were not bright.

Finally, the preservation of independence—independence from the Soviet Union. This might rest primarily with the Yugoslavs, but, as intimated at the very beginning of this chapter, it remained a matter of great concern to the United States and the West in general. What was needed was flexibility, patience, and understanding on the part of Western governments and legislatures and of institutions like the IMF and the World Bank. To all of these, Yugoslavia would remain a problem, often intractable and infuriating. But all have to understand what is at stake here. Since 1948 Yugoslavia, to repeat and underline what has already been said, has represented a clear advantage for the Western powers in their relationship with the Soviet Union. Until the East-West relationship basically changes—if it ever does—this advantage has to be preserved. Yugoslavia has declined in practically every respect since the hopeful years in the 1960s. But it is precisely the decline that lent urgency to its importance for the West and its attractions for the Soviet Union. Yet again, the danger is "sly infiltration," to which Yugoslavia is so vulnerable and the West so inattentive.

How many Yugoslavs thought Yugoslavia worth saving? From short visits to the country the answer seemed to be not many. If impressions like these were put together with the concrete fact that since 1948—i.e., long enough for two whole generations to have been born and grown —the existence of Yugoslavia had never been threatened, then there seemed grounds for believing that a fatal disaffection had taken hold. If danger now came in the form of an enemy plain and tangible, then a hidden loyalty might still be tapped and the will to resist brought forth once again. But the enemy now was not going to appear like that. What Yugoslavia needed now was loyalty *toward* it, not just the spin-off of a loyalty *against* something else—a loyalty that was positive not merely negative. The opportunity to achieve this seemed to be passing.

12   Albania

In the West only experts or eccentrics have been interested in Albania as a subject. As an object, however, Albania has attracted a wider interest. Its not inconsiderable energy and mineral resources have drawn geologists and enquirers. But it has been Albania's strategic significance, attracting soldiers and diplomats alike, that has made it important. Situated at the entrance to the Adriatic, just over forty miles from Italy, it has held a key position in southeastern Europe. As a partial wedge between Greece and Yugoslavia it has also beckoned any power wishing to control the western half of the Balkan peninsula.

Small wonder, therefore, that Albania has brought out the acquisitive or the competitive instincts in others. In fact, it only owed its establishment as a sovereign principality in 1913 to the Austrian determination to deny Serbia access to the Adriatic. It emerged as a frail but fully independent state only after World War I in 1920. It was a client state almost by definition, being neither militarily nor economically strong enough to be viable. Yugoslavia, Italy, and Greece vied with one another in efforts to occupy, control, or dismember it. First, it fell under Yugoslav influence, but then, under the northern Albanian chieftain Ahmed Zogu, first president and later king, it became increasingly dominated by fascist Italy. In the 1930s Albania became Mussolini's first satellite, dominated to a degree greater than ever in its history. It was a fatal embrace that culminated in the Italian military occupation of the country in 1939.

During World War II Albania was occupied first by the Italians and then by the Germans. Of the three serious resistance groups it was the least likely communist-dominated movement that, through its exertions, support from Tito and the British, and the necessary slice of luck, became the most powerful force. But it was completely under

Yugoslav tutelage. Thus, though the actors were different, the situation remained the same as before the war. Albania remained a satellite. Yugoslav Tito was the patron and the communist Enver Hoxha the client.

Enver Hoxha and His Legacy

Enver Hoxha, therefore, began his career as Albanian leader as a Yugoslav client. He was to end it forty years later as pater patriae and the deadly enemy of Yugoslavia. He had become Albanian party leader in 1941 at the age of thirty-three. Before that, in the 1930s, he had spent six years in Western Europe as did many scions of wealthy prewar Albanian families, including several of his later party associates.

No assessment of Hoxha can begin without reference to his inhumanity, his ruthless elimination of political opponents. Yet he cannot just be moralistically written off as a monster. For one thing he seemed to have been spared that element of personal evil that dogged some of his contemporaries, Mátyás Rákosi, for example, in Hungary; and for sheer ferocity he was nothing compared with Mehmet Shehu, Albanian premier for twenty-seven years till 1981. As for his political crimes, he was the creature of both his environment and his time. He had less blood on his hands than Tito or, probably, Milovan Djilas. The difference, though, was that while Djilas repented and Tito mellowed, Hoxha's paranoia continued unabated, and his personal reputation has duly suffered.

But he was more than just the last Stalinist paranoid. He became an Albanian nationalist who secured and assured his country's independence with extraordinary skill and audacity. Albanian independence may have seemed fairly self-evident by the end of the 1980s, but it had been far from such forty years earlier. Hoxha changed all this. By the time he died, Albania was an accepted fact of international life. Over one hundred countries recognized it, and none threatened it.[1]

It was an extraordinary feat. But Hoxha should not be seen primarily or originally as a nationalist or even as a communist. He was above all a survivor, bent on keeping his own power and his own life. He could have lost both in 1948 had not the Tito-Stalin break intervened. He could have lost both in 1956 when Tito, supported by Khrushchev, tried to get rid of him.

It was the survival instinct that inspired both his political philosophy and his strategy. By inclination he may have tended toward left-wing extremism, as many Balkan communists originally did. But what made him embrace it as a fighting creed for life was Tito's policy as it emerged after 1948. Tito, though he remained at least a Leninist, adopted a radically new "revisionist" policy. With his archenemy doing this, therefore, and being denounced by his new protector Stalin, the only tactical path for Hoxha was the one that led to the opposite end of the communist spectrum. And there he remained, showing his real political mettle a few years later when Stalin's successor, Khrushchev, must have seemed to him seduced by Tito, with both bent on his destruction. Other earmarked victims might try accommodation. But realizing that such a course would signify weakness Hoxha insisted both on the correctness of his own course and on the baseness of his enemies. His boldness was rewarded by survival, and this was soon to be guaranteed by the emergence of China as a challenger to the Soviet Union.[2]

It was by 1961, when the open break came with Khrushchev, that Hoxha's metamorphosis from formidable opportunist to national savior was completed and publicly acclaimed.[3] But he and Albania had survived through the parading and manipulation of a hard-line Stalinist dogmatism. And this hard-line dogmatism was to remain policy for the next quarter of a century—the second most important part of the Hoxha legacy after the securing of his country's independence.

But it is probably only in retrospect that both Albania and Hoxha seemed safe after 1961. For the next twenty years many things happened that could have disturbed any Albanian leader, even one without the paranoid tendencies Hoxha was increasingly to display. Khrushchev fell in 1964, a matter of satisfaction till his successors more clearly emerged. In any case, his prime enemy, Tito, was still flourishing. In 1968 the invasion of Czechoslovakia must have given cause for genuine alarm: at last Albania took the legalistic precaution of formally leaving the Warsaw Pact, feeling safer outside than inside it. The decade of East-West détente opened up unsettling possibilities; even more the transformation of the Chinese leadership and policy. The death of Tito in 1980, itself the occasion of ungracious jubilation in Tirana, made Yugoslavia less predictable than before. Finally, there was the death, debility, and disarray in the Kremlin itself between 1982 and 1984. All Albania's points of reference were changing radically.

The continued uncertainty abroad probably reinforced Hoxha's determination to maintain tight personal or centralized control over political and economic life at home. Albania was doomed to the hard line —with occasional flurries of Mao-like militancy, it is true, but these too were closely supervised. There was no Red Guard spontaneity in Albania. Toward the end of his life Hoxha even introduced changes in agriculture that destroyed whatever vestiges of material incentive had remained.[4] China may have become prostituted along with the rest, but Albania would preserve its communist virginity.

It is intriguing—and may be instructive—to compare Hoxha's personality and practices with those of Nicolae Ceauşescu in Romania (see chapter 8). Hoxha, of course, predated Ceauşescu in power by a good twenty years, and with Gheorghe Gheorghiu-Dej, the Romanian leader till 1965, he had precious little in common. But with Ceauşescu the similarities are tantalizing: the megalomania; the paranoia; the personality cult; the highly personalized rule; the rigid centralism and hard-line domestic policy. There have been enough similarities to pose the question whether they represent just personal coincidences, whether they could partly derive from the circumstances where, *toutes proportions gardées*, both leaders have pursued a policy of independence from the Soviet Union and isolation from the Soviet bloc, or whether they also derive from historic aspects of Balkan ruling practice.

Hoxha as Nation-Builder?

Stavro Skendi, probably Albania's greatest historian, saw King Zog in the role of nation-builder. "Whatever his flaws," Skendi wrote, "he made a nation and a government where there had been a people and anarchy."[5] Obviously Zog, who dominated Albanian public life for a decade and a half, gave his country an international profile and a degree of internal unity it had never had. It is reasonable to question, though, how much the Albanians had acquired a feeling of nationhood in the modern sense by the spring of 1939 when Zog and his entourage left the country, never to return. Albanians, it should be stressed, had always had a sense of their identity, their "Albanianism." They were proud of their descent from the ancient Illyrians, of their Skanderbeg heritage, and their differences from Slavs, Turks, and Greeks. They have also had a sense of racial superiority over these nations (and have known that these nations have looked down on them).[6]

This was the inchoate legacy Zog inherited, and he molded it into something firmer and more definite. But he hardly finished the job of nation-building. During the wartime occupation, first by Italians and then by Germans, there had been hardly any united resistance. Such resistance as there was came from three distinct groups who, like the Chetniks and Partisans in Yugoslavia, tended to fight each other as well as the foreigner. (There was also some active and much passive cooperation with the occupier.) However, one development of great historic and symbolic significance did occur during the wartime occupation. That was the incorporation of the Kosovo area of Yugoslavia as well as the predominantly Albanian parts of Macedonia and Montenegro into greater Albania. Albania, therefore, though not free, was historically whole for the first time since 1912, and this gave something of the same stimulus to Albanian national sentiment as the wartime existence of the Slovak republic did for the Slovaks. (Kosovo is discussed at length in chapters 12 and 14. To reduce repetition it will not be discussed here. But its impact on the Albanian national psyche should not be ignored.)

After World War II the Albanian communists seemed to present the poorest credentials possible for nation-building. They were part of a movement ostensibly transcending nationality but which had become firmly identified with Russian national interests as determined by Stalin. Within Albania itself the communist party was largely a Tosk movement originating in the southern part of the country. The Tosks of Albania spoke a different dialect from the other tribal composite, the Gegs, of the northern part. These two tribes also had different social structures, and their members are often of different appearance. The Tosks have tended to be quieter farming people. The Gegs (of whom King Zog had been a spectacular example) were more flamboyant mountaineers with a social organization reminiscent of the medieval Highlands of Scotland and the custom of the blood feud that militated against even the crudest type of civic organization. Traditionally the Gegs had despised the Tosks, and it has been plausibly argued that one reason for the relative communist strength in the Tosk areas was their identification with ethnic equality.[7] Numerically Gegs outnumbered Tosks by nearly two to one.

Just as the Geg clan chiefs dominated Albanian politics during the Zog era, after 1945 it was Tosk communists who largely took over, and, though proclaiming a break from the past, they too brought some traditional characteristics with them, notably the familiar system. The wives of Enver Hoxha, Mehmet Shehu, and Hysni Kapo, who were to become the three top men in the regime, were prominent central committee members, and Shehu, in particular, was to flank himself with several powerful family members.[8]

Hoxha, after he had consolidated his domestic power, appears to have tried to reduce the strong Geg fears that a communist Albania would mean discrimination against them by the victorious Tosks. Many Gegs assumed powerful positions in the party, state, and economic bureaucracy. His eventual designated successor, Ramiz Alia, is a Geg. But the perceived differences have continued to be very much part of the popular psyche, as has the Geg sense of victimization. One of the most widespread of Geg suspicions against Hoxha was that he neglected to press Albania's irredenta regarding Kosovo because the Albanians in Yugoslavia (Kosovars) are Gegs and their incorporation would mean an overwhelming Geg preponderance in a new greater Albania.[9]

But if Hoxha could never bridge a chasm that still preoccupied many Albanians, the adventures of his long period of rule gave them a sense of identity as never before. The perils they faced together were themselves a unifying factor, especially when skillfully dramatized. And, like all demagogues, Hoxha could project dangers to himself as mortal dangers to his country. What was good (or bad) for Enver Hoxha was good (or bad) for Albania. His own survival in 1948 and 1956, for example, became matters of survival for his country.

In domestic affairs the centrifugal forces that previously dominated Albanian public life were smashed and replaced by a forced multifaceted centralism in political, social, economic, and cultural life. Society also became heavily militarized. A rigid ideological doctrine was the only one tolerated. Hoxha saw organized religion in Albania, in its three varieties of Islam, Orthodox, and Catholicism, not only as an alternative domestic source of power and ideology but also as an actual or potential foreign fifth column. He therefore suppressed it in 1967.[10] The personality cult was also a cohesive force. Finally, the spectacular purges of the late 1950s and then the 1970s, with the victims denounced as foreign agents, helped to increase that sense of threat and the need to unite against it.[11]

Thus Hoxha's predilections and idiosyncracies, combined with his remarkable political perceptiveness, helped build Albanian nationhood. A momentous phase in the history of a tiny nation produced a man whose virtues as well as his vices helped it through from near-extinction to relative safety. One may assume Hoxha seldom worked from a conscious program of action. No leader consciously sets out on a policy of nation-building. This, after all, is the historical by-product as well as the climax of a whole series of everyday actions that are both the stuff of leadership and the preoccupation of those engaged in it. Hoxha in this context should be seen as a pragmatist using hard-line policies for specific short-term purposes. Much of his policy took on an ideological coloration. But the motives behind it were severely practical.

In his choice of successor, however, Hoxha obviously did make a longer-term calculation. In doing so he brought on one of the most dramatic episodes in his long, action-packed rule.

On 18 December 1981 the Albanian media announced that Mehmet Shehu, prime minister for twenty-seven years, had killed himself in a "state of agitation."[12] It was later claimed by Hoxha that the man who had been his closest political associate for forty years and had always been regarded as the nation's number two man had in reality been, from his earliest youth, an agent working for *four* enemy secret services: the American, British, Soviet, and Yugoslav. Hoxha also revealed what he claimed had been the final abortive efforts of Shehu to assassinate him and take his place.[13] The whole concoction was so bizarre that the only possible recipients of sympathy were the Albanian people, whose intelligence was so grievously insulted. More than anything it revealed Hoxha's Stalinist paranoia: his version matches, even exceeds, anything from the Soviet show trials of the 1930s or the Soviet and East European show trials of the late 1940s and early 1950s. It also reveals the continuing clan nature of Albanian politics. (Shehu's family following has already been mentioned.) With both the interior and defense ministers as supporters through kin, Shehu may well have felt strong enough to pressure even Hoxha into giving a commitment that he would be recommended to succeed him. Alternatively, knowing Hoxha had settled for Ramiz Alia, the Shehu clan may have tried not to oust Hoxha totally but to kick him upstairs to the state presidency on the grounds of ill health. At any rate, the Shehu group failed and paid dearly for their temerity with either their lives or their liberties. Hoxha had his way and died peacefully, mourned with massive sincerity and succeeded by Ramiz Alia.[14]

Hoxha bequeathed Alia a totally different land from the one he had begun to lead forty years before. It was now a nation-state that had asserted its identity and independence. The question, though, was whether Albania could achieve a stable viability with the legacy he had left behind him.

The End of the China Connection

In China, Albania had found the ideal patron. This patronage would pay in several ways. Yet China was far away and only asked for what Hoxha was ready to give anyway: unstinting support against the Soviet Union. True, China could not defend Albania militarily, but there seemed little danger of this being needed. The Chinese turned out to be the longest-standing patrons in Albanian history—for seventeen years, taking 1961 as the beginning and 1978 as the end of its patronage, longer even than Italian patronage between the two world wars.

Estimates of Chinese economic and financial aid vary. In a study for the Joint Economic Committee of the U.S. Congress Michael Kaser has put total Chinese financial aid at about $885 million between 1959 and 1975, well over half of this coming in the five-year plan period of 1971 to 1975.[15] But Albania's reliance on Chinese aid after 1961 was measurable not only in dollars. For example, thousands of Albanian specialists and students went to China, for varying periods, for study and training. Hundreds of Chinese experts came to Albania to help build industrial projects, including the radio-television center and the powerful broadcasting transmitters that have made Radio Tirana's somewhat single-minded foreign language services so boringly audible. There was a Sino-Albanian shipping company and a weekly Tirana-Peking flight connection.[16] Finally, Albania became dependent on Chinese military hardware. It is impossible to put a price on this, but, taking into account Tirana's incessant propaganda about military preparedness, it must have been considerable. In 1986 Albania's total armed forces numbered about 40,400, and, while most of their heavy armament was originally of Soviet provenance, the Chinese themselves had made much of the Albanians' lighter armament and equipment.[17]

But on 11 July 1978, a date that might turn out to be the most fateful in the whole of Albanian history, the Chinese announced they had cut off all aid to Albania. Vitriolic polemics between China and Albania (together with its "true," splinter-party Marxist-Leninist allies) had been waged for more than a year before, ostensibly over Peking's "Three Worlds Theory." This theory, originally conceived by Mao himself, was based on the division of the world into three groups of states—the two superpowers, the developed countries, and the developing countries.[18] It was bitterly attacked by the Albanians as "revisionist," but, as usual, communist theory was simply the thin cover for differences involving national interest. From the Albanian point of view the militant support of the Chinese had been useful in its anti-Soviet and especially its anti-Yugoslav phase. But now that post-Mao China was in the process of drastically revising both its foreign and domestic policy and drawing what must have seemed dangerously close to Yugoslavia, it was necessary for the Albanians to renounce their alliance of convenience.

It was time for Albania to move on. But, unlike twenty years before, there was now nowhere to go. Moreover, Albania had painted itself into a tight corner by a constitutional law of 1976 that forbade any present or future regime to raise international loans. Such a self-disbarment was yet another factor making Albania unique among the world's states. It was also the culminating point in the mythology of self-reliance that Hoxha had been developing since the break with Khrushchev in 1961.

But mythology never makes good policy. "Going it alone," taken literally, was always impossible. What Hoxha appears to have had in mind was a policy that, taking "self-reliance" as the cornerstone, would add to it three other components: (1) a further intensification of economic relations with the Third World; (2) a partial restoration of economic relations with China; (3) a greater development of economic relations with the West.

This seemed the best combination of alternatives over the short run, and before Hoxha died all three of these external possibilities were being implemented. The picking up of trade relations with China might be surprising after the bitterness of the polemics such a short time before. But it was another small example of Hoxha's pragmatism, and, in any case, the scale of relations was very much lower than in the days of Chinese patronage.[19]

There were two other alternatives that were indignantly dismissed by the Albanian leadership. These were rapprochements with Yugoslavia and the Soviet Union. Despite the political enmity, Yugoslavia remained Albania's biggest single trading partner, whereas direct economic relations with the Soviet Union were completely discontinued after 1961. But the trade with Yugoslavia was "mutually beneficial" and was on a strictly commercial basis. It could be increased, but any basic improvement in the relations between the two countries that would have a major impact on the Albanian economy was rejected by Tirana on the grounds of the concessions it might involve. Thus, the completion of the railway between Shkodër and Titograd in Montenegro, which connected Albania with the European rail system for the first time, had nothing but symbolic significance.[20] As for the Soviet Union, it continually held out the olive branch, which just as continually was spurned by the Albanians.[21]

But what most intrigued Albania watchers even before Hoxha died, but especially after, was the possibility of a general rapprochement with the West. Albania enjoyed full diplomatic relations with several economically advanced West European countries, notably Italy, France, and Austria. When Hoxha was still alive the first signs of an Albanian Westpolitik became discernible.

Perhaps the most striking development was the remarkable improvement of relations with Greece, culminating in 1987 with the formal ending of the state of war between the two countries, which had technically lasted more than forty years. Previous attempts to improve relations had been vitiated not just by Albanian obduracy: Greece had territorial claims on parts of southern Albania, which it referred to as "Northern Epirus." But even when these claims had been quietly dropped Greek resentment continued at alleged persecution of members of the Greek minority in this territory. This minority probably numbered about 50,000, but some Greek sources claimed it was over 300,000. Despite this important bone of contention, however, inter-government relations at a high level had developed and flourished.[22]

Relations with Italy had always been better than with any other Western country. They took a step further when a three-times-a-month ferry service between Durrës and Trieste was inaugurated in 1983—a small financial disaster for the Italians who were paying for it, but worth the loss for its diplomatic and political potential. Visits by Italian officials and businessmen increased, as did important visits from France. With Great Britain there had been contacts to try to break the deadlock arising from the Corfu channel incident in 1946 when two British destroyers were struck by mines with considerable loss of life. As a result, Britain had impounded some Albanian gold. There was a steady optimism that a solution could be found.[23] Informal contacts had also been made with Washington. But the key role in any broader Albanian Westpolitik would necessarily be played by the Federal Republic of Germany. Contacts between the two countries began apparently in the late 1970s. Some of these were well publicized like the visit of the Bavarian premier, Dr. Franz-Josef Strauss, in 1984. Others were secret and more meaningful, like the visit of the Albanian Academy of Sciences chairman, Professor Aleks Buda, to Bonn in 1983. The Albanians were at first insisting on a West German payment of a "war reparations" bill for DM 4 million as an earnest of good intentions, but this appeared to have been considerably modified after Ramiz Alia took power.[24] So much so that in 1987 the two countries agreed to assume diplomatic relations. The breakthrough had been made.

The Need for a New Look

The future of relations with the West would, of course, depend on how literally the Albanians took Hoxha's self-reliance principle. The real crux lay in the 1976 self-disbarment from credits. How long would it be before this needed to be modified? The resolutions and the tenor of the ninth congress of the Albanian (communist) Party of Labor in November 1986 were hardly encouraging. But Ramiz Alia has subsequently given some reason to believe that this was a hurdle that could eventually be vaulted or circumvented.

As expected, the congress was dominated by the dead Hoxha. No one expected anything else. Nor need anyone expect any public "de-Enverization" for a long time—if ever. But, assuming Alia is not just an interim leader and shows enough strength to assert his control, it might be expected that, under the rubric of "creatively applying" the Hoxha tradition, new policies will gradually be introduced and some old taboos lifted, especially in the economy. Already in the first year after Hoxha's death there was talk in Albania of a general relaxation of the atmosphere, which inevitably caused complaints about the "erosion of discipline."[25] Whether this was the prelude to significant changes was difficult to say. But if Albania were not just to survive but also prosper in the twenty-first century, some veritable revolutions in policy would be needed. And no matter how these were presented they would involve shedding the Hoxha legacy.

The first essential was a slowdown in the population growth, which was the fastest in Europe. In 1961 when Albania broke with the Soviet Union the population was 1.6 million. In 1986 it was over 2.9 million. By the end of the century it was expected to be 4 million. One of the main planks in Hoxha's policy had been rapid population growth. Large families were actively encouraged. Abortion was forbidden, other forms of birth control discouraged. Emigration was impossible.

Albania simply could not sustain such a growth. Most of the country is mountainous, uninhabitable, and/or infertile. It was estimated to have only about 600,000 hectares of arable land, and even if the population were to be considerably lower in A.D. 2000 than the estimated 4 million, a revolutionary change would in any case have to be made in agricultural policy.[26] It would involve the introduction of material incentives. Private plots needed enlarging and encouraging. Private animal breeding needed to be reintroduced and a free market in agricultural produce permitted.[27]

But if it were not just a case of avoiding the worst, but getting the best, then a new economic strategy would be needed. This would involve discontinuing much of Albania's heavy manufacturing industry. True, a complete change would be virtually impossible, since heavy industry in Eastern Europe and the Soviet Union had become synonymous with socialism. But for Albania especially the products of this obsession with industrialization were almost totally unsalable. A much simpler economy based on natural resources and agriculture might facilitate real viability.

With an annual oil production of about 2.5 million tons in 1985 Albania supplied its own needs and exported to Italy, Greece, and Yugoslavia. It also had considerable reserves of natural gas. It was the third largest producer in the world of chrome and the second largest chrome exporter, mainly to the West. It also had large reserves of copper and nickel, exporting large quantities of the latter. Its own energy requirements were mainly supplied by hydroelectric power, which it also exported to Yugoslavia and Greece.[28] These reserves were not infinite, and the existing oil deposits could well run out by the end of this century. After 1984 in any case the international price of oil slumped badly. But there would still be time for an intelligent and profitable exploitation of these natural resources to be made the basis of a modest and appropriate industry. As it stood, the Albanian economy was dominated by a bizarre gigantomania expressed in a few large metallurgical and light industrial combines, grossly overmanned and totally unprofitable.

Albania's fully collectivized agriculture, too, was chronically overmanned and inefficient. But still, in the first half of the 1980s agriculture accounted for about 30 percent of the country's total exports. Albanian tomatoes, for example, were known in many parts of Western Europe. What was needed was the encouragement of greater personal incentive, already mentioned, and greater financial support for those branches with an export potential. Khrushchev, during his visit to Tirana in the summer of 1959, urged the Albanians to make their country a "flourishing garden."[29] It was part of his campaign to induce the Southern Tier to cast aside comprehensive industrialization, and it foundered on both the nationalist and socialist aspirations of his audiences. Some thirty years later some may have been begun timorously acknowledging that he had a point.

Eventually Albania also needed to begin fully participating in international trade. (Indeed this should be the prelude to change rather than the climax of it.) But to participate in international trade it would need credits—and this brings the argument back once again to the 1976 provision. If it remained untouchable for long, this culminating gesture of Hoxha's isolationism could become a sentence of death on Albania as a nation-state. The East European experience with credits in the 1970s may have been unfortunate. But any long-term Albanian existence without them could be fatal.[30]

Albania's future, therefore, looked woeful but not hopeless if the country were served by strong and imaginative leadership. What was needed, if public "de-Enverization" was not possible, was a partial, creeping "de-Enverization." If the essence of Hoxha's legacy—the building of the Albanian nation-state—was to be preserved and built upon, then the errors of that legacy would have to be discarded.

13   Social Problems in Perspective

Social analysis is difficult. First, an enormous number of subjects fall within its purview. Second, there is the problem—especially for an outsider to the country or countries concerned—of assessing their relative importance. Third, there is the danger of lapsing into a catalog of problems that, however accurately compiled, gives a distorted view of the society concerned. Fourth, no analysis, however well-judged and discriminating, can convey what it is like to live in any society. Only a sustained period of residence and even participation can do that; and this is an experience few outsiders are ever privileged to enjoy where Eastern Europe is concerned.

Attempting to tackle the subject in a few pages is probably both presumptuous and foolhardy. The subject warrants a book in its own right. But any East European survey would be culpably incomplete without some attempt to depict the societal landscape in which the principal actions of public life take place. It is a landscape that helps shape those actions and is in turn shaped by them.

What follows is one writer's arbitrary view of some of the more important social factors at work in Eastern Europe for the quarter of a century between 1960 and 1985. It does not seek to minimize the social problems besetting East European societies. But neither does it seek to exaggerate their impact, or see them exclusively as symptoms of communist-induced degeneracy. It may be an oversimplified view in that it sometimes makes regional generalizations at the expense of the strict country-by-country analysis. Statistics are kept to barest essentials in the text, not because they are deemed unimportant—they are part of the very stuff of the subject—but because too many would give a distorting image of a complex situation. Some relevant tables are given in appendix III.

Environment

It is right to begin with the engulfing factor of the environment. As the second half of the twentieth century has worn on, environmental problems have steadily outstripped most if not all others in importance in Europe. Public awareness of the dimensions of the problems was slow in developing. For many years the problems lacked urgency in the popular mind. Nature had for centuries been exploited rather than protected. Economic growth superseded all considerations of conservation, health, and public hygiene. Only when it was almost too late were thoughts, then words, then deeds turned to remedy, care, and caution.

In the summer of 1986 any discussion of the environment in Eastern Europe had to begin with Chernobyl. Barring any more such accidents, the terror caused by the radiation dangers (real or imagined) emanating from that disaster would have receded in a few years' time. The Soviet and East European governments had confirmed their determination to continue with their ambitious nuclear energy programs[1] (see appendix III, table 20). But it only needed one more accident even approaching the scale of Chernobyl to cause an unrest that could have serious political as well as social consequences in addition to calling into question the whole future of nuclear energy. In the meantime Chernobyl might even have its benefits. It could alert public opinion to ecological problems generally, and this could strengthen the role of public opinion on the whole range of issues that directly affect it.

Environmental protection crept almost unseen into East European statute books in the early 1960s. In Czechoslovakia, for example, some measures were first enacted in March 1966. But at that time legislation on the matter was a formality throughout the region. It was not till much later that its magnitude and public misgivings about it converged into genuine concern. Among regime circles, the deterioration of the environment had often been held to be a phenomenon of capitalist societies, which exploited nature as ruthlessly as they exploited man. Socialist society, on the other hand, which protected both, was held to be largely immune from the danger.

Obviously few believed such simple generalizations, neither the purveyors nor the victims of the propaganda. But there was, nevertheless, a general complacency about the subject. It *was* a problem—that was occasionally admitted—but not so serious that it could not wait. There was also the view, widely held in countries that are less advanced economically, that pollution was the price of progress. Industrialization meant progress, and pollution was its unavoidable concomitant. Pollution, therefore, was even regarded with a degree of pride as a sure sign of steady advance. (More recently this has become an opinion found in Third World countries.) Warnings by Westerners of its dangers and of the possibility of avoiding the West's mistake in this regard were sometimes even resented, being taken as a ploy to keep others languishing in backwardness.

Twenty years later all but a few East Europeans would have agreed that the price paid had been too great. Every country in the region was suffering environmental deterioration on a scale comparable with anything in Western Europe.[2] What had begun as a problem had been allowed in many areas to become a disaster. The worst affected area was in the more industrialized Northern Tier, covering a large triangle in which were included parts of Czechoslovakia, the GDR, and Poland. In North Bohemia, for example, an observer has estimated that 55 percent of all the forests would have died by the end of the century.[3] Parts of the once lush Erzgebirge Mountains, which straddle the Czech-East German border, presented a macabre picture to the traveler. The once flourishing town of Most in North Bohemia consisted in the early 1980s of one huge crater and a sixteenth-century Gothic church.[4] The tragedy of Most is a telling example of the dangers to a town when no thought is given to its protection. Though relatively small (some 60,000 inhabitants) it was proportionally one of the most industrialized centers in Europe, with large chemical and metallurgical works. Even more fatal was the fact that it was near a large brown coal mining area, the subsidence of which was mainly responsible for killing the town by making the huge crater. Most's population had to be billeted in high-rise apartment blocks nearby, and in 1985 the possibility of moving the church was also being discussed.

In the GDR there may have been nothing so directly tragic as Most, but perhaps even a larger area than in Czechoslovakia was seriously affected. Beginning as far north as Halle and proceeding south through an area containing cities like Leipzig and Karl-Marx-Stadt (Chemnitz), there were abnormally high levels of pollution.[5] In Poland the situation was similar. Large cities like Katowice and Zabrze and practically the whole of the Silesian Basin were, in the opinion of many travelers, unfit for habitation because of air pollution.[6] Many of the citizens, for their part, had become accustomed, or resigned, to the prevailing conditions.

Obviously these areas were worse than the others. But they did affect three different countries. In fact, in terms of air pollution the GDR and Poland have often been considered as the worst countries in the world, and North Bohemia and North Moravia were considered two of the worst areas. Air pollution was also becoming a serious and obvious problem in Prague, Cracow, and Budapest. Belgrade, too, was becoming notorious for its thick coat of smog.

The air pollution was mainly caused by the extensive use for electrical energy of soft brown coal, which emits sulfur dioxide. The increasing motorization was an important secondary factor. A few figures from the GDR may give some idea of the dimensions of the problem. In 1982, 276 million tons of brown coal were used in order to meet 63 percent of the country's prime energy requirements. In that same year almost 5 million tons of sulfur dioxide were emitted. A comparison with the Federal Republic is illuminating. There, on a territorial surface more than twice as big as that of the GDR, 3 million tons of sulfur dioxide were emitted.[7] Indeed, it was the use of soft brown coal, which, except for Poland, is virtually the only kind of coal mined in Eastern Europe, that was the main single reason for the environmental disasters in the whole region.

But polluted air caused by sulfur dioxide was by no means the only aspect of the problem. Earth subsidence caused by mining operations has already been mentioned in the case of Most. Several other sizable towns in Central Europe were affected by this to varying degrees, and there was even considerable evidence suggesting that the historic Bohemian spa of Karlovy Vary (Karlsbad) could also be affected in this way.[8] Open cast coal mining, most notably in Poland, gouged out huge craters in the countryside in some areas.

But perhaps the disaster most frequently cited next, after the all-pervasive air pollution, was the poisoning of rivers, streams, and lakes. By 1985 Lake Balaton in Hungary suffered serious pollution as did large sections of the Danube, the Vistula in Poland, the Sava in Yugoslavia, and the Maritsa in Bulgaria. Almost any river near an industrial site had some degree of pollution, often due to the indiscriminate dumping of chemical waste. Public water supplies in many cities and towns were affected.

Some of the wider effects of this deterioration were not at first apparent. It was not just a case of smog-laden cities, poisoned rivers, polluted plant life, and forests destroyed by acid rain. The price in human health was also becoming very high. Many cases of respiratory disease, infant mortality, even suicides were believed to have a direct connection with the deterioration of the environment. Certainly such cases in the districts affected by heavy pollution were considerably higher than the relevant national average. In the Most district, for example, the incidence of infant mortality in 1980 was 12 percent higher than in the rest of Czechoslovakia. The percentage of babies falling sick was nearly four times higher. Respiratory diseases, psychic ailments, and even suicides were also appreciably higher. There were figures showing a similar tendency in the GDR and Poland. What was happening, therefore, was a deterioration of both the human, the material, and the natural condition in many parts of Eastern Europe.

By the beginning of the 1980s the deterioration, spreading and accelerating, had begun to arouse serious public unease. The environment became yet another issue on which public opinion could focus and around which groups of dedicated citizens could coalesce. What had previously been the concern of the experts was now taken over by the laymen. In Czechoslovakia Charter 77 distributed and had smuggled to the West a report from the Czechoslovak Academy of Sciences that described the environmental situation in terms of catastrophe.[9] In the GDR the environment became one of the main social concerns of the Evangelical church, which reflected and articulated the mounting concern. Here, too, from across the border, the great publicity attracted by the West German "Greens" and their considerable electoral successes had an obvious stimulating effect. In Hungary a group of citizens, clearly modeling itself on the West German Greens, began voicing concern over the local situation and gained a certain international prominence by its organized opposition to the Gabčikovo-Nagymaros hydroelectric dam project on the Danube at the Hungarian-Czechoslovak border (see also chapter 6). Opposition to this project induced cooperation between Hungarian, Austrian, and Swiss environmental activists, and a petition, signed by several thousand Hungarian citizens, induced the Hungarian authorities to postpone for a time the beginning of work on the project on its side of the border in early 1985.[10] (Work was later resumed, however.) In Poland the environmental cause was taken up by several intellectual supporters of Solidarity, and after the declaration of martial law in December 1981 it continued to be featured in the publications of the underground press.

What of regime response, both to the magnitude of the problem and the growing public concern? Some measures were taken, but for most observers they looked like too little too late. The Czechoslovak government approved a comprehensive ecological rehabilitation program in 1985 that was incorporated into the five-year economic plan for 1986–90. The program was mainly concerned with air and water pollution. The Hungarian government began converting residential heating from coal to gas. It was also trying to clean up Lake Balaton. The GDR and Czechoslovakia agreed to cut the volume of sulfur dioxide emissions by 30 percent by 1993, with 1980 as the base year. Many piecemeal efforts were being made throughout Eastern Europe, and many conscientious officials were applying themselves resourcefully to their task. It would be churlish to dismiss such efforts. But there was little sign of any consistent, large-scale, international effort to tackle these admittedly very complicated problems, especially the problem caused by the burning of brown coal.

Indeed, the deterioration, at least in Czechoslovakia, the GDR, and Poland, appeared to be gathering momentum in the mid-1980s. Instead of slow but effective progress toward remedy, what seemed more likely was a steadily quickening retreat toward disaster.

In the first place, the evils of brown coal, instead of being mitigated, looked as if they might be multiplied. This was primarily due to the reduction of oil supplies from the Soviet Union, in response to which countries such as the GDR and Czechoslovakia would have to fall back on their own main energy resource.[11] Eventually, of course, if the world price of oil remained fairly low after the precipitous falls of 1985 and 1986, then the use of oil might be continued and increased. Increased use of gas could also help. Ultimately, nuclear power might be the best answer. But there were uncertainties connected with all these possible solutions. Moderately priced oil might not be available in sufficient quantities. Conversion to gas takes time and is not free of problems. And, though almost all the East European states had reaffirmed after Chernobyl their determination to persist with nuclear energy, another big accident might lead to a change of policy.

The baleful effects of brown coal can be mitigated through a whole variety of filters, separation equipment, and the like. But these cost money—and that exposes the crux of the whole issue. It can be summarized by the well-known cliché, "economy before ecology." As long as economic life continues to be oriented almost exclusively on production, then ecological issues will be relegated to the fringe, or beyond it. Furthermore, the dismissive attitude toward the environment will apply on every level of industry. At the national level there will be no sustained effort since this would mean budget reallocations and a policy that for several years could incur slowing, even halting, the rate of production increase. At the factory level the manager, with his plan to meet, is loath to spend anything on antipollution devices unless forced to. And he knows this will be highly unlikely. Even if threatened with fines for infringing ecology regulations, he would often prefer to pay the fine than buy the preventive installations involved. Most workers, too, would support nothing that reduced their wages and bonuses. (In this, as in many other issues, it is the workers who are the most conservative of all.) Thus at all levels of the production process there is a conspiracy to avoid taking the necessary steps. This, it should be stressed, is not necessarily the fault of "real, existing socialism" alone. It occurs under capitalism and under variations of reform or market socialism, as Yugoslavia's far from satisfactory record indicates. What would be required for change would be a determination at the top to reorder priorities, to impose incentives and penalties, and, with the help of the necessary publicity, gradually transform habits and attitudes throughout society. If this meant working with those groups in society conscious of, and concerned about the problem, so much the better.

There has been little sign of this basic change on the part of the East European governments. Not surprisingly, it has been the Hungarian government that has shown the most awareness. Not only did it tolerate some degree of social action on ecological issues, but it also occasionally seemed ready itself to face up to the measure of the problem. There were also some encouraging hints—though not much action—from Bulgaria and some of the Yugoslav republics. As for Czechoslovakia and the GDR, two of the countries most directly affected, the official response seemed mainly one of evasion rather than action. The official press of both countries was sometimes frank in its reporting of the problem. But the main aim of much of the commentary seemed to be to try to absolve the regime from any blame. The party periodicals carried not so much open discussion but instructions to the faithful on how to explain them to an uneasy public. Both the Czechoslovaks and East Germans repeatedly pointed, for example, to acid rain coming from the West, taking comfort in reminding readers that the problem has a very long history in all industrialized areas. They relished referring to the ecological catastrophes that had occurred in many capitalist or "nonsocialist" countries. Scientific explanations for different phenomena were painstakingly propounded. In fact, everything was done to divert attention from the regime's own share of the responsibility for what has happened in its own country.[12]

This official dilemma is easily understood. The environmental disasters in Eastern Europe were immovable evidence, not of the party's wisdom, but of its errors and neglect. Other errors could somehow be set right—or they could be made to appear so. The early atrocities of power could be blamed on Stalin and his henchmen. Economic policies could be changed, and those responsible for past errors blamed. But the environment offers no such easy avenue of escape. The damage done to it can only be effectively remedied if there is an admission of guilt for causing the damage.

This would be difficult enough. But it is made the more difficult because there is, indeed, little prospect of the damage being effectively repaired. This situation does not lend itself to the familiar sequence of acknowledging error, exposing the "guilty," initiating a new policy, basking in self-congratulation. Even if the regimes could break out of their production ethos and mold new attitudes, there would simply not be the means to initiate anything but the slowest recovery. The cause has anyway already been preempted by societal groups—the church in the GDR and Charter 77 in Czechoslovakia, for example—demonstrating that "spontaneity" all Leninists have feared and mistrusted. It is doubtful whether the present order in Eastern Europe can cope with this dilemma. In the meantime Eastern Europe goes on, day by day, destroying its heritage.

Population, Urbanization, and Housing

In all the capitals of Eastern Europe and in most of the larger cities the shortage of housing is usually at the top of the list of popular complaints. The problem has remained serious throughout the region, especially in the larger cities. In most countries housing in rural areas improved considerably after about 1970. Hungary was probably the best example. Here the liberal system operating in most agricultural collectives helped stimulate housing construction, which was encouraged by the central government in its effort to stem the influx into the cities, especially into Budapest, where the population grew to 2 million out of a population of about 10.7 million.[13]

It is always difficult to come to precise conclusions or comparisons about housing because official statistics are often unreliable or based on different criteria. But, allowing for some very bad areas in Romania, housing conditions were probably the worst in Poland, a fact largely due to a combination of three factors: regime incompetence, a relatively rapid birthrate, and a poor housing performance in rural areas because of peasant inability and regime reluctance. But the situation in Poland is by no means atypical; it would certainly be recognized in both Hungary and Czechoslovakia and in many areas throughout the region. It is, therefore, worth giving some idea of the dimensions of the problem there.

As usual, estimates of the housing shortage in Poland and the projected need have tended to differ greatly. It was not simply a contrast of official and unofficial, or semiofficial, estimates; government estimates themselves have differed widely in different years. But a government report of 1984 estimated that 4.5 million new housing units needed to be built by 1990. This represented the combined total of the apartment deficit existing in 1980 (1.75 million), the apartments needed to match demographic increase (1.5 million), and the apartments needed to replace those condemned as unfit for further habitation (1.3 million).[14]

By themselves such figures mean little. More telling was a 1986 estimate that 3 million Poles were on the waiting lists for cooperative apartments, the predominant form of residential construction in urban areas. One expert estimated that, in the Warsaw area, this meant a twenty-six-year waiting period. In Łodz, a city of 850,000, cooperatives had a waiting list of 110,000. The existing housing was greatly overcrowded as it was. Official statistics put the number of persons per room at 1.2 in 1978. Some experts considered this as too favorable, but it still made Poland one of the worst-off countries anywhere in Europe. In Hungary the overall figure was even worse at 1 to 1.5, but the almost catastrophic situation in overcrowded Budapest seriously affected this ratio.[15]

What this situation in Poland meant in terms of human frustration is not difficult to imagine. It partly contributed to other social problems, like divorce, alcoholism, etc., not to mention the nervous and psychic complications it helped generate. Moreover, the housing itself, when constructed, was often of very low quality. Planning concepts, too, so often led to the construction of apartment house complexes that, apart from their gross aesthetic failings, led to a serious deterioration in social life, a situation that blighted many Western cities as well.

But housing amenities were often far below the standards normally accepted in the more advanced Western countries. Piped water, for example, was totally inadequate except in the GDR and Czechoslovakia. Romania was clearly the worst off in this respect, as it was in the statistics for electric light. As for housing units with telephones, all the countries throughout the region were very badly supplied, with Poland, Yugoslavia, and Romania—not to mention Albania—the worst off.[16]

The main reason for the very serious housing situation was the unwillingness of governments to allocate the necessary resources. After about 1965 privately purchased cooperative housing grew at the expense of direct state-subsidized housing, but, as in the case of Poland, it was simply not able to meet the growing need. In the long run the situation looked the most promising in Hungary, where a combination of public and private initiative made for an economically based construction program. But even here whether new construction could keep up with the deterioration of already existing buildings was open to question.

But the roots of the housing problem in the East European cities went deeper. They had to be sought in the urbanization process that was already under way by the end of World War I but accelerated greatly after World War II, with great stimulus being added by communist economic policies. The process has been the most dramatic in the less-developed countries of the Southern Tier, but the more-developed northern countries also saw similar changes. In Bulgaria about 20 percent of the population lived in cities before 1940, but by the second half of the 1970s the figure was estimated at about 56 percent.[17] At the same time the proportion of the population engaged in agriculture fell from 81.9 percent in 1948, to 33.4 percent in 1971. In Czechoslovakia, the most advanced East European state in several respects, the proportion of the population living in towns of over 10,000 was 23 percent in 1930; in 1970 the figure was 39.1 percent. Between 1955 and 1972 the proportion of the Czechoslovak population engaged in agriculture dropped from 30.9 percent to 14.2 percent.[18] Generally, however, the urban population in Czechoslovakia and the GDR, two advanced industrial countries with relatively small populations, has expanded much less than elsewhere in the region.

Once the first great wave of industrialization had been completed, however, the intensity of internal migration in all the East European countries slackened. It has been estimated, for example, that whereas about 2.1 million people migrated in Bulgaria, Czechoslovakia, the GDR, Hungary, and Poland in 1970, the number of such internal migrants in the same countries fifteen years earlier had been twice as large.[19] The urbanization "problem" had, therefore, stabilized by the early 1970s. But urbanization itself still continued. In Czechoslovakia it was the strongest in Slovakia, where the "urbanization gap" with the Czech

Lands was considerably narrowed between 1960 and 1980. In the GDR there was a rise from 22 percent to nearly 26 percent in the population of cities of 100,000 or more.[20] In Hungary during the same period the population living in rural areas declined from 55.7 percent to 46.8 percent, with a corresponding increase for the urban areas except Budapest.[21] In Budapest, which had expanded rapidly after World War II, the influx had peaked in the 1960s. But the strain of this internal migration on urban social services of all kinds had still not been overcome by the mid-1980s and showed little sign of being so. And it was in the housing sector where the strain was the most immediate and obvious.

As for the population as a whole, the total figure for the eight East European countries together in 1980 was nearly 134 million. In 1950 it had been 105,504,000. The annual growth rates for all the countries except Albania and the GDR have been termed low to moderate by world standards (between 0.5 percent to 1.2 percent annually). Albania was the exception at the top end of the scale with an annual growth rate of 2.6 percent, the highest birthrate in the whole of Europe. In 1950 its population was 1,990,000; in 1980 it was 2,644,000;[22] and in 1985 it was estimated at 2,841,000. (The growth rate of Albanians in Kosovo, in Yugoslavia, was similar if not slightly higher.) At the bottom end of the scale stood the GDR, which was the only East European country to have a lower population in 1980 than in 1950. This was mainly due to the large losses by emigration to the Federal Republic before the building of the Berlin Wall in 1961. But the GDR has also experienced a net loss of population since the Wall. Between 1970 and 1980 the population declined by a total of 335,000, largely because of a lower birthrate and increasing mortality.[23] In Hungary, though the population grew slightly between 1960 and 1980, the underlying demographic situation was similar. The population growth in both countries was seriously affected by two world wars. Both have aging populations. In Hungary the number of persons aged over sixty-five increased by 22 percent between 1970 and 1980, and those aged over seventy-five increased by as much as one-third.[24] The next highest annual rate of population increase after Albania between 1950 and 1980 was recorded in Poland, where it was 1.2 percent. In 1950 the Polish population, seriously affected by the course and consequences of World War II, stood at 24,613,000, and in 1980 at 35,413,000.[25] Between 1950 and 1960 there were sharp annual increases, but the tendency after 1965 was downward. After 1975 there was some improvement.[26]

Among the factors affecting the birthrate in Eastern Europe none has aroused more controversy or affected the sensibilities of more people than the practice of abortion. The laws on abortion were liberalized throughout the region after the communists took power. This happened as many more women were coming into the work force and as religious belief and the old traditions in family life, as well as family life itself, were being weakened in many ways. At the end of the 1950s material living standards began to rise to an unprecedented level, and in countries like Czechoslovakia, the GDR, and Hungary abortion became a significant element in the whole birth control process. It provoked the vehement opposition of the Catholic church in Poland and, to a lesser extent, from churches everywhere. The primitive barbarities that accompanied many abortion operations also caused unease among many sections of the population, especially in Hungary where they received the greatest publicity. The whole issue acquired a broad emotional dimension. Finally, the communist regimes themselves, which had originally brought in the abortion legislation, became alarmed at the decline in the birthrates to which it was undoubtedly contributing—though by how much was a matter of dispute. The laws were considerably amended, making abortions much more difficult to obtain. At about the same time generous maternity benefits were introduced to stimulate the birthrate. These did have some effect, especially in Hungary and Czechoslovakia. But no one was sure how much the real abortion rate had been cut. Reliable statistics on the subject are not available in either East or West. The general assumption was that it was cut, but that the abortion industry was simply driven underground and the ghastly conditions characterizing some parts of it persisted. In Romania, however, Ceauşescu's savage legislation against it in the 1970s probably did act as a real deterrent. But even there the underground practice continued. Abortion had become an established and quite widespread practice.

Future population trends have varied from country to country according to projected levels of fertility and on the age and sex structure. Albania would certainly lead the way in population growth by a large margin. Poland would be next but at a considerably lower rate of increase than between 1950 and 1980. Romania would probably be not much less than Poland, but Hungary would be in last place, possibly even experiencing a negative birthrate by the end of the century.[27] Projections for the GDR were almost as gloomy, the only consolation for the East German authorities being that some of the projections for the Federal Republic were even worse!

The Plight of Pensioners

Eastern Europe's aging population will bring the situation of old age pensioners more to the center of the national stage than it has ever been. Whether it will become a serious political issue, however, is open to question. As in the West, so in the East, pensioners carry little or no political weight. They are expendable, and they realize it. But because so many families—probably a higher percentage in Eastern Europe than in Western Europe or North America—are directly concerned with, or responsible for, the care of the aged, the problem will assume greater proportions and in the course of doing so could take on political overtones.

The GDR and Hungary, for the reasons mentioned above, will face the severest problems soonest. The East German pension provisions are better than the Hungarian, and, in any case, the presence of the Federal Republic acts as a cushion for the considerable number of elderly East Germans able to rest on it. The East Berlin authorities place no barriers for pensioners wishing to travel to the Federal Republic; if they stay, so much the better. And they certainly place no obstacles to deutsche marks coming into the GDR to help pensioners.

Hungarian pensioners, except the comparatively few who get support from relatives in the West, have no such cushion. They are dependent on a state with very few reserves and a society growing more materialist and less cohesive. A review of their condition might, therefore, be instructive, giving, as it does, a fair idea of the pensioners' lot throughout the region.

In the middle of 1985 there were 2,260,000 Hungarian pensioners out of a population of 10,651,000.[28] This meant there were forty-four retirees to every hundred active workers—the highest proportion in Europe. Between 1970 and 1984 the proportion of pensioners to the total population had grown from 13.4 percent to 20.7 percent. About 70 percent of the pensioners received a pension of 3,000 forint a month, and 48 percent received one of less than 2,500 forint (the realistic exchange rate was about eighty forint to the dollar). According to a survey made in 1982, the Hungarian subsistence level was 2,150 forint for pensioners in general and about 2,700 for those over seventy-five years old and living alone.

Obviously, many pensioners were forced to try to find work to supplement their incomes, and, under the terms of a 1983 decree, they could work 1,250 hours a year and could generally earn up to 60,000 forint. In some jobs there were no limits on either the number of hours worked or the income derived—a reflection of the shortage of labor in many branches of the Hungarian economy. In early 1985 there were 50,000 pensioners employed in industry, 45,000 in agriculture, 40,000 in the public health services, and 30,000 in trade. In the countryside many of the private plots of collective farmers were worked by the retired members of the family.

Altogether, out of the total of 2,260,000 pensioners, about 400,000 were working in 1985. It was readily conceded that they played a vital role in a highly stretched economy. The food trade, for example, could not have coped without them, and the service sector was to a large degree dependent on their contribution. It Budapest in particular, which, despite its growth after 1945, was constantly short of labor of various kinds, there was a big demand for pensioners' labor. Out of the 400,000 pensioners living in the capital about one-quarter were working.[29]

Not all pensioners in Hungary were badly off by any means. People in professional occupations who retired on a high-scale pension and then took on part-time work often did quite well. But these were relatively few. For most it was a continuous struggle to cope with an economy where inflation had been running fairly high since the middle of the 1970s. As early as 1971 the authorities had introduced an automatic pension increase of 2 percent per annum—a sort of poor man's *scala mobile*. But after September 1974, as a result of fuel price increases, additional monthly increments were added. There were also several other types of supplements to which most pensioners were entitled but some of these were known only to a few because of the labyrinthine bureaucratic complexities in which they were embedded.

Generally women pensioners were worse off than men, mainly because they had worked for a shorter time and had usually been in jobs that paid less. There were also more widows than widowers. On the whole, a woman's pension was only three-quarters of that of a man.

One of the basic problems of pensioners, not only in Hungary but throughout Eastern Europe, was that people retired too early. The retirement age in Hungary for men was sixty and for women fifty-five.

These were unrealistically low for a country that could not generate the wealth to provide adequate services and which had a serious labor shortage to boot. But the enlightened compassion that inspired the setting of such early retirement ages was considered one of the proud hallmarks of socialism. In some parts of the economy raising the retirement age could also lead to overcrowding. As one Hungarian official delicately put it: raising the retirement age would not suit the "employment policy objectives" of the regime.[30]

Another problem for many pensioners was that the sense of family responsibility for them was weakening, in Hungary as well as everywhere else. Many were still cared for by their families, not just materially but also with love and concern. But many old people were simply neglected. The old adage about one parent providing more easily for six children than six children can provide for one parent cruelly applied. With the vastly increased social mobility that overtook Eastern Europe, families were increasingly splitting up, and many parents simply lost touch with their children. It was such pensioners whose plight could be often truly desperate. So-called "social homes" existed for those in need. But they were woefully inadequate both in numbers and in facilities, and many of them were in a disgraceful condition. In general, social facilities for pensioners—home helps, recreation clubs, etc. —were grossly inadequate.

In the 1970s and 1980s there was usually more publicity about the plight of pensioners in Hungary than in any other East European country. This was partly because of the high proportion of pensioners in society as a whole. It was also because the consciences of many were becoming worried by their condition. Nor was the regime unmindful of the situation. This problem was discussed extensively at the thirteenth party congress in March 1986. It was also raised at many trade union meetings and at meetings of the Patriotic People's Front (the national front organization). But many pensioners rightly became cynical about the words, instead of money, being spent on them. The same proposals, they claimed, the same horror stories, as well as the same excuses, were repeated year after year. Basically, the problem in many cases was that neither of the responsible parties—the state and the family—was doing its share, and both tended to duck their responsibilities by leaving them to the other. By the mid-1980s it had become a grim and shameful situation that was going to get worse.

The pensioners' plight may have been less dramatic or poignant in other East European countries. In Romania the situation of many pensioners in the cities was probably worse than in Hungary, and regime policy on the issue seemed as insensitive and even bizarre as in other walks of life.[31] But traditional family life in the rural areas had survived more in Romania than in Hungary, and many Romanian pensioners were consoled by a certain family security, miserable though their material plight might be. In Bulgaria pensioners were probably better off than in any other southeast European country. In Poland conditions in the cities were often as bad as anything in Hungary, but the Catholic church did extraordinary social work for the aged. In Czechoslovakia and the GDR the provisions and material conditions were the best in Eastern Europe, with the GDR, as mentioned earlier, having the Federal Republic as an important supportive factor. But Hungary was no great exception. Conditions there in many cases may have been worse, but the picture was not essentially different. East European pensioners would be familiar with the Hungarian situation and would probably not be shocked by it, and, like their Hungarian counterparts, they knew that, though they might expect some relief, their problems would never be satisfactorily resolved. Until pensioners could mount their own 1956 revolution or organize their own Solidarity, no regime was going to pay them the attention they deserved.

The Situation Among Youth

Nowhere is the danger of distortion more real than when discussing the situation among youth—whether in Eastern Europe or anywhere else. And nowhere is there a greater danger of simply compiling a catalog of evils and then wringing one's hands. Youth captures the headlines by its excesses. The faults of the few are generalized, and the virtues of the many often ignored.

Western views of East European youth are all too often dominated by a few statistics indicating an alarming deterioration in behavior —drugs, vandalism, alcohol, etc. The figures on all three of these evils are indeed alarming, and it would be folly to underestimate their gravity. But they are often generalized to depict a whole generation debauched and demoralized by communist rule. It is a misleadingly one-dimensional picture. The youth scene is much more varied than that.

What has happened is that many East European youth have joined —some with an almost pathetic determination—the transnational movement in which the behavioral tone and pace is set by their Western counterparts. One of the great achievements of Soviet rule in Eastern Europe has been to make the citizens of the region feel more Western than they ever did. As discussed in chapter 3, for most of the adults this has probably meant a growing identity with Western Europe, but for many of their children it has meant looking ultimately to the United States. Their contacts may be mainly with Western Europe, but it is from New York and California that their inspiration ultimately derives. The few young East Europeans who visit the United States are usually bowled over by it. The contrast with just a couple of generations ago is great indeed. As the world has become smaller, the horizons of most of its citizens have become incomparably wider.

It is this development that has worried Eastern Europe's rulers. Years of effort at ideological conversion appear to have been wasted. Enthusiasm for "socialist values," evident among many young people in the early years of communist rule, steadily declined. Communism may have once seemed a shortcut to a more equitable future. But it had become a dead end of disappointment and broken promises. The brutalities that some earlier had seen as a means to a better end had become an end in themselves. And what they indeed achieved was a travesty of what had been promised and expected. Many youth, therefore, so quick to see hypocrisy and inconsistency, turned angrily against both the ideology and the system that had promoted it.

But not only Eastern Europe's rulers were worried by this development: many of Eastern Europe's parents were also. The rejection of communism did not worry them at all, but they were uneasy about the vacuum of values that had followed it. Communist indoctrination had sought to rid young people of the value systems of previous generations based on church, country, and family, and for some years after 1945 it had seemed that it was at least partially succeeding. Now, with the speedy evaporation of communism's attractions, there was nothing left. And the amorphous youthful transnationalism that was moving into the vacuum, together with behavior that was not just antisocialist but sometimes antisocial, left many members of society just as anxious as the officials of state—if for diametrically opposed reasons.

But this is yet another generalization riddled with exceptions. Some values persisted strongly. For example, where nationalism and religion were mutually reinforcing—as in Poland, Croatia, and Slovakia—they both tended to remain strong (see chapter 3). But during the 1970s there was also a renewed interest in religion itself among a section of the youth in most parts of Eastern Europe. In the GDR, though religious belief as such was hardly reviving, the Evangelical church became an important center of youthful concern and aspirations. It was also in the GDR that transnational or, in this case, transborder, contacts between East and West were seen in striking reality with the ties with West German youth. The East German "peace movement" and the movement to preserve the environment were directly influenced by similar movements in the Federal Republic. Such issues united many young Germans, in East and West, and established links that would probably survive even if the East German regime preferred to make physical contact as difficult as possible. Here the churches in the two countries might well be called upon to play an increasingly important role in keeping youthful contacts alive.

Also, as mentioned earlier, the Chernobyl disaster seemed likely to sustain and increase public concern over the dangers of nuclear energy. In the immediate aftermath of Chernobyl large numbers of young people in Poland, Hungary, and Czechoslovakia, as well as the GDR, openly expressed their concern. It was they who, after all, would have to face the consequences of the nuclear age into which their rulers were leading them. It was perhaps too much to talk about the "greening" of Eastern Europe after Chernobyl, but the catastrophe made more young people more socially aware and public-spirited than before. Some two and a half years before Chernobyl, in early 1984, many East German and Czechoslovak youth had been roused by the Soviet decision to install new nuclear missiles on their territories as a response to the Federal Republic's deployment of American Pershing II and cruise missiles. Here public expressions of opposition had to be much more subdued because of Soviet sensitivities. Under the Chernobyl cloud there were fewer inhibitions, and after the cloud had dispersed, much of the concern, the solidarity, and civic resolve remained.

But, though numerous young East Europeans became concerned and even active over contemporary issues, the majority—like the majority everywhere—remained inactive if not indifferent. Who were this majority, and what motivated or activated them?

Most of them, like their Western counterparts, tended to conform in varying degrees to the prevailing models. Some of these were traditional, others contemporary; some had grown organically, others had been imposed. Most young people, from a variety of motives, were keen to make a career and anxious to avoid activity that might prejudice it. Nearly everybody, including some engaged directly in the state or party apparatus, rejected the communists, but they conformed in order to progress, working mainly for themselves and their immediate families. They often appeared cynical and self-serving, but they were no more so than many of their Western counterparts.

In the universities and other higher educational establishments, before the grind of life begins, there has generally been considerable nonconformity. In most universities there has always been a core of antiregime or generally militant sentiment that has occasionally erupted according to the issues exciting campus opinion. These issues have often narrowly focused on students' material concerns. But they have also affected questions of academic freedom generally, thus broadening into important political issues. The student disturbances in Yugoslavia and Poland in 1968 were classic examples. After periods of frenetic political activity in the student milieux a period of "bourgeois" calm has usually followed, with emphasis put on serious study and career orientation. (Again the similarities with the West, especially with the United States, in the 1970s and 1980s are striking.) This was the case in Czechoslovakia after 1968. In Poland, however, after the imposition of martial law in December 1981 student life was very slow in getting back to normal. Downright apathy became the prevailing mood of many, a contracting out of public life and a strong desire to emigrate.

In their spare time most East European youth do things most youth everywhere do—and there is nothing much wrong with them. What struck a visitor most forcefully was the passion for sport and the facilities provided for it. Again, it is possible to view this phenomenon skeptically. Sport in communist lands, it may be argued, is a deliberately engineered mass distraction, the second leg of the "bread and circuses" syndrome, a new "opium of the people." It may be all these things and more. But many East Europeans look at it in simpler, less sophisticated, or cynical terms. They may have little time for the party, military, or government organizations promoting sport, but they have not allowed this to affect the pleasure they derive from it. Most East Europeans also take pride in the achievements of their teams and individual champions in the international arena. In fact, their most effusive and boisterous demonstrations of patriotism have often been reserved for international sporting occasions, especially when the Russians are the opponents. They see their teams representing, not the socialist way of life, but their country. The phenomenal success of East German athletes has done more to kindle GDR patriotism than anything Ulbricht or Honecker ever devised. There is nothing in Eastern Europe like the attitude of South African blacks who, when South Africa used to take part in international competitions, supported the other side. No outsider, therefore, can afford to ignore the popularity and the significance of sport in Eastern Europe.

Nor can any outsider afford to ignore—however much he or she might wish to—the extraordinary appeal of pop music to the young generation. Here, more conspicuously and loudly than in any other sphere, many East European young people have shown themselves determined to jump on the carousel their Western counterparts have set in motion. From the Sopot Festival in Poland down to the pop cellars of Varna, the mania had fully caught on by the end of the 1960s and was showing no sign of abating some twenty years later. Not so much a form of music as a way of life, it encompassed dress, ornamentation, manner of speech, and behavior. Unlike sport, which was approved by both regime and large sections of the population, the pop culture was widely regarded as politically, culturally, socially, and morally subversive. In Czechoslovakia, especially, it was construed as a symbol of antiregime defiance, and some groups were persecuted with a paranoid intensity.[32] In response, prominent cultural figures took up its cause not only inside Czechoslovakia but in exile too.[33]

Finally, the pop culture has played a considerable role in prompting the demand for sound and video cassettes. In the year 2000 this and other aspects of the revolution in communications will need to take up an important part of any study of Eastern Europe. And this revolution will affect not only, or even primarily, the youth, or the social or the cultural scene. It will have a direct impact on political life and the way the East European countries are run, presenting their rulers with some of the most intractable problems they will have yet faced. This would have happened without the pop craze and its Western gravitational pull. But pop's role in the early stages of this revolutionary process will have to be recognized and admitted. In the words of one observer: "It was not until about 1983 that the first winds of the video revolution, already rampant in the West, reached Eastern Europe, and since then they have become a major storm, which is still gathering strength."[34]

The Spread of Corruption

Since the beginning of the 1970s many East Europeans traveling to the West have stressed the serious growth of corruption in their countries.

Corruption, they would argue, has not become just a way of life: it has become the essential means for life to go on.

When most East Europeans refer to growing corruption they mean not so much the malfeasance of the powerful, which they usually take for granted, but the increasing necessity to bribe (to use "sliding money") in order to obtain a whole range of economic, social, professional, and medical services. Many doctors and dentists, for example, began to demand bribes for professional attention. Those not prepared to bribe were either not attended to at all or were given poor or offhand attention. Similarly, a whole range of services from plumbing to legal advice was only given even halfway efficiently if the client was ready to pay extra for the job. Without bribery little or nothing got done. Bribery made wheels turn and hence made many important aspects of life more tolerable (or less intolerable) than they would otherwise be. This kind of bribery also extended to service in shops. Goods were kept under the counter for customers who could pay extra or who could render a reciprocal service to the seller—"service corruption." It was not that bribery had simply become common; it had been densely woven into national life, which it helped "arrange" and order.

It was significant that many complaints about everyday bribery came from citizens of the two countries that had no proud tradition of corruption, namely, Czechoslovakia and Hungary. For them, therefore, what may be described as "service corruption" was something relatively new. In both countries there was a tradition of decent administration, and in the Czech Lands, especially, an honest bureaucracy with few rivals anywhere in the world had existed. Of the other countries the GDR could look back to a Prussian legacy of efficiency and honesty. It was the countries of southeastern Europe that presented a totally different historical picture. Heirs to an Ottoman system of rule, they carried into independence many of the mores of the old empire. Nowhere was this more evident than in Romania, but many-sided corruption was also rampant in Serbia and other parts of Yugoslavia that were once under Ottoman rule. In Bulgaria, also for five hundred years under the Turkish yoke, there appeared to be less blatant corruption, but there was enough for numerous complaints both from regime officials and private citizens.

In Czechoslovakia and Hungary, therefore, it is difficult to see this "service corruption" as anything but a development associated with communism. Whereas in the Southern Tier it may simply have been continued under communist rule, in the Northern Tier it appears largely to have been created under it. George Schöpflin, in a masterly essay on East European corruption written in 1984, gives various reasons for the development and aggravation of service corruption under communism.[35] Two of them date back to various aspects of the de-Stalinization process that started after 1953. The first relates to the depoliticization of a "certain, though undefined, range of economic activities." The party no longer made explicit claim to control the whole of society, and certain areas of economic activity were left relatively free from close supervision. The creation of such opportunities, together with steady dismantling of much of the apparatus of terror, were important preconditions for the growth of corruption. The absence of terror led to the development of what Schöpflin calls "immunity mechanisms" in society. The various molds of officially induced behavior into which society was pressed under Stalin now cracked and were replaced by other forms of behavior antagonistic to officialdom and often antagonistic to one another as well.

A third reason is the population's basic lack of identification with the governing system as such and, in the case of many, a growing alienation from it. This became intensified when, as in the case of Hungary in 1956 and Czechoslovakia in 1968, a movement with which many citizens identified and that gave the promise of closer rapport between rulers and ruled was crushed. The ensuing disappointment and disillusion were conducive to the spread of corruption. Czechoslovakia, especially, after 1968 was a classic example of this, and it was in the early 1970s that massive corruption appears to have taken hold there.

The interaction of basic consumer shortages and rising demand also played a key role. In all East European countries the basic condition has been one of scarcity. But in all countries, also, the long periods of scarcity have been interspersed with shorter periods of relative plenty. Rising expectations have ensued. When periods of relative plenty were followed by a reimposition of the opposite, then corruption tended to accelerate. And, having accelerated, it never seemed to lose pace. Corruption, wherever it takes hold, is always gathering pace, spreading even into the nooks and crannies of public and private life.

It is the "scarcity–rising expectations" syndrome that also accounts for the growth and virtual indispensability of the black market. Indeed, this is an institution that has become so prevalent that many Eastern Europeans would be reluctant to see it as a form of corruption. In any case, the demarcation lines between the black market, gray market, and officially sanctioned free market have often been difficult to draw.

The general public was often envious of the incomes made in all the nonstate economic sectors, legal or illegal, and reserved a special disdain for black market operators, many of whom became part of organized crime networks. But at the same time it tolerated them because they represent not just the sugar on the cake but often the cake as well. The most obvious forms of black marketeering were in Western currencies and Western consumer goods. Few Western visitors could avoid pestering from currency exchangers or fail to be confused by the variety of rates being offered. And not many avoided the requests for Western cigarettes. More than a few taxi fares have been remitted with them.

The more spectacular forms of corruption were available only to those in sufficiently high positions in the party or state bureaucracy. They involved the misuse of public funds on a large scale. They took on innumerable forms, but generally there were two main types. The first pertained to direct fraud and/or embezzlement by officials. There were spectacular cases of this in all East European countries after the beginning of the 1960s, amounting to racketeering on a considerable scale. Some aspect of foreign (Western) trade was usually involved, and the main culprits were often employed in the foreign trade sector. But the network of criminal conspiracy often spread beyond one particular sector as it became necessary to involve others to increase returns or escape detection. Schöpflin mentions the case of Gheorghe Stefanescu in Romania in 1983 who led a racket in foreign trade and apparently escaped detection for a decade. Stefanescu was executed and his case given publicity *pour encourager les autres*. But there were other big cases in Romania and elsewhere that received little publicity. There must also have been many that have received none at all, many more that escaped detection altogether.

The other main type of "abuse of office" corruption was what Max Weber called "sultanism": rewards granted on the basis of political loyalty. This involves the extensive misuse of public funds for private aggrandizement and/or pleasure, with the connivance of authority. Thanks to unofficial and official revelations after 1980, Edward Gierek's regime in Poland had an excellently documented record of this activity.[36] But the bureaucracy "took care of its own" in every East European country, with officialdom in the GDR—the "Red Prussia"—probably preserving the best record of public and private probity.

Finally, there have been the "secondary" or "indirect" forms of corruption operated through networks based on family, clan, a particular geographic area, or a shared experience. Ceauşescu's nepotism in Romania is an extravagant and pathological example of the family relationship, but there have been other, more discreet examples. Albania is the best remaining example of power based on clan and locality, but while Gierek was in power in Poland in the 1970s a remarkable number of officials in the central government came from his old power base in Silesia. As for shared experiences, there have been many, but none could ever equal the Partisan network in Yugoslavia, especially the "Club of 41," members of which had flocked to Tito at the beginning of the resistance struggle and kept their headlock on Yugoslav public life for a generation afterward.

Most Westerners reading this last paragraph will be struck by the parallels in their own countries. There must also be similarities, mutatis mutandis, between East and West in the other types of corruption cited earlier. The decline in the level of integrity and in standards of public behavior in Great Britain since 1945, to mention only one example, should be enough to deter complacent judgments. Corruption may be "different" in Eastern Europe, and some aspects of it may be more prevalent. Some may also have been exacerbated by communism or stimulated by it. But few originated with communism, and none is confined to it.

Equality, Social Mobility, and Society

A discussion of corruption can lead to a consideration of the basic assumptions on which society is based. It is a subject so big, multifaceted, and important that to try to treat it in a few paragraphs is presumptuous and foolhardy. But even by simply addressing the subject one can perhaps give some idea, not only of the complexities of communist societies, but also the degree of contradiction between premise and practice in them.

There is no more basic premise of communist society than equality. As Ivan Völgyes has written:

> One of the primary claims of the East European communist regimes and their most frequently used argument for legitimacy has been that only communist rule can achieve the cherished ambition of equality. Since communist regimes could claim to give only restricted political liberties to the people and had promoted class-hatred rather than brotherhood, the communist theorists

had only equality left on which to claim kinship with their progressive forefathers in the French Revolution and the three great revolutionary principles of liberty, equality, and fraternity.[37]

When the communists assumed power the societies they were to transform differed considerably from country to country. Czechoslovakia and Bulgaria were, for example, relatively egalitarian societies, while Poland and Hungary were marked by huge social and economic differences. It was fairly easy to eliminate most of the traditional inequalities — at least in the superficial sense. It was done through expropriation. Industry was nationalized, and in theory everybody became a shareholder in property that was now owned by the state. In agriculture the land was first divided up among the peasants. Later many of the peasants were forced into collectives, but, despite the unpopularity and often inhumanity of this action, it tended to strengthen the egalitarian character of agriculture.

So far, so good. But the new communist regimes had promised not only equality but also higher living standards and economic progress. It was in the pursuit of these goals that the task of preserving equality was eventually realized to be impossible. Equality was a relatively simple matter when there appeared to be enough wealth to go round, but it was another matter when new wealth had to be created.

This did not become apparent for several years. First, there was the task of expropriation and redivision. Second, in a region still stunned by the effects of a devastating war most citizens were simply glad to be alive and were grateful for whatever work and sustenance were to be obtained. Third, the Stalinist command economic system itself imposed a certain egalitarianism. Fourth, Stalinist terror forced acceptance of the egalitarianism his system imposed.

But with the disintegration of Stalinism the days of this enforced equality were numbered. Economic reforms were suggested, and some even enacted, that created opportunities for differentiation in industry, agriculture, and services. Just as important, the terror was lifted and individual assertiveness and even acquisitiveness gradually came forward. The "rigorous" egalitarianism of the immediate postwar period, therefore, irretrievably broke down. From the very first, of course, there had been demonstrable inequality where party and government elites were concerned. Many of the new commissars lived in a style reminiscent of the old aristocrats, sometimes with a consumption just as conspicuous and always with a bodyguard vastly more numerous. But these were relatively few; the vast majority of citizens lived in a gray, austere equality that became the hallmark of East European socialism.

The need to create new wealth and the measures, however inadequate, to meet it brought in a new inequality. This applied to all the East European countries — perhaps with the exception of Albania. Society began to be differentiated according to income and economic potential. Later social criteria for differentiation reappeared that caused further and deeper divisions. Embryonic economic and social classes emerged, often with competing and sometimes with mutually antagonistic interests. Later, these classes became more sharply defined. Nowhere has this been more evident than in Yugoslavia, where Djilas achieved world fame with his book *The New Class*, and in Hungary, and it was no coincidence that it has been precisely in these two countries where economic reform, despite all the failings and inconsistencies, has been applied more comprehensively and successfully than anywhere else. Economic reform, then, has been the motor of the new inequality in Eastern Europe.

In Yugoslavia there has been a wider range of incomes than anywhere else in Eastern Europe. But because of the peculiar nature of its political and economic development and the *Gastarbeiter* phenomenon (see chapter 11), Yugoslavia fell into a category by itself. Hungary, though distinctive, represented a better standard for judgment. Völgyes has given some facts illustrating the divide between incomes, and these only reinforce the picture painted in chapter 6. In 1984, according to official figures, the average wage in Hungary was 4,800 forint per month (about $975 according to the official exchange rate but only about $600 according to the free market exchange rate). To illustrate his point, Völgyes mentions that Professor Ernö Rubik, inventor of the world-famous Rubik's Cube, despite a savings deposit of $70 million legally earned from royalties, was still not among the three hundred richest individuals in the People's Republic of Hungary. At the other end of the scale 28.2 percent of the Hungarian population in 1983 had an income below what was officially considered to be the "poverty level" of 2,500 forint. By any standard it would, according to Völgyes, be safe to say that in 1984 at least a quarter of the Hungarian population was living in poverty.[38]

The composition of the new classes in Eastern Europe was much more heterogeneous and diverting than that of the anciens régimes. The upper crust in Horthy's Hungary, for example, would have had little in common with their counterpart in Kádár's Hungary (and would doubtless have been quick to disclaim any). Hungary's new rich now included:

> lawyers, engineers, writers, party *apparatchiki*, bureaucrats, house-painters, collective farmers, electricians and business contractors. Among them are those who have worked hard for their money, working in the second economy legally and paying their taxes accordingly. They also include, however, for example doctors who routinely accept payments for services they are supposed to perform freely. Such earnings may be legal but they go untaxed. There are also boutique owners, small manufacturers, building contractors, and a host of individuals specialising in goods or skills that are in short supply.[39]

Hungary was special because of economic reform. The New Economic Mechanism had tapped a large reserve of latent entrepreneurial instinct. But Hungary was not entirely unrepresentative of the rest of Eastern Europe. As mentioned, Yugoslavia was even less egalitarian. But in Poland, the GDR, and even in Romania new elites had developed that were taking on some of the characteristics of economic and social classes. The Czechoslovak regime had always prided itself on a strict egalitarianism: in terms of salary, coalminers, followed by building workers, constituted the new elite. But even there the need for more complex differentiation was realized, however belatedly. During the 1970s some Czechoslovak collective farmers made sizable incomes, as did many doctors and members of the professions. There was nothing like the *enrichessez-vous* mood that prevailed in Hungary, but the old forced egalitarianism was eroding.

Societies generally were reverting to the classic division of "haves" and "have nots," and it was highly unlikely that this process would ever be reversed. But it was causing an increasing bitterness among the growing numbers of "have nots." These included not only those living in poverty or just above it but also workers who resented losing their one-time privileged positions and who still carried much political force and influence. Often tending toward conservatism, they were likely targets for manipulation by demagogic, dogmatic elements in the political process.

Indeed, one of the most important social and political developments in Eastern Europe during the 1970s was the solidification of a more static working class. Except in the Czech Lands and in what is now the GDR, the working class in Eastern Europe had always been

relatively small. In the first years of Communist rule it expanded rapidly through the twin policies of rapid industrialization and rural collectivization. Large numbers of peasants moved into industry. At the
same time the growing industry required managers and professionals
of various kinds and, though many of the old managers had to be
retained or taken back temporarily because their skills were unique,
the new top and middle ranks of the economy were filled from the
more able and forceful members of the working class.

Thus, as Walter D. Connor has argued:

> At the top, the ambitious, the intelligent, and even opportunistic . . .
> were coopted into the new privileged groups. At the bottom, peas-
> ants and their offspring, unused to city life and industrial disci-
> pline but eager to escape the harsh rural life, entered in increasing
> numbers. . . . The frame of reference of the members of the new
> intelligentsia was that of the working class from which they had
> risen; that of the new workers, the peasant world they had left.[40]

For peasants and workers, therefore, there was much social and
professional mobility. And this mobility had its political implications.
To quote Connor again:

> For the peasant, mobility into the working class—into the urban
> environment, to a job with bounded hours, steady work and regu-
> lar pay—represented an individual solution. For working class
> offspring not content to settle for their fathers' status, the expan-
> sion of educational opportunities and the demand for profes-
> sional cadres held out the prospect, once again, of *individual*
> advancement. These high mobility prospects militated against a
> readiness to seek *collective* solutions to problems—a readiness
> more likely to arise when individuals are convinced that their
> membership in a particular class is a "life sentence."[41]

As Connor argues, this may have been one of the reasons for the
political "neutrality" of many sections of the working class in many
parts of Eastern Europe. But beginning in the 1970s, that is, well over a
generation after this process of mobility began, the social situation
began to settle down. Industrialization began to slow down, and,
although the migration from countryside to the urban areas continued
well after collectivization had been completed, what had once been a
torrent now became more of a drift. Moreover, the new economic and
technical intelligentsia would mainly reinforce themselves and often

be succeeded by their own offspring. A new structure was, therefore, forming and a working class was, willy-nilly, solidifying—the first mass working class in Eastern Europe.

It was forming at about the same time as a deteriorating economic situation was forcing most of the regimes to embrace some kind of economic reforms that would encourage economic differentiation, the profit motive, and entrepreneurial talent. Some members of the working class might thrive in the new atmosphere and get relatively rich. But these would be very few. The vast majority would have to watch while others enriched themselves, and for many of them the only way even to make ends meet was to work long, exhausting hours of overtime or in the second economy. It must have been particularly galling in some countries for workers to see so many peasants making a good income down on the farm for the first time in history.

By the middle of the 1980s a social situation conducive to conflict was developing in Eastern Europe. The "have nots" were seeing their upward escape route increasingly barred, and many of them could only maintain their families, their economic level, and their social self-respect by extra labor that was taking its toll on health, nerves, and temper. The "haves" seemed to be getting more and often flaunted their wealth provocatively. They were, in short, "using" the system. The "have nots" saw the system as "using" them.

A Faute de Mieux Society?

Several times in this chapter comparisons with the West have been made. These comparisons serve to emphasize the similar underlying problems in all societies, regardless of the political structures involved, that have passed a certain point in economic and social development. In many respects Eastern Europe in the early 1980s was similar to Western Europe in the 1950s.

But the vital differences should not be forgotten either. Much of Eastern Europe's economic progress, especially its industrialization, has been telescoped into a much shorter period than was the case with the West, rapid though the development was there. The problems associated with modern life, therefore, have appeared all the sharper and harder to tackle. Just as important is the fact that, though many societal problems, in both East and West, arise from varying degrees of alienation from the established order, that alienation goes much deeper in Eastern Europe than in the West.

Finally, the evils of social life in the West are generally exposed, analyzed, and agonized over in an atmosphere of freedom of discussion. This may not bring their solution any nearer, but it creates a healthier and franker environment in which they can be discussed. It also gives Western life a resilience that does not exist in Eastern Europe. True, social problems have now begun to be discussed there with more frankness than ever before, particularly in Hungary and Poland. But there is nothing like the frankness existing in the West. The days when all social evils were said to have either originated in the West or were due to surviving bourgeois traces at home are over. But all too often the East European media handle these evils as if they are ideologically ashamed of them.

Still, life goes on in Eastern Europe, and, though most would like to change it, they are durable enough to make the best of it. Some have always found it tolerable; others have become reconciled to it; still others are resigned to it. They are denied basic freedoms that in the West are all too often taken for granted. But in the shadow of this denial they live everyday lives that may be full of difficulties but also have their compensations. A perceptive analyst has summed up the situation as follows:

> While ensuring a little for everyone, the communist system severely restricts the choice and quality of goods available to the consumer and on top of that makes acquiring these goods very arduous. The market-based systems, on the other hand, tend to satisfy consumers in terms of quality and choice but have so far failed to extend full participation in such benefits to all members of the community. It may well be that there are people who would rather stick to what they have got than risk having the superior Western consumerist pattern but with the price-tag of insecurity; conversely, it is conceivable that there are people in the West who might opt for the Eastern version of consumerism in order to increase job security. The point is, however, that the former have no choice over the matter.[42]

It might also be added that most of the older generation in Eastern Europe have known life to be much worse than it has been since the beginning of the 1970s. They have a high threshold of endurance. But the younger generations did not experience the war years or the miseries of reconstruction and Stalinist transformation. They are not satisfied with the "things are much better now" argument.

On the contrary, they are provoked by it. Their impatience could be an important ingredient in an unstable, even explosive, future mix. The instabilities of political life in Eastern Europe could be heavily reinforced in the future by those that are developing in social life.

14 The National Minorities and Their Problems

Eastern Europe has never been rich in natural resources, but it has always been rich in nations. It covers an area about two-thirds the size of Western Europe. But, whereas Western Europe is more or less exclusively covered by five large nations—the Germanic, French, Hispanic, Anglo-Celtic, and Italian—Eastern Europe has more than fifteen nations jostling within its boundaries. Nor are many of these nations compact units: many have sizable minorities of other nations in their own midst and members of their own nation enveloped by others. The patchwork quilt has been produced by historical events that still embitter the atmosphere in many parts of the region today, often evoking nationalism in its more virulent forms.

The whole course of East European history has made its contribution to this patchwork quilt, beginning with the great migrations before the tenth century that gave the region its lasting ethnic complexion. They were followed by the golden age of medieval empires, which buried itself deep in the historical subconscious of many East European peoples to reemerge centuries after when modern nationalism fought its winning battles with alien imperialisms. These imperialisms —the Ottoman, tsarist Russian, Habsburg, and, more latterly, the Prussian—dominated Eastern Europe between the end of the fourteenth and the beginning of the twentieth centuries. After World War I they disappeared, and for a fleeting twenty years nationalism triumphed in Eastern Europe. But the self-determination principle of the Paris peace treaties, noble and naive, brought resentment as well as fulfillment. What was historic justice for some was, for others, an injustice often harder than anything they had suffered before. The divisions and the bitterness these two decades generated were one reason (though not the only one) why Eastern Europe again fell an easy prey, first to the new German imperialism, and then, after its defeat, to the new Soviet Russian domination that has continued to the present.

These vicissitudes of history have made the minority problem in Eastern Europe today. The problem is an offshoot of the nationalism that foreign imperialism submerged but did not obliterate. Imperialism fosters nationalism, which, in turn, fosters minority problems. More recently, communist Eastern Europe has inherited some, though not all, of the minority problems of nationalist Eastern Europe of the interwar years. Because of the tragedies of Nazism, war, and the postwar settlements, these problems are now fewer, smaller, and not as acute. East European Jewry, for example, was virtually annihilated; the large German minorities were almost totally expelled from every country except Romania and Hungary; Poland, without the Jews and almost all its interwar Ukrainians, achieved ethnic homogeneity for the first time.

A cursory survey of contemporary Eastern Europe shows Poland and the GDR to be virtually free of minorities.[1] Poland, it is true, still has some 180,000 to 200,000 Ukrainians and a few hundred thousand citizens wholly or partly of Germanic origin, concentrated mainly in Silesia. The GDR has a very small Slavic Wend population in its southeastern corner, concentrated in the Bauzen area. Hungary has a minority population of about 300,000, of which probably the Slovaks, numbering about 80,000 to 100,000, are politically the most important.

Albania has about 50,000 Greeks in Southern Albania, or "Northern Epirus" in Greek irredentist terminology. (Nationalist Greeks claim there are many more, and that many of them are persecuted, although most of these claims should be viewed skeptically.)[2] Otherwise, the minority that Albanians are most preoccupied with is the one made up of their own countrymen in neighboring Yugoslavia. There are some 1.8 million members of the Albanian minority in Yugoslavia, most of them in Kosovo, adjacent to the Albanian border, where by the middle of the 1980s they constituted about 80 percent of the total population. But there also has always been a large Albanian community, numbering over 300,000, in the republic of Macedonia and a smaller one in Montenegro.

Poland, the GDR, Albania, and Hungary, therefore, are countries without minorities that could cause serious domestic or international problems. The other four countries, however—Czechoslovakia, Romania, Bulgaria, and Yugoslavia—have large minorities. The first Czechoslovak republic had a German population numbering over 3 million; in the early 1920s this was slightly larger than the whole Slovak population.[3] Many left toward the end of World War II; almost all the rest were expelled. But a large Hungarian community remained in Slovakia, the result of a thousand years of Hungarian rule. The original intention appears to have been to expel the Hungarians also, and up to 200,000 were actually expelled or left beforehand.[4] But a Hungarian minority of some 600,000 has remained in Slovakia, the prime responsibility for governing it resting with the Slovak authorities in Bratislava, rather than the Czechoslovak authorities in Prague. The largest Hungarian minority, however, is in Romania, officially numbering about 1.7 million or more, mainly in the area loosely known as Transylvania. As in the case of Slovakia, this was territory that had been part of greater Hungary for ten centuries until 1918. Romania also has a large German minority that, before World War II, numbered almost 700,000. Today, mainly as a result, not of expulsion, but of migration and loss of territory resulting from war, there are about 380,000 left, with many of these Germans wanting to leave for the Federal Republic. The most numerous minority in Bulgaria has been the Turkish, a remnant of Ottoman rule numbering, until very recently, about 800,000 or nearly 10 percent of the population.

Communist Yugoslavia, as a recognized multinational state, was the only one of Moscow's immediate postwar satellites to adopt the Soviet-type federal form of government. (In October 1968, in its own special circumstances, Czechoslovakia also became a federal state.) In view of this federalization, some Yugoslavs would object to any of their nationalities being designated as minorities. But in the context of this discussion it is appropriate to consider both the Albanians and the Hungarians living in Yugoslavia as such. The Albanians have already been mentioned. The Hungarians, living mainly in the autonomous province of Vojvodina, adjacent to the Hungarian border, number about 480,000 and also live on territory formerly part of Hungary.

In the case of Yugoslavia, therefore, discussions will be confined to these two nationalities, although many might argue that this is not enough. Most Bulgarians, for example, would claim that the Macedonians—whom they refuse to recognize as a nation, claiming them to be really Bulgarian—should also be added. Yugoslavs, on the other hand, claim there is a Macedonian minority in Bulgaria—in "Pirin Macedonia" —which the Bulgarians did once briefly recognize.

The Muslims in Yugoslavia form a special, rather complicated category. By 1985 there were just under 4 million of them in the country as a whole. About 1.7 million of these were the Albanians of Kosovo, Macedonia, and Montenegro referred to above. But there were also just over 2 million Muslims who were Slavic by race, over 1.6 million of them in Bosnia-Herzegovina. These Slavic Muslims (all Sunnis) are descended from either Serbs or Croats converted to Islam under the Turkish occupation. In the interwar Yugoslav kingdom and for some time under Tito, the Serbs regarded them as Serbs and the Croats regarded them as Croats. To end this dispute Tito decided in 1961 to create a Muslim nation. Since then, Muslim with a capital M has denoted ethnic Muslim while muslim with a small m has denoted muslim in the religious sense. Followers of Islam in Bosnia-Herzegovina are, therefore, both Muslim and muslim (or Muslim muslims), while Albanians in Kosovo are just plain muslims.[5]

Finally a word—and regretfully only that—on traditionally the most oppressed minority of all: the Gypsies. Nowhere are they given the status of a national minority, being regarded more as a social problem than anything else. By the beginning of the 1980s there were probably about 2.5 million Gypsies in Eastern Europe (and about 250,000 in the Soviet Union). It is difficult to arrive at a precise number. Official statistics are often greatly misleading. In the 1971 census in Yugoslavia, for example, their number was put at 78,485, but six years later it was estimated that there were over 300,000 living in the country.[6] Even allowing for their very high birthrate they could hardly have increased so quickly in so short a time. The discrepancy can only be explained by Gypsies choosing to register during a census as nationals of the republic where they happened to live, or happened to be camping.

Numerically, Eastern Europe's Gypsies have recovered from the decimation of World War II when they formed one of the main targets of Hitler's genocidal schemes. At least half a million of them perished in the Nazi camps. The main reason for this resurgence is their diligence in reproducing themselves. In Hungary, for instance, the majority of Gypsy families have three or more children, and some Hungarian demographers have estimated that they will account for 10 percent of the population by the year 2000.[7]

Generally the Gypsies have been fairly tolerantly treated by the communist regimes—at least by some of the standards of the twentieth century. Only in Czechoslovakia is their nomadic way of life a statutory offense, although it must be said that the Czechoslovak government has done more than any other in Eastern Europe for the Gypsies in the way of social and material benefits. But that precisely is what many

Gypsies do not want, preferring the traditional nomadic life. A Gypsy and the "new socialist man" tend to be incompatible types. This is partly why so many Gypsies violate the law in many respects and are punished for it. Many Gypsies are also involved in crime of various sorts. Public sentiment (it is often nothing more than racial prejudice) against Gypsies has increased strikingly in Eastern Europe since 1970, especially in Hungary, where it has been the subject of considerable concern.[8]

Types of National Minorities

In Eastern Europe, as elsewhere, there are different types of national minorities, and it is worth examining them before going on to discuss the policies toward them.

Minorities have often been classified in geographic terms, i.e., according to their location. Thus the first and most significant category covers those minorities living adjacent to the frontiers of the state occupied or dominated by their own nation.[9] This includes most members of the Hungarian minorities: those living in Slovakia, in Transylvania, and Vojvodina. Many Hungarians (or Szeklers) living in Transylvania proper are, of course, a considerable distance from the Hungarian border, from which they are separated by some districts that have Romanian majorities. But, by and large, this "adjacency" is a characteristic of Hungarian national minorities and what has made them, since the Treaty of Trianon in 1920, a disturbing and sometimes explosive factor in East European politics. This was especially so in the interwar years when successive Budapest governments were preoccupied with irredentism, aided and abetted by Fascist Italy and Nazi Germany. Even now, with irredentism loudly disowned by the Hungarian communist regime, the geographic location of the minorities makes them objects of suspicion in Bratislava and Bucharest—even in Belgrade, also, despite the relative tranquility in Vojvodina.

Also in this category of geographic adjacency are over half the Turkish minority in Bulgaria, in the southeast part of the country next to Turkey. The same applies to the Kosovar Albanians, situated in the southwest part of Yugoslavia next to the Albanian frontier. But since the end of the Ottoman Empire successive governments in Ankara have had few irredentist ambitions. The postwar communist regime in Tirana, on the other hand, though professing no territorial claims, has often seemed less than sincere. And the possibility that it might one day change its line adds a dangerous dimension, not only to antagonism in Kosovo itself, but also to the future of Yugoslavia as a whole.[10]

A second category of minorities covers those situated at longer or shorter distances from the state occupied or dominated by their own nation.[11] Up to 1939 this was an important category, since it applied to practically all the German minorities in Eastern Europe and in parts, first of Russia, and then the Soviet Union. (The minority in the Czech Lands, falling into the first category, was a crucial exception.) Up to the Nazi period these minorities made a notable contribution to the public life of their host countries. After 1933 Hitler sought to use them as a German fifth column. Some Germans in Eastern Europe were ready accomplices, others not. But after World War II they were expelled without distinction from most parts of the region, and it was this expulsion that drastically reduced the importance of this whole category of minorities in the East European context.

Finally, there are two categories worth mentioning, although they have had little or no significance for East European politics or international relations. One includes single, usually small and isolated minorities, like the Wends in the GDR. The second covers veritable hotchpotches of small groups of minorities living cheek-by-jowl in a relatively confined area. The best examples of this were parts of prewar Macedonia (then part of Serbia) and Bessarabia (then part of Romania).[12] Time, the ravages of war, assimilation, migration, change of sovereignty, and statistical manipulation have all served to disperse these colorful agglomerations.

So much for the categories based primarily on geography. Obviously they are important, but there are at least three other factors even more meaningful. They are (1) the different historical antecedents of the minority concerned; (2) the attitudes of different minorities to the state in which they live and to the predominant nation (*Staatsvolk* or "nation of state") in it; and (3) their attitudes to integration or assimilation into the state, or by the "nation of state" concerned. Obviously these categories are often closely interrelated. But they are also worth examining separately.

1. *Historical antecedents.* Some ethnic groups, especially those recently pushed into minority status, were at one time an integral part of an imperial nation—not just a *Staatsvolk* but a *Herrenvolk*. This applies not so much to Germans as to Turks, Hungarians, and—within the Yugoslav context—Serbs. Other ethnic groups have historically been at the oppressed end of the power spectrum: Vlachs, Albanians

(until recently in Yugoslavia), not to mention Gypsies—with the Jews occupying a special position invoking envy, hatred, respect, fear, or primitive superstition. This is to mention only a few. There have been several tiny minorities, almost unrecorded, in East European history that have never known anything but subjugation.

2. *Minority attitudes*. It follows that members of the once "imperial" minority will tend to have a superior, often arrogant and disdainful attitude to the new "nation of state," since this was formerly one of the nations they themselves dominated. This is clearly the case with the Hungarians in relation to the Slovaks and the Romanians. During the days of their domination most Hungarians looked down on both Slovaks and Romanians. The Germans, too, left no one in doubt about their superior attitude, but since they in most cases had not been the "nation of state," their behavior was not so potentially destabilizing as the Hungarian. Still, the old Siebenbürger Saxon chestnut about speaking German to each other, Hungarian to their horses, and Romanian to their cattle sums up an attitude that characterized—and did not endear—most Germans east of the Fatherland. It had also characterized the Serbs—and most Yugoslavs for that matter—in their attitude to Albanians. This, together with the fact that Kosovo, which the Serbs have had steadily to leave under pressure, was the heartland of the great Serbian medieval empire does much to explain the bitterness aggravating relations with Albania.

3. *Attitudes to integration*. Some minorities, most notably the Jews, have often shown a willingness and an ability to integrate into the dominant nation. Their success in doing this, of course, has not depended on them alone. The attitudes and mores of the dominant society concerned have been crucial. In general, it was Hungarian society that the Jews found easiest and most congenial to enter.[13] But here again generalization can lead to oversimplification. It was educated Jews who found assimilation most easy and attractive. Many Jews, poorer and less educated, preferred to live their own lives and be left alone in dignity. This was an attitude they shared with most other subordinated—but less talented—minorities like the Bosniaks and Pomaks, the Muslim converts in Yugoslavia and Bulgaria, respectively, not to mention the Gypsies. In this category must also fall the Turks in Bulgaria and the rest of the Balkans. Though members of a former imperial nation that ruled all the Balkans for at least four hundred years, they have shown few of the characteristics of the Hungarians, Germans, and Serbs. They have simply sought toleration to pursue

their own way of life, something the authorities in Bulgaria, where most of them have lived, were not prepared to grant them.

Communist Principles and Policies

In few areas of East European public life over the last four decades has there been such a contradiction between communist principles, sometimes even ideals, and practice as in the treatment of national minorities.

Marx himself was little interested in nationalism or national minorities. The class question for him was more important than the national.[14] Solve the former and the latter would take care of itself. The national question in all its aspects, therefore, was of peripheral concern, although he did originate the famous slogan of the national "right of self-determination," a principle ostentatiously espoused by the Russian Bolsheviks before they came to power and brazenly ignored afterward. For his part, Lenin was an instinctive Russian chauvinist. This showed in his contempt for the non-Russian peoples of the tsarist empire and later of the Soviet Union and, more practically, after 1917 in his insistence that the Russians remain the "nation of state" in the new state. Before 1917 he saw the importance for the revolution of exploiting national feeling, and he disturbed internationalists, like Rosa Luxemburg, with his bounteous promises of self-determination and even a "privileged" position for minorities. After the Bolsheviks had come to power it was Stalin who formulated the official view on nationalism in his famous "Marxism and the National Question" in 1920. In this work Stalin put forward four criteria for the definition of a nation. It should (1) speak the same language; (2) occupy a compact territory; (3) have the same economic system; (4) be united by the same psychological makeup that could be subsumed under the expression "culture."[15] (This last criterion has caused difficulty for Marxists in that it could cover nonmaterialist elements that they could neither digest nor even accept.) But, in the context of the national question, Stalin's major contribution was to be his dilution, to the point of eradication, of any practical application of the right of "self-determination." The young provincial Georgian was to become one of the great Russian metropolitan nationalists.[16]

But this Russian nationalism was disguised—even hidden from many not affected by it—by a large and impressive mask of concessions to the non-Russian nationalities. First of all, the Soviet Union became a federal state in structure. Within this federal framework national cultures and native national languages were encouraged. Administration and education could be conducted in local languages. Many of these concessions were more impressive on paper than in practice; but they did allow many members of the Soviet nationalities an opportunity for education and advancement that had not existed before. What they certainly did not allow, however, was nationalism.

When the communist regimes were installed in power in Eastern Europe after World War II, Stalin clearly expected them to take the Soviet Union as a model. This became especially urgent after the break with Tito in 1948 that showed the dangers of even a little latitude. The result was that though only Yugoslavia, with its plethora of nations, adopted the Soviet model of federation, all governments with sizable minorities granted them, however reluctantly, similar concessions to those allegedly prevailing in the Soviet Union. These concessions, written into the constitution, affected education, publishing, use of language, and the right to form cultural organizations. Again, these fell short of what many members of the minorities in Eastern Europe would have wanted. But they represented a considerable improvement on the treatment most minorities had received in the interwar years. Indeed, this relatively better treatment, combined with the support the communists had often given—and received from—the minorities before the war, led to more initial acceptance of the new regimes by the minorities than by the population as a whole.[17]

Among the communist leaders in the countries concerned there was, despite the distaste of some, a strong show of support by all for the Soviet-inspired policy toward minorities. But, in reality, divisions of attitude and policy were present that were subsequently to surface. Generally speaking, those leaders, called "Muscovites" because of their training in the Soviet Union, were often more liberally inclined toward minorities than the "home" communists; at least their prejudices were fewer. None more so than Jewish "Muscovites," many of whom had embraced communist internationalism ardently and sincerely. The "home" communists, however, who had remained in their own countries and who were thus more affected by local feeling and prejudice, tended to share the popular hostility toward minorities. Leading Slovak Communists, for example, like Vladímir Clementis, Gustáv Husák and Laço Novomeský were known for their strong anti-Hungarian views, as was Lucreţiu Pătrăşcanu, one of the top Romanian "home" communists. But, again, there were important exceptions to these generalizations. Vulko Chervenkov, a "Muscovite" who would become the "little Stalin" of Bulgaria, showed little internationalism when it came to the Macedonian question, and even Georgi Dimitrov, former secretary-general of the Comintern, is said to have (privately) described the partial expulsions of Turks from Bulgaria in the late 1940s as the final steps in his country's deliverance from the "Turkish yoke." But as long as the law was laid down from Moscow as rigidly as it was in Stalin's last years, it was Soviet doctrine that had to be followed. And after 1948 the "home" communists in practically every East European country were submerged in favor of the "Muscovites."

After Stalin's death, however, there was a steady reversal. Both "Muscovites" and real "internationalists" began falling into eclipse, their place initially taken by those "home" communists who had physically survived the earlier decimations. Subsequently a new generation of "home" communists was to emerge whose active careers had, mostly or entirely, been spent after communism had come to power. Both of these generations of "home" communists tended toward a nationalist attitude to minorities and began to show it. Their coming to power coincided with an increasing freedom, of autonomy in minority policy, as well as many other aspects of domestic affairs, that the East European states have gained from the Soviet Union since Stalin's death. Minority policy, especially, seemed well fitted to give East European leaderships a degree of popular legitimacy they sorely needed. As for Moscow, legitimacy began to be identified—or confused—with stability, and it was not going to stop anything that increased it.

Thus three factors have been crucial in the steadily mounting pressure on national minorities in Eastern Europe. They are (1) the emergence of ruling elites holding the same "nation of state" attitudes toward, and historical prejudices against, minorities as those of most of the population; (2) the possibility of greater popular legitimacy for the ruling elites by exploiting the minority issue in a "nationalist" way; (3) the greater domestic autonomy allowed—deliberately or unavoidably—by Moscow to the East European regimes.

Other factors, of course, played a role. For example, the support many Hungarians in Romania gave the Hungarian Revolution in 1956 led to savage repression for a short time and probably induced the regime to undertake the reorganizations in education and administration that affected them afterward. It subsequently emerged also that some Hungarians in Slovakia had been restive in 1956.[18] But in Slovakia it was the events of 1968 that helped lead to a perceptible change for the worse in the status and rights of the Hungarian minority. The intoxicating freedom Slovakia enjoyed along with the Czech Lands in 1968 allowed both an assertiveness in favor of more freedom by the Hungarians and an open expression by many Slovaks of their anti-Hungarian feelings. There is no doubt that the Hungarian attitude alarmed many Slovaks, and, after Slovakia acquired its federal status in October 1968, the Slovak authorities felt much freer to pursue a more restrictive policy toward the Hungarian minority. And they had no doubt that they had the majority of their own nation behind them.

It should not be thought, however, that the restrictive trend after the 1950s followed an inexorable, undeviating course. Periods of discrimination were followed by periods of relative tolerance. For example, in the 1960s the Hungarian minority in Czechoslovakia was generally left alone. In his first five years as party leader in Romania, Ceauşescu was looked at with hope by many Hungarians after the policies of Gheorghe Gheorghiu-Dej, his predecessor.[19] Some Hungarians looked on him as almost a protector and, when official Romanian policy began to harden, persisted for some time in excusing him from their complaints. The tide of restriction ebbed and flowed, therefore. But the sea did not retreat and over the years has come to threaten ever more closely the separate positions to which the minorities cling.

Forms of Discrimination and Pressure

Against this background it is worth discussing the various types of restriction, the forms of pressure, manipulation, and discrimination central governments have used against minorities. It is communist governments, of course, that are the subject of this discussion, but it should not be forgotten that their predecessors used identical or similar methods, often in a cruder and more brutal form.

These methods may be itemized as follows:

1. *Expulsion or forced emigration.* This was used in the immediate postwar period, often in the heat of revenge and retribution against a former enemy. Thus an estimated 5 million Germans were expelled from Poland, Czechoslovakia, Yugoslavia, and partly from Hungary. About 200,000 Hungarians were expelled from Slovakia to Hungary amid calls from Czechoslovakian democratic and communist politicians alike that all should go.[20] Beginning in the late 1940s about 180,000 Turks were expelled from Bulgaria, and, again, the original intention appears to have been to expel them all. (Subsequently, after

1964, a trickle of orderly emigration was allowed with the agreement of the Turkish government.)[21]

2. *Census manipulations*. This is a time-honored practice in East-Central Europe going back to the very first censuses under the Habsburgs. Usually, as in Slovakia, the aim has been to reduce the real numbers of those being ruled. It could be claimed that many Hungarians were really Slovaks or—as before 1914—vice versa. Some plausibility to these gambits was lent by the fact that many Slovaks became Hungarianized, and, more recently, some Hungarians in Slovakia have become Slovakized. Bulgaria has blatantly manipulated the Macedonian column of its censuses to fit the changing course of its relations with Belgrade over the future of Macedonia itself. The authorities in Sofia were happy to record over 200,000 Macedonians as living in Bulgaria (almost exclusively in Pirin Macedonia adjoining the Yugoslav frontier) as long as there was some hope in the early postwar years of achieving a Balkan federation in which Macedonia would hew ever more closely to Bulgaria. When the futility of this hope was realized, the number of Macedonians officially recorded in the 1965 census as living in Bulgaria dropped calamitously to under 9,000. At the next decennial census they disappeared altogether, leading many Yugoslavs to allude cynically to "statistical genocide."[22]

3. *The "creation" of new nations*. This is "statistical procreation," the opposite of "statistical genocide." On the two occasions it has been massively used it has been to settle nationality and territorial disputes with a neighboring power. Thus, though the existence of a territory known as Macedonia has never been in doubt, the Yugoslavs had to "create," or at least "induce," a Macedonian nation—which they proceeded to do after 1941.[23] Sound arguments exist for suggesting that a Macedonian nation did exist in antiquity. But in modern times most ethnographers have held that the people living in Macedonia were mainly of Bulgarian stock. Certainly, little was heard of a Macedonian nation (as opposed to various Macedonian organizations) in the nineteenth century and before World War II—not from Athens, Sofia, or even Belgrade. But it was Tito's way of solving a difficult national and international problem, and he sacrificed neither time, nor effort, nor expense to launch the Macedonian nation. He was brilliantly successful. Whether the Soviet Union has been as successful in creating a Moldavian nation out of the large Romanian majority in Bessarabia is not so clear. They, like the Yugoslavs, have used all the historical, linguistic, cultural, and anthropological—not to mention coercive

—means at their disposal to distinguish the Romanians on their side of the River Pruth from the Romanians on the other side. Their efforts began soon after their recovery of Bessarabia after World War II. More recently, the first phase of their work presumably completed, they have been at pains to justify themselves with scientific, cultural, and historical arguments. Whether this is in response to Romanian efforts arguing the opposite or mainly in response to the palpable lack of Moldavian consciousness on the part of the Bessarabians is hard to say.[24]

4. *Compulsory "denationalization."* The most blatant example of "denationalization" has been the treatment of the Turkish minority in Bulgaria. Beginning in the 1970s moves were made by the Bulgarian authorities to break down the exclusiveness of the Turkish minority in the interests of a unitary state. Many Turks were pressured to renounce their names and their religion and were often subjected to violence. This culminated in the compulsory name-change campaign at the end of 1984 and in early 1985. The Turks, probably numbering about 800,000, had always been recognized by the Bulgarian regime itself as ethnically Turkish. (As such they had been distinguished from the Pomaks, who numbered between 150,000 and 200,000 and were the descendants of ethnic Bulgarians converted to Islam during the Ottoman occupation.) But now, in a short, well-prepared campaign all members of the Turkish minority were given Bulgarian names and were declared Bulgarian. More than this, they were declared to have been always ethnically Bulgarian but to have been "Turkicized" in Ottoman times. Now they were just being "re-Bulgarianized"! The regime, therefore, totally reversed a stand that it shared with previous "bourgeois" governments; that these were Turks, a residual of the "Turkish yoke." Small wonder that this crude and cruel denationalization provoked strong opposition among the Turkish minority that resulted in many deaths. It was a cynical, primitive maneuver that further reduced sympathy for Bulgaria beyond its borders.[25]

5. *Administrative-territorial "reorganizations" in minority areas.* What is meant here is the gerrymandering of geographical units of local government so as to break up the compactness of minority concentrations. Both the Czechoslovak and Romanian authorities have indulged in this type of manipulation. The first administrative-territorial reorganization introduced by the communist regime in Czechoslovakia in 1948 divided Slovakia into six districts (*kraje*). These divisions effectively broke up the compactness of the Hungarian minority, which is

mainly located on an east-to-west axis in the south of Slovakia. The main Hungarian concentration is in the Dunajská Streda and Komárno areas, and this was split between the Bratislava and Nitra districts. A later administrative-territorial reorganization in 1960 appears further to have eroded the compactness of Hungarian population concentrations. It now divided Slovakia into three large regions. Both these reorganizations made administrative sense, but they also heightened the Slovak demographic preponderance over the Hungarians.[26]

In Romania developments were similar, except that the position the Hungarians originally enjoyed was much more privileged; hence their subsequent frustration has been all the greater. For Romania was the only East European state, other than Yugoslavia, to establish an autonomous administrative region for a minority on the Soviet model. The Hungarian (Magyar) Autonomous Region was established in Transylvania in 1952 with considerable administrative freedom for the nearly 600,000 Hungarians who lived there. (Note, however, that only about a third of Romania's Hungarian population *did* live there.) But this privileged position lasted only till 1960 when two counties with strong Hungarian majorities were moved out of the Autonomous Region and three counties with strong Romanian majorities formerly outside the region were moved into it. The percentage of Hungarians now in the region was reduced from 77 to 62 percent. At the same time the name of the region was changed to the Mures Hungarian Autonomous Region, thus taking away the distinctively Hungarian appelation it had once enjoyed. In 1968 a new reorganization affecting the whole country abolished the autonomous region altogether. In only Harghita and Kovasna of the newly formed thirty-nine counties (*judeţe*) did the Hungarians have a majority. It is true the majorities were overwhelming; in Harghita Hungarians made up nearly 90 percent of the population and in Kovasna nearly 80 percent. But the significant point is that, instead of making *one* large county in the area concerned (as had originally been promised) made up of more than half a million citizens, mainly Hungarian, the Bucharest authorities chose to divide this large Hungarian concentration between the *two* counties mentioned above. Other counties created under the reorganization had populations of well over half a million, but these were in the ethnically Romanian parts of the country. Thus what happened to the Hungarians in Slovakia in 1960 happened to the Hungarians in Romania in 1968.[27]

It can be argued, of course, that these reorganizations were not carried out solely, or even primarily, to fragment the Hungarian minority. Especially in the Slovak case there were sound economic and geographical reasons for the changes made in 1960. The Romanian reorganization of 1968 can also be defended on similar grounds. But the Romanian aim, steadily and patiently pursued, of dismantling the Hungarian Autonomous Region was evident soon after the Hungarian Revolution of 1956, with its dangerous impact in Transylvania. And the point is that whether the anti-Hungarian aim of the Slovak and Romanian changes was primary or secondary, its impact was obvious. No one would claim this impact was wholly incidental—still less accidental.

6. *Erosion of rights and privileges.* This has been going on ever since the then progressive provisions for minorities were first embodied in law after the communists gained power. As mentioned earlier, the process has not been steady or consistent throughout. The pace has quickened and slackened, with periods when official respect for minority rights has even appeared to increase. But in Bulgaria separate Turkish educational facilities were abolished in 1958, and all along there were almost no Turkish newspapers and periodicals. By contrast, the privileges and facilities of the Hungarians in both Czechoslovakia and Romania were impressive. Indeed, they have remained impressive, despite the erosion, by the standards of minority treatment elsewhere in the world. But it is precisely the erosion, and not the original generosity, that is uppermost in the minds of the Hungarian minority. Probably the most frustrating has been the steady closing of schools for Hungarian children in both countries. This was accelerated in the 1970s. A natural corollary to the school closings has been the reduction in the number of subjects in advanced education that are available in Hungarian.

The most striking single example of educational discrimination was the abolition in 1959 of the Hungarian "Bolyai" University in Cluj in Romania. This was done in typical fashion by merging it with the Romanian "Babes" University in the same city. At the time of the merger numerous assurances were given that education in Hungarian would be fully respected at the new institution, now called the "Babes-Bolyai" University. Steadily, however, what was intended came about. The university quickly became much more Babes than Bolyai, until by the mid-1980s it was a thoroughly Romanianized institution with no subjects, except Hungarian philology and literature, being taught in Hungarian.[28] Generally, in Romania educational facilities for Hungarians have been elbowed aside more unceremoniously than in Slovakia.

Indeed, the strength of Hungarian opposition to proposed changes in a Slovak law on higher education in 1985 succeeded in preventing (or postponing) measures that could have begun the gradual abolition of specifically Hungarian higher educational facilities.[29]

Hungarians in Romania and Slovakia have felt so strongly about these educational facilities because it is on their retention that the survival, not just of Hungarian culture, but of a *distinct Hungarian identity* depends. Hence, their grievances over this issue have been deeper and more bitter than those over cultural facilities like the supply of newsprint, newspapers and journals, and cultural amenities in general. These are important, but it is on education that the national identity ultimately depends. Similarly, though Hungarians in both Romania and Czechoslovakia have genuine complaints about their lack of proportionate representation in central party, executive, and legislative posts and in local government positions—sometimes when the Hungarian population is in a clear majority—they feel less strongly about these than about being able to educate their children as ethnic Hungarians.

These generalizations, it should be noted, apply to Romania and Slovakia. They do not generally apply to Vojvodina in Yugoslavia. Here, for well over thirty years, ethnic Hungarians have enjoyed rights, privileges, and facilities that probably make them the best-treated large minority in the communist world. But many Hungarians in the Vojvodina feel a certain unreality or impermanance about their situation. A purge of the Hungarian cultural press in Novi Sad, the capital of Vojvodina, in 1984 caused considerable nervousness, and there have been cases of excesses by both Serbs and by the Hungarians themselves. Indeed, the situation since the beginning of the 1980s may have deteriorated. But this should also be seen against the political, economic, and psychological deterioration in Yugoslavia as a whole. There is little or no comparison between Vojvodina, on the one side, and Romania and Slovakia, on the other, and the national minority question, as it is known elsewhere in Eastern Europe, still hardly exists there.

7. *Selective industrialization.* This is a broad and controversial question deserving of more exhaustive treatment. To put it briefly, a centrally directed strategy of industrial location by authorities in Bucharest or in Prague (or Bratislava) can adversely affect the situation of Hungarian minorities, even when it is ostensibly bringing more prosperity. There have been several cases in both Romania and Czechoslo-

vakia of the introduction of new industries into minority areas that will make for economic benefit eventually. But these new industries also serve to undermine the traditional Hungarian way of life and are another means of eroding the compactness of the population. This is because the central authorities insist on bringing in many Romanian or Slovaks, as the case may be, to work in the new factories and, very often, to manage them. This last also means that qualified Hungarians who could have been used as managers have to take lower positions or go elsewhere.

8. *Direct repression.* There have been many genuine examples of this—as well as many cases of inaccuracies, exaggerations, distortion, and sheer invention. Some of the latter originate in the countries affected; others stem from émigré circles abroad. On the other hand, there must be many genuine cases that never get reported at all. Instances of physical repression have certainly increased over the years as the pressure on most minorities has roused active or passive resistance. Nothing, however, has ever come near equaling the wholesale slaughters, mainly of Germans and Hungarians, that occurred immediately after World War II. (This, of course, was the revenge of the victorious or liberated peoples for the years of savagery they themselves had had to endure.) Still, the massacres of Turks in Bulgaria in 1984–85 for resisting "Bulgarization" showed that wholesale killings were not quite a thing of the past, even though the scale was smaller. But what has become frequent in Transylvania—less so in Slovakia —have been arrests, short-term imprisonment, detention without trial, and just plain beatings. Few such cases ever become known in the West, or even outside the local community where they occur. Only when they affect well-known personalities like the Slovak-Hungarian poet Miklós Duray, who was imprisoned twice in the early 1980s, and András Sütö, the son of the well-known Transylvanian writer, István Sütö, do they arouse some attention.[30] But, again, despite the growing numbers of cases of physical repression, some sense of proportion should be maintained. Except in the case of the Turks in Bulgaria, most minorities have been free of the blatant persecution that was common in many parts of Eastern Europe in the interwar years.

It should also be pointed out that, at least in Transylvania, many Romanians who bear little or no resentment against Hungarians began, after about 1975, to feel a growing aggressiveness on the part of the latter. There also apparently have been many cases of Romanians being beaten up by Hungarians. Some Romanians are convinced that the alleged Hungarian aggressiveness comes from their feeling that Hungary has the support of the Soviets on the minority question because Moscow wishes to punish Ceaușescu for his independence policy. In the midst of such bitterness it is a pleasure to read an eyewitness account, by one of the leaders—a Hungarian—of the Jiu Valley miners strike in 1977 in which Romanian and Hungarian miners stood together with no rivalry or mutual hostility.[31]

The Human and Historical Aspects

The points just itemized are useful as analytical indicators showing the scope of the minorities problem and the measures taken to deal with it. But, taken alone, they give little idea of the human and historical background of the situation that they dissect, or of the atmosphere in which national—or race—relations in Eastern Europe take place. Nor can they reflect those elements of the instinctive, or often the irrational, that pervade and sometimes dominate these relations. These are all things that can best be felt or sensed rather than analyzed. To describe them adequately is almost impossible, but perhaps some idea of them can be conveyed.

Some nations in Eastern Europe have mingled with one another over the centuries; others have lived side by side, keeping themselves largely to themselves. Thus Hungarians and Slovaks and Hungarians and Croats mingled considerably over the centuries of Hungarian dominance. In Transylvania there was less interaction among the races. Germans and Hungarians generally kept separate from one another and from the despised Romanians. In Kosovo, Serbs tried to keep rigidly separate from Albanians, and in Bulgaria relations between Bulgarians and Turks were always uneasy and distant. Bulgaria had a generally good record in its treatment of minorities. The royal government during World War II saved the country's Jews from deportation, and subsequently all Jews wishing to do so could emigrate to Israel. About 340,000 Turks left the country between 1912 and the beginning of World War II.[32] After the callous plans for total expulsion in the late 1940s were scrapped, government policy was generally to leave the remaining Turks alone. Bulgarian society also did the same. The Turkish minority, concentrated in two main areas, in the northwest and southeast of the country, was overwhelmingly agrarian by occupation; in southeast Bulgaria many grew tobacco. There were villages that were wholly Turkish, and many Turks rarely saw a Bulgarian. Only in the towns was there some interaction, and here the Bulgarians were generally tolerant, although many as a result of education in both home and school harbored the same resentment as Dimitrov against these reminders of the "Turkish yoke."

These varying degrees of closeness obviously resulted in varying degrees of knowledge and understanding. Slovaks and Hungarians in Slovakia, for example, often knew each other very well, while Bulgarians and Turks in Bulgaria knew each other hardly at all. Many Slovaks spoke Hungarian—under Hungarian rule this was compulsory for some jobs. Not as many Hungarians could speak Slovak; but plenty could. Very few Bulgarians could ever speak Turkish.

It should not be thought, however, that where mutual understanding existed, as between Slovaks and Hungarians, this brought friendship or even tolerance. Hungarians in Slovakia were generally contemptuous of Slovaks, and the official pre-1914 Budapest policy of assimilation through "Magyarization," though it brought considerable benefits to those prepared to submit to it, aroused a humiliated resentment among the steadily growing Slovak intelligentsia, which had to accept "Magyarization" or vegetate—or emigrate. Thus "anti-Hungarianism" became one of the mainsprings of Slovak nationalism. This was true of the clerical fascists of the Father Tiso variety, of democratic nationalists, as well as of communists like Clementis and Husák. Vladímir Mináč, an elderly Slovak writer, put it poignantly and emotionally in 1964: "Should one touch healed wounds? Are the wounds really healed? National antagonism is a tough flower; if we do not talk about it, that does not signify it does not exist. Our relationship to the Hungarians not only molded our national fate but also formed our way of thinking; it formed the soul of our nation."[33]

After the humiliations under Hungarian rule many Slovaks then went on to experience the repulsive aspects of Hungarian irredentism in the 1930s and of the subsequent Hungarian occupation of some parts of their country. Croats experienced much the same from the Hungarians, and their feelings toward them were similar. (For Croats, however, Serbs were to become the prime enemy—in a way that the Czechs never became for most Slovaks.) There are parallels for such relationships in other parts of Europe: between Poles and Germans in Silesia, for example, and between Irish and English. The hatreds of the past color attitudes and policies of the present, and prejudices are passed on from one generation to another. Obviously they become diluted in time. Younger Slovaks, Croats, and Romanians are generally not as preoccupied with Hungarians as were their fathers and grandfathers. Similarly, younger Bulgarians are not as resentful as their elders over Macedonia. But passions can easily be rekindled. The assertiveness of the *Csemadok*, the Hungarian cultural organization in Slovakia, in 1968 raised the hackles of Slovaks of all generations,[34] and recent complaints by members of both the Hungarian minority in Romania, as well as by the Budapest government itself, have caused general offense in Romania. On this point most Romanians, for once, solidly supported their governmental line as expressed in the media, just as most Bulgarians have supported their government's anti-Turkish campaign. The most innocent and reasonable pleas by members of the Hungarian minorities are denounced as the prelude to irredentism. It is a depressing response but, in the light of history, a perfectly understandable one. And the cause of the Hungarian minorities is not helped by the shrillness of some exile organizations in the West, some of whose members have indeed never resigned themselves to the losses of Trianon.

The Impact on State Relations

Minority questions are primarily a domestic matter for the government of the state concerned. These governments have always, almost without exception, insisted that they are *exclusively* a matter of domestic concern and have rejected any representation or even observation on the subject from abroad as interference and even a breach of their sovereignty. But those who lead these governments are only too sensitively aware that, given the complexities of Eastern Europe's history, no cocoon, however protective, can shield from outside attention a policy toward one group of citizens who have conationals and their own historic homeland, not just elsewhere, but often next door.

It is necessary, therefore, to consider the attitudes and reactions of the "metropolitan" states toward the treatment of their former citizens abroad. The states concerned are Hungary, Turkey in relation to the Bulgarian Turks, and Serbia in relation to the fate of Serbs in Kosovo.

The Serbian case is unique. First, because Serbia is a republic within a larger federation and, second, because Kosovo is part of the republic of Serbia. But Kosovo is an autonomous province that enjoys self-government and, within the Yugoslav federation, practically all the rights, including that of veto, enjoyed by the six republics. Nor is it the government of Kosovo, dominated by relatively pliable Albanian officials, that has caused the national troubles. The national troubles in Kosovo are caused by the Albanian popular movement there. It is, as previously mentioned, the result of a rapid population growth that has made the Albanians some 80 percent of the population, of a resurgence of Albanian national feeling, and of a memory of cruel Serbian domination—a domination much more recent than either the Hungarian or the Turkish domination elsewhere. All this makes the Serb case unique. But it is precisely this resurgence of a former *Untermensch* minority—now a "nation of state"—against the previous dominant nation—now a minority—that makes the Kosovo case relevant despite its special characteristics.[35]

The Serb reaction to the humiliation in Kosovo has so far consisted of fulminations in Belgrade (see chapter 11). Serbian leaders as well as Yugoslav leaders at the federal level have deplored the Serbian exodus and have plainly alluded to direct Albanian responsibility for it. The Belgrade press has often expressed its alarm, and the authorities in Pristina, the capital of Kosovo, have been criticized for their alleged inaction.

But it is difficult to see what can be done against a trend that appears inexorable. Although Serbian numerical preponderance in Kosovo had disappeared more than two hundred years before, Serbian power in Kosovo ended only with the fall of Alexander Ranković in 1966. Violent Albanian demonstrations took place in 1968, and demands increased subsequently for the granting of full republic status for Kosovo. Tito himself, who appeared to have considerable sympathy for Albanian demands in Kosovo, nevertheless adamantly rejected the claims for republic status. He probably realized, as many more have subsequently done, that republican status for Kosovo could well start the unraveling of the whole Yugoslav federation (see chapter 11). The Albanian population in both Macedonia and Montenegro would certainly want to join such a new republic. These two republics would strongly oppose this and, farther north, similar demands by the *prečani* Serbs to join Serbia could lead to serious trouble in Croatia. And many Yugoslavs would, in any case, feel that full republic status for Kosovo was the last step before demands for incorporation into Albania proper, especially if serious instability were to engulf Yugoslavia. But during the 1970s the demand for republic status grew more widespread in Kosovo, and before the end of the decade it had become clear that the now huge Albanian numerical preponderance in the province was leading to an intolerable situation for most of the Serbs remaining.

Then, just as Ranković's removal had sparked off the first important postwar disturbances in Kosovo, the death of Tito sparked off the second in 1981. But these were much more serious, resulting in many more deaths than the official number of thirteen. Since then, thanks to judicial repression and much tightened police control, the situation has remained outwardly quiet. But no one would be surprised if the tension did not again erupt into bloody disturbances.

In addition to those reasons given above, one of the main reasons why Tito and his successors refused Kosovo republic status was fear of Serbian reaction. At the very foundation of the federation Serbian leaders had objected to even provincial or regional status for Kosovo. Again, the historical heritage intervenes; it is difficult for non-Serbs—most of all Westerners—to appreciate the emotional and romantic attachment of Serbs, whatever their station or education, to this historical homeland where Serbia's culture and Christian faith matured and where the Serbian empire flourished and then perished at the emotion-drenched battle of Kosovo in 1389. The very presence of Albanians in this region —not to mention their preponderance—is resented by most Serbs. And now it is the Serb presence there that is coming to an end—an end more ignominious than glorious.[37] Moreover, the humiliation in Kosovo is only one aspect, albeit the hardest to bear, of a general sense of Serb frustration over several trends in the present Yugoslav situation. From a position of dominance of prewar Yugoslavia, Serbia has obviously slipped to, at best, a primus inter pares status; and even this is a status most non-Serbs reject and most Serbs doubt. In such a mood of national pessimism (or self-pity) it would need only a few serious incidents in Kosovo in which Serbs were the sufferers to provoke a national demand for vengeance there. This could even lead to Serbian soldiery simply moving in and cutting a broad punitive swath in parts of the province. At the very least, serious tension can be expected in 1989, the six hundredth anniversary of the Battle of Kosovo.

The reaction of Turkey to the Bulgarization of Turks needs only a brief discussion. With the final demise of the Ottoman Empire and with Kemal Atatürk's creation of the new modern Turkey, Turkish political interest in Europe sharply declined. The loss of its European possessions had been a drawn-out process that came to be regarded as inevitable long before the last one was lost. There was little sense of nostalgia, therefore, or even of humiliation. Not that the new Turkey ignored its large residue of empire scattered up and down the Balkan peninsula. The big exchange of population with Greece in the 1920s and the repeated offers to repatriate Turks from Bulgaria were evidence of that. In the years since World War II more than 200,000 Bulgarian Turks have gone back to Turkey, some by expulsion, others by agreement. But Turkey's interest in the remainder was neither aggressive nor even inquisitive.

But, obviously, what began happening in late 1984 could not be ignored by any Turkish government.[37] Even so, Turkish reaction was at first quite restrained. This may have been partly due to a desire not to jeopardize a growing economic relationship with Bulgaria, to a wish to avoid strained relations with Sofia as well as with Athens, and to a Turkish embarrassment over the whole question of minorities in view of their own atrocious record in dealing with Armenians and even Kurds. But growing public anger, fueled by often sensationalist rumors in the domestic press, forced the government into a series of protests and strong public statements. These in turn were strenuously rejected by Sofia on the predictable grounds that they violated Bulgaria's sovereignty. Anyway, the members of the Turkish minority had suddenly realized they had always been Bulgarian and had voluntarily agreed to change their names! That was Sofia's story, and it stuck to it.

Finally, the Hungarian reaction. This is the most centrally important of all in the context of East-Central Europe and of relations between communist states. The Turkish-Bulgarian interaction is marginal to Eastern Europe and has fewer possible repercussions. The possible Serb reaction to Kosovo could, as discussed above, have widespread ramifications. But the Hungarian reaction already affects three East European states—Hungary itself, Romania, and Czechoslovakia—and, if the lot of Hungarians there were to worsen, could also affect a fourth, Yugoslavia. It also affects the relations among communist states and tests the validity of a crucial communist axiom concerning nations and international relations. Last, it could affect even Soviet policy in Eastern Europe since the question of national minorities could become so sensitive as to necessitate Moscow's intervention.

Any discussion of Hungarian reaction must begin by emphasizing that irredentism is no longer considered a viable proposition in either Hungary itself or in the lost lands of St. Stephen. Obviously many would embrace (or re-embrace) it if the international situation were to be radically transformed in a potentially favorable way. (Some Hungarian intellectuals privately admit this.) But no one except a warped romantic (though some still exist) believes in such a possibility. There are also many Hungarians, however, who reject irredentism less because of its impracticality as because of its immorality. Hungary's behavior in the 1930s and during the war, the suffering it caused to other countries and to itself, the lasting damage it did to Hungary's name—the bad memory of all this led to a considerable moral revulsion against irredentism.

Hungary's communist leaders, for additional or quite different reasons, also rejected irredentism. Obviously they could never have questioned the Soviet-prescribed international order in Eastern Europe, but there are also indications that very few were inclined to. The "internationalist-Muscovite" leadership group, dominated by Mátyás Rákosi, never cared for even Hungary's legitimate interests anyway. Imre Nagy, who obviously did, was certainly against irredentism, as were all but a surrealistic few of the thousands of active revolutionaries in 1956. Indeed, mainly through clandestine radio broadcasts, the revolutionaries were anxious to repudiate Soviet-inspired charges that they longed for pre-Trianon Hungary. Later, the Soviet-installed Kádár regime repeated time and again its denials that Hungary had any territorial claims on its neighbors. As for Kádár himself, personally as well as ideologically, he appears to be revolted by the idea of nationality strife and is thought to have long resisted efforts by several of his senior colleagues to conduct a more aggressively active policy toward Romania and Czechoslovakia to gain better treatment for the Hungarians there.

But the rejection of irredentism has not meant any lack of concern, and the concern has grown with the pressure on the minorities. Thus the minorities issue in Hungary has been a classic example of a regime first having to respond to public pressure and then taking up the issue with some energy. Beginning in 1956 with no legitimacy whatever and then gaining some through its pragmatic, conciliatory, and successful policies, the Kádár regime could well have frittered it away in the 1970s had it not followed public opinion on this score. It was the intellectuals, mostly the writers—the traditional voice (or conscience) of the nation—who first turned the minority question into a public issue. Gyula Illyés, the dean of Hungarian writers, made himself the champion of the cause of Hungarians abroad in the late 1960s. He appears to have considered this the work that would crown his life's achievement, and he quickly gathered support from fellow writers—some close to the regime, others not—and a much larger group of educated people of different age groups. Illyés is several times unofficially reported to have used his great prestige to pressure the political leadership, including apparently Kádár himself, to take a stronger stand on the minority issue.[38] Occasionally Illyés was the target for vitriolic attacks in the Romanian press for his pains.[39]

After Illyés's death in 1984 his place was taken by Sandor Csoóri, considered by some an even greater writer than Illyés. Csoóri has shown himself even more vigorous in publicizing and protesting cases of discrimination against members of the minorities. In 1985 he wrote the introduction to a book by Miklós Duray on the Hungarian minority in Slovakia. After Czechoslovak representations, the Hungarian regime felt obliged to act, and Csoóri was barred from publishing for a year.[40]

The Csoóri case shows the Hungarian regime's dilemma. Ideally it has wanted the whole subject to go away. Convinced that it would not, it realized not only that it would have to do something, but also that it be seen to do something. But though it could take the subject up, it could never take it over. The fact that it had to take even nominal cognizance of Czechoslovak protests in the Csoóri-Duray case showed the limits to what it could do. There were reports that it made representations in Prague, Bratislava, as well as Bucharest on the minorities issue and got little satisfaction. It also inspired or allowed articles in the press that referred to the minorities, often in the guise of historical discussions. But for many years the rules of the Soviet alliance allowed it to do nothing publicly, and, as in the Csoóri case, it had at least to make the appearance of restraining its own firebrands.

The Hungarians have pressed their case more strenuously with Romania than with Czechoslovakia—and rather more openly. This is because the sheer size of the Hungarian minority there, as well as the sharper edge of Romanian policy, have given them more to complain about. Also Romania's often strained relations with the Soviet Union and unique position within the alliance made circumspection less necessary. As already mentioned, many Romanians—and not only they—have speculated whether Hungarian moves on the minority question had not been inspired by Moscow in efforts to warn Romania. Was it, for example, coincidence that the then Hungarian Politburo member, Zoltán Komócsin, obliquely but obviously referred to the condition of the Hungarian minority in 1971 shortly after Ceauşescu had completed a visit to China that infuriated Moscow?[41] Certainly the Romanians saw no coincidence, and, judging from occasional references by Ceauşescu himself, they have suspected Soviet complicity in Hungarian actions on several occasions. After allowing for Romanian paranoia, they would seem to be right. In the same way the Soviets have sometimes inspired or allowed the Bulgarians to step up their propaganda on Macedonia when their own relations with Yugoslavia have been tense. But, if Soviet complicity is accepted, then it must be stated that they appear to have used this weapon with some restraint, almost halfheartedly.

Such restraint would indeed be understandable. First, it would be a weapon difficult to control since the "socialist camp" is studded with actual or potential minority, national, and territorial issues—not least in the Soviet Union itself. Second, Hungary's complaints extend to Slovakia as well; and Slovakia is part of a country that has been one of Moscow's most loyal allies, needing, especially since 1968, all the stability it could get. Finally, once the precedent has been set of encouraging one country to interfere in the affairs of another, it may be difficult to set the limits deemed appropriate. This would particularly apply to an emotional issue like national minorities.

As it was, during the 1970s it appeared that, as the minority issue became more acute and as the Soviet grip on Eastern Europe slackened, the Hungarian government did show more initiative and independence. The issue led to a series of direct Hungarian-Romanian confrontations, not perhaps serious but certainly unseemly as between fraternal socialist states, with the Soviet role apparently inconspicuous to the point of irrelevance. (The same applied to Sofia's policy on Macedonia. It acquired an exclusively Bulgarian character and ceased to be an unerring weather vane of Soviet-Yugoslav relations.) Representations were made directly to the Romanian government on several occasions. At a meeting between Kádár and Ceaușescu in 1979 some promises appear to have been made by the Romanian side that were not kept. As the situation deteriorated, Hungarian public opinion pressed the regime for more direct action.[42] This culminated in the minority issue being raised at the Hungarian party congress in March 1985, the first time this had been done. Though the references made to it might seem bland to an observer, they were an important symptom.[43] Feeling on the subject increased subsequently. It has led to a serious deterioration in Hungarian-Romanian relations and could eventually lead to the same in Hungarian relations with Czechoslovakia.

For many years the Budapest regime has pleaded that the Hungarian minorities abroad should be a "bridge" between Hungary and the three countries concerned. They should help open up the borders and facilitate the socialist international atmosphere to which all were striving. To strengthen its case, Hungary has taken pains to give its own several, small minorities exemplary conditions. (This was partly also to preempt the familiar Slovak argument—from Tito to Husák—that Budapest should take care of its Slovaks before asking Bratislava to take care of its Hungarians.) But only Yugoslavia so far has gone even part of the way to building that bridge. Czechoslovakia and Romania have both regarded the very concept of a bridge as a means of keeping the image and memory of Hungary always bright and of alienating the minorities from their proper loyalties. Hungarian concessions to its own minorities are spurned as irrelevant, even hypocritical, because there is no such problem in Hungary. The minority issue charges relations between the three countries with hatred, suspicion, and paranoia. It is a wedge between countries, not a bridge, and it may indeed only be time before it so threatens East European unity that Gorbachev, or his successor, finds it placed squarely in his unwelcoming lap.

An Insoluble Problem

The problem appears insoluble because a satisfactory solution for the minorities, as minorities, is in contrast with the prevailing notion of national unity and integrity. Even assuming that the passions of history that infuse the problem could be exorcised, the problem would remain. This is because modern national leaderships refuse to accept any notion of the distinctiveness of groups of citizens living within their state boundaries to which they should accord treatment that only perpetuates that distinctiveness. In the East European case the Bulgarian, Romanian, and Czechoslovak (Slovak) leaders have often stated that they would gladly give all their citizens the same rights and privileges, expecting from them in return the same loyalties and responsibilities. But they balk at separate treatment for separate citizens, which, in effect, would put them in a privileged position. The citizen body is indivisible.

It is, therefore, the Bulgarian regime that, ironically enough, has been the most direct, consistent, and apparently successful in reaching this goal. From Bulgarian history it inherited Turkish, Pomak, and Gypsy minorities as well as the Macedonian "problem." It solved the Macedonian problem by a statistical sleight of hand. It then proceeded to reduce the Gypsies to as much conformity as possible and then absorbed the submissive Pomaks. The Turks were a more difficult problem, and the process of harassment and forced integration appears to have begun in the early 1970s. The 1984–85 name-changing episode was, therefore, the last phase and was apparently prompted by the approaching decennial census designed to show a completely integrated nation.

The Bulgarians set about their task quietly, almost stealthily. They were able to do so because Bulgaria is a tucked-away backwater, little visited and seldom noticed. It would be impossible for either the Bucharest or the Bratislava regime to reach their desired goal so easily or quickly. In the first place the international uproar would be much greater. It would also create a crisis in the Warsaw Pact alliance that the Soviet Union would have to settle. Finally, in the Romanian case the problem is on a different scale from the Bulgarian. There is not only the large Hungarian minority but also the German. In the latter case Ceauşescu appears to have reversed his early opposition to emigration. Now he is quite willing for Germans to buy themselves out—at prices ranging from DM 10,000 to 30,000. This problem seems on its way to a gradual—if not very dignified—solution. Most young Germans want to go, and all the older ones will die.[44] The Hungarians are quite a different proposition. Here intermarriage, the steady breaking down of the compactness of the Hungarian-populated areas, economic policies, and, perhaps eventually, a breakdown of Hungarian morale are what the Romanian regime is evidently counting on. In Slovakia the obstacles to integration are fewer. Certainly the regimes in both Bucharest and Bratislava are hoping for a steady process of assimilation, arguing in the meantime that their policies for comprehensive development cannot be undermined by sectional considerations and that it is in the long-term interests of their Hungarian minorities to enter the mainstream of national life.

The End of Empire

In historical perspective the question of national minorities in Eastern Europe constitutes the final act—perhaps more the epilogue—in the great drama that began in the early nineteenth century and ended after World War I. This drama saw the retreat and then the defeat of the great empires that had dominated Eastern Europe and the rise of modern national states in their place. The Ottoman, the Habsburg, and the German empires all disappeared but left in their wake larger and smaller settlements of people whose status changed from masters to minorities. Similarly, the Hungarians, first a part and then a partner of the Habsburg empire, dominated the lands of St. Stephen and then saw their territory dismembered. The Serbs, too, after liberation from the Turks, became themselves an imperial power seeking to dominate the peoples who now formed Yugoslavia. They also have recently suffered the indignities of frustration and constriction. (Only the Russian empire is the great exception. It too suffered total defeat in 1917, but then revived and, in a different guise and with different methods, now dominates almost the entire region. But the Russian empire, unlike the others, never left Russian communities in its wake—at least in the West. Russian minorities in Asia are a different question.)

In the place of the old imperial nations, new "nations of state" have emerged, vigorous in their nationalism, self-conscious, sensitive, and often resentful. The Slovaks, Romanians, Croats, Bulgarians, and Albanians all have these characteristics in some degree. They are pressing their old masters. They have more will and are determined to make the territory in which they live their own. And the very fact that most of them live under Soviet domination makes them all the more eager to exercise their sovereignty and domination wherever they can.

But it would be unwise for these new nations, richly deserving of their sovereignty though they are, to push their dominance too fast and too far. Certainly a nation like the Serbs should never be provoked too far. Nor should the Hungarian will to survive be underestimated. National survival has, of course, always been part of the Hungarian mystique—constantly invoked. But many Hungarians today see the survival of their compatriots abroad as essential to the survival of the whole nation. Many thoughtful young Hungarians are devoting themselves to working for the preservation of the Hungarian identity. They have no ill will toward any nation but are just part of a most complex situation that could unfold in a tragedy affecting not one but several nations.

Finally—to show how old and apparently intractable the problem is—a passage from Harold Temperley's *History of Serbia*. He is referring to the many Serbs who historically lived in greater Hungary:

> During the eighteenth century the Serbs had been subjected by the Hungarian Government to oppression, on account of their religious and civil independence. Speaking generally, they had maintained their religious independence, but had lost all political rights. But during the twenty years previous to 1848 they were subjected to a new pressure, that of forcible nationalisation—that is, of Magyarisation. The policy of the Magyar Government had, in

the eighteenth century, been purely religious in its oppression, and had persecuted Serbs who had refused to become Catholics. Now it assumed a more dangerous form, and persecuted Serbs who refused to become Magyars. The policy was national and Chauvinistic in the highest degree; official pressure was applied to destroy the Serb language and to stamp out the Serb nationality in Hungary. Put shortly, a Serb who declared himself a Magyar was well treated, a Serb who refused to do so was not. Then in the year 1848 came the great uprising, when revolution and freedom were everywhere and every king in Europe trembled on his throne. Headed by Kossuth, the Magyars hastened to extort a pledge of complete self-government from the Austrian Emperor. Liberation and political rights were in everyone's mouth. It was natural that the Hungarian Serbs should think that the Magyars, who spoke so loudly of liberty, would be willing to grant some concessions to them. A deputation of Hungarian Serbs waited on Kossuth in April 1848, and held an interview which has become famous.

They demanded the recognition of their language in public documents, and of their rights as a nation. "What," said Kossuth, "do you understand by 'nation'?" "A race," said the head of the deputation, "which possesses its own language, customs, and culture, and self-consciousness enough to preserve them." "A nation," said Kossuth, "must have its own Government." "We do not go so far," said the head of the deputation. "One nation can live under several different Governments, and again several nations can form a single State!" The discussion outlined clearly the two views — the Magyar unable to conceive a nation unless as a unified government, the Serb conceiving a nation as a linguistic unity. The views were irreconcilable, and Kossuth, recognising the fact, dismissed the deputation with the famous words, "In that case, the sword will decide!" It did, though not in the way anticipated either by Magyar or by Serb.[45]

Today the solutions may be somewhat less radical than Kossuth prescribed. But a few decades ago they were infinitely worse, immeasurably worse than anybody in the nineteenth century could have contemplated. The problem, however, has not gone away. More broadly, what this passage from Temperley shows is that Eastern Europe's history, despite its repudiation by the communists, has the habit of catching up on them all too often.

A Summing-Up

In October 1986 the thirtieth anniversary of the Hungarian Revolution was commemorated in the West and in Hungary. Perhaps the poignant event was marked most by the issuance of a joint appeal signed by over a hundred intellectuals in the GDR, Poland, Czechoslovakia, Hungary itself, and in Romania, too. The signatories evoked the national and human freedoms that were the ideals of 1956 and that remained "our common heritage and inspiration."

All the signatories could be described as "dissidents" whose activities made them objects of police attention and often persecution. How representative were they? In some respects not very; yet these "dissidents" unmistakably voiced the yearnings of most of their contemporaries. They were carrying on, often in unromantic circumstances, the East-Central European tradition of intellectuals speaking for the nation. Everybody knew that the realities of East European life, of which the fate of the Hungarian Revolution had been the cruelest reminder, made the aims of the 1986 appeal seem impossible to attain—at least for the indefinite future. Moreover, the prosaic demands of everyday life in Eastern Europe made other tasks vastly more urgent and relevant. But, in spite of all this, the 1986 appeal still expressed the deep-seated aspirations of most East Europeans as well as their deep-seated dissatisfaction. At least in this, the dissidents and the silent majority were one.

What the October 1986 signatories wanted, what the revolutionaries of 1956 wanted, is dismissed by many in the West as "excessive." The demands of Solidarity, even the very existence of Solidarity, were similarly labeled, as was the whole Prague Spring for that matter. The sophisticated gloss on such views is that national and human rights in Eastern Europe could weaken European stability and eventually world peace. Therefore, what Westerners regard as their birthright is too risky a proposition for East Europeans, too risky in a game whose rules are laid down by the Soviet Union.

Obviously there is logic to such Western attitudes. (They are infinitely more serious than those residues of racial prejudice, the bearers of which hold that East Europeans are unfit for democracy and who are grateful for the "Pax Sovietica.") But many Westerners, in their justifiable concern about European stability, often forget the degree of realism that has developed in Eastern Europe, too. No one there wants freedom on a heap of radioactive ruins. Nor is there any expectation —certainly not among those signing the October 1986 appeal—of any quick achievement of their aspirations. There is also less illusion in Eastern Europe about Soviet power and determination than there is in the West. But, while accepting (however reluctantly) the Soviet Union's interest in Eastern Europe, most East Europeans do not accept the Soviets' self-appointed role as sole arbiter of the region's destiny. And while recognizing the contrast between dreams and reality, they also insist they have as much moral right to freedom as anybody else. The ideal should not be abandoned. The "lack" of East European moderation has been little more than the mirror image of Soviet rigidity in insisting on a system as unviable as it is unethical.

Few would find much irresponsibility about such an attitude. Indeed, the remarkable thing about reform and dissent in Eastern Europe over the last thirty years has been its restraint. The provocation has come from authority, not from those trying to modify, reform, or regenerate authority.

But descending now from aspirations to realities, it remains to sum up in a few points Eastern Europe's past and present under communist rule and then hazard a guess at some likely future developments.

In the late 1940s and early 1950s the Stalinist system was imposed on Eastern Europe. It made revolutionary transformations that were to be lasting:

1. It changed a region of mostly agrarian economies into one of industrialized economies.
2. It totally reorientated Eastern Europe's economic relations toward the Soviet Union.
3. It involved total dominance by the Soviet Union.
4. It transformed the social structure and culture in most countries

from peasant-dominated to worker-dominated, creating at the same time much upward, professional, and social mobility.
5. It imposed a political system of one-party control and one accepted ideology with an economic structure characterized by state ownership and control.

It was Stalinism that set the pattern for development in both the Soviet Union and Eastern Europe, and since Stalin's death in 1953 most of domestic policy in both regions has been dominated by his legacy. *Despite efforts to modify and even dismantle the Stalinist system, it still dominates Soviet and East European public life.* One vital ingredient of it—systematic terror—has been drastically limited, but the institutions of Stalinism have survived.

Stalinism to most East Europeans meant:

a. The suppression of personal freedoms.
b. Economic policies causing great hardship.
c. The suppression of national independence.

Because of this, it encountered opposition based on the often inseparable factors of popular dissatisfaction and nationalism:

1. *Popular dissatisfaction* manifested itself as early as 1953, above all in East Germany, Czechoslovakia, and even in Bulgaria. It culminated in the revolution in Hungary and the near-revolution in Poland in 1956. With the outstanding exception of Poland (1968, 1970, and 1980–81), active expressions of popular dissatisfaction tended to diminish after the climax of 1956.
2. *Nationalism*. Yugoslav nationalism in 1948 and Albanian nationalism in 1961 resulted in these two countries leaving the Soviet alliance. Hungary tried and failed to leave it in 1956. Romania successfully carved out a considerable degree of foreign policy autonomy beginning in the 1960s and had generally preserved this autonomy a quarter of a century later. The popular upheavals in Poland were also strongly tinged with nationalism.

Khrushchev's first de-Stalinization campaign, an important part of which was his attempted rapprochement with Yugoslavia, was a direct onslaught, not so much against the Stalinist system, as against its methods. It hastened the upheavals in Hungary and Poland. Both were defeated: the Hungarian Revolution by direct means, the Polish October first by seeming to accept it, then by eroding it, mainly with the aid of the leader, Władysław Gomułka, who had been originally hailed as its symbol.

Each in its own way, the Hungarian Revolution and the Polish October were expressions of that *spontaneity* that the Soviet system, whether at home or in Eastern Europe, has considered to be its most serious threat. The former, of course, was a direct assault on the system. The latter was more insidious in that, had it been allowed to proceed unhindered, it would have led to systemic reform in both the economic and political fields, with unpredictable consequences.

What Khrushchev was prepared to tolerate, and even to urge energetically, was reform directed and controlled from above. The reform encompassed:

1. Intrabloc relations, using the Warsaw Pact and Comecon as instruments. The aim was to make Soviet–East European relations more equitable by replacing Stalinist exploitation with a policy of Soviet economic support and by at least the appearance of more genuine diplomatic cooperation. At the same time closer cohesion would make ultimate Soviet control more effective.
2. Domestic affairs, through the initiating in most countries of controlled economic reforms, the abandonment of mass terror, and the introduction of more political relaxation.

Khrushchev's new system of relations with Eastern Europe was only partially successful. He failed to develop suitable integrating mechanisms within the alliance. His overtures to Yugoslavia failed, and the deepening of the schism with China facilitated the total defection of Albania and the partial defection of Romania. Even with the GDR, relations with the Ulbricht regime after the building of the Berlin Wall in 1961 (itself literally a concrete measure against spontaneity) were slowly becoming strained. In most East European countries the economic reforms were implemented less than thoroughly. But there was little popular dissatisfaction because living standards in the 1960s were rising rapidly, and in all countries there were varying degrees of political relaxation.

In Czechoslovakia, however, the pressure for more effective economic reform coincided with a period of growing political flux. Despite the real differences between the Prague Spring and the Polish October, both were pressing for systemic changes in the economy and politics, and both had the element of spontaneity that proved difficult to control. Thus the period between 1956 and 1968 began and ended with

expressions of East European spontaneity. One—the Hungarian (1956)
—was in the form of a popular uprising. The two others—Poland
(1956) and Czechoslovakia (1968)—were efforts at self-regeneration by
the regimes concerned, conducted with the enthusiastic support of
large sections of the population. They were both suppressed—one by
attrition, the other by invasion—because of their incompatibility with
the Soviet system.

The fate of the Prague Spring put paid to many hopes inside Eastern
Europe and to many expectations outside it. A quarter of a century ago
many Western analysts believed (this writer among them) that
de-Stalinization, nationalism, and the need for economic reform were
pushing the system in Eastern Europe toward more pluralism both
internally and in bloc relations. Three factors, however, were under-
played or ignored in this optimism:

1. The determination and repressive abilities of the Soviet Union.
2. The conservatism of many of the elites in Eastern Europe itself and
   the strength of their coercive powers.
3. The difficulty in maintaining a steady, gradual process of change
   without the process being punctuated by upheaval.

August 1968 shattered this optimism, and yet twenty years later the
urge for change is still there, and the need for it is even greater. The
crucial question is—or is going to be—how long can the Soviets and
the East European elites resist it, or how long will they continue to
think there is still more to be gained by resisting the urge than accommodating to it or even embracing it?

The suppression of the Prague Spring set the course of East European development for twenty years:

1. It was the last effort by an East European regime to radically change
   its system of rule and, therefore, itself.
2. It marked the end of the Marxist-Leninist ideology as a live and
   generative force.
3. Change of the system, if any, would now have to emanate more from
   outside pressure than from inside ferment.
4. The Soviet Union, by its action and its theoretical justification for it
   in the Brezhnev Doctrine, lost whatever very slim chance it may
   have had of containing East European nationalism in a system where
   it was respected even if it could not be fulfilled.

The "Brezhnev era" in Eastern Europe really began after the invasion of Czechoslovakia. It was characterized in these ways:

1. Soviet attempts to reshape the alliance and establish a new East European system that would obviate the likelihood of a new Prague Spring and the consequent need to suppress it. This system was not inimical to change as such but to spontaneous manifestations of it.
2. The resumption on a much bigger scale of East-West détente. Soviet determination to press détente was such that they were prepared to jettison the East German leader, Ulbricht, who saw dangers to it for the GDR.
3. Détente, in turn, was to have profound effects in Eastern Europe. In economic terms it led to a period of massive Western financial lending to Eastern Europe that had serious economic effects.
4. Upheavals in Poland in 1970 and 1980, the second of which, Solidarity, was an unprecedented demonstration of popular will.
5. The initiation and continuance of economic reform in Hungary that contained at least the potential for systemic innovation. Though inconsistently and, in some respects, unsuccessfully implemented, this reform became symbolic of a general relaxation making Hungary the yardstick by which developments in other countries were often measured.

In the meantime in Yugoslavia the reforms of the middle and late 1960s were immediately followed by spontaneous outbursts of liberalism and nationalism. These were put down and followed by a period of reaction and disintegration leading to serious questions about the very future of Yugoslavia.

In the first half of the 1970s it seemed to many that the situation in Eastern Europe had become stabilized, largely through Soviet control, Western credits, and rising standards of living. But this stability was short-lived. It was undermined by a serious economic downturn caused by:

1. Drastic increases in Soviet energy prices as a result of the two world oil price explosions of the 1970s.
2. Overindulgence in Western credits, often necessitating further credits to service existing debts.
3. The impact of worldwide economic recession.
4. Incompetent and/or inflexible economic management involving, with the exception of Hungary, the refusal to initiate economic reform.

The destabilizing effects of this economic downturn were aggravated by a number of political considerations:

1. The slackening of the Soviet grip on Eastern Europe.
2. The impact of détente that encouraged societal assertions and tended to moderate regime reaction to it. Included here is the election of a Polish pope in 1978.
3. Rising sociopolitical discontent, especially in Poland, caused by the disappointment of rising expectations combined with perceived regime ineffectiveness.
4. Enfeeblement and then disarray in the Kremlin caused by the death of three leaders in three years.

It was no surprise that, when the East European upheaval came, it came in Poland and in the form of a societal assault on the system. Solidarity, the outcome of this assault, first a trade union and then a national movement, looked for a deceptive few months as if it could eventually change the whole recent history of Eastern Europe. But it was eventually smashed by Poland's own army and police, in a display of force that was a numbing reminder of how efficient even the domestic forces of coercion in Eastern Europe can be.

Eastern Europe seemed now to be mainly dominated by an awareness that change was both inevitable and necessary, but also by some apprehensiveness over the form it would take. The awareness was prompted by:

1. Gorbachev's accession to power in Moscow.
2. The impending departure of several Eastern European leaders.
3. A general political uncertainty.
4. A bad economic situation.

Two more points should be added here. The first was uncertainty over the future of relations with the West. All East European states were interested in either improving Western contacts or at least maintaining them. The summer of 1984 when the GDR publicly begged to differ with the Soviet Union over relations with Bonn still remained vividly in the mind. (And since then even Czechoslovakia and Poland had dropped their opposition to closer Western contacts.) But Eastern Europe was uncertain about how much leeway Gorbachev would be prepared to give them in international relations and how far the West would be interested in resuming them after the financial debacle of the late 1970s.

The second point, which had now begun to impress itself on many East Europeans, was the threat to the environment. This was still not given anywhere near the importance it deserved. Chernobyl certainly dramatized the problem. But the damage Chernobyl caused was only one aspect of a danger that could progressively become more lethal, not only for the quality of life, but also for life itself.

Communist rule in Eastern Europe has been vitiated by the clash of incompatibles. The Soviet dilemma of cohesion and viability in Eastern Europe has been mentioned several times in this book and by the author elsewhere. But this dilemma provides only the larger frame within which efforts to harmonize other incompatibles have so far foundered: nationalism and internationalism, legitimacy and control, initiative and discipline, incentive and equality.

Toward the end of the 1980s these incompatibilities were causing real concern about the future of the system. But this concern only raised in turn the most basic question of all: whether the *system* could survive *systemic* reform. This was Gorbachev's main dilemma. It was a dilemma that could be ducked, rather than tackled, by resorting to changes of procedure, organizational reform, reordering priorities, modernization. But if the ducking did not stop sometime, then the only future was one of inexorable decay.

Gorbachev's decisions about the Soviet future will not be made any easier because of their possible impact on Eastern Europe. If he were to duck the dilemma and choose reordering, reorganizing, and modernizing, he would gain a politician's respite. But this would be briefer in Eastern Europe than at home because the need for change there is more urgent. But if he were to tackle it and go for real systemic reform, then the instability would be greater in Eastern Europe than in the Soviet Union. This is quite simply because—allowing for the growing dissatisfaction of many kinds in the Soviet Union itself—the system has always been thinner and shallower in Eastern Europe. Systemic reform might go a long way toward strengthening both the Soviet state and the Soviet system. But what nearly forty years of communist rule has shown is that what might be good for the Soviet Union is not necessarily good for Eastern Europe. Again, the incompatibility syndrome!

Unless the present system in Eastern Europe were to be replaced, or allowed to evolve into one allowing the expression of the popular will and the realization of national aspirations, then the future would consist of a mixture of stagnation and instability, punctuated by upheaval.

Many Soviet observers realize this. So do some Soviet leaders. Gorbachev might well bring all of his energy, ability, and imagination to bear on forging yet more "socialist relations of a new type." But he would soon learn that there was little meeting ground between Soviet interests and East European aspirations.

Appendixes

I Chronology of Main Events in Eastern Europe Since 1969

The choice of "main events" is always arbitrary. Some readers will look for events that are not included. Some will wonder at the inclusion of others. But the choice was not made lightly, and the author tried to make it as catholic as possible. The year of commencement, 1969, was chosen because it followed the watershed year of 1968, which changed the course of East European history.

1969

January
Suicide of Jan Palach.

March
Meeting of political-consultative committee of Warsaw Pact in Budapest renews call for European security conference.
Romanian Defense Council reconstituted. Ceauşescu becomes chairman. (Took place immediately before Warsaw Pact meeting.)
Ninth Yugoslav party congress held in Belgrade.

April
Comecon summit session.
Husák replaces Dubček as Czechoslovak party leader. Dubček becomes chairman of the Federal Assembly. Husák to Moscow.

April and May
Elections for all legislative bodies in Yugoslavia. For first time there was a choice of two or more candidates for most of the seats.

May
Gomułka expresses wish to negotiate normalization of Polish relations with FRG on basis of recognition of the Oder-Neisse frontier.
Romanian party leader Ceauşescu and Premier Ion Gheorghe Maurer visit Moscow.
Agreement signed between Soviet Union and Bulgaria allowing for Bulgarian workers to be recruited for work in Soviet Union. (By the end of 1972 between 25,000 to 30,000 Bulgarian workers in Soviet Union.)

June

International conference of communist parties in Moscow.

August

Agreement comes into force on repatriation to Turkey of 10,000 to 15,000 Bulgarian Turks.

President Nixon visits Romania.

Former Romanian Premier Chivu Stoica and former first party secretary Gheorghe Apostol lose posts in Standing Presidium of party. (Ceauşescu's position strengthened.)

October

Ceauşescu fails to attend celebrations in East Berlin marking twentieth anniversary of founding of GDR.

December

Warsaw Pact summit meeting in Moscow.

Czechoslovak radio stations report appointment of Dubček as ambassador to Turkey.

Two prominent Hungarian economic officials call for common, convertible Comecon currency.

1970

January

Tax benefits for private artisans in Hungary.

Yugoslav Central Committee session discusses Croatian nationalism.

Bloc Central Committee secretaries for ideology meet in Sofia. (Typical of post-1968 "consensus" politics inside Soviet alliance.)

Important modifications of the 1968 federalization statute in Czechoslovakia involving greater centralization.

March

Chancellor Brandt and GDR Premier Willi Stoph meet in Erfurt (GDR).

April

Bulgarian Central Committee plenum decides on establishment of agro-industrial complexes.

May

Brandt and Stoph meet in Kassel (FRG).

Yugoslavia and Hungary agree to conduct their future bilateral trade on a convertible currency basis. (This actually began in January 1973, and the currency used was dollars.)

Thirty-million dollar Euro-loan for Hungary. (First Western loan to Hungary had been a $10 million investment loan from Lazards. The May 1970 loan was Hungary's fourth Western loan and brought the country's total Western debt to $70 million.)

Establishment of Comecon Investment Bank. Romania originally not a member but joined when the bank commenced operations in January 1971.

Catastrophic floods in Romania: 162 dead, 78,000 homeless.

Dubček officially recalled as Czechoslovak ambassador to Ankara; also stripped of his last public position, that of deputy to the Federal Assembly.

August

West German–Soviet treaty "normalizing" relations between the two countries.

September

Zhivkov and Ceauşescu meeting on the Danube marks beginning of intensive personal contacts between these two leaders.

October

Romanian Premier Maurer suffers serious injuries in car accident.

December

Polish–West German treaty "normalizing" relations signed in Warsaw.

Polish government decree announcing steep increases in food prices followed by serious rioting in Baltic coast towns resulting in many deaths.

Gierek replaces Gomułka as Polish party leader in extensive leadership reshuffle. Jaroszewicz replaces Cyrankiewicz as premier.

Warsaw Pact summit in East Berlin.

1971

January

Publication in Prague of the "Lessons from the Crisis in the Development of Party and Society . . ." (directed against Dubček and the Prague Spring reformers).

Gierek as new Polish party leader visits Gdansk and Szczecin and succeeds in ending strikes there.

February

Polish Central Committee condemns Gomułka, Zenon Kliszko, and Bolesław Jaszczuk.

March

Negotiations begin between Czechoslovakia and West Germany on "normalization" agreement.

New Polish Premier Jaroszewicz meets Cardinal Wyszyński.

New Soviet ambassador Stanislav Pilotovich arrives in Warsaw.

March–April

Twenty-fourth CPSU congress in Moscow.

April

Tenth Bulgarian party congress.

May

Ulbricht forced to resign as East German party leader. Replaced by Erich Honecker.

June

Amendment to Yugoslav constitution adopted providing for more self-management and greater power for the republics at expense of federal center.

Ceauşescu visits China, North Korea, and North Vietnam. Angers Soviets.

Mieczysław Moczar removed as Polish Central Committee secretary.

June–July

Top-level polemics between Hungarian Politburo member Zoltán Komócsin and Romanian Politburo member Paul Niculescu-Mizil on situation of Hungarian minority in Transylvania.

July

Ceauşescu initiates Romania's "minicultural revolution," thought to have been inspired by his visit to China the previous month.

August

First meeting of Brezhnev with top East European leaders in the Crimea. (Up to 1976 the meetings were held collectively in the Crimea. After 1976 and up to 1982 Brezhnev held bilateral meetings in the Crimea with the East European leaders.)

September

Four-power agreement on Berlin.

Paul Goma's *Ostinato* published in West Germany—the "Romanian Solzhenitsyn."

Brezhnev visits Yugoslavia.

November

Tito visits United States.

December

Tito meets Croatian leaders—Tripalo, Dabčević-Kučar, and Pirker—at Karadjordjevo. Attacks their separatist nationalism and, in effect, forces their resignation. The "Croatian crisis" at an end.

Sixth Polish United Workers' party congress appears to set Poland on a reform course. Jaruzelski becomes full Politburo member.

1972

January

"Passport-free" and "currency-free" travel between GDR and Poland instituted. Lasted one year.

February

Western media report execution of Romanian General Ion Şerb allegedly for passing secrets to the Soviets.

May

Israel's premier, Golda Meir, visits Romania.

Ceauşescu and Tito inaugurate Iron Gates hydroelectric and navigation system.

July

Beginning of wave of political trials in Czechoslovakia, which had had no parallel since the end of the 1950s.

September

Strike of Romanian coal miners in Petroşani. Ceauşescu visits scene and pacifies them.

October

Tito forces purge of liberals from Serbian party leadership.

Gierek visits Paris and begins his contact with Western capitals.

"Experimental" changes announced in Polish system of economic planning and management.

Liviu Ciulei, great Romanian theater director, ousted from directorship of the Bulandra Theatre in Bucharest.

November

Hungarian Central Committee plenum that began slowdown and partial reversal of New Economic Mechanism.

December

"Basic Treaty" regulating relations between West Germany and the GDR.

Czechoslovakia's first nuclear energy plant begins operation at Jaslovske Bohuniče.

1973

January

First Industrial Agricultural Complex established in Bulgaria.

Czechoslovak official says Gabčikovo-Nagymaros hydroelectric dam to begin construction in 1976 and due for completion 1984–85.

Hungarian trade union leadership calls for protection of workers against those seeking to exploit New Economic Mechanism (one of the early signs of worker reservations about NEM).

Radical reorganization of local government at parish level in Poland.

May

West German–Czechoslovak "normalization" document signed after six rounds of negotiations starting in March 1971. (Treaty finally signed December 1973.)

June

Helsinki conference on security and cooperation in Europe opens. (To last two years.)

Ceauşescu visits West Germany (the first East European communist leader to do so).

Elena Ceauşescu made full member of the RCP Executive Committee.

Albanian Central Committee plenum gives signal for purges that were to last over two years and affect prominent cultural, military, and economic leaders.

August

Hungary admitted to GATT after having first applied in 1969.

Death of Walter Ulbricht. Willi Stoph replaces him as chairman of GDR Council of State, and Horst Sindermann replaces Stoph as premier.

December

Ceauşescu visits the United States.

Appointment of first Hungarian, Czechoslovak, and Bulgarian ambassadors to West Germany.

1974

January

Josef Smrkovský, one of the heroes of the Prague Spring, dies.

New Yugoslav constitution promulgated.

February

Reports about trial of a Turkish teacher in Bulgaria for stirring up "Turkish nationalism." New Yugoslav constitution promulgated.

Albanian Central Committee plenum condemns "cultural liberalism" of purged officials Fadil Pacrami and Todi Lubonya.

March

Reszö Nyers, the "father" of the Hungarian NEM, loses his position as Central Committee secretary. Gyorgy Aczél and Lájos Fehér, both strong reformers, also lose Central Committee Secretary posts.

May

Tenth Yugoslav party congress held in Belgrade.

First section of Prague subway goes into operation.

West German concern Siemens announces it will start up joint company with Hungary.

Polish Politburo member and Central Committee secretary Franciszek Szlachcic loses both those positions and is demoted to deputy premier (often regarded as second to Gierek in the regime).

July

Ivan Abadzhiev, Bulgarian Politburo member and Central Committee secretary, loses both these positions (regarded by many as Zhivkov's "heir apparent").

Announcement in Hungary of price increases on a whole range of domestic goods. Prices to come into force only on 1 January 1975.

Agreement on permanent working contacts between Polish government and the Vatican.

Purge of Albanian Defense Minister Beqir Balluku and chief of staff Petrit Dume.

August

Labor unrest reported in Polish ports of Gdansk and Gdynia over new work norms.

September

First Bulgarian nuclear plant completed at Kozloduy.

Bulgarian Politburo member and deputy premier Ivan Popov visits United States (the highest-ranking Bulgarian *ever* to visit the United States).

Hungarian writer Antal Végh publishes "Why Hungarian Soccer Is Sick" (overnight succès de scandale).

October

Gierek visits United States.

GDR constitution of 1968 changed drastically in some aspects. "New" constitution of 1974 emerges.

November

Henry Kissinger makes one-day visit to Yugoslavia.

Romanian communist party's eleventh congress. Ceauşescu declines secretary-general post for life.

1975

January

Antonin Novotný, former Czechoslovak president and party leader, dies.

February

Chivu Stoica, former Romanian premier, dies.

March

Eleventh Hungarian party congress. Nyers loses Politburo seat.
György Lázár promoted to Politburo. (Later to become Hungarian premier.)
Yugoslav Premier Dzemal Bijedić visits Washington.

April

American-Romanian trade agreement gives MFN privileges to Romania.
Yugoslav Premier Dzemal Bijedić visits Moscow.

May

Polish Central Committee plenum decides on radical reform of territorial administration.
Hungarian Premier Jenö Fock resigns. Succeeded by György Lázár.
Party leader Gustáv Husák replaces the ailing Ludvík Svoboda as president of Czechoslovakia.
Death of Cardinal Mindszenty.
Albanian Central Committee plenum on economic affairs results in purge of Politburo members Abdyl Këllezi and Koço Theodhosi.

June

Lyudmila Zhivkova named head of committee on art and culture in Bulgaria.
First congress of the proregime Pacem in Terris Catholic organization in Czechoslovakia.

July

Manea Manescu replaces Ion Gheorghe Maurer as Romanian premier.
President Gerald Ford visits Poland.
Greek premier Konstantin Karamanlis visits Bulgaria. (First visit at that level since World War II.)
CSCE summit meeting in Helsinki.

August

President Gerald Ford visits Romania.
Chinese premier Chou En-lai gives famous interview to the Zagreb *Vjesnik* (28 August), in which, amid conjecture about a Chinese-led Romanian-Yugoslav-Albanian grouping, he quotes the proverb "Distant waters cannot quench fire."

October

Long-term Treaty of Friendship, Cooperation, and Mutual Assistance between GDR and Soviet Union.

December

Seventh Polish United Workers' party congress.

Protest of fifty-nine Polish intellectuals against proposed amendments to the constitution involving greater stress on party control and on alliance with the Soviet Union.

Todor Zhivkov visits West Germany. First Bulgarian head of state to visit FRG.

1976

January

New system of economic regulation introduced in Hungary.

Romania admitted to Group of 77 developing countries.

February

Austrian Chancellor Bruno Kreisky visits Czechoslovakia (first visit by an Austrian government leader since World War II).

All East European party leaders at CPSU twenty-fifth congress in Moscow.

March

Monsignor Lászlo Lékai enthroned as archbishop of Esztergom (primate of Hungary), replacing Cardinal Mindszenty (April 1976 Lékai named cardinal).

April

Todor Zhivkov visits Greece.

May

Ninth SED congress in East Berlin. Honecker strengthens grip on party, but Willi Stoph returns as premier in place of Sindermann. Erich Mielke, minister of state security, elected to Politburo. Honecker becomes chairman of State Council (head of state).

June

Todor Zhivkov visits Turkey.

Gierek visits West Germany.

Workers' riots and demonstrations in Poland lead to immediate withdrawal of proposed food price increases.

June–July

Conference of European communist parties in East Berlin.

September

Committee of intellectuals formed in Poland to provide "legal, financial, and medical aid for workers subjected to repression and physical terror" during the June 1976 disturbances. Committee became known as KOR (Committee for the Defense of the Workers).

October

President Giscard d'Estaing makes "unofficial" visit to Poland and consults with Gierek.

New Yugoslav law—Associated Labor Law—passed providing framework for "model democracy."

November

Brezhnev visits Yugoslavia.

Brezhnev visits Romania.

Romania becomes first Comecon country to conclude individual agreement with the European Community.

Seventh Albanian party congress. Sixty percent of Central Committee members purged. Definite signs of cooling relations with China.

Wolf Biermann, East German troubador, deprived of GDR citizenship while on visit to West Germany. Arouses storm of East German intellectual opposition.

December

Milan Huebl, Jiři Mueller, Jaroslav Šabata, and Antoni Rusek released in Czechoslovakia. (These were the last four Dubček supporters sentenced in 1972 to be released.)

Hungarian bishops issue collective warning about "basis communities"—spontaneous Catholic groups at the parish level.

Inauguration of Huta Katowice, huge and controversial new Polish metallurgical plant.

1977

January

Founding of Charter 77 in Czechoslovakia.

Thirty-four Hungarian intellectuals express their support for Charter 77.

February

Festivities connected with fifteenth anniversary of Friendship Pipeline on Czechoslovak territory.

March

ROPCiO (Committee for the Defense of Human and Civil Rights) formed in Poland. (Another dissident group, less socialist and more nationalist than KOR.)

Earthquake hits Bucharest (4 March). Over 1,500 killed.

Romanian Orthodox Patriarch Justinian dies.

April

Rainer Kunze, prominent East German writer, leaves GDR.

May

Bulgarian Politburo member and Central Committee secretary Boris Velchev dropped from both positions.

Czechoslovak dramatist and dissident Václav Havel released from custody after having been detained since January 1977 on unspecified charges.

Celebration of centenary of Romanian independence.

June

Archbishop František Tomášek, apostolic administrator of Prague, created cardinal.

Kádár visits Italy and the Vatican.

Kádár and Ceauşescu meet on Romanian-Hungarian border, agree to open consulates in Debrecen and Cluj.

Justin Moisescu appointed Romanian patriarch.

July

Kádár visits West Germany.

Albanian party daily *Zëri i popullit* carries 7,000-word attack on China.

August

Tibor Déry, "grand old man" of Hungarian literature, dies.

Strike of Romanian coal miners in the Jiu Valley. Ceauşescu goes to scene and pacifies them, but only with difficulty. Substantial concessions in wages and work conditions followed by ruthless victimization.

September

"Partial agreement" between Vatican and Czechoslovak government. Tomášek to be archbishop of Prague; independent Slovak church province established.

Former Romanian Central Committee member Károly Király (ethnic Hungarian) sends letter to Politburo and Central Committee secretary Ilie Verdeţ complaining about treatment of Hungarian minority.

Tito visits China and North Korea.

November

Dissident Romanian writer Paul Goma arrives in West.

December

Rubik's Cube first sold in Hungary.

President Jimmy Carter visits Poland.

Proposal adopted in Yugoslavia to increase maximum size of private holdings in agriculture up to twenty hectares in hilly country.

Centenary of Hungarian Institute for Rabbinical Studies (only such institute in either Soviet Union or Eastern Europe).

1978

January

Minor economic experiment begun in Czechoslovakia to improve quality and variety of goods ("complex experiment of effectiveness and quality control").

United States returns Crown of St. Stephen to Hungary.

Tenth anniversary of beginning of Hungarian NEM.

Ceauşescu celebrates sixtieth birthday amid great official adulation.

February

Unofficial "Flying University" begins semester in Warsaw.

March

Meeting between GDR head of state and party leader Erich Honecker and Bishop Albrecht Schoenherr, head of East German Evangelical church. "Concordat" agreed upon involving concessions to Christians in GDR.

Romanian politician Ilie Verdeţ loses Central Committee secretaryship but becomes chairman of State Planning Commission and a first deputy premier. Cornel Burtícă loses Central Committee secretaryship. Stefan Andrei replaces Gheorghe Macovescu as foreign minister.

One hundredth anniversary of Treaty of San Stefano. Bulgarian and Yugoslav media clash over differing interpretations, especially over Macedonia.

April

Béla Biszkú dismissed as Hungarian Central Committee secretary responsible for cadres and mass organization affairs (was considered number two man to Kádár).

Gierek visits Moscow amid some evidence of tension between Moscow and Warsaw.

Ceauşescu visits United States.

May

Hungarian Society for Sociologists founded.

Romanian official Mihnea Gheorghiu attacks article by Hungarian writer Gyula Illyés on Hungarian minority in Romania.

July

Western agencies report that China stops aid to Albania.

Albanian letter attacking China.

Ion Pacepa (lieutenant general in Romanian security service) defects to West.

August

The Marcali blue jeans factory begins operation in Hungary; result of cooperation with and sponsorship by Levi Strauss Company of United States.

Hua Kuo-Feng, leader of Chinese communist party, visits Romania and Yugoslavia.

Polish and Czechoslovak dissidents urge mutual cooperation.

September

Compulsory military education introduced in GDR.

Comecon Executive Committee discusses aid for Vietnam.

Cardinals Wyszyński and Wojtyła lead powerful Polish church delegation to West Germany.

October

Election of Karol Cardinal Wojtyła as Pope John Paul II.

November

Warsaw Pact summit meeting in Moscow. Ceauşescu refuses Soviet demand to increase military expenditure and makes dispute public when he returns home.

Illichovsk-Varna ferry link between Soviet Union and Bulgaria established.

1979

January

On occasion of her sixtieth birthday Elena Ceauşescu referred to as chairman of Central Committee Commission for Party and State Cadres.

Western media report Romania asking Saudi Arabia for delivery of 3 million tons of oil a year. (Romania had previously been importing 5 million tons a year from Iran.)

Thirtieth anniversary of founding of Comecon.

Brezhnev visits Bulgaria with Chernenko, thereby strengthening speculation that the latter is his designated heir.

Bulgarian New Economic Mechanism begins in agriculture.

February
Eduard Kardelj dies.

March
Ilie Verdeţ becomes Romanian prime minister in place of Manea Mănescu.

May
Tito's last visit to Moscow.
Collective state presidency inaugurated in Yugoslavia.
Death of Istvan Bibó in Hungary, advocate of "The Third Road."

June
John Paul II makes first visit to Poland as pope.
Elena Ceauşescu enters Romanian cabinet as chairman of the National Council of Science and Technology.

July
Lyudmila Zhivkova becomes member of Bulgarian Politburo.

August
West German Chancellor Helmut Schmidt visits Poland.
East European motor tourists to Romania ordered to pay for their gasoline in hard currency.

September
Confederation for an Independent Poland (KPN) founded as dissident group in Poland (a right-wing, nationalist split-off from ROPCiO).
Ludvik Svoboda, former president of Czechoslovakia, dies.
Hoxha speech indicating some willingness to develop relations with Western countries.
Hysni Kapo, number three man in Albanian regime, dies.

October
Czechoslovak writer-dissident Pavel Kohout forced into exile.
Sentences passed on six Czechoslovak Charter 77 members and human rights activists. (Two hundred fifty-four Hungarian intellectuals protest in November at these sentences.)

November
Twelfth Romanian CP congress ends with unprecedented outburst against Ceauşescu by former Politburo member Constantin Pîrvulescu.

December
Chernenko visits Bulgaria.
"Adria" oil pipeline inaugurated (Hungarian, Yugoslav, Czechoslovak project).

1980

January
Bratislava overtakes Brno as second largest city in Czechoslovakia, itself a sign of Slovakia's growth.

February
Eighth congress of Polish United Workers' party. Jaroszewicz voted out of Politburo. Edward Babiuch succeeds him as premier.

March
Ernö Gerö, leader of Hungarian party at time of 1956 revolution, dies.
Twelfth Hungarian party congress endorses continuation of reform.
"Set of Measures" approved in Czechoslovakia designed to "improve the system of planned management."

April
Hungarian consulate in Cluj reportedly opened after great delay. (Had been agreed upon between Kádár and Ceauşescu in June 1977.)

May
Tito dies (4 May).

June
Unofficial document calling for extensive political reform circulating in Poland. Prepared by the DiP group (Experience and the Future). (Same group had issued a similar document calling for reform in May 1979.)
Károly Király addresses a second letter to Verdeţ, now Romanian premier, complaining about treatment of Hungarian minority (see September 1977).

July
Western bankers, faced with a request for another Polish loan, question Poland's credit-worthiness for the first time.
Local strikes in Poland in anticipation of meat price increases.

August
Strikes in Gdansk, Szczecin, and Baltic coast spread throughout Poland.
On 31 August Gdansk Agreement signed by government representative and strikers' representatives led by Lech Wałęsa. Birth of the trade union Solidarity.
Babiuch out as premier. Replaced by Józef Pinkowski.
East German government doubles minimum amount West German and other foreigners are obliged to spend per day in GDR.

September
Stanisław Kania replaces Gierek as Polish party leader.

October
Cesław Miłosz awarded Nobel Prize for Literature.
GDR head of state and party leader Honecker in a speech in Gera gives four essential points for normalization of relations with West Germany. Most important point is recognition by Bonn of East German citizenship.

November
Helsinki CSCE follow-up conference opens in Madrid.

December
Summit meeting of Warsaw Pact members in Moscow to discuss situation in Poland. Kania and Pinkowski attend for Poland.

1981

February
General Wojciech Jaruzelski succeeds Pinkowski as Polish premier.

March
Serious incident at Bydgoszcz in Poland involving beating up by police of several trade unionists. General strike narrowly averted.

March–April
Serious rioting in Yugoslav autonomous province of Kosovo.

April
Polish government formally recognizes Rural Solidarity.
Sixteenth Czechoslovak party congress sees practically no change. Brezhnev present.
Tenth SED congress. Honecker presents proposals for economic reform.

May
Cardinal Wyszyński dies (28 May).

June
Brezhnev addresses critical letter about situation in Poland to all members of the Polish Central Committee, Kania, and the Politburo.
Grisha Filipov succeeds Stanko Todorov as Bulgarian premier.
Hungarian meat prices go up 10 percent after only a four-day warning.

July
Extraordinary Polish party congress held.
Monsignor Józef Glemp named to succeed Wyszyński as Polish primate.
Polish Sejm passes greatly liberalized censorship law (came into operation October 1981).
Czechoslovak Premier Štrougal calls for more specialization in Comecon ("We must invest in a more selective fashion and we must complement each other").
Lyudmila Zhivkova dies.
Amendment to Yugoslav constitution providing for a four-year term for the prime minister and the possibility of two successive four-year terms for members of the government.

September
Soviet ambassador Aristov sends letter to Polish regime complaining about "anti-Soviet actions" in Poland.
Solidarity congress takes place in Poland. Jaruzelski in speech to Sejm (24 September) speaks of preparations of both interior ministry forces and the military for emergency. KOR (Polish dissident group) formally disbands.

October
Bulgaria celebrates 1,300th anniversary of foundation of first Bulgarian state.
Hungarian underground publication *Hirmondó* (The Talker) first appears.
Jaruzelski becomes Polish party leader. (Now combines positions of party leader, premier, and minister of defense.) Deployment of special local task force in Poland to cover actual and potential trouble spots.

December

Martial law declared in Poland (12–13 December). Riot police backed by troops soon succeed in pacifying country. Worst incident occurs at Wujek mine, near Katowice, where eight miners killed and 39 miners and police reported injured.

Radio Tirana (18 December) announces "suicide" of Albanian Premier Mehmet Shehu.

1982

January

Bulgarian "New Economic Mechanism" (NEM) begins operation in entire economy.

March

Satirical drawing of Ceauşescu appears in Hungarian party daily *Nepszabadsag* (13 March).

Declaration of Vatican's Sacred Congregation for the Clergy forbidding active participation by priests in politics. (Aimed against Pacem in Terris movement in Czechoslovakia.)

April

Underground Solidarity organizes "interim coordinating committee" (TKK). Zbigniew Bujak of Warsaw named leader.

Ceauşescu visits China and North Korea.

Soviet foreign minister Gromyko visits Belgrade.

Professor Robert Havemann, famous East German dissident, dies.

May

New Yugoslav government installed with Mrs. Milka Planinc as premier.

Constantin Dăscălescu replaces Ilie Verdeţ as Romanian premier.

Underground Solidarity organizes May Day parade on 1 May.

July

Stefan Olszowski and Hieronim Kubiak dropped from Polish Central Committee Secretariat.

September

Władysław Gomułka dies (1 September).

Founding of Patriotic Movement of National Rebirth (PRON) in Poland.

"Shield-82" Warsaw Pact maneuvers held in Bulgaria, involving Soviet, East German, Polish, Czechoslovak, and Hungarian troops plus Romanian staff officers.

October

Cornel Burtică (former Romanian Central Committee secretary) purged, allegedly for irregularities in foreign trade. Ilie Verdeţ made vice-president of State Council.

November

Death of Leonid Brezhnev (10 November). Replaced by Yuri Andropov.

Release of Lech Wałęsa from internment.

Seventy-one Hungarian intellectuals send protest to Premier Lázár about treatment of Hungarian ethnic intellectuals in Transylvania.

Ramiz Alia becomes formal Albanian head of state.

December
Hungary's first nuclear reactor commissioned at Paks, on Danube 115 kilometers south
of Budapest.

1983

January
Death of Croatian leader and Yugoslav statesman Vladimir Bakarić.
Polish Primate Józef Glemp made cardinal.
New official Polish trade unions begin operating.

February
Yugoslavia negotiates new trade and economic agreement with EEC.
Trial of Míklos Duray, ethnic Hungarian dissident in Slovakia, for "antistate activities."

April
Death of Polish writer Jerzy Andrzejewski.

May
Chinese party secretary-general Hua Yaobang visits Romania and Yugoslavia.
Petr Abrasimov recalled as Soviet ambassador to GDR (was ambassador 1962–71 and
then 1975–83).
Literaturnaya Gazeta attacks novel by Dumitru Popescu, member of Romanian Political-
Executive Committee.

June
Second visit by Pope John Paul II to Poland.

July
Martial law formally lifted in Poland.
Amendment to electoral law introduced in Hungary making multiple candidacies oblig-
atory in national and local elections.
Charter 77 publishes Document No. 26 of 1 July 1983 on Czechoslovakia facing ecologi-
cal disaster.

September
American Vice-President George Bush visits Romania.
Bulgarian Politburo member and Central Committee secretary Alexander Lilov "resigns"
(considered another possible successor to Zhivkov).

October
Simultaneous announcement in Czechoslovakia and GDR about stationing of new Soviet
rockets on their territories in response to West German intention of stationing
cruise and Pershing missiles (INF controversy).
Lech Wałęsa awarded Nobel Peace Prize.
Inauguration of Albanian-Italian ferry connection between Durrës and Trieste.

November
Romanian parliament criticizes stationing of new medium-range missiles in both Eastern and Western Europe.

Jaruzelski relinquishes post of minister of defense but is voted chairman of the newly
structured National Defense Committee.

December
Nicu Ceauşescu (son of Nicolae and Elena) becomes head of Young Communists' League
and automatically minister of youth with a seat in the cabinet.

1984

February
Andropov dies. Succeeded as Soviet party leader by Chernenko.
Joint statement on human rights issued by KOR and Charter 77.
British Premier Margaret Thatcher visits Hungary.

May
Danube–Black Sea canal inaugurated in Romania.
Ecological movement formed in Hungary to protest the Gabčikovo-Nagymaros dam
project.

June
First Comecon summit meeting since April 1969.
Ceauşescu lays foundation stone for House of the Republic and Victory of Socialism
Boulevard in Bucharest. (Beginning of giant new "socialist" architectural complex.)

July–August
Public airing of differences between Soviet Union, on the one side, and the GDR, Hungary,
and Romania, on the other, over relations with West Germany. Honecker and Zhivkov
forced by Soviet pressure to cancel their planned visits to West Germany.

August
Romania the only Warsaw Pact country to participate in the Los Angeles Olympics.
Father Gheorghe Calciu, dissident Romanian Orthodox priest, released from prison.
(Had been sentenced to ten years in 1979.)
Amnesty declared in Poland for most Solidarity leaders and advisers.
Hungarian deputy premier Lájos Faluvégi refers to problem of Hungarian minority in
Transylvania in a public speech marking Romanian Liberation Day. (First time a
Hungarian government official had referred to the issue *publicly*.)
Yugoslav premier Milka Planinc visits Bulgaria.

September
First reports of series of bomb outrages in Bulgaria.
Celebration of 1,300th anniversary of founding of the Croatian church.
Li Xiannian, Chinese head of state, visits Yugoslavia.

October
Ceauşescu visits West Germany after Honecker and Zhivkov had had to cancel their
visits.
Father Jerzy Popiełuszko murdered in Poland by members of the security apparatus.
Czechoslovak writer Jaroslav Seifert awarded Nobel Prize for Literature.
GDR celebrates thirty-fifth anniversary.

November

Joint statement by the Charter 77 members and about the same number of East German peace activists. Timed for one year after the stationing of Soviet SS 21s and 22s on Czechoslovak and East German territory. A carefully worded protest against nuclear weapons, superpower politics, and the denial of human rights.

December

Beginning of government operation in Bulgaria forcing Turkish minority to "Bulgarize" their names. Operation completed by February 1985. Officially claimed that Turkish minority does not exist.

1985

February

Father Popiełuszko's murderers convicted and sentenced to long jail terms.
Honecker meets Bishop Johannes Hempel, leader of Evangelical church in GDR.

March

Chernenko dies. Succeeded as Soviet party leader by Gorbachev.
Thirteenth Hungarian party congress. Reform course confirmed. Károly Németh appointed deputy party leader to Kádár. Károly Grósz elected to full Politburo membership.

April

Gorbachev attends Warsaw Pact summit in Warsaw. Warsaw Treaty renewed for a further twenty years with option of renewal for a further ten.
Enver Hoxha dies (11 April). Succeeded by Ramiz Alia as party leader.
Honecker received in Vatican by Pope John Paul II.

May

Trial begins in Rome of Bulgarian air line official Serge Antonov accused of complicity in attempt to assassinate the pope in 1981.

June

Parliamentary and local government elections in Hungary based on multiple candidate system.

July

Soviet ambassador to Bulgaria, Grekov, criticizes Bulgarian economy in interview with a Sofia magazine.
Celebrations of 1,100th anniversary of death of St. Methodius culminate in service at Velehrad, Czechoslovakia.

August

Hungarian government finally decides to go ahead with the Gabčikovo-Nagymaros dam project.

September

French foreign ministry delegation visits Tirana.

October

Polish parliamentary (Sejm) elections produce a reliably estimated 70 percent turnout. Solidarity had urged boycott.

Kádár visits Britain.

Gorbachev visits Bulgaria.

October–November

European Cultural Forum, under CSCE auspices, held in Budapest.

November

Bulgarian Premier Grisha Filipov visits Yugoslavia.

Zbigniew Messner becomes Polish premier replacing Jaruzelski, who becomes chairman of the State Council (head of state). Olszowski resigns from Politburo and ministry of foreign affairs. Rakowski resigns as deputy premier. New Polish foreign minister is Marian Orzechowski.

Stefan Andrei replaced as Romanian foreign minister. Becomes a Central Committee secretary.

December

Six Albanians seek refuge in the Italian embassy in Tirana bringing Italo-Albanian relations to a halt.

Comecon summit publishes "Comprehensive Program on Technical and Scientific Cooperation."

American Secretary of State Shultz visits Romania and warns regime about its poor human rights record.

Bulgarian decennial census held. Aimed at showing a totally integrated state.

1986

March

Filipov replaced as premier by Georgi Atanasov in Bulgaria; becomes Central Committee secretary.

Seventeenth Czechoslovak party congress. No significant changes.

April

Thirteenth Bulgarian party congress. In spite of some speculation Zhivkov retains all positions.

Czechoslovaks sign cultural and scientific exchange agreement with the United States.

Eleventh SED congress. Gorbachev present. Honecker exudes self-satisfaction.

Gorbachev calls for "new economic mechanism" within Comecon.

June

Tenth Polish party congress. Gorbachev gives strong endorsement to Jaruzelski.

Hungarian primate Cardinal Lékai dies.

July

Amnesty law introduced in Poland.

Hungarian journal publishes a speech by CC secretary Szürös claiming special international role for small nations.

August

Church in Poland calls for month of alcoholic abstinence.

Rail link between Titograd in Yugoslavia and Shkodër in Albania finally completed. Albania becomes part of European rail system.

September

All Polish political prisoners officially announced as released.

Hungary promulgates Eastern Europe's first bankruptcy law.

Greek Premier Papandreou visits Romania and Bulgaria.

Serbian Academy issues memorandum critical of Yugoslav situation; refers to "serious situation" of Serbian nation.

October

GDR leader Honecker officially visits China—sign of important attempts at rapprochement between Soviet bloc and China.

Thirtieth anniversary of Hungarian Revolution marked by major efforts of Hungarian dissident groups to reinterpret the event. Joint statement by more than 120 East European dissidents calls for democratization throughout Eastern Europe.

Ceaușescu reaffirms Romanian foreign policy at Warsaw Pact foreign ministers' meeting in Bucharest.

November

Ceaușescu rejects Soviet-sponsored reform measures for Comecon.

Ninth congress of Albanian Workers party. Ramiz Alia's position strengthened.

CSCE follow-up conference in Vienna opens.

Split in Hungarian Writers Union; all but a few party members ousted from executive board.

December

"Social-consultative council" set up in Poland; designed to increase societal participation.

Czechoslovak Party Central Committee indicates receptivity to reform.

1987

January

Reform of Hungarian banking system goes into effect.

Jaruzelski visits Italy and makes official visit to Vatican for talks with John Paul II.

Charter 77 marks tenth anniversary with message to Czechoslovak public.

Meeting of bloc Central Committee secretaries for ideology and foreign relations.

Ceaușescu, in speech on his sixty-ninth birthday, continues to resist Soviet pressures for reform.

U.S. Deputy Secretary of State John C. Whitehead visits Poland amid indications of normalization of relations between the two countries.

Gorbachev outlines broad reform outline at CPSU Central Committee meeting.

February

Soviet Foreign Minister Shevardnadze visits Prague.

American sanctions against Poland lifted.

Wage freeze in Yugoslavia sets off unprecedented wave of strikes that lasts six weeks.

March

Celebrations in Hungary (commemorating revolution of 15 March in 1848); an occasion
for dissident marches and demonstrations.

Polish government sharply increases prices of food and fuel.

Husák confirms Czechoslovak party's recent commitment to reform.

Ceauşescu rejects Hungarian "interference" in Romania's minority policy.

Zhivkov outlines comprehensive reform program for Bulgaria.

Hungarian Central Committee Secretary Szürös visits United States.

April

Gorbachev makes official visit to Czechoslovakia.

In speech to trade union congress Honecker reaffirms GDR's rejection of reforms.

Honecker declines to attend West Berlin's opening celebration of 750th anniversary of
founding of Berlin.

May

Gorbachev makes official visit to Romania; differences with Ceauşescu as great as ever.

CPSU Politburo member and CC Secretary Ligachev visits Hungary; reaffirms "own roads
to socialism."

June

Pope John Paul II makes third visit to Poland.

Chinese Premier Zhao Ziyang begins visit to five East European countries: Poland, GDR,
Czechoslovakia, Hungary, and Bulgaria.

Hungarian-Romanian party talks on minority issues fail to produce agreement.

GDR leader Honecker visits Netherlands.

Bulgarian leader Zhivkov visits FRG.

Yugoslav party Central Committee holds plenum on Kosovo.

Major Hungarian party and state leadership reshuffle; Grósz replaces Lázár as premier.

July

West German Foreign Minister Hans-Dietrich Genscher visits Bulgaria.

U.S. Congress affirms six months' suspension of MFN status for Romania. Reagan had
asked for a six-month extension.

Hungarian Premier Grósz on "working visit" to Moscow.

Polish state and church leaders agree on way to support private farmers with U.S.
financial aid; ends four and a half years of impasse.

Zhivkov announces major administrative and political reform in Bulgaria.

Ramiz Alia asserts need for economic reform in Albania.

August

Charter 77 issues call for reconciliation and democratization in Czechoslovakia on anniversary of Soviet invasion.

Demonstration of youths in East Berlin against Wall.

First International Gypsy Folklore Meeting held in Hungary.

Joint meeting of Czechoslovak and Polish dissidents issue communiqué calling for East
European freedom.

Greece ends de jure state of war (since 1940) with Albania.

Israeli Premier Shamir visits Bucharest.

September

GDR leader Honecker pays official visit to FRG.

Meeting in Sofia of Soviet bloc Central Committee secretaries responsible for Comecon.

"Agrokomerc" scandal breaks in Yugoslavia.

Albania announces establishment of diplomatic relations with FRG.

Hungarian Premier Grósz announces economic stabilization including introduction of income tax.

United States announces resumption of relations at ambassadorial level with Poland.

II Biographical Sketches of East European Leaders

What follows are biographical details about the party leaders and prime ministers of the eight East European communist countries. (As explained later, there is no biography of the Yugoslav party leader because the annual rotation system affecting that office makes the incumbent a slippery fish indeed.)

An attempt has been made to avoid duplication by concentrating here more on the personal aspects of the individuals' careers; the policy aspects have been considered in the appropriate country chapters. Obviously there is some overlap, but hopefully the material is not too repetitive.

At a time when several East European party leaders are aging and/or ailing, writing biographies is a risky business. By the time this book appears some may have left the political or even the earthly scene. As a precaution, it would have been possible to include shorter biographies of their putative successors. But this would have been an even riskier business. In East European communist politics the crown prince of today is often the ambassador or even the collective farm chairman of tomorrow. Better, therefore, to let discretion be the better part of valor and stick with incumbents, however moribund.

As for prime ministers, in terms of power wielded only a few deserve to be preserved for posterity this way. But because of their office and the public exposure this brings, not only at home but also abroad, it is worthwhile setting down a few facts about them. The tendency in recent years has been for premiers to be primarily economic-technical officials; Messner in Poland and Lázár in Hungary are good examples of that category. In the first generation of communist rule they were mostly stronger characters, however, personally and politically. Mehmet Shehu in Albania was an example, but so also were József Cyrankiewicz in Poland (if in his own special way) and certainly Ion Gheorghe Maurer in Romania, not to mention the tragic Imre Nagy in Hungary. But even more recently Piotr Jaroszewicz in Poland wielded considerable power, as did—more constructively—Jenö Fock in Hungary. Today only Willi Stoph of the GDR, Branko Mikulić in Yugoslavia, and perhaps Lubomir Štrougal in Czechoslovakia are real political personalities. Mikulić is probably the strongest political personality in Yugoslavia.

The trend, therefore, is (roughly and erratically) toward economist prime ministers. The new party leaders will also be a new breed, very different in many ways from the old. Most of those still in office are part of the prewar generation, active in the communist underground in peace or war. Their successors will have been formed and groomed under the "socialist system." They will be primarily political managers, machine politicians, well educated in terms of letters and diplomas. They will be the East European Gorbachevs, an improvement on their predecessors in many ways, except perhaps in terms of human stature. They will be more predictable, probably less interesting as personalities. How responsive they will be to the pressures of their countrymen is difficult to say. Precisely on this point some may turn out considerably less predictable than they look.

Bulgaria

Todor Zhivkov
President of the State Council and General Secretary
of the Bulgarian Communist Party

Todor Zhivkov was born in September 1911 in the village of Pravets, a short distance north of Sofia. His family were poor peasants. After only a few years of elementary education in his native village he went to Sofia where he began a long career as a printer in the State Printing Office.

In 1928, when he was seventeen, Zhivkov joined the underground Young Communist League and joined the Communist party itself in 1932, working his way through various branches of the Sofia party organization. During the war he fought in the small Bulgarian communist resistance movement, ending his service as deputy commander of one of the Sofia operation zones.

In 1945 he began his quite meteoric rise in the party. He became a candidate-member of the Central Committee in that year and in 1948 was promoted to full membership. He became especially powerful in Sofia where for a time he held the top positions in local government and in the party organization. Although a "home" communist at a time of "Muscovite" dominance in the party leadership, he did not seem to suffer from it. Traicho Kostov, the leading "home" communist, was executed in 1949 and many others sentenced to terms of imprisonment. But Zhivkov, on the contrary, was made a Central Committee secretary and a candidate-member of the Politburo in 1950, moving up a year later to full membership status. He then appeared to have reached the top of his career ladder, and few were prepared for his election as first secretary at the sixth party congress in 1954.

It was all part of the de-Stalinization game of musical chairs that was being played in practically every East European country. Vulko Chervenkov, Bulgaria's "little Stalin," had to give up either the party leadership or the premiership, and he gave up the former. This in turn had to go to a "home" communist, and it went to Zhivkov, not because of any presumed leadership qualities but because he was considered safe, mediocre, and malleable.

He may have been all three in 1954, but he was not the man people thought he was. His political instinct developed, his skills grew, and, above all, his luck held. Within a decade he was the undisputed master of Bulgaria and on his way to becoming both an international figure and a national institution.

Zhivkov embodies some of the characteristics traditionally associated with the Bulgarian peasant: he is patient, wry, dogged, industrious, shrewd to the point of cunning, canny to the point of suspicious. Combined with these are the political skills mentioned above and an ability to be ruthless when necessary against opponents, actual or deemed potential. He has always been a poor speaker, although he improved over the years. Among the masses he can turn his lack of education to an advantage, although he has often made heavy weather of his attempts at popular humor. Like some uneducated men he wishes to be taken seriously by intellectuals and has often been resentful when he was not. Although not ostentatious in his style of living, he likes to live well. Like many East European proletarian leaders he developed almost a passion for the aristocratic pastime of hunting. With most people he has always been known as a friendly person, fond of good food, drink, and company. He has survived at least two severe illnesses through sheer physical strength. His wife, Mara Maleeva, died in 1971. She was a doctor by profession and a highly respected woman. Afterward both Zhivkov's affection and patronage were showered on his daughter, Lyudmila (see chapter 10). Her death ten years later had a most severe personal effect on him.

His active career must soon be drawing to an end. He will have ruled Bulgaria longer than anyone in its history as a modern independent state, longer than the thirty-one years of King Ferdinand between 1887 and 1918. Ferdinand, a German prince, has gone down in history as "Foxy" Ferdinand. Zhivkov, the Bulgarian peasant, is more deserving of the sobriquet and, whatever his failings, has been vastly less unsuccessful than Ferdinand.

Georgi Atanasov
Chairman of the Bulgarian Council of
Ministers (prime minister)

Georgi Atanasov was born near Plovdiv in July 1933. He is, therefore, very much of the "in-power" generation of Bulgarian communists. He actually joined the party only in 1956 after graduating with a degree in history from Sofia University.

Atanasov began his party career with the Komsomol (youth organization) and in 1961 was leader of the Sofia city Komsomol committee. The following year he became a candidate-member of the party Central Committee and in 1965 became the national leader (first secretary) of the Bulgarian Komsomol. It was on the strength of his Komsomol position that he was elected a full member of the party Central Committee in 1966. After leaving the Komsomol he headed the Central Committee's Science and Education Department (1968–76) and between 1976 and 1979 was head of the Central Committee's powerful Administrative Department. He had already been made a Central Committee secretary in 1977 and was to hold this position until his elevation to the premiership in March 1986 to succeed Grisha Filipov. In the same month that he became premier, Atanasov was also elected to full membership of the Politburo in which he had sat as a candidate-member since 1984.

Atanasov's appointment as premier came as a surprise. He had mostly been associated with party work, although between 1981 and 1984 he had concurrently served as a deputy chairman of the State Council and chairman of the (watchdog) Committee on State and People's Control. He is, however, not an economist, unlike his predecessor, Filipov, and contrary to the general East European prime ministerial custom. But a series of reorganizations and other appointments soon made it clear that Atanasov's duties as premier would primarily need to be administrative.

Atanasov has made little personal impact on most foreigners he has met. Though he has traveled quite extensively in both East and West on Komsomol and party business, with a degree in history to boot, he gives some the impression of a narrow apparatchik.

But, depending on the pitfalls he avoids during his premiership, he will undoubtedly play a big role in the post-Zhivkov era.

Czechoslovakia

Gustáv Husák
President of Czechoslovakia and General Secretary
of the Communist Party of Czechoslovakia
Husák was born into a middle-class family in Bratislava in 1913. He joined the Czecho-slovak communist party in 1933, the year he began his law studies in Bratislava, which lasted four years. During World War II Husák worked in the Slovak communist under-ground, while on the surface working in the legal profession. His wartime activities have since been the subject of controversy on two accounts: his membership of a Slovak delegation invited by the Nazis to investigate the Katyn massacre of Polish officers; and his personal friendship with Alexander (Šemó) Mach, interior minister in the puppet Slovak fascist republic. Speculation based on these facts that Husák was more a German collaborator than a communist resister can, however, be dismissed as either stretching or twisting the evidence.

Similarly, the fact that Husák was associated with the 1941 Slovak party program advocating the establishment of a Slovak Soviet Socialist Republic has led to the charge that, despite pretensions to Slovak nationalism, he was throughout his career first and foremost a servant (even an agent) of the Soviet Union. It would need several pages to discuss this accusation. All that can be said here is that it is simplistic to the point of irrelevant in trying to assess the mainspring of Husák's beliefs and career. He was a leader of a Slovak national-communist circle in Bratislava that believed, at least at that time, the Soviet Union to be both the protector and the fulfillment of its aspirations.

After the war Husák rose rapidly. In 1946 he was a member of the Slovak party Politburo (or presidium) and chairman of the Slovak Board of Commissioners (the semi-autonomous Slovak government body). He was also a member of the Czechoslovak party Central Committee. In 1951, however, in part of the great ongoing purge in the Czecho-slovak party, he was arrested on charges of Slovak "bourgeois nationalism." It was not, however, till 1954 that he was sentenced to life imprisonment along with his friend, Laço Novemeský. Another close friend, Vladímir (Vlado) Clementis, had previously been exe-cuted. Husák's sentence occurred early in the career of Antonín Novotný as Czechoslo-vak party leader, and the enmity between the two men lasted till Novotný's political demise in 1968.

Husák was released under an amnesty in 1960 after nine courageous years in prison. He worked as a clerk in a Bratislava office till 1963 when he was completely rehabilitated and regained his party membership. For the next five years he worked as a researcher at the Slovak Academy of Sciences. In April 1968 in the Prague Spring, which he then fully supported, he became one of the Czechoslovak deputy premiers.

An assessment of the rest of his career—his role shortly after the Soviet invasion, his assumption of the party leadership in place of Dubček, and his subsequent "normal-ization" policy—can be found in chapter 9. The motives for his behavior during the months after the Soviet invasion may have had some similarities with those of János Kádár during and immediately after the Hungarian Revolution. But those who have known Husák, while respecting his political ability and intelligence and recognizing his role in restraining those demanding political trials of the Prague Spring leaders, would see in him a ruthlessness and driving ambition that Kádár did not possess.

Husák's policy since 1969 has had its defenders, who argue that things could have been worse. This is true, but many more would argue that, despite all the constraints, Husák could have made them better. This is what has made his career, despite his personal triumphs, something of a tragedy. He had the attributes for something bigger than just a successful personal career.

Lubomir Štrougal
Chairman of the Czechoslovak Federal Council
of Ministers (prime minister)

Born in 1924 in southern Bohemia, Štrougal graduated in law from the Charles University in Prague in 1949. He began his party work in the České Budějovice regional organization in southern Bohemia and rose to first party secretary there. He is, therefore, an early member of the postwar generation of communist leaders.

In 1958, by virtue of his potential and the importance of the party organization he led, he was elected to the Czechoslovak party Central Committee. Štrougal thus began a rapid career as an all-round bureaucrat. Between 1959 and 1961 he was minister of agriculture, and between 1961 and 1965 he was minister of the interior, replacing Rudolf Barák. In 1965 Štrougal became a Central Committee secretary.

In view of his successful career it was not surprising that Štrougal was considered something of a Novotnýite. But he survived during the Prague Spring. He lost his post as Central Committee secretary in April 1968 but was immediately appointed chairman of the new Economic Council aimed at reviving the lagging economy. There was a strong feeling against him, however, among most reformers and, at the clandestine extraordinary congress held immediately after the Soviet-led invasion in August 1968, he was dropped from the Central Committee entirely. He was not, however, accused of collaborating with the Soviets.

In November 1968 Štrougal was comprehensively returned to favor. He became a member of the party Presidium (Politburo) and a Central Committee secretary, making statements indicating his full support for the new order without, however, joining forces with the hard-line conservatives urging vengeance on the supporters of the Prague Spring.

In 1970 Štrougal became federal premier and assumed overall responsibility for the Czechoslovak economy. He can hardly claim to have discharged his duties with any great distinction, but he has had to act under ideological and political restraints that never gave him a chance to show what his real abilities were. In fact, toward the end of the 1970s Štrougal's speeches were marked by cautious indications that he thought some injection of flexibility in economic policy at home, as well as in intra-Comecon relations, was increasingly necessary. He became regarded as one of the leaders favoring reform if and when the time was right—and safe.

A high-level career apparatchik, Štrougal has survived several upheavals in Czechoslovak politics and could conceivably survive another, provided it were not too long delayed. He has been enabled to do this, partly because of political opportunism but also because of intelligence and ability. No precisian in private life, he has kept a lot of friends, partly because of his position, but also partly because of his refreshing lack of personal or political vindictiveness.

German Democratic Republic

Erich Honecker
Chairman of the GDR State Council
General Secretary, Socialist Unity Party (SED)

Erich Honecker was born in August 1912 in the Neunkirchen district of the Saarland, the son of a coal miner. He was one of six children. Neunkirchen was a traditional bastion of the German Communist party, and even as late as the 1980s the communist vote there was considerably higher than the national average.

His father was a left-socialist who eventually joined the communist party. The young Erich grew up in a heavily political, left-wing household and joined the communist Young Pioneer's association when he was barely twelve. He was apprenticed as a roof slater but never finished his apprenticeship. After leaving school he joined the communist youth organization and in 1929, at the age of 17, the party itself. He became communist youth secretary in the Saarland, spent a year at the Lenin School in Moscow, and then became a member of the central committee of the communist youth organization. When the Nazis came to power in 1933 the communist party went underground, but Honecker was arrested and spent the years 1935–45 in prison.

Honecker is, therefore, technically a "home" communist. But he missed the drama and danger of anti-Nazi underground work. Had he not, however, been in jail during this crucial period he might have been in Moscow with Walter Ulbricht and many other German communists. Either way he missed experiences that had a profound effect on many older German and East European communists.

After the war he rose quickly in what became the German Democratic Republic. Between 1946 and 1955 he was chairman of the communist youth association, Freie Deutsche Jugend (FDJ), and also became a member of the party Central Committee in 1946. In 1950 he became a candidate-member of the Politburo and in 1958 a full member. It was also in 1958 that he became Central Committee secretary responsible for security affairs, and it was in that capacity that he supervised the building of the Berlin Wall in 1961. In 1971 he replaced Walter Ulbricht as first secretary of the party, a title that was changed to general secretary in 1976. In 1971 he also became head of the National Defense Council. In 1976 he became chairman of the State Council (head of state).

Honecker's policies since he became party leader are discussed in chapter 7. In the fifteen years concerned he has made an impact on his country just as big in its way as that made by Ulbricht. His most important contribution has been to give the GDR international status. Domestically the contrast between him and his predecessor is very strong. Personally, whereas Ulbricht was cold, distant, and feared, Honecker is approachable and sociable, though by no means charming. Politically, he has done more to raise living standards than Ulbricht and has allowed a far more relaxed atmosphere to develop. For this he has gained considerable respect. But he has still not achieved what he obviously regards as the goal of his career—to win popular legitimacy for both the GDR and the communist system. He had given the GDR international status, but he has not won for it national acceptance.

In September 1987 Honecker finally made an official visit to West Germany and revisited his Saarland home. It was a personally moving episode in a politically successful visit.

Willi Stoph
Chairman of the GDR Council of Ministers (prime minister)

Willi Stoph, a native Berliner, was born in July 1914, the son of a building worker. After an elementary school education he became an apprentice bricklayer. At the age of fourteen he joined the communist youth organization, joined the party three years later, and was an active trade unionist.

Between 1933 and 1945 Stoph, according to official GDR biographies, was engaged in the "illegal antifascist resistance struggle." That may be so, but he did his peacetime military service between 1935 and 1937 and during the war served with an artillery unit in the Wehrmacht.

After the war he made a rapid career in the GDR, starting out in industrial administration. He then went to work for the economy department of the party and already in 1950 was a Central Committee secretary. In 1952, however, he embarked on a new specialty when he became minister of the interior. Four years later he was moved to the ministry of defense. In 1962 he became first deputy premier, and in this post he actually assumed responsibility for running the government because of the terminal illness of the official premier, Otto Grotewohl. On Grotewohl's death he became prime minister in 1964. It was as premier that Stoph had his two historic meetings with Federal Chancellor Willy Brandt in Erfurt and Kassel in 1970.

In 1973, however, just two years after Honecker replaced Ulbricht as party leader, Stoph was kicked upstairs to be GDR head of state on Ulbricht's death. He was replaced by the technocrat, Horst Sindermann. Stoph appeared to be sick at the time and may not have minded the demotion to a much quieter post. But Sindermann proved incompetent as premier, and Stoph came back to his old job in 1976.

Over a decade later he was still at his post despite rumors that he might be replaced by the economic expert Gunther Mittag. By this time he had become a rarity in East European politics: a prime minister who really counted for something. Stoph is sometimes referred to as the "Red Prussian" or the (really) "Good Soldier Stoph." He served Ulbricht well and, whatever he may have felt about Honecker's preferment to him, he has worked for, and with, him with dedication and discipline. His rumored differences with Honecker on certain matters of policy have not degenerated into factionalism or intrigue. It is not surprising he has had few enemies. He is, in fact, a rarity in East European politics in another sense: an old communist whom office has not apparently corrupted.

Hungary

János Kádár
General Secretary of the Hungarian Socialist
Workers' Party (HSWP)

János Kádár was born in May 1912 in what was then the Hungarian Adriatic seaport of Fiume and is now, as Rijeka, part of Yugoslavia. His mother, to whom he was always very devoted, was a working-class woman; he never knew his father. Kádár was brought up in desperately poor circumstances in a village in Somogy county in Hungary itself. In 1918 his mother took him to Budapest to live along with his brother, Mihály, who later emigrated to Canada.

Kádár grew up an active boy, a very good chess and soccer player and an avid reader. He was drawn into underground communist circles in the early 1930s. From then on, until 1945, he was constantly under police surveillance, spending some four years in prison. In 1942 he entered the party's underground Central Committee and in 1943 became a Central Committee secretary. By the end of World War II he was second in importance in the underground only to his close friend László Rajk.

It was Mátyás Rákosi, however, returning from Moscow who became leader of the party after the war, and it was the "Muscovites" who dominated the party leadership. Kádár, however, was a Politburo member from 1946–51. But Rákosi was determined to oust the "home" communists from the leadership, and his prime target was Rajk, who was arrested, tried, and executed on trumped-up charges of plotting with Western security agencies, charges that were to become familiar in the series of Stalinist trials in Eastern Europe.

Kádár is believed to have visited Rajk on the eve of his trial and urged him to plead guilty in the greater interests of the party. But he himself later fell victim to the purge of "home" communists and was arrested in May 1951, cruelly tortured, and sentenced to an indeterminate prison sentence. After the death of Stalin he was freed, "rehabilitated," and resumed his party work, quickly reclimbing the hierarchical ladder. In October 1956, shortly after the beginning of the revolution, he took over the party leadership from the universally hated Ernö Gerö, who had only replaced Rákosi four months earlier. Kádár's role in the revolution became part of history. Rather than see the communist system crushed—which it undoubtedly would have been—he requested Soviet troops to begin their fatal attack.

After the crushing of the revolution the "Kádár era" in Hungarian history began. Its main points and essential characteristics are described in chapter 6. What should be repeated here is the essential role Kádár's diplomatic skill with the Soviets, political ability at home, quiet but firm leadership, and his reassuring personality have played in Hungarian history since 1956. Kádár became admired and liked by the majority of Hungarians at home, and in the Soviet alliance he became a respected elder statesman to whose advice the Russians listened, if they did not always heed it.

Yet Kádár's successful emergence into fame and popularity cannot obliterate the three great evils with which his career was associated between 1948 and 1958: his part in the downfall of Rajk; his role in the revolution; and his acceding to the execution of Imre Nagy, premier during the revolution, in 1958. His communist convictions, of course, can square these acts with his own conscience. But many Hungarians, when they recall those days, find them unforgivable. And Kádár's own innate decency might have sometimes caused him to regret, not just the situations that he thought necessitated these deeds, but even the very fact that he had done them.

György Lázár
Chairman of the Hungarian Council
of Ministers (prime minister) 1975–87
György Lázár was born in 1924 into a worker's family. He is a whole generation younger than Kádár and missed the experience of the underground and any active role in either the Stalinist period or the 1956 revolution.

He received a good economic and technical education. Between 1948 and 1958 he was, successively, a clerk, deputy department chief, and then department chief in the National Planning Office. Between 1958 and 1970 he was deputy chairman of the same office. From 1970 to 1973 he was minister of labor. From 1973 to his elevation to the premiership in 1975 he held four important posts simultaneously: deputy premier; Hungary's chief representative to Comecon; chairman of the National Planning Office; and chairman of the State Planning Committee.

Lázár's promotion to the premiership was part of an important change in Hungarian politics at the time. He replaced Jenö Fock, a colorful, popular figure, but above all a *political* leader prominent in the politics of economic reform and the whole policy of relaxation in Hungary. Fock lost the premiership the year after Rezsö Nyers, known as "the father" of the New Economic Mechanism, as well as other exponents of reform were demoted. These personnel changes took place at a time when economic reform appeared to have been shelved, partly because of Soviet suspicions.

But Lázár, who entered the Politburo in 1975, was in no sense opposed to the reform. He was always, in fact, much more a civil servant than a politician. As such he is generally considered to have been an able prime minister, in command of his job. He can hardly be blamed for the decline in the economy during the second half of his premiership, although he has occasionally been candid in self-criticism. This, plus persistent reports about his bad health, have led to periodic speculation about his retirement. But in June 1987, rather than retiring, Lázár relinquished the premiership and became deputy head of the party under Kádár. This, however, was seen not as leading to a new political lease on life for Lázár but rather as indicating what a sinecure the deputy party leader's job really was.

Károly Grósz
Chairman of the Hungarian Council of
Ministers (prime minister) 1987–

Károly Grósz was born in Miskolc in 1930 into a worker's family of strong left-wing tendencies. He became a printer but later attended university in Budapest and qualified as a teacher. He joined the party in 1945 and in 1950 began working in the party central apparatus, although in the early 1950s he also served in the army as a commissioned officer. In 1956 he began his local association with the Borsód county party organization. He was first a member of its agitprop department and was later editor of the communist newspaper there.

In 1962 Grósz became secretary of the party committee of the central Hungarian radio and television, a post he held for six years. Between 1968 and 1984 he alternated between important party posts in the central committee apparatus and in the provinces. Between 1979 and 1984 he was first secretary in Borsód county, which became his strong local base of power. In 1980 he became a Central Committee member and in 1984 became first secretary of the Budapest party committee, a post of great power and responsibility. In 1985, at the thirteenth party congress, he, not unexpectedly, was elected to the Politburo. In the extensive leadership reshuffle in June 1987 he took the premier's position from György Lázár, who had suffered bad health for several years.

There can be no doubting the impact Grósz has made on the Hungarian leadership. An able, forceful man he will have had, with his service as prime minister, a unique all-around governing experience. The assumption of the premiership could mean that a man's career is being deliberately diverted or sidetracked. It could be the case with Grósz who, though not reactionary, has sometimes been considered too critical of regime policy. He has certainly issued powerful warnings about reform in Hungary hurting large numbers of workers and creating poverty as well as prosperity. But it would be unwise to write Grósz off totally as Kádár's eventual successor. He will pick up more patronage as premier, and he does not seem a man who is easily sidetracked.

Poland

Wojciech Jaruzelski
Chairman of the Polish State Council; First Secretary
of the Polish United Workers' Party (PUWP)

Wojciech Jaruzelski was born in July 1923 near Pulawy in the Lublin voivodship to a family of landed gentry. From the scant information available about his early years, it would appear that he studied at a Jesuit boarding school. His life changed completely, however, as it did for all Poles, with the German/Soviet invasion of Poland in September 1939. According to his official biographers, Jaruzelski suddenly "found himself," with his family, in the Soviet Union. Whether they fled there to escape the Germans or were deported there by the Russians along with the 1.5 million other Poles has never been divulged. His father apparently died in the Soviet Union during the war, and his mother and sister returned to Poland in 1946.

Jaruzelski himself is said to have worked as a laborer till 1943. Then, however, he began his military career: he entered a Soviet military school at Ryazan, which trained officers for the Polish contingents, led by General Berling, which later entered Poland with the Red Army. Jaruzelski fought with Berling's army during the whole Soviet westward campaign.

Immediately after the war he was active in putting down anticommunist partisans on Polish territory. He was then sent to the infantry officers' school and then on to the General Staff Academy, from which he graduated in 1955, and the following year became the youngest general in the Polish army. The political and military aspects of Jaruzelski's career were soon to become closely intertwined. In 1960 he became head of the Main Political Administration of the Armed Forces and a deputy minister of defense. In April 1968, when Gomułka's close associate Marian Spychalski became titular head of state, Jaruzelski replaced him as minister of defense. Very shortly after he had the invidious task of arranging for Polish participation in the Soviet-led invasion of Czechoslovakia.

A party member since 1947, Jaruzelski entered the Central Committee in 1964, a promotion obviously in connection with his post as the military's chief political officer. In December 1970, after the worker riots had toppled Gomułka, he became a candidate-member of the Politburo in the new Gierek leadership and exactly a year later achieved full member status.

It now appeared that Jaruzelski, as minister of defense and full Politburo member, had reached the pinnacle of his career. But no one anticipated the democratic landslide that engulfed Poland in 1980 and 1981. In February 1981 he became prime minister in place of Józef Pinkowski and the following October became party leader in the place of Stanisław Kania. Never in Polish history had any man had such a combination of titles: first party secretary, prime minister, defense minister, and head of the military council.

Two months later came the military putsch that destroyed many things, including

Jaruzelski's reputation among the Polish people. The events surrounding and following the coup are discussed in chapter 5. What remains here is to try to assess the man whose name is so irrevocably linked with them.

Right up to the very eve of his military coup Jaruzelski enjoyed a very high prestige among his nation, probably more so among noncommunists than communists. His assumption of the premiership was seen as a reassurance and was greeted by Lech Wałęsa himself. After the coup his name was excoriated as that of a traitor. Previous stories referring to his patriotism and sense of honor, once accepted as true, were now dismissed as propaganda myths. But more recently, after about the beginning of 1985, the nation's general assessment of him seemed to have improved. Many, of course, especially Poles abroad, remained unrelenting, but many others, probably correctly, saw him as a spartan, distant figure trying to do what he thought best for the cause (communism) and the country (Poland) he served. His personal integrity should never have been doubted. What Jaruzelski should have realized all along, however, was the incompatibility between cause and country, an incompatibility that was never more obvious than after December 1981. He will remain a controversial, tragic, and mysterious figure. His reputation in history may well be higher than it has been during his turbulent years as Polish leader.

Zbigniew Messner
Chairman of the Polish Council of Ministers
(prime minister)

Zbigniew Messner was born in 1929 in the city of Stryj, in the Lwow district, which is now part of the Soviet Union. But he has been associated for most of his life with the city of Katowice. He studied economics there and in Cracow and received a doctorate from the Katowice Academy of Economics in 1961. He had already been a lecturer at the same academy since 1950. In 1972 he reached professorial rank and in 1977 became professor ordinarius. By this time he had been active several years in academic administration and in 1968 had become one of the Katowice Academy's pro-rectors. Between 1975 and 1982 he was rector of that institution.

Like Józef Cyrankiewicz, one of his predecessors as premier, Messner began his political career as a socialist and was a member of a socialist-sponsored youth organization. This later merged with the communist Union of Polish Youth. In 1953 Messner joined the Polish United Workers' (communist) party and was active in the Katowice Academy's party organization. But he soon branched out into Katowice city and regional politics. He was a member of the Katowice city party committee in the 1970s and of the Katowice voivodship (regional) party executive between 1980 and 1982. But it was the ninth (central) party congress in Warsaw in July 1981 that marked his debut in the highest ranks. There he leapfrogged over many others into full Central Committee and Politburo membership. At the same time he was building up his power base in his industrial stronghold at Katowice. Between December 1981 and December 1983 he was both first secretary of the voivodship party committee there and chairman of the voivodship people's council, the organ of local government.

After the military coup in December 1981 Messner emerged as one of Jaruzelski's strongest supporters. He was transferred to central government duties in November 1983 when he became deputy premier and eventually chairman of the government's economic reform commission. He was now virtually in charge of the whole economy.

Many were expecting that when Jaruzelski decided to step aside from the premiership it would be Messner who would take his place. This happened in 1985.

By the end of 1987 Messner had still not cut any real figure of his own in the prime ministerial post. Nor had any real ability, or lack of it, been revealed. It was still difficult to get any unbiased appraisal of him. He had made his way in Katowice when Edward Gierek was satrap there but came to prominence only when Gierek had gone to Warsaw as party leader. He has presumably always been a competent economist but obviously owed some of his academic preferment to his party positions. It was difficult also to tell where he stood on economic reform. What few indications there were pointed to his being a technician rather than a reformer. He is a man of energy (in spite of a broken back reportedly incurred when a wild boar crashed into his car in 1984), but apparently an executor of policy rather than a man of ideas. In this he was far from unique in the Jaruzelski regime.

Romania

Nicolae Ceauşescu
President of the State Council and General Secretary
of the Romanian Communist Party

Nicolae Ceauşescu was born in 1918 to a poor peasant family in Scorniceşti, a once obscure village in Oltenia that has since become a booming secular shrine. According to his official biographies, which not surprisingly tend toward hagiography, Ceauşescu joined the illegal communist party in 1933 and immediately became active in its youth movement. Both before and during World War II he spent a considerable time in various prisons. He became well known in revolutionary circles, made the acquaintance of Gheorghe Gheorghiu-Dej, the future head of the party, and other future regime leaders.

In 1945 he began his senior party career as a candidate-member of the Central Committee and secretary of the Union of Communist Youth. After two years' experience as a regional apparatchik he joined the now fully communist government as a deputy minister of agriculture (1948–50). In 1951 he was transferred to the army with the rank of major-general and became a deputy minister of the armed forces. The following year he was listed as head of the Armed Forces Political Directorate and in September 1953 became first deputy minister of the armed forces.

As a "home" communist and as one already with considerable experience behind him, Ceauşescu benefited greatly from the fall of the Jewish "Muscovite" Ana Pauker and her group in 1952. He proceeded up the party ladder and in 1954 was made a candidate-member of the Politburo and a Central Committee secretary.

In December 1955 Ceauşescu achieved full Politburo status and in a matter of two years became the second most important man in the party after Gheorghiu-Dej. Although several others had more seniority and prestige, it was becoming evident that Gheorghiu-Dej was grooming him as his successor. But even more basic to his strength was his position as Central Committee secretary for party organization and cadres. This classic stepping-stone to leadership gave him a power, and hence a following, that nobody could match. He began to accompany Gheorghiu-Dej on important missions abroad, most notably to the Soviet Union, but also to other countries, communist and noncommunist as well. At the same time he began acquiring the reputation of a nationalist and emerged as a stout champion, sometimes the front-runner, of Romania's campaign against supranational Comecon integration.

When Gheorghiu-Dej died in March 1965 Ceauşescu's accession to the party leadership came as little surprise. What followed is described and analyzed at some length in chapter 8. His accession was generally welcomed by the population, and the first five years of his rule constituted Romania's best period under communist rule. But the next fifteen years witnessed an accelerating downward spiral that cannot be explained solely in political or rational terms. It cannot be defended at all.

Constantin Dăscălescu
Chairman of the Romanian Council of Ministers
(prime minister)

Constantin Dăscălescu was born in 1920 near Piteşti to a worker's family. He began his party career as a provincial apparatchik and in 1958 was recorded as a secretary of the Piteşti regional party committee. Six years later he was a secretary of the party committee in Galaţi, and in 1965 he was first secretary of the same committee, serving at the same time as a deputy to the Grand National Assembly (parliament) for a constituency in the Galaţi region. In 1965 he was made a full member of the party Central Committee. Galaţi, however, the region containing the huge new Romanian metallurgical complex, continued to be his power base, and for several years he was both head of the party and head of the regional people's council there.

Dăscălescu's first important post in Bucharest was as a Central Committee department chief in 1974, and in 1976 he jumped into prominence as chairman of the National Union of Agricultural Cooperatives and, more important, a Central Committee secretary. In 1978 he was made a member of the party's Political Executive committee and chairman of the Council of Economic-Social Organizations, another of those bureaucracy-swelling bodies in which Ceauşescu appeared to delight. But much more important for his career was his emergence in the same year as Central Committee secretary in charge of party organization and his promotion toward the end of 1979 to membership in the topmost party body, the Standing Bureau. Dăscălescu was now in the first rank of princelings under Nicolae and Elena Ceauşescu and was believed to be a personal favorite of both. He was certainly beginning to outshine—in prominence if not in talent—some of the earlier members of the ruling coterie.

Still, it was a surprise in May 1982 when Dăscălescu succeeded Ilie Verdeţ as prime minister. At sixty-two he was relatively old for the job, and he was without much governmental experience. But he had the favor of his superiors and the virtue of obedience. Though without much education, he is apparently not without either qualities or profile, but in the stifling governing atmosphere of Bucharest he has been able to show very little of either. He looks as if he will be remembered solely for being nominal head of Romania's government during one of the most blighted periods in its history.

Albania

Ramiz Alia
President of the Albanian State Council (head of state)
and First Secretary of the Albanian Party of Labor

Ramiz Alia was born in October 1925 in Shkodër (Scutari) of poor Geg Muslim parents. He joined the communist-dominated National Liberation Army in 1944. Though he finished the war as a divisional political commissar with the rank of lieutenant-colonel, Alia was neither one of the founder-members of the Albanian party nor one of the core of communist resistance fighters.

He began his political career with the party's youth organization and between 1949 and 1955 was president of the Albanian Union of Working Youth, becoming a full member of the party Central Committee in 1954. Between 1955 and 1958 he was minister of education. A candidate-member of the Politburo after 1956, he became a full member in 1961. But before this Alia had begun to broaden his interests and experience considerably. He held the posts of chairman of the Foreign Affairs Commission of the People's Assembly (parliament) in 1958 and in the same year was a member of the Central Committee's agitation and propaganda department. In 1960 he became a Central Committee secretary.

It was already evident, therefore, by 1960, when Alia was only thirty-five, that he was the most promising and versatile of the younger generation of Albanian leaders. The question was whether he could keep clear of the paranoid vindictiveness of Enver Hoxha and/or premier Mehmet Shehu. He was able to do this quite triumphantly. While others were being struck down, Alia quietly got on with his various duties and, at least judging from the scanty information available, never seems to have been in real danger.

Indeed, in the course of the 1970s he steadily became more visible. He was obviously growing in Hoxha's favor and it was during the second half of the 1970s that seasoned Albania watchers began to regard him as Hoxha's annointed successor. He must, therefore, have found himself in the middle of a growing feud between Hoxha and Shehu, with the latter wanting to succeed and the former determined to prevent him from doing so. This led to Shehu's dramatic death at the end of 1981 (see chapter 12), which cleared the way for a smooth succession. In 1982 Alia became president of the State Council (titular head of state) and, as Hoxha's health deteriorated and he began to spend much of his time on his multivolumed memoirs, the running of the party more and more fell to Alia. It was no surprise, therefore, that he succeeded Hoxha when the latter died in April 1985 (despite the fact that he was a Geg in a regime many Albanians considered a Tosk conspiracy).

Ramiz Alia's greatest political success up to 1985 was as a survivor. Now, however, he would need to show broader, more outer-oriented talents. People who knew him spoke well of his intelligence and his personality. He suffered a serious personal loss in 1986 with the death of his wife. It was expected that, if Alia could consolidate his position and really assert his mastery, Albania would gradually step out of her (very hard) shell.

Adil Çarçani
Chairman of the Albanian Council of
Ministers (prime minister)

Adil Çarçani was born in May 1922. He was brought up in Shkodër (Scutari) but is reportedly not of Geg origin but the son of Tosk parents who had come north to live. He served in the National Liberation Army during the war and became a political commissar.

After the war and the communist triumph he began his career in the Tirana party organization. But subsequently he made a career in the government rather than the party side of the regime and almost exclusively in economic posts. He was deputy minister of commerce in 1948 and minister of industry in 1951. In 1955 he was minister of industry and mines. He was also rising in the party during this period and was made a candidate-member of the Politburo in 1956 and a full member in 1961.

Çarçani's elevation to the Politburo in 1961—at the same party congress that saw Ramiz Alia's elevation—indicates his full support for Hoxha and his anti-Soviet line. He became a deputy premier in 1965 and first deputy premier in 1974, all the while under Mehmet Shehu as head of the government. During this period one of Çarçani's more noteworthy tasks was to travel to China twice to negotiate credit agreements with the Chinese government. It was ironical, therefore, that he was a member of the commission to draft the new Albanian constitution of 1976 that prohibited the contracting of foreign debts.

Çarçani had to wait till the spectacular demise of Shehu to become prime minister, which he did in January 1982. He is of the same vintage and from the same home town as Ramiz Alia, and their careers have been parallel. Little is known about his personality or abilities, but if Albania extends its foreign economic relations the chances are that he will soon become less a distant cardboard figure and more the object of considerable Western curiosity.

Yugoslavia

The office rotation system with which Yugoslavia has been plagued since even before the death of Tito has made it pointless to give the biographies of either the head of state or the party leader since the allotted term in office for both is one year. What the rotation system actually created was an oligarchy, with top offices, especially in party and state, being shuffled around among about fifteen top representatives from the different republics and provinces. It has been an unsatisfactory system, but the question increasingly being asked was not so much when it would be changed but whether any change attempted might not destabilize the situation even further. It was yet another case of many being united on the need for change but even more fearing the consequences of it.

Only in the case of the office of prime minister (president of the Federal Executive Council) has some degree of stability seemed assured. The term of office here was fixed at four years. The first premier under this new dispensation was Veselin Djuranović and then Milka Planinc (born 1920) whose term lasted from 1982–86. The following is a brief biography of her successor, who is due to remain in office till 1990.

Branko Mikulić
President of the Federal Executive Council
of Yugoslavia (prime minister)
Branko Mikulić, a Croat, was born to a peasant family in the village of Pogradje in Bosnia-Herzegovina in June 1928. In 1943 he joined Tito's partisans, but little is known about his war record.

After the war he graduated from the Economic High School in Zagreb and then went into party work in Bosnia. He was secretary of the Yugoslav youth federation in two localities and then was organizational secretary of the district party committees of Bugojno and Jacje. He was later secretary of the district party committees in Livno and Zenica. His first senior office came in 1965 when he was elected a member of the Bosnian-Herzegovinian Central Committee and secretary of its Executive Committee.

By the beginning of the 1970s Mikulić was already considered one of the emerging men in Yugoslav politics, and in 1974, at the tenth party congress, he was elected a member of the Yugoslav Central Committee and of its Presidium. In October 1978 he became chairman of the Presidium of the Central Committee for a one-year period and was then succeeded by Stevan Doronjski (of Serbia).

After serving his one-year term as head of the federal party, Mikulić became part of the new official oligarchy. He was representative for Bosnia-Herzegovina in the collective state presidency and was due to become president of that body (i.e., titular head of state) for the period from May 1988 to May 1989. But, to the surprise of some, he was nominated for the premiership early in 1986 and assumed office in May of that year.

Mikulić is typical of that able group of younger Yugoslav politicians who wasted as little time in Belgrade federal politics as possible and carefully tended their power base at the republic level. For many years party and then government leader in Bosnia-Herzegovina, he became the virtual dictator of that republic, which has always been considered one of the most primitive in the whole of Yugoslavia.

Mikulić has always been a doer rather than a thinker or a reader. He is a hard-headed, often hard-hearted, pragmatist whose attitudinal lineage can be traced back to Alexander Ranković, although he has never been guilty of (or had the opportunities for) the "deformations" that finally ended Ranković's career. As such, Mikulić is the opposite from the Djilas-Kardelj type of Yugoslav leader—thinkers, ideologists, doctrinaire rather than practical.

Under Mikulić Bosnia-Herzegovina became a model of law and order with a strong leadership, unsympathetic to intellectuals and liberals, and decidedly inimical to all political dissent or unorthodoxy. This "no-nonsense" atmosphere has not been without its economic rewards: it has, in fact, attracted considerable Western industrial investment. Without Mikulić it would also have been hard to see Sarajevo bidding for the 1984 Winter Olympics, let alone getting them. And, in the event, thanks to a last-minute deluge of snow and to good organization that showed that Yugoslavia (or at least Bosnia) could "do it" after all, the games were a success and Mikulić's reputation enhanced.

He faced a grimmer task now. Yugoslavia's problems are certainly beyond the abilities of one man to solve, however impressive he might be. Indeed, after only one year in office Mikulić was already being criticized for several lapses of judgment. But he is determined, and has character. The question was whether he would be pragmatic enough to listen to those who saw Yugoslavia's deliverance in greater daring and vision.

III Selected Demographic, Social, and Economic Data on Eastern Europe

Table 1 Area

Country	Population (millions)	sq. km.	sq. miles	Density (per sq. km.)
Albania	2.84	28,700	10,600	99
Bulgaria	8.94	110,912	43,325	81
Czechoslovakia	15.41	127,877	49,952	121
German Democratic Republic	16.70	108,178	42,257	154
Hungary	10.69	93,030	36,340	115
Poland	36.57	312,677	122,139	117
Romania	22.55	237,500	92,773	95
Yugoslavia	22.85	255,804	99,923	89

Source: U.N. Demographic Yearbook, 1983.

Table 2 Those Aged 0–19 Years as a Percentage of the Total Population, 1960, 1980, and 2000

	1960	1980	2000
Albania	50.8	48.6	37.7
Bulgaria	33.6	29.0	27.5
Czechoslovakia	35.1	31.1	30.3
German Democratic Republic	28.3	27.9	23.7
Hungary	32.8	27.6	27.2
Poland	40.1	31.8	29.5
Romania	35.5	32.9	30.4
Yugoslavia	38.3	32.7	28.1

Source: World Health Organization, Regional Publications, European Series no. 17 (Copenhagen, 1984), Demographic Trends in the European Region: Health and Social Implications, p. 139.

Table 3 Employed Civilian Labor Force, by Main
Sectors, 1982

	Agriculture		Industry		Other		Total
	(in thou-sands)	(%)	(in thou-sands)	(%)	(in thou-sands)	(%)	(in thou-sands)
Albania[1,2]	128	21.9	221	37.8	235	40.3	584
Bulgaria[1]	929	22.8	1,406	34.5	1,741	42.7	4,076
Czechoslovakia	1,039	14.0	2,806	37.7	3,590	48.3	7,435
German Democratic Republic[1]	339	4.3	3,525	44.9	3,979	50.8	7,843
Hungary	1,144	22.9	1,605	32.1	2,248	45.0	4,997
Poland	5,357	31.4	5,015	29.4	6,671	39.2	17,043
Romania	3,025	29.0	3,813	36.6	3,590	34.4	10,428
Yugoslavia[1]	302	5.0	2,461	41.2	3,217	53.8	5,980
United States	3,571	3.6	22,742	22.9	73,213	73.5	99,526

[1]Socialized sector.
[2]1978.
Sources: ILO Yearbook of Labor Statistics, 1983; Europa Yearbook, 1984.

Table 4 Female Labor Force as Percentage of Total
Labor Force, 1975 and 1984

	Women in total labor force	
	1975	1984
Albania	n/a	n/a
Bulgaria	47	49
Czechoslovakia	45	46
German Democratic Republic	50	52
Hungary	40	45
Poland	42	43
Romania	36	40
Yugoslavia	38	39
United States	39	43

Source: The Economic Role of Women in the ECE Region (New York: United Nations, 1985), p. 13.

Table 5 Percentage Distribution of Economically Active Men and Women, by Major Economic Sectors, for Years around 1950, 1960, 1970, and 1980

	Men			Women		
	Agri-culture	Industry	Services	Agri-culture	Industry	Services
Bulgaria						
1956	55	25	20	78	10	12
1965	36	41	23	55	23	22
1975	21	48	31	26	37	37
1980	26	46	28	24	37	39
Czechoslovakia						
1947	30	43	27	53	27	30
1961	21	54	25	30	37	33
1970	17	54	29	17	40	43
1980	15	57	28	12	40	48
German Democratic Republic						
1964	15	53	32	15	37	49
1971	12	57	31	11	39	49
1980	14	64	23	9	37	54
Hungary						
1949	55	27	18	61	18	21
1960	39	40	21	42	29	29
1970	26	49	25	23	40	37
1980	22	46	32	15	41	44
Poland						
1950	46	29	25	68	14	18
1960	37	37	26	59	17	24
1970	32	44	24	46	24	30
1980	12	59	29	6	43	51
Romania						
1956	59	24	16	83	7	9
1966	45	35	20	72	12	16
1970	8	57	35	3	43	54
1980	9	57	34	3	49	48
Yugoslavia						
1953	65	21	14	82	8	10
1961	54	28	18	69	14	17
1971	44	35	21	57	20	23
1980	6	58	36	3	41	57

Source: The Economic Role of Women in the ECE Region (New York: United Nations, 1985), p. 39.

Table 6 Infant Mortality, 1977–1981 (deaths of children less than one year old per 1,000 live births)

	1977	1978	1979	1980	1981
Bulgaria	24.0	22.2	19.8	20.2	19.5[1]
Czechoslovakia	19.7	18.8	17.7	16.6	16.8[1]
German Democratic Republic	13.1	13.1	12.9	12.1	12.3[1]
Hungary	26.2	24.4	24.0	23.2	20.6[1]
Poland	24.6	22.5	21.1	21.3	20.6[1]
Romania	31.2	30.3	31.6	29.3	([2])

[1] Denotes provisional.
[2] Denotes not available.
Source: Elizabeth M. Clayton, "Consumption, Living Standards, and Consumer Welfare in Eastern Europe," in *East European Economies: Slow Growth in the 1980s*, vol. 1. Selected Papers Submitted to the Joint Economic Committee, Congress of the United States (Washington, D.C.: U.S. Government Printing Office, 1985), p. 257.

Table 7 Daily Food Consumption per Capita, 1977

	Calories	Protein (grams)
Bulgaria	3,578	105.1
Czechoslovakia	3,457	98.5
German Democratic Republic	3,644	99.9
Hungary	3,520	91.9
Poland	3,619	111.4
Romania	3,448	103.4
United States	3,578	106.4

Source: Elizabeth M. Clayton, "Consumption, Living Standards, and Consumer Welfare in Eastern Europe," in *East European Economies: Slow Growth in the 1980s*, vol. 1. Selected Papers Submitted to the Joint Economic Committee, Congress of the United States (Washington, D.C.: U.S. Government Printing Office, 1985), p. 259.

Table 8   Radios, Televisions, and Telephones in Use, 1980

	Radio receivers		TV receivers		Telephones	
	(in thou-sands)	(per thou-sand popu-lation)	(in thou-sands)	(per thou-sand popu-lation)	(in thou-sands)	(per thou-sand popu-lation)
Albania[1]	202	74	10	3.7	n.a.	n.a.
Bulgaria[2]	2,149	242	1,652	186	1,255	141
Czechoslovakia[2]	4,693	307	4,292	280	3,150	206
German Democratic Republic[2]	6,409	383	5,731	342	3,156	189
Hungary	2,700[1]	252	2,766[2]	258	1,261	118
Poland[2]	8,666	244	7,954	224	3,387	95
Romania[2]	3,205	144	3,714	167	1,196[3]	56[3]
Yugoslavia[2]	4,851	217	4,442	199	2,139	95
Soviet Union[1]	130,000	490	81,000	305	23,707[4]	89
United States[1]	477,800	2,099	142,000	624	180,424	788
United Kingdom[1]	53,000	947	22,600	404	26,651	477

[1]Estimated number of receivers in use.
[2]Number of licenses issued or sets declared.
[3]1975.
[4]Excludes telephone systems of the military forces.
Sources: UNESCO *Statistical Yearbook, 1984*; *U.N. Statistical Yearbook, 1981*; in George Schöpflin, ed., *The Soviet Union and Eastern Europe* (London: Muller, Blond and White, 1986), p. 167.

Table 9 Warsaw Pact Defense Expenditure, 1980

	Defense expenditure		GNP	Defense expenditure
	($ million)	($ per capita)	($ per capita)	(as % of GNP)
Bulgaria	1,180	133	4,219	3.2
Czechoslovakia	2,750	180	5,821	3.1
German Democratic Republic	6,020	360	7,226	5.0
Hungary	1,100	103	4,200	2.4
Poland	4,300	121	3,929	3.1
Romania	1,350	61	3,851	1.6
Soviet Union	130,000	490	4,564	10.7

Source: "World Military and Social Expenditures, 1983," in George Schöpflin, ed., *The Soviet Union and Eastern Europe* (London: Muller, Blond and White, 1986), p. 152.

Table 10 Exchange Rates of East European Currencies per Dollar (as of November 1984)

	Official bank rate	Free market rate (approximate)
Albania (new lek)	8.40	n/a
Bulgaria (leva)	1.02	3
Czechoslovakia (koruna [crown])	6.77	25
German Democratic Republic (ostmark)	3.05	11
Hungary (forint)	49.75	80
Poland (złoty)	125.39	600
Romania (leu)	5.04	n/a
Yugoslavia (dinar)	222.20	300
Soviet Union (ruble)	0.83	4

Source: George Schöpflin, ed., *The Soviet Union and Eastern Europe* (London: Muller, Blond and White, 1986), p. 153.

Table 11   Per Capita Net Material Product at Constant Prices, 1972–1979
(1975 = 100)

	1972	1973	1974	1976	1977	1978	1979
Albania	n.a	n.a	n.a	n.a	n.a	n.a	n.a
Bulgaria	80	86	93	107	114	121	126
Czechoslovakia	87	90	95	103	107	110	113
German Democratic Republic	85	91	97	106	111	113	115
Hungary	84	89	95	102	110	115	117
Yugoslavia[1]	87	91	98	103	110	117	124
Poland	79	86	94	106	110	113	109
Romania	75	83	92	110	119	127	133
Soviet Union	86	93	96	104	109	113	114
United States[2]	99	103	102	105	109	113	115
United Kingdom[2]	95	102	101	104	105	109	110

[1]Gross material product.

[2]Gross Domestic Product (GDP) at constant prices.

Sources: *U.N. Statistical Yearbook, 1981*; in George Schöpflin, ed., *The Soviet Union and Eastern Europe* (London: Muller, Blond and White, 1986), p. 151.

Table 12   Increases in Net Material Product, Utilized National Income and Investment, 1971–1984 (in percentages)

	1971–75*	1976–80*	1981	1982	1983	1984
Net material product						
Bulgaria	7.8	6.1	5.0	4.2	3.0	4.6
Czechoslovakia	5.7	3.7	− 0.1	0.2	2.4	2.8
German Democratic Republic	5.4	4.1	4.8	2.6	4.4	5.5
Hungary	6.2	3.2	2.5	2.6	0.3	2.5
Romania	11.2	7.3	2.2	2.7	3.4	7.7
Poland	9.8	1.2	− 12.0	− 5.5	6.0	5.6
Utilized national income						
Bulgaria	8.6	2.8	7.7	1.9	1.2	2.8
Czechoslovakia	6.1	2.2	− 3.4	− 1.6	0.7	1.5
German Democratic Republic	4.7	3.6	1.3	− 3.4	0.3	3.3
Hungary	5.6	1.9	0.7	− 1.1	− 2.7	− 0.6
Poland	11.6	− 0.2	− 10.5	− 10.5	5.4	5.0
Romania	n.a.	6.9	− 5.7	− 2.2	0.7	3.4
National income used for net investment (accumulation fund)						
Bulgaria	12.9	0.1	14.8	− 3.3	− 3.6	1.4
Czechoslovakia	8.4	1.4	− 21.7	− 3.6	− 7.2	− 3.3
German Democratic Republic	2.9	3.0	− 3.4	− 19.9	− 1.9	− 0.6
Hungary	8.1	− 2.0	− 8.6	− 12.4	− 20.4	− 11.3
Poland	18.1	− 11.8	− 27.6	− 6.6	4.9	6.3
Romania	n.a.	6.6	− 22.1	− 4.3	2.0	2.4

*Average annual rate of growth.

Source: Keith Crane, *The Soviet Economic Dilemma of Eastern Europe* (Santa Monica: Rand, May 1986).

Table 13 Net Material Product Plan Targets and Performance, 1981–1985 (annual average percentage volume change)

	1981–85 (plan)	1983 (plan)	1983 (actual)	1984 (plan)	1984 (est'd)	1985 (plan)
Albania	6.0–6.4					
Bulgaria	3.7	3.8	3.0	3.8	4.6	4.1
Czechoslovakia	2.0–2.6	2.0	2.2–2.7	3.0	3.2	3.2
German Democratic Republic	5.1	4.2	4.4	4.4	5.4	4.4
Hungary	2.7–3.2	0.5–1.0	−0.5	1.5–2.0	2.0–2.5	2.3–2.8
Poland	3.4–3.9	2.5	6.0	2.6	5.0–6.0	3.0–3.5
Romania	7.1	5.0	3.4	7.3	—	—
Yugoslavia (gross social product)[1]	4.0–4.5	1.0	−1.3	2.0	1.5	3+

[1]Special Yugoslav definition includes some nonproductive services.

Source: Economist Intelligence Unit, *Regional Review: Eastern Europe and the USSR, 1985* (London: EIU, 1985), pp. 37, 45, 52, 62, 71, 84, 92, 117.

Table 14 Comparative Economic Growth Rates, 1960–1985 (compound annual rates of growth of total Gross National Product)

	1960–61	1965–70	1970–75	1976	1977
German Democratic Republic	2.9	3.1	3.5	2.0	3.0
Czechoslovakia	2.4	3.4	3.4	1.8	4.3
Hungary	3.9	3.0	3.3	0.3	6.3
Poland	4.5	4.0	6.5	2.5	1.9
Bulgaria	6.4	5.1	4.7	3.0	−1.0
Romania	5.4	4.9	6.7	10.8	2.5
Eastern Europe Total	3.8	3.7	4.9	3.2	2.8
Eastern Europe excluding Poland	3.6	3.7	4.1	3.6	3.3

Source: Lincoln Gordon, *Eroding Empire: Western Relations with Eastern Europe* (Washing

1978	1979	1980	1981	1982	1983	1984	1985
1.7	2.8	2.1	2.1	− 0.4	1.8	3.2	2.4
1.6	0.8	2.3	− 0.5	2.0	1.5	2.7	1.7
2.4	0.3	1.0	0.7	3.7	− 1.0	2.7	− 0.9
3.5	− 1.8	− 2.4	− 5.3	− 1.0	4.9	3.4	1.6
2.2	3.8	− 2.9	2.7	3.2	− 1.8	2.9	− 0.8
4.7	3.6	− 1.5	0.2	2.6	0.0	4.6	1.8
2.8	1.0	− 0.3	− 1.0	0.9	1.8	3.3	1.4
2.5	2.2	0.7	0.9	1.8	0.5	3.3	1.3

., Brookings Institution, 1987), p. 331, appendix table A-2.

Table 15   Total External Trade, 1983

	Imports		Exports		Balance[1]
	$ million	$ per capita	$ million	$ per capita	$ million
Albania	n.a.	n.a.	n.a.	n.a.	n.a.
Bulgaria	12,164	1,360	12,130	1,357	− 34
Czechoslovakia	16,325	1,059	16,522	1,072	+ 197
German Democratic Republic	21,524	1,289	23,793	1,425	+ 2,268
Hungary	8,503	795	8,696	813	+ 193
Poland	9,995	273	10,951	299	+ 956
Romania[2]	9,836	436	11,714	519	+ 1,877
Yugoslavia	11,104	492	9,038	401	− 2,067
Soviet Union	80,410	295	91,336	335	+ 10,927
United States	269,878	1,155	200,538	858	− 69,341

[1] + denotes export surplus, − denotes import surplus.
[2] 1982.
Source: *U.N. Monthly Bulletin of Statistics*, May 1985.

Table 16 Soviet Trade Surpluses with Eastern Europe (millions of rubles)

Year	Bulgaria	Czecho-slovakia	German Democratic Republic	Hungary	Poland	Romania
1970	− 128.5	− 27.8	181.2	36.7	80.0	− 29.4
1971	− 100.7	13.4	− 11.6	101.0	54.9	− 82.5
1972	− 102.4	− 118.5	− 363.9	− 74.5	− 188.9	− 112.1
1973	− 93.2	− 51.6	− 252.5	− 112.3	− 110.3	− 92.1
1974	52.9	− 7.3	13.9	− 13.3	92.8	− 33.8
1975	128.4	127.8	337.2	41.7	41.1	− 121.6
1976	87.9	97.7	438.6	181.0	265.2	− 59.5
1977	164.1	243.5	594.9	156.0	323.8	− 18.4
1978	147.0	− 56.6	270.8	331.0	− 150.4	− 18.0
1979	139.0	179.5	299.5	576.0	2.0	34.0
1980	221.3	112.2	546.8	696.0	809.7	5.0
1981	677.6	277.5	371.5	519.0	1117.0	13.0
1982	596.5	315.6	643.4	594.0	651.0	− 23.0
1983	457.5	451.2	202.1	424.0	490.0	− 91.0
1984	516.4	574.3	114.2	400.0	772.4	52.0

Source: Keith Crane, *The Soviet Economic Dilemma of Eastern Europe* (Santa Monica: Rand, May 1986), p. 31.

Table 17 Soviet Oil Export Prices and Terms of Trade (per metric ton)

Year	Soviet oil prices (transferable rubles) CMEA (1)	World market (2)	Soviet terms of trade with the CMEA (3)	with the West (4)	Ratio of (3) to (4)
1970	15.3	11.9	100.0	100.0	1.00
1971	15.4	15.5	100.6	112.5	.89
1972	15.7	17.7	100.1	83.7	1.20
1973	16.0	21.1	100.8	96.4	1.05
1974	18.1	60.7	101.0	120.1	.84
1975	33.8	63.5	106.6	129.9	.82
1976	37.1	70.2	110.2	145.2	.76
1977	46.9	73.7	114.9	154.6	.74
1978	55.9	68.9	118.0	159.8	.74
1979	63.6	93.4	120.5	209.0	.58
1980	74.7	159.7	122.2	244.6	.50
1981	95.0	192.5	133.5	250.2	.53
1982	117.4	179.4	148.3	n.a.	n.a.
1983	138.8	159.5	n.a.	n.a.	n.a.

Source: Keith Crane, *The Soviet Economic Dilemma of Eastern Europe* (Santa Monica: Rand, May 1986), p. 16.

Table 18   Estimates of Gross and Net Hard Currency Debt (in billions of dollars)

	1971	1975	1976	1977	1978	1979	1980	1981	1982	1983
Soviet Union										
gross	1.8	10.6	14.7	15.6	16.4	18.1	17.6	20.9	20.1	20.0
net	0.6	7.5	10.0	11.2	10.4	9.3	9.3	12.4	10.1	8.4
Bulgaria										
gross	0.7	2.6	3.2	3.7	4.3	4.4	3.5	3.1	2.8	2.5
net	0.7	2.3	2.8	3.2	3.7	3.7	2.7	2.2	1.8	1.4
Czechoslovakia										
gross	0.5	1.1	1.9	2.6	3.2	4.1	4.9	4.4	4.0	3.5
net	0.2	0.8	1.4	2.1	2.5	3.1	3.6	3.5	3.3	2.6
German Democratic Republic										
gross	1.4	5.2	5.9	7.1	8.9	10.9	14.4	14.7	13.1	12.3
net	1.2	3.5	5.0	6.2	7.5	9.0	11.8	12.5	11.1	8.9
Hungary										
gross	1.1	3.1	4.1	5.7	7.5	8.5	9.1	8.7	7.7	8.3
net	0.8	2.2	2.9	4.5	6.5	7.3	7.0	7.0	6.6	6.7
Poland										
gross	1.1	8.0	11.5	14.0	17.8	22.7	25.1	25.5	25.2	26.4
net	0.8	7.4	10.7	13.5	17.0	21.5	24.5	24.7	24.2	25.2
Romania										
gross	1.2	2.9	2.0	3.6	5.2	7.0	9.4	10.2	9.8	8.9
net	1.2	2.4	2.5	3.3	4.8	6.5	9.1	9.8	9.4	8.4
Yugoslavia										
gross				8.4	10.7	13.5	17.4	19.0	18.5	18.9
net				6.4	8.4	12.2	16.1	17.4	17.7	17.9

Source: Economist Intelligence Unit, *Regional Review: Eastern Europe and the USSR, 1985* (London: EIU, 1985), p. 16.

Table 19 Gross Fixed Agricultural Investment and Its Share in Total Investment

	Indexes of gross fixed agricultural investment (preceding period = 100)					Agriculture's share in total investment (%)				
	1966–70	1971–75	1976–80	1981	1982	1966–70	1971–75	1976–80	1981	1982
Bulgaria[1]	139	135	124	116	81	16.1	15.3	13.3	12.4	10.7
Czechoslo-vakia[2]	103	139	131	106	98	11.1	10.8	10.6	10.9	11.0
German Democratic Republic[3]	162	121	109	103	91	14.1	12.2	10.4	9.8	9.5
Hungary[4]	182	143	104	n.a	n.a	15.9	14.5	11.2	14.3	15.1
Poland[5]	170	165	146	87	88	17.4	15.2	16.2	18.6	18.4
Romania[6]	153	149	154	110	n.a	15.5	14.0	13.4	15.4	n.a
Yugoslavia[7]	152	162	129	n.a	n.a	9.2	9.3	9.1	n.a	n.a

[1]State and collective farms' investment in leva at 1962 and 1971 prices.
[2]Total investment in agriculture in crowns, 1966–75 at 1967 prices; 1976–82 at 1977 prices.
[3]Agriculture includes forestry and investment in marks, 1966–75 at 1967 prices; 1976–82 at 1975 prices.
[4]Investment in forints, 1966–75 at 1968 prices; 1976–80 at 1976 prices; 1981–82 at current prices.
[5]Investment in złotys, 1966–75 at 1971 prices; 1976–82 at 1977 prices.
[6]Investment in lei, 1966–75 at 1963 prices; 1976–81 at 1977 prices.
[7]Investment including private farming, 1966–75 in dinars; 1976–80 is an estimate.
Source: Gregor Lazarcik, "Comparative Growth of Agricultural Output, Inputs, and Productivity in Eastern Europe, 1965–82," in *East European Economies: Slow Growth in the 1980s*, vol. 1. Selected Papers Submitted to the Joint Economic Committee, Congress of the United States (Washington, D.C.: U.S. Government Printing Office, 1985), p. 417.

Table 20 Nuclear Reactors in East European Comecon Countries

	Reactor name and location	Type	Capacity in megawatts	Date operable
Bulgaria	Kozlodui 1	PWR[1]	440	1974
	Kozlodui 2	PWR	440	1975
	Kozlodui 3	PWR	440	1978
	Kozlodui 4	PWR	440	1979
	unnamed			1990
	unnamed	PWR	plans include 440 and 1000	1990
	unnamed			1990
	unnamed			1990
Czechoslovakia	Bohunice A-1	GCHWR[2]	150	1972
	Bohunice V-1	PWR	440	1978
	Bohunice V-1	PWR	440	1980
	Bohunice V-2	PWR	440	1982
	Bohunice V-2	PWR	440	1983
	Dukovany	PWR	4×440	1983–85
	Mochovce	PWR	4×440	1986–90
	Malovice	PWR	4×1000	1990–2000
German Democratic Republic	Rheinsberg 1	PWR	70	1966
	Griefswald-Nord 1-1	PWR	440	1973
	Griefswald-Bruno Leuschner	PWR	440	1974
	Griefswald-Nord 2-1	PWR	440	1978
	Griefswald-Nord 2-2	PWR	440	1980
	Griefswald	PWR	4×440	1980–90
Poland	Zernowiec (near Gdansk)	PWR	440	1984
	Zernowiec	PWR	440	1985
	Kujawy	PWR	3×1000	1990
Hungary	Paks	PWR	440	1981
	Paks	PWR	440	1982
	Paks	PWR	440	1984
	Paks	PWR	440	1985
	(more planned)			1990
Romania[3]	Cernavoda	PWR	600	1985
	(14 more reactors planned)	PWR	600	1987

[1]Pressurized (light) water reactor, VVER type.

[2]Gas-cooled heavy water reactor.

[3]After a period of hesitation Romania opted out of the Comecon nuclear energy cooperation system and pursued an independent line by installing two Canadian Candu reactors.

Source: Vladimir Sobell, *The Red Market: Industrial Co-operation and Specialization in Comecon* (Aldershot, England: Gower, 1984), p. 70.

Notes

1 The Course of Political Development

1 See Robert R. King, *Minorities under Communism* (Cambridge, Mass.: Harvard University Press, 1973), esp. pp. 5–50.

2 Hugh Seton-Watson, *Eastern Europe between the Wars* (Hamden, Conn.: Archon Books, 1946). For a longer perspective on Eastern Europe, see Joseph Rothschild, *East Central Europe between the Wars* (Seattle and London: University of Washington Press, 1983).

3 The immediate postwar phase is well covered by Hugh Seton-Watson in *The East European Revolution,* (New York: Praeger, 1951).

4 Zbigniew K. Brzezinski, *The Soviet Bloc: Unity and Conflict* (Cambridge, Mass.: Harvard University Press, 1960), pp. 40–103.

5 For these cases, see Adam Ulam, *Titoism and the Cominform* (Cambridge, Mass.: Harvard University Press, 1952), pp. 173–99 (for Gomułka), pp. 199–217 (for Kostov).

6 His ideas on Balkan federation were criticized in *Pravda* 28 January 1948. For Stalin's private treatment of him, see Milovan Djilas, *Conversations with Stalin* (London: Methuen, 1962), pp. 128–33, 154–68.

7 The literature on the break is huge. Dennison Rusinow has a fine chapter on it in his incomparable *The Yugoslav Experiment, 1948–1974* (London: C. Hurst, for the Royal Institute of International Affairs, 1977), pp. 32–80.

8 See J. F. Brown, *The New Eastern Europe: The Khrushchev Era and After* (New York: Praeger, 1966).

9 On this point regarding the broader implications of the Soviet destruction of the Prague Spring, see Philip Windsor, *Change in Eastern Europe* (London: Royal Institute of International Affairs, 1980).

10 See J. F. Brown, *Relations between the Soviet Union and Its East European Allies: A Survey* (Santa Monica: Rand, 1975).

11 For a brief analysis of the cause of Poland's economic crash, and one that has general application for the situation in other East European countries, see Włodzimierz Brus, "Economics and Politics: The Fatal Link," in Abraham Brumberg, ed., *Poland: Genesis of a Revolution* (New York: Random House, 1981), pp. 26–41.

12 No better book on Solidarity has been published so far than Timothy Garton Ash, *The Polish Revolution: Solidarity* (New York: Scribner's, 1984).

13   Windsor, *Change in Eastern Europe*, discusses this point with great insight.

14   For a favorable and optimistic assessment of Gorbachev, see Archie Brown: "Gorbachev: New Man in the Kremlin," *Problems of Communism* (May–June 1985).

15   For an excellent discussion of legitimacy in Eastern Europe, see Sarah Meiklejohn Terry, "The Implications of Economic Stringency and Political Succession for Stability in Eastern Europe in the Eighties," in U.S. Congress, Joint Economic Committee, *East European Economies: Slow Growth in the 1980's* (Washington, D.C.: U.S. Government Printing Office, 1985), vol. 1, pp. 502–40.

16   Richard Lowenthal, "The Ruling Party in a Mature Society," in Mark G. Field, ed., *Social Consequences of Modernization in Communist Societies* (Baltimore: Johns Hopkins University Press, 1976), pp. 106–13.

17   Wolfgang Leonhard, *Child of the Revolution* (London: Collins, 1959).

18   For a more comprehensive summary, though dealing mainly with the Soviet Union, see Marcus Wheeler, "Ideology and Politics," in George Schöpflin, ed., *The Soviet Union and Eastern Europe—A Handbook*, 2d ed. (London: Muller, Blond and White, 1986), pp. 208–18.

19   See Carl Beck, "Leadership Attributes in Eastern Europe," in Carl Beck, Frederic J. J. Fleron, Jr., et al., *Comparative Communist Political Leadership* (New York: David McKay, 1973), pp. 86–153.

20   See Ferenc Fehér et al., *Dictatorship over Needs: An Analysis of Soviet Societies* (London: Blackwell, 1983). Also Leszek Kołakowski, "The Intelligentsia," in Brumberg, *Poland*, pp. 54–67.

21   See J. Adelman, ed., *Communist Armies in Politics* (Boulder, Colo.: Westview Press, 1982); D. Herspring and I. Völgyes, eds., *Civil-Military Relations in Communist Systems* (Boulder, Colo.: Westview Press, 1978).

22   See W. D. Connor, "Social Change and Stability in Eastern Europe," *Problems of Communism* (November–December 1977).

23   See, for example, Jürgen Tampke, *The Peoples' Republics of Eastern Europe* (London: Croom Helm, 1983).

24   *Protokoly tzw Komisji Grabskiego* (Paris: Instytut Literacki, 1986). I am grateful to Wiesława Surazska of Wolfson College, Oxford, for drawing my attention to this.

25   Romuald Spasowski, *The Liberation of One* (New York: Harcourt Brace Jovanovich, 1986), p. 492. Gierek had worked for many years in French and Belgian coal mines.

26   See Herspring and Völgyes, *Civil-Military Relations*.

27   See A. Ross Johnson, *The Role of the Military in Yugoslavia: An Historical Sketch* (Santa Monica: Rand, January 1978).

28   J. F. Brown, *Communist Rule in Bulgaria* (New York: Praeger, 1970), pp. 173–87.

29   Michael Shafir, "Romania," in Martin McCauley and Stephen Carter, eds., *Leadership and Succession in the Soviet Union, Eastern Europe and China* (London: Macmillan, 1986), pp. 129–33.

2   Soviet–East European Relations

1   For a fuller discussion, see Brzezinski, *The Soviet Bloc*; J. F. Brown, *Relations between the Soviet Union and its Eastern European Allies: A Survey* (Santa Monica: Rand, 1975); John Van Oudenaren, *The Soviet Union and Eastern Europe: Options for the 1980's and Beyond* (Santa Monica, Rand, 1984); Robert L. Hutchings, *Soviet–East*

European Relations: Consolidation and Conflict, 1968–1980 (Madison: University of Wisconsin Press, 1983); John C. Campbell, *"Soviet Policy in Eastern Europe: An Overview,"* in Sarah Meiklejohn Terry, ed., *Soviet Policy in Eastern Europe*, (New Haven and London: Yale University Press, 1984); Richard Lowenthal, "Changing Soviet Policies and Interests," in *Soviet-American Relations and World Order: The Two and the Many* (Adelphi Papers no. 66, London, Institute for Strategic Studies, March 1970), pp. 11–23.

2   Paul Marer addresses this subject directly in his chapter, "The Political Economy of Soviet Relations with Eastern Europe," in Terry, *Soviet Policy in Eastern Europe*, pp. 171–85.

3   Paul Marer, "Intrabloc Economic Relations and Prospects," in David Holloway and Jane M. O. Sharp, eds., *The Warsaw Pact: Alliance in Transition?* (Ithaca, N.Y.: Cornell University Press, 1984), pp. 215–37. See also Morris Bornstein, "Soviet–East European Economic Relations," in Morris Bornstein, Zvi Gitelman, and William Zimmerman, eds., *East-West Relations and the Future of Eastern Europe: Politics and Economics* (London: George Allen and Unwin, 1981), esp. pp. 106–10.

4   Zdeněk Mlynář, *Nightfrost in Prague* (New York: Karz, 1980), pp. 239–40.

5   See the excellent discussion of this in Van Oudenaren, *The Soviet Union and Eastern Europe*, pp. 3–17.

6   Helpful in this connection are the following: Melvin Croan, "Entwicklung der Politischen Beziehungen zur Sowjetunion seit 1955," and Gerhard Wettig, "Warschauer Pakt," in Hans Adolf Jacobsen, Gerd Leptin, Ulrich Scheuner, and Eberhard Schultz, eds., *Die Jahrzehnte Aussenpolitik der DDR* (Munich: R. Oldenbourg, 1979), pp. 347–85 and 559–73, respectively.

7   See James F. Brown, *Soviet Relations with the Northern Tier in East Europe*, EAI Paper no. 9, Spring 1985 (Marina del Rey, Calif., European American Institute for Security Research) pp. 5–9.

8   In view of the virtual unanimity on this subject in Eastern Europe, it is stimulating to find a vigorously argued dissenting view by, of all people, a Pole. See Edmund Osmanczyk (well-known journalist and member of the Sejm) in *Die Zeit*, 9 August 1984.

9   See Gerhard Wettig, "The Present Soviet View on Trends in Germany," in Harry Gelman, ed., *The Future of Soviet Policy toward Western Europe* (Santa Monica, Rand, 1985).

10   See Brown, *Soviet Relations with the Northern Tier*, pp. 42–47.

11   See Jiři Valenta, *Soviet Intervention in Czechoslovakia: An Anatomy of a Decision* (Baltimore: Johns Hopkins University Press, 1979), pp. 125–28.

12   See David J. Dallin, *Soviet Foreign Policy after Stalin* (New York: J. P. Lippincott, 1961), pp. 364–65; J. F. Brown: *The New Eastern Europe: The Khrushchev Era and After* (New York: Praeger, 1969), p. 187.

13   The deterioration of the Soviet position in the Balkans is vividly described in Paul Lendvai, *Eagles in Cobwebs: Nationalism and Communism in the Balkans* (New York: Doubleday, 1969).

14   See J. F. Brown: "The Balkans: Soviet Ambitions and Opportunities," *The World Today* (June 1984).

15   Ibid. This article was written before Hoxha died in April 1985, but the points it makes about Albania's future remain relevant.

16 See F. Stephen Larrabee, "Papandreou: National Interests Are the Key," *Atlantic Monthly* (March 1983).

17 See Hutchings, *Soviet–East European Relations*, pp. 160–68.

18 Mlynář, *Nightfrost in Prague*, pp. 194–96.

19 They were certainly—and understandably—favorites of the Soviet ambassador, Chervenenko. See Jiří Valenta: "Soviet Policy toward Hungary and Czechoslovakia," in Terry, ed., *Soviet Policy in Eastern Europe*, p. 114.

20 For this brief discussion of the Warsaw Pact I have depended greatly on Robert L. Hutchings, *Foreign and Security Policy Coordination in the Warsaw Pact* (Berichte des Bundesinstituts für ostwissenschaftliche und internationale Studien, Cologne, no. 15, 1985). See also Malcolm Mackintosh: "The Warsaw Treaty Today," *Survival* (May–June 1974), and "The Warsaw Treaty Organization: A History," in Holloway and Sharp, eds., *The Warsaw Pact*, pp. 41–58; A. Ross Johnson, "The Warsaw Pact: Soviet Military Policy in Eastern Europe," in Terry, ed., *Soviet Policy in Eastern Europe*, pp. 255–83; Teresa Rakowska-Harmstone et al., *Warsaw Pact: The Question of Cohesion* (Ottawa: Operational Research and Analysis Establishment, 1984).

21 MTI (Hungarian News Agency), 4 April 1984.

22 *Pravda*, 16 September 1965.

23 The Romanian counterproposals (officially denied in Bucharest) were reported in the *New York Times*, 16 May 1966. For Czechoslovak views, see Alexander Alexiev, "The Czechoslovak Military," in A. Ross Johnson, Robert W. Dean, and Alexander Alexiev, *East European Military Establishments: The Warsaw Pact Northern Tier* (New York: Crane Russak, 1982), pp. 114–21.

24 Hutchings, *Foreign and Security Policy Coordination*, pp. 44–45.

25 Ibid., p. 34.

26 Ibid., p. 37. Confirming and greatly strengthening the point about Soviet control over the East European national armies is the information contained in the interview given by Colonel Ryszard J. Kuklinski, a senior Polish staff officer, to the Paris-based Polish exile magazine, *Kultura*, and published in its April 1987 edition. Kuklinski, who defected to the West in November 1981, refers to the "Statute of Joint Armed Forces [of the Warsaw Pact] and Organs of Their Command in Wartime," which stipulates that in wartime the leadership of the armed forces of the East European countries is to be assumed completely by the "Supreme and Highest Command," which is, in effect, the Soviet High Command. Only Romania refused to accept this statute. (See also chapter 5, n. 38.)

27 See Brown, *Relations between the Soviet Union and Its Eastern European Allies*, pp. 9–10.

28 Ibid., pp. 10–15.

29 See Fritz Ermarth, *Internationalism, Security and Legitimacy: The Challenge to Soviet Interests in East Europe, 1964–1968* (Santa Monica, Rand, 1969).

30 See William E. Griffith, *Albania and the Sino-Soviet Rift* (Cambridge, Mass.: MIT Press, 1963); Bernhard Tönnes, *Sonderfall Albanien* (Munich: F. Oldenbourg, 1980). Tönnes argues powerfully for the historical continuity of the Hoxha regime.

31 Of the several books written on the origins of the Romanian deviation, the most stimulating is Kenneth Jowitt, *Revolutionary Breakthroughs and National Development: The Case of Rumania* (Berkeley and Los Angeles: University of California Press, 1971).

32 See the massive and outstanding work by H. Gordon Skilling, *Czechoslovakia's Interrupted Revolution* (Princeton, N.J.: Princeton University Press, 1976).

33 For details of Bulgaria's apparent willingness for closer relations with Bonn, see J. F. Brown, *Communist Rule in Bulgaria* (New York: Praeger, 1970), pp. 284–86.

34 For a fuller discussion by the author, see Brown, *Relations between the Soviet Union and Its Eastern European Allies*, pp. 16–31.

35 Especially helpful in this particular context is Henry Wilcox Schaefer, *Comecon and the Politics of Integration* (New York: Praeger, 1972).

36 See William F. Robinson, *The Pattern of Reform in Hungary* (New York: Praeger, 1973), p. 181.

37 Giuseppe Boffa, "Special Relations in the Eastern European Bloc: Origins, Effects, Connections with the Communist Movement," *The International Spectator* (Rome) no. 1 January–March 1986, p. 32.

38 In the early 1980s there was considerable speculation about a new world conference, with the Czechoslovak party being particularly insistent on the need for one. By 1986, however, it seemed that the idea, if not abandoned entirely, had been very much put on the back burner.

39 See Andrzej Korbonski, "Soviet Policy toward Poland," in Terry, ed., *Soviet Policy in Eastern Europe*, pp. 61–71.

40 See John P. Hardt, "Soviet Energy Policy toward Eastern Europe," in Terry, ed., *Soviet Policy in Eastern Europe*, pp. 189–220.

41 See Włodzimierz Brus, "Economics and Politics: The Fatal Link," in Abraham Brumberg, ed., *Poland: Genesis of a Revolution* (New York: Random House, 1983), pp. 26–41. The author has relied heavily on Brus in writing about both the Polish economy and the economic-political link.

42 See Timothy Garton Ash, *The Polish Revolution: Solidarity* (New York: Scribner's, 1983), passim. Also Jan B. de Weydenthal, Bruce D. Porter, and Kevin Devlin, *The Polish Drama 1980–1982* (Lexington, Mass.: Lexington Books, 1983), pp. 101–44 and 283–98.

43 Elizabeth Ann Goldstein, "Soviet Economic Assistance to Poland, 1980–81," in John P. Hardt, ed., *Soviet Economy in the 1980s: Problems and Prospects*, pl. 2, selected papers submitted to the Joint Economic Committee, Congress of the United States (Washington, D.C.: U. S. Government Printing Office, 1983), p. 567. Cited by Korbonski, "Soviet Policy toward Poland," p. 85 n. 38. This figure includes "at least 3.1 billion dollars in bloc assistance (almost all of it Soviet) and 1.5 billion dollars Polish trade deficit with the Soviet Union." It excludes the Soviet subsidy on energy exports. In 1982, i.e., after the imposition of martial law, direct Soviet assistance was marginal.

44 See Bruce Porter, "Warsaw Pact Maneuvers and Poland: The Political Implications," *Radio Liberty Background Report* (Munich), 17 March 1981.

45 Published in the Polish party daily, *Trybuna Ludu*, 11 June 1981.

46 PAP (Polish News Agency) 18 September 1981.

47 Bruce Porter, "The USSR and Poland on the Eve of the PUWP's Ninth Congress," *Radio Liberty Background Report* (Munich), 13 July 1981.

48 See Valenta, "Soviet Policy toward Hungary and Czechoslovakia," pp. 123–28.

49 Timothy Garton Ash in *The Polish Revolution*, pp. 326–27, argues that some kind of compromise might have been possible in the first few months of Solidarity's existence. See chapter 5.

50 See Melvin Croan: "A New Afrika Corps," the *Washington Quarterly* (Winter 1980).

51 See Sonia A. Winter, "Czechoslovakia's Trade with the West," *Radio Free Europe Research Background Report* (Munich), 4 August 1983.

52 See Edwina Moreton, "Foreign Policy Goals," in Holloway and Sharp, eds., *The Warsaw Pact*, pp. 141–60.

53 Ibid., pp. 146–48.

54 For a good survey of initial East European reaction to Gorbachev's reform pronouncements, see R. St., "Osteuropäische Stimmen zu Gorbatschew's Kurs," *Neue Zürcher Zeitung* (Fernausgabe) 22–23 February 1987. The announcement of the Bulgarian reforms was made after the publication of this article. See chapter 10, p. 328.

55 Carried in Charles Gati, *Hungary and the Soviet Bloc* (Durham, N.C.: Duke University Press, 1986), p. 135. For assessments of Soviet–East European relations under Gorbachev, see Gati's article, "Gorbachev and Eastern Europe," *Foreign Affairs* (June 1987); also Seweryn Bialer, *The Soviet Paradox: External Expansion, Internal Decline* (New York: Knopf, 1986), pp. 173–231; and Ivan Völgyes, "Troubled Friendship or Mutual Dependence? Eastern Europe and the USSR in the Gorbachev Era," *Orbis* (Summer 1986).

3 Relations with the West and the Impact of Détente

1 A Bulgarian intellectual in conversation with the author in 1978 described the eagerness with which any possibility of Western travel was sought after. So much so that the Soviet embassy became concerned that few intellectuals or academics wanted to go to the Soviet Union and so many wanted to go West.

2 See, for example, Kundera's speech on receiving the Jerusalem Prize for Literature, published in *New York Review of Books*, 13 June 1985. Also his interview in *New York Times Magazine*, 19 May 1985, and in *Granta* (Cambridge, England), no. 11, 1984. For Konrád, see György Konrád, *Antipolitics* (New York: Harcourt Brace Jovanovich, 1984).

3 See William E. Griffith, *The Ostpolitik of the Federal Republic of Germany* (Cambridge, Mass.: MIT Press, 1978), passim.

4 For an excellent, balanced discussion of the Rapacki Plan, see Helga Haftendorn, *Sicherheit und Entspannung, Zur Assenpolitik der Bundesrepublik Deutschland* (Baden-Baden: Nomos, 1983), pp. 110–16.

5 See, for example—although he does not specifically mention the Rapacki Plan —Otto Schily's contribution to the published symposium, *Reden über des eigene Land: Deutschland 2* (Munich: Bertelsmann, 1984), p. 50.

6 See Horst Lambrecht, "Entwicklung der Wirtschaftsbeziehungen zur Bundesrepublik Deutschland," in Jacobsen et al., *Die Jahrzehnte Aussenpolitik*, pp. 453–72.

7 See Josef Joffe, "The Tacit Alliance: Bonn's Policy in Central and Eastern Europe," in Lincoln Gordon, *Eroding Empire: Western Relations with Eastern Europe* (Washington, D.C.: Brookings Institution, 1987).

8 See Brown, *Communist Rule in Bulgaria*, pp. 284–86.

9 See Pierre Hassner, "The View from Paris," in Gordon, *Eroding Empire*.

10 See his article in the *Observer* (London), 11 May 1980 on the twenty-fifth anniversary of Austria's independence.

11 See *Radio Free Europe Hungarian Situation Report*, no. 4, 6 April 1985.

12 For more on Austria's political and economic policy in Eastern Europe, see J. F. Brown, "The Views from Vienna and Rome," in Gordon, *Eroding Empire*. Also Friedrich Levcik and Jan Stankovsky, *A Profile of Austria's East-West Trade in the 1970s and 1980s*, a study prepared for ECE/UN (Vienna: Vienna Institute for International Comparative Economic Studies, May 1985).

13 The best history of the Vatican's Eastern policy is Hansjakob Stehle, *Die Ostpolitik des Vatikans* (Munich: Piper, 1975).

14 Of the many books about Pope John Paul II one of the most perceptive remains George Blazynski, *John Paul II: A Man from Cracow* (London: Weidenfeld and Nicolson, 1979); see especially pp. 25–104.

15 For a good discussion of this issue, see Vladimir Kusin, "Czechoslovakia's Proregime Priests Contest Vatican Decree," *Radio Free Europe Background Report*, 14 July 1982.

16 See R. St., "Heitere Demonstration des Glaubens in Mähren," *Neue Zürcher Zeitung* (Fernausgabe), 11 July 1985.

17 See, for example, "Der Papst mahnt den ungarischen Episkopat," *Frankfurter Allgemeine Zeitung*, 6 January 1979.

18 See Josef Schmitz van Vorst, "Ungarn hat den Vatikan überspielt," *Frankfurter Allgemeine Zeitung*, 4 April 1979.

19 See Christopher Cviic, "The Church," in Brumberg, *Poland: Genesis of a Revolution*, especially pp. 96–102.

20 See Stehle, *Die Ostpolitik des Vatikans*, pp. 305–48.

21 Ibid.

22 See chap. 5, pp. 185–86, for a discussion of Glemp's characteristics. The pope was known to be personally close to several of Solidarity's advisers.

23 For a perceptive but sympathetic view of Glemp's strategy, see Jörg Bremer, "Weder Unbesonnenheit noch Feigheit," *Frankfurter Allgemeine Zeitung*, 24 October 1985.

24 Archbishop Sarić of Sarajevo, for example, collaborated with the Nazis. In Bosnia the situation was especially complicated because of the racial and religious mixture. Only about 20 percent of the population was Croat and Catholic.

25 There was much tension over the issue of Catholic education. See Zdenko Antić, "Catholic Schools and Education in Yugoslavia," *Radio Free Europe Research Report*, 26 January 1979.

26 Tanjug (Yugoslav News Agency), 19 December 1980. There may have been no inconsistency here because of the independence enjoyed and flaunted by the republican capital, Zagreb, as against the Federal center, Belgrade. But Jure Bilić, one of Croatia's top party and state leaders, indicated early in January 1981 that church–state relations in Croatia were satisfactory (Tanjug, 12 January 1981).

27 This was in a speech by Jakov Blazević, Croatia's titular head of state, on the publication of his memoirs. Blazević had been the public prosecutor at Stepinac's trial. See Zdenko Antić, "Catholic Church under Fire in Croatia," *Radio Free Europe Research Report*, 20 February 1981.

28 See CVK, "Kirchenfeiern in Kommunistischen Kroatien," *Neue Zürcher Zeitung* (Fernausgabe), 16–17 September 1984.

29 See Kevin Devlin, "The Challenge of Eurocommunism," *Problems of Communism* (January–February 1977).

30 For a different view, see Jiři Valenta, "Eurocommunism and Eastern Europe," *Prob-*

lems of Communism (March–April 1978).

31 On the Eurocommunist view of Eastern Europe, see Eric Willenz, "Eurocommunist Perceptions of Eastern Europe: Ally or Adversary?" in Vernon A. Aspaturian, Jiři Valenta, and David P. Burke, eds., *Eurocommunism between East and West* (Bloomington: Indiana University Press, 1980), pp. 254–70.

32 The most quoted of Kádár's pronouncements on Eurocommunism was in response to a denunciation made by the Bulgarian leader, Todor Zhivkov, who described Eurocommunism as "anti-Soviet" (*Rabotnichesko Delo*, 1 December 1976). In a reply to the Associated Press on 7 December 1976 Kádár dissociated himself from this view. The dissociation was clear enough but it should be remembered that Kádár made the statement while in the West (a visit to Finland) to a Western agency. In Budapest he would certainly have been more cautious.

33 For a good brief summary of the East Berlin conference, see Hutchings, *Soviet–East European Relations*, pp. 208–12; also Kevin Devlin, "The Decline and Fall of Conciliar Communism: Pan-European Miscalculations," *Radio Free Europe Background Report*, 6 July 1984.

34 The best running commentaries in the West on Yugoslav relations with the West are in the *Neue Zürcher Zeitung, Süddeutsche Zeitung, Frankfurter Allgemeine Zeitung,* and *Le Monde.*

35 See Brown, *Relations between the Soviet Union and Its East European Allies,* pp. 82–84.

36 See Siegfried Kupper, "Politische Beziehungen zur Bundesrepublik Deutschlands 1955–1977," in Jacobsen et al., *Die Jahrzehnte Aussenpolitik*, pp. 435–43.

37 David Childs, *The GDR: Moscow's German Ally* (London: George Allen and Unwin, 1983), pp. 86–87.

38 See Hajek and Niznansky, "Signing of the FRS-Czechoslovak Treaty: The Thorny Road to Normalization," *Radio Free Europe Research Background Report*, 7 December 1973.

39 See Jane M. O. Sharp, "Security through Détente and Arms Control," in Holloway and Sharp, *The Warsaw Pact*, pp. 165–75; also Charles Andras, "The 'Freer Flow' Issue at Helsinki," *Radio Free Europe Research Background Report*, 22 August 1975.

40 Consensus was not achieved at the CSCE "Cultural Forum" in Budapest in November–December 1985 or at the "Human Rights" Forum in Berne in July 1986. For the best coverage of the Helsinki follow-up conferences see Vojtech Mastny, *Helsinki, Human Rights and European Security: Analysis and Documentation* (Durham, N.C.: Duke University Press, 1986). This is partly based on the excellent series of Radio Free Europe/Radio Liberty reports by Roland Eggleston.

41 The best expert discussion of this subject is in David Buchan, *Western Security and Economic Strategy Towards the East* (London: International Institute for Strategic Studies, Adelphi Paper no. 192, 1984).

42 For a good review of the progress of East European indebtedness through the 1970s and into the 1980s, see the *Neue Zürcher Zeitung* (Fernausgabe), 2–3 December 1984, analysis of the *Economic Bulletin for Europe*, vol. 36, United Nations, 1984.

43 See Childs, *The GDR*, pp. 218–27.

44 Ibid, pp. 104–5.

45 See the Minutes of the Grabski Commission cited in chap. 1, p. 26, n. 24.

46 For Romanian and Bulgarian initiatives during this period see J. F. Brown, *Commu-*

nist Rule in Bulgaria (New York: Praeger, 1970), pp. 269–73.

47 See Patrick Moore, "The Diplomatic Scene," in the chapter entitled "Balkan Sources of International Instability," in Vojtech Mastny, ed., *Soviet East European Survey, 1983–1984: Selected Research and Analysis from Radio Free Europe/Radio Liberty* (Durham, N.C.: Duke University Press, 1985), pp. 259–65.

48 These points are taken from J. F. Brown, "The Soviet Union View of East European Détente in the Aftermath of the Polish Crisis," in Harry Gelman, ed., *The Future of Soviet Policy Toward Western Europe* (Santa Monica: Rand, 1985), pp. 103–16.

49 Ibid., pp. 104–5.

50 *Frankfurter Allgemeine Zeitung,* 24 July 1984.

51 *East Berlin and Moscow: the Documentation of a Dispute,* compiled and introduced by Ronald C. Asmus (Munich: RFE Occasional Papers, Radio Free Europe, 1985), p. 9.

52 *Társadalmi Szemle* (Budapest), no. 1, January 1984, translated and printed in Asmus, ibid., pp. 21–24.

53 It is worth noting, not least for the sake of irony, that Hungary and Romania could unite on this point at a time when relations between them were deteriorating sharply over the Hungarian minority question in Transylvania. The irony is heightened by the fact that Szürös himself became one of the sharpest Hungarian official critics on this issue. See "Situation of Ethnic Hungarians in Romania Viewed with Mounting Concern," *Radio Free Europe Research Hungarian Situation Report,* 25 February 1986.

54 Speech to SED Central Committee plenum, reported in *Neues Deutschland,* 26–27 November 1983, translated and reprinted in Asmus, *East Berlin and Moscow,* pp. 19–21.

55 Michal Stefanak and Ivan Hlivka, "The National and the International in the Policy of the CPCS," *Rúde Právo,* March 1984, translated and printed in Asmus, ibid., pp. 25–27.

56 Interview with *Magyar Hirlap,* 4 April 1984, translated and printed in Asmus, ibid., pp. 27–30.

57 L. Bezymensky, "In the Shadow of American Missiles," *Pravda,* 27 July 1984, translated and printed in Asmus, ibid., pp. 46–49.

58 See Asmus, ibid., pp. 49–54.

59 See *Bureau of the Census, Historical Statistics of the United States: Colonial Times to 1970* (Washington, D.C.: U. S. Government Printing Office, 1975), pp. 105–6. These statistics are reproduced in Lincoln Gordon et al., *Eroding Empire: Western Relations with Eastern Europe* (Washington D.C.: Brookings Institution, 1987), p. 68 n. 2. Gordon's book, to which this author also contributed, is the most current and authoritative review of Western policy and contains chapters on German, French, and British policy as well as American. In writing this review of American policy the author has depended heavily on Gordon's book. He has also extensively used Raymond L. Garthoff's excellent chapter, "Eastern Europe in the Context of U. S.-Soviet Relations," in Terry, *Soviet Policy in Eastern Europe,* pp. 315–48.

60 Gordon, *Eroding Empire,* p. 67.

61 Ibid.

62 Ibid.

63 For German Ostopolitik, see Josef Joffe, "The View from Bonn: The Tacit Alliance," in Gordon, *Eroding Empire,* pp. 129–87.

64 Department of State Bulletin, vol. 83 (November 1983), pp. 19–23, carried by Garthoff, pp. 338–39.

65 See statistical table in Gordon, *Eroding Empire*, p. 75.

66 Since the Jackson-Vanik amendment to the Trade Act of 1974 making the granting of MFN annually dependent on the emigration policy of the recipient, Romanian behavior has been almost constantly under critical inspection. It has somehow passed the test every time, but there is no certainty this will continue.

67 See Garthoff, p. 318 and n. 5.

68 For an excellent discussion of the realities of American policy in the early postwar years and after, see Bennet Kovrig, *The Myth of Liberation: East-Central Europe in U.S. Diplomacy and Politics since 1941* (Baltimore: Johns Hopkins University Press, 1973).

69 Zbigniew Brzezinski and William E. Griffith, "Peaceful Engagement in Eastern Europe," *Foreign Affairs*, July 1961. See also Brzezinski's *Alternative to Partition: For a Broader Concept of America's Role in Europe* (New York: McGraw-Hill for Council on Foreign Relations, 1965).

70 In an address at a closed meeting in London to American ambassadors in Europe in December 1975, the then State Department counselor, Helmut Sonnenfeldt, called for an "organic" relationship between the Soviet Union and the East Europeans. This was later distorted in parts of the American press, particularly by Evans and Novak, "A Soviet-East European 'Organic Union,'" *Washington Post*, 22 March 1976. Actually, Sonnenfeldt said nothing particularly new or startling, although what he said was bound to be subject to leaks and distortions and might have been phrased more felicitously.

71 For example, Kissinger was reported ready to consider the closing of Radio Free Europe as a bargaining chip in return for Soviet concessions in other areas. The author was told this by several Washington sources.

72 Zbigniew Brzezinski, *Power and Principle: Memoirs of the National Security Adviser, 1977–1981* (New York: Farrar, Straus and Giroux, 1983), pp. 300, 541, quoted by Gordon, *Eroding Empire*, p. 82.

73 Gordon, *Eroding Empire*, p. 82.

74 These impressions were gained by the author when he worked for Radio Free Europe. He had many encounters with American diplomats during this period, encounters not always free of controversy, but always free of acrimony.

4 An Economic Overview

1 Alan H. Smith, "The Eastern Bloc Economic Model," in EIU (The Economist Intelligence Unit) Regional Review, *Eastern Europe and the USSR 1985* (London: Economist Publications, 1985), p. 6. See also the same author's *The Planned Economies of Eastern Europe* (London: Croom Helm, 1983), esp. pp. 18–53.

2 Ibid., p. 5.

3 *Pravda*, 9 September 1962.

4 Smith, *Eastern Europe and the USSR 1985*, p. 7. See also Brown, *The New Eastern Europe*, pp. 81–124.

5 Morris Bornstein, "Economic Reform in Eastern Europe," in John P. Hardt, ed., *East European Economies Post-Helsinki*, papers submitted to the Joint Economic Com-

mittee, (Congress of the United States, Washington, D.C.: GPO, 1977), pp. 109–10. See also the same author's *Plan and Market: Economic Reform in Eastern Europe* (New Haven: Yale University Press, 1973).

6 Smith, *Eastern Europe and the USSR 1985*, p. 7.

7 Ibid., pp. 7–8.

8 Stanislaw Gomulka, *Growth, Innovation and Reform in Eastern Europe* (Brighton, England: Wheatsheaf Books, 1986), pp. 271–98.

9 Ibid., p. 274.

10 Smith, *Eastern Europe and the USSR 1985*, p. 10.

11 Romolo Caccavale, "Is There Chance for Reforms in the East?" *L'Unità* (Rome), 26 October 1983, quoted in Kevin Devlin, "Are the East Bloc Regimes Reformable? Leftists Ask," *Radio Free Europe Research Background Report*, 3 November 1983.

12 Włodzimierz Brus, "Political System and Economic Efficiency: The East European Context," in Gomulka, *Growth, Innovation and Reform*, p. 28.

13 Ibid., pp. 28–29.

14 Keith Crane, *The Soviet Economic Dilemma of Eastern Europe* (Santa Monica: Rand, September 1984), p. 5.

15 Laura d'Andrea Tyson, *Economic Adjustment in Eastern Europe* (Santa Monica: Rand, September 1984), p. 5.

16 John M. Kramer; "Soviet-CEMA Energy Ties," *Problems of Communism*, July–August 1985.

17 Tyson, *Economic Adjustment in Eastern Europe*, p. 15.

18 Kosygin's promise was made at the June 1980 Comecon Council Meeting in Prague. See John P. Hardt, "Soviet Energy Policy in Eastern Europe," in Terry, *Soviet Policy in Eastern Europe*, p. 212.

19 See Alexander Nicoll, "East Europeans Welcomed back to the Fold," *Financial Times*, 18 March 1986.

20 See chap. 8, pp. 285–86.

21 See Crane, *The Soviet Economic Dilemma*, pp. 15–42.

22 Ibid., pp. 37–38.

23 Gregor Lazarcik, "Comparative Growth of Agricultural Output, Inputs and Productivity in Eastern Europe, 1965–82," in *East European Economies: Slow Growth in the 1980's*, vol. 1, Economic Performance and Policy, pp. 391–92, table 1.

24 Everett M. Jacobs, "Agriculture," in Schöpflin (ed.), *The Soviet Union and Eastern Europe*, p. 431.

25 Ibid., p. 434.

26 Karl E. Wädekin, "East European Agriculture Trends and Prospects: A European Perspective," in *East European Economies*, vol. 1, p. 432.

27 Ibid., p. 432.

28 Lazarcik, "Comparative Growth of Agricultural Output," pp. 391–92, table 1.

29 Jacobs, "Agriculture," p. 440. In 1982 the Bulgarian private plots appear to have had a share of nearly 40 percent of total animal production, Wädekin, "East European Agriculture," p. 442.

30 Wädekin, "East European Agriculture," p. 443.

31 Ibid., p. 444.

32 Crane, *The Soviet Economic Dilemma*, p. 3, table 1.

33 Michael Marrese and Jan Vaňous, *Soviet Subsidization of Trade with Eastern Europe:*

A Soviet Perspective (Berkeley: Institute of International Studies, University of California, 1983).

34   Raimund Dietz, "Advantages and Disadvantages in Soviet Trade with Eastern Europe," in *East European Economies: Slow Growth in the 1980's*, vol. 2, Foreign Trade and International Finance, p. 288. Dietz makes a comprehensive criticism of the methods used by Marrese and Vaňous and argues especially that "forgone gains are by no means subsidies, although they may, in some cases, in fact, imply that subsidies are being paid" (p. 294).

35   Paul Marer, "Intrabloc Economic Relations and Prospects," in Holloway and Sharp, *The Warsaw Pact*, pp. 215–37; Jozef M. Van Brabant, "The USSR and Socialist Economic Integration—A comment," *Soviet Studies* (January 1984).

36   Crane even suggests that it was possible that neither the Soviets nor the East Europeans actually perceived a subsidy (p. 15). He notes Dietz's observation that the Soviets made no complaint on this subject till 1979 and then again in 1981 during the Polish crisis (Dietz, "Advantages and Disadvantages in Soviet Trade," pp. 295–96).

37   Crane, *The Soviet Economic Dilemma*, pp. 32–33.

38   See, for example, Ceauşescu's speech at the Romanian party anniversary, 7 May 1986 (*Scînteia*, 8 May 1966).

39   For Albania see William E. Griffith, *Albania and the Sino-Soviet Rift* (Cambridge, Mass: MIT Press, 1963), pp. 46–47; for Poland see examples quoted by Kramer, "Soviet-CEMA Energy Ties," p. 37.

40   Hardt, *East European Economies Post-Helsinki*, pp. 189–94; Kramer, "Soviet-CEMA Energy Ties," p. 33.

41   Hardt, *East European Economies*, p. 192.

42   Ibid., pp. 196–98.

43   Kramer, "Soviet-CEMA Energy Ties," p. 44.

44   See Leslie Colitt and David Buchan, "Oil Price Plunge Hits East Europe," *Financial Times*, 19 February 1986.

45   Marvin Jackson, "When is a Price a Price? The Levels and Patterns of Prices in the CEMA," *Radio Free Europe Research Background Report*, 24 August 1985; reproduced by Kramer, "Soviet-CEMA Energy Ties," p. 42.

46   Hardt, *East European Economies Post-Helsinki*, pp. 206–7.

47   See Colitt and Buchan, *Financial Times* 19 February 1986. It should be stated, however, that serious doubts have been raised about these figures for East German oil exports. See *PlanEcon Report*, vol. 2, no. 9, 3 March 1986, pp. 9–12.

48   Crane, *The Soviet Economic Dilemma*, p. 30.

49   Ibid., p. 42.

50   See Michael Kaser, *Comecon: Integration Problems of the Planned Economics* (London: Oxford University Press, 1965), pp. 9–38.

51   There is enough evidence to suggest that Khrushchev wished both Bulgaria and Albania to adopt policies similar to those advocated for Romania. On his visit to Tirana in 1959, for example, he openly urged Albania to become a "flourishing garden" (see chap. 11, p. 382, n. 29). For Bulgaria the evidence is mainly from unofficial sources. Bulgaria, however, proceeded with full-scale industrialization, with Soviet permission.

52   See Hutchings, *Soviet–East European Relations*, pp. 169–92.

53   Ibid., p. 190.

54 Daniel Franklin, EIU Regional Review, *Eastern Europe and the USSR 1985*, p. 20.
55 Vladimir Sobell, *The Red Market: Industrial Cooperation and Specialization in Comecon* (Aldershot, England: Gower, 1984), p. 6.
56 Ibid., p. 8.
57 Ibid., p. 9.
58 The news of a Comecon summit after fifteen years brought forth several good articles in the Western press. Two of the best were in the *Neue Zürcher Zeitung* (Fernausgabe): A. O., "Beschwörung der Integration am Comecon-Gipfel," 17–18 June 1984, and "Harte Haltung Moskaus am Comecon Gipfel," 22 June 1984. On the East-West trade aspect see also David Buchan, "Comecon Looks to Loosen Western Ties," *Financial Times*, 12 June 1984.
59 Franklin, *Eastern Europe and the USSR 1985*, p. 21.
60 See Vladimir Sobell, "Mikhail Gorbachev Takes Charge of the CMEA," *Radio Free Europe Research Background Report*, 20 December 1985.

5 Poland

1 For an amplification of these points, see J. F. Brown, "The Significance of Poland," in Lawrence L. Whetten, ed., *The Present State of International Communism* (Lexington, Mass.: Lexington Books, 1983).
2 See Brzezinski, *The Soviet Bloc*, pp. 333–57.
3 For a (perhaps overly sympathetic) biography of Gomułka see Nicholas Bethell, *Gomulka, His Poland and his Communism* (London: Longmans, 1969). Also Hansjakob Stehle, *The Independent Satellite* (New York: Praeger, 1963).
4 See A. Ross Johnson, "Polish Perspectives Past and Present," *Problems of Communism* (July–August 1971).
5 For Moczar see George Blazynski, *Flashpoint Poland* (New York: Pergamon Press, 1979), pp. 27–28.
6 See Jack Bielasiak, "The Party: Permanent Crisis," in Brumberg, *Poland: Genesis of a Revolution*, pp. 12–15.
7 Jacques Rupnik in a brilliant essay on the military in Poland deals with the various phases through which it has passed during the communist period: "The Military and Normalisation in Poland," in Paul Lewis, ed., *Eastern Europe: Political Crisis and Legitimation* (London: Croom Helm, 1984), pp. 154–71, esp. pp. 159–61. See also A. Ross Johnson's excellent chapter on the Polish military in A. Ross Johnson, Robert W. Dean, and Alexander Alexiev, *East European Military Establishments: The Warsaw Pact Northern Tier* (New York: Crane Russak, 1982), pp. 17–61.
8 Some of Glemp's more unfortunate comments, the anti-Semitic implications of which were obvious, were made in Brazil in March 1984, where he called some Solidarity advisers "Trotskyites" with little in common with true Poles. As occasionally was the case after his statements to the press, he subsequently sought to soften his remarks (AP, 21 March 1984, and Reuters, 23 March 1984).
9 For the Polish and East German roles in the Czechoslovak crisis see Erwin Weit, *Eyewitness* (London: Andre Deutsch, 1973), pp. 196–210. Weit, who subsequently came to live in the West, had been Gomułka's interpreter.
10 This is all in marked contrast to the longevity of southern tier leaders—Zhivkov, Tito, Hoxha, Ceauşescu—not to mention Kádár.

11 For a good character sketch of Gierek, see Blazynski, *Flashpoint Poland*, pp. 79–86.

12 See ibid., chap. 3, "A Year of Agonizing Reappraisals 1971," pp. 32–78.

13 Romuald Spasowski, *The Liberation of One*, p. 492.

14 Blazynski, *Flashpoint Poland*, p. 69.

15 Brus, "Economics and Politics: The Fatal Link," in Brumberg, *Poland: Genesis of a Revolution*, pp. 31–37.

16 Ibid., p. 34.

17 Ibid., pp. 35–37.

18 In Terry, ed., *Soviet Policy in Eastern Europe*, pp. 69–71.

19 Brus, "Economics and Politics: The Fatal Link," p. 27.

20 See Aleksander Smolar, "The Rich and the Powerful," in Brumberg, *Poland: Genesis of a Revolution*, pp. 42–53.

21 Bielasiak, "The Party: Permanent Crisis," p. 16.

22 See "Reform of Territorial Administration" and "Appointment of Voivodship Party Secretaries," *Polish Situation Reports*, Radio Free Europe Research, 16 May 1975 and 16 June 1975, respectively.

23 I am grateful to Wiesława Surazska on this point. See also chap. 1, p. 26, n. 24.

24 See Thomas E. Heneghan, "The Summer Storm in Poland," *Radio Free Europe Research Background Report*, 16 August 1976.

25 See Smolar, "The Rich and the Powerful," pp. 42–47.

26 Ibid., p. 43.

27 Brus, "Economics and Politics: The Fatal Link," p. 37. The discussion about Poland's credit policy is based wholly on Professor Brus's chapter.

28 Leszek Kołakowski, "The Intelligentsia," in Brumberg, *Poland: Genesis of a Revolution*, p. 63.

29 For the origins of both these groups see, "KOR Broadens its Horizons" and "Workers Defence Committee Renamed and Scope Broadened," *Polish Situation Reports*, Radio Free Europe Research of 20 May 1977 and 13 October 1977, respectively.

30 See "The New Dissident Group," *Polish Situation Report*, Radio Free Europe Research, 13 September 1979.

31 There appeared, however, to be a not unsurprising lack of cordiality after the food price fiasco of June 1976. Meeting almost immediately afterward at the European Communist party conference in East Berlin the two men were described by the Polish news agency PAP on June 29 as having had a "friendly talk." The term "brotherly" was not used, as it was to describe Brezhnev's conversations with other allied leaders.

32 For a good assessment of Olszowski see Gert Baumgarten, "Ein unbequemer Minister geht zum zweiten Mal von Bord," *Stuttgarter Zeitung*, 13 November 1985.

33 For an admirable chronology of the strikes leading to the formation of Solidarity, see *August 1980: The Strikes in Poland* (Munich: Radio Free Europe Research, 1980). RFE Research provided the best ongoing coverage of the Solidarity period.

34 Sermon at Czestochowa on 26 August which was carried on Warsaw television the same evening.

35 The Deutsche Presse Agentur (dpa), the West German news agency, carried this statement in full on 28 August 1980. For Wyszyński's meeting with Wałęsa see the *New York Times*, 8 September 1980.

36 See J. B. de Weydenthal, "Poland on the Eve of the PUWP's Extraordinary Ninth Party Congress," *Radio Free Europe Research Background Report*, 14 July 1981. Also A. Ross Johnson, *Poland in Crisis* (Santa Monica: Rand, July 1982). Johnson is particularly good where he stresses that it was Solidarity's organizational threat to the party and not the few examples of "verbal excess" by its leaders that made the regime determined to suppress it.

37 Moczar, however, sought to divest himself of his anti-Semitic reputation and paid a tribute to the Jewish role in Polish history; *Trybuna Ludu*, 4 November 1980. Anti-Semitism continued to be a weapon used against some of Solidarity's intellectual advisers.

38 In this case the revelations of former Colonel Ryszard J. Kuklinski, see chapter 3, n. 26, are informative. In an interview published in the Paris *Kultura* in April 1987 Kuklinski, who was privy to much of the military planning to counter Solidarity, says that Jaruzelski was all along determined to crush Solidarity but was desperately anxious that it be done by Poles, not Russians. Kuklinski, whose version of events is not always consistent, cites Kania as the only Polish leader who genuinely wanted negotiations with Solidarity.

39 Garton Ash, *The Polish Revolution: Solidarity*, pp. 326–27.

40 Zmotoryzowane Odwody Milicji Obywatelskiej—ZOMO (Motorized Detachments of the Citzen's Militia). Many members of this body were also young peasants. The same units could be quickly transferred by air from one trouble spot to another. It was widely suspected that before going into action many ZOMOs were plied with alcohol or drugs.

41 Radio Warsaw, 1 February 1984.

42 See Eric Bourne, "New Polish Unions Assert their Power," *Christian Science Monitor*, 24 January 1984.

43 See "Poland: Alienated Youth," *Polish Situation Report*, Radio Free Europe Research, 7 April 1984.

44 For a good review of the church's position after December 1981, see Hansjakob Stehle, "Poland: Can the Church Point the Way?," *The World Today* (February 1981).

45 See Jan B. de Weydenthal et al., "The Torun Trial," in Vojtech Mastny, ed., *Soviet–East European Survey 1984–1985* (Durham, N.C.: Duke University Press, 1986), pp. 166–73.

46 For example, Jerzy Urban, the Polish government spokesman, claimed that American sanctions had done $15-billion damage to the Polish economy. *Rzeczpospolita* (Warsaw), 29 October 1985. But everything Urban said was dubious. His figure should best be taken as a rough indicator.

47 *United States Policy Toward Poland: A Conference Report* (Santa Monica: Rand, April 1987), pp. 1–2.

6 Hungary

1 As the thirtieth anniversary of the Revolution approached, however, the regime began to treat it with much greater candor than ever before. Television, radio, and press implied a greater understanding for the popular mood in both 1956 and 1986. See, for example, Leslie Colitt, "Hungary Lifts the Lid on 1956 Uprising," *Financial Times*, 12 September 1986.

2 See Bennet Kovrig, "Decompression in Hungary—Phase Two," in Peter A. Toma, ed.,

The Changing Face of Communism (Tucson: University of Arizona Press, 1970), pp. 193–213; Charles Gati, "The Kádár Mystique," *Problems of Communism,* May–June 1974; George Schöplin, "Hungary Between Prosperity and Crisis," *Conflict Studies,* no. 136, 1981.

3   Reported in *Népszabadság,* 10 December 1961.

4   Hungarian underground literature is strewn with such accusations, but there have also been many implied, indirect references in official literature and the press.

5   A Hungarian foreign ministry official had to deny he was resigning. *Kurier* (Vienna), 30 October 1964.

6   See Alfred Reisch, "Laszlo Rajk Remembered," *Radio Free Europe Research Background Report,* 17 April 1984.

7   For further discussion on this point, see J. F. Brown, "Die ungarische Aussenpolitik im Schatten des Bundnisses," *Europa-Archiv* (Bonn), no. 15, 1967, pp. 541–50.

8   The German Press Agency correspondent in Budapest, Kurt Gebauer, in his dispatch of 8 October 1968 had the fullest report on this.

9   Probably the best, most direct source for Soviet opposition is former Central Committee secretary Rezsö Nyers himself; for example, his interview in *Corriere della Sera* (Milan), 29 July 1984. Nyers subsequently protested about the way *Corriere della Sera* had used his remarks, but he did not specifically deny any of them (*Corriere della Sera,* 17 August 1984). Evidence that opposition persisted in some senior Soviet circles is evident from the ambiguity in the speech of Politburo member and Central Committee Secretary Grigorii Romanov to the thirteenth Hungarian party congress in March 1986. See "CPSU Fails Formally to Endorse Hungary's Economic Reform," *Hungarian Situation Report,* Radio Free Europe Research, 27 April 1985. (Romanov was later purged by Gorbachev.)

10 The pioneering study on the NEM is by William F. Robinson, *The Pattern of Reform in Hungary* (New York: Praeger, 1973). For later discussions, see Paul Hare, Hugo Radice, and Nigel Swain, eds., *Hungary: A Decade of Economic Reform* (London: George Allen and Unwin, 1981); and Rudolf Tökes, "Hungarian Reform Imperatives," *Problems of Communism* (September–October 1984).

11 Robinson, *The Pattern of Reform,* pp. 3–69.

12 Ibid., pp. 79–80.

13 Ibid., pp. 78–79.

14 Hans-Georg Heinrich, *Hungary: Politics, Economics and Society* (London: Frances Pinter, 1986), pp. 45–47.

15 Robinson, *The Pattern of Reform,* pp. 49–80.

16 Heinrich, *Hungary: Politics, Economics and Society,* pp. 46–47.

17 See Nyers, *Corriere della Sera,* 29 July 1984. Bilak was reported to have criticized the Hungarian reforms in a speech to the Czechoslovak Central Committee in October 1971 (*Corriere della Sera,* 14 February 1972). Bilak subsequently denied this report (*Rúde Právo,* 20 April 1972).

18 See Paul Marer, "Economic Reform in Hungary: From Central Planning to Regulated Market," in *East European Economies: Slow Growth in the 1980's,* vol. 3, Country Studies on Eastern Europe and Yugoslavia, Selected Papers submitted to the Joint Economic Committee, Congress of the United States (Washington, D. C.: U.S. Government Printing Office, 1986), pp. 239–46. People like myself have been indebted to Professor Marer for many years for his expert and clear writings on the East European economies.

19 Marer, "Economic Reform in Hungary," pp. 246–47.

20 Heinrich, *Hungary: Politics, Economics and Society*, p. 41. See Laura D'Andrea Tyson, *Economic Adjustment in Eastern Europe* (Santa Monica: Rand, 1984), pp. 39–63.

21 Marer, "Hungary's Balance of Payments Crisis and Response, 1977–1984," in *East European Economies: Slow Growth in the 1980's*, vol. 3, p. 301.

22 Keith Crane, *The Soviet Economic Dilemma of Eastern Europe* (Santa Monica: Rand, May 1986), p. 31.

23 John P. Hardt and Richard F. Kaufman, "Policy Highlights," "A Regional Economic Assessment of Eastern Europe," *East European Economies*, vol. 1, p. viii.

24 "Shadows behind the Shop-Window," The *Economist* (London), 14 June 1986.

25 See R. St., "Ein Stellvertreter für János Kádár," *Neue Zürcher Zeitung* (Fernausgabe), 30 March 1985.

26 Havasi's stature emerges in an interview with Christian Schmidt-Häuer, *Die Zeit* (Hamburg), 28 May 1986.

27 Heinrich, *Hungary: Politics, Economics and Society*, pp. 147–49.

28 "Eastern Europe and the USSR" (The Economist Intelligence Unit, London, 1985), p. 70.

29˙ *Népszabadság*, 28 March 1986.

30 R. St., "Mehr Raum für Privatinitiative in Ungarn," *Neue Zürcher Zeitung* (Fernausgabe), 14–15 March 1982.

31 Heinrich, *Hungary: Politics, Economics and Society*, p. 161. See also Dietmar Stützer, "In Ungarn Landwirtschaft eine Universalbeschäftigung," *Süddeutsche Zeitung*, 1 September 1986.

32 Ibid., p. 162.

33 "Financial Markets and Trends" (OECD), quoted in Alexander Nicol, "East Europeans Welcomed Back to the Fold," *Financial Times*, 18 March 1986.

34 *Financial Times*, 11 September 1986.

35 Crane, *The Soviet Economic Dilemma*, p. 31.

36 The 70 percent figure was given to the author by a private source. Keith Crane has assured me of the plausibility of the information, which is also confirmed in PlanEcon Report of 11 November 1985.

37 *Financial Times*, 12 September 1986.

38 See "Enterprises Run by New Types of Management," *Hungarian Situation Report*, Radio Free Europe Research, 2 February 1985.

39 See "On the Eve of the 1985 National Elections" and "Election Results and their Assessment," *Hungarian Situation Report*, Radio Free Europe Research, 21 June 1985. András Hegedüs was enthusiastic about the electoral reform, saying that it represented "the embryo of an alternative socialist model"; see Kevin Devlin, "Hegedüs tells Rinascità, Hungarian Electoral Reforms Are Something New," *Radio Free Europe Research Background Report*, 1 July 1985. A thoughtful, sober view is by Judy Dempsey, "Hungary's Elections: A Half-Step towards Pluralism?," *The World Today* (August–September 1985).

40 See "Kippen und Schwellen," *Der Spiegel*, 17 December 1984.

41 Statisztikai Evkönyv (Budapest: Központi Statisztikai Hivatal, 1986).

42 Népszabadsáy, 26 March 1985.

43 Heinrich, *Hungary: Politics, Economics and Society*, p. 88.

44 R. St., "Personelle Änderungen in Budapest," *Neue Zürcher Zeitung* (Fernausgabe),

26 June 1987.

45 Ibid.

7 The German Democratic Republic

1 See A. James McAdams, *East Germany and Détente: Building Authority after the Wall* (Cambridge: Cambridge University Press, 1985). This book is excellent in putting East German domestic policy in the context of relations with the Federal Republic and East-West relations in Europe.

2 See David Childs, *The GDR: Moscow's German Ally* (London: George Allen and Unwin, 1983), pp. 41–42.

3 Ibid., pp. 195–228.

4 As late as October 1984, in spite of the emigration of about 1,500 political prisoners during that year, it was estimated that there were still about ten thousand political prisoners in the GDR: dpa (German Press Agency) 24 October 1984.

5 Brown, *The New Eastern Europe*, p. 101.

6 See Peter Christian Ludz, *The Changing Party Elite in East Germany* (Cambridge, Mass.: MIT Press, 1972); Thomas A. Baylis, *The Technical Intelligentsia and the East German Elite* (Berkeley: University of California Press, 1974).

7 Apel committed suicide at the end of 1965. Some suspected it was because the Soviets prevented a westward shift in GDR trade policy that he was advocating.

8 See also Carola Stern, *Ulbricht: eine politische Biographie* (Cologne and West Berlin: Verlag für Politik und Wirtschaft, 1963); Brown, *The New Eastern Europe*, pp. 262–64.

9 McAdams, *East Germany and Détente*, pp. 79–81.

10 Ibid., p. 81. See also Melvin Croan, "East Germany: The Soviet Connection," *The Washington Papers* (Beverly Hills: Sage, 1976), p. 10.

11 See Irwin Weit, *Eyewitness* (London: André Deutsch, 1973), pp. 196–210.

12 See Hutchings, *Soviet–East European Relations*, pp. 62–64.

13 *Trybuna Ludu*, 18 May 1969.

14 Terry, ed., *Soviet Policy in Eastern Europe*, p. 39.

15 McAdams, *East Germany and Détente*, pp. 118–19.

16 Ibid., p. 119.

17 Ibid., p. 125. For tables showing visits from the FRG and from West Berlin to the GDR during the 1970s, see Childs, *The GDR*, pp. 89–90.

18 McAdams, *East Germany and Détente*, p. 18.

19 Ibid.

20 See Anders Åslund, *Private Enterprise in Eastern Europe* (London: Macmillan in Association with St. Antony's College, Oxford, 1985), pp. 182–96.

21 On Stoph, see Peter Jochen Winters, "Vielleicht der einzige rote Preusse: Willi Stoph, der Ministerprasident der DDR, wird 70," *Frankfurter Allgemeine Zeitung*, 9 July 1984. Also appendix 2, p. 485.

22 On Hoffmann, see Ws., "Vater der National Volksarmee," *Frankfurter Allgemeine Zeitung*, 3 December 1985.

23 Mielke has remained a mystery man with a shadowy past. See Karl Wilhelm Fricke, "Ein politischer Mord vor fünfzig Jahren: Erich Mielke und das Attentat auf dem Berliner Bulowplatz," *Frankfurter Allgemeine Zeitung*, 5 August 1981.

24 This "social contract" side of Honecker's policy is well brought out by McAdams, *East Germany and Détente*, pp. 137–39.

25 John M. Kramer, "Soviet–CEMA Energy Ties," *Problems of Communism* (July–August 1985).

26 *Neue Zürcher Zeitung* (Fernausgabe), 27 March 1985, citing a report by the Vienna Institute for Comparative International Economics.

27 For the "swing" provision (and a critical view of its durability), see Peter Hort, "Hoffnungsvolle Blicke auf den 'Swing,'" *Frankfurter Allgemeine Zeitung*, 21 March 1985.

28 Analysis of the Central Intelligence Agency, *East European Economies: Slow Growth in the 1980's*, vol. 2: Foreign Trade and International Finance, Selected Papers submitted to the Joint Economic Committee Congress of the United States (Washington, D.C.: U.S. Government Printing Office, 1986), p. 170. See also Maria Haendke-Hoppe, "DDR—Aussenhandel im Zeichen schrumpfender Westimporte," *Deutschland-Archiv*, no. 10, 1983.

29 Manfred Melzer and Arthur A. Stahnke, "The GDR Faces the Economic Dilemmas of the 1980's: Caught Between the Need for New Methods and Restricted Options," in *East European Economies: Slow Growth in the 1980's*, vol. 3: Country Studies on Eastern Europe and Yugoslavia, pp. 132–35 and p. 166.

30 Quoted by Doris Cornelsen, "Die Wirtshaft der DDR 1981–1985," *Politik und Zeitgeschichte* (Beilage zur Wochenzeitung *Das Parlament*, 25 January 1986), p. 3.

31 Ibid., p. 4.

32 Cornelsen, "Die Wirtschaft der DDR," p. 5.

33 Actually some Kombinaten, centrally directed, had existed since 1973; see Melzer and Stahnke, "The GDR Faces Economic Dilemmas," pp. 139–42.

34 For a profile of one of them, see Peter Jochen Winters, "Siegfried Porsche, ein Wirtschaftskapitan der DDR," *Frankfurter Allegmeine Zeitung*, 8 August 1983; also "What It Takes to Be Boss" (an article on Wolfgang Biermann, director of Carl Zeiss Jena), in the *Economist*, 22 February 1986.

35 Melzer and Stahnke, "The GDR Faces Economic Dilemmas," p. 166 and pp. 132–35. For an expert review of the situation in 1985 and future prospects, see *Plan Econ Report*, vol. II, no. 9, 3 March 1986. See also B. V. Flow: "The East German Economy: What is Behind the Success Story?," *Radio Free Europe Research Background Report*, 15 March 1985.

36 Melzer and Stahnke, "The GDR Faces Economic Dilemmas," p. 133.

37 See "It's a Long Way from Prussia to Russia," the *Economist*, 22 February 1986.

38 For the types of shops, see Childs, *The GDR*, pp. 144–46.

39 An excellent article on the whole GDR policy on this issue is by Albert Hunze, "Ein Warteschlange von unbekannter Laenge," *Süddeutsche Zeitung*, 19 January 1985. Some of the immigrants to the Federal Republic wanted to return, a fact over which the GDR authorities made a huge propaganda campaign; see Helmut Lölhöffel, "Der stille Treck ins andere Deutschland," *Süddeutsche Zeitung*, 8 March 1985.

40 See Barbara Donovan, "Inter-German Relations: Political and Cultural Aspects," *Radio Free Europe Background Report*, 8 May 1987, esp. n. 2.

41 Rudolph Bahro, an SED member since 1954, was arrested in 1977 on charges of antistate activity. His real crime was having had a book published in West Germany strongly critical of socialist practice in the GDR. He was allowed to go to the Federal Republic in 1978.

42 See sk., "Der Situation der Katholischen Kirche in der DDR," *Neue Zürcher Zeitung* (Fernausgabe), 15 December 1983.

43 For example, in 1985 only one in four children was baptized. Only one out of three

marriages was celebrated in church. The numbers on the church register of *Land* Mecklenburg dropped between 1975 and 1985 from 782,000 "souls" to 555,129. Karl-Heinz Baum, "Zahlen der Ernüchterung und des Aufbruchs," *Frankfurter Rundschau*, 25 March 1985.

44 See Ronald D. Asmus, "Is There a Peace Movement in the GDR?," *Orbis*, Summer 1983. Also B. V. Flow, "The East German Protestant Church: Variations on the Theme of Peace," *Radio Free Europe Research Background Report*, 21 November 1985.

45 See Matthew Boyse, "Increased Militarization of East German Society," *Radio Free Europe Research Background Report*, 23 August 1986.

46 See Ws., "Keine Nachteile für Verweigerer Paramilitärische Lehrlingsausbildung," *Frankfurter Allgemeine Zeitung*, 8 March 1986.

47 So much so that some observers have tended to see the church as essentially doing a service for the regime. See, for example, James M. Markham, "East German Clerics: Defenders of Marxist Faith," *New York Times*, 9 October 1984.

48 For an excellent review, up to 1980, of religion generally in the GDR, see Sharon L. Kegerreis, "A Church within Socialism: Religion in the GDR Today," *Radio Free Europe Research Background Report*, 8 October 1980.

49 See B. V. Flow, "A Major Biography Caps Bismarck's Rehabilitation in the GDR," *Radio Free Europe Research Background Report*, 26 March 1986. Also Ronald D. Asmus, "The Portrait of Bismarck in the GDR," *Radio Free Europe Research Background Report*, 24 July 1984.

50 The best treatment of this is by Ronald D. Asmus, "The GDR and Martin Luther," *Survey* (London), vol. 28 (Summer 1984).

51 The point is well brought out by Timothy Garton Ash in his brilliant "Which Way Will Germany Go?" *New York Review of Books*, 31 January 1985. See also Ferdinand Hurni, "Deutscher als die Bundesrepublik?" *Neue Zürcher Zeitung*, 27 July 1987.

8 Romania

1 *Scînteia*, 22 August 1968.

2 See David Sherman Spector, *Romania at the Paris Peace Conference: A Study of the Diplomacy of Ioan C. Bratianu* (New York: Bookman Associates, 1962).

3 This was not the first implicit Romanian claim to Bessarabia. In 1964 the Romanians published Karl Marx's ruminations on the subject, which clearly supported their historical claim. A. Oţetea and S. Schwann, eds., *K Marx—Insemnari Despre Romani* (Bucharest: R. P. R. Academy of Sciences, 1964).

4 Paul Lendvai, *Eagles in Cobwebs: Nationalism and Communism in the Balkans* (New York: Doubleday, 1969), p. 273.

5 Ibid. Some aspects of Premier Ionel Bratianu's policy in the 1920s were later evoked in the communist period. See ibid., p. 272.

6 This is best argued in John Michael Montias, *Economic Development in Communist Romania* (Cambridge, Mass.: MIT Press, 1967).

7 Nikita S. Khrushchev, *Khrushchev Remembers: The Last Testament*, ed. Strobe Talbott (Boston: Little, Brown, 1976), pp. 227–29.

8 See Ghiţa Ionescu, *Communism in Romania 1944–1962* (London: Oxford University Press, 1964), pp. 1–46.

9 There is an English translation of this document in William E. Griffith, *Sino-Soviet*

Relations (Cambridge, Mass.: MIT Press, 1967), p. 282.

10 See, for example, his speech on the forty-fifth anniversary of the founding of the Romanian Communist party, *Scînteia*, 7 May 1968. See also J. F. Brown, "Rumänien unter Nicolae Ceauşescu," *Osteuropäische Rundschau*, July 1967.

11 This was especially true in the early stages of the conference; see, for example, Hannes Gamillschlag, "In der Konferenzpause beginnt die Arbeit," *Frankfurter Rundschau*, 23 March 1984.

12 Hutchings, *Soviet–East European Relations*, pp. 98–100.

13 See *Romanian Situation Report*, Radio Free Europe Research, 31 December 1983.

14 Interview to Hsinhua, New China News Agency, reported in *Scînteia*, 3 May 1983.

15 At the end of 1986 both Honecker and Jaruzelski had already visited China.

16 See, for example, Richard Homan, "Romanians Block Unity at Warsaw," *Washington Post*, 20 April 1974.

17 Practically on the eve of this meeting (November 1978) Chinese troops had invaded Vietnam on a "punitive mission."

18 See Charles Andras, "A Summit with Consequences," *Radio Free Europe Background Research Report*, 14 December 1978. Also Anneli Ute Gabanyi, "Bucharest schert wieder aus," *Osteuropa*, no. 3, 1979.

19 See R. St., "Plebiszit uber Rustungsabbau in Rumänien" *Neue Zürcher Zeitung* (Fernausgabe), 23 October 1986.

20 See, for example, *Frankfurter Allgemeine Zeitung*, 29 January 1980.

21 See Anneli Ute Gabanyi, "Friedenspolitik zwischen autonomiestreben und Blockzwang. Uberlegungen zum rumänischen Abrustungsmodell," *Südosteuropa* (Munich), no. 1, 1984.

22 Three articles in *Le Monde* (Paris) by Jan Krauze sum up Ceauşescu's domestic and foreign policy at least as well as anything yet written. "Le Style, c'est l'homme," 28 February 1987; "Vingt-deux millions de fourmis et quelques cigales," 29 February 1984; "Quelques murmures isolés dans la foule," 1 March 1984.

23 In several conversations Kenneth Jowitt has persuasively argued the similarities.

24 See, for example, Michael Shafir, *Romania: Politics, Economics and Society* (London: Frances Pinter, 1985).

25 Apostol and Bîrlădeanu did not reveal their disgust in public. About Voitec, a former president of the Grand National Assembly, there remains considerable doubt despite unofficial reports of his opposition to Ceauşescu in 1980. See R. E., "Where Is Stefan Voitec?," and Dan Ionescu, "Stefan Voitec: The Death of a Long-Distance Runner," *Romanian Situation Reports*, Radio Free Europe Research, 20 January 1981 and 14 December 1984, respectively.

26 Kenneth Jowitt explains this "party familialization" (his term) mainly by sociology. In scarcity-conditioned peasant societies the corporate family becomes a basic self-defense unit. Posts, and wealth, are given to those one trusts, i.e., to family members, and these are expected to protect the patron and each other. See Kenneth Jowitt, *The Leninist Response to National Dependency* (Berkeley: Institute of International Studies, University of California, 1978).

27 See *Süddeutsche Zeitung*, 7 February 1983. For analyses of the Romanian military, see Alex Alexiev, *Party Military Relations in Romania* (Santa Monica: Rand, 1977); Ivan Völgyes, *The Political Reliability of the Warsaw Pact Armies: The Southern Tier* (Durham, N.C.: Duke Policy Studies, 1982).

28 Jowitt, *The Leninist Response.*

29 See W. M. Bacon, "The Military and the Party in Romania," in Dale R. Herspring and Ivan Völgyes, eds., *Civil-Military Relations in Communist Systems* (Boulder, Colo.: Westview Press, 1978), pp. 170–71.

30 See Robert R. King, *History of the Romanian Communist Party* (Stanford, Calif.: Hoover Institution Press, 1980), p. 88.

31 See Ceauşescu's speech in August 1983 in which he criticized even leading cadres who "argue whether or not to fulfill a task, whether or not to acquiesce in leaving a certain county." (*Scînteia,* 5 August 1983).

32 See Dan Ionescu, "Destruction of Old Bucharest Continues," *Romanian Situation Report,* Radio Free Europe Research, 13 August 1985. This piece contains several illustrations of the historic buildings to be destroyed. A good, indignant article on the subject is by Carl-Gustav Ströhm, "Denkmäle für den Parteichef oder die Zerstörung des alten Bucharest," *Die Welt,* 18 December 1985.

33 Speech at the November 1985 Central Committee meeting, *Scînteia,* 21 November 1985. Subsequently, at a Central Committee meeting in April 1986, Ceauşescu criticized the existing economic mechanism but gave no indication of any attempts at reform (*Scînteia,* 3 April 1986). In fact, after Ceauşescu's speech in November 1985 there appears to have been a campaign in the specialized press against economic reform. See "Romania Continues to Renounce Economic Reform," *Romanian Situation Report,* Radio Free Europe Research, 11 August 1986.

34 See *Romanian Situation Reports,* Radio Free Europe Research, of 10 December 1980 and 9 April 1985.

35 Ibid., 13 March 1985.

36 Laura D'Andrea Tyson, *Economic Adjustment in Eastern Europe* (Santa Monica: Rand, September 1984), pp. 84–92.

37 Ibid., pp. 83–84.

38 Ibid., pp. 85–86.

39 Joseph Brada and Marvin Jackson, "Romania: Crisis or Turning Point?," Wharton Econometric Forecasting Associates, Special Report, 1981, quoted by Tyson, p. 89.

40 Figures given by the Vienna Institute for Comparative International Economics, quoted in *Neue Zürcher Zeitung* (Fernausgabe), 27 March 1985.

41 See Paul Gafton, "Chernobyl and Romania's Debt to Western Banks," *Romanian Situation Report,* Radio Free Europe Research, 17 July 1986.

42 See Vladimir Socor, "Romanian Food Exports to the USSR Rising Sharply," *Radio Free Europe Research Background Report,* 19 August 1986.

43 See also Paul Gafton, "The Electricity Crisis," *Romanian Situation Report,* Radio Free Europe Research, 17 December 1985; also Leslie Colitt, "Romanian Economy Troubled by Winter Energy Cuts," *Financial Times,* 26 March 1986.

44 Figures given by the Vienna Institute for Comparative International Economics, quoted in *Neue Zürcher Zeitung* (Fernausgabe), 5–6 April 1985.

45 See F. Stephen Larrabee, *The Challenges to Soviet Interests in Eastern Europe: Romania, Hungary, East Germany* (Santa Monica: Rand, December 1984), pp. 33–46.

46 Many of the striking miners were Hungarian nationals, but there was apparently a strong unity between Romanian and Hungarian miners during the strike. See chap. 14, p. 432.

47 See Larrabee, p. 36 n. 24.

48 Viktor Meier, "Widerstand in der rumänischen Armee," *Frankfurter Allgemeine Zeitung*, 27 December 1985; Harry Schleicher, "Rumäniens Armee ist ins Kreuzfeuer geraten," *Frankfurter Rundschau*, 7 January 1986. Olteanu was by no means disgraced when he lost the defense ministry. He became mayor of Bucharest and kept up a high profile. He was believed to be a favorite of Elena Ceauşescu.

49 See Anneli Maier, "Press Retouching Photographs of Ceauşescu," *Romanian Situation Report*, Radio Free Europe Research, 11 September 1985.

50 For an expert analysis, see Michael Shafir, "Coalitions and Political Succession in Communist Systems: A Comparative Analysis of the Future of the Romanian leadership," *Südosteuropa*, no. 3–4, 1986.

9 Czechoslovakia

1   The literature on the Prague Spring is huge, and most of it is of good quality. But Gordon Skilling's monumental work is never likely to be surpassed: H. Gordon Skilling, *The Interrupted Revolution* (Princeton, N.J.: Princeton University Press, 1976). The best eyewitness account is Zdeněk Mlynář, *Nightfrost in Prague: The End of Human Socialism* (New York: Karz, 1980).

2   Vladimir V. Kusin, "Husak's Czechoslovakia and Economic Stagnation," *Problems of Communism*, May–June 1982. See also the same author's *From Dubcek to Charter 77* (New York: St. Martin's Press, 1978).

3   Kusin, "Husak's Czechoslovakia."

4   Crane, *The Soviet Economic Dilemma*, p. 32.

5   Kusin, "Husak's Czechoslovakia."

6   Men who knew him say it made him less derogatory about Russians.

7   For a survey of Slovakia during and after the Prague Spring, see Eugen Steiner, *The Slovak Dilemma* (London: Cambridge University Press, 1973).

8   Generally these led to the strengthening of the federal government in Prague. See "Which Way Federation in Czechoslovakia?," *Radio Free Europe Background Research Report*, 11 March 1970.

9   See Viktor Meier, "Die Slowakei is Selbstbewusster," *Frankfurter Allgemeine Zeitung*, 13 December 1984.

10 It has been very difficult to verify many of the reports about the victimization of clergy and some of the atrocities against them. Many are carried in the German-language Catholic news agencies, KNA and Kathpress. Some are undoubtedly exaggerated, but there is no reason to doubt the basic truth of many of them.

11 *Ekonomický Časopis*, no. 5, May 1975. See also, "Slovakia Catching Up," *Czechoslovak Situation Report*, Radio Free Europe Research, 4 September 1974.

12 Kusin, "Husak's Czechoslovakia."

13 Ibid.

14 At the end of 1984 Czechoslovakia's net hard-currency debt was put at $2.5 billion. Poland's was $24.9 billion, *Neue Zürcher Zeitung* (Fernausgabe), 27 March 1985.

15 *Rúde Právo*, 13 November 1972. Bilak waxed sarcastic about those who were, so soon after the trauma of 1968, allegedly already seeing "blue skies" when none existed.

16 Radio Prague, 19 June 1985.

17 Radio Prague, 17 February 1986.

18   *Rúde Právo*, 25 March 1986.

19   At the seventeenth Czechoslovak party congress in March 1986 Štrougal spelled out his reform ideas fairly clearly, *Rúde Právo*, 26 March 1986. See "Strougal Announces Economic Reforms," *Czechoslovak Situation Report*, Radio Free Europe Research, 16 April 1986.

20   Leslie Colitt, "West Woos Orders from Prague," *Financial Times*, 17 September 1985.

21   The changes involved far fewer regulations and much less subsidization. State and collective farms now had only two requirements to meet: to fulfill their quotas for the state purchase of grain and slaughter animals.

22   H. Gordon Skilling, "Independent Currents in Czechoslovakia," *Problems of Communism* (January–February 1985). Much of the information on current trends in society in this chapter is taken from this article.

23   For the early years of the charter, see H. Gordon Skilling, *Charter 77 and Human Rights in Czechoslovakia* (London: George Allen and Unwin, 1981). For a list of Charter papers for 1983 alone, see "Charter 77 in 1983: Documents," *Radio Free Europe Research Background Report*, 24 January 1984.

24   See Bradley Graham, "After Brief Thaw, Czechoslovak Ties to Church Frozen Again," *Washington Post*, 3 March 1985; also Hansjakob Stehle, "Ein Rest von Hoffnung: Prags Kafkaesk Angst vor dem Vatikan," *Die Zeit*, 29 June 1984.

25   Interview with Bradley Graham, *Washington Post*, 3 May 1984.

26   See the three excellent analyses under the general title "Saints Cyril and Methodius": (1) "Controversy over the Saints and Celebrations," (2) "Government to Interfere in Church's Commemoration," (3) "The Brother Saints in the Context of Czechoslovak History," in *Czechoslovak Situation Report*, Radio Free Europe Research, 19 April 1985.

27   See Skilling, "Independent Currents in Czechoslovakia."

28   Ibid. See also Harry Schleicher, "Auch Tschechen gegen Raketen," *Frankfurter Rundschau*, 23 December 1983.

29   Skilling, "Independent Currents in Czechoslovakia."

30   See "Drogensucht in der Tschechoslowakei," anonymous article, originating in Czechoslovakia, in *Neue Zürcher Zeitung* (Fernausgabe), 16 March 1985.

31   Vilem Prečan, *Vyvoj Charty, Zaznam z Konference ve Franken* (The Charter's Progress, Record of a Conference in Franken), *Index*, Cologne 1981, quoted by Skilling, "Independent Currents in Czechoslovakia."

10   Bulgaria

1   See J. F. Brown, *Bulgaria under Communist Rule* (New York: Praeger, 1970), pp. 23–28.

2   Ibid., pp. 53–82 and 96–142.

3   Ibid., pp. 173–89. See also Paul Lendvai, *Eagles in Cobwebs: Nationalism and Communism in the Balkans* (New York: Doubleday, 1969), pp. 235–39.

4   For a fuller discussion of leadership rivalries and factionalism, see J. F. Brown, "Bulgaria," in Martin McCauley and Stephen Carter, eds., *Leadership and Succession in the Soviet Union, Eastern Europe, and China* (London: Macmillan, 1986), pp. 136–56.

5   For an excellent discussion see Keith Crane, *The Soviet Economic Dilemma of Eastern Europe* (Santa Monica: Rand, 1986), passim.

6 A *Financial Times* survey on Bulgaria of 7 September 1984, quoting Wharton Econometrics, states that in the previous three years Bulgaria had made a profit of $2.2 billion on the re-export of refined or chemically reprocessed Soviet oil.

7 See, for example, *Financial Times*, 26 October 1984, commenting on the meeting of Comecon premiers in Havana.

8 See Brown, *Bulgaria under Communist Rule*, pp. 116–19.

9 On postwar relations with the Yugoslavs, see Paul Shoup, *Communism and the Yugoslav National Question* (New York: Columbia University Press, 1968), especially pp. 144–83.

10 Brown, *Bulgaria under Communist Rule*, pp. 126–29.

11 For excellent histories of the BCP, see Joseph Rothschild, *The Communist Party of Bulgaria: Origins and Development, 1883–1936* (New York: Columbia University Press, 1959); Nissan Oren, *Bulgarian Communism: The Road to Power, 1934–1944* (New York: Columbia University Press, 1971).

12 By far the best biographical sketch of Zhivkova is by Yordan Kerov (pseudonym), "Lyudmila Zhivkova—Fragments of a Portrait," *Radio Free Europe Research Background Report*, 27 October 1980.

13 There appears to have been some Bulgarian-Soviet (or Ukrainian) rivalry over the 1,300th anniversary of the first Bulgarian state and celebrations marking the 1,500th anniversary of Kiev. The Bulgarian celebrations were in 1981. The Soviets marked Kiev's 1,500th anniversary a year later. True, the Soviets had announced three years before that the anniversary of Kiev would be held in 1982, but this was after the Bulgarian preparations had begun and there seemed to be no genuine grounds, anyway, for celebrating Kiev's 1,500th anniversary in 1982.

14 *Agence France Presse* (AFP), 19 September 1984.

15 *Neue Zürcher Zeitung* (Fernausgabe), 5 and 6 April 1985, quoting figures on the performance of all the European Comecon states supplied by the Vienna Institute for Comparative International Economics.

16 For the end of 1984, the *Neue Zürcher Zeitung* (Fernausgabe) (30 November 1985) put the net debt at $0.7 billion.

17 Brown, *Bulgaria under Communist Rule*, pp. 143–72.

18 See R. N., "Bulgaria's Agro-Industrial Complexes after Seven Years," *Radio Free Europe Research Background Report*, 14 February 1977.

19 See "Bodyul Promotion Signals Move to Create Agroindustrial Complex," FB15 Background Paper, 14 January 1981.

20 For two well-informed analyses—skeptical to a greater or lesser degree—see Harry Schleicher, "Von Reform zu Reden wäre Übertreibung," *Frankfurter Rundschau*, 28 September 1984; and R. St., "Bulgariens Vortasten zu neuen Wirtschaftsmechanismen," *Neue Zürcher Zeitung* (Fernausgabe), 3-4 June 1984.

21 See "Small and Medium-sized Enterprises," *Bulgarian Situation Report*, Radio Free Europe Research, 16 January 1985; and "Small is Beautiful," the *Economist*, 4–11 November 1983.

22 Ivan Iliev, head of the State Planning Commission, *Rabotnichesko Delo*, 13 December 1985.

23 For a detailed report on Bulgaria's economic progress for 1985 and the first quarter of 1986, see *PlanEcon Report*, vol. 2, no. 24, 13 (June 1986).

24 See Harry Schleicher, "Frühjahrsputz mit Vagen Oberbegriffen," *Frankfurter*

Rundschau, 7 April 1986.

25 See R. St., "Bulgarian für einen 'neuen Sozialismus,'" *Neue Zürcher Zeitung* (Fernausgabe) 21 August 1987.

26 See "A Review of Bulgarian-Soviet Relations," *Bulgarian Situation Report*, Radio Free Europe Research, 7 November 1985.

27 In an otherwise excellent chapter called "The Bulgarian Stumbling Block," in his *Small-State Security in the Balkans* (London: Macmillan, 1983), pp. 179–230, Aurel Braun perhaps tends to neglect the element of "own" interest in Sofia's willingness to act as Moscow's proxy in the Balkans. For a general view of Bulgaria stressing its self-assertiveness, see Christian Schmidt-Häuer, "Bulgarien, das sich im Sozialismus geschickt eingerichtet hat, sucht grössere Eigenständigkeit," *Die Zeit*, 10 May 1984.

28 See "The Athens Conference and Regional Cooperation in the Balkans," in Robert R. King and James F. Brown, eds., *Eastern Europe's Uncertain Future* (New York: Praeger, 1977), pp. 31–45.

29 See Patrick Moore, "The Diplomatic Scene," in Vojtech Mastny, ed., *Soviet/East European Survey, Selected Research and Analysis from Radio Free Europe/Radio Liberty* (Durham, N.C.: Duke University Press, 1985), pp. 259–65.

30 The most dramatic of these was the murder of George Markov, the exiled Bulgarian playwright, with a poison-tipped umbrella in London in 1978. A similar attempt was also made on the life of another Bulgarian exile, the former regime journalist Vladimir Kostov. See Kostov's *Le parapluie bulgare* (Paris: Stock, 1986).

31 *Frankfurter Allgemeine Zeitung*, 19 April 1986.

11 Yugoslavia

1 The best economic coverage of Yugoslavia over the years has been by the *Neue Zürcher Zeitung* (Fernausgabe). See fjc, "Ungunstiges Gesamtbild der Jugoslawischen Wirtschaft," 13 September 1986.

2 For a detailed account of the aspects and development of the self-management system see Harold Lydall, *Yugoslav Socialism: Theory and Practice* (Oxford: Clarendon Press, 1984). For an excellent brief summary of the system see Paul Lendvai, *Eagles in Cobwebs: Nationalism and Communism in the Balkans* (New York: Doubleday, 1969), pp. 89–100. As a general guide to the history of communist Yugoslavia, see Dennison Rusinow, *The Yugoslav Experiment 1948–1974* (London: C. Hurst for the Royal Institute of International Affairs, 1977). This is probably the best book written on any East European communist country and, as those familiar with it will see, I relied heavily on it in writing this chapter. It should be read shortly before or shortly after reading Duncan Wilson, *Tito's Yugoslavia* (Cambridge: Cambridge University Press, 1979). Wilson's book provides signposts through Rusinow's detail. For the Yugoslav "atmosphere," the interaction between East, West, communism, and the Balkans, none is better than Dusko Doder, *The Yugoslavs* (London: George Allen and Unwin, 1979).

3 See Andreas Kohlschütter, "Titos Erben sind bankrott—Nur Resignation verhindert den Ausbruch von Arbeiterunruhen," *Die Zeit*, 17 January 1986.

4 Doder, *The Yugoslavs*, pp. 42–60, has an excellent discussion on social classes.

5 This progressive "confederalization" of Yugoslavia has been analyzed many times. See the books by Rusinow and Wilson, for example, cited above. A good, brief, more

up-to-date comment is by one of the best-informed writers on Yugoslavia, Viktor Meier, "Jugoslawien als Konföderation," *Frankfurter Allgemeine Zeitung*, 14 May 1984.

6   See Jean-Claude Pomonti, "La Yougoslavie sans Tito," (1) "Le Recours à la palabre"; (2) "Confiance et incertitudes," *Le Monde*, 5–6 March 1981.

7   See Heiko Flottau, "Wie heisst Jugoslawiens Präsident?," *Süddeutsche Zeitung*, 16 April 1984.

8   On the Serb "problem" see Milovan Djilas, "Serbian Strains Tug at Yugoslav Unity," *Wall Street Journal* (European edition), 22 May 1986; Viktor Meier, "Serbien fühlt sich eingeengt," *Frankfurter Allgemeine Zeitung*, 16 April 1986; Pedro Ramet, "Concern about Serbian Nationalism," *Yugoslav Situation Report*, Radio Free Europe Research, 27 March 1986. An extreme (not untypical) manifestation of Serb nationalist resentment appeared in September 1985 in Belgrade in the form of a book, *The Allies and the Yugoslav War Drama* by the well-known Serb historian Veselin Djuretić, arguing that the whole Partisan movement and the whole history of Yugoslav communism had been based on an anti-Serb platform. In the autumn of 1986 many members of the Serbian Academy of Sciences prepared a seventy-page memorandum with strong nationalist overtones, complaining about the "Vietnamization" of Serbia. See R. St., "Streit um ein Standortbestimung in Belgrad," *Neue Zürcher Zeitung* (Fernausgabe), 12 November 1986.

9   Wilson, *Tito's Yugoslavia*, pp. 140–45.

10 See, for example, Viktor Meier, "Belgrad über Macht der Republiken besorgt," *Frankfurter Allgemeine Zeitung*, 4 November 1985.

11 There are several good histories of Yugoslavia and the Balkans generally that bring out this point. For example, Fred Singleton, *Twentieth Century Yugoslavia* (New York: Columbia University Press, 1976); L. S. Stavrianos, *The Balkans since 1453* (New York: Rinehart, 1958); R. W. Seton-Watson, *The Rise of Nationality in the Balkans* (London: Constable, 1917); Robert Lee Wolff, *The Balkans in our Time* (New York: Norton, 1978); Barbara Jelavich, *History of the Balkans — Twentieth Century* (Cambridge: Cambridge University Press, 1983); Charles Jelavich and Barbara Jelavich, eds., *The Balkans in Transition* (Berkeley and Los Angeles: University of California Press, 1963).

12 One of its earliest and most exemplary champions was the Croat bishop Josip-Jurai Strossmayer. Viktor Meier has written much on this illustrious churchman. See, for example, his "Ein Bischof des 'Jugoslawismus,'" *Frankfurter Allgemeine Zeitung*, 26 July 1983.

13 Vladimir Bakarić, the Croatian political leader, in an interview with the *Frankfurter Rundschau*, 17 December 1971, put the proportion of Serbian officers in the army at "70% at most."

14 For the most recent study, see Jim Seroka and Rados Smiljković, *Political Organizations in Socialist Yugoslavia* (Durham, N.C.: Duke University Press, 1986).

15 See Rusinow, *The Yugoslav Experiment*, pp. 81–137.

16 Two of the most prominent were Krsto Crvenkovski and Kiro Gligorov, both of whom emerged as liberals in the 1960s and generally supported the Croat and Slovene positions; see Rusinow, ibid., p. 136.

17 *Politika* (Belgrade), 29-30 August 1970, referred to by Rusinow, *The Yugoslav Experiment*, pp. 281 and 312.

18 Doder, *The Yugoslavs*, is excellent on the impact of the *Gastarbeiter*. See especially

pp. 78–93.

19   Albanian irredentism was never far below the surface, however. This was well expressed by Premier Mehmet Shehu as early as 1958 when he said—as if trying to point out Tirana's reasonableness, "We are not at present asking that Kosovo join with Albania," *Zëri i popullit* (Tirana), 20 October 1958. It was a sign of Yugoslav nervousness on this subject that nearly twenty-eight years later a Yugoslav commentator threw this statement back at Tirana in a commentary denouncing alleged claims by Albania to Yugoslav territory. Milo Djukić, Tanjug (Yugoslav news agency), 10 July 1986. (I am grateful to Louis Zanga for telling me this.)

20   I am grateful to Zdenko Antić who, in our many conversations about Yugoslavia, spelled out these points clearly.

21   Rusinow, *The Yugoslav Experiment*, p. 195.

22   Wilson, *Tito's Yugoslavia*, p. 141, quoting Tito's remarks to delegates from the High School of Political Science.

23   Rusinow, *The Yugoslav Experiment*, p. 206.

24   Doder, *The Yugoslavs*, p. 145.

25   Rusinow, *The Yugoslav Experiment*, pp. 259–309.

26   Ibid., p. 285.

27   Ibid., p. 330.

28   Michael Dobbs, "Workers' Experiment Falters in Yugoslavia," *Washington Post*, 17 September 1985. See also Wilson, *Tito's Yugoslavia*, pp. 234–36.

29   Doder, *The Yugoslavs*, p. 106, quotes a sociologist as confirming these fears.

30   See Slobodan Stanković, *The End of the Tito Era: Yugoslavia's Dilemmas* (Stanford, Calif.: Hoover Institution Press, 1981), pp. 65–74.

31   Ibid., pp. 115–18.

32   On Mikulić see Georg von Huebbenet, "Tätendrang in kunftiger Regierung Jugoslawiens," *Stuttgarter Zeitung*, 18 April 1986. See also appendix 2, pp. 493–94.

33   Stanković, *End of the Tito Era*, pp. 34–36.

34   Rusinow, *The Yugoslav Experiment*, p. 299.

35   Under the terms of both the federal constitution of 1974 and a Croatian law of January 1971, the invitation or acceptance of outside "enemy" forces is forbidden. But whether laws like this would have any effect in a crisis is doubtful indeed.

36   *Politika*, 24 September 1971.

37   Tanjug, 16 November 1976.

38   Rusinow, *The Yugoslav Experiment*, p. 320.

39   See Laura Tyson, *The Yugoslav Economic System and its Performance in the 1970's* (Berkeley, Calif.: Institute of International Studies, 1980).

40   Ibid., p. 89.

41   Rusinow, *The Yugoslav Experiment*, p. 319.

42   In this connection, Kardelj's warning to Slovenia about the dangers of getting too involved with the West is significant; Rusinow, *The Yugoslav Experiment*, pp. 320–21.

43   Twenty-eight intellectuals were arrested by police at a private meeting at which the speaker should have been Milovan Djilas. Djilas himself was temporarily detained. Six were eventually brought to a trial which finally ended in February 1985. Three defendants were convicted and given relatively light sentences. The trial, which was widely reported in the West, was a legal farce because the evidence was so thin and it became obvious that it was an entirely trumped-up political affair. On the atmo-

sphere at the end of the trial, see James M. Markham, "Despite Trial, Talk is Lively in Yugoslavia," *New York Times*, 13 February 1985. On the campaign against the Catholic church, see Viktor Meier, "Kampagne gegen Kirche in Kroatien und Bosnien Verschärft sich," *Frankfurter Allgemeine Zeitung*, 5 February 1985.

12 Albania

1 For a general review of Albania since 1964 see Peter R. Prifti, *Socialist Albania since 1944: Domestic and Foreign Developments* (Cambridge, Mass.: MIT Press, 1978); Nicholas C. Pano, *The People's Republic of Albania* (Cambridge, Mass.: MIT Press, 1968). See also Lendvai, *Eagles in Cobwebs*, pp. 173–205.

2 See Griffith, *Albania and the Sino-Soviet Rift*, especially pp. 20–60.

3 For a study that stresses the historical nationalist roots of Hoxha's policy see Bernhard Tönnes, *Sonderfall Albanien* (Munich: R. Oldenbourg, 1980).

4 Michael Kaser, "Albania under and after Enver Hoxha," in *East European Economies: Slow Growth in the 1980's*, vol. 3, pp. 17–21; Paul Lendvai, *Das einsame Albanien* (Zurich: Edition Interfrom, 1985), pp. 73–76.

5 Quoted by Lendvai, *Eagles in Cobwebs*, p. 181.

6 See Anton Logoreci, *The Albanians: Europe's Forgotten Survivors* (Boulder, Colo.: Westview Press, 1977).

7 R. V. Burks, *The Dynamics of Communism in Eastern Europe* (Princeton, N.J.: Princeton University Press, 1964), pp. 144–49.

8 Lendvai, *Das einsame Albanien*, pp. 37–38.

9 This suspicion is particularly strong among the Kosovars, who have the freedom to voice it and often do.

10 For examples and effects of the ban on religion see Lendvai, *Das einsame Albanien*, pp. 42–50.

11 For analyses of these important purges see the two Radio Free Europe research background reports by Louis Zanga: "Changes in Albanian Leadership Signify Struggle for Succession to Power," 24 November 1975; and "The Congress of the Great Purge," 9 November 1976. Zanga's analyses of Albanian developments since the early 1960s have provided the best regular Western coverage.

12 Radio Tirana and ATA (Albanian Telegraphic Agency), 18 December 1981. For speculation in the following weeks see Louis Zanga, "More on Albanian Premier's Mysterious Death," *Radio Free Europe Research Background Report*, 21 January 1982.

13 Enver Hoxha, *The Titoites* (Tirana: "8 Nëndori" Publishing House, 1982, English translation), pp. 578–633.

14 On Alia see Louis Zanga, "Ramiz Alia—Albania's New Strongman," *Radio Free Europe Research Background Report*, 13 July 1983.

15 Kaser, "Trade and Aid in the Albanian Economy," in *East European Economics Post-Helsinki*, submitted to the Joint Economic Committee, U.S. Congress, 25 August 1977 (Washington, D.C.: U.S. Government Printing Office), pp. 1327–28.

16 Louis Zanga, "China Stops Aid to Albania," *Radio Free Europe Research Background Report*, 13 July 1978.

17 *The Military Balance 1985–1986* (London: The International Institute for Strategic Studies, 1985), p. 62.

18 Louis Zanga, "The Sino-Albanian Ideological Dispute Enters a New Phase," *Radio*

Free Europe Research Background Report, 15 November 1977.

19   AFP (Peking), on 4 December 1985, quoted Albanian diplomats in the Chinese capital as saying that the 1986–1990 treaty involved about $20 million of business a year.

20   See R. St., "Lokaltermin in Tuzi: Der Schwerige Eisenbahnbau von Titograd nach Albanien," *Neue Zürcher Zeitung* (Fernausgabe), 22 November 1984.

21   But much better relations began again with the GDR in 1984. See, for example, Ws. "Ost-Berlin Werben um Albanien," *Frankfurter Allgemeine Zeitung*, 30 November 1984; and Louis Zanga, "Closer Relations between Tirana and East Berlin," *Radio Free Europe Research Background Report*, 29 August 1986.

22   See, for example, R. St., "Griechisch-albanische Annäherung," *Neue Zürcher Zeitung* (Fernausgabe), 1 February 1985.

23   John Cooley, "Albania Expected to Resume Secret Talks with Britain," *Christian Science Monitor*, 26 August 1985.

24   Louis Zanga, "West German-Albanian Economic Cooperation," *Radio Free Europe Research Background Report*, 15 November 1985.

25   For an excellent survey of developments since Hoxha's death, see Elez Biberaj, "Albania after Hoxha: Dilemmas of Change," *Problems of Communism* (November–December 1985).

26   See Kaser (1986), pp. 19–21.

27   Ibid., p. 21.

28   Lendvai, *Das einsame Albanien*, pp. 71–72.

29   Hoxha himself quotes Khrushchev on this point in *The Krushchevites* (Tirana: "8 Nëndori" Publishing House, 1980), p. 375.

30   In a private conversation in Bonn in 1985 a West German official indicated the readiness of the FRG to give financial assistance to Tirana. This official was aware of the constitutional inhibitions but would not elaborate on how they might be overcome.

13   Social Problems in Perspective

1   The Radio Free Europe Research Department's coverage of the effects of Chernobyl on Eastern Europe was excellent. See, for example, "Eastern Europe and Chernobyl: The Initial Response," *Radio Free Europe Research Background Report*, 23 May 1986. For a thorough review of the nuclear energy situation in Eastern Europe, see Henrik Bischof, *Nach Tschernobyl—Stand und Perspektiven der Atomenenergiepolitik Kommunistischer Länder* (Bonn: Friedrich-Ebert-Stiftung, February 1986).

2   See Henrik Bischof, *Umweltschutz-probleme in Osteurope* (Bonn: Friedrich-Ebert-Stiftung, February 1986).

3   Reiner Klingholz, *Die Zeit*, 30 October 1984.

4   Ibid.

5   See B. V. Flow, "The Environmental Crisis in the GDR," *Radio Free Europe Research Background Report*, 3 September 1984.

6   The most spectacular example of environmental disaster in Poland was probably the open-cut lignite mine at Belchatow, southwest of Warsaw. It had been described as "Europe's biggest environmental time bomb" by Kay Withers, "Poland Ecological Time Bomb," *Baltimore Sun*, 17 February 1984.

7   sk, "Alarmierende Umweltzerstörung in der DDR," *Neue Zürcher Zeitung* (Fernaus-

gabe), 3 August 1985.

8 See "Is the Spa at Karlovy Vary Threatened by Coal Mining?," *Czechoslovak Situation Report*, Radio Free Europe Research, 13 August 1985.

9 *Die Zeit*, 30 May 1984 quoted passages from this report. It was Charter 77 Document no. 36 of 12 December 1983. See also the excellent report by Frank Pohl, "Environmental Deterioration in Czechoslovakia," *Radio Free Europe Research Background Report*, 6 May 1983.

10 See "Kippen und Schwellen," *Der Spiegel*, 17 December 1984.

11 The GDR, for example, planned to increase slightly production of brown coal to 300 million tons by 1990, which would cause sulfur dioxide emissions to rise to four million tons. *Deutsche Institut für Wirtschaftforschung* (DIW) Wochenbericht no. 4, 1983.

12 For a perceptive view of East German official attitudes, see sk., "Wachsende Umweltzerstörung in der DDR," *Neue Zürcher Zeitung* (Fernausgabe), 28 November 1984.

13 For a good brief survey see Sophia M. Miskiewicz, "Housing in Eastern Europe: A 'Social Right' Abandoned," *Radio Free Europe Research Background Report*, 12 June 1986.

14 "Government Struggles with the Housing Crisis," *Polish Situation Report*, Radio Free Europe Research, 4 April 1986. The statistics used for housing in Poland are derived from this source.

15 UN Annual Bulletin of Housing and Building Statistics for Europe, 1983.

16 Elizabeth M. Clayton, "Consumption, Living Standards, and Consumer Welfare in Eastern Europe," in *East European Economies: Slow Growth in the 1980's*, vol. 1, p. 253, table 2.

17 Robert R. King, "The Impact of Urbanization on National Identity in Eastern Europe," paper delivered at the Pennsylvania State University Conference on the Impact of Communist Modernization on National Identity and State Integration in Eastern Europe, 30–31 October 1975.

18 Ibid.

19 A. D. Lopez, "Demographic Change in Europe and its Health and Social Implications," in *Demographic Trends in the European Region* (Copenhagen: World Health Regional Office for Europe, 1984), p. 57.

20 Ibid., p. 10.

21 Ibid.

22 Godfrey Baldwin, "Population Estimates and Projections for Eastern Europe, 1950–2000," *East European Economies: Slow Growth in the 1980's*, vol. 1, p. 268, table 1.

23 Lopez, "Demographic Change in Europe," p. 10.

24 Ibid.

25 Baldwin, "Population Estimates," p. 268, table 1.

26 Ibid., p. 269, table 1.

27 Ibid., pp. 270–71, table 3.

28 The following account is based on the excellent report by Eva Lengyel, "The Unresolved Plight of Pensioners," *Hungarian Situation Report*, Radio Free Europe Research, 8 June 1985. The statistics given are all taken from this source.

29 The demand, however, slackened off in 1985. See "No Substantial Relief for Pensioners," *Hungarian Situation Report*, Radio Free Europe Research, 25 March 1986.

30 Lengyel, "The Unresolved Plight of Pensioners."

31 In a speech on 11 September 1985 (Radio Bucharest of that date) Ceauşescu rumi-nated about settling an undisclosed number of urban pensioners in the country-side, "enabling them to develop a certain useful activity or to preserve their physical and mental health." In 1985 there were more than three million pensioners in Romania.

32 See "Rock and the Regime," *Czechoslovak Situation Report,* Radio Free Europe Research, 26 March 1986. Also T. Havel, "Soviet-Bloc Rock on the Offensive," *Radio Free Europe Research Background Report,* 5 September 1986.

33 Josef Škvorecký, one of the greatest modern Czech writers, now in exile, has regu-larly taken up the cudgels for persecuted jazz and rock musicians in his native land. See, for example, his article "Hipness at Noon," *New Republic,* 17 December 1984.

34 Steven Koppany, "Unprepared Regime Scrambles to Meet Challenges of the Video Era," *Hungarian Situation Report,* Radio Free Europe Research, 4 September 1985.

35 George Schöpflin, "Korruption, Infomalismus, Irregularität in Osteuropa: Eine politische Analyse" (text in English) *Südosteuropa* (Munich), vols. 7–8, 1984.

36 Aleksander Smolar has an excellent chapter on this form of corruption in Gierek's Poland, in Abraham Brumberg, *Poland: Genesis of a Revolution,* pp. 42–53.

37 Ivan Völgyes, "The Burden of Equality: Kadar's Hungary Today," *Radio Free Europe Research Background Report,* 23 November 1984. (This is a brilliant essay deserving wider distribution.) The most comprehensive and erudite study of this subject is by Pierre Kende and Zdenek Strmiska, *Égalité et Inégalités en Europe de l'Est* (Paris: Presses de la Fondation Nationales des Sciences Politiques, 1984). A very useful work is Daniel Nelson, ed., *Communism and the Politics of Inequalities* (Lexington, Mass.: Lexington Books, 1984).

38 Völgyes, "The Burden of Equality."

39 Ibid.

40 Walter D. Connor, "Dissent in Eastern Europe: A New Coalition," *Problems of Communism* (January–February 1980).

41 Ibid.

42 Vladimir Sobell, "A Reflection on the Czechoslovak Standard of Living," *Czechoslovak Situation Report,* Radio Free Europe Research, 24 September 1985.

14 The National Minorities and Their Problems

1 George Schöpflin has a very good survey (with a helpful map) of minorities in Eastern Europe in his essay on "National Minorities in Eastern Europe," in Schöpflin, ed., *The Soviet Union and Eastern Europe,* pp. 302–12. See also Walker Connor, *The National Question in Marxist-Leninist Theory and Strategy* (Princeton N.J.: Princeton University Press, 1984).

2 The Greek minority in Albania became a fairly serious domestic political issue in Greece when the Papandreou government tried to improve relations with Tirana. Opposition parties and the Greek Orthodox church opposed better relations with-out improvement in the condition of the minority. See, for example, "Opposition gegen Papandreou's Albanienkurs," *Neue Zürcher Zeitung* (Fernausgabe), 6 Septem-ber 1986.

3 See Robert R. King, *Minorities under Communism: Nationalities as a Source of Tension among Balkan Communist States* (Cambridge, Mass.: Harvard University

Press, 1973), p. 92. (King includes Slovakia in his survey.) I have drawn heavily on King's excellent book for parts of this chapter.

4   Ibid., pp. 53–56.

5   See C. Sr., "Die Muslime in Bosnien-Herzegowina," *Neue Zürcher Zeitung* (Fernausgabe), 31 October 1985.

6   *Politika* (Belgrade), 11 September 1977 (special supplement).

7   Radio Budapest, 7 July 1977.

8   See "Dim Prospects for Improving the Plight of Gypsies," *Hungarian Situation Report*, Radio Free Europe Research, 4 September 1985.

9   See Seton-Watson, *Eastern Europe between the Wars*, pp. 269–70; Rothschild, *East Central Europe between the Two World Wars*, pp. 10–14 and passim. See also Seton-Watson, *Nations and States: An Enquiry into the Origins of Nations and the Politics of Nationalism* (London: Methuen, 1977), chaps. 4 and 12.

10 An excellent, brief analysis of the situation is to be found in Jens Reuter, *Die Albaner in Jugoslawien* (Munich: R. Oldenbourg, 1982). The best regular coverage is to be found in the *Neue Zürcher Zeitung* and the *Frankfurter Allgemeine Zeitung*.

11 Seton-Watson, *Eastern Europe between the Wars*, p. 270.

12 Ibid. pp. 270–71.

13 See William O. McCagg, Jr., *Jewish Nobles and Geniuses in Modern Hungary* (New York: Columbia University Press, 1986).

14 King, *Minorities under Communism*, p. 15.

15 Ibid., p. 101.

16 Ibid., p. 23.

17 In the interwar years several minorities in Eastern Europe had shown some support for the local communist parties on account of the latter's promises on the subject. See R. V. Burks, *The Dynamics of Communism in Eastern Europe* (Princeton, N.J.: Princeton University Press, 1961), especially pp. 73–87.

18 King, *Minorities under Communism*, pp. 80–81.

19 Several Hungarian visitors to the West from Transylvania in the middle and late 1960s reported this in conversation.

20 King, *Minorities under Communism*, pp. 53–55.

21 Brown, *Bulgaria under Communist Rule*, pp. 294–95.

22 King, *Minorities under Communism*, pp. 91–99.

23 Ibid., pp. 95–108.

24 Ibid., pp. 97–108.

25 Western press coverage of this episode was massive. See especially Viktor Meier, "Sofia gefahrdet seine Beziehungen zu Ankara," *Frankfurter Allgemeine Zeitung*, 14 February 1985; also "Officials Say There Are No Turks in Bulgaria," *Bulgarian Situation Report*, Radio Free Europe Research, 28 March 1985; and "Recent Developments in the Turkish Issue," *Bulgarian Situation Report*, Radio Free Europe Research, 29 June 1985.

26 King, *Minorities under Communism*, pp. 111–14.

27 Ibid., pp. 154–63. See also George Schöpflin, "National Minorities in Eastern Europe," pp. 309–12.

28 See "Babes-Bolyai in Cluj: A Tale of Two Universities," *Romanian Situation Report*, Radio Free Europe Research, 9 July 1982.

29 See "Dispute and Education of Hungarian Minority," *Czechoslovak Situation Report*, Radio Free Europe Research, 4 May 1984; "Hungarian Minority Protests Against

Proposals to Change Language Instruction in Czechoslovakia," *Hungarian Situation Report*, Radio Free Europe Research, 8 May 1984. For a well-informed, more relaxed view of the situation of the Hungarian minority in Slovakia, see, "Hungarian Minority in Czechoslovakia: Equal or Oppressed?," *Czechoslovak Situation Report*, Radio Free Europe Research, 13 August 1985. For a brilliant, emotional description of the situation of Hungarians in Slovakia, see Suzanne Satory, "Les Hongrois silencieux de Bratislava," *Le Monde*, 4–5 November 1984.

30   Duray's case became internationally known. He joined the Czechoslovak Charter 77 movement in early 1984. In March 1985, when he was detained without trial, his case was taken up in the United States by Congressman Tom Lantos, who organized a petition signed by thirty-nine congressmen and sent to Husák. Duray was later released. András Sutö was severely beaten up by Romanian police in 1984.

31   See Vladimir Socor, "Eyewitness on the 1977 Miners' Strike in Romania's Jiu Valley," *Radio Free Europe Research Background Report*, 13 August 1986. This paper is based on an extensive interview given to Radio Free Europe and broadcast by both its Hungarian and Romanian services.

32   John R. Lampe, *The Bulgarian Economy in the Twentieth Century* (London: Croom Helm, 1986), p. 18 n. 6.

33   *Kulturný Zivot* (Bratislava), 15 October 1965; quoted in King, *Minorities under Communism*, pp. 177–78.

34   King, *Minorities under Communism*, pp. 120–23.

35   See Reuter, *Die Albaner in Jugoslawien*, passim. Among the many excellent articles, one of the most outstanding is Cyrill Stieger, "Latent Unrest in Kosovo," *Neue Zürcher Zeitung* (Fernausgabe), 28 August 1985.

36   See Viktor Meier, "Das Kosovo werht sich gegen Serbien," *Frankfurter Allgemeine Zeitung*, 31 December 1984.

37   One of the best analyses on this subject is by David Blanchard and David Buchan, "Ankara Tries to Temper Outcry over Effort to 'Bulgarize' Turks," *Financial Times*, 20 February 1985.

38   See Harry Schleicher, "Gyula Illyés und die Ungarische Nation," *Frankfurter Rundschau*, 20 June 1978.

39   For example, by Minhea Gheorghiu, *Luceafărul*, cited in Shafir, *Romania*, p. 186.

40   Csúori's publication ban was not reported at the time. A reference was made to it in the Budapest library journal *Elet és Irodalom*, 16 September 1983.

41   *Népszabadság*, 25 June 1971.

42   An excellent survey is by Viktor Meier, "Budapest und Bukarest Verbergen die Spannungen Nicht Mehr," *Frankfurter Allgemeine Zeitung*, 29 December 1984.

43   For example, in the Central Committee report to the party congress the following was stated: "we consider it to be a natural requirement that citizens of Hungarian nationality in neighbouring countries should be able to cultivate their mother tongue and develop their national culture," Hungarian Television, 25 March 1985.

44   The West German press has followed the fate of the Germans in Romania closely. One of the most moving articles has been Christian Zinsser, "In Rumänien geht ein stuck deutscher Geschichte seinem Ende" *Frankfurter Allgemeine Zeitung*, 7 October 1983.

45   H. M. V. Temperley, *History of Serbia*, 2d impression (London: G. Bell and Sons, 1919), pp. 229–30.

Bibliography

This book is based almost entirely on secondary sources. I have read extensively the BBC (Caversham) world monitoring reports and the FBIS (Foreign Broadcast Information Service) daily reports for Eastern Europe. As will be evident from the notes, the research reports of the Radio Free Europe Research and Analyses Departments have been indispensable.

Western journals dealing specifically or often with Eastern European topics have often been consulted. These include mainly *Problems of Communism, Studies in Comparative Communism, Slavic Review, The World Today, Survey, Soviet Studies, Osteuropa, Europa-Archiv, Südosteuropa, Deutschland-Archiv, Aussenpolitik, Osteuropäische Rundschau, Est et l'Ouest, Orbis*, and *The International Spectator*. References to specific articles are given in the notes.

Several daily newspapers proved essential. Most of them have been German, or at least written in German. They include the *Neue Zürcher Zeitung*, the *Frankfurter Allgemeine Zeitung*, the *Frankfurter Rundschau*, the *Süddeutsche Zeitung*, *Die Presse, Die Zeit* (a weekly), and the *Stuttgarter Zeitung*. These papers are able to give space to Eastern Europe that few others can. But *Le Monde* is excellent and *Figaro* is worth reading for its Polish coverage. In Italy the Communist party daily, *l'Unità*, has consistently excellent coverage. *Corriere della Sera* and *La Stampa* are often very good. The English language press is less helpful, not because of the quality of the correspondents, which is generally high, but because coverage is much thinner. Still, one cannot do without the *New York Times*, the *Washington Post*, and the *Los Angeles Times*, and occasionally the *Wall Street Journal* and the *Christian Science Monitor*. In Great Britain the lack of public interest in Eastern Europe is reflected in the press coverage, although reports and analyses in *The Times* used to be of a high order. Generally, however, the *Financial Times* has had the most consistently good coverage. *The Economist* tackles subjects tersely but almost always with discernment.

Finally, various handbooks and collections of papers have been extremely helpful, above all the papers on the East European economies submitted to the Joint Economic Committee of the Congress of the United States. I have used these extensively and many specific references are made in the notes. Various studies by the United Nations Economic Commission for Europe (ECE, Geneva), publications by the Organization for European Cooperation and Development (OECD, Paris), Plan Econ (Washington), and the Vienna Institute for Comparative Economic Studies have also been consulted. The Economist Intelligence Unit (EIU) publications combine economic expertise with readability. The EIU's *Regional Review: Eastern Europe and the USSR, 1985* turned out to be worth much more than the rather steep sum I paid for it.

The list that follows includes those books and studies that I can recall as having been of the most direct use to me in writing this book. It would be much longer—and very eclectic indeed—if it covered those books that had been of indirect help.

Adelman, Jonathan R., editor. *Communist Armies in Politics*. Boulder, Colo.: Westview Press, 1982.

Alexander, Stella. *Church and State in Yugoslavia since 1945*. Cambridge: Cambridge University Press, 1979.

Allison, Graham T. *Essence of Decision: Explaining the Cuban Missile Crisis*. Boston: Little, Brown, 1971.

Anderson, M. S. *The Eastern Question, 1774–1923*. London: Macmillan, 1966.

Ash, Timothy Garton. *The Polish Revolution: Solidarity*. New York: Scribners, 1984.

Åslund, Anders. *Private Enterprise in Eastern Europe*. London: Macmillan, 1985.

Asmus, Ronald D. *East Berlin and Moscow: The Documentation of a Dispute*. Munich: Radio Free Europe, 1985.

Aspaturian, V. V., J. Valenta, and D. Burke, editors. *Eurocommunism between East and West*. Bloomington: Indiana University Press, 1980.

Baylis, Thomas. *The Technical Intelligentsia and the East German Elite*. Berkeley and Los Angeles: University of California Press, 1974.

Beck, Carl, et al. *Comparative Communist Political Leadership*. New York: David McKay, 1973.

Beloff, Nora. *Tito's Flawed Legacy*. London: Victor Gollancz, 1985.

Bender, Peter. *East Europe in Search of Security*. Baltimore: Johns Hopkins University Press, 1972.

Bialer, Seweryn. *The Soviet Paradox: External Expansion, Internal Decline*. New York: Knopf, 1986.

Blazynski, George. *Flashpoint Poland*. New York: Pergamon Press, 1979.

Bornstein, Morris. *Plan and Market: Economic Reform in Eastern Europe*. New Haven: Yale University Press, 1973.

Bornstein, Morris, Zvi Gitelman, and William Zimmerman, editors. *East-West Relations and the Future of Eastern Europe*. London: Allen and Unwin, 1981.

Braun, Aurel. *Small-State Security in the Balkans*. London: Macmillan, 1983.

Bromke, Adam, and Derry Novak, editors. *The Communist States in the Era of Détente, 1971–1977*. Oakville, Ontario: Mosaic Press, n.d.

Bromke, Adam, and Teresa Rakowska-Harmstone, editors. *The Communist States in Disarray, 1965–1971*. Minneapolis: University of Minnesota Press, 1972.

Bromke, Adam, and Philip Uren, editors. *The Communist States and the West*. New York: Praeger, 1967.

Brown, Archie, and Jack Gray, editors. *Political Culture and Political Change in Communist States*. London: Macmillan, 1977.

Brown, J. F. *Bulgaria under Communist Rule*. New York: Praeger, 1970.

———. *The New Eastern Europe: The Khrushchev Era and After*. New York: Praeger, 1966.

———. *Relations between the Soviet Union and Its Eastern European Allies: A Survey*. Santa Monica: Rand, 1975.

————. *Soviet Relations with the Northern Tier in East Europe*. European American Institute Paper, no. 9. Marina del Rey, Calif.: European American Institute for Security Research, 1985.

Brown, J. F., and A. Ross Johnson. *Challenges to Soviet Control in Eastern Europe: An Overview*. Santa Monica: Rand, 1984.

Brumberg, Abraham, editor. *Poland: Genesis of a Revolution*. New York: Random House, 1983.

Brzezinski, Zbigniew K. *The Soviet Bloc: Unity and Conflict*. Cambridge: Harvard University Press, 1960.

Burks, R. V. *The Dynamics of Communism in Eastern Europe*. Princeton, N.J.: Princeton University Press, 1961.

Carter, April. *Democratic Reform in Yugoslavia: The Changing Role of the Party*. Princeton, N.J.: Princeton University Press, 1982.

Casaroli, Agostino. *Der Heilige Stuhl und die Völkergemeinschaft*. Berlin: Duncker and Humblot, 1981.

Checinski, Michael. *Poland: Communism, Nationalism, Anti-Semitism*. New York: Karz-Cohl, 1982.

Childs, David. *East Germany*. London: Ernest Benn, 1969.

————. *The GDR: Moscow's German Ally*. London: Allen and Unwin, 1983.

Crane, Keith. *The Soviet Economic Dilemma of Eastern Europe*. Santa Monica: Rand, May 1986.

Croan, Melvin. *East Germany: The Soviet Connection*. Washington Paper, vol. 4, no. 36. Beverly Hills: Sage, 1976.

Davies, Norman. *God's Playground: A History of Poland*. 2 vols. Oxford: Clarendon Press, 1981.

————. *Heart of Europe: A Short History of Poland*. Oxford: Oxford University Press, 1986.

Dawisha, Karen, and Philip Hanson, editors. *Soviet-East European Dilemmas: Coercion, Competition, and Consent*. London: Heinemann, 1981.

Dean, Robert W. *West German Trade with the East: The Political Dimension*. New York: Praeger, 1974.

Dellin, L. A. D., and Herman Gross, editors. *Reforms in the Soviet and East European Economies*. Lexington, Mass.: D. C. Heath, Lexington Books, 1972.

Deutsch, Karl W. *The Analysis of International Relations*. Englewood Cliffs, N.J.: Prentice-Hall, 1968.

Djilas, Milovan. *Tito: Eine Kritische Biographie*. Vienna: Verlag Fritz Molden, 1980.

Doder, Dusko. *The Yugoslavs*. London: Allen and Unwin, 1979.

Dornberg, John. *The Other Germany*. New York: Doubleday, 1968.

Ermarth, Fritz. *Internationalism, Security, and Legitimacy: The Challenge to Soviet Interests in Eastern Europe, 1964–1968*. Santa Monica: Rand, March 1969.

Feiwel, George R. *Growth and Reforms in Centrally Planned Economics: The Lessons of the Bulgarian Experience*. New York: Praeger, 1977.

Fischer-Galati, Stephen. *The New Rumania: From People's Democracy to Socialist Republic*. Cambridge, Mass.: MIT Press, 1967.

————, editor. *Eastern Europe in the 1980's*. Boulder, Colo.: Westview Press, 1981.

Fleron, Frederic J., Jr. *Communist Studies and the Social Sciences*. Chicago: Rand McNally, 1969.

Floyd, David. *Rumania: Russia's Dissident Ally*. New York: Praeger, 1965.

Fox, Annette Baker. *The Power of Small States*. Chicago: University of Chicago Press, 1959.

Gati, Charles. *Hungary and the Soviet Bloc*. Durham, N.C.: Duke University Press, 1986.

————, editor. *The International Politics of Eastern Europe*. New York: Praeger, 1976.

Gelman, Harry. *The Brezhnev Politburo and the Decline of Détente*. Ithaca, N.Y.: Cornell University Press, 1984.

Gilberg, Trond. *Modernization in Romania since World War II*. New York: Praeger, 1975.

Golan, Galia. *Reform Rule in Czechoslovakia: The Dubcek Era, 1968–1969*. Cambridge: Cambridge University Press, 1973.

————. *The Czechoslovak Reform Movement: Communism in Crisis, 1962–1968*. Cambridge: Cambridge University Press, 1971.

Gomulka, Stanislaw. *Growth, Innovation, and Reform in Eastern Europe*. Brighton, England: Harvester Press, 1986.

Griffith, William E. *Albania and the Sino-Soviet Rift*. Cambridge, Mass.: MIT Press, 1963.

————. *The Ostpolitik of the Federal Republic of Germany*. Cambridge, Mass.: MIT Press, 1978.

————. *The Sino-Soviet Rift*. London: Allen and Unwin, 1964.

————, editor. *Communism in Europe: Continuity, Change, and the Sino-Soviet Dispute*. 2 vols. Cambridge, Mass.: MIT Press, 1964 and 1966.

Hacker, Jens. *Der Ostblock: Enstehung, Entwicklung und Struktur*. Baden-Baden: Nomos Verlagsgesellschaft, 1983.

Hanhardt, Arthur M., Jr. *The German Democratic Republic*. Baltimore: Johns Hopkins University Press, 1968.

Heinrich, Hans-Georg. *Hungary: Politics, Economics, and Society*. London: Frances Pinter, 1986.

Herspring, Dale, and Ivan Völgyes, editors. *Civil-Military Relations in Communist Systems*. Boulder, Colo.: Westview Press, 1978.

Holloway, David, and Jane M. O. Sharp, editors. *The Warsaw Pact: Alliance in Transition*. Ithaca, N.Y.: Cornell University Press, 1984.

Hoxha, Enver. *The Khrushchevites*. Tirana: The "8 Nëndori," 1980.

————. *The Titoites*. Tirana: The "8 Nëndori," 1982.

Hutchings, Robert L. *Soviet-East European Relations: Consolidation and Conflict, 1968–1980*. Madison: University of Wisconsin Press, 1983.

Ionescu, Ghiṭa. *The Breakup of the Soviet Empire in Eastern Europe*. Harmondsworth, England: Penguin, 1965.

————. *Communism in Rumania, 1944–1962*. London: Oxford University Press, 1964.

Jacobsen, Hans-Adolf, et al., editors. *Drei Jahrzehnte Aussenpolitik der DDR*. Munich: R. Oldenbourg Verlag, 1979.

Janos, Andrew C., editor. *Authoritarian Politics in Communist Europe: Uniformity and Diversity in One-Party States*. Berkeley: Institute of International Studies, University of California, 1976.

Jelavich, Barbara. *History of the Balkans*. 2 vols. Cambridge: Cambridge University Press, 1983.

Jelavich, Charles and Barbara, editors. *The Balkans in Transition: Essays on the Development of Balkan Life and Politics since the Eighteenth Century*. Berkeley and Los Angeles: University of California Press, 1963.

Johnson, A. Ross. *The Impact of Eastern Europe on Soviet Policy toward Western Europe*. Santa Monica: Rand, March 1986.

————. *The Transformation of Communist Ideology: The Yugoslav Case, 1948–1953*. Cambridge, Mass.: MIT Press, 1972.

Johnson, A. Ross, Robert W. Dean, and Alexander Alexiev. *East European Military Establishments: The Warsaw Pact Northern Tier*. New York: Crane Russak, 1980.

Johnson, John J. *The Role of the Military in Under-developed Countries*. Princeton, N.J.: Princeton University Press, 1962.

Jones, Christopher D. *Soviet Influence in Eastern Europe: Political Anatomy and the Warsaw Pact*. New York: Praeger, 1980.

Jowitt, Kenneth. *Revolutionary Breakthroughs and National Development: The Case of Romania, 1944–1965*. Berkeley and Los Angeles: University of California Press, 1971.

Karpiński, Jakub. *Countdown: The Polish Upheavals of 1956, 1968, 1970, 1976, 1980 . . .* New York: Karz-Cohl, 1982.

Kaser, Michael. *Comecon: Integration Problems of the Planned Economies*. London: Oxford University Press, 1965.

Kende, Pierre, and Zdenek Strmiska. *Égalité et Inégalités en Europe de L'Est*. Paris: Presses de la Fondation Nationale des Sciences Politiques, 1984.

King, Robert R. *History of the Romanian Communist Party*. Stanford, Calif.: Hoover Institution Press, 1980.

————. *Minorities under Communism: Nationalities as a Source of Tension among Balkan Communist States*. Cambridge: Harvard University Press, 1973.

King, Robert R., and James F. Brown, editors. *Eastern Europe's Uncertain Future*. New York: Praeger, 1977.

Kolkowicz, Roman. *The Soviet Military and the Communist Party*. Princeton, N.J.: Princeton University Press, 1967.

Korbonski, Andrzej, and Roman Kolkowicz, editors. *Soldiers, Politicians, and Bureaucrats*. London: Allen and Unwin, 1981.

Kusin, Vladimir. *From Dubček to Charter 77: A Study of "Normalization" in Czechoslovakia, 1968–1978*. New York: St Martin's Press, 1978.

Labedz, Leopold, editor. *International Communism after Khrushchev*. Cambridge, Mass.: MIT Press, 1965.

Lampe, John R. *The Bulgarian Economy in the Twentieth Century*. London: Croom Helm, 1986.

Larrabee, F. Stephen. *Balkan Security*. Adelphi Papers, no. 35. London: International Institute for Strategic Studies, 1976.

————. *The Challenge to Soviet Interests in Eastern Europe: Romania, Hungary, East Germany*. Santa Monica: Rand, December 1984.

Lavigne, Marie. *Les Relations économiques est-ouest*. Paris: Presses Universitaires de France, 1979.

Lendvai, Paul. *Anti-Semitism in Eastern Europe*. London: Macdonald, 1971.

————. *Eagles in Cobwebs: Nationalism and Communism in the Balkans*. New York: Doubleday, 1969.

————. *Das einsame albanien*. Zurich: Edition Interfrom, 1985.

Lengyel, Emil. *Nationalism—The Last Stage of Communism*. New York: Funk and Wagnalls, 1969.

Letgers, Lyman, editor. *The German Democratic Republic: A Developed Socialist Society*. Boulder, Colo.: Westview Press, 1978.

Linden, Ronald H., editor. *Foreign Policies of Eastern Europe*. New York: Praeger, 1980.

Ludz, Peter Christian. *Parteielite im Wandel*. Cologne: Westdeutscher Verlag, 1970.

Lydall, Harold. *Yugoslav Socialism: Theory and Practice*. Oxford: Clarendon Press, 1984.

McAdams, A. James. *East Germany and Détente: Building Authority after the Wall*. Cambridge: Cambridge University Press, 1985.

McCagg, William O., Jr. *Jewish Nobles and Geniuses in Modern Hungary*. New York: Columbia University Press, 1986.

McCauley, Martin. *The German Democratic Republic since 1945*. London: Macmillan, 1984.

McCauley, Martin, and Stephen Carter. *Leadership and Succession in the Soviet Union, Eastern Europe, and China*. London: Macmillan, 1986.

Mackintosh, Malcolm. *The Evolution of the Warsaw Pact*. Adelphi Papers, no. 58. London: International Institute of Strategic Studies, 1969.

Marer, Paul, and John M. Montias, editors. *East European Integration and East-West Trade*. Bloomington: Indiana University Press, 1980.

Marrese, Michael, and Jan Vaňous. *Implicit Subsidies and Non-Market Benefits in Soviet Trade with Eastern Europe*. Berkeley and Los Angeles: University of California Press, 1983.

Mastny, Vojtech, editor. *Soviet/East European Survey, 1983–1984*. Durham, N.C.: Duke University Press, 1985.

———. *Soviet/East European Survey, 1984–1985*. Durham, N.C.: Duke University Press, 1986.

Meier, Jens, and Johann Hawlowitsch, editors. *Die Aussenwirtschaft Südosteuropas*. Cologne: Verlag Wissenschaft und Politik, 1970.

Meier, Reinhard and Karhtin. *Sowjetrealität in der Ära Breschnew*. Stuttgart: Seewald Verlag, 1981.

Meissner, Boris, and Georg Brunner, editors. *Gruppeninteressen und Entscheidungsprozess in der Sowjetunion*. Cologne: Verlag Wissenschaft und Politik, 1975.

Meyer, Alfred G. *Communism*. New York: Random House, 1967.

Mićunović, Veljko. *Moscow Diary*. New York: Doubleday, 1980.

Mlynář, Zdeněk. *Krisen und Krisenbewältigung im Sowjetblock*. Cologne: Bund-Verlag, and Vienna: Wilhelm Braumüller-Verlag, 1983.

———. *Nightfrost in Prague*. New York: Karz-Cohl, 1980.

Montias, John Michael. *Economic Development in Communist Romania*. Cambridge, Mass.: MIT Press, 1967.

Moreton, N. Edwina. *East Germany and the Warsaw Alliance: The Politics of Détente*. Boulder, Colo.: Westview Press, 1978.

Moreton, Edwina, and Gerald Segal, editors. *Soviet Strategy toward Western Europe*. London: Allen and Unwin, 1984.

Morrison, James F. *The Polish Peoples Republic*. Baltimore: Johns Hopkins University Press, 1968.

Narkiewicz, Olga. *Eastern Europe: 1968–1984*. London: Croom Helm, 1986.

Nelson, Daniel N. *Democratic Centralism in Romania: A Study of Local Government Politics*. Boulder, Colo.: East European Monographs, 1980.

———, editor. *Romania in the 1980s*. Boulder, Colo.: Westview Press, 1981.

Neuburg, Paul. *The Hero's Children: The Post-War Generation in Eastern Europe*. London: Constable, 1972.

Oren, Nissan. *Bulgarian Communism: The Road to Power, 1933–1944*. New York: Columbia University Press, 1971.

―――. *Revolution Administered*. Baltimore: Johns Hopkins University Press, 1973.

Palmer, Stephen E., and Robert R. King. *Yugoslav Communism and the Macedonian Question*. Hamden, Conn.: Archon Books, 1971.

Pano, Nicholas C. *The People's Republic of Albania*. Baltimore: Johns Hopkins University Press, 1968.

Polonsky, Antony. *The Little Dictators: The History of Eastern Europe since 1918*. London: Routledge and Kegan Paul, 1975.

Prifti, Peter R. *Socialist Albania since 1944: Domestic and Foreign Developments*. Cambridge, Mass.: MIT Press, 1978.

Rakowska-Harmstone, Teresa, editor. *Communism in Eastern Europe*. 2d revised edition. Bloomington: Indiana University Press, 1984.

Remington, Robin Alison. *The Warsaw Pact: Case Studies in Communist Conflict Resolution*. Cambridge, Mass.: MIT Press, 1971.

Reuter, Jens. *Die Albaner in Jugoslawien*. Munich: R. Oldenbourg Verlag, 1982.

Révész, László. *Staat und Kirche im "realen" Sozialismus*. Berne: Verlag SOI, and Munich: Günter Olzog Verlag, 1986.

Robinson, William F. *The Pattern of Reform in Hungary*. New York: Praeger, 1973.

―――, editor. *August 1980: The Strikes in Poland*. Munich: Radio Free Europe, October 1980.

Rothschild, Joseph. *The Communist Party of Bulgaria: Origins and Development, 1883–1936*. New York: Columbia University Press, 1959.

―――. *East Central Europe between the Two World Wars*. Seattle: University of Washington Press, 1983.

Rusinow, Dennison. *The Yugoslav Experiment 1948–1974*. London: C. Hurst, 1977.

Schaefer, Henry Wilcox. *Comecon and the Politics of Integration*. New York: Praeger, 1972.

Schöpflin, George. *The Soviet Union and Eastern Europe*. Revised edition. Handbooks to the Modern World. London: Muller, Blond and White, 1986.

Schulz, Eberhard, and Peter Danylow. *Bewegung in der deutschen Frage?* Bonn: Forschungsinstitut der Deutschen Gesellschaft für Auswärtige Politik, 1985.

Seton-Watson, Hugh. *Eastern Europe between the Wars*. Hamden, Conn.: Archon Books, 1962.

―――. *The East European Revolution*. New York: Praeger, 1962.

―――. *Nations and States: An Inquiry into the Origins of Nations and the Politics of Nationalism*. London: Methuen, 1977.

Shafir, Michael. *Romania, Politics, Economics, and Society*. London: Frances Pinter, 1985.

Shawcross, William. *Crime and Compromise: Janos Kadar and the Politics of Hungary since the Revolution*. New York: Dutton, 1974.

―――. *Dubcek*. London: Weidenfeld and Nicolson, 1970.

Shoup, Paul. *Communism and the Yugoslav National Question*. New York: Columbia University Press, 1968.

Simon, Jeffrey, and Trond Gilberg. *Security Implications of Nationalism in Eastern Europe*. Carlisle Barracks, Pa.: U.S. Army War College, 1985.

Sinanian, Sylva, Istvan Deak, and Peter C. Ludz, editors. *Eastern Europe in the 1970s*. New York: Praeger, 1972.

Sirć, Ljubo. *The Yugoslav Economy under Self-Management*. New York: St. Martin's Press, 1979.

Skilling, H. Gordon. *Czechoslovakia's Interrupted Revolution*. Princeton, N.J.: Princeton University Press, 1976.

————. *The Governments of Communist East Europe*. New York: Thomas Y. Crowell, 1966.

Smith, Alan H. *The Planned Economies of Eastern Europe*. London: Croom Helm, 1983.

Smith, Jean Edward. *Germany Behind the Wall*. Boston: Little, Brown, 1965.

Sobell, Vladimir. *The Red Market: Industrial Cooperation and Specialization in Comecon*. Aldershot, England: Gower, 1984.

Sodaro, Michael J., and Sharon L. Wolchik, editors. *Eastern Europe in the 1980s: Aspects of Domestic and Foreign Policy*. New York: St. Martin's Press, 1983.

Spasowski, Romuald. *The Liberation of One*. New York: Harcourt Brace Jovanovich, 1986.

Spulber, Nicholas. *The Economics of Communist Eastern Europe*. Cambridge, Mass.: MIT Press, 1957.

Stanković Slobodan. *The End of the Tito Era: Yugoslavia's Dilemmas*. Stanford, Calif.: Hoover Institution Press, 1981.

Stehle, Hansjakob. *The Eastern Politics of the Vatican, 1917–1979*. Athens: University of Ohio Press, 1981.

————. *The Independent Satellite*. New York: Praeger, 1965.

Stern, Carola. *Ulbricht: Eine politische Biographie*. Cologne: Verlag für Politik und Wirtschaft, 1963.

Talbott, Strobe, editor. *Khrushchev Remembers*. Boston: Little, Brown, 1970.

Tampke, Jürgen. *The People's Republics of Eastern Europe*. London: Croom Helm, 1983.

Terry, Sarah Meiklejohn, editor. *Soviet Policy in Eastern Europe*. New Haven: Yale University Press, 1984.

Tökes, Rudolf, editor. *Opposition in Eastern Europe*. London: Macmillan, 1979.

Tönnes, Bernhard. *Sonderfall Albanien*. Munich: R. Oldenbourg Verlag, 1980.

Triska, Jan, and Paul Cocks, editors. *Political Development in Eastern Europe*. New York: Praeger, 1977.

Triska, Jan F., and Charles Gati, editors. *Blue-Collar Workers in Eastern Europe*. London: Allen and Unwin, 1981.

Tucker, Robert C., editor. *Stalinism: Essays in Historical Interpretation*. New York: W. W. Norton, 1977.

Tyson, Laura D'Andrea. *Economic Adjustment in Eastern Europe*. Santa Monica: Rand, September 1984.

Urban, G. R., editor. *Communist Reformation: Nationalism, Internationalism, and Change in the World Communist Movement*. New York: St. Martin's Press, 1979.

Van Brabant, Jozef M. *Socialist Economic Integration: Aspects of Contemporary Economic Problems in Eastern Europe*. Cambridge: Cambridge University Press, 1980.

Van Oudenaren, John. *The Soviet Union and Eastern Europe: Options for the 1980s and Beyond*. Santa Monica: Rand, March 1984.

Weit, Erwin. *Eyewitness*. London: André Deutsch, 1973.

Weydenthal, Jan B. de. *The Communists of Poland: An Historical Outline*. Stanford, Calif.: Hoover Institution Press, 1978.

Weydenthal, Jan B. de, Bruce D. Porter, and Kevin Devlin. *The Polish Drama, 1980–1982*. Lexington, Mass.: D. C. Heath, Lexington Books, 1983.

Whetten, Lawrence L., editor. *The Present State of Communist Internationalism*. Lexington, Mass.: D. C. Heath, Lexington Books, 1983.

Wilczynski, J. *Technology in Comecon*. London: Macmillan, 1974.

Wilson, Duncan. *Tito's Yugoslavia*. Cambridge: Cambridge University Press, 1979.

Windsor, Philip. *Change in Eastern Europe*. Chatham House Papers, no. 9. London: Royal Institute of International Affairs, 1980.

Windsor, Philip, and Adam Roberts. *Czechoslovakia, 1968: Reform and Resistance*. New York: Columbia University Press, 1969.

Zaninovich, M. George. *The Development of Socialist Yugoslavia*. Baltimore: Johns Hopkins University Press, 1968.

Index

Library of Congress Cataloging-in-Publication Data
Brown, J. F. (James F.), 1928–
Eastern Europe and communist rule.
Bibliography: p.
Includes index.
1. Europe, Eastern—History—1945–
2. Communist countries—History.   I. Title.
DJK50.B77   1988   947   87-30572
ISBN 0-8223-0810-X
ISBN 0-8223-0841-X (pbk.)

The Author

J. F. (Jim) Brown was educated at Manchester University (England), the University of Michigan, Columbia University, and Radio Free Europe. After serving as a Flying Officer in the Royal Air Force and after periods first in schoolteaching and then in industry, he joined the staff of Radio Free Europe in Munich in 1957. He worked with RFE for twenty-six years, becoming head of research in 1969 and director of the radio section in 1978. He resigned in 1983. He is a consultant to the Rand Corporation and the Stiftung Wissenschaft und Politik in the Federal Republic of Germany.

He is the author of *The New Eastern Europe* (1966) and *Bulgaria under Communist Rule* (1970) as well as numerous chapters in books and articles in scholarly journals and popular magazines. He recently contributed three chapters to Lincoln Gordon's *Eroding Empire: Western Relations with Eastern Europe* (Washington, D.C.: Brookings Institution, 1987).

Mr. Brown's home is in Oxford. In 1988 he is a Visiting Fellow at the UCLA/Rand Center for the Study of Soviet International Behavior. He is also writing a book on superpower rivalry in the Balkans.

Eastern Europe and Communist Rule

J. F. Brown analyzes the major political and economic developments in Eastern Europe over the last
quarter century, discussing both the region as a
whole and its components. He gives individual coverage to the six Warsaw Pact nations plus Yugoslavia and Albania. Brown also surveys common
themes among these countries—political and economic development, relations with the USSR and the
West, social and cultural life, and the treatment of
minorities.

In addition, Brown provides a summary chapter
and three appendixes: a chronology of main events
since 1969; biographical sketches of key leaders;
and selected demographic, social, and economic
data.

J. F. Brown has been both Director and Research
Director of Radio Free Europe. He is currently a
Visiting Fellow with the Rand/UCLA Center for the
Study of Soviet International Behavior.

"This is the volume specialists in the field have
awaited since Brown's *The New Eastern Europe.*

"*Eastern Europe and Communist Rule* contains
material that is not readily available elsewhere; it
also ventures a balanced yet analytical approach to
the past experience of Eastern Europe and its future prospects." —Melvin Croan, University of
Wisconsin-Madison

Sponsored by The Joint Committee on Eastern
Europe Publication Series of the American Council
of Learned Societies, The Social Science Research
Council.

ISBN 0-8223- 0841-X

Duke University Press
6697 College Station   Durham, North Carolina
27708